T0336763

Embedded Computing Systems:

Applications, Optimization, and Advanced Design

Mohamed Khalgui
Xidian University, China

Olfa Mosbahi
University of Carthage, Tunisia

Antonio Valentini
O3neida Europe, Belgium

Information Science
REFERENCE

Managing Director:	Lindsay Johnston
Editorial Director:	Joel Gamon
Production Manager:	Jennifer Yoder
Publishing Systems Analyst:	Adrienne Freeland
Assistant Acquisitions Editor:	Kayla Wolfe
Typesetter:	Erin O'Dea
Cover Design:	Jason Mull

Published in the United States of America by
Information Science Reference (an imprint of IGI Global)
701 E. Chocolate Avenue
Hershey PA 17033
Tel: 717-533-8845
Fax: 717-533-8661
E-mail: cust@igi-global.com
Web site: http://www.igi-global.com

Library of Congress Cataloging-in-Publication Data

Embedded computing systems : applications, optimization, and advanced design / Mohamed Khalgui, Olfa Mosbahi and Antonio Valentini, editors.
    pages cm
  Summary: "This book brings together theoretical and technical concepts of intelligent embedded control systems and their use in hardware and software architectures by highlighting formal modeling, execution models, and optimal implementations"--Provided by publisher.
  Includes bibliographical references and index.
  ISBN 978-1-4666-3922-5 (hardcover) -- ISBN 978-1-4666-3923-2 (ebook) -- ISBN 978-1-4666-3924-9 (print & perpetual access) 1. Embedded computer systems. I. Khalgui, Mohamed. II. Mosbahi, Olfa, 1976- III. Valentini, Antonio, 1980-
  TK7895.E42E564 2013
  006.2'2--dc23
                                2012051534

British Cataloguing in Publication Data
A Cataloguing in Publication record for this book is available from the British Library.

All work contributed to this book is new, previously-unpublished material. The views expressed in this book are those of the authors, but not necessarily of the publisher.

Associate Editors

Table of Contents

Detailed Table of Contents

NaiQi Wu, Guangdong University of Technology, China
MengChu Zhou, New Jersey Institute of Technology, USA
Feng Chu, Université d'Evry Val d'Essonne, France
Said Mammar, Université d'Evry Val d'Essonne, France

The process of an oil refinery contains both discrete event and continuous variables and can be characterized as a hybrid system. It is extremely challenging to schedule such a system. The short-term scheduling problem of crude oil operations addressed in this chapter is one of the most difficult parts. With jobs to be scheduled being unknown at the beginning, heuristics and meta-heuristics are unable to be applied. Thus, by the existing methods, this problem is formulated as a mathematical programming problem and solved by using exact methods. However, because it is NP-hard in nature, mathematical programming is not computationally efficient and cannot be applied in practice. Up to now, there is no software designed to this problem. In this chapter, for the first time, the problem is studied in a control theory perspective. The problem is modeled by a type of hybrid Petri nets. Based on the model, a two-level control architecture is presented. At the lower level, it solves the schedulability and detailed scheduling problem in a hybrid control theory perspective. At the upper level, it solves a refining scheduling problem, a relative simple problem, with the schedulability conditions as constraints. Consequently, it results in a breakthrough solution such that the large practical application problem can be solved.

Osman Hasan, National University of Sciences and Technology, Pakistan
Sofiène Tahar, Concordia University, Canada

The accurate reliability assessment of embedded systems has become a concern of overwhelming importance with their increasingly ubiquitous usage in safety-critical domains like transportation, medicine, and nuclear power plants. Traditional reliability analysis approaches of testing and simulation cannot guarantee accurate result and thus there is a growing trend towards developing precise mathematical models of embedded systems and to use formal verification methods to assess their reliability. This chapter is mainly focused towards this emerging trend as it presents a formal approach for the reliability assessment of embedded computing systems using a higher-order-logic theorem prover (HOL). Besides providing the formal probability theory based fundamentals of this recently proposed technique, the chapter outlines a generic reliability analysis methodology for embedded systems as well. For illustration purposes, two case studies have been considered, i.e., analyzing the reparability conditions for a reconfigurable memory array in the presence of stuck-at and coupling faults and assessing the reliability of combinational logic based digital circuits.

Chapter 3

Kamel Barkaoui, CEDRIC-CNAM – Paris, France

This chapter deals with the structure theory of Petri nets. The authors define the class of P/T systems, namely K-systems, for which the equivalence between controlled-siphon, deadlock-freeness, and liveness properties holds. Using the new structural notions of ordered transitions and root places, they revisit the non-liveness characterization of P/T systems satisfying the cs-property and define by syntactical manner new and more expressive subclasses of K-systems where the interplay between conflict and synchronization is relaxed.

Chapter 4

David Parker, University of Hull, UK
Martin Walker, University of Hull, UK
Yiannis Papadopoulos, University of Hull, UK

The scale and complexity of computer-based safety critical systems pose significant challenges in the safety analysis of such systems. In this chapter, the authors discuss two approaches that define the state of the art in this area: failure logic modelling and behavioural modelling safety analyses. They also focus on Hierarchically Performed Hazard Origin and Propagation Studies (HiP-HOPS)—one of the advanced failure logic modelling approaches—and discuss its scientific and practical contributions. These include a language for specification of inheritable and reusable component failure patterns, a temporal logic that enables assessment of sequences of faults in safety analysis as well as algorithms for top-down allocation of safety requirements to components during design, bottom-up verification via automatic synthesis of Fault Trees and Failure Modes and Effects Analyses, and dependability versus cost optimisation of systems via automatic model transformations. The authors summarise these contributions and discuss strengths and limitations in relation to the state of the art.

Chapter 5

Najet Zoubeir, Institut Supérieur d'Informatique, Tunisia
Adel Khalfallah, Institut Supérieur d'Informatique, Tunisia
Samir Benahmed, Faculté des Sciences de Tunis, Tunisia

The definition of the semantics of visual languages, in particular Unified Modeling Language (UML) diagrams, using graph formalism has known a wide success, since graphs fit the multi-dimensional nature of this kind of language. However, constraints written in Object Constraint Language (OCL) and defined on these models are still not well integrated within this graph-based semantics. In this chapter, the authors propose an integrated semantics of OCL constraints within class diagrams, using graph transformation systems. Their contribution is divided into two parts. In the first part, they introduce graph constraint patterns, as the translation into graphs of a subset of OCL expressions. These patterns are validated with experimental examples using the GROOVE toolset. In the second part, the authors define the relation between OCL and UML models within their graph transformation system.

The chapter deals with UML-based design of Reconfigurable Embedded Control Systems (RECS). The different software architectural configurations of the control system are described as a set of interconnected software components. A software agent is defined in order to handle dynamic reconfiguration scenarios. The agent has the ability to interact with users and to monitor the system's environment in order to apply valid reconfiguration scenarios at different levels of the system's architecture. In order to address all possible forms of reconfiguration, three architectural levels are defined. A set of UML-compliant metamodels are proposed in order to describe the knowledge about the reconfiguration agent, the system architecture, the reconfiguration scenarios, and the reconfiguration events. The validity of the reconfiguration scenarios is checked by using a UML-based environment that allows evaluation of the architectural and reconfiguration constraints. The proposed reconfiguration approach is applied to two industrial production systems, FESTO and ENAS.

This chapter proposes an approach for reusing specification patterns for the development of automated systems composed of two components: the controller and the controlled parts. The first is a software component controlling the second one that models the physical device and its environment. Specification patterns are design patterns that are expressed in a formal specification language. Reusing a specification pattern means instantiating it and the proofs associated. This chapter shows through a case study how to define specification patterns in Event-B, how to reuse them, and also how to reuse the proofs associated with specification patterns.

The number of computer-controlled systems has increased dramatically in our daily life. Processors and microcontrollers are embedded in most of the devices we use every day, such as mobile phones, cameras, media players, navigators, washing machines, biomedical devices, and cars. The complexity of such systems is increasing exponentially, pushed by the demand of new products with extra functionality, higher performance requirements, and low energy consumption. To cope with such a complex scenario, many embedded systems are adopting more powerful and highly integrated hardware components, such as multi-core systems, network-on-chip architectures, inertial subsystems, and special purpose co-processors. However, developing, analyzing, and testing the application software on these architectures is not easy, and new methodologies are being investigated in the research community to guarantee high predictability and efficiency in next generation embedded devices. This chapter presents some recent approaches proposed within the real-time research community aimed at achieving predictability, high modularity, efficiency, and adaptability in modern embedded computing systems.

Chapter 9

Luis Gomes, Universidade Nova de Lisboa, Portugal & UNINOVA-CTS, Portugal

Anikó Costa, Universidade Nova de Lisboa, Portugal & UNINOVA-CTS, Portugal

João Paulo Barros, Instituto Politécnico de Beja, Portugal & UNINOVA-CTS, Portugal

Filipe Moutinho, Universidade Nova de Lisboa, Portugal & UNINOVA-CTS, Portugal

Fernando Pereira, Instituto Politécnico de Lisboa, Portugal & UNINOVA-CTS, Portugal

Design of distributed embedded controllers can benefit from the adoption of a model-based development attitude, where Petri nets modeling can provide support for a comprehensive specification and documentation of the system together with verification capabilities and automatic deployment into implementation platforms. This chapter presents a Petri nets-based development flow based on composition and decomposition of Petri net models, using Input-Output Place-Transition Petri nets (IOPT nets) as the underlying formalism, allowing reusability of models in new situations through a net addition operation, as well as partitioning of the model into components using a net splitting operation. Distributed embedded controllers are addressed adding the concept of time domains to IOPT nets. Finally, a tool chain framework is presented supporting the whole development process, from specification to implementation, including property verification, simulation, and automatic code generation for deployment into implementation platforms (considering hardware-based implementation and VHDL coding or software-oriented implementation and C coding).

Chapter 10

Atef Gharbi, University of Carthage, Tunisia

Hamza Gharsellaoui, University of Carthage, Tunisia

Antonio Valentini, O3neida Europe, Belgium

Mohamed Khalgui, University of Carthage, Tunisia & CNR Research Council, Italy
     & Xidian University, China

The authors study the safety reconfiguration of embedded control systems following component-based approaches from the functional level to the operational level. At the functional level, a Control Component is defined as an event-triggered software unit characterized by an interface that supports interactions with the environment (the plant or other Control Components). They define the architecture of the Reconfiguration Agent, which is modelled by nested state machines to apply local reconfigurations. The authors propose technical solutions to implement the agent-based architecture by defining UML meta-models for both Control Components and also agents. At the operational level, a task is assumed to be a set of components having some properties independently from any real-time operating system. To guarantee safety reconfigurations of tasks at run-time, the authors define service and reconfiguration processes for tasks and use the semaphore concept to ensure safety mutual exclusions. They apply the priority ceiling protocol as a method to ensure the scheduling between periodic tasks with precedence and mutual exclusion constraints.

Chapter 11

Pranab K. Muhuri, South Asian University, India

K. K. Shukla, Banaras Hindu University, India

In real-time embedded systems, timeliness of task completion is a very important factor. In such systems, correctness of the output depends on the timely production of results in addition to the logical outcome of computation. Thus, tasks have explicit timing constraints besides other characteristics of general systems, and task scheduling aims towards devising a feasible schedule of the tasks such that timing constraints, resource constraints, precedence constraints, etc. are complied. In real-time embedded systems, the most important timing constraint of a task is the deadline, as tasks must be completed within this time. The next important timing constraint is the processing time, because a task occupies a processor only for this duration of time. However, in the early phase of real-time embedded systems design only an approximate idea of the tasks and their characteristics are known. As a result, uncertainty or impreciseness is associated with the task deadlines and processing times; hence, it is appropriate to use fuzzy numbers to model deadlines and processing times in real-time embedded systems. The chapter introduces a new method using mixed cubic-exponential Hermite interpolation technique for intuitively defining smooth Membership Functions (MFs) for fuzzy deadlines and processing times. The effect of changes in parameterized MFs on the task schedulability and task priorities are explained. Examples are given to demonstrate the significant features and better performance of the new technique.

This chapter deals with Reconfigurable Uniprocessor embedded Real-Time Systems to be classically implemented by different OS tasks that we suppose independent, asynchronous, and periodic in order to meet functional and temporal properties described in user requirements. The authors define a schedulability algorithm for preemptable, asynchronous, and periodic reconfigurable task systems with arbitrary relative deadlines, scheduled on a uniprocessor by an optimal scheduling algorithm based on the EDF principles and on the dynamic reconfiguration. Two forms of automatic reconfigurations are assumed to be applied at run-time: Addition-Remove of tasks and just modifications of their temporal parameters: WCET and/or Periods. Nevertheless, when such a scenario is applied to save the system at the occurrence of hardware-software faults, or to improve its performance, some real-time properties can be violated. The authors define a new semantic of the reconfiguration where a crucial criterion to consider is the automatic improvement of the system's feasibility at run-time by using an Intelligent Agent that automatically checks the system's feasibility after any reconfiguration scenario to verify if all tasks meet the required deadlines. Indeed, if a reconfiguration scenario is applied at run-time, then the Intelligent Agent dynamically provides otherwise precious technical solutions for users to remove some tasks according to predefined heuristic (based on soft or hard task), or by modifying the Worst Case Execution Times (WCETs), periods, and/or deadlines of tasks that violate corresponding constraints by new ones, in order to meet deadlines and to minimize their response time. To handle all possible reconfiguration solutions, they propose an agent-based architecture that applies automatic reconfigurations in order to re-obtain the system's feasibility and to satisfy user requirements. Therefore, the authors developed the tool RT-Reconfiguration to support these contributions that they apply to a Blackberry Bold 9700 and to a Volvo system as running example systems and we apply the Real-Time Simulator Cheddar to check the whole system behavior and to evaluate the performance of the algorithm (detailed descriptions are available at the Website: http://beru.univ-brest.fr/~singhoff/cheddar). The authors present simulations of this architecture where they evaluate the agent that they implemented. In addition, the authors present and discuss the results of experiments that compare the accuracy and the performance of their algorithm with others.

Chapter 13

Abderrazak Jemai, University of Tunis El Manar, Tunisia & University of Carthage, Tunisia
Kamel Smiri, University of Tunis El Manar, Tunisia & University of Kairouan, Tunisia
Habib Smei, ISET de Rades, Tunisia

Task migration has a great consideration is MPSoC design and implementation of embedded systems in order to improve performance related to optimizing execution time or reducing energy consumption. Multi-Processor Systems-on-Chip (MPSoC) are now the leading hardware platform featured in embedded systems. This chapter deals with the impact of task migration as an alternative to meet performance constraints in the design flow. The authors explain the different levels of the design process and propose a methodology to master the migration process at transaction level. This methodology uses some open source tools like SDF3 modified to provide performance estimation at transaction level. These results help the designer to choose the best hardware model in replacement of the previous software implementation of the task object of migration. Using the SDF3 tool, the authors model a multimedia application using SDF graphs. Secondly, they target an MPSoC platform. The authors take a performance constraint to achieve 25 frames per second.

Chapter 14

Ricardo Moraes, Universidade Federal de Santa Catarina, Brazil
Francisco Vasques, Universidade do Porto, Portugal

During the last few years, the demand for Real-Time (RT) communication has been steadily increasing due to a wide range of new applications. Remarkable examples are VoIP (Voice over IP) and Networked Control Systems (NCS). For such RT applications, the support of timely communication services is one of the major requirements. The purpose of this chapter is to survey the state-of-the-art on RT communication in CSMA-based networks and to identify the most suitable approaches to deal with the requirements imposed by next generation communication systems. This chapter focuses on one of the most relevant solutions that operate in shared broadcast environments, according to the CSMA medium access protocol, the IEEE 802.11 standard. From this survey, it becomes clear that traditional CSMA-based networks are not able to deal with the requirements imposed by next generation communication systems. More specifically, they are not able to handle uncontrolled traffic sources sharing the same broadcast environment.

Chapter 15

Mohamed Wassim Jmal, University of Sfax, Tunisia
Oussema Ghorbel, University of Sfax, Tunisia
Olfa Gaddour, University of Sfax, Tunisia
Mohamed Abid, University of Sfax, Tunisia

Wireless Sensor Networks (WSNs) are currently attracting great interest and the number of its application domains is varying and increasing. However, some of these applications are very sensitive to the execution time and require huge memory and computation resources, which contrast to the nature of sensor motes with limited capabilities. There have been a lot of software solutions that aim to optimize the memory consumption and to reduce the execution time of WSN applications, but few previous research efforts considered a hardware/software optimization of the sensor mote resources. The limitation of studies on hardware optimization on WSN motivated the authors to write this chapter, with the objective to design a new HW architecture with FPGA technology that allows extending the sensor mote capabilities. An optimal routing protocol to efficiently route messages between motes was chosen. It enables the reduction of different communication problems such as message unreachability, long paths, and traffic congestion. The authors first study one of WSN applications that require great resources, image processing. They demonstrate how the memory and processing capabilities of classical sensor motes are not sufficient for the treatment of this application, and the point-to-point routing cannot be applied in such applications. The authors then survey the most important routing protocols for WSNs in order to select the best routing algorithm. They finally propose a reconfigurable HW/SW architecture based on FPGA for critical WSN applications. Results show that the proposed solution outperforms the performance of the classical sensor motes, and is extensible for application to other WSN applications.

Chapter 16

In recent years, the automotive industry has witnessed an exponential growth in the number of vehicular embedded applications, leading to the adoption of distributed implementations for systems in the powertrain and chassis domains. The Controller Area Network (CAN) protocol has been a de facto standard for intra-vehicular communications, while the FlexRay Communication System is being promoted as the future de facto standard for network interconnections of applications related to X-by-wire systems. Due to the characteristics of CAN and FlexRay, the coexistence of both protocols in the same vehicle is expected, leading to the use of gateways to manage the information exchange between electronic control units connected to different network segments. This chapter describes the main characteristics of CAN and FlexRay protocols, surveying the literature addressing schedulability and time analysis in both FlexRay and CAN protocols. The chapter also outlines the state-of-the-art in research about gateways for intra-vehicular communication networks.

Chapter 17

The evolution of industrial networks can be summarized as a constant battle to define the universal technology that integrates field devices and applications. Since the Fieldbus wars in the 1980s, diverse wired solutions have been proposed. However, this scenario has been changing due to the introduction of industrial wireless sensor networks. In the last 10 years, the development of deterministic scheduling techniques, redundant routing algorithms, and energy saving issues has brought wireless sensor networks into the industrial domain. This new communication paradigm is governed by a de facto standard, the IEEE 802.15.4, and more recently also by the IEEE 802.15.5. However, there are signs of a new battle on the horizon with the new publicly available specifications of WirelessHART, ISA100.11a, and IEC 62601. In this chapter, to the authors analyze the advantages and drawbacks of these emerging technologies for industrial wireless sensor networks.

Fethi H. Bellamine, University of Waterloo, Canada & National Institute of Applied Sciences and Technologies, Tunisia

Aymen Gdouda, National Institute of Applied Sciences and Technologies, Tunisia

Developing fast and accurate numerical simulation models for predicting, controlling, designing, and optimizing the behavior of distributed dynamic systems is of interest to many researchers in various fields of science and engineering. These systems are described by a set of differential equations with homogenous or mixed boundary constraints. Examples of such systems are found, for example, in many networked industrial systems. The purpose of the present work is to review techniques of hybrid soft computing along with generalized scaling analysis for the solution of a set of differential equations characterizing distributed dynamic systems. The authors also review reduction techniques. This paves the way to control synthesis of real-time robust realizable controllers.

Ricardo Chessini Bose, University of Mons, Belgium

Georgios Fourtounis, University of Mons, Belgium

Naim Harb, University of Mons, Belgium

Laurent Jolczyk, University of Mons, Belgium

Paulo Da Cunha Possa, University of Mons, Belgium

Carlos Valderrama, University of Mons, Belgium

Multiple processors, microcontrollers, or DSPs have been used in embedded systems to distribute control and data flow according to the application at hand. The recent trends of incorporating multiple cores in the same chip significantly expands the processing power of such heterogeneous systems. However, these trends demand new ways of building and programming embedded systems in order to control cost and complexity. In this context, the authors present an overview on multi-core architectures and their inter-core communication mechanisms, dedicated cores used as accelerators, and hardware reconfiguration providing flexibility on today's multi-core embedded systems. Finally, they highlight tools, frameworks, and techniques for programming multi-cores and accelerators in order to take advantage of their performance in a robust and cost effective manner.

Elisavet Konstantinou, University of the Aegean, Greece

Panayotis E. Nastou, University of the Aegean, Greece

Yannis C. Stamatiou, University of Patras, Greece

Christos Zaroliagis, University of Patras, Greece

Embedded computing devices dominate our everyday activities, from cell phones to wireless sensors that collect and process data for various applications. Although desktop and high-end server security seems to be under control by the use of current security technology, securing the low-end embedded computing systems is a difficult long-term problem. This is mainly due to the fact that the embedded systems are constrained by their operational environment and the limited resources they are equipped with. Recent research activities focus on the deployment of lightweight cryptographic algorithms and security protocols that are well suited to the limited resources of low-end embedded systems. Elliptic Curve Cryptography (ECC) offers an interesting alternative to the classical public key cryptography for embedded systems (e.g., RSA and ElGamal), since it uses smaller key sizes for achieving the same security level, thus making ECC an attractive and efficient alternative for deployment in embedded systems. In this chapter, the processing requirements and architectures for secure network access, communication functions, storage, and high availability of embedded devices are discussed. In addition, ECC-based state-of-the-art lightweight cryptographic primitives for the deployment of security protocols in embedded systems that fulfill the requirements are presented.

Strong security is a necessity in the modern IT world and is broadly provided though Hardware Security Modules (HSM) capable of realizing a wide variety of security algorithms and protocols. Such modules are no longer only found in expensive computer systems like servers, corporate PC, or laptops but also in every device where security is required, including embedded systems like smart cards or smart grid, smart environment, automobile, game station, and aviation processors. The chapter provides to the reader the necessary information on how strong security is structured in a hardware embedded system environment from cryptographic engineering point of view. The focus is efficient design on symmetric, asymmetric cryptography and hash function systems, and design approaches that can be used in order to provide strong security to the embedded system user.

NAND Flash memories gained a solid foothold in the embedded systems domain due to its attractive characteristics in terms of size, weight, shock resistance, power consumption, and data throughput. Moreover, flash memories tend to be less confined to the embedded domain, as it can be observed through the market explosion of flash-based storage systems (average growth of the NVRAM is reported to be about 69% up to 2015). In this chapter, the authors focus on NAND flash memory NVRAM. After a global presentation of its architecture and very specific constraints, they describe the different ways to manage flash memories in embedded systems which are 1) the use of a hardware Flash Translation Layer (FTL), or 2) a dedicated Flash File System (FFS) software support implemented within the embedded operating system kernel.

EAST-ADL is an Architecture Description Language (ADL) initially defined in several European-funded research projects and subsequently refined and aligned with the more recent AUTOSAR automotive standard. It provides a comprehensive approach for defining automotive electronic systems through an information model that captures engineering information in a standardized form. Aspects covered include vehicle features, requirements, analysis functions, software and hardware components, and communication. The representation of the system's implementation is not defined in EAST-ADL itself but by AUTOSAR. However, traceability is supported from EAST-ADL's lower abstraction levels to the implementation level elements in AUTOSAR. In this chapter, the authors describe EAST-ADL in detail, show how it relates to AUTOSAR as well as other significant automotive standards, and present current research work on using EAST-ADL in the context of fully-electric vehicles, the functional safety standard ISO 26262, and for multi-objective optimization.

Preface

Reconfigurable Embedded Control Systems exist in all aspects of our personal and professional modern life due to many applications of their use. Tomorrow, telecommunication systems will employ numerous reconfigurable embedded systems from telephone switches to mobile phones at the end-user. Computer networking will uses dedicated intelligent reconfigurable embedded controllers-based routers and network bridges to route data with a perfect intelligence. Consumer electronics will be based also on reconfigurable autonomous controllers from Personal Digital Assistants (PDAs), mp3 players, mobile phones, videogame consoles, to digital cameras, DVD players, GPS receivers, and printers. Many future household intelligent devices, such as televisions, microwave ovens, washing machines and dishwashers, will include reconfigurable autonomous embedded electronics to provide flexibility, efficiency, and features. Moreover, Advanced Heating, Ventilating, and Air Conditioning (HVAC) systems use networked thermostats to more accurately and efficiently control temperature that can change by time of day and season. Home automation will use wired- and wireless-networking that can be used to automatically control lights, climate, security, audio/visual, surveillance, etc. with a perfect intelligence, all of which use reconfigurable adaptive embedded controllers for sensing and controlling. Today, all the intelligent transportation systems from flight, maritime to automobiles, motorcycles, and bikes increasingly use reconfigurable adaptive embedded electronics for control and supervision. The future airplanes will contain advanced avionics such as intelligent inertial guidance systems and adaptive GPS receivers that should have considerable intelligent safety requirements. Tomorrow, various electric motors brushless DC motors, induction motors and DC motors will use electric/electronic motor controllers. Future smart and autonomous adaptive automobiles, electric vehicles, and hybrid vehicles will increasingly use embedded systems to maximize efficiency and reduce pollution. Other automotive safety systems include intelligent Antilock Braking System (ABS), Electronic Stability Control (ESC/ESP), Traction Control (TCS), and automatic intelligent four-wheel drive. Tomorrow, medical equipment will continue to advance with more reconfigurable intelligent embedded software solutions for vital signs monitoring, electronic stethoscopes for amplifying sounds, and various medical imaging (PET, SPECT, CT, MRI) for non-invasive internal inspections. In addition to commonly described embedded systems based on small computers, a new class of intelligent miniature wireless devices called motes are quickly gaining popularity as the field of autonomous adaptive wireless sensor networking rises. Intelligent Wireless sensor networking, WSN, couples full autonomous wireless subsystems to sophisticated intelligent sensors, enabling people and companies to measure a myriad of things in the physical world and act on this information through monitoring and control controllers. These motes are completely self-contained, and will typically run off a battery source for many years before the batteries need to be changed or charged. The current book deals with reconfigurable intelligent embedded control systems, where several interesting chapters are presented to discuss valuable theoretical and practical contributions related to formal modeling and verification, scheduling, execution models, optimal implementations and feasible simulations of future reconfigurable intelligent centralized/distributed adaptive architectures.

In Chapter 1, it is assumed that the process of an oil refinery contains both discrete event and continuous variables, and can be characterized as a hybrid system. It is extremely challenging to schedule such a system. The short-term scheduling problem of crude oil operations addressed in this chapter is one of the most difficult parts. With jobs to be scheduled being unknown at the beginning, heuristics and meta-heuristics are unable to be applied. Thus, by the existing methods, this problem is formulated as a mathematical programming problem and solved by using exact methods. Up to now, there is no software designed to this problem. In this chapter, for the first time, the problem is studied in a control theory perspective. The problem is modeled by a type of hybrid Petri nets. Based on the model, a two-level control architecture is presented. At the lower level, it solves the schedulability and detailed scheduling problem in a hybrid control theory perspective. At the upper level, it solves a refining scheduling problem, a relative simple problem, with the schedulability conditions as constraints. Consequently, it results in a breakthrough solution such that large practical application problem can be solved.

The accurate reliability assessment of embedded systems has become a concern of overwhelming importance with their increasingly ubiquitous usage in safety-critical domains like transportation, medicine, and nuclear power plants. Traditional reliability analysis approaches of testing and simulation cannot guarantee accurate result and thus there is a growing trend towards developing precise mathematical models of embedded systems and to use formal verification methods to assess their reliability. Chapter 2 is mainly focused towards this emerging trend as it presents a formal approach for the reliability assessment of embedded computing systems using a higher-order-logic theorem prover (HOL). Besides providing the formal probability theory based fundamentals of this recently proposed technique, the chapter outlines a generic reliability analysis methodology for embedded systems as well. For illustration purposes, two case studies have been considered, i.e., analyzing the repairability conditions for a reconfigurable memory array in the presence of stuck-at and coupling faults and assessing the reliability of combinational logic based digital circuits.

Chapter 3 deals with the structure theory of Petri nets. The author defines the class of P/T systems namely K-systems for which the equivalence between controlled-siphon, deadlock freeness, and liveness properties holds. Using the new structural notions of ordered transitions and root places, the author revisits the non liveness characterization of P/T systems satisfying the cs-property and defines by syntactical manner new and more expressive subclasses of K-systems where the interplay between conflict and synchronization is relaxed.

The scale and complexity of computer-based safety critical systems pose significant challenges in the safety analysis of such systems. Chapter 4 discusses two approaches that define the state of the art in this area: failure logic modelling and behavioural modelling safety analyses. The authors focus on Hierarchically Performed Hazard Origin and Propagation Studies (HiP-HOPS)—one of the advanced failure logic modelling approaches—and discuss its scientific and practical contributions. These include a language for specification of inheritable and reusable component failure patterns, a temporal logic that enables assessment of sequences of faults in safety analysis as well as algorithms for top-down allocation of safety requirements to components during design, bottom-up verification via automatic synthesis of Fault Trees and Failure Modes and Effects Analyses, and dependability versus cost optimization of systems via automatic model transformations.

The definition of the semantics of visual languages, in particular Unified Modeling Language (UML) diagrams, using graph formalism has known a wide success, since graphs fit the multi-dimensional nature of this kind of languages. However, constraints written in Object Constraint Language (OCL) and defined on these models are still not well integrated within this graph-based semantics. In chapter 5, the authors propose an integrated semantics of OCL constraints within class diagrams, using graph transformation systems. The contribution is divided into two parts: In the first part, the authors introduce graph constraint patterns, as the translation into graphs of a subset of OCL expressions. These patterns are validated with experimental examples using the GROOVE toolset. In the second part, they explicit the relation between OCL and UML models within our graph transformation systems.

Chapter 6 deals with UML-based design of Reconfigurable Embedded Control Systems (RECS). The different software architectural configurations of the control system are described as a set of interconnected software components. A software agent is defined in order to handle dynamic reconfiguration scenarios. The agent has the ability to interact with users and to monitor the system's environment in order to apply valid reconfiguration scenarios at different levels of the system's architecture. In order to address all possible forms of reconfiguration, three architectural levels are defined. A set of UML-compliant metamodels are proposed in order to describe the knowledge about the reconfiguration agent, the system architecture, the reconfiguration scenarios, and the reconfiguration events. The validity of the reconfiguration scenarios is checked by using a UML-based environment which allows to evaluate architectural and reconfiguration constraints.

Chapter 7 proposes an approach for reusing specification patterns for the development of automated systems composed of two components: the controller and the controlled parts. The first is a software component controlling the second one that models the physical device and its environment. Specification patterns are design patterns that are expressed in a formal specification language. Reusing a specification pattern means instantiating it and the proofs associated. The chapter shows through a case study how to define specification patterns in Event-B, how to reuse them, and also how to reuse the proofs associated with specification patterns.

Nowadays, many embedded systems are adopting more powerful and highly integrated hardware components, such as multi-core systems, network-on-chip architectures, inertial subsystems, and special purpose co-processors. However, developing, analyzing, and testing the application software on these architectures is not easy, and new methodologies are being investigated in the research community to guarantee high predictability and efficiency in next generation embedded devices. Chapter 8 presents some recent approaches proposed within the real-time research community aimed at achieving predictability, high modularity, efficiency, and adaptability in modern embedded computing systems.

Design of distributed embedded controllers can benefit from the adoption of a model-based development attitude, where Petri nets modeling can provide support for a comprehensive specification and documentation of the system together with verification capabilities and automatic deployment into implementation platforms. Chapter 9 presents a Petri nets-based development flow based on composition and decomposition of Petri net models, using Input-Output Place-Transition Petri nets (IOPT nets) as the underlying formalism, allowing reusability of models in new situations through a net addition operation, as well as partitioning of the model into components using a net splitting operation.

The authors in chapter 10 study the safety reconfiguration of embedded control systems following component-based approaches from the functional level to the operational level. At the functional level, a Control Component is defined as an event-triggered software unit characterized by an interface that supports interactions with the environment (the plant or other Control Components). They define the architecture of the Reconfiguration Agent which is modelled by nested state machines to apply local reconfigurations. They propose technical solutions to implement the whole agent-based architecture, by defining UML meta-models for both Control Components and also agents. At the operational level, a task is assumed to be a set of components having some properties independently from any real-time operating system. To guarantee safety reconfigurations of tasks at run-time, they define service and reconfiguration processes for tasks and use the semaphore concept to ensure safety mutual exclusions. The chapter applies the priority ceiling protocol as a method to ensure the scheduling between periodic tasks with precedence and mutual exclusion constraints.

Chapter 11 develops a new model for task scheduling in real-time embedded systems using fuzzy numbers with different membership functions. Here, the fuzzy real-time scheduling problem is explained in detail, where task deadlines and processing times are represented by fuzzy numbers in parametric representation. This allows fuzzy deadlines and processing times not to be restricted to any particular membership function and shape. The uncertainties associated with these important timing parameters of real-time tasks can be modeled from a wide variety of possible membership functions and shapes according to the nature and environment of tasks and systems giving the schedule designer considerable flexibility. Thus, the chapter introduces a new method using mixed cubic-exponential Hermite interpolation technique for intuitively defining smooth Membership Functions (MFs) for fuzzy deadlines and processing times. The effect of changes in parameterized MFs on the task schedulability and task priorities are explained.

The research work in chapter 12 deals with Reconfigurable Uniprocessor embedded Real-Time Systems to be classically implemented by different OS tasks that we suppose independent, asynchronous, and periodic in order to meet functional and temporal properties described in user requirements. The authors define a schedulability algorithm for preemptable, asynchronous, and periodic reconfigurable task systems with arbitrary relative deadlines, scheduled on a uniprocessor by an optimal scheduling algorithm based on the EDF principles and on the dynamic reconfiguration.

Task migration has a great consideration is MPSoC design and implementation of embedded systems in order to improve performance related to optimizing execution time or reducing energy consumption. Multi-Processor Systems-on-Chip (MPSoC) are now the leading hardware platform featured in embedded systems. Chapter 13 deals with the impact of task migration as an alternative to meet performance constraints in the design flow. A methodology is proposed to master the migration process at transaction level. This methodology uses some open source tools like SDF3 modified to provide performance estimation at transaction level. These results help the designer to choose the best hardware model in replacement of the previous software implementation of the task object of migration.

During the last few years, the demand for Real-Time (RT) communication has been steadily increasing due to a wide range of new applications. Remarkable examples are VoIP (Voice over IP) and Networked Control Systems (NCS). For such type of RT applications, the support of timely communication services is one of the major requirements. The purpose of Chapter 14 is to survey the state-of-the-art on RT communication in CSMA-based networks and to identify the most suitable approaches to deal with the requirements imposed by next generation communication systems. The chapter focuses in one of the most relevant solutions that operate in shared broadcast environments, according to the CSMA medium access protocol—the IEEE 802.11 standard. From this survey, it becomes clear that traditional CSMA-based networks are not able to deal with the requirements imposed by next generation communication systems. More specifically, they are not able to handle uncontrolled traffic sources sharing the same broadcast environment.

Chapter 15 discusses Wireless Sensor Networks (WSNs) which are currently attracting great interest and the number of its application domains is varying and increasing. However, some of these applications are very sensitive to the execution time and require huge memory and computation resources, which contrast to the nature of sensor motes with limited capabilities. There have been a lot of software solutions that aim to optimize the memory consumption and to reduce the execution time of WSN applications; but few previous research efforts considered a hardware/software optimization of the sensor mote resources. The limitation of studies on hardware optimization on WSN motivates to write this chapter, with the objective to design a new HW architecture with FPGA technology, which allows extending the sensor mote capabilities. An optimal routing protocol to efficiently route messages between motes was chosen. It enables to reduce different communication problems such as message unreachability, long paths, and traffic congestion. The authors first study one of WSN applications that require great resources, image processing. They demonstrate how the memory and processing capabilities of classical sensor motes are not sufficient for the treatment of this application, and the point-to-point routing cannot be applied in such applications. They then survey the most important routing protocols for WSNs in order to select the best routing algorithm. They finally propose a reconfigurable HW/SW architecture based on FPGA for critical WSN applications.

Chapter 16 discusses the automotive industry, which has witnessed an exponential growth in the number of vehicular embedded applications, leading to the adoption of distributed implementations for systems in the powertrain and chassis domains. The Controller Area Network (CAN) protocol has been a *de facto* standard for intra vehicular communications, while the FlexRay Communication System is being promoted as the future *de facto* standard for network interconnections of applications related to X-by-wire systems. Due to the characteristics of CAN and FlexRay, it is expected the coexistence of both protocols in the same vehicle, leading to the use of gateways to manage the information exchange between electronic control units connected to different network segments. This chapter describes the main characteristics of CAN and FlexRay protocols, surveying the literature addressing schedulability and time analysis in both FlexRay and CAN protocols. The chapter also outlines the state-of-the-art in research about gateways for intra-vehicular communication networks.

Chapter 17 analyzes the evolution of industrial networks which can be summarized as a constant battle to define the universal technology that integrates field devices and applications. Since the Fieldbus wars in the 1980s, diverse wired solutions have been proposed. However, this scenario has been changing due to the introduction of industrial wireless sensor networks. In the last 10 years, the development of deterministic scheduling techniques, redundant routing algorithms, and energy saving issues has brought wireless sensor networks into the industrial domain. This new communication paradigm is governed by a *de facto* standard, the IEEE 802.15.4, and more recently also by the IEEE 802.15.5. However, there are signs of a new battle on the horizon with the new publicly available specifications of WirelessHART, ISA100.11a, and IEC 62601. This chapter intends to analyze the advantages and drawbacks of these emerging technologies for industrial wireless sensor networks.

Chapter 18 is interested in developing fast and accurate numerical simulation models for predicting, controlling, designing, and optimizing the behavior of distributed dynamic systems. These systems are described by a set of differential equations with homogenous or mixed boundary constraints. Examples of such systems are found, for example, in many networked industrial systems. The purpose of the present work is to review techniques of hybrid soft computing techniques along with generalized scaling analysis for the solution of a set of differential equations characterizing distributed dynamic systems. The chapter also reviews reduction techniques. This paves the way to control synthesis of real-time robust realizable controllers.

Chapter 19 discusses the multiple processors, microcontrollers, or DSPs which have been used in embedded systems to distribute control and data flow according to the application at hand. The recent trends of incorporating multiple cores in the same chip significantly expands the processing power of such heterogeneous systems. However, these trends demand new ways of building and programming embedded systems in order to control cost and complexity. In this context, the chapter presents an overview on multi-core architectures and their inter-core communication mechanisms, dedicated cores used as accelerators, and hardware reconfiguration providing flexibility on today's multi-core embedded systems. Finally, it highlights tools, frameworks, and techniques for programming multi-cores and accelerators in order to take advantage of their performance in a robust and cost effective manner.

Chapter 20 is interested in embedded computing devices, which dominate our everyday activities, from cell phones to wireless sensors that collect and process data for various applications. Although desktop and high-end server security seems to be under control by the use of current security technology, securing the low-end embedded computing systems is a difficult long-term problem. This is mainly due to the fact that the embedded systems are constrained by their operational environment and the limited resources they are equipped with. Recent research activities focus on the deployment of lightweight cryptographic algorithms and security protocols that are well suited to the limited resources of low-end embedded systems. Elliptic Curve Cryptography (ECC) offers an interesting alternative to the classical public key cryptography for embedded systems (e.g., RSA and ElGamal), since it uses smaller key sizes for achieving the same security level, thus making ECC an attractive and efficient alternative for deployment in embedded systems. In this chapter, the processing requirements and architectures for secure network access, communication functions, storage, and high availability of embedded devices are discussed. In addition, ECC-based state-of-the-art lightweight cryptographic primitives for the deployment of security protocols in embedded systems that fulfill the requirements are presented.

Chapter 21 discusses the strong security, which is a necessity in the modern IT world and is broadly provided though Hardware Security Modules (HSM) capable of realizing a wide variety of security algorithms and protocols. Such modules are no longer only found in expensive computer systems like servers, corporate PC, or laptops but also in every device where security is required, including embedded systems like smart cards or smart grid, smart environment, automobile, game station, and aviation processors. The goal is to provide to the reader, the necessary information on how strong security is structured in a hardware embedded system environment from cryptographic engineering point of view. The focus is efficient design on symmetric, asymmetric cryptography and hash function systems and design approaches that can be used in order to provide strong security to the embedded system user.

Chapter 22 discusses NAND Flash memories, which gained a solid foothold in the embedded systems domain due to its attractive characteristics in terms of size, weight, shock resistance, power consumption, and data throughput. Moreover, flash memories tend to be less confined to the embedded domain, as it can be observed through the market explosion of flash-based storage systems. This chapter focuses on NAND flash memory NVRAM. After a global presentation of its architecture and very specific constraints, the chapter describes throughout some examples the different ways to manage flash memories in embedded systems, which are: 1) the use of a hardware Flash Translation Layer (FTL), or 2) a dedicated Flash File System (FFS) software support implemented within the embedded operating system kernel.

Finally, Chapter 23 is interested in EAST-ADL which is an Architecture Description Language (ADL) initially defined in several European-funded research projects and subsequently refined and aligned with the more recent AUTOSAR automotive standard. It provides a comprehensive approach for defining automotive electronic systems through an information model that captures engineering information in a standardized form. Aspects covered include vehicle features, requirements, analysis functions, software and hardware components and communication. The representation of the system's implementation is not defined in EAST-ADL itself but by AUTOSAR. However, traceability is supported from EAST-ADL's lower abstraction levels to the implementation level elements in AUTOSAR. This chapter describes EAST-ADL in detail, show how it relates to AUTOSAR as well as other significant automotive standards and presents current research work on using EAST-ADL in the context of fully-electric vehicles, the functional safety standard ISO 26262 and for multi-objective optimization.

Mohamed Khalgui
Xidian University, China

Olfa Mosbahi
University of Carthage, Tunisia

Antonio Valentini
O3neida Europe, Belgium

Chapter 1
Modeling and Scheduling of Crude Oil Operations in Refinery:
A Hybrid Timed Petri Net Approach

NaiQi Wu
Guangdong University of Technology, China

Feng Chu
Université d'Evry Val d'Essonne, France

MengChu Zhou
New Jersey Institute of Technology, USA

Said Mammar
Université d'Evry Val d'Essonne, France

ABSTRACT

The process of an oil refinery contains both discrete event and continuous variables and can be characterized as a hybrid system. It is extremely challenging to schedule such a system. The short-term scheduling problem of crude oil operations addressed in this chapter is one of the most difficult parts. With jobs to be scheduled being unknown at the beginning, heuristics and meta-heuristics are unable to be applied. Thus, by the existing methods, this problem is formulated as a mathematical programming problem and solved by using exact methods. However, because it is NP-hard in nature, mathematical programming is not computationally efficient and cannot be applied in practice. Up to now, there is no software designed to this problem. In this chapter, for the first time, the problem is studied in a control theory perspective. The problem is modeled by a type of hybrid Petri nets. Based on the model, a two-level control architecture is presented. At the lower level, it solves the schedulability and detailed scheduling problem in a hybrid control theory perspective. At the upper level, it solves a refining scheduling problem, a relative simple problem, with the schedulability conditions as constraints. Consequently, it results in a breakthrough solution such that the large practical application problem can be solved.

DOI: 10.4018/978-1-4666-3922-5.ch001

1. INTRODUCTION

With increasingly global competition, the profit and productivity enhancement technology for process industry has attracted more and more research interest in recent years. Oil refinery is one type of such processes. In operating a plant of refinery, there are three levels: production planning, production scheduling, and process control. It is believed that when the plant is well operated it may increase profit by $10 per ton of product or more (Moro, 2003). Thus, for competitiveness, considerable attention has been paid to the development of effective techniques for the operation of refinery for the last two decades. Up to now, at the process control level, advanced control systems have been installed for unit control to optimize production objectives in most oil refineries, leading to significant productivity gains in these units. Nevertheless, the optimization of the production units does not mean the global economic optimization of the plant. Usually the objectives of the individual units are conflicting and thus lead to a suboptimal and sometimes infeasible overall operation.

At the planning level, the potential benefits of optimization for process operations in oil refineries have long been observed, and linear programming has been applied in crude oil blending and product pooling (Symonds, 1955). Oil refineries are increasingly concerned with improving the planning of their operations. Faced with global market competition, companies should assess the potential impact of dynamical changes such as demands for final product specifications, prices, and crude oil compositions. For this purpose, Coxhead (1994) identifies several applications of planning models in the refining and oil industry, including crude selection, crude allocation for multi-refinery situations, and operations planning. With the availability of LP-based commercial software for refinery production planning, such as PIMS (Process Industry Modeling System — Bechtel, 1993), general production plans of the whole

refinery can be found. As pointed out by Pelham and Pharris (1996), the planning technology can be considered well-developed and its drastic progress should not be expected. Additional advances in this area may be based on model refinement through the use of nonlinear programming.

Short-term scheduling is at the middle level. As pointed by Shobrys and White (2000), to effectively operate a process plant, the three levels should work together. In fact, the need for integration has been a frequent topic since the 1960s (Mesarovic et al., 1970; Jaikumar, 1974; Baker and Shobrys, 1985; Bodington, 1995; Pinto et al., 2000; and Honkomp et al., 2000). Thus, with the techniques for planning and process control well-developed, it is crucial to develop effective techniques for short-term scheduling.

There are mainly two types of industries: discrete manufacturing industry and process industry. It is believed that scheduling discrete manufacturing operations is well-established (Baker, 1974) and there is a large body of literature on this field. Because of the NP-hard nature for the general scheduling problem, usually heuristics and metaheuristics, such as simulated annealing algorithms, genetic algorithms, and tabu algorithms, are applied (Sabuncuoglu and M. Bayiz, 1999; Ponnambalam et al., 1999; Mattfeld and Bierwirth, 2004; Yang and Wang, 2001; Czerwinski and Luh, 1994; and Chen et al., 1998).

Process industry can be further divided into two categories: batch and continuous processes. In batch process industry, the materials are processed in batches. These discrete batches can be treated as jobs just as in the discrete manufacturing systems. Nevertheless, the materials are transferred between devices continuously as fluid, and hence, they are characterized as continuous variables. Great effort has been made in scheduling of a batch process by using rule-based algorithms (Kudva et al., 1994; Stephanopoulos and Han, 1996), search algorithms (Ku and Karimi, 1991; and Murakami et al., 1997), and mixed integer programming (Pinto and Grossmann, 1997; Realff and Stephanopoulos, 1998; Kondili et al., 1993; Pantelides, 1994; Mendez and J. Cerda, 2002 and 2003; Ierapetritou and Floudas, 1998; Mendez et al., 2006; and Liu and Karimi, 2008).

Oil refinery belongs to continuous process industry. Short-term scheduling for crude oil operations is one of the most difficult scheduling problems in operating an oil refinery plant. Thus, there is great research interest in developing effective techniques for this problem. As pointed out in (Wu et al., 2008a), heuristics and meta-heuristics cannot be applied to this problem. The mathematical programming models used for batch processes are modified for the short-term scheduling of crude oil operations. When mathematical programming models are used, the key is how the time is described. There are mainly two categories of models: discrete and continuous-time ones. The former divides the scheduling horizon into a number of time intervals with uniform time durations. An event, such as start and end of an operation, should happen at the boundary of a time interval. Then, an exact solution method is used to obtain an optimal short-term schedule. The representative work can be found in (Shah, 1996; Lee *et al.*, 1996; Pinto *et al.*, 2000; Glismann and Gruhn, 2001; Jia *et al.*, 2003; Rejowski and Pinto, 2003; Saharidisa *et al.*, 2009; and Mendez *et al.* 2006). By such models, the uniform time interval must be small enough so as to obtain acceptable accuracy. This leads to a huge number of binary variables for real-world applications that are difficult or even impossible to solve (Floudas and Lin, 2004).

To reduce the number of discrete variables, continuous-time models are adopted in (Jia and Ierapetritou, 2003, 2004; Li et al., 2002; Karuppiah et al., 2008; and Shah et al., 2009). With these methods, although the number of discrete variables is significantly reduced, the drawback is that there are nonlinear constraints in it (Pinto *et al.*, 2000). Thus, it is also difficult to solve by exact solution methods. Furthermore, it needs to know the number of discrete events that occur during the scheduling horizon. In fact, it is not known at the beginning. Thus, iterative methods are necessary to determine such a number (Floudas and Lin, 2004). Hence, it is not applicable to real-world problems either.

Notice that both discrete and continuous-time models use exact solution methods to solve the problem. With combinatorial nature (Floudas and Lin, 2004), it is sure that only small-size problem can be solved by using exact solution methods. Thus, up to now, it lacks effective techniques and software tools for the short-term scheduling of crude oil operations. To solve the problem, the short-term scheduling problem for crude oil operations is decomposed into two sub-problems in a hierarchical way as shown in Figure 1 (Wu *et al.*, 2008b, 2009, 2010a, and 2010b). A hybrid timed Petri net model is developed to describe the dynamic behavior of the system (Wu et al., 2007). With this model, at the lower level, the schedulability is analyzed in a control theory perspective and schedulability conditions are given. These schedulability conditions provide a very efficient way to find the detailed schedule that realizes a given refining schedule. Also, with the schedulability conditions as constraints at the upper level, it finds the realizable refining schedule to optimize the objectives without involving in the detailed schedule (Wu et al., 2011). In this way,

Figure 1. The architecture of short-term scheduling for crude oil operations

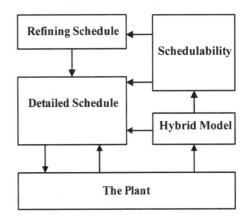

large-scale practical application problems can be solved efficiently. Based on our prior work (Wu *et al.*, 2007, 2008b, 2009, 2011), this chapter introduces this novel method for short-term scheduling of crude oil operations.

2. THE PROCESS AND ITS SHORT-TERM SCHEDULING

Generally, the processes of an oil refinery contain three stages: crude oil operations, production, and final product delivering. In terms of refinery scheduling, the most challenging problem is to schedule crude oil operations. This chapter addresses such a challenging short-term scheduling problem of crude oil operations. Before presenting the method, this section briefly introduces crude oil operations and the short-term scheduling problem.

2.1. Crude Oil Operations in Refinery

A general refinery process is illustrated in Figure 2. Crude oil is carried to the port by crude oil tankers, where crude oil is unloaded into storage tanks by the port. The crude oil in the storage tanks is transported to charging tanks in the refinery plant through a pipeline. From the charging tanks, oil is fed into distillers for distillation. The middle products from the distillers are then sent to other production units for fractionation and reaction. The products after fractionation and reaction are blended to produce the final products that are ready for delivery. Here, we address only short-term scheduling problem for crude oil operations from a tanker to distillers.

In a refinery, various types of crude oil are processed. The components are different with different types of crude oil. Crude oil can be unloaded into only an empty storage tank unless the same type of crude oil is in it. After filling a storage or charging tank, crude oil must stay in it for a certain amount of time to separate the brine, and then can be transported to charging tanks via the pipeline. We call this time delay oil Residency Time (RT). When crude oil is transported through a pipeline to charging tanks in a refinery plant, different types of crude oil may be mixed to obtain suitable components for distillation with the oil transportation. However, we do not consider the mixing here for a mixture can be treated just as a new type of crude oil. Usually, a pipeline takes tens of kilometers long with capacity of tens of thousand cubic meters. It is full of crude oil all the time and cannot be emptied. Crude oil in the pipeline should be taken as inventory and cannot be neglected. Notice that all the types of oil are transported from storage tanks to charging tanks via the pipeline. To do so, it needs to switch from one type of oil to another from time to time. There

Figure 2. The illustrative view of the refinery process

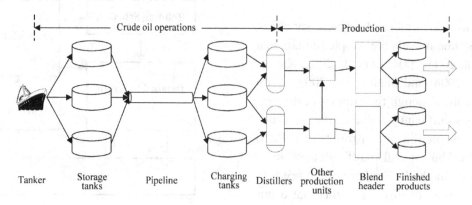

may be a number of crude oil segments in the pipeline with each segment having different types of crude oil. When crude oil is transported, the pipeline can feed one charging tank at a time.

Some crude oil types have fusion point higher than 30°C and it is in a solid state under ordinary temperature. To prevent such crude oil from being frozen in the pipeline, the pipeline and the crude oil that is being transported must be kept to be hot enough. The pipeline can be heated only by hot crude oil that is flowing through it. Thus, before high fusion point crude oil is to be transported from storage tanks to charging tanks through the pipeline, a certain amount of hot crude oil with low fusion point should be transported via the pipeline so that the pipeline can be heated first. After the pipeline is heated in this way, then, the heated high fusion point crude oil can be sent to charging tanks through the pipeline. After a parcel of high fusion point crude oil is sent to the pipeline, another parcel of crude oil with low fusion point must be sent to the pipeline so that the high fusion point crude oil can go out of the pipeline. This results in high set up cost for transporting high fusion point crude oil. Thus, in scheduling crude oil operations, when high fusion point crude oil is transported from storage tanks to charging tanks, it is desired that it can transport as much as possible, or at least an expected amount by a single set up. Often, in determining a refining schedule, a planner wants to know if a given amount of high fusion crude oil in the storage tanks can be transported to charging tanks for processing by a single set up.

Each charging tank can hold one type of crude oil at a time as well. Besides, a tank cannot receive and send oil simultaneously for both storage and charging tanks. Crude oil can also be mixed when it is charged into distillers. Notice that when a charging tank feeds a volume ξ of crude oil into a distiller in time interval (τ_1, τ_2), this tank must be dedicated to the distiller and cannot be charged in (τ_1, τ_2). Thus, if crude oil is mixed in crude oil feeding, two or more charging tanks should be

used to serve one distiller at the same time. In this way, a large number of charging tanks are required for distiller feeding. Hence, crude oil is not mixed when feeding distillers due to the limited number of charging tanks. Thus, only one tank is needed to feed one distiller at a time unless it switches from one charging tank to another tank for feeding a distiller. In refining, all distillers work concurrently and no distiller can be interrupted unless its maintenance is required.

In summary, to schedule crude oil operations includes the following resource and process constraints. The former include: 1) the limited number of storage and charging tanks and the capacity of each tank; 2) the limited flow rate of oil unloading and pipeline; and 3) the volume of various crude oil types available in storage and charging tanks, and in coming tankers. The latter include: 1) a distiller should be kept in working all the time uninterruptedly; 2) at least one charging tank should be dedicated to a distiller at any time for feeding it; 3) a tank cannot be charged and discharged simultaneously; 4) oil residency time constraint must be met; and 5) high fusion crude oil transportation constraint must be met.

2.2. Short-Term Scheduling

A crude oil operation process is composed of a series of operations. The questions are when an operation should take place, what should be done, and how it should be done. For each operation to take place, a decision should be made to answer these questions. To describe a short-term schedule, we first present the definition of an Operation Decision (OD).

Definition 2.1: $OD = (COT, \zeta, S, D, INT = (a, b))$ is defined as an operation decision, where COT = crude oil type; ζ = volume of crude oil to be unloaded from a tanker to a storage tank, or transported from a storage tank to a charging tank, or fed from a charging tank to a distiller; S = the source from which the crude oil is to be delivered; D = the destination to which the crude oil is to be delivered; and *INT* is a time interval in which a and b are the start and end time points of the operation.

The flow rate in delivering crude oil in (a, b) can be variable. However, to ease the operations, in reality, it is kept as a constant for a single operation. Thus, given volume ζ and time interval (a, b) in an *OD*, $\zeta/(b - a)$ is determined and used as its flow rate. Each *OD* is a command that transfers the system from a state to another.

There are three types of *OD*s: crude oil unloading, transportation, and feeding, denoted by *ODU*, *ODT*, and *ODF*, respectively, and their time interval is denoted as (α, β), (λ, μ) and (ω, π), respectively. For *ODU*, S is a tanker and D is a storage tank. For *ODT*, S is a storage tank, D is a charging tank, and the transportation must be conducted through a pipeline. For *ODF*, S is a charging tank and D is a distiller. We use ODF_{ki} to denote the i-th *OD* for feeding distiller k during the schedule horizon. Let $\Gamma = (\tau_s, \tau_e)$ be the schedule horizon that often lasts for a week or ten days and $g = \zeta/(\beta - \alpha)$, $f = \zeta/(\mu - \lambda)$, and $h = \zeta/(\pi - \omega)$ denote flow rates for a tanker unloading, pipeline transportation, and distiller feeding decided by *OD*s. Given the system state at τ_s, i. e., the inventory of crude oil and state of all the devices, and information of tanker arrival, the short-term scheduling problem is to find a series of *OD*s described as follows.

$$SCHD = \{ODU_1, ..., ODU_w, ODT_1, ..., ODT_z, ODF_1, ..., ODF_K\} \qquad (2.1)$$

Subject to

$$\omega_{k1} = \tau_s, \pi_{k1} = \omega_{k2}, ..., \pi_{k(i-1)} = \omega_{ki}, ..., \text{ and } \pi_{kn} = \tau_s, \text{ for } \forall k \in K \qquad (2.2)$$

as well as all the resource and process constraints mentioned before.

Constraint (2.2) requires that the schedule should cover the entire scheduling horizon and a distiller cannot be stopped.

2.3. Safeness and Schedulability

A schedule for crude oil operations may not be feasible. Consider the situation shown in Figure 3. Assume that there are one distiller and two charging tanks with the same capacity, and initially at time τ_1, tank #1 is full and #2 is empty. This system is scheduled such that at τ_1 it starts to feed the distiller by tank #1 with feeding rate f and at the same time it starts to charge tank #2 through the pipeline with charging rate f that is equal to the feeding rate. At τ_2, tank #1 is emptied and #2 is full, and #2 is scheduled to feed the distiller and it starts to charge #1 both with the same rate

Figure 3. The illustration of an infeasible schedule

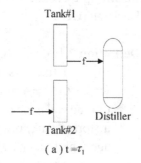

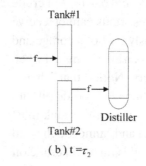

f. It can be sure that at $\tau_3 = \tau_2 + (\tau_2 - \tau_1)$ tank #2 will be emptied and tank #1 will be full. Thus, this process can be repeated until the end of the scheduling horizon if there is enough crude oil in the storage tanks. It seems that the above schedule is feasible, but, in fact, it is not due to the oil residency time constraint on #2. At τ_2, when #1 is emptied and #2 is full, the crude oil in #2 cannot be fed into the distiller immediately due to the RT constraint. It implies that during the time interval $(\tau_2, \tau_2 + \Lambda)$ there is no crude oil to be fed into the distiller, where Λ is the time delay required by RT. This is not feasible for oil refinery because a distiller cannot be interrupted.

It follows from the short-term schedule given in (2.1) that an operation decision *OD* in a schedule is, in fact, a control. In other words, a short-term schedule is composed of a series of controls. These controls act on the system sequentially. Clearly, they transfer the system from one state to another as shown in Figure 4.

Definition 2.2: If a state is reached such that one or more constraints are violated, this state is said to be an infeasible state.

For example, at time τ_2, the system shown in Figure 3 is in an infeasible state. If a state is not infeasible, it must be feasible. With the definition of infeasible state, we can define unsafe state.

Definition 2.3: Assume that, at time τ, after the action of $OD_1, OD_2, \ldots$, and OD_i, the system is transferred from state S_1 to S_i, and S_i itself is feasible. However, no matter what *OD*s

are applied after time τ, the system will enter an infeasible state. Then, state S_i is called an unsafe state.

For example, at time τ_1, the system shown in Figure 3 is in an unsafe state. If a state is not unsafe, it must be safe. As shown in Figure 4, if a short-term schedule SCHD $= (OD_1, OD_2, \ldots, OD_n)$ is obtained such that OD_1 transfer the system from S_1 to S_2, OD_2 from S_2 to S_3, $\ldots$, and OD_n from S_n to S_{n+1}, and all the states $S_1, S_2, \ldots, S_{n+1}$ are safe, the schedule is feasible. On the other hand, at any time, if the system is in a safe state, there must exist a short-term schedule such that the system is always in a safe state.

To make the short-term scheduling problem of crude oil operations tractable, the key is safeness of the system just as it does in discrete event systems. For example, when S_1 is known and safe, we can create OD_1 easily. Then, with the one-step look ahead policy, we can find S_2. If S_2 is also safe, OD_1 must be feasible. By doing so, a short-term schedule SCHD $= \{OD_1, OD_2, \ldots, OD_n\}$, which is feasible, can be found by a computationally efficient algorithm. Thus, it is very meaningful to make effort in studying the safeness (schedulability) problem of the system to present the conditions to identify a safe state set. Of course, this problem itself must be NP-hard. However, we can manage to find a set of conditions that is sufficient but neither conservative nor necessary, such that the problem is tractable. Since the most difficult part in short-term scheduling for crude oil operations is to find the *ODT*s and *ODF*s, this work focuses on analyzing the safeness of the states that are affected by *ODT*s and *ODF*s.

3. HYBRID PETRI NET MODELING

For crude oil operations, an activity in a schedule contains its start time, source and destination. These variables are discrete event variables. How-

Figure 4. State transitions under the action of a schedule

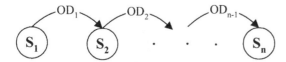

ever, the volume to be delivered in an activity is a continuous variable. Thus, crude oil operations belong to a hybrid process, and a hybrid model suitable for short-term scheduling is needed. Although there are Petri Net (PN) models for a hybrid process, for instance (Chen and Hanisch, 2001; David and Alla, 2001; Silva and Recalde, 2002), they cannot be applied in oil refining process directly because of the special constraints and requirements discussed above. For example, in their work, a pipeline is treated just as a tank, but it is not suitable to do so for the scheduling purpose. Here the segments of different oil types in a pipeline should be identified. Besides, the operation of an oil refinery process is governed by the decisions given in a short-term schedule. In other words, the process is under control. Thus, a model should describe these decisions (commands). A new hybrid Petri net model is developed for this purpose. A reader is referred as to (Zhou and Venkatesh, 1998; and Wang 1998) for the basic knowledge of Petri nets.

The PN model used here is a kind of colored-timed PN (CTPN) defined as CTPN $= (P=P_D \cup P_C,$ $T=T_D \cup T_T \cup T_C,$ $I, O, \Phi, M_0)$, where P_D and P_C are sets of discrete and continuous places; T_D, T_T, and T_C are sets of discrete, timed, and continuous transitions; I and O are input and output functions; $\Phi(p)$ and $\Phi(t)$ represent the color sets of the places in P and transitions in T; and M_0 is the initial marking. The icons are shown in Figure 5.

3.1. Device Modeling

The devices in the system are modeled as modules, and based on the modules the PN model for the overall system can be easily developed. The devices considered here are tanks (storage and charging tanks) and pipeline only. A tank is modeled by a PN shown in Figure 6 with the interpretation of places and transitions in Table 1. A token in a discrete place is a discrete token and acts just as that in ordinary PN. A token in a continuous place represents a type of materi-

als with a real number of volume, called token volume for short. A discrete transition acts just as that in ordinary PN. When a timed transition fires, it delivers a token from a place to another with a constant time delay. When a continuous transition fires, some type of material represented by a token is delivered from a place to another with a known flow rate determined by an *OD*. Whether the token is completely removed from its input place is determined by its firing duration of the transition.

In Figure 6, continuous places p_s and p_c that can hold at most one token at a time model the state of a tank. A token in them represents that there is crude oil in the tank. However, a token in p_s represents that the oil in the tank is not ready for discharging, and it is ready only if p_c has a token and p_s is empty. Continuous transitions t_1 and t_3 model the processes of filling to and discharging from a tank. The time delay in t_2 models

Figure 5. Icons in the model

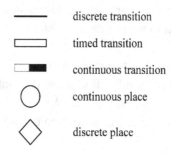

Figure 6. Petri net of a tank

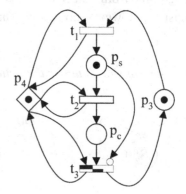

Table 1. The interpretation of places and transitions in Figure 6

Places		Transitions	
p_s	Continuous place, a token in it represents that there is oil in a tank and the oil is not ready for discharging	t_1	Continuous transition for tank charging
p_c	Continuous place, a token in it represents that there is oil in a tank and the oil is ready for discharging	t_2	Timed transition for guaranteeing oil residency time constraint
p_3	Continuous place, a token in it represents the remaining capacity of a tank	t_3	Continuous transition for tank discharging
p_4	Discrete place for controlling the charging and discharging of a tank		

the oil Residency Time (RT) constraint. Thus, when charging oil to a tank is done, a token representing a type of crude oil must stay in p_s for some time. After the time delay specified by t_2, a token with a real number of volume moves from p_s to p_c, and is ready to be discharged from a tank. Discrete place p_4 is used to control the firing of t_1, t_2, and t_3 such that the constraints on a tank can be satisfied. Because there is only one token in discrete place p_4, only one of transitions t_1 and t_3 can fire at a time. This guarantees that a tank cannot be filled and discharged at the same time. The self-loop between p_4 and t_2 together with the inhibitor arc (p_s, t_3) guarantees the RT requirement of the oil in the tank before it can be discharged. Notice that t_1, t_2, and t_3 are not immediate transitions, their firing takes time. Whenever, one of them is firing, p_4 is emptied. The volume associated with the token in continuous place p_3 models the capacity of the tank available at the current marking. Thus, the behavior of the charging and discharging of a tank is exactly described. There-

after, by $K_i(p_s), K_i(p_c)$, and $K_i(p_s, p_c)$ (or K_i in short) we mean places p_s, p_c, and the model for tank i.

The PN model in Figure 7 describes the behavior of the pipeline and Table 2 describes all the places and transitions. The behavior of a segment in the pipeline for holding one type of crude oil is described by the PN shown in Figure 7(a). Place p is a continuous one that can hold at most one token at a time. However, the volume of the token can be a positive real number. Transitions t_1 and t_2 are immediate transitions. This implies that when t_1 is enabled and fires, a token in p is removed immediately, and when t_2 is enabled and fires, a token enters p immediately.

The PN model for the pipeline that holds three different types of crude oil is shown in Figure 7(b). Continuous places p_1, p_2, and p_3 are connected by discrete transitions in a serial way to model three different crude oil segments in the pipeline. Continuous transitions t_{11} to t_{1k} and t_{O1} to t_{Ok} are used to model the behavior that crude oil flows into and out of the pipeline with a given

Figure 7. The PN model for the pipeline

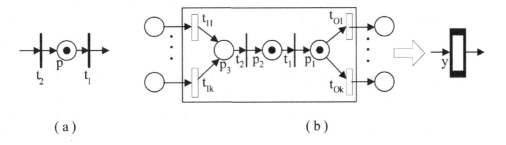

(a)   (b)

Table 2. The interpretation of places and transitions in Figure 7

Places		Transitions	
p_1, p_2, p_3	Continuous places, each one for a segment of different type of crude oil	$t_{11}, ..., t_{1k}$	Continuous transitions for pipeline charging in oil transportation
		$T_{O1}, ..., t_{Ok}$	Continuous transitions for pipeline discharging in oil transportation
		t_1, t_2	Discrete transitions for oil flowing in the pipeline
		y	The macro-transition for the pipeline

flow rate. Let $T_I = \{t_{11}, ..., t_{1k}\}$ and $T_O = \{t_{O1}, ..., t_{Ok}\}$. When one of transition in T_O is firing, the token volume in p_1 is continuously decreasing, until p_1 is emptied. Then, t_1 is enabled and fires, the token in p_2 is moved into p_1 immediately, so one transition in T_O can fire continuously. When one transition in T_I, say t_{11}, fires, a token goes into p_3 immediately. With the continuous firing of t_{11}, the token volume in p_3 increases continuously. Because we do not consider crude oil mixing here in transportation through the pipeline, only one transition in T_I and one transition in T_O can fire at a time. The number of continuous places in the model means the number of segments of crude oil of different types in the pipeline. It can be set as the largest number of crude oil segments that may occur. Since a transition in T_I and a transition in T_O should fire with the same flow rate, we model the pipeline by a macro transition y. Then, place p_1 in y can be denoted as $p_1(y)$. When y fires, it implies that one transition in T_I and one transition in T_O fire with the same rate simultaneously, or crude oil is delivered from a storage tank to the pipeline (a place in y) by a transition in t_I, and at the same time crude oil in $p_1(y)$ is being delivered into a charging tank by a transition in T_O.

3.2. The Model for the Whole System

The PN for the whole system with two storage and charging tanks, respectively, is shown in Figure 8(a). For the reason of simplicity, a simplified one is obtained and shown in Figure 8(b) by omitting the discrete places and its associated arcs, and

the inhibitor arc in a tank PN model. It should be pointed out that, by omitting these places and arcs, it does not mean that the omitted places and arcs are useless in the model. These places and arcs are used to control the correct firing of the transitions in the model. For example, p_{14} and arc (p_{1s}, y) are used to guarantee that t_{11}, t_{12}, and y cannot fire simultaneously. Even though they are omitted, we must keep such control rules in mind while achieving the purpose to make the model look structurally simple. Thereafter, the simplified one is used for schedulability analysis. Crude oil in a storage tank is discharged through the pipeline, and then transition y for the pipeline is the discharging transition for every storage tank. Similarly, y is the charging transition for every charging tank. Thus, $\{t_{11}, t_{12}, y, p_{1s}, p_{1c}, p_{13}\}$ and $\{t_{21}, t_{22}, y, p_{2s}, p_{2c}, p_{23}\}$ are for the two storage tanks, respectively, and $\{y, t_{31}, t_{32}, p_{3s}, p_{3c}, p_{33}\}$ and $\{y, t_{41}, t_{42}, p_{4s}, p_{4c}, p_{43}\}$ for the two charging tanks, respectively. Transition t_1 creates a token when a tanker arrives. If a tanker carries k types of crude oil, then k tokens are created with their respective volumes. However, a token can be moved into p_1 from t_1 only if p_1 is empty. Places p_3 and p_4 represent two distillers. It should be pointed out that the PN model shown in Figure 8 just describes the structure of the system, but not the dynamics of crude oil flow. From the definition of a short-term schedule, we know that firing of a continuous transition in the PN model must be triggered by an *OD*. Thus, the dynamics of crude oil flow in the PN model should be governed by the flow rate given in an *OD*. This can be modeled by the transition enabling and firing rules that are defined below.

We use $^\bullet t$ ($^\bullet p$) to denote the set of input places of transition t (input transitions of place p) and $t^\bullet$ ($p^\bullet$) the set of output places of t (output transitions of p). Let $V(M(p))$ denote the volume of material in p at marking M.

Definition 3.1: A discrete transition (including discrete ones in y) t is said to be enabled at marking M if $M(p) \geq 1$, $p \in {^\bullet t}$ and $M(p) = 0$, $p \in t^\bullet$. When t fires, M is changed into M' with $M'(p) = M(p) - 1$, $p \in {^\bullet t}$ and $M'(p) = M(p) + 1$, $p \in t^\bullet$.

Compare with the transition enabling and firing rules for regular PN, it requires that t's output places are empty, just like that for a finite capacity PN. Notice that, in a general PN, tokens are discrete, but the tokens in the PN model here may be discrete or continuous. However, to fire a discrete transition, all tokens in the model are treated as discrete one. By Definition 3.1, when some part of oil in p_1 in Figure 7 is discharged, there is still a token in p_1 and transition t_1 cannot fire, and thus a token in p_2 cannot go to p_1. Only when all the oil in p_1 is discharged such that p_1 is empty, then can t_1 fire and a token in p_2 can go to p_1. In this way, it guarantees that each continuous place in Figure 7 can hold one type of crude oil. A timed transition is used only in the PN for a tank

Figure 8. The PN model for the whole system: (a) the complete one; and (b) the simplified one

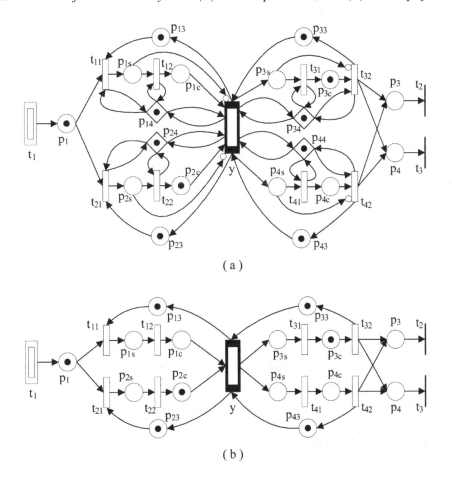

(a)

(b)

to guarantee the RT before oil in a tank can be discharged. Assume that the time associated with a timed transition is Ψ, then, the enabling and firing rule for a timed transition is defined as follows.

Definition 3.2: A timed transition t is said to be enabled at marking M if $M(p_i) \geq 1$, $p_i \in {}^\bullet t$. When t fires at time τ, M is changed into M' such that: 1) at time τ, $M'(p_i) = M(p_i) - 1$, if $p_i \in {}^\bullet t$ and $p_i \in P_D$, and $M'(p_i) = M(p_i)$ if $p_i \in {}^\bullet t$ and $p_i \in P_C$; and 2) at time $\tau + \Psi$, $M'(p_i) = M(p_i) - 1$ and $V(M'(p_i)) = 0$, $p_i \in {}^\bullet t$ and $p_i \in P_C$, and $M'(p_j) = 1$, $V(M'(p_j)) = V(M(p_j)) + V(M(p_i))$, $p_j \in t^\bullet$.

Notice that before a timed transition t fires there may be a token in its output place p_j. After the firing of t, the token in the input place p_i of t moves into p_j, these two tokens merge into one with the volume being the sum. This definition is used to describe such a fact that when a tank is neither full nor empty, this tank can still be charged. When it is charged, the volume of oil should be added. Meanwhile, the time delay associated with the timed transition guarantees the RT constraint. In this way, the behavior of a tank is precisely modeled by the PN.

Because there are multiple types of crude oil, it is necessary to distinguish them. To do so, colors are introduced into the PN model. We use φ to denote the color of crude oil and say that a token in place p representing crude oil of type i has color φ_i and the number tokens in p with color φ_i at marking M is denoted by $M(p, \varphi_i)$, and the volume for this token at marking M is denoted by $V(M(p, \varphi_i))$. When $V(M(p, \varphi_i)) = 0$, it implies that the number of tokens with color φ_i in p is zero. If a continuous transition t is firing to move crude oil type i from a place to another, we say that t is firing with color φ_i. A continuous transition must fire with a color. As discussed above, the volume of a token in p_3 in Figure 6 models the capacity of a tank available. Let Θ denote the color for such a

token. In other words, p_3 in each tank's PN model has the same color as the token in p_s and/or p_c.

Definition 3.3: A continuous transition (including t_I and t_O in y) t is said to be enabled with color φ_i at marking M if: a) $M(p, \varphi_i) \geq 1$ or $M(p, \Theta) \geq 1$, for any $p \in {}^\bullet t$; and b) $K_j(p_s) \in t^\bullet$ for some j, then $M(K_j(p_s), \varphi_i) \geq 1$ or $M(K_j(p_c), \varphi_i) \geq 1$, or $M(K_j(p_s)) = M(K_j(p_c)) = 0$ must hold.

$M(K_j(p_s), \varphi_i) \geq 1$ or $M(K_j(p_c), \varphi_i) \geq 1$ say that the oil in $K_j(p_s)$ has color φ_i that is same as that in $p \in {}^\bullet t$. This implies that if there is crude oil in a tank, only the same type of crude oil can be filled into it. However, if a tank is empty, any type of crude oil can be filled into it. When a continuous transition t is enabled and triggered by an OD, it can then fire. This firing must be associated with a flow rate given in OD, i.e., the flow of crude oil is governed by the flow rate. The transition firing rules below describe this dynamics. We assume that t's firing with color φ_i begins at time τ_1, ends at time τ_2, $\tau \in (\tau_1, \tau_2)$, and the flow rate is f. Then, the marking changes as follows. At τ_1, if $p \in {}^\bullet t$ and p is a discrete place

$$M'(p) = M(p) - 1 \tag{3.1}$$

At τ_2, if $p \in t^\bullet$ and p is a discrete place

$$M'(p) = M(p) + 1 \tag{3.2}$$

At $\tau \in (\tau_1, \tau_2)$, if p is t's input continuous place, and there is a token with color φ_i

$$V(M'(p, \varphi_i)) = V(M(p, \varphi_i)) - (\tau - \tau_1)f \tag{3.3}$$

If p is t's input continuous place, and there is a token with color Θ

$$V(M'(p, \Theta)) = V(M(p, \Theta)) - (\tau - \tau_1)f \tag{3.4}$$

If p is t's output continuous place, and there is a token with color φ_i

$$V(M'(p, \varphi_i)) = V(M(p, \varphi_i)) + (\tau - \tau_1)f \qquad (3.5)$$

Because any firing of a continuous transition leads to a crude oil operation determined by an *OD*, expressions (3.1) through (3.5) describe the dynamics of crude oil flow in the PN model for the system. Up to now, we have completed the modeling of the system. It should be pointed out that only one of the output transitions of p_1 in Figure 8 and one of input transitions of a place representing a distiller can fire at a time. Transition y can fire with only one input and one output transition. Further, the starting time and duration of a transition firing should be determined by a control policy. Thus, to run the above PN model, a control policy is necessary and is discussed in the next section.

4. SCHEDULABILITY AND DETAILED SCHEDULING FOR A ONE DISTILLER SYSTEM

With the PN model developed for crude oil operations above, schedulability analysis can be carried out. It is shown that schedulability depends on the number of storage and charging tanks and their capacity, the crude oil inventory at the beginning of the scheduling horizon, the maximal transportation flow rate of the pipeline, and the feeding rate to distillers. Assuming that there is always enough crude oil in the storage tanks to be processed, the schedulability is independent of the number of storage tanks and their capacity.

Definition 4.1: A system of crude oil operations with initial state S_0 is said to be schedulable if there exists a feasible short-term schedule for a horizon $\Gamma = (0, \infty)$.

Notice that the key here is the schedule horizon $\Gamma = (0, \infty)$, because the operation of distillers cannot be interrupted. The existence of a feasible short-term schedule $\text{SCHD}_1 = \{OD_1, OD_2, ..., OD_n\}$ for a schedule horizon $(0, a)$ does not guarantee that a feasible short-term schedule $\text{SCHD}_2 = \{OD_1, OD_2, ..., OD_n, OD_{n+1}, ..., OD_{n+k}\}$ with $\text{SCHD}_1 \subset \text{SCHD}_2$ for schedule horizon $(0, b)$, with $b > a$, can be found.

Definition 4.2: A state S of a system of crude oil operations is said to be safe if, with S as initial state, the system is schedulable.

Therefore, with Definitions 4.1 and 4.2, to analyze the schedulability of crude oil operations is to analyze the safeness of the system. The analysis is carried out with a different number of distillers in the system. First, we consider the situation with one distiller. Let f_{ds}, f_{pmax}, and Ψ denote the feeding rate to the distiller, the maximal oil transportation rate of the pipeline, and the residency time for charging tanks, respectively.

Theorem 4.1: Assume that there is a single distiller with feeding rate f_{ds}, the maximal crude oil transportation rate of the pipeline is $f_{pmax} > f_{ds}$, and $\Psi > 0$. If there is only one charging tank in the plant, the system is not schedulable.

Proof: It is obvious and omitted.

This situation can be modeled and well explained by the PN shown in Figure 9 where $K(p_s, p_c)$ and p_1 for the charging tank and distiller, respectively. In fact, in this situation, even if $f_{pmax} = \infty$, the system is not schedulable. Assume that $f_{pmax} = \infty$, at time τ_1, $M(p_s) = 1$ and $V(M(p_s)) = \zeta$. Thus, transition t_1 is enabled and can fire. It takes Ψ time units for t_1 to complete its firing, or only at $\tau_2 = \tau_1 + \Psi$, the token in p_s can enter p_c. This implies that in the time interval (τ_1, τ_2) with $\tau_2 >$

τ_1, the operation of the distiller is interrupted, or there is no feasible short-term schedule.

It shows that RT is one of the causes of non-schedulability. When $\Psi = 0$ and $f_{pmax} = \infty$, the system is schedulable. However, if $f_{pmax} < \infty$ the system is not schedulable even if $\Psi = 0$, for, in this case, it takes time to fill p_s. This shows that f_{pmax} affects the schedulability of a system. Now, we consider the situation with two charging tanks. Let $\xi = \dfrac{\Psi \times f_{p\,max} \times f_{ds}}{f_{p\,max} - f_{ds}}$ and φ is the color of crude oil type if only one type of oil is considered. We use p_{is} and p_{ic} in the PN model for charging tank CTK_i and p_i for distiller i.

Theorem 4.2: Assume that: 1) there is a single distiller with feeding rate f_{ds} in the refinery plant; 2) the maximal crude oil transportation rate of the pipeline is $f_{pmax} > f_{ds}$; 3) there are two charging tanks CTK_1 and CTK_2 in the plant with capacity greater than or equal to ξ; 4) one type of crude oil is to be processed; and 5) initially there is crude oil ready for charging with volume ζ in tank CTK_1, and CTK_2 is empty. Then, the system is schedulable if and only if: $\zeta \geq \xi$ (4.1)

Proof: Sufficiency. This situation can be modeled by the PN shown in Figure 10. By assumption, at the beginning (time τ_0), we have $M(p_{1c}) = 1$ and $V(M(p_{1c}, \varphi)) = \zeta$ as shown in Figure 10(a). Then, t_{12} can fire with rate f_{ds} for feeding the distiller. Because it processes one type of crude oil, there is enough

crude oil to fill p_{2s}. At time $\tau_1 = \tau_0 + \zeta/f_{pmax}$, $M(p_{2s}) = M(p_{1c}) = 1$, $V(M(p_{2s}, \varphi)) = \zeta$, and $V(M(p_{1c}, \varphi)) = \zeta - (\tau_1 - \tau_0) \times f_{ds} > 0$ as shown in Figure 10(b). At time $\tau_2 = \tau_0 + \zeta/f_{ds}$, $M(p_{1c}) = 0$ and $V(M(p_{1c})) = 0$. This time, we have

$$\tau_2 - \tau_1 = \frac{\varsigma}{f_{ds}} - \frac{\varsigma}{f_{p\,max}} = \frac{f_{p\,max} - f_{ds}}{f_{p\,max} \times f_{ds}} \times \varsigma \geq$$

$$\frac{f_{p\,max} - f_{ds}}{f_{p\,max} \times f_{ds}} \times \frac{\Psi \times f_{p\,max} \times f_{ds}}{f_{p\,max} - f_{ds}} = \Psi, \quad \text{or we}$$

have $M(p_{2c}) = 1$ and $V(M(p_{2c}, \varphi)) = \zeta$ as shown in Figure 10(c). At this marking, t_{22} can fire with rate f_{ds} and the distiller can continue its operation without interruption. Meanwhile, p_{1s} can be charged by firing y with rate f_{pmax}. By assumption, it processes one type of crude oil and there is enough oil in the storage tanks to be processed, this process can be repeated infinitely, or there exists a feasible short-term schedule for a horizon $(0, \infty)$.

Necessity: Assume that $\zeta < \xi$. If y fires with rate f_{pmax} to fill p_{2s} from τ_0 to $\tau_1 = \tau_0 + \zeta/f_{pmax}$ such that $M(p_{2s}) = 1$ and $V(M(p_{2s}, \varphi)) = \zeta$, at time $\tau_2 = \tau_0 + \zeta/f_{ds}$, marking M is reached such that $M(p_{1c}) = 0$ and $V(M(p_{1c})) = 0$, and $\tau_2 - \tau_1 = \dfrac{\varsigma}{f_{ds}} - \dfrac{\varsigma}{f_{p\,max}} =$

$$\frac{f_{p\,max} - f_{ds}}{f_{p\,max} \times f_{ds}} \times \varsigma \leq \qquad \frac{f_{p\,max} - f_{ds}}{f_{p\,max} \times f_{ds}} \times \xi =$$

$$\frac{f_{p\,max} - f_{ds}}{f_{p\,max} \times f_{ds}} \times \frac{\Psi \times f_{p\,max} \times f_{ds}}{f_{p\,max} - f_{ds}} = \Psi. \text{ This means}$$

Figure 9. The PN model for the proof of Theorem 4.1

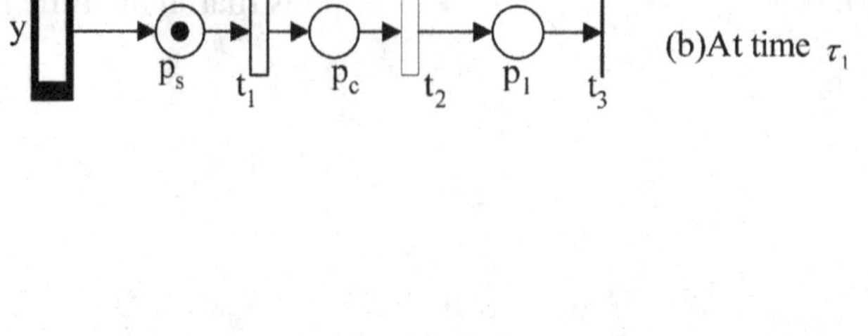

(a) At time τ_0

(b) At time τ_1

Figure 10. The PN model for the proof of Theorem 4.2

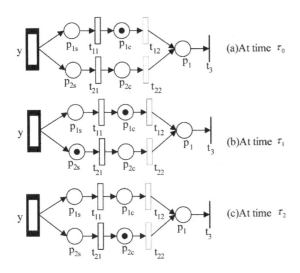

that, at time τ_2, $M(p_{2c}) = 0$, an infeasible marking. It may fire y to fill p_{2s} from τ_0 to τ_1 such that $\tau_1 = \tau_0 + V/f_{ds} - \Psi$. Thus, at $\tau_2 = \tau_0 + \zeta/f_{ds}$, the system reaches a marking M such that $M(p_{1c}) = 0$, $V(M(p_{1c})) = 0$, $M(p_{2c}) = 1$, and $V(M(p_{2c}, \varphi)) = \zeta_1$, a feasible marking. However, $\zeta_1 < \zeta$ must hold. Then, the next time, CTK_1 must be filled with volume ζ_2. In this way, at the k-th time, it fills with volume ζ_k, and we have $\zeta > \zeta_1 > \zeta_2 > \ldots > \zeta_k > \ldots$. Thus, $\zeta_k \to 0$ when $k \to \infty$. This implies that, at time $\tau = \infty$, there is no crude oil to feed the distiller. According to Definition 4.1, in this case, the system is not schedulable.

When there are two charging tanks and one distiller with known f_{pmax} and f_{ds}, this theorem presents the necessary crude oil inventory in charging tanks that is ready for feeding. It gives when it can begin to feed a distiller. It should be noticed that if there is oil in CTK_2 at time τ_0, it takes less time to fill CTK_2 to ζ, or the system is schedulable. However, if the difference $f_{pmax} - f_{ds}$ is small, according to (4.1), ζ may be too large to be realized, for it requires charging tanks to have very large capacity and high crude oil inventory.

Theorem 4.3: Assume that: 1) there is a single distiller with feeding rate f_{ds} in the refinery

plant, the maximal crude oil transportation rate of the pipeline is $f_{pmax} > f_{ds}$; 2) there are only two charging tanks CTK_1 and CTK_2 with capacity ξ_1 and ξ_2, respectively, and $\xi_1 > \xi_2 > \Psi \times f_{ds} = \alpha$; 3) one type of crude oil is to be processed; and 4) there is oil with volume $\zeta = \xi_2$ ready to be fed in one of the charging tanks. Then, it is schedulable if and only if

$$f_{p\max} \geq \frac{\xi_2}{\xi_2 - \Psi \times f_{ds}} \times f_{ds} \qquad (4.2)$$

Proof: Sufficiency. Assume that initially (at time τ_0) there is crude oil with volume $\zeta = \xi_2$ in CTK_1 ready for feeding and CTK_2 is empty. Similar to the proof of Theorem 4.1, we have 1) at time τ_0, $M(p_{1c}) = 1$ and $V(M(p_{1c}, \varphi)) = \xi_2$, and t_{12} can fire with rate f_{ds}; 2) at time $\tau_1 = \tau_0 + \xi_2/f_{pmax}$, $M(p_{2s}) = M(p_{1c}) = 1$, $V(M(p_{2s}, \varphi)) = \xi_2$, and $V(M(p_{1c}, \varphi)) = \xi_2 - (\tau_2 - \tau_1) \times f_{ds} > 0$, t_{12} can continue its firing; 3) At time $\tau_2 = \tau_0 + \xi_2/f_{ds}$, $M(p_{1c}) = 0$, $V(M(p_{1c}, \varphi)) = 0$, $M(p_{2s}) = 0$, $M(p_{2c}) = 1$, and $V(M(p_{2c}, \varphi)) = \xi_2$ for $\tau_2 - \tau_1 = \dfrac{\xi_2}{f_{ds}} - \dfrac{\xi_2}{f_{p\max}} \geq \dfrac{\xi_2}{f_{ds}} -$

$$\frac{\xi_2}{\xi_2 \times f_{ds} / (\xi_2 - t_r \times f_{ds})} = \Psi.$$ This implies

that, at τ_2, t_{22} can fire, or the operation of the distiller is not interrupted, or it is schedulable.

Necessity: Assume that

$$f_{p\max} < \frac{\xi_2}{\xi_2 - t_r \times f_{ds}} \times f_{ds}.$$

If transition y fires with rate f_{pmax} to fill p_{2s} from τ_0 to $\tau_1 = \tau_0 + \zeta/f_{pmax}$ such that $M(p_{2s}) = 1$ and $V(M(p_{2s}, \varphi)) = \xi_2$, at time $\tau_2 = \tau_0 + \zeta/f_{ds}$ the system reaches a marking such that $M(p_{1c}) = 0$ and $V(M(p_{1c})) = 0$, and $\tau_2 - \tau_1 = \dfrac{\xi_2}{f_{ds}} - \dfrac{\xi_2}{f_{p\max}} \leq \dfrac{\xi_2}{f_{ds}} -$

$\dfrac{\xi_2}{\xi_2 \times f_{ds} / (\xi_2 - \Psi \times f_{ds})} = \Psi$. This means that, at time τ_2, $M(p_{2c}) = 0$, an infeasible marking. It may fire y to fill p_{2s} from τ_0 to τ_1 such that $\tau_1 = \tau_0 + \xi_2/f_{ds} - \Psi$. Thus, at $\tau_2 = \tau_0 + \zeta/f_{ds}$, the system reaches a marking such that $M(p_{1c}) = 0$, $V(M(p_{1c})) = 0$, $M(p_{2c}) = 1$, and $V(M(p_{2c}, \varphi)) = \zeta_1$, a feasible marking. However, $\zeta_1 < \xi_2$ must hold. Then, next time, CTK_1 must be filled with volume ζ_2. In this way, at the k-th time, it fills with volume ζ_k, and we have $\xi_2 > \zeta_1 > \zeta_2 > \ldots > \zeta_k > \ldots$. Thus, $\zeta_k \to 0$ when $k \to \infty$. This implies that, at time $\tau = \infty$, there is no crude oil to feed the distiller. According to Definition 4.1, in this case, the system is not schedulable.

Theorem 4.3 shows that, with f_{ds} given, if we want to reduce the capacity requirement of charging tanks and initial crude oil inventory ready for feeding in charging tanks, the maximal pipeline transportation rate f_{pmax} must be high enough. From Theorems 4.2 and 4.3, we have the following corollaries.

Corollary 4.1: Assume that: 1) there is a single distiller with feeding rate f_{ds} in the refinery plant, the maximal crude oil transportation rate of the pipeline is $f_{pmax} > f_{ds}$; 2) there are only two charging tanks CTK_1 and CTK_2 with capacity ξ_1 and ξ_2, respectively; 3) one type of crude oil is processed; and 4) at time τ_0, CTK_1 is feeding the distiller with volume $\zeta_1 \geq \Psi \times f_{ds} = \alpha$ remaining and CTK_2 is being charged with ζ_2 in it. Then, it is schedulable

if $\min\{\xi_1, \xi_2, \zeta_2 + \left(\dfrac{\varsigma_1}{f_{ds}} - \Psi\right) \times f_{p\max}\} = \zeta \geq$

$\dfrac{\Psi \times f_{p\max} \times f_{ds}}{f_{p\max} - f_{ds}}$.

Proof: Assume that $\zeta_2 + \left(\dfrac{\varsigma_1}{f_{ds}} - \Psi\right) \times f_{p\max} = \zeta$,

$\xi_1 \geq \zeta$ and $\xi_2 \geq \zeta$ hold. Then, $V(M(p_{2c}, \varphi)) = \zeta$ must hold when the PN shown in Figure 10 reaches a marking such that $M(p_{1c}) = 0$,

$M(p_{2c}) = 1$. It follows from Theorem 4.2 that the system is schedulable. If $\xi_1 = \zeta$ or $\xi_2 = \zeta$, at $\tau_1 < \tau_0 + \zeta_1/f_{ds} - \Psi$, $M(p_{1c}) = 1$, $V(M(p_{1c})) > 0$, $M(p_{2s}) = 1$, and $V(M(p_{2s}, \varphi)) = \zeta$. Hence, $M(p_{2c}) = 1$ and $V(M(p_{2c}, \varphi)) = \zeta$ must hold, when $M(p_{1c}) = 0$, $V(M(p_{1c})) = 0$ at $\tau_2 = \tau_0 + \zeta_1/f_{ds}$. In other words, the system is schedulable.

Notice that for all the cases discussed above it is required that $f_{pmax} > f_{ds}$, hence we have the following corollary immediately.

Corollary 4.2: If there are only two charging tanks for feeding one distiller in the plant and $f_{pmax} \leq f_{ds}$, the system is not schedulable.

Assume that $f_{pmax} > f_{ds}$ and

let $\xi = \dfrac{\Psi \times f_{p\max} \times f_{ds}}{f_{p\max} - f_{ds}}$,

then we have the following corollary.

Corollary 4.3: If there are only two charging tanks with capacity $\xi_1 \geq \xi$ and $\xi_2 \geq \xi$ in the plant for feeding one distiller and there is a volume $\zeta < \xi$ remaining for one type of crude oil in the storage tanks, then this volume of oil cannot be refined unless it is mixed with other types of oil.

Proof: Let φ_1 denote the color for the crude oil type being processed, and φ_2 be the color for the crude oil type to be processed next. Consider the PN model shown in Figure 10 and assume, without loss of generality, that, at time τ_0, marking M is reached such that $M(p_{1c}) = 1$, $V(M(p_{1c}, \varphi_1)) = \xi$, $M(p_{2s}) = 0$, $M(p_{2c}) = 0$, and it begins to fire t_{12} for feeding p_1 and y with color φ_1 for charging p_{2s}. Then, at time $\tau_1 = \tau_0 + \zeta/f_{pmax}$, we have $M(p_{1c}) = 1$, $M(p_{2s}) = 1$, $V(M(p_{2s}, \varphi_1)) = \zeta < \xi$, $M(p_{2c}) = 0$, and there is no more oil with color φ_1 to fill p_{2s}, and thus y must stop firing. At time $\tau_2 = \tau_0 + \xi/f_{ds}$ with $\tau_2 - \tau_1 > \Psi$, $M(p_{1c}) = 0$,

$M(p_{2s}) = 0$, $M(p_{2c}) = 1$, $V(M(p_{2c}, \varphi_1)) = \zeta$ $< \xi$. At this marking, t_{22} can fire to feed p_1 and y can fire with color φ_2 to charge p_{1s}. However, it follows from Theorem 4.2 that the system is not schedulable.

Corollary 4.3 shows that if there are only two charging tanks for feeding one distiller, some crude oil must be mixed with other type of crude oil, and otherwise the system is not schedulable. This is undesirable. On one hand, crude oil mixing may degrade one type of oil, leading to a loss. On the other hand, a mixture of two types of crude oil should be treated as a new type of crude oil, which increases the number of switches from one type to another type in distillation, leading to another loss. In distillation, the operation condition is determined by the components of the crude oil to be processed. When two types of crude oil are mixed, the components are changed and it should be treated as a new type.

The results obtained above present the safe and unsafe states when there are two charging tanks for feeding one distiller. It specifies the relation among initial crude oil inventory in charging tanks, the pipeline transportation rate, distiller feeding rate, and the charging tank capacity. It is also seen that, with two charging tanks, to make the system safe there are restrictions on it. Next, consider three charging tanks to feed one distiller.

Theorem 4.4: Assume that: 1) there is a single distiller with feeding rate f_{ds} in the refinery plant, the maximal crude oil transportation rate of the pipeline is $f_{pmax} = f_{ds}$; 2) there are three charging tanks $CTK_{1\text{-}3}$ with capacity $\xi_{1\text{-}3}$ ($\xi_i \geq 2\alpha$); 3) one type of crude oil is to be processed; and 4) initially there is crude oil $\zeta_1 \geq 2\alpha$ available for feeding the distiller in CTK_1 and the other tanks are empty. Then, the system is schedulable.

Proof: The PN model for this case is shown in Figure 11. Then, by assumption, initially at marking M_0 (time τ_0) we have $M_0(p_{1c}) = 1$ and $M_0(p_{1s}) = M_0(p_{2s}) = M_0(p_{2c}) = M_0(p_{3s})$ $= M_0(p_{3c}) = 0$, and $V(M_0(p_{1c}, \varphi)) = 2\alpha$, and $V(M_0(p_{1s})) = V(M_0(p_{2s})) = V(M_0(p_{2c})) = V(M_0(p_{3s})) = V(M_0(p_{3c})) = 0$. This time we fire t_{12} and y to feed p_1 and charge p_{2s} by rate f_{ds}, respectively. At time $\tau_1 = \tau_0 + \Psi$, M_1 is reached such that $M_1(p_{1c}) = M_1(p_{2s}) = 1$ and $V(M_1(p_{1c}, \varphi)) = V(M_1(p_{2s}, \varphi)) = \alpha$. At this time, t_{12} continues its firing and the firing of y switches to charge p_{3s}, and meanwhile t_{21} starts to fire. Then, at time $\tau_2 = \tau_0 + 2\Psi$, M_2 is reached such that p_{1c} is emptied, $M_2(p_{2c}) = M_2(p_{3s}) = 1$, and $V(M_2(p_{2c}, \varphi)) = V(M_2(p_{3s}, \varphi)) = \alpha$. At M_2, t_{22} is fired to feed p_1 and y is fired to charge p_{1s}, t_{31} starts to fire. At time $\tau_3 = \tau_0 + 3\Psi$, M_3 is reached such that p_{2c} is emptied, $M_3(p_{3c}) = M_3(p_{1s})$ $= 1$, and $V(M_3(p_{3c}, \varphi)) = V(M_3(p_{1s}, \varphi)) = \alpha$. By assumption, only one type of crude oil

Figure 11. The PN model for three charging tanks and one distiller

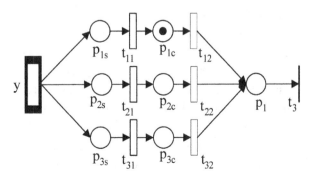

is to be processed and there is always crude oil in the storage tanks. Thus, this process can be repeated continuously, and this forms a short-term schedule. In other words, the system is schedulable.

In the proof, we assume that only one type of crude oil is to be processed and there is always crude oil in the storage tanks. The assumption that only one type of crude oil is to be processed will be relaxed late. While the assumption that there is always crude oil in the storage tanks is guaranteed by the distiller refining schedule discussed late. Notice that, with three charging tanks, the system is schedulable under assumption $f_{pmax} = f_{ds}$. By $f_{pmax} = f_{ds}$, it means that the system reaches its maximal production rate. It follows from Theorem 4.3 that when $f_{pmax} = f_{ds}$, the condition that there are three charging tanks is necessary. This is important that the production rate in a refinery is often required to run near the maximal rate. There is no question that if $f_{pmax} > f_{ds}$ the system is schedulable. From Theorem 4.4, we have the following corollary immediately.

Corollary 4.4: In Theorem 4.4, if the volume of oil in CTK_1 $\zeta_1 \geq \alpha$, the volume of oil in CTK_2 $\zeta_2 \geq \alpha$, the oil in one of the tanks CTK_1 and CTK_2 is ready for feeding, and the other conditions are unchanged, the system is schedulable.

Corollary 4.4 shows that, with three charging tanks, to make the system safe, at any state there must be at least oil volume 2α in the charging tanks. It should be pointed out that it is easy to show that such a condition is also necessary. Often Ψ lasts for several hours only, so $\alpha = \Psi \times f_{ds}$ is not huge. This implies that the condition given in Corollary 4.4 is easy to be satisfied. Further, the volume of oil to be charged into a charging tank is 2α. In other words, it requires capacity 2α for each charging tank, a small capacity requirement. Furthermore, we have the following result.

Theorem 4.5: Assume that: 1) there is a single distiller with feeding rate f_{ds} in the refinery plant, and the maximal crude oil transportation rate of the pipeline is $f_{pmax} = f_{ds}$; 2) there are three charging tanks CTK_{1-3} with capacity ξ_{1-3} ($\xi_i \geq 3\alpha$); 3) initially there is crude oil $\zeta_1 \geq 3\alpha$ available for feeding the distiller from CTK_1 and the other tanks are empty, and 4) there is volume $\zeta_0 < \alpha$ of crude oil type same to that in CTK_1 remaining in the storage tanks and then it should switch to process another type of crude oil. Then, the system is schedulable and ζ_0 can be used up without mixing with other type of crude oil.

Proof: Assume that initially the volume of crude oil in CTK_1 is 3α. Consider the PN model shown in Figure 11. Initially, at time τ_0, $M_0(p_{1c}) = 1$ and $V(M_0(p_{1c}, \varphi_1)) = 3\alpha$, and all other places are empty. At this time, transition t_{12} fires to feed p_1 and meanwhile y fires with color φ_1 to charge p_{2s} with volume ζ_0. At time $\tau_1 = \tau_0 + \zeta_0/f_{pmax}$, M_1 is reached such that $M_1(p_{1c}) = M_1(p_{2s}) = 1$, $V(M_1(p_{1c}, \varphi_1)) = 3\alpha - \zeta_0 > 2\alpha$, and $V(M_1(p_{2s}, \varphi_1)) = \zeta_0$. At M_1, t_{12} continues firing to feed p_1, the firing of y switches to charge p_{3s} with color φ_2, and t_{21} fires. At $\tau_2 = \tau_1 + 2\Psi$, M_2 is reached such that $M_2(p_{1c}) = M_2(p_{2c}) = M_2(p_{3s}) = 1$, $V(M_2(p_{1c}, \varphi_1)) = \alpha - \zeta_0 > 0$, $V(M_2(p_{2c}, \varphi_1)) = \zeta_0$, and $V(M_2(p_{3s}, \varphi_2)) = 2\alpha$. At M_2, t_{12} continues firing to feed p_1, we stop the firing of y, and meanwhile t_{31} fires. At $\tau_3 = \tau_2 + (\alpha - \zeta_0)/f_{ds}$, M_3 is reached such that p_{1c} is emptied, and we fire t_{22} to feed p_1. At $\tau_4 = \tau_2 + \Psi$, M_4 is reached such that p_{2c} is emptied, $M_4(p_{3c}) = 1$, and $V(M_4(p_{3c}, \varphi_2)) = 2\alpha$. At M_4, t_{32} fires to feed p_1 and y fires to charge p_{1s}. Then, it follows from Theorem 4.4 that the system is schedulable and the refining process can continue. In this way, the oil $\zeta_0 < \alpha$ in p_{2c} is used up without mixed with other oil type.

Often, an oil refinery can process multiple types of crude oil. Thus, a distiller needs to switch from processing one type of crude oil to another type from time to time, which can lead to a small volume $\zeta_0 < \alpha$ of some type of crude oil. It is highly desirable that such a small volume can be processed without being mixed with other type of crude oil, because an undesired mix of crude oil often results in loss. It follows from Theorem 4.5 that such a small volume can be processed without being mixed with other type of crude oil if there are three charging tanks. It should also be pointed out that after processing such a small volume of crude oil, the volume of crude oil in the charging tanks is reduced. To overcome this problem, we can schedule the system such that f_{ds} is slightly less than f_{pmax}.

Theorem 4.6: Assume that: 1) there is a single distiller with feeding rate f_{ds} in the refinery plant, and the maximal crude oil transportation rate of the pipeline is $f_{pmax} > f_{ds}$; 2) there are three charging tanks $CTK_{1\text{-}3}$ with capacity $\xi_{1\text{-}3}$ ($\xi_i \geq 2\alpha$); 3) one type of crude oil is to be processed; and 4) initially there is crude

oil $\zeta_1 \geq \dfrac{\alpha \times \left(f_{p\max} + f_{ds}\right)}{f_{p\max}}$ available for feed-

ing the distiller in CTK_1 and the other tanks are empty. Then, the system is schedulable.

Proof: Consider the PN model shown in Figure 11. By assumption, at time τ_0 (marking M_0), we have $M_0(p_{1c}) = 1$, $V(M_0(p_{1c}, \varphi)) = \dfrac{\alpha \times \left(f_{p\max} + f_{ds}\right)}{f_{p\max}}$, and all other places are empty. At this marking, t_{12} fires to feed the distiller and y fires to charge p_{2s}. At time $\tau_1 = \tau_0 + \alpha/f_{pmax}$, y switches to charge p_{3s} and marking M_1 is reached such that $M_1(p_{1c}) = 1$, $M_1(p_{2s}) = 1$, and $V(M_1(p_{2s}, \varphi)) = \alpha$. At this marking, t_{21} fires. At time $\tau_2 = \tau_0 + \dfrac{\varsigma_1}{f_{ds}}$, we

have $\tau_2 - \tau_1 = \dfrac{\varsigma_1}{f_{ds}} - \dfrac{\alpha}{f_{p\max}} \geq$

$\dfrac{\alpha \times \left(f_{p\max} + f_{ds}\right)}{f_{p\max} \times f_{ds}} - \dfrac{\alpha}{f_{p\max}} = \Psi$. Thus, mark-

ing M_2 is reached such that $M_2(p_{1c}) = 0$, $M_2(p_{2c}) = 1$, $V(M_2(p_{2c}, \varphi)) = \alpha$, $M_2(p_{3s}) = 1$, and $V(M_2(p_{3s}, \varphi)) = f_{p\max} \times t_r > \alpha$. With M_2 as an initial state, then, it follows from Corollary 4.4, the system is schedulable.

Theorem 4.6 shows that if $f_{pmax} > f_{ds}$, it requires less crude oil in the charging tanks and the volume of oil in the charging tanks can increase continuously. Notice that, in practice, the capacity of a charging tank is much greater than 3α. Thus, if there are three charging tanks with one distiller, we can schedule the system such that f_{ds} is slightly less than f_{pmax} and the amount of oil in the charging tanks can fill two tanks to capacity. When it switches to process from one type of oil to another, it needs to process a small amount of oil that is less than α, the total volume of crude oil in the charging tanks is reduced. However, because $f_{pmax} > f_{ds}$, two tanks will be full again after some time. In this way, the system remains always in a safe state and the production rate is near the maximal one. Clearly, if there are four charging tanks for a single distiller the system is schedulable.

In summary, if there is only one distiller with two charging tanks, to guarantee the system to be in safe state, f_{pmax} and the tank capacity must be large enough, and initially there is enough oil in the tanks. Even though when it needs to switch from processing one type of crude oil to another and there is a small amount of the first type oil, such a small amount of oil should be processed by mixing with another type of oil. This is undesirable. However, with three or more charging tanks usable, it is easy to keep the system always in a safe state.

The schedulability conditions given above guarantee the safeness of the system. Thus, by the conditions, at a safe state, one can create an *OD* such that, after the *OD* is executed, the system is still safe. Then, based on the new state another feasible *OD* can be created. In this way, it can create the *OD*s one by one such that the system is always in the safe state. These *OD*s form a feasible detailed schedule. It implies that, by the schedulability analysis, an effective method to derive a detailed schedule is obtained.

5. SCHEDULABILITY AND DETAILED SCHEDULING FOR SYSTEM WITH MULTIPLE DISTILLERS

To analyze the schedulability problem for a multiple-distiller system, we first discuss the problem for a two-distiller system. The results are then generalized.

5.1. Two-Distiller System

It follows from the discussion for one distiller situation that the schedulability is greatly dependent on the number of charging tanks in the system. Thus, the problem is discussed based on the number of charging tanks. From the prior section, the system must not be schedulable if there are only two charging tanks. Hence, we consider cases with three or more charging tanks.

5.1.1. Case 1: Three Charging Tanks

Consider the safeness condition when there are three charging tanks. Let f_{ds1} and f_{ds2} denote the feeding rate to distiller DS_1 with crude oil of type #1 and distiller DS_2 with crude oil of type #2, and

$\alpha_1 = \Psi \times f_{ds1}$ and $\alpha_2 = \Psi \times f_{ds2}$, respectively. In the PN model shown in Figure 12, for $i = 1, 2$, and 3, $\{p_{is}, p_{ic}, t_{id}, t_i\}$ is for charging tank CTK_i, and p_i is for distiller DS_i.

Theorem 5.1: Assume that: 1) there are three charging tanks CTK_{1-3} for feeding two distillers DS_1 and DS_2; and 2) $f_{pmax} = f_{ds1} + f_{ds2}$. Then, the system is not schedulable.

Proof: Without loss of generality, assume that, initially, there is crude oil of type #1 (color φ_1) with volume $\zeta_1 > \alpha_1$ in tank CTK_1 and crude oil of type #2 (color φ_2) with volume $\zeta_2 > \alpha_2$ in CTK_3 ready for feeding, and $\zeta_1/f_{ds1} < \zeta_2/f_{ds2}$. This implies that, for the PN model shown in Figure 12, at the initial marking M_0 (time τ_0) we have $M_0(p_{1c}) = M_0(p_{3c}) = 1$, $V(M_0(p_{1c}, \varphi_1)) = \zeta_1$, and $V(M_0(p_{3c}, \varphi_2)) = \zeta_2$. Thus, transitions t_1 and t_3 can fire with colors φ_1 and φ_2 to feed p_1 (DS_1) and p_2 (DS_2), respectively. Because $\zeta_1/f_{ds1} < \zeta_2/f_{ds2}$, at this marking, we fire y with color φ_1 to charge p_{2s}. To guarantee the feasibility, at time $\tau_1 = \tau_0 + (\zeta_1 - \alpha_1)/f_{ds1}$, transition y must stop firing and $M_1(p_{2s}) = 1$. At time $\tau_2 = \tau_0 + \zeta_1/f_{ds1}$, marking M_1 is reached such that $M_1(p_{1c}) = 0$ and $M_1(p_{2c}) = 1$. Hence, t_2 can fire with color φ_1 to feed p_1 and y can fire with color φ_2 to p_{1s}. During (τ_1, τ_2), p_{1c}, p_{2s} and p_{3c} are not empty, y cannot fire, leading

Figure 12. The PN model with three charging tanks for feeding two distillers

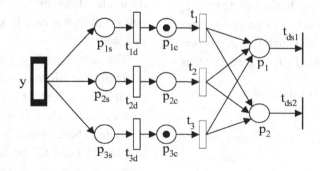

to the decrease of crude oil in the charging tanks by $(\tau_2 - \tau_1) \times f_{pmax}$. Similarly, before ζ_2 in p_{3c} is used up, y should stop firing for charging p_{3s}, leading to a reduction of crude oil in the charging tanks. In this way, the crude oil in the charging tanks will be less and less, until an infeasible sate is reached. This implies the system is not schedulable.

The key here is that to meet the oil residency time requirement, y must stop firing for some time because of the limited number of charging tanks, and not large enough f_{pmax}. Hence, if f_{pmax} is large enough, the system may be schedulable as shown next.

Theorem 5.2: Assume that: 1) there are two distillers DS_1 and DS_2 with $f_{ds1} = f_{ds2} = f_{ds}$ and three charging tanks CTK_{1-3} with capacity $\xi_1 \geq 4\alpha$, $\xi_2 \geq 4\alpha$, and $\xi_3 \geq 4\alpha$ ($\alpha = \Psi \times f_{ds}$); 2) initially, there is oil volume 4α of type 1 in CTK_1, volume 2α of type 2 in CTK_2 ready for feeding, and CTK_3 is empty, and 3) $f_{pmax} \geq 4f_{ds}$. Then, the system is schedulable.

Proof: Consider the Petri net model shown in Figure 12, at τ_0, $M_0(p_{1c}) = 1$, $M_0(p_{2c}) = 1$, $V(M_0(p_{1c}, \varphi_1)) = 4\alpha$, and $V(M_0(p_{2c}, \varphi_2)) = 2\alpha$. At M_0, t_1 and t_2 fire with colors φ_1 and φ_2 to feed $p_1(DS_1)$ and $p_2(DS_2)$, respectively. At the same time, y fires with color φ_2 to charge p_{3s}. At $\tau_1 = \tau_0 + \Psi$, M_1 is reached such that $M_1(p_{1c}) = M_1(p_{2c}) = M_1(p_{3s}) = 1$, $V(M_1(p_{1c}, \varphi_1)) = 3\alpha$, $V(M_1(p_{2c}, \varphi_2)) = \alpha$, and $V(M_1(p_{3s}, \varphi_2)) = 4\alpha$, because $f_{pmax} \geq 4f_{ds}$. At M_1, y stops firing, t_1 and t_2 continue their firing for feeding p_1 and p_2, and at the same time t_{3d} fires. At $\tau_2 = \tau_0 + 2\Psi$, M_2 is reached such that $M_2(p_{1c}) = M_2(p_{3c}) = 1$, $V(M_2(p_{1c}, \varphi_1)) = 2\alpha$, and $V(M_2(p_{3c}, \varphi_2)) = 4\alpha$. At M_2, t_1 and t_3 fire with colors φ_1 and φ_2 to feed p_1 and p_2, respectively, and y fire with color φ_1 to charge p_{2s}. At $\tau_3 = \tau_0 + 3\Psi$, M_3 is reached such that $M_3(p_{1c}) = M_3(p_{3c}) = M_3(p_{2s}) = 1$,

$V(M_3(p_{1c}, \varphi_1)) = \alpha$, $V(M_3(p_{3c}, \varphi_2)) = 3\alpha$, and $V(M_3(p_{2s}, \varphi_1)) = 4\alpha$. At M_3, t_1 and t_3 continue their firing, but y stop firing, and t_{2d} fires. Then, at $\tau_4 = \tau_1 + 4\Psi$, M_4 is reached such that $M_4(p_{2c}) = M_4(p_{3c}) = 1$, $V(M_4(p_{2c}, \varphi_1)) = 4\alpha$, and $V(M_4(p_{3c}, \varphi_2)) = 2\alpha$. This marking is equivalent to M_0. Therefore, such a process can be repeated, or the system is schedulable.

Let $\nu > \alpha$ and $V(M_0(p_{1c}, \varphi_1)) = 4\nu$, and $V(M_0(p_{2c}, \varphi_2)) = 2\nu$, the system can be scheduled in a similar way. The key here is that $f_{pmax} \geq 4f_{ds}$ and initially $V(M_0(p_{2c}, \varphi_2)) = V(M_0(p_{1c}, \varphi_1))/2 = 2\alpha$. Suppose that, initially at time τ_0, $V(M_0(p_{2c}, \varphi_2)) = V(M_0(p_{1c}, \varphi_1)) = 4\alpha$. At this marking, t_1 and t_2 fire with colors φ_1 and φ_2 to feed p_1 and p_2, respectively, and at the same time y fire with color φ_2 to charge p_{3s}. At $\tau_1 = \tau_0 + \Psi$, M_1 is reached such that $M_1(p_{1c}) = M_1(p_{2c}) = M_1(p_{3s}) = 1$, $V(M_1(p_{1c}, \varphi_1)) = V(M_1(p_{2c}, \varphi_2)) = 3\alpha$, and $V(M_1(p_{3s}, \varphi_2)) = 4\alpha$. At M_1, firing y is stopped, t_{3d} fires, and t_1 and t_2 continue their firing with colors φ_1 and φ_2 to feed p_1 and p_2, respectively. Then, at $\tau_2 = \tau_0 + 2\Psi$, M_2 is reached such that $M_2(p_{1c}) = M_2(p_{2c}) = M_2(p_{3c}) = 1$, $V(M_2(p_{1c}, \varphi_1)) = V(M_2(p_{2c}, \varphi_2)) = 2\alpha$, and $V(M_2(p_{3c}, \varphi_2)) = 4\alpha$. At M_2, if we continue fire t_1 and t_2 with colors φ_1 and φ_2, at $\tau_3 = \tau_0 + 3\Psi$, M_3 is reached such that $M_3(p_{1c}) = M_3(p_{2c}) = M_3(p_{3c}) = 1$, $V(M_3(p_{1c}, \varphi_1)) = V(M_3(p_{2c}, \varphi_2)) = \alpha$, and $V(M_3(p_{3c}, \varphi_2)) = 4\alpha$. It is easy to verify that this is an unsafe state, for it will enter an infeasible state. To make the schedule feasible, at M_2, one should stop t_2 with color φ_2, but fire t_3 with color φ_2 to feed p_2. At the same time, y should be fired with color φ_1 to charge p_{2s} so that when p_{1c} is emptied there is oil with color φ_1 in p_{2c} to feed p_1. However, to do so, it needs to mix the two types of oil for $M_2(p_{2c}) \neq 0$, leading to a violation of process constraints. This implies that M_0 is an unsafe sate.

It should also be pointed out that if $f_{ds1} \neq f_{ds2}$ and when a distiller switches from processing one type of oil to another, the situation becomes complicated. Thus, although, with three charging tanks, there may exist a feasible schedule, the strict initial condition is very difficult to be satisfied. Furthermore, it requires $f_{pmax} \geq 4f_{ds}$, leading to a great reduction of the production rate.

5.1.2. Case 2: Four Charging Tanks

Now, we discuss the schedulability when there are four charging tanks for feeding two distillers. The PN for this case is shown in Figure 13.

Theorem 5.3: It can be shown based on Figure 13 (a). Assume that: 1) the feeding rate for the two distillers DS_1 and DS_2 is $f_{ds1} = f_{ds2} = f_{ds}$ and $\alpha = \Psi \times f_{ds}$; 2) there are four charging tanks CTK_{1-4} with capacity $\xi_1 \geq 2K\alpha$, $\xi_2 \geq 2K\alpha$, $\xi_3 \geq 2K\alpha$, and $\xi_4 \geq 2K\alpha$, $K \in \{1, 2, ...\}$, and CTK_1 and CTK_2 are for DS_1, CTK_3 and CTK_4 for DS_2; 3) $f_{pmax} = 2f_{ds}$; 4) initially, the volume of oil type 1 in CTK_1 and CTK_2 is $\zeta_1 = 2K\alpha$ and $\zeta_2 = \alpha$, and the volume of oil type 2 in CTK_3 and CTK_4 is $\zeta_3 = 2K\alpha$ and $\zeta_4 = 0$, and the oil in CTK_2 and CTK_3 is ready for feeding. Then, the system is schedulable.

Proof: With the Petri net model shown in Figure 13, the system can be scheduled as follows. At M_0 (at time τ_0), $M_0(p_{2c}) = M_0(p_{3c}) = 1$, $M_0(p_{1s}) = 1$ or $M_0(p_{1c}) = 1$, $V(M_0(p_{2c}, \varphi_1)) =$ α, $V(M_0(p_{1s}, \varphi_1)) + V(M_0(p_{1c}, \varphi_1)) = 2K\alpha$, and $V(M_0(p_{3c}, \varphi_2)) = 2K\alpha$. At this marking, fire t_2 and t_3 with colors φ_1 and φ_2 to feed p_1 and p_2, respectively, and at the same time fire y with color φ_2 to charge p_{4s}. At $\tau_1 = \tau_0 + \Psi$, p_{2c} is emptied, there must be a token in p_{1c} while p_{1s} must be empty, resulting in M_1 such that $M_1(p_{2c}) = M_1(p_{1s}) = 0$, $M_1(p_{1c}) = M_1(p_{3c}) = M_1(p_{4s}) = 1$, $V(M_1(p_{1c}, \varphi_1)) = 2K\alpha$, $V(M_1(p_{3c}, \varphi_2)) = (2K-1)\alpha$, and $V(M_1(p_{4s}, \varphi_2)) = 2\alpha$. At M_1, fire t_1 with color φ_1 to feed p_1, and continue t_3's firing with color φ_2 to feed p_2, and y's firing with color φ_2 to charge p_{4s}. At $\tau_2 = \tau_1 + (K-1)\Psi = \tau_0 + Kt_r$, M_2 is reached such that $M_2(p_{3c}) = M_2(p_{1c}) = M_2(p_{4s}) = 1$, $V(M_2(p_{3c}, \varphi_2)) = K\alpha$, $V(M_2(p_{4s}, \varphi_2)) = 2K\alpha$, $V(M_2(p_{1c}, \varphi_1)) = (K+1)\alpha$. Continue firing t_1 and t_3 with colors φ_1 and φ_2 to feed p_1 and p_2, respectively, and fire y with color φ_1 to charge p_{2s}. Then, at $\tau_3 = \tau_2 + K\Psi = \tau_0 + 2K\Psi$, marking M_3 is reached such that $M_3(p_{3c}) = M_3(p_{4s}) = 0$, $M_3(p_{4c}) = M_3(p_{1c}) = M_3(p_{2s}) = 1$, $V(M_3(p_{4c}, \varphi_2)) = V(M_2(p_{2s}, \varphi_1)) = 2K\alpha$, $V(M_3(p_{1c}, \varphi_1)) = \alpha$. Notice that this marking is equivalent to M_0. Hence, the previous process can be repeated. This means that the system is schedulable.

Figure 13. The PN model with four charging tanks for feeding two distillers

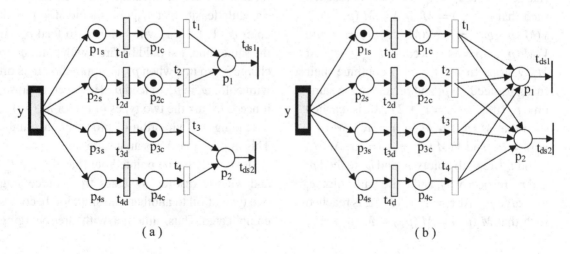

(a)   (b)

If the PN model has the structure as shown in Figure 13 (b), it is more flexible to dynamically assign the charging tanks for feeding the distillers. Hence, it must be schedulable. It should be pointed out that, at any time, two charging tanks are used for distiller feeding, and the other two are charging. Thus, in the sense of schedulability, these two PN models are equivalent. In the prior section, it is shown that a system is not schedulable if there are only two charging tanks for feeding one distiller and $f_{pmax} = f_{ds}$. Notice that, in the situation given in Theorem 5.3, one distiller can be assigned only two charging tanks. However, by Theorem 5.3, the system is schedulable when the production rate reaches its maximal one (f_{pmax}). The reason is that after p_{4s} (CTK_4) is just charged, then, while the oil in p_{4s} stays here for the residency time, y can be used to charge p_{1s}.

In Theorem 5.3, if α is replaced by $\beta \geq \alpha$, the system can be scheduled in the same way, or it is schedulable. Assume that for the capacity of the tanks we have $\xi_1 \geq \xi_4$, $\xi_2 \geq \xi_4$, and $\xi_3 \geq \xi_4$. Then, it follows from the proof of Theorem 5.3 that we can utilize only the capacity ξ_4 for each tank. In Theorem 5.3, it is assumed that $f_{ds1} = f_{ds2}$. The question is that whether the system is schedulable if $f_{ds1} \neq f_{ds2}$ and $f_{pmax} = f_{ds1} + f_{ds2}$. The answer is negative as shown in the following theorem.

Theorem 5.4: Assume that: 1) the feeding rate for two distillers DS_1 and DS_2 is $f_{ds1} > f_{ds2}$, $\alpha_1 = \Psi \times f_{ds1}$, and $\alpha_2 = \Psi \times f_{ds2}$; 2) there are four charging tanks CTK_{1-4} with capacity $\xi_1 \geq 2\alpha_1$, $\xi_2 \geq 2\alpha_1$, $\xi_3 \geq 2\alpha_1$, and $\xi_4 \geq 2\alpha_1$, and CTK_1 and CTK_2 are for DS_1, CTK_3 and CTK_4 for DS_2; 3) $f_{pmax} = f_{ds1} + f_{ds2}$; 4) initially, the volume of oil type 1 in CTK_1 and CTK_2 is $\zeta_1 = 2\alpha_1$ and $\zeta_2 = \alpha_1$, and the volume of oil type 2 in CTK_3 and CTK_4 is $\zeta_3 = 2\alpha_2$ and $\zeta_4 = 0$, and the oil in CTK_2 and CTK_3 is ready for feeding. Then, the system is not schedulable.

Proof: At M_0 (time τ_0), we have $M_0(p_{1s}) = M_0(p_{2c}) = M_0(p_{3c}) = 1$, $V(M_0(p_{1s}, \varphi_1)) = 2\alpha_1$, $V(M_0(p_{2c}, \varphi_1)) = \alpha_1$, $V(M_0(p_{3c}, \varphi_1)) = 2\alpha_2$, and other places are empty. At this marking, we can fire t_2 and t_3 with colors φ_1 and φ_2 to feed p_1 and p_2, respectively. At the same time, we fire y with color φ_2 to charge p_{4s}. Notice that, only Ψ time units later when p_{2c} is emptied can we charge p_{2s}. Thus, at $\tau_1 = \tau_0 + \Psi$, M_1 is reached such that $M_1(p_{1c}) = M_1(p_{3c}) = M_1(p_{4s}) = 1$, $V(M_1(p_{1c}, \varphi_1)) = 2\alpha_1$, $V(M_1(p_{3c}, \varphi_2)) = \alpha_2$, and $V(M_1(p_{4s}, \varphi_2)) = \alpha_1 + \alpha_2$. At M_1, we fire t_1 and t_3 with colors φ_1 and φ_2 to feed p_1 and p_2. At the same time, we fire y with color φ_1 to charge p_{2s}. Notice that, at $\tau_2 = \tau_0 + 2\Psi$, y must stop firing for charging p_{2s} so as to guarantee the oil residency time requirement. At $\tau_2 = \tau_0 + 2\Psi$, M_2 is reached such that $M_2(p_{1c}) = M_2(p_{2s}) = M_2(p_{4c}) = 1$, $V(M_2(p_{1c}, \varphi_1)) = \alpha_1$, $V(M_2(p_{2s}, \varphi_1)) = \alpha_1 + \alpha_2$, and $V(M_2(p_{4c}, \varphi_2)) = \alpha_1 + \alpha_2$. At M_2, we can fire t_1 and t_4 with colors φ_1 and φ_2 to feed p_1 and p_2, and at the same time, fire y with color φ_2 to charge p_{3s}. Then, at $\tau_3 = \tau_0 + 3\Psi$, M_3 is reached such that $V(M_3(p_{2c}, \varphi_1)) = \alpha_1 + \alpha_2$. Notice that $(\alpha_1 + \alpha_2)/f_{ds1} < 2\Psi$. This must be an unsafe state, or the system is not schedulable.

Now, consider the schedulability when a distiller needs to switch from processing one type of oil to another type.

Theorem 5.5: Assume that: 1) two distillers DS_1 and DS_2 have the identical feed rate $f_{ds1} = f_{ds2} = f_{ds}$ and $\alpha = \Psi \times f_{ds}$; 2) there are four charging tanks CTK_1, CTK_2, CTK_3, and CTK_4 with capacity $\xi_1 \geq 2\alpha$, $\xi_2 \geq 2\alpha$, $\xi_3 \geq 2\alpha$, and $\xi_4 \geq 2\alpha$, and CTK_1 and CTK_2 are for DS_1, CTK_3 and CTK_4 for DS_2; 3) $f_{pmax} = 2f_{ds}$; 4) initially, the volume of oil type 1 in CTK_1 and CTK_2 is $\zeta_1 = 2\alpha$ and $\zeta_2 = \alpha$, and the volume of oil type 2 in CTK_3 and CTK_4 is $\zeta_3 = 2\alpha$ and $\zeta_4 = 0$, and the oil in CTK_2 and CTK_3 is ready for feeding; 5) after processing the oil of type 2, DS_2 needs to process oil type 3 and the remaining volume of oil type 2 in the storage tanks is $\beta < \alpha$, Then, the system is not schedulable unless the volume β is mixed with oil type 3.

Proof: Consider the PN shown in Figure 13, at marking M_0 (time τ_0), we have $M_0(p_{1s})$ = $M_0(p_{2c}) = M_0(p_{3c}) = 1$, $V(M_0(p_{1s}, \varphi_1)) = 2\alpha$, $V(M_0(p_{2c}, \varphi_1)) = \alpha$, and $V(M_0(p_{3c}, \varphi_2))$ = 2α. At this marking, we can fire t_2 and t_3 with colors φ_1 and φ_2 to feed p_1 and p_2, fire y with color φ_2 and volume β to charge p_{4s}. At time $\tau_1 = \tau_0 + \Psi$, M_1 is reached such that $V(M_1(p_{1c}, \varphi_1)) = 2\alpha$, $V(M_1(p_{3c}, \varphi_2)) = \alpha$, and $M_1(p_{4s}, \varphi_2) = \beta < \alpha$. This marking is still feasible, for we can fire t_1 with color φ_1 to feed p_1 and t_3 with color φ_2 to feed p_2, and fire y with color φ_1 to charge p_{2s}. At $\tau_2 = \tau_0$ $+ 2\Psi$, M_2 is reached such that $V(M_2(p_{1c}, \varphi_1))$ = α, $V(M_2(p_{2s}, \varphi_1)) = 2\alpha$, $V(M_2(p_{4c}, \varphi_2)) = \beta$, and other places are empty. At M_2, t_1 and t_4 fire with colors φ_1 and φ_2 to feed p_1 and p_2, y fires with φ_3 to charge p_{3s}. Then, at $\tau_3 = \tau_2 + \beta/f_{ds}$, M_3 is reached such that $V(M_3(p_{3s}, \varphi_3)) = 2\beta$, $V(M_3(p_{4c})) = 0$. No transition can fire to feed p_2, an infeasible state. In other words, it is not schedulable.

Theorem 5.5 shows that with four charging tanks for two distillers, it is difficult to deal with the situation that a distiller needs to switch from processing one type of oil to another. In summary, with four charging tanks for two distillers, feasible schedules may exist, but require very restricted conditions to be met.

5.1.3. Case 3: Five Charging Tanks

The PN model with five charging tanks for two distillers is shown in Figure 14. In this situation, it is no question that the system is schedulable when $f_{ds1} = f_{ds2} = f_{ds}$ and $f_{pmax} \geq 2f_{ds}$. The question is that whether the system is schedulable if $f_{ds1} \neq f_{ds2}$ and $f_{pmax} = f_{ds1} + f_{ds2}$. The answer is yes and we have the following result.

Theorem 5.6: Assume that: 1) the feeding rate for the two distillers DS_1 and DS_2 is $f_{ds1} > f_{ds2}$, $\alpha_1 = \Psi \times f_{ds1}$, and $\alpha_2 = \Psi \times f_{ds2}$; 2) there are five charging tanks CTK_{1-5} with capacity $\xi_1 \geq 2\alpha_1$, $\xi_2 \geq 2\alpha_1$, $\xi_3 \geq 2\alpha_1$, $\xi_4 \geq 2\alpha_2$, and $\xi_5 \geq 2\alpha_2$; 3) $f_{pmax} = f_{ds1} + f_{ds2}$; 4) initially, the volume of oil type 1 in CTK_1 and CTK_2 is

Figure 14. The PN model with five charging tanks for feeding two distillers

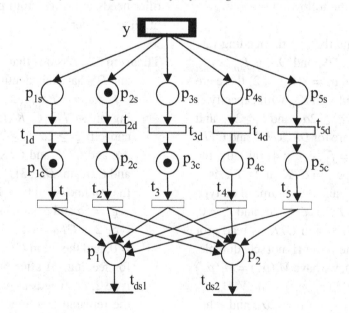

$\zeta_1 = \zeta_2 = 2\alpha_1$, and the volume of oil type 2 in CTK_4 is $\zeta_4 = 2\alpha_2$, CTK_3 and CTK_5 are empty, and the oil in CTK_1 and CTK_4 is ready for feeding. Then, the system is schedulable.

Proof: With the PN model shown in Figure 14, the system can be scheduled as follows. Initially, at marking M_0 (time τ_0), we have $M_0(p_{1c}) = M_0(p_{2s}) = M_0(p_{4c}) = 1$, $V(M_0(p_{1c}, \varphi_1)) = V(M_0(p_{2s}, \varphi_1)) = 2\alpha_1$, $V(M_0(p_{4c}, \varphi_2)) = 2\alpha_2$, and other places are empty. At this marking, we fire t_1 and t_4 with colors φ_1 and φ_2 to feed p_1 and p_2, respectively. At the same time, we fire y with color φ_2 during time interval $(\tau_0, \tau_0 + 2\alpha_2/f_{pmax})$ to charge p_{5s} and fire y with color φ_1 during time interval $(\tau_0 + 2\alpha_2/f_{pmax}, \tau_0 + 2\Psi)$ to charge p_{3s}. In this way, at $\tau_0 + 2\alpha_2/f_{pmax}$, t_{5d} can start to fire and at $\tau_0 + 2\Psi$, the firing of t_{5d} must have ended, because $2\alpha_2/f_{pmax} < (\alpha_1 + \alpha_2)/f_{pmax} = (f_{ds1} + f_{ds2})\Psi/f_{pmax} = \Psi$. Thus, at time $\tau_1 = \tau_0 + 2\Psi$, marking M_1 is reached such that $M_1(p_{2c}) = M_1(p_{5c}) = M_1(p_{3s}) = 1$, $V(M_1(p_{2c}, \varphi_1)) = V(M_1(p_{3s}, \varphi_1)) = 2\alpha_1$, and $V(M_1(p_{5c}, \varphi_2)) = 2\alpha_2$, and other places are empty. This marking is equivalent to the initial marking M_0 so the previous process can be repeated. In other words, the system is schedulable.

In Theorem 5.6, if α is replaced by $\beta > \alpha$, a similar and feasible schedule can be obtained. Notice that in this situation, initially, two tanks must be filled with crude oil of type 1 and only one tank is filled with crude oil of type 2. With such a feasible schedule, it must transport crude oil type 2 first and then crude oil type 1. In this way, it keeps three charging tanks for feeding p_1, and only two charging tanks can be used to feed p_2. Thus, if p_2 needs to switch from processing one type of oil to another and there is a small amount of oil $\beta < \alpha_2$, such a small amount of oil cannot be used up unless it is mixed with other type of oil.

However, if $f_{pmax} = 2f_{ds1}$, a different feasible schedule can be obtained as follows. Assume that, at M_0, we have $M_0(p_{1c}) = M_0(p_{2s}) = M_0(p_{3c}) = 1$, $V(M_0(p_{1c}, \varphi_1)) = V(M_0(p_{2s}, \varphi_1)) = 2\alpha_1$, and $V(M_0(p_{3c}, \varphi_2)) = 2\alpha_2$. At this marking, we fire t_1 and t_3 with colors φ_1 and φ_2 to feed p_1 and p_2, respectively. At the same time, we fire y with color φ_2 during time interval $(\tau_0, \tau_0 + \Psi)$ to charge p_{4s} and during time interval $(\tau_0 + \Psi, \tau_0 + 2\Psi)$ to charge p_{5s} sequentially. At $\tau_1 = \tau_0 + 2\Psi$, M_1 is reached such that $M_1(p_{2c}) = M_1(p_{4c}) = M_1(p_{5s}) = 1$, $V(M_1(p_{2c}, \varphi_1)) = 2\alpha_1$, and $V(M_1(p_{4c}, \varphi_2)) = V(M_1(p_{5s}, \varphi_2)) = 2\alpha_2$. At this marking, we fire t_2 and t_4 with colors φ_1 and φ_2 to feed p_1 and p_2, respectively. At the same time, we fire y with color φ_1 during time interval $(\tau_1, \tau_1 + \Psi)$ to charge p_{1s} and during time interval $(\tau_1 + \Psi, \tau_1 + 2\Psi)$ to charge p_{3s} sequentially. Then, at $\tau_2 = \tau_1 + 2\Psi$, M_2 is reached such that $M_2(p_{1c}) = M_2(p_{3s}) = M_2(p_{5c}) = 1$, $V(M_2(p_{1c}, \varphi_1)) = V(M_2(p_{3s}, \varphi_1)) = 2\alpha_1$, and $V(M_2(p_{5c}, \varphi_2)) = 2\alpha_2$. This marking is equivalent to M_0, and the process can be repeated in a cycle way, or we obtain a feasible schedule.

5.1.4. Case 4: Six Charging Tanks

When there are six charging tanks for two distillers, each distiller can be assigned three charging tanks. In Section 4, if there are three charging tanks for one distiller, the system is schedulable under some weak conditions. Furthermore, in this case, the system can reach its maximal production rate. Now we discuss the situation of six charging tanks for two distillers. The PN model for this case is shown in Figure 15.

Theorem 5.7: Assume that: 1) the feeding rate for the two distillers DS_1 and DS_2 is $f_{ds1} > f_{ds2}$, $\alpha_1 = \Psi \times f_{ds1}$, and $\alpha_2 = \Psi \times f_{ds2}$; 2) there are six charging tanks CTK_{1-6} with capacity $\xi_1 \geq \alpha_1, \xi_2 \geq \alpha_1, \xi_3 \geq \alpha_1, \xi_4 \geq \alpha_2, \xi_5 \geq \alpha_2$, and $\xi_6 \geq \alpha_2$; 3) $f_{pmax} = f_{ds1} + f_{ds2}$; 4) initially, the volume of oil type 1 in CTK_1 and CTK_2 is $\zeta_1 = \zeta_2 = \alpha_1$, and the volume of oil type 2 in CTK_4 and CTK_5 is $\zeta_4 = \zeta_5 = \alpha_2$, CTK_3 and CTK_6 are empty, and the oil in CTK_1 and

Figure 15. PN with six charging tanks for two distillers

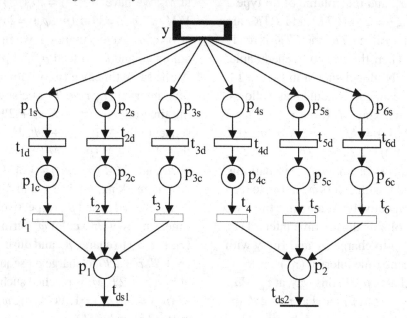

CTK_4 is ready for feeding. Then, the system is schedulable.

Proof: With the PN model shown in Figure 15, the system can be scheduled as follows. At M_0 (time τ_0), we have $M_0(p_{1c}) = M_0(p_{2s})$ $= M_0(p_{4c}) = M_0(p_{5s}) = 1$, $V(M_0(p_{1c}, \varphi_1)) =$ $V(M_0(p_{2s}, \varphi_1)) = \alpha_1$, $V(M_0(p_{4c}, \varphi_2)) = V(M_0(p_{5s}, \varphi_2)) = \alpha_2$, and all other places are empty. At this marking, we fire t_1 and t_4 with colors φ_1 and φ_2 to feed p_1 and p_2, respectively. At the same time, we fire y with color φ_1 in the time interval $(\tau_0, \tau_0 + (f_{ds1}/f_{pmax})\Psi)$ to charge p_{3s} and with color φ_2 in $(\tau_0 + (f_{ds1}/f_{pmax})\Psi, \tau_0 + \Psi)$ to charge p_{6s}. Then, at time $\tau_0 + \Psi$, M_1 is reached such that $M_1(p_{2c}) = M_1(p_{3s}) = M_1(p_{5c})$ $= M_1(p_{6s}) = 1$, $V(M_1(p_{2c}, \varphi_1)) = M_1(p_{3s}, \varphi_1) =$ α_1, $V(M_1(p_{5c}, \varphi_2)) = V(M_1(p_{6s}, \varphi_2)) = \alpha_2$, and all other places are empty. This marking is equivalent to M_0, and thus the process can be repeated in a cyclic way and a feasible schedule is obtained.

It follows from Theorem 5.7 that the system is schedulable and it can reach its maximal production rate if there are three charging tanks for each distiller even if either distiller has different feeding rate. In the proof of Theorem 5.7, we fire y to charge p_{3s} first and then p_{6s}. It is easy to verify that we can do that in other order, or for example, one can charge p_{6s} first then p_{3s}. This implies that the condition in Theorem 5.7 is less restrictive than that in Theorem 5.6. Further, we have the following result.

Theorem 5.8: Assume that: 1) the feeding rate for two distillers DS_1 and DS_2 is $f_{ds1} > f_{ds2}$, $\alpha_1 = \Psi \times f_{ds1}$, and $\alpha_2 = \Psi \times f_{ds2}$; 2) there are six charging tanks CTK_{1-6} with capacity ξ_1 $\geq 2\alpha_1$, $\xi_2 \geq 2\alpha_1$, $\xi_3 \geq 2\alpha_1$, $\xi_4 \geq 2\alpha_2$, $\xi_5 \geq 2\alpha_2$, and $\xi_6 \geq 2\alpha_2$; 3) $f_{pmax} = f_{ds1} + f_{ds2}$; 4) initially, the volume of oil type 1 in CTK_1 and CTK_2 is $\zeta_1 = \zeta_2 = 2\alpha_1$, and the volume of oil type 2 in CTK_4 is $\zeta_4 = 2\alpha_2$, CTK_3, CTK_5, and CTK_6 are empty, and the oil in CTK_1 and CTK_4 is ready for feeding; 5) the volume of crude oil of type 2 remaining in storage tanks is $\beta <$ α_2, and after processing this amount of oil type 2, distiller DS_2 should switch to process oil type 3. Then, the system is schedulable and the volume β of oil type 2 can be used up without being mixed with other oil type.

Proof: With the PN model shown in Figure 15, the system can be scheduled as follows. Initially, at M_0 (time τ_0), we have $M_0(p_{1c}) = M_0(p_{2s}) = M_0(p_{4c}) = 1$, $V(M_0(p_{1c}, \varphi_1)) = V(M_0(p_{2s}, \varphi_1)) = 2\alpha_1$, $V(M_0(p_{4c}, \varphi_2)) = 2\alpha_2$, and all other places are empty. At this marking, we fire t_1 and t_4 with colors φ_1 and φ_2 to feed p_1 and p_2, respectively. At the same time we fire y with color φ_2 in the time interval $(\tau_0, \tau_0 + \beta/f_{pmax})$ to charge p_{5s}, with color φ_3 in the time interval $(\tau_0 + \beta/f_{pmax}, \tau_0 + 2\alpha_2/f_{pmax})$ to charge p_{6s}, and with color φ_1 in $(\tau_0 + 2\alpha_2/f_{pmax}, \tau_0 + 2\Psi)$ to charge p_{3s}. Thus, at time $\tau_1 = \tau_0 + 2\Psi$, M_1 is reached such that $M_1(p_{2c}) = M_1(p_{3s}) = M_1(p_{5c}) = M_1(p_{6c}) = 1$, $V(M_1(p_{2c}, \varphi_1)) = V(M_1(p_{3s}, \varphi_1)) = 2\alpha_1$, $V(M_1(p_{5c}, \varphi_2)) = \beta$, and $V(M_1(p_{6c}, \varphi_2)) = 2\alpha_2 - \beta$, and all other places are empty. At this marking, we fire t_2 with color φ_1 to feed p_1, fire t_5 with color φ_2 in time interval $(\tau_1, \tau_1 + \beta/f_{ds2})$ to feed p_2 and fire t_6 with color φ_3 in $(\tau_1 + \beta/f_{ds2}, \tau_1 + 2\Psi)$ to feed p_2. We fire y with color φ_3 in $(\tau_1, \tau_1 + 2\alpha_2/f_{pmax})$ to charge p_{4s} and with color φ_1 in $(\tau_1 + 2\alpha_2/f_{pmax}, \tau_1 + 2\Psi)$ to charge p_{1s}. Then, at $\tau_2 = \tau_1 + 2\Psi$, M_2 is reached such that $M_2(p_{3c}) = M_2(p_{1s}) = M_2(p_{4c}) = 1$, $V(M_2(p_{3c}, \varphi_1)) = V(M_2(p_{1s}, \varphi_1)) = 2\alpha_1$, $V(M_2(p_{4c}, \varphi_3)) = 2\alpha_2$, and all other places are empty. This marking is equivalent to M_0 in Theorem 5.6. Hence, it is a safe state. Thus, the system is schedulable.

Notice that, for the system with three charging tanks for one distiller, when a volume of oil less than α is to be processed, the total oil in the charging tanks is reduced. This situation does not occur here.

5.2. Systems with More than Two Distillers

Now, we discuss the situation with more than two distillers and generalize the two-distiller results. In scheduling a system, it is desired that maximal production rate can be reached. Thus, in the following discussion we require that $f_{p\max} = \sum_{k=1}^{K} f_{dsk}$. Besides, in a refinery, in general, feeding rates of different distillers are different. Hence, thereafter, we always assume that $f_{dsi} \neq f_{dsj}$, $i \neq j$.

5.2.1. Three-Distiller System

First, we consider a system with three distillers. It follows from the discussion above that if each distiller can be assigned only two charging tanks and the feeding rates are different, the system cannot reach its maximal production rate. Thus, a system with six charging tanks for three distillers is not schedulable if maximal production rate is required to reach. Now, we consider the system with seven charging tanks for three distillers and the Petri net model is shown in Figure 16.

Theorem 5.9: Assume that: 1) the feeding rate for the three distillers DS_{1-3} is $f_{ds1} > f_{ds2} > f_{ds3}$, $\alpha_1 = \Psi \times f_{ds1}$, $\alpha_2 = \Psi \times f_{ds2}$, and $\alpha_3 = \Psi \times f_{ds3}$; 2) there are seven charging tanks CTK_{1-7} with capacity $\xi_1 \geq 3\alpha_1$, $\xi_2 \geq 3\alpha_1$, $\xi_3 \geq 3\alpha_1$, $\xi_4 \geq 3\alpha_2$, $\xi_5 \geq 3\alpha_2$, $\xi_6 \geq 3\alpha_3$, and $\xi_7 \geq 3\alpha_3$; 3) $f_{pmax} = f_{ds1} + f_{ds2} + f_{ds3}$; 4) initially, the volume of oil type 1 in CTK_1 and CTK_2 is $\zeta_1 = \zeta_2 = 3\alpha_1$, the volume of oil type 2 in CTK_4 is $\zeta_4 = 3\alpha_2$, and the volume of oil type 3 in CTK_6 is $\zeta_6 = 3\alpha_3$, CTK_3, CTK_5, and CTK_7 are empty, and the oil in CTK_1, CTK_4, and CTK_6 is ready for feeding. Then, the system is schedulable.

Proof: With the Petri net model shown in Figure 16, the system can be scheduled as follows. Initially, at M_0 (time τ_0), we have $M_0(p_{1c}) =$

Figure 16. PN with seven charging tanks for three distillers

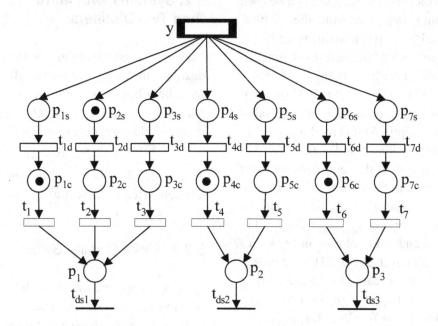

$M_0(p_{2s}) = M_0(p_{4c}) = M_0(p_{6c}) = 1$, $V(M_0(p_{1c}, \varphi_1)) = V(M_0(p_{2s}, \varphi_1)) = 3\alpha_1$, $V(M_0(p_{4c}, \varphi_2)) = 3\alpha_2$, $V(M_0(p_{6c}, \varphi_3)) = 3\alpha_3$, and all other places are empty. At this marking, we fire t_1, t_4, and t_6 with colors φ_1, φ_2, and φ_3 to feed p_1, p_2, and p_3, respectively. At the same time, we fire y with color φ_3 in the time interval $(\tau_0, \tau_0 + 3\alpha_3/f_{pmax})$ to charge p_{7s}, with color φ_2 in $(\tau_0 + 3\alpha_3/f_{pmax}, \tau_0 + 3(\alpha_2 + \alpha_3)/f_{pmax})$ to charge p_{5s}, with color φ_1 in $(\tau_0 + 3(\alpha_2 + \alpha_3)/f_{pmax}, \tau_0 + 3\Psi)$ to charge p_{3s}. Notice that $\tau_0 + 3(\alpha_2 + \alpha_3)/f_{pmax} = \tau_0 + 3\Psi - 3\alpha_1/f_{pmax} < \tau_0 + 3\Psi - \Psi = \tau_0 + 2\Psi$. This implies that t_{5d} can start to fire at time $\tau_0 + 3(\alpha_2 + \alpha_3)/f_{pmax}$ and this firing must have been completed before time $\tau_0 + 3\Psi$. Thus, at $\tau_1 = \tau_0 + 3\Psi$, M_1 is reached such that $M_1(p_{2c}) = M_1(p_{3s}) = M_1(p_{5c}) = M_1(p_{7c}) = 1$, $V(M_1(p_{2c}, \varphi_1)) = V(M_1(p_{3s}, \varphi_1)) = 3\alpha_1$, $V(M_1(p_{5c}, \varphi_2)) = 3\alpha_2$, $V(M_1(p_{7c}, \varphi_3)) = 3\alpha_3$, and all other places are empty. This marking is equivalent to M_0, and thus the process can be repeated in a cyclic way to form a feasible schedule.

This situation is similar to that given in Theorem 5.6 where it has five charging tanks and two distillers. Similar to the situation with five charging tanks for two distillers, for this situation, if distiller j, $1 \le j \le 3$, needs to switch from processing one type of oil to another and a remaining small volume $\beta_j < \alpha_j$ in storage tanks should be processed, the volume β_j cannot be done, unless it is mixed with other type of oil. However, if there are eight charging tanks, this problem can be solved as shown next.

Theorem 5.10: Assume that: 1) the feeding rate for the three distillers DS_{1-3} is $f_{ds1} > f_{ds2} > f_{ds3}$, $\alpha_1 = \Psi \times f_{ds1}$, $\alpha_2 = \Psi \times f_{ds2}$, and $\alpha_3 = \Psi \times f_{ds3}$; 2) there are eight charging tanks CTK_{1-8} with capacity $\xi_1 \ge 3\alpha_1$, $\xi_2 \ge 3\alpha_1$, $\xi_3 \ge 3\alpha_1$, $\xi_4 \ge 3\alpha_2$, $\xi_5 \ge 3\alpha_2$, $\xi_6 \ge 3\alpha_2$, $\xi_7 \ge 3\alpha_3$, and $\xi_8 \ge 3\alpha_3$; 3) $f_{pmax} = f_{ds1} + f_{ds2} + f_{ds3}$; 4) initially, the volume of oil type 1 in CTK_1 and CTK_2 is $\zeta_1 = \zeta_2 = 3\alpha_1$, the volume of oil type 2 in CTK_4 is $\zeta_4 = 3\alpha_2$, and the volume of oil type 3 in CTK_6 is $\zeta_6 = 3\alpha_3$, and CTK_3, CTK_5, $CTK7$, and CTK_8 are empty, and the oil in CTK_1,

CTK_4, and CTK_6 is ready for feeding; 5) the volume of crude oil of type 3 remaining in storage tanks is $\beta < \alpha_3$, and after processing this amount of oil type 3, distiller DS_3 should switch to process oil type 4. Then, the system is schedulable and the volume β of oil type 3 can be used up without being mixed with other oil type.

Proof: The PN for a system with eight charging tanks for three distillers is shown in Figure 17. With Figure 17, the system can be scheduled as follows. Initially, at marking M_0 (time τ_0), $M_0(p_{1c}) = M_0(p_{2s}) = M_0(p_{4c}) = M_0(p_{6c}) = 1$, $V(M_0(p_{1c}, \varphi_1)) = V(M_0(p_{2s}, \varphi_1)) = 3\alpha_1$, $V(M_0(p_{4c}, \varphi_2)) = 3\alpha_2$, $V(M_0(p_{6c}, \varphi_3)) = 3\alpha_3$, and the other places are empty. At this marking, we fire t_1, t_4, and t_6 with colors φ_1, φ_2, and φ_3 to feed p_1, p_2, and p_3, respectively. At the same time, we fire y with color φ_3 in $(\tau_0, \tau_0 + \beta/f_{pmax})$ to charge p_{7s} with volume β, with color φ_4 in $(\tau_0 + \beta/f_{pmax}, \tau_0 + 3\alpha_3/f_{pmax})$ to charge p_{8s} with volume $3\alpha_3 - \beta$, with color φ_2 in $(\tau_0 + 3\alpha_3/f_{pmax}, \tau_0 + 3(\alpha_2 + \alpha_3)/f_{pmax})$ to charge p_{5s} with volume $3\alpha_2$, and with color φ_1 in $(\tau_0 + 3(\alpha_2 + \alpha_3)/f_{pmax}, \tau_0 + 3\Psi)$ to charge

p_{3s} with volume $3\alpha_1$. Thus, at $\tau_1 = \tau_0 + 3\Psi$, M_1 is reached such that $M_1(p_{2c}) = M_1(p_{3s}) = M_1(p_{5c}) = M_1(p_{7c}) = M_1(p_{8c}) = 1$, $V(M_1(p_{2c}, \varphi_1)) = V(M_1(p_{3s}, \varphi_1)) = 3\alpha_1$, $V(M_1(p_{5c}, \varphi_2)) = 3\alpha_2$, $V(M_1(p_{7c}, \varphi_3)) = \beta$, $V(M_1(p_{8c}, \varphi_4)) = 3\alpha_3 - \beta$, and the other places are empty. At this marking, we fire t_2 and t_5 with colors φ_1 and φ_2 to feed p_1 and p_2, respectively, fire t_7 with color φ_3 in $(\tau_1, \tau_1 + \beta/f_{ds3})$ and then fire t_8 with color φ_4 in $(\tau_1 + \beta/f_{ds3}, \tau_1 + 3\Psi)$ to feed p_3. We fire y with color φ_4 in $(\tau_1, \tau_1 + 3\alpha_3/f_{pmax})$ to charge p_{6s} with volume $3\alpha_3$, with color φ_2 in $(\tau_1 + 3\alpha_3/f_{pmax}, \tau_1 + 3(\alpha_2 + \alpha_3)/f_{pmax})$ to charge p_{4s} with volume $3\alpha_2$, and with color φ_1 in $(\tau_1 + 3(\alpha_2 + \alpha_3)/f_{pmax}, \tau_1 + 3\Psi)$ to charge p_{1s} with volume $3\alpha_1$. Then, at $\tau_2 = \tau_1 + 3\Psi$, M_2 is reached such that $M_2(p_{3c}) = M_2(p_{1s}) = M_2(p_{4c}) = M_2(p_{6c}) = 1$, $V(M_2(p_{3c}, \varphi_1)) = V(M_2(p_{1s}, \varphi_1)) = 3\alpha_1$, $V(M_2(p_{4c}, \varphi_2)) = 3\alpha_2$, $V(M_2(p_{6c}, \varphi_4)) = 3\alpha_3$, and the other places are empty. This marking is equivalent to M_0 and thus the process can be repeated in cyclic way. In other words, a feasible schedule can be obtained.

Figure 17. Petri net with eight charging tanks for three distillers

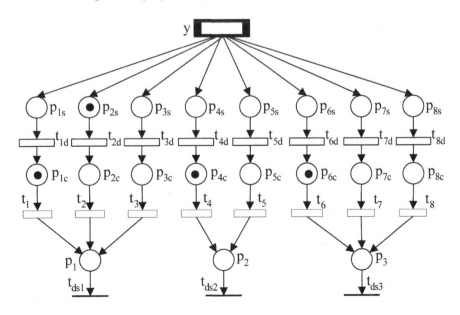

Notice that if two distillers switch from processing one type of crude oil to another at the same time it needs one more charging tank. It follows from the proof of Theorems 5.9 and 5.10 that the order of place charging by firing y is important; and otherwise one may reach an unsafe marking. This restricts the scheduling freedom. With more charging tanks, one has more scheduling freedom.

Theorem 5.11: Assume that: 1) the feeding rates for the three distillers $DS_1, DS_2,$ and DS_3 are $f_{ds1} > f_{ds2} > f_{ds3}$, $\alpha_1 = \Psi \times f_{ds1}$, $\alpha_2 = \Psi \times f_{ds2}$, and $\alpha_3 = \Psi \times f_{ds3}$; 2) there are nine charging tanks CTK_{1-9} with capacity $\xi_1 \geq \alpha_1, \xi_2 \geq \alpha_1,$ $\xi_3 \geq \alpha_1, \xi_4 \geq \alpha_2, \xi_5 \geq \alpha_2, \xi_6 \geq \alpha_2, \xi_7 \geq \alpha_3,$ $\xi_8 \geq \alpha_3,$ and $\xi_9 \geq \alpha_3$; 3) $f_{pmax} = f_{ds1} + f_{ds2} + f_{ds3}$; 4) initially, the volume of oil type 1 in CTK_1 and CTK_2 is $\zeta_1 = \zeta_2 = \alpha_1$, the volume of oil type 2 in CTK_4 and CTK_5 is $\zeta_4 = \zeta_5 = \alpha_2$, the volume of oil type 3 in CTK_7 and CTK_8 is $\zeta_7 = \zeta_8 = \alpha_3$, $CTK_3, CTK_6,$ and CTK_9 are empty, and the oil in $CTK_1, CTK_4,$ and CTK_7 is ready for feeding. Then, the system is schedulable.

Proof: This situation can be scheduled similarly to that shown in Theorem 5.7.

In Theorem 5.11, it requires much less crude oil in the charging tanks and the order of place charging by firing y has no effect on the schedule feasibility. Also, maximal production rate is reached. Thus, it has more scheduling freedom. In Theorem 5.11, if $\zeta_1 \geq 2\alpha_1, \zeta_4 \geq 2\alpha_2, \zeta_7 \geq 2\alpha_3,$ $CTK_2, CTK_3, CTK_5, CTK_6, CTK_8,$ and CTK_9 are empty, it follows from the proof of Theorem 5.7 that, when $CTK_1, CTK_4,$ and CTK_7 are emptied, CTK_2 and CTK_3 are charged up to more than α_1, CTK_5 and CTK_6 up to more than α_2, CTK_8 and CTK_9 up to more than α_3. Thus, from Theorem 5.11, we have the following Corollary.

Corollary 5.1: Assume that: 1) the feeding rates for the three distillers $DS_1, DS_2,$ and DS_3 are

$f_{ds1} > f_{ds2} > f_{ds3}$, $\alpha_1 = \Psi \times f_{ds1}$, $\alpha_2 = \Psi \times f_{ds2}$, and $\alpha_3 = \Psi \times f_{ds3}$; 2) there are nine charging tanks CTK_{1-9} with capacity $\xi_1 \geq \alpha_1, \xi_2 \geq \alpha_1,$ $\xi_3 \geq \alpha_1, \xi_4 \geq \alpha_2, \xi_5 \geq \alpha_2, \xi_6 \geq \alpha_2, \xi_7 \geq \alpha_3, \xi_8$ $\geq \alpha_3,$ and $\xi_9 \geq \alpha_3$; 3) $f_{pmax} = f_{ds1} + f_{ds2} + f_{ds3}$; 4) initially, the volume of oil type 1 in CTK_1 is $\zeta_1 \geq 2\alpha_1$, the volume of oil type 2 in CTK_4 is $\zeta_4 \geq 2\alpha_2$, the volume of oil type 3 in CTK_7 is $\zeta_7 \geq 2\alpha_3$, $CTK_2, CTK_3, CTK_5, CTK_6, CTK_8,$ and CTK_9 are empty, and the oil in $CTK_1,$ $CTK_4,$ and CTK_7 is ready for feeding. Then, the system is schedulable.

5.2.2. K-Distiller System

Up to now, all the results obtained are for a given number of distillers and it does not show if the results are applicable to the general case. In the follows, we present the results that are applicable to a general case.

Theorem 5.12: Assume that: 1) the feeding rate for the $K (\geq 2)$ distillers DS_{1-K} is $f_{ds1} > f_{ds2} > ... >$ f_{dsK}, $\alpha_1 = \Psi \times f_{ds1}$, $\alpha_2 = \Psi \times f_{ds2}, ...,$ and $\alpha_K = \Psi \times f_{dsK}$; 2) there are $2K + 1$ charging tanks $CTK_{1-(2K+1)}$ with capacity $\xi_1 \geq K\alpha_1, \xi_2 \geq K\alpha_1,$ $\xi_3 \geq K\alpha_1, \xi_4 \geq K\alpha_2, \xi_5 \geq K\alpha_2, ..., \xi_{2i} \geq K\alpha_i,$ $\xi_{2i+1} \geq K\alpha_i, ...,$ and $\xi_{2K} \geq K\alpha_K, \xi_{2K+1} \geq K\alpha_K$; 3) $f_{pmax} = f_{ds1} + f_{ds2} + ... + f_{dsK}$; 4) initially, the volume of oil type 1 in CTK_1 and CTK_2 is $\zeta_1 = \zeta_2 = K\alpha_1$, the volume of oil type 2 in CTK_4 is $\zeta_4 = K\alpha_2, ...,$ the volume of oil type i in CTK_{2i} is $\zeta_{2i} = K\alpha_i, ...,$ the volume of oil type K in CTK_{2K} is $\zeta_{2K} = K\alpha_K$, the other tanks are empty, and the oil in $CTK_1, CTK_4, ...,$ $CTK_{2i}, ...,$ and CTK_{2K} is ready for feeding. Then, the system is schedulable.

Proof: Let a charging tank CTK_i be modeled by $\{p_{is}, p_{ic}, t_{id}, t_i\}$ and distiller DS_i be modeled by p_i in the PN. Then, this system can be scheduled as follows. Initially, at M_0 (time τ_0), $M_0(p_{1c}) = M_0(p_{2s}) = 1$, $M_0(p_{(2i)c}) = 1$, $i =$ 2, 3, ..., K, $V(M_0(p_{1c}, \varphi_1)) = V(M_0(p_{2s}, \varphi_1))$ $= K\alpha_1$, $V(M_0(p_{(2i)c}, \varphi_i)) = K\alpha_i$, $i = 2, 3, ...,$

K, and the other places are empty. At this marking, we fire t_1 with color φ_1 to feed p_1, and t_{2i} with color φ_i to feed p_i, $i = 2, 3, \ldots$, K, respectively. Meanwhile, we fire y in the following order: with color φ_K to charge $p_{(2K+1)s}$ with volume $K\alpha_K \to$ with color φ_{K-1} to charge $p_{(2K-1)s}$ with volume $K\alpha_{K-1} \to \ldots \to$ with color φ_i to charge $p_{(2i+1)s}$ with volume $K\alpha_i \to \ldots \to$ with color φ_2 to charge p_{5s} with volume $K\alpha_2 \to$ with color φ_1 to charge p_{3s} with volume $K\alpha_1$. Notice that

$$\frac{K\alpha_1}{f_{p\max}} = \frac{K \times f_{ds1} \times \Psi}{f_{ds1} + \cdots + f_{dsK}} \geq \frac{(f_{ds1} + \cdots + f_{dsK}) \times \Psi}{f_{ds1} + \cdots + f_{dsK}} = \Psi.$$

This implies that charging p_{5s} stops before time $\tau_0 + (K-1)\Psi$. Hence, the firing of t_{5d} can start before $\tau_0 + (K-1)\Psi$ and must end before $\tau_1 = \tau_0 + K\Psi$. Thus, at τ_1, marking M_1 is reached such that $M_1(p_{2c}) = M_1(p_{3s}) = 1$, $M_1(p_{(2i+1)c}) = 1$, $i = 2, 3, \ldots, K$, $V(M_1(p_{2c}, \varphi_1)) = M_1(p_{3s}, \varphi_1) = K\alpha_1$, $V(M_1(p_{(2i+1)c}, \varphi_i)) = K\alpha_i$, $i = 2, 3, \ldots, K$, and the other places are empty. This marking is equivalent to M_0. Hence, the process can be repeated in a cyclic way and a feasible schedule can be obtained.

Consider the situation that a tank switches from processing one type of crude oil to another and there is a small volume of the former crude oil type. We have the following result.

Theorem 5.13: Assume that: 1) the feeding rate for the K (≥ 2) distillers DS_{1-K} is $f_{ds1} > f_{ds2} > \ldots > f_{dsK}$, $\alpha_1 = \Psi \times f_{ds1}$, $\alpha_2 = \Psi \times f_{ds2}$, $\ldots$, and $\alpha_K = \Psi \times f_{dsK}$; 2) there are $2K + 2$ charging tanks $CTK_{1-(2K+2)}$ with capacities $\xi_1 \geq K\alpha_1$, $\xi_2 \geq K\alpha_1$, $\xi_3 \geq K\alpha_1$, $\xi_4 \geq K\alpha_2$, $\xi_5 \geq K\alpha_2$, $\ldots$, $\xi_{2i} \geq K\alpha_i$, $\xi_{2i+1} \geq K\alpha_i$, $\ldots$, and $\xi_{2K} \geq K\alpha_K$, $\xi_{2K+1} \geq K\alpha_K$, $\xi_{2K+2} \geq K\alpha_K$; 3) $f_{pmax} = f_{ds1} + f_{ds2} + \ldots + f_{dsK}$; 4) initially, the volume of oil type

1 in CTK_1 and CTK_2 is $\zeta_1 = \zeta_2 = K\alpha_1$, the volume of oil type 2 in CTK_4 is $\zeta_4 = K\alpha_2$, $\ldots$, the volume of oil type i in CTK_{2i} is $\zeta_{2i} = K\alpha_i$, $\ldots$, the volume of oil type K in CTK_{2K} is $\zeta_{2K} = K\alpha_K$, the other tanks are empty, and the oil in $CTK_1, CTK_4, \ldots, CTK_{2i}, \ldots$, and CTK_{2K} is ready to feed; 5) the volume of crude oil of type K remaining in storage tanks is $\beta < \alpha_K$, and after processing this amount of oil type K, distiller DS_K should switch to process oil type j. Then, the system is schedulable and the volume β of oil type K can be used up without being mixed with other oil type.

Proof: Initially, at M_0 (time τ_0), we have $M_0(p_{1c}) = M_0(p_{2s}) = 1$, $M_0(p_{(2i)c}) = 1$, $i = 2, 3, \ldots$, K, $V(M_0(p_{1c}, \varphi_1)) = V(M_0(p_{2s}, \varphi_1)) = K\alpha_1$, $V(M_0(p_{(2i)c}, \varphi_i)) = K\alpha_i$, $i = 2, 3, \ldots, K$, and the other places are empty. At this marking, we fire t_1 with color φ_1 to feed p_1, and t_{2i} with color φ_i to feed p_i, $i = 2, 3, \ldots, K$, respectively. Meanwhile, we fire y in the following order: with color φ_K to charge $p_{(2K+1)s}$ with volume β, and then with color φ_j to charge $p_{(2K+2)s}$ with volume $K\alpha_K - \beta \to$ with color φ_{K-1} to charge $p_{(2K-1)s}$ with volume $K\alpha_{K-1} \to \ldots \to$ with color φ_i to charge $p_{(2i+1)s}$ with volume $K\alpha_i \to \ldots \to$ with color φ_2 to charge p_{5s} with volume $K\alpha_2 \to$ with color φ_1 to charge p_{3s} with volume $K\alpha_1$. Thus, at $\tau_1 = \tau_0 + K\Psi$, M_1 is reached such that $M_1(p_{2c}) = M_0(p_{3s}) = 1$, $M_1(p_{(2i+1)c}) = 1$, $i = 2, 3, \ldots, K$, $M_1(p_{(2K+2)c}) = 1$, $V(M_1(p_{2c}, \varphi_1)) = V(M_1(p_{3s}, \varphi_1)) = K\alpha_1$, $V(M_1(p_{(2i+1)c}, \varphi_i)) = K\alpha_i$, $i = 2, 3, \ldots, (K-1)$, $V(M_1(p_{(2K+1)c}, \varphi_K)) = \beta$, $V(M_1(p_{(2K+2)c}, \varphi_j)) = K\alpha_K - \beta$, and the other places are empty. At M_1, we fire t_2 with color φ_1 to feed p_1; fire t_{2i+1} with color φ_i to feed p_i, $i = 2, 3, \ldots$, $K-1$; fire t_{2K+1} with color φ_K to feed p_K with volume β and then fire t_{2K+2} with color φ_j to feed p_K with volume $K\alpha_K - \beta$. Meanwhile, we fire y in the following order: with color φ_j to charge $p_{(2K)s}$ with volume $K\alpha_K \to$ with color φ_{K-1} to charge $p_{(2K-2)s}$ with volume $K\alpha_{K-1} \to \ldots \to$ with color φ_i to charge $p_{(2i)s}$ with volume

$Ka_i \to \dots \to$ with color φ_2 to charge p_{4s} with volume $Ka_2 \to$ with color φ_1 to charge p_{1s} with volume Ka_1. Thus, at $\tau_2 = \tau_1 + K\Psi$, M_2 is reached such that $M_2(p_{3c}) = M_2(p_{1s}) = 1$, $M_2(p_{(2i)c}) = 1$, $i = 2, 3, \dots, K$, $V(M_2(p_{3c}, \varphi_1)) = V(M_2(p_{1s}, \varphi_1)) = Ka_1$, $V(M_2(p_{(2i)c}, \varphi_i)) = Ka_i$, $i = 2, 3, \dots, K\text{-}1$, $V(M_2(p_{(2K)c}, \varphi_j)) = Ka_K$, and the other places are empty. This marking is equivalent to M_0 in Theorem 5.12. It follows from Theorem 5.12 that the system is schedulable.

In Theorems 5.12 and 5.13, it is required that the capacity of a charging tank and the volume of crude oil in a charging tank are greater or equal to Ka_i. It seems that it is difficult to be satisfied. However, in practice, it is not a serious restriction. In practice, in general, there are no more than four distillers in most refineries. Similarly, feeding rate for a distiller is no more than 650 tons per hour. Generally, Ψ is from four to six hours. Thus, we have $4 \times 650 \times 6 = 15{,}500$ tons that is less than the capacity of a general charging tank. If each time a tank is charged with a small amount of oil, in feeding a distiller, frequent switch from one charging tank to another is necessary. This is undesirable in practice for there is a switch loss. Hence, it is desirable to fill the charging tanks as full as possible. To do so, we can replace α_i by $\beta_i > \alpha_i$ in the previously obtained results.

Theorem 5.14: Assume that: 1) the feeding rates for the K (≥ 2) distillers $DS_{1\text{-}K}$ are $f_{ds1} > f_{ds2} > \dots > f_{dsK}$, $\alpha_1 = \Psi \times f_{ds1}$, $\alpha_2 = \Psi \times f_{ds2}$, $\dots$, and $\alpha_K = \Psi \times f_{dsK}$; 2) there are $3K$ charging tanks $CTK_{1\text{-}3K}$ with capacity $\xi_1 \geq \alpha_1$, $\xi_2 \geq \alpha_1$, $\xi_3 \geq \alpha_1$, $\dots$, $\xi_{3i+1} \geq \alpha_{i+1}$, $\xi_{3i+2} \geq \alpha_{i+1}$, $\xi_{3(i+1)} \geq \alpha_{i+1}$, $1 \leq i \leq K\text{-}1$; 3) $f_{pmax} = f_{ds1} + \dots + f_{dsK}$; 4) initially, the volume of oil type 1 in CTK_1 and CTK_2 is $\zeta_1 = \zeta_2 = \alpha_1$, $\dots$, the volume of oil type i in CTK_{3i+1} and CTK_{3i+2} is $\zeta_{3i+1} = \zeta_{3i+2} = \alpha_i$, $1 < i \leq K\text{-}1$, the other tanks are empty, and the oil in CTK_1, CTK_{3i+1}, $1 < i \leq$

$K\text{-}1$, is ready for feeding. Then, the system is schedulable.

Proof: The system can be scheduled as follows. Initially, at M_0 (time τ_0), we have $M_0(p_{1c}) = M_0(p_{2s}) = 1$, $M_0(p_{(3i+1)c}) = M_0(p_{(3i+2)s}) = 1$, $1 \leq i \leq K\text{-}1$, $V(M_0(p_{1c}, \varphi_1)) = V(M_0(p_{2s}, \varphi_1)) = \alpha_1$, $V(M_0(p_{(3i+1)c}, \varphi_{i+1})) = V(M_0(p_{(3i+2)s}, \varphi_{i+1})) = \alpha_{i+1}$, $1 \leq i \leq K\text{-}1$, and other places are empty. At this marking, we fire t_1 with color φ_1 to feed p_1, t_{3i-2} with color φ_i to feed p_i, $2 \leq i \leq K$. At the same time, we fire y with the following order: with color φ_1 to charge p_{3s} with volume $\alpha_1 \to \dots \to$ with color φ_i to charge $p_{(3i)s}$ with volume $\alpha_i \to \dots \to$ with color φ_K to charge $p_{(3K)s}$ with volume α_K. Then, at $\tau_1 = \tau_0 + \Psi$, M_1 is reached such that $M_1(p_{2c}) = M_1(p_{3s}) = 1$, $M_1(p_{(3i+2)c}) = M_1(p_{(3i+3)s}) = 1$, $1 \leq i \leq K\text{-}1$, $V(M_1(p_{2c}, \varphi_1)) = V(M_1(p_{3s}, \varphi_1)) = \alpha_1$, $V(M_1(p_{(3i+2)c}, \varphi_{i+1})) = V(M_1(p_{(3i+3)s}, \varphi_{i+1})) = \alpha_{i+1}$, $1 \leq i \leq K\text{-}1$, and other places are empty. This marking is equivalent to M_0, and thus the process can be repeated in a cyclic way and a feasible schedule can be obtained.

It should be pointed out that when $K = 1$, Theorem 5.13 is not meaningful. The factors that affect the safeness of the system include the number of charging tanks and their capacity, the amount of crude oil of each type in the charging tanks, transportation rate of the pipeline, and production rate. Theorems 5.12-5.14 present the relationship among these factors under the assumption that maximal production rate is reached. Clearly, when the production rate is not required to reach the maximal one, these results are applicable as well.

Notice that, in Theorems 5.12 and 5.13, the volume of oil required in a charging tank is Ka_i, or it depends on the number of distillers. However, in Theorem 5.14, the volume of oil required in a charging tank is α_i, or it is independent of the number of distillers. In fact, Theorems 5.12 and 5.13 present the safeness boundary in the sense of the number of charging tanks if the maximal production rate is required. In this case, the feasible space is small. Thus, if there are $3K$ charging tanks for K distillers, the system operates at a point in the feasible space that is away from the boundary with a distance in the sense of the number of charging tanks. Hence, we have more freedom to find a feasible solution. In practice, most refineries have more than $3K$ charging tanks with K distillers and thus allow more scheduling freedom.

The conditions in Theorem 5.14 present the safeness boundary under the assumption that there are $3K$ charging tanks for K distillers. Under these conditions, each time, a charging tank is filled with a small amount of crude oil. This leads to frequent switch from transporting one type of crude oil to another, and frequent switch from one to another for feeding a distiller. This is undesirable, because such a switch results in a loss. Notice that α_i is the smallest amount of crude oil required to be filled into a charging tank. Clearly if, each time, $\beta_i > \alpha_i$ is filled into a charging tank, the system is in the safeness space. Thus, in practice, we fill a charging tank as full as possible when it is charged. When each charging tank is full if it is required to be filled with oil in the conditions given in Theorem 5.14, the system must be in a safe state that is far away from the safeness boundary because the capacity of a tank is much greater than α_i. Therefore, in this situation, to schedule the system we need to check only if a system status crosses the safeness boundary.

It follows from Theorems 5.12 to 5.14 that if there are more charging tanks, the feasible space becomes large, and it is easier to find a feasible schedule. However, by mathematical programming models for short-term scheduling of refinery, adding a charging tank leads to the addition of more constraints and creates much more discrete variables. Hence, it greatly increases the computational burden. Clearly, the proposed method can be used to solve large practical application problems as contrary to a mathematical programming method. The results obtained are derived by using

the Petri net models developed in this chapter. It seems that these results may be difficult to be applied because one lacks effective analysis tool for such a type of Petri nets. Notice that, although these results are derived by using the models, the schedulability conditions are independent of the models. We will see how a refining scheduling problem can be solved by using these conditions as constraints next.

With the safeness conditions given in Theorems 5.12-5.14, at any safe state for a system, one can create an operation decision such that when it is executed, the system is transferred into another safe state. This implies that if the initial state is known and a refining schedule is given, we can check if a refining schedule is realizable. Furthermore, if it is schedulable, a detailed schedule can be found by creating the operation decisions one by one by following the proofs of the results. In this way, the starting time, the amount of oil and its type to be delivered, and the flow rate for an operation decision can be easily determined, and the time can be any continuous time point. In conclusion, the most difficult problem faced by mathematical programming models is solved. Then, the safeness conditions are used as constraints to find a realizable refining schedule.

6. REFINING SCHEDULING

With the schedulability analysis done for the problem at the lower level, we can discuss the problem at the upper level for finding a refining schedule such that it is optimal and realizable.

6.1. The Refining Scheduling Problem

Let $\Gamma = (\tau_s, \tau_e)$ denote the scheduling horizon that often lasts for a week or ten days with τ_s and τ_e being the start and end time points. A short-term schedule for crude oil operations should provide all the activities in every detail. For general scheduling problems, there are a set of jobs and a number of servers. The jobs are well-defined, or they are often assumed to consume deterministic processing time. The scheduling problem is to assign the jobs to servers and determine the processing sequence for each server. For refining scheduling, the servers are the set of distillers in a refinery plant. However, the jobs to be scheduled are not known before a schedule is obtained. All the information we know is the scheduling horizon $\Gamma = (\tau_s, \tau_e)$ and the initial state of the process at τ_s. The initial state is characterized by:

1. **The production state:** For a distiller i, it gives
   a. The type of crude oil that is being processed by distiller i;
   b. The production rate with which crude oil is being processed by distiller i;
   c. The charging tank that is feeding distiller i.
2. **The state of tanks:** A storage or charging tank must be in one of the four states: a) idle and empty; b) idle with oil in it; c) in charging; and d) in discharging
   a. State b), one has the information of the crude oil type and amount in it;
   b. State c), the crude oil type that is being charged, the charging rate, and amount of oil in the tank at the moment are given;
   c. State d), the crude oil type and amount remained in the tank, and the discharging rate are given.
3. **The state of a pipeline:** A pipeline must be in one of the states: a) idle; and b) transporting crude oil from storage tanks to charging tanks
   a. For both states a) and b), one has the number of different segments of crude oil in the pipeline, the crude oil type

and amount for each segment at the moment;
   b. State b), one has the rate with which crude oil is being transported.
4. **The information of tanker arrivals:** It includes the number of ships that will arrive during the scheduling horizon, and for each ship, one has
   a. Arrival time;
   b. The types of crude oil in the ship and the amount of oil for each type; and
   c. The oil unloading rate.

With the initial state for a process, a refining schedule is to determine, at any time point for the entire scheduling horizon, the production rate and the type of crude oil to be processed for every distiller in the system. In a refinery, processing different types of crude oil produces different products. To meet the market demands, various types of crude oil should be processed. Thus, for a distiller, it needs to switch from processing one type of crude oil to another type. Thus, the main decision for a refining scheduling is when such switches take place and the types of crude oil for each switch. To describe a refining schedule, we define a feeding parcel of crude oil (*FP*).

Definition 6.1: $FP = (COT, \zeta, (\alpha, \beta))$ is defined as a feeding parcel of crude oil, where COT = crude oil type to be fed into a distiller; ζ = volume of crude oil to be fed into a distiller; and (α, β) is a time interval in which α and β are the start and end time points for feeding this parcel of crude oil.

The flow rate for feeding such a parcel of oil during (α, β) can vary. However, when it changes, the set point for the distillation process should change as well, which leads to some loss. Thus, in practice, the flow rate for an *FP* is set to be a constant and can be calculated by $f = \dfrac{\varsigma}{\beta - \alpha}$.

Thereafter, if the same type of crude oil is fed into a distiller with different flow rate, we can simply treat it as a different *FP*. Let $FP_{ij} = (COT_{ij}, \zeta_{ij}, (\alpha_{ij}, \beta_{ij}))$ denote the *j*th *FP* for feeding distiller *i*. Assume that it needs *Q FPs* for distiller *i* during the scheduling horizon. Then its refining schedule for distiller *i* can be denoted as $RS_i = \{FP_{i1}, FP_{i2}, ..., FP_{iQ}\}$. Further, assume that there are K distillers in the system and let $DS = \{1, 2, ..., K\}$ be the set of distillers and $f_{ij} = \zeta_{ij}/(\beta_{ij} - \alpha_{ij})$. Then, the refining scheduling problem is to find an ordered set of *FPs* $RS = \{RS_1, RS_2, ..., RS_K\}$ such that the following conditions are satisfied.

$$\tau_s = \alpha_{i1}, \beta_{i1} = \alpha_{i2}, ..., \beta_{ij} = \alpha_{i(j+1)}, ..., \beta_{i(Q-1)} = \alpha_{iQ},$$
$$\text{and } \beta_{iQ} = \tau_e, \forall i \in DS \qquad (6.1)$$

$$F_{i(MIN)} \leq f_{ij} \leq F_{i(MAX)}, \forall i \in DS \qquad (6.2)$$

where $F_{i(MIN)}$ and $F_{i(MAX)}$ are the allowable minimal and maximal flow rate for feeding distiller *i*. An illustrative refining schedule is shown in Figure 18, where there are three distillers and two *FPs* for each distiller with a ten-day scheduling horizon.

Feasibility is essential for scheduling the crude oil operations. It requires that a refining schedule must be realizable by a detailed schedule. It should be pointed out that conditions (6.1) and (6.2) are not enough to guarantee the feasibility of a refining schedule *RS*. An oil refining process is a continuous process and it has an operation require-

ment as follows. If, at the initial state, charging tank CTK_A is feeding distiller DS_1 with a type of crude oil #k, a refining process starting from time τ_s should be scheduled such that distiller DS_1 should continue to refine crude oil #k in CTK_A until CTK_A is emptied. If a refining schedule can meet this requirement, it is said that such a refining schedule is compatible with the initial state. Hence, the feasibility of a refining schedule is defined as follows.

Definition 6.2: A refining schedule for crude oil operations in a refinery is said to be feasible if 1) It is compatible with the initial state; and 2) There exists a detailed schedule that implements it such that all the constraints are satisfied.

Next, based on Definitions 6.1 and 6.2 and the schedulability conditions obtained in prior sections, a novel method for refining scheduling is presented.

6.2. Analysis of Refining Scheduling

Some objectives should be optimized when the crude oil operations are scheduled. Thus, we need to determine the objectives first. In the literature, the objectives include: 1) minimization of crude oil inventory cost, tanker waiting cost, and crude oil unloading cost (Lee *et al.*, 1996; Jia *et al.*, 2003

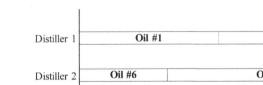

Figure 18. An illustrative refining schedule

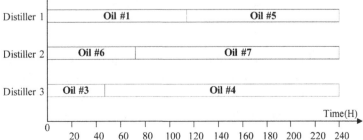

and 2004); 2) maximization of production rate and minimization of the number of tanks used (Pinto *et al.*, 2000); 3) minimization of changeover cost (Lee *et al.*, 1996); and 4) minimization of heels (Shah, 1996). Among them, the minimization of crude oil inventory and changeover costs, and the maximization of production rate are related to the refining scheduling, while the others should be pursued at the detailed scheduling level. Notice that, for refining scheduling, the amount of crude oil available at the beginning of the scheduling horizon and the amount of crude oil that will arrive during the scheduling horizon are independent of the scheduling. Thus, with the initial crude oil inventory and oil arrival information, if the crude oil operations are scheduled such that the production rate is maximized, the crude oil inventory during the scheduling horizon must be minimized. Hence, by maximizing the production rate, it minimizes the crude oil inventory cost at the same time. Besides maximization of the production rate and minimization of crude oil inventory, the cost caused by assigning crude oil types to distillers for processing should be minimized when crude oil operations are scheduled. In a refinery, although a type of crude oil can be processed by a number of distillers, the cost effectiveness is different when it is processed by different distillers. Therefore, it needs to assign crude oil types to appropriate distillers for processing. Thus, it needs to find a refining schedule such that the production rate is maximized, and changeover and crude oil type assignment costs are minimized. Further, to make a refining schedule realizable, the schedulability conditions should be satisfied. The problem is how these conditions are included in the models as constraints such that a feasible refining schedule can be obtained.

It follows from the initial state information that some crude oil arrives at the port at time t with $\tau_s < t < \tau_e$. This implies that only after time point $\tau > t$ can such crude oil be ready to feed a distiller. With time point t, the oil unloading rate,

the oil residency time, and the oil transportation rate from a storage tank to a charging tank known, τ can be calculated. Thus, when Q tankers arrive during the scheduling horizon at times $t_1, t_2, \ldots,$ and t_Q, respectively, with $\tau_s < t_1 < t_2 < \ldots < t_Q < \tau_e$, we can obtain $\tau_1, \tau_2, \ldots,$ and τ_Q with $\tau_s < \tau_1 < \tau_2 < \ldots < \tau_Q < \tau_e$ such that the crude oil in the tanker that arrives at t_i can be available for feeding after τ_i. Hence, we assume that $\tau_1, \tau_2, \ldots,$ and τ_Q are known. In this way, the scheduling horizon is divided into $Q+1$ time buckets $(\tau_s, \tau_1), (\tau_1, \tau_2),$ $\ldots, (\tau_{Q-1}, \tau_Q)$ and (τ_Q, τ_e). Alternatively, they can be called buckets 0, 1, $\ldots,$ and Q, respectively.

To describe the cost effectiveness to process a crude oil type by a distiller, a cost associated with a type of crude oil and a distiller can be set. If it is the best to process crude oil type i by distiller j, small cost is set. We can order the crude oil types that can be processed by a distiller from the best to the worst and set the cost in an increasing way. If crude oil type i cannot be processed by distiller j the cost is set to be a very large number. To develop the refining scheduling approach, we need the following notation.

Parameters:

- Λ: The number of crude oil types (COT) to be processed during the scheduling horizon;
- $COT = \{1, 2, \ldots, \Lambda\}$: The set of crude oil types;
- Π: The number of distillers in the plant;
- $DS = \{1, 2, \ldots, \Pi\}$: The set of distillers;
- Q: The number of tankers that will arrive during the scheduling horizon;
- $BUK = \{0, 1, \ldots, Q\}$: The set of buckets that begin at $\tau_s, \tau_1, \ldots,$ and τ_Q, respectively;
- C_{ij}: The cost if crude oil type i is processed by distiller j, $i \in COT$ and $j \in DS$;
- V_p: The capacity of the pipeline;
- V_{i-c}: The volume of crude oil type i in the charging tanks at time τ_s, $i \in COT$;

- W_{ij}: The remaining volume of crude oil type i in the charging tank that is feeding distiller j at time τ_s, $i \in COT$ and $j \in DS$;
- $V_{i\text{-}p}$: The volume of crude oil type i in the pipeline at time τ_s, $i \in COT$, with $\sum_{i \in COT} V_{i(pipe)} = V_{pipe}$;
- $V_{i\text{-}s}$: The volume of crude oil type i in the storage tanks at time τ_s, $i \in COT$;
- V_{ik}: The volume of crude oil type i that is available for feeding after time τ_k, $i \in COT$ and $k \in BUK$;
- $F_{i(MAX)}$: The maximal feeding rate allowed for distiller $i \in DS$;
- $F_{i(MIN)}$: The minimal feeding rate allowed for distiller $i \in DS$;
- F_{pmax}: The maximal oil transportation rate via the pipeline;
- Ω_i: The set of crude oil types that can be processed by distiller i, $i \in DS$;

Variables:

- f_{ij}: The oil feeding rate to distiller i during bucket j, $i \in DS$ and $j \in BUK$.

The proposed scheduling approach is a three-phase one. In Phase 1, it determines the production rate to maximize the production. The amount of crude oil to be processed for each distiller during each bucket is therefore found. Then, in Phase 2, the crude oil types and amount of crude oil are assigned to the distillers to minimize the crude oil type assignment cost. In Phase 3, the result obtained in Phase 2 is adjusted, and the crude oil parcels and their sequence are determined to minimize the changeover cost.

6.3. Determination of Production Rate

In the follows, a model is presented to solve the problem of Phase 1. To maximize the production is to maximize the crude oil feeding rate for each distiller.

Problem P1: Maximize J $= \sum_{j=0}^{Q} \sum_{i \in DS} f_{ij}$ (6.3)

Subject to

$$F_{i(MIN)} \leq f_{ij} \leq F_{i(MAX)}, i \in DS \text{ and } j \in BUK \quad (6.4)$$

$$\sum_{i \in DS} f_{ij} \leq F_{pmax}, j \in BUK \quad (6.5)$$

$$\sum_{i \in \Omega_j} V_{i\text{-}c} + \sum_{i \in \Omega_j} V_{i\text{-}p} + \sum_{i \in \Omega_j} V_{i\text{-}s} \geq (\tau_1\text{-}\tau_s) f_{j0}, j \in DS \quad (6.6)$$

$$\sum_{i \in COT} V_{i\text{-}c} + \sum_{i \in COT} V_{i\text{-}p} + \sum_{i \in COT} V_{i\text{-}s} \geq (\tau_1\text{-}\tau_s) \sum_{j \in DS} f_{j0} \quad (6.7)$$

$$\sum_{i \in \Omega_j} V_{i\text{-}c} + \sum_{i \in \Omega_j} V_{i\text{-}p} + \sum_{i \in \Omega_j} V_{i\text{-}s} + \sum_{i \in \Omega_j} \sum_{k=1}^{n} V_{ik} \geq (\tau_1\text{-}\tau_s) f_{j0} + \sum_{k=1}^{n} (\tau_{k+1} - \tau_k) f_{jk}, j \in DS \text{ and } 1 \leq n \leq Q\text{-}1 \quad (6.8)$$

$$\sum_{i \in COT} V_{i\text{-}c} + \sum_{i \in COT} V_{i\text{-}p} + \sum_{i \in COT} V_{i\text{-}s} + \sum_{i \in COT} \sum_{k=1}^{n} V_{ik} \geq (\tau_1\text{-}\tau_s) \sum_{j \in DS} f_{j0} + \sum_{j \in DS} \sum_{k=1}^{n} (\tau_{k+1} - \tau_k) f_{jk}, 1 \leq n \leq Q\text{-}1 \quad (6.9)$$

$$\sum_{i \in \Omega_j} V_{i\text{-}c} + \sum_{i \in \Omega_j} V_{i\text{-}p} + \sum_{i \in \Omega_j} V_{i\text{-}s} + \sum_{i \in \Omega_j} \sum_{k=1}^{Q} V_{ik} \geq (\tau_1\text{-}\tau_s) f_{j0} + \sum_{k=1}^{Q-1} (\tau_{k+1} - \tau_k) f_{jk} + (\tau_e\text{-}\tau_Q) f_{jQ}, j \in DS \quad (6.10)$$

$$\sum_{i \in COT} V_{i\text{-}c} + \sum_{i \in COT} V_{i\text{-}p} + \sum_{i \in COT} V_{i\text{-}s} + \sum_{i \in COT} \sum_{k=1}^{Q} V_{ik} - V_p \geq (\tau_1\text{-}\tau_s) \sum_{j \in DS} f_{j0} + \sum_{j \in DS} \sum_{k=1}^{Q-1} (\tau_{k+1} - \tau_k) f_{jk} + \sum_{j \in DS} (\tau_e - \tau_Q) f_{jQ} \quad (6.11)$$

Objective (6.3) maximizes the production, and meanwhile it minimizes crude oil inventory cost as well. Constraint (6.4) states that for every distiller the crude oil feeding rate should be in an allowable range. It follows from the schedulability conditions that the total production rate for the system cannot be greater than the maximal flow rate of the pipeline. This is guaranteed by Constraint (6.5). In bucket 0, only the crude oil in charging tanks, pipeline, and storage tanks can be usable. Constraint (6.6) says that f_{j0}'s should be set such that there is enough crude oil to be processed at each distiller, which implicitly gives the constraint that there is enough crude oil in the charging tanks at the beginning of the scheduling horizon as required by the schedulability conditions. Because a type of crude oil can be processed by more than one distiller, the satisfaction of Constraint (6.6) cannot guarantee that there is enough crude oil to be processed for the entire system in bucket 0. Thus, Constraint (6.7) is introduced. Similarly, Constraints (6.8) and (6.9) are introduced to guarantee that there is enough crude oil to be processed for each distiller and the entire system in the buckets 0, 1, ..., n with $1 \leq n \leq Q\text{-}1$. By Constraints (6.10) and (6.11), it means that, during the entire scheduling horizon, there is enough crude oil for each distiller and the whole system, respectively. Notice that, at the end of the scheduling horizon, the pipeline should be full of oil, and thus, it subtracts V_p from the left size in Constraint (6.11).

It can be seen that, in the model, f_{ij}'s are the decision variables and they are continuous variables and there is no discrete variable at all. Thus, Problem P1 is formulated as a linear programming and is easy to solve.

6.4. Assignment of Crude Oil to Distillers

With the production rate obtained by solving Problem P1, the amount of crude oil to be processed by each distiller is known. Then, it needs to divide the amount of crude oil to be processed during the scheduling horizon into a number of parcels and assign these parcels into the distillers. This problem is called Problem P2. Moreover, the number of parcels of crude oil is not known and needs to be determined by the scheduler. Thus, it seems that such a problem is a combinatorial problem and is hard to solve. However, if we treat the types of crude oil as suppliers and the distillers as demanders, this problem can be formulated as a transportation problem. It is sure that, by solving such a transportation problem, a number of parcels of crude oil with different types are assigned to each distiller. By merging the parcels of the same type of crude oil, a schedule can be formed for each distiller. In this way, this problem can be solved easily.

Let Θ_{ij}, $i \in DS$ and $j \in BUK$, denote bucket j of distiller i; $\Phi_{i\text{-}c}$, $i \in COT$, crude oil type i in the charging tanks; $\Phi_{i\text{-}p}$, $i \in COT$, crude oil type i in the pipeline; $\Phi_{i\text{-}s}$, $i \in COT$, crude oil type i in the storage tanks; Φ_{ij}, $i \in COT$ and $j \in BUK$, crude oil type i available after τ_j, the transportation problem model for P2 is presented in Table 3.

To make a refining schedule feasible, crude oil that is available after τ_j cannot be assigned to a distiller for processing in a bucket k with $k < j$, or Φ_{ij} cannot be assigned to Θ_{hk} with $k < j$. Thus, big M is set in the intersection of Φ_{ij} and Θ_{hk}. In fact, this is why the scheduling horizon is divided into a number of buckets when the problem is modeled. It should also be pointed out that a C_{ij} may be equal to M, meaning that crude oil type i cannot be processed by distiller j.

To make a refining schedule compatible with the initial state, if a charging tank with crude oil type i in it is feeding distiller j at the initial state, the remaining oil in that tank should be fed into distiller j in the schedule. This implies that such crude oil should be assigned into distiller j in the schedule. In a refinery plant, the number of distillers is less than the number of crude oil types. Hence, without loss of generality, we assume that the crude oil type being fed into distiller j is j at the initial state, and the remaining volume is W_{jj}. Further, assume that $(\tau_1\text{-}\tau_s)f_{j0} \geq W_{jj}$. Thus, the demand of Θ_{j0} is $(\tau_1\text{-}\tau_s)f_{j0} - W_{jj}$ as shown in the model. If $(\tau_1\text{-}\tau_s)f_{j0} \geq W_{jj}$ is not satisfied, we

Table 3. The transportation model for Problem P2

Crude oil	Distillers or pipeline												Supply
	Θ_{10}	•	$\Theta_{\Pi0}$	Θ_{11}	•	$\Theta_{\Pi1}$	•	Θ_{1Q}	•	$\Theta_{\Pi Q}$	Pipeline	DM-DS	
$\Phi_{1\text{-}c}$	C_{11}	•	$C_{1\Pi}$	C_{11}	•	$C_{1\Pi}$	•	C_{11}	•	$C_{1\Pi}$	M	M	$V_{1\text{-}c} - W_{11}$
•••													•••
$\Phi_{\Lambda\text{-}c}$	$C_{\Lambda1}$	•	$C_{\Lambda\Pi}$	$C_{\Lambda1}$	•	$C_{\Lambda\Pi}$		$C_{\Lambda1}$	•	$C_{\Lambda\Pi}$	M	M	$V_{\Lambda\text{-}c}$
$\Phi_{1\text{-}p}$	C_{11}	•	$C_{1\Pi}$	C_{11}	•	$C_{1\Pi}$	•	C_{11}	•	$C_{1\Pi}$	M	M	$V_{1\text{-}p}$
•••													•••
$\Phi_{\Lambda\text{-}p}$	$C_{\Lambda1}$	•	$C_{\Lambda\Pi}$	$C_{\Lambda1}$	•	$C_{\Lambda\Pi}$		$C_{\Lambda1}$	•	$C_{\Lambda\Pi}$	M	M	$V_{\Lambda\text{-}p}$
$\Phi_{1\text{-}s}$	C_{11}	•	$C_{1\Pi}$	C_{11}	•	$C_{1\Pi}$	•	C_{11}	•	$C_{1\Pi}$	0	0	$V_{1\text{-}s}$
•••													•••
$\Phi_{\Lambda\text{-}s}$	$C_{\Lambda1}$	•	$C_{\Lambda\Pi}$	$C_{\Lambda1}$	•	$C_{\Lambda\Pi}$	•	$C_{\Lambda1}$	•	$C_{\Lambda\Pi}$	0	0	$V_{\Lambda\text{-}s}$
Φ_{11}	M	•	M	C_{11}	•	$C_{1\Pi}$	•	C_{11}	•	$C_{1\Pi}$	0	0	V_{11}
•••													•••
$\Phi_{\Lambda1}$	M	•	M	$C_{\Lambda1}$	•	$C_{\Lambda\Pi}$		$C_{\Lambda1}$	•	$C_{\Lambda\Pi}$	0	0	$V_{\Lambda1}$
Φ_{12}	M	•	M	M	•	M	•	C_{11}	•	$C_{1\Pi}$	0	0	V_{12}
•••													•••
$\Phi_{\Lambda2}$	M	•	M	M	•	M	•	$C_{\Lambda1}$	•	$C_{\Lambda\Pi}$	0	0	$V_{\Lambda2}$
•••													•••
Φ_{1Q}	M	•	M	M	•	M	M	C_{11}	•	$C_{1\Pi}$	0	0	V_{1Q}
•••													•••
$\Phi_{\Lambda Q}$	M	•	M	M	•	M	M	$C_{\Lambda1}$	•	$C_{\Lambda\Pi}$	0	0	$V_{\Lambda Q}$
Demand	$(\tau_1-\tau_s)f_{10} - W_{11}$	•	$(\tau_1-\tau_s)f_{\Pi0} - W_{1\Pi}$	$(\tau_2-\tau_1)f_{11}$	•	$(\tau_2-\tau_1)f_{\Pi1}$	•	$(\tau_e-\tau_Q)f_{1Q}$	•	$(\tau_e-\tau_Q)f_{\Pi Q}$	V_{pipe}	Z	

can just set the demand of Θ_{j0} to be zero and the demand of Θ_{j1} to be $(\tau_2-\tau_1)f_{j1} + (\tau_1-\tau_s)f_{j0} - W_{jj}$. Correspondingly, the supply of Φ_{j-c} becomes $V_{j-c} - W_{jj}$ as shown in the model.

At the end of the scheduling horizon, the pipeline must be full of crude oil. Thus, there is a "crude oil demand" for filling the pipeline with amount V_p.

To guarantee the existence of a solution for a transportation problem, the total demand must be equal to the total supply. By Problem P1, the total supply is greater than or equal to the total demand. Thus, a dummy distiller denoted by DM-DS is necessary and its demand is

$$Z = \sum_{i\in COT} V_{i-c} + \sum_{i\in COT} V_{i-p} +$$
$$\sum_{i\in COT} V_{i-s} + \sum_{i\in COT}\sum_{k=1}^{Q} V_{ik} - V_p - (\tau_1-\tau_s)$$
$$\sum_{j\in DS} f_{j0} - \sum_{j\in DS}\sum_{k=1}^{Q-1}(\tau_{k+1}-\tau_k)f_{jk} -$$
$$\sum_{j\in DS}(\tau_e-\tau_Q)f_{jQ}.$$

According to the schedulability conditions, it needs at least three charging tanks for a distiller to make a refining schedule realizable, which is not included in P1 as a constraint. Hence, this constraint should be considered in P2. In a refinery plant, if all the charging tanks are usable, this condition can be easily satisfied. In general, in a refinery plant, $\sum_{i\in COT} V_{i-c} + \sum_{i\in COT} V_{i-p}$ is less than the total amount for processing during the scheduling horizon. Thus, to guarantee the condition that there are three charging tanks for a distiller satisfied, all the charging tanks with oil in it at τ_s should be usable during the scheduling horizon. This implies that all the crude oil in the charging tanks at τ_s cannot be assigned to the dummy distiller DM-DS, and such crude oil is impossible to assign to the pipeline. The crude oil in the pipeline at τ_s takes spaces of charging tanks and cannot be assigned to dummy distiller DM-DS either. Hence, the corresponding costs are set to be big M.

With the above analysis, by solving the transportation model given in Table 3, a feasible refining schedule can be obtained. It is well-known that a transportation problem is easier to be solved

than a linear programming and there are standard commercial software tools, such as CPLEX and LINGO, for this purpose. Thus, Problem P2 can be solved very efficiently. Notice that the solution is composed of a number of crude oil parcels distinguished by oil types. It should be pointed out that the great challenge of scheduling crude oil operations results from the hybrid property of the process. Although Problem P2 is a continuous optimization problem, its solution is composed of a number of discrete crude oil parcels. Thus, P2 implicitly solves a hybrid optimization problem.

6.5. Sequencing Parcels

To minimize the changeover cost, it is best to assign crude oil in a charging tank to a single distiller. However, by solving the transportation problem given in Table 3, crude oil in a charging tank at τ_s may be assigned to more than one distiller. For example, there is volume V of crude oil in a charging tank at τ_s, it may assign V_1 to Distiller 1 and V_2 to distiller 2 with $V_1 + V_2 = V$. For this case, if possible, it is better to adjust the assignment such that V is assigned to distiller 1 or 2 only. It can be done as follows.

1. Assume that another crude oil type, say type 2, is assigned to distiller DS_1 and meanwhile there is crude oil type that can be processed by distiller DS_2, say type 3, and is assigned to DM-DS with volume $V_3 \geq V_2$. Then, we can reassign the crude oil by: a) V is assigned to DS_1; b) take V_2 of crude oil type 3 from DM-DS to DS_2; and c) take V_2 of crude oil type 2 from DS_1 to DM-DS.

2. Assume that another crude oil type, say type 2, is assigned to DS_1 and crude oil type 2 can be processed by DS_2 too. Then, we can reassign the crude oil by: a) V is assigned to DS_1; and b) take V_2 of crude oil type 2 from DS_1 to DS_2.

The computational complexity of the above algorithm can be analyzed as follows. Assume that there are *N* charging tanks in which there is crude oil at the initial state. By requirement, such crude oil should be processed during the next scheduling horizon. Further, assume that the crude oil type in different charging tank is different and each type of crude oil can be assigned to at most *G* distillers with *G* equal to or less than $\prod$, the number of distillers in the plant. For a charging tank, only *G*-1 adjustments are needed to complete the above algorithm. Thus, there are no more than $N\times(G-1)$ adjustments, which is of polynomial complexity.

Notice that, in solving the transportation problem given in Table 3, the crude oil from the charging tanks, pipeline, storage tanks, and so on is treated as being from different suppliers. However, two parcels of crude oil assigned to a distiller from different suppliers may be of the same type. These parcels should be merged if they can be processed one after another such that changeover cost is reduced. Because the number of crude oil types is limited, the parcel merging is very simple.

With crude oil reassigned and parcel merging, we need only to sequence the parcels of crude oil for each distiller according to the order of available time to obtain a feasible refining schedule.

Up to now, we have presented the approach for refining scheduling. By this three-phase approach, we successfully discompose a hybrid optimization problem into sub-problems such that each sub-problem contains only continuous or discrete variables. Also, multiple objectives are effectively handled in different phases. To solve the problem, it needs to solve a linear programming problem, a transportation problem, and adjusting and sequence the parcels. In this way, the sub-problems in all the phases can be efficiently solved. Thus, the proposed approach for refining scheduling is computationally efficient and can be used for practical applications. Furthermore, by combining the approaches for detailed schedule presented above, a short-term schedule for crude oil operations can be efficiently found. This is a significant advancement in this research field.

7. AN INDUSTRIAL CASE STUDY

An industrial case problem is given here to show the application of the proposed approach. It arises from a practical application scenario of a refinery. The refinery has three distillers DS_1, DS_2, and DS_3. Three times each month, a short-term schedule should be created for the next 10 days. For the considering scheduling horizon, there are six types of crude oil to be processed. Crude oil type #1 can be processed by only DS_1 and Crude oil #2 by only DS_2. Crude oil #3 can be processed by all three distillers, however, it is best to be processed by DS_1, then by DS_3, and it is the worst if it is processed by DS_2. Crude oil types #4, #5, and #6 can be processed by both DS_2 and DS_3 with different cost. Such cost associated with crude oil types and distillers is given in Table 4, where "*M*" means that a type of oil cannot be processed by the corresponding distiller.

During the scheduling horizon, there are nine charging tanks available. Initially, there is crude oil in Charging Tanks #129, #128, #116, #117, and #115, and the others are empty. At this state, Tanks #129, #128, and #116 are feeding Distillers DS_1, DS_2, and DS_3, respectively. The initial state of the charging tanks is shown in Table 5. The capacity of the pipeline is 12,000 tons and the pipeline is full of crude oil type #2. There are 28,000 tons of crude oil #3, 54,000 tons of crude oil #2, and 64,000 tons of crude oil #1 in the storage tanks. During the scheduling horizon, a tanker will arrive with 132,000 tons of crude oil #6. Assume that $\tau_s = 0h$, then we can obtain $\tau_l = 96h$, or after time 96h, the oil in the tanker can be used for distillation. Hence, the scheduling horizon is divided into two buckets (0, 96) and (96, 240).

The minimal production rates for three distillers are 312.5 tons, 205 tons, and 458 tons per hour, and maximal production rates are 375 tons, 230 tons, and 500 tons per hour, respectively. The maximal flow rate of the pipeline is $f_{pmax} = 1,250$ tons per hour. Six hours are required for oil residency time.

Table 4. The cost associated with crude oil types and distillers

	DS$_1$	DS$_2$	DS$_3$
Crude oil #1	1	*M*	*M*
Crude oil #2	*M*	1	*M*
Crude oil #3	4	10	6
Crude oil #4	*M*	8	3
Crude oil #5	*M*	5	10
Crude oil #6	*M*	8	5

For this case problem, there are three distillers with $\alpha_1 \le 375 \times \Psi = 375 \times 6 = 2250$, $\alpha_2 \le 230 \times \Psi = 1380$, and $\alpha_3 \le 500 \times \Psi = 3000$. Initially, Tank #129 with crude oil 27000 tons is feeding DS$_1$, or we have $2\alpha_1 < 27000$. Also the volume of oil in Tanks #128 and #116 that are feeding DS$_2$ and DS$_3$ is greater than $2\alpha_2$ and $2\alpha_3$, respectively. This implies that the initial condition given in Corollary 5.1 (i.e. the initial condition in Theorems 5.11 and 5.14) is satisfied. In other words, there is enough crude oil in the charging tanks for obtaining a realizable refining schedule. Further, there are nine charging tanks available. Hence, if all the oil in the charging tanks is processed during the scheduling horizon, the number of charging tanks required by Theorems 5.11 and 5.14 is met. Thus, there are enough charging tanks for scheduling the system. Therefore, the proposed approach can be used to find a realizable refining schedule.

By using the initial state information, it is easy to write down the linear programming model of problem P1 for this case problem as follows.

Maximize $J = f_{10} + f_{20} + f_{30} + f_{11} + f_{12} + f_{13}$

Subject to $96f_{10} \le 64000 + 55000 = 119000$

$96f_{20} \le 84000 + 55000 + 27000 + 55000 = 233000$

$96f_{30} \le 55000 + 27000 + 55000 = 137000$

$96(f_{10} + f_{20} + f_{30}) \le 64000 + 55000 + 27000 + 55000 + 84000 = 297000$

$96f_{10} + 144f_{11} \le 119000$

$96f_{20} + 144f_{21} \le 353000 + 12000 = 365000$

$96f_{30} + 144f_{31} \le 269000$

$96(f_{10} + f_{20} + f_{30}) + 144(f_{11} + f_{12} + f_{13}) \le 417000$

Table 5. The initial state of the charging tanks

Tank	Capacity (Ton)	Type of oil filled	Volume (ton)	Distiller feeding
Tank #129	34,000	Crude oil #3	27,000	DS$_1$
Tank #128	34,000	Crude oil #2	30,000	DS$_2$
Tank #116	34,000	Crude oil #4	27,000	DS$_3$
Tank #117	34,000	Crude oil #5	30,000	
Tank #115	34,000	Crude oil #5	25,000	
Tank #127	34,000			
Tank #182	20,000			
Tank #180	20,000			
Tank #181	20,000			

$312.5 \leq f_{10} \leq 375$

$312.5 \leq f_{11} \leq 375$

$205 \leq f_{20} \leq 230$

$205 \leq f_{21} \leq 230$

$458 \leq f_{30} \leq 500$

$458 \leq f_{31} \leq 500$

$f_{10} + f_{20} + f_{30} \leq 1250$

$f_{11} + f_{12} + f_{13} \leq 1250$

Then, by solving P1, we obtain $f_{10} = f_{11} = 375$ tons/h, $f_{20} = f_{21} = 230$ tons/h, and $f_{30} = f_{31} = 500$ tons/h. This is the maximal production rate for the system and the crude oil inventory is also minimized. With the production rate for each distiller in each bucket, the amount of crude oil to be processed by each distiller in each bucket can be obtained as shown in Table 6.

At the initial state, Charging Tanks #129, #128, and #116 are feeding Distillers DS_1 - DS_3, respectively. Thus, to make a refining schedule compatible with the initial state, the 27,000 tons of type #3 oil, 30,000 tons of type #2 oil, and 27,000 tons of type #4 oil should be assigned to bucket 0 of DS_1 - DS_3, respectively. With this assignment, the modified amount of crude oil to be processed by each distiller in each bucket is shown in Table 7. Notice that 22,080 tons of crude oil to be processed by DS_2 in bucket 0 is less than the amount in Charging Tanks #128. Hence, the amount of oil to be processed by DS_2 in bucket (96, 240) is modified as 25,200 tons.

Then, we can build the transportation problem model for Problem P2 as shown in Table 8. The following result of crude oil assignment is obtained by solving P2.

DS$_1$: 27,000 tons of type #3 oil in Tank #129 (parcel P_{11}), 9,000 tons of type #1 oil from

storage tanks (parcel P_{12}), and 54,000 tons of type #1 oil from storage tanks (parcel P_{13});

DS$_2$: 30,000 tons of type #2 oil in Tank #128 (parcel P_{21}), 13,200 tons of type #5 oil in Tanks #117 and #115 (parcel P_{22}), and 12,000 tons of type #2 oil in the pipeline (parcel P_{23});

DS$_3$: 27,000 tons of type #4 oil in Tank #116 (parcel P_{31}), 21,000 and 20,800 tons of type #5 oil in Tanks #117 and #115 (parcels P_{32} and P_{33}), and 51,200 tons of type #6 oil (parcel P_{34}).

After this assignment, 1,000 tons of type #1 oil, 54,000 tons of type #2 oil, 28,000 tons of type #3 oil, and 80,800 tons of type #6 oil remain. By P_{22}, P_{32}, and P_{33}, it assigns the oil in Tanks #117 and #115 to more than one distiller such that the oil in one tank is divided into two parcels, leading to the changeover cost. Thus, according to the method proposed, this can be adjusted: 1) move P_{22} from Distiller 2 to Distiller 3; 2) create a P_{24} with 13,200 tons of type #2 oil from the storage tanks; and 3) take 13,200 tons of oil from P_{34}. Then, we merge: 1) P_{12} and P_{13}; 2) P_{23} and P_{24} with P_{23} processed before P_{24}; and 3) P_{32}, P_{33} and P_{22}, for they are the same type of crude oil. In this way, a realizable refining schedule is obtained as shown in Figure 19. It can be seen that although it

Table 6. The amount (ton) of crude oil to be processed in each bucket

Bucket	DS$_1$	DS$_2$	DS$_3$
(0, 96)	36,000	22,080	48,000
(96, 240)	54,000	33,120	72,000

Table 7. The modified amount (ton) of crude oil to be processed in each bucket

Bucket	DS$_1$	DS$_2$	DS$_3$
(0, 96)	9,000	0	21,000
(96, 240)	54,000	25,200	72,000

Table 8. The transportation problem model for problem P2

	Θ_{10}	Θ_{20}	Θ_{30}	Θ_{11}	Θ_{21}	Θ_{31}	Pipeline	DM-DS	Supply
$\Phi_{5\text{-}c}$	M	5	10	M	5	10	M	M	55,000
$\Phi_{2\text{-}p}$	M	1	M	M	1	M	M	M	12,000
$\Phi_{1\text{-}s}$	1	M	M	1	M	M	0	0	64,000
$\Phi_{2\text{-}s}$	M	1	M	M	1	M	0	0	54,000
$\Phi_{3\text{-}s}$	4	10	6	4	10	6	0	0	28,000
Φ_{61}	M	M	M	M	8	5	0	0	132,000
Demand	9,000	0	21,000	54,000	25,200	72,000	12,000	151,800	

is the best for DS_2 to process crude oil type #5, it is assigned to DS_3; and otherwise there would be no enough oil for DS_3 to process during bucket (0, 96) thereby an infeasible solution. Also, 28,000 tons of oil type #3 is not used though it can be processed by all the distillers. It is meaningful to keep this type of crude oil for DS_1 to process for the next scheduling horizon, and otherwise there is no oil that can be processed by DS_1 during that time. Thus, the obtained refining schedule is a very good one.

With the solution obtained, we have $\alpha_3 = 3000 > \alpha_1 = 2250 > \alpha_2 = 1380$. This implies that the capacity of all the charging tanks is greater than α_3, the largest one. Further, $(f_{10} + f_{20} + f_{30}) = (f_{10} + f_{20} + f_{30}) = 1105 < f_{pmax} = 1250$. As pointed out above, there are enough charging tanks and crude oil at the initial state. Thus, in obtaining the refining schedule, all the schedulability conditions given in Theorem 5.11 or Theorem 5.14 are satisfied. Thus, a detailed schedule can be found to realize the refining schedule. Hence, accordingly,

we can schedule the filling of the charging tanks such that each tank is as full as possible when a charging tank is charged. The detailed schedule is found by creating the ODTs and ODFs one by one in following the proposed method. For example, we have the following ODTs: 20000 tons of oil #2 into Tank #180 → 20000 tons of oil #2 into Tank #181 → 34000 tons of oil #1 into Tank #127 → 20000 tons of oil #1 into Tank #182, and the following ODFs for feeding DS_1: 27000 tons of oil #3 in Tank #129 → 34000 tons of oil #1 in Tank #127 → 20000 tons of oil #1 in Tank #182 → 9000 tons of oil #1 in Tank #129. The Gant Charts of charging tank filling and distiller feeding are shown in Figures 20 and 21, respectively. It can be seen that all the constraints, including crude oil residency time constraint, are satisfied.

It should be pointed out that this case problem is from practical applications with all the constraints considered. It is extremely difficult for an existing mixed integer mathematical programming model to solve such large problems if it is not

Figure 19. The refining schedule for the case study

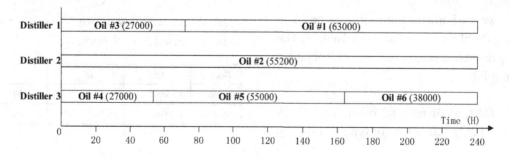

impossible. However, by the method presented here, a short-term schedule is easily found.

CONCLUSION

The short-term scheduling problem of crude oil operations is characterized as a hybrid system containing discrete event and continuous variables such that it is extremely challenging. Moreover, at the beginning of the scheduling horizon, we know only the initial state of the system and the jobs to be scheduled are undecided. This makes that heuristics and meta-heuristics that are widely used in scheduling for discrete manufacturing cannot be applied. Thus, mathematical programming models are formulated for the short-term scheduling problem of crude oil operations and exact solution methods are developed. With the combinatorial nature of the problem, the mathematical programming models can solve only small-size problems, but cannot be applied to large practical application problems.

This chapter presents a novel approach for the short-term scheduling problem of crude oil operations. The system is modeled by a hybrid Petri net. Based on the model, we analyze the schedulability in a control theory perspective such that a feasible detailed schedule can be easily found. Meanwhile, by using the schedulability conditions as constraints, an optimal and realizable refining schedule can be efficiently found. In this way, the problem is decomposed into sub-problems in a hierarchical way such that it can be efficiently solved to obtain the optimal solution.

The schedulability analysis presented in this chapter is based on the developed hybrid Petri nets. However, up to now, there is no tool available for modeling and analysis of such a kind of Petri nets. Thus, it is meaningful to explore further such a method and computer-aided design tools for such models.

Different refineries may have different configurations and the configuration given in Figure 2 is for some parts of refineries. Also, in scheduling crude oil operations, there are much more objec-

Figure 20. The detailed schedule of charging tank filling

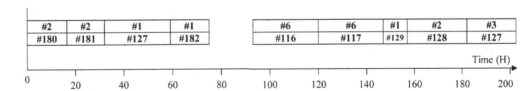

Figure 21. The detailed schedule of distiller feeding for the case study

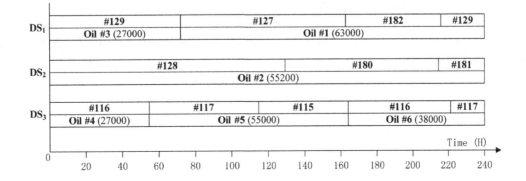

tives to be optimized (Wu et al., 2005). Thus, there is more work to be done, which includes:

1. Based on the hybrid Petri net model and the architecture, searching for effective methods to optimize other objectives in scheduling crude oil operations;
2. Extending the approach to the short-term scheduling for the entire refinery; and
3. Exploring the possibility for applying the proposed approach to the short-term scheduling for other process industries.

REFERENCES

Baker, T. E., & Shobrys, D. E. (1985). *The integration of planning, scheduling, and control.* Paper presented at the National Petroleum Refiners Association Computer Conference. New Orleans, LA.

Bechtel. (1993). *PIMS (process industry modeling system) user's manual, version 6.0.* Houston, TX: Bechtel Corp.

Bodington, C. E. (1995). *Planning, scheduling, and control integration in the process industries.* New York: McGraw-Hill.

Chen, H., & Hanisch, H.-M. (2001). Analysis of hybrid system based on hybrid net condition/event system model. *Discrete Event Dynamic Systems: Theory and Applications, 11*(1-2), 163–185.

Chen, H. X., Chu, C. B., & Proth, J. M. (1998). An improvement of the Lagrangian relaxation approach for job shop scheduling: A dynamic programming method. *IEEE Transactions on Robotics and Automation, 14*(5), 786–795. doi:10.1109/70.720354.

Coxhead, R. E. (1994). Integrated planning and scheduling systems for the refining industry. In Ciriani, T. A., & Leachman, R. C. (Eds.), *Optimization in industry (Vol. 2*, pp. 185–199). New York: Wiley.

Czerwinski, C. S., & Luh, P. B. (1994). Scheduling products with bills of materials using an improved Lagrangian relaxation technique. *IEEE Transactions on Robotics and Automation, 10*(2), 99–110. doi:10.1109/70.282535.

David, R., & Alla, H. (2001). On hybrid Petri nets. *Discrete Event Dynamic Systems: Theory and Applications, 11*(1-2), 9–40.

Floudas, C. A., & Lin, X. (2004). Continuous-time versus discrete-time approaches for scheduling of chemical processes: A review. *Computers & Chemical Engineering, 28*(11), 2109–2129. doi:10.1016/j.compchemeng.2004.05.002.

Glismann, K., & Gruhn, G. (2001). Short-term scheduling and recipe optimization of blending processes. *Computers & Chemical Engineering, 25*(4), 627–634. doi:10.1016/S0098-1354(01)00643-3.

Honkomp, S. J., Lombardo, S., Rosen, O., & Pekny, J. F. (2000). The curse of reality – Why process scheduling optimization problems are difficult in practice. *Computers and Chemical Engineering, 24*(2-7), 323-328.

Ierapetritou, M. G., & Floudas, C. A. (1998). Effective continuous-time formulation for short-term scheduling, 1: Multipurpose batch processes. *Industrial & Engineering Chemistry Research, 37*(11), 4341–4359. doi:10.1021/ie970927g.

Jaikumar, R. (1974). An operational optimization procedure for production scheduling. *Computers & Operations Research, 1*(2), 191–200. doi:10.1016/0305-0548(74)90045-8.

Jia, Z., & Ierapetritou, M. (2004). Efficient short-term scheduling of refinery operations based on a continuous time formulation. *Computers & Chemical Engineering, 28*(6-7), 1001–1019. doi:10.1016/j.compchemeng.2003.09.007.

Jia, Z., Ierapetritou, M., & Kelly, J. D. (2003). Refinery short-term scheduling using continuous time formation: Crude oil operations. *Industrial & Engineering Chemistry Research, 42*(13), 3085–3097. doi:10.1021/ie020124f.

Karuppiah, R., Furmanb, K. C., & Grossmann, I. E. (2008). Global optimization for scheduling refinery crude oil operations. *Computers & Chemical Engineering, 32*(11), 2745–2766. doi:10.1016/j.compchemeng.2007.11.008.

Kondili, E., Pantelides, C. C., & Sargent, R. W. H. (1993). A general algorithm for short-term scheduling for batch operations—1: MILP formulation. *Computers & Chemical Engineering, 17*(2), 211–227. doi:10.1016/0098-1354(93)80015-F.

Ku, H., & Karimi, I. (1991). Evaluation of simulated annealing for batch process scheduling. *Industrial & Engineering Chemistry Research, 30*(1), 163–169. doi:10.1021/ie00049a024.

Kudva, G. A., Elkamel, A., Pekny, J. F., & Reklaitis, G. V. (1994). A heuristic algorithm for scheduling multiproduct plants with production deadlines, intermediate storage limitations, and equipment changeover cost. *Computers & Chemical Engineering, 18*, 859–875. doi:10.1016/0098-1354(93)E0018-5.

Lee, H., Pinto, J. M., Grossmann, I. E., & Park, S. (1996). Mixed integer linear programming model for refinery short-term scheduling of crude oil unloading with inventory management. *Industrial & Engineering Chemistry Research, 35*(5), 1630–1641. doi:10.1021/ie950519h.

Li, W. K., Chi, W. H., & Hua, B. (2002). Scheduling crude oil unloading, storage, and processing. *Industrial & Engineering Chemistry Research, 41*(26), 6723–6734. doi:10.1021/ie020130b.

Liu, Y., & Karimi, I. A. (2008). Scheduling multistage batch plants with parallel units and no interstage storage. *Computers & Chemical Engineering, 32*(4-5), 671–693. doi:10.1016/j.compchemeng.2007.02.002.

Mattfeld, D. C., & Bierwirth, C. (2004). An efficient genetic algorithm for job shop scheduling with tardiness objectives. *European Journal of Operational Research, 155*(2), 616–630. doi:10.1016/S0377-2217(03)00016-X.

Mendez, C. A., & Cerda, J. (2002). An efficient MILP continuous time formulation for short-term scheduling of multiproduct continuous facilities. *Computers & Chemical Engineering, 26*(4-5), 687–695. doi:10.1016/S0098-1354(01)00789-X.

Mendez, C. A., & Cerda, J. (2003). Dynamic scheduling in multiproduct batch plants. *Computers & Chemical Engineering, 27*(8-9), 1247–1259. doi:10.1016/S0098-1354(03)00050-4.

Mendez, C. A., Cerda, J., Grossmann, I. E., Harjunkoski, I., & Fahl, M. (2006). State-of-the-art review of optimization methods for short-term scheduling of batch processes. *Computers & Chemical Engineering, 30*(5-6), 913–946. doi:10.1016/j.compchemeng.2006.02.008.

Mendez, C. A., Grossmann, I. E., Harjunkoski, I., & Kabore, P. (2006). A simultaneous optimization approach for off-line blending and scheduling of oil-refinery operations. *Computers & Chemical Engineering, 30*(4), 614–634. doi:10.1016/j.compchemeng.2005.11.004.

Mesarovic, M. D., Macko, D., & Takahara, Y. (1970). *Theory of hierarchical multilevel systems.* New York: Academic Press.

Moro, L. F. L. (2003). Process technology in the petroleum refining industry – Current situation and future trends. *Computers & Chemical Engineering, 27*(8-9), 1303–1305. doi:10.1016/S0098-1354(03)00054-1.

Murakami, Y., Uchiyama, H., Hasebe, S., & Hashimoto, I. (1997). Application of repetitive SA method to scheduling problem in chemical processes. *Computers & Chemical Engineering, 21*(supplement), 1087–1092.

Pantelides, C. C. (1994). Unified frameworks for optimal process planning and scheduling. In *Proceedings of the 2nd International Conference on Foundations of Computer* (pp. 253-274). CACHE Publications.

Pelham, R., & Pharris, C. (1996). Refinery operation and control: a future vision. *Hydrocarbon Processing, 75*(7), 89–94.

Pinto, J. M., & Grossmann, I. E. (1997). A logic-based approach to scheduling problem with resource constraints. *Computers & Chemical Engineering, 21*(8), 801–818. doi:10.1016/S0098-1354(96)00318-3.

Pinto, J. M., Joly, M., & Moro, L. F. L. (2000). Planning and scheduling models for refinery operations. *Computers & Chemical Engineering, 24*(9-10), 2259–2276. doi:10.1016/S0098-1354(00)00571-8.

Ponnambalam, S. G., Jawahar, N., & Aravindan, P. (1999). A simulated annealing algorithm for job shop scheduling. *Production Planning and Control, 10*(8), 767–777. doi:10.1080/095372899232597.

Realff, M. J., & Stephanopoulos, G. (1998). On the application of explanation-based learning to acquire control knowledge for branching and bound algorithms. *INFORMS Journal on Computing, 10*(1), 56–71. doi:10.1287/ijoc.10.1.56.

Rejowski, R., & Pinto, J. M. (2003). Scheduling of a multiproduct pipeline system. *Computers & Chemical Engineering, 27*(8-9), 1229–1246. doi:10.1016/S0098-1354(03)00049-8.

Sabuncuoglu, I., & Bayiz, M. (1999). Job shop scheduling with beam search. *European Journal of Operational Research, 118*(2), 390–412. doi:10.1016/S0377-2217(98)00319-1.

Saharidisa, G. K. D., Minouxb, M., & Dallery, Y. (2009). Scheduling of loading and unloading of crude oil in a refinery using event-based discrete time formulation. *Computers & Chemical Engineering, 33*(8), 1413–1426. doi:10.1016/j.compchemeng.2009.02.005.

Shah, N. (1996). Mathematical programming techniques for crude oil scheduling. *Computers & Chemical Engineering, 20*(Suppl.), S1227–S1232. doi:10.1016/0098-1354(96)00212-8.

Shah, N., Saharidis, G. K. D., Jia, Z., & Ierapetritou, M. G. (2009). Centralized–decentralized optimization for refinery scheduling. *Computers & Chemical Engineering, 33*(12), 2091–2105. doi:10.1016/j.compchemeng.2009.06.010.

Shobrys, D. E., & White, D. C. (2000). Planning, scheduling and control systems: why can they not work together. *Computers & Chemical Engineering, 24*(2-7), 163-173.

Silva, M., & Recalde, L. (2002). Petri nets and integrality relaxations: a view of continuous Petri net models. *IEEE Transactions on Systems, Man, and Cybernetics. Part C, 32*(4), 317–327.

Stephanopoulos, G., & Han, C. (1996). Intelligence systems in process engineering: A review. *Computers & Chemical Engineering, 20*(6-7), 743–791. doi:10.1016/0098-1354(95)00194-8.

Symonds, G. H. (1955). *Linear programming: The solution of refinery problems*. New York: Esso Standard Oil Company.

Wang, J. (1998). *Timed petri nets: Theory and application*. Dordrecht, The Netherlands: Kluwer Academic Publishers.

Wu, N. Q., Bai, L. P., & Chu, C. B. (2007). Modeling and conflict detection of crude-oil operations for refinery process based on controlled-colored-timed Petri net. *IEEE Transactions on Systems, Man, & Cybernetics. Part C, 37*(4), 461–472.

Wu, N. Q., Bai, L. P., & Zhou, M. C. (2011). *A three-stage method to find refining schedules of crude oil operations in refinery*. Paper presented at the 2011 IEEE International Conference on Service Operations and Logistics, and Informatics. Beijing, China.

Wu, N. Q., Chu, F., Chu, C. B., & Zhou, M. C. (2008b). Short-term schedulability analysis of crude oil operations in refinery with oil residency time constraint using Petri net. *IEEE Transactions on Systems, Man, and Cybernetics. Part C, 38*(6), 765–778.

Wu, N. Q., Chu, F., Chu, C. B., & Zhou, M. C. (2009). Short-term schedulability analysis of multiple distiller crude oil operations in refinery with oil residency time constraint. *IEEE Transactions on Systems, Man, and Cybernetics. Part C, 39*(1), 1–16.

Wu, N. Q., Chu, F., Chu, C. B., & Zhou, M. C. (2010a). Hybrid Petri net modeling and schedulability analysis of high fusion point oil transportation under tank grouping strategy for crude oil operations in refinery. *IEEE Transactions on Systems, Man, and Cybernetics. Part C, 40*(2), 159–175.

Wu, N. Q., Chu, F., Chu, C. B., & Zhou, M. C. (2010b). Tank cycling and scheduling analysis of high fusion point oil transportation for crude oil operations in refinery. *Computers & Chemical Engineering, 34*(4), 529–543. doi:10.1016/j.compchemeng.2009.11.007.

Wu, N. Q., Zhou, M. C., & Chu, F. (2005). Short-term scheduling for refinery process: bridging the gap between theory and applications. *International Journal of Intelligent Control and Systems, 10*(2), 162–174.

Wu, N. Q., Zhou, M. C., & Chu, F. (2008a). A Petri net based heuristic algorithm for realizability of target refining schedules in oil refinery. *IEEE Transactions on Automation Science and Engineering, 5*(4), 661–676. doi:10.1109/TASE.2008.916737.

Yang, S. X., & Wang, D. W. (2001). A new adaptive neural network and heuristics hybrid approach for job-shop scheduling. *Computers & Operations Research, 28*(10), 955–971. doi:10.1016/S0305-0548(00)00018-6.

Zhou, M. C., & Venkatesh, K. (1998). *Modeling, simulation and control of flexible manufacturing systems: A Petri net approach*. Singapore: World Scientific.

Chapter 2
Formal Reliability Analysis of Embedded Computing Systems

Osman Hasan
National University of Sciences and Technology, Pakistan

Sofiène Tahar
Concordia University, Canada

ABSTRACT

The accurate reliability assessment of embedded systems has become a concern of overwhelming importance with their increasingly ubiquitous usage in safety-critical domains like transportation, medicine, and nuclear power plants. Traditional reliability analysis approaches of testing and simulation cannot guarantee accurate result and thus there is a growing trend towards developing precise mathematical models of embedded systems and to use formal verification methods to assess their reliability. This chapter is mainly focused towards this emerging trend as it presents a formal approach for the reliability assessment of embedded computing systems using a higher-order-logic theorem prover (HOL). Besides providing the formal probability theory based fundamentals of this recently proposed technique, the chapter outlines a generic reliability analysis methodology for embedded systems as well. For illustration purposes, two case studies have been considered, i.e., analyzing the reparability conditions for a reconfigurable memory array in the presence of stuck-at and coupling faults and assessing the reliability of combinational logic based digital circuits.

INTRODUCTION

Reliability analysis involves the usage of probabilistic techniques for the prediction of reliability related parameters, such as a system's resistance to failure and its ability to perform a required function under some given conditions. This information is in turn utilized to design more reliable and secure systems. The reliability analysis of embedded computing systems has been conducted since their early introduction. However, the ability to efficiently analyze the reliability of embedded systems has become very challenging nowadays because of their growing sizes and the complex nature of hardware software interaction.

DOI: 10.4018/978-1-4666-3922-5.ch002

Traditionally, simulation has been the most commonly used computer based reliability analysis technique for embedded systems. Most simulation based reliability analysis software provide a programming environment for defining functions that approximate random variables for probability distributions. The environmental behavior and the input patterns of embedded systems are random quantities and are thus modeled by these functions and the system is analyzed using computer simulation techniques, such as the Monte Carlo Method, where the main idea is to approximately answer a query on a probability distribution by analyzing a large number of samples. Statistical quantities, such as expectation and variance, may then be calculated, based on the data collected during the sampling process, using their mathematical relations in a computer. Due to the inherent nature of simulation coupled with the usage of computer arithmetic, the reliability analysis results attained by the simulation approach can never be termed as 100% accurate.

The accuracy of reliability analysis results has become imperative these days because of the extensive usage of embedded systems in safety critical areas. Some examples of safety-critical embedded systems include aircraft flight control systems, surgical robotics and patient monitoring system used in hospitals and instrumentation and control systems found in nuclear power plants. Erroneous reliability analysis in these kinds of areas could have serious consequences, such as loss of human lives.

Formal methods are capable of conducting precise system analysis and thus overcome the above mentioned limitations of simulation (Hall, 2007). The main principle behind formal analysis of a system is to construct a computer based mathematical model of the given system and formally verify, within a computer, that this model meets rigorous specifications of intended behavior. Two of the most commonly used formal verification methods are model checking (Baier, 2008) and higher-order-logic theorem proving (Harrison,

2009). Model checking is an automatic verification approach for systems that can be expressed as a finite-state machine. Higher-order-logic theorem proving, on the other hand, is an interactive verification approach that allows us to mathematically reason about system properties by representing the behavior of a system in higher-order logic.

A number of elegant approaches for the formal analysis of embedded systems can be found in the literature (Balarin, 1996, Ulrich 2006). However, most of this existing formal verification literature is focused towards analyzing the functional verification aspects instead of reliability properties. Recently, both model checking and theorem proving has been extended with probabilistic reasoning support (Baier, 2003, Hurd, 2002) and thus a few formal reliability analysis approaches for embedded systems have been reported (e.g. Hasan, 2009, Hasan, 2011). Probabilistic model checking is automatic but is limited to systems that can only be expressed as probabilistic finite state machines or Markov chains. Another major limitation of using probabilistic model checking to analyze reliability of embedded systems is state space explosion (Baier, 2008) due to the large size of system models and complex hardware software interactions in embedded systems. Similarly, to the best of our knowledge, it has not been possible to use probabilistic model checking to precisely reason about most of the statistical quantities, such as expectation and variance, which are an integral component of every reliability analysis. On the other hand, the higher-order-logic theorem proving based technique tends to overcome the above mentioned limitations of probabilistic model checking. Due to the formal nature of the higher-order-logic models and properties and the inherent soundness of the theorem proving approach, reliability analysis carried out in this way is free from any approximation and precision issues. Similarly, the high expressiveness of higher-order logic allows us to analyze both hardware and software components of an embedded system along with their uncertainties without any modeling limitations, such as infinite state-space or the limitedness to Markovian chain models.

Thanks to the recent developments in the formalization of probability theory concepts in higher-order-logic (Hurd, 2002; Hasan, 2008), we are now at the stage where we can handle the reliability analysis of a variety of embedded systems in a higher-order-logic theorem prover with reasonable amount of modeling and verification efforts. The main idea is to use higher-order logic to develop a precise model of the given embedded system, while expressing its random or unpredictable elements in terms of formalized random variables, and to formally represent the system reliability properties in terms of probabilistic and statistical characteristics of the underlying random variables. These properties can then be verified based on deductive reasoning within the sound core of a mechanical theorem prover.

This chapter provides a brief overview of existing higher-order-logic formalizations that facilitate the formal modeling of embedded systems and formal reasoning about their reliability properties. We show how these capabilities fit into the overall formal reliability analysis framework and also point out some of the missing links that need further investigations. In order to illustrate the practical effectiveness and utilization of the presented approach, we discuss the formal reliability analysis of two real-world embedded systems, namely, reconfigurable memory arrays and combinational logic based digital circuits.

FORMAL RELIABILITY ANALYSIS USING HOL THEOREM PROVER

The reliability analysis of an embedded system mainly involves a description of the system behavior and a set of reliability properties and the goal is to check if the given embedded system satisfies these given properties. Since reliability of a system is dependent upon many nondeterministic and unpredictable factors thus the system behavior is usually expressed mathematically in terms of appropriate random variables and the system properties are represented in terms of probabilistic and statistical characteristics.

The first step in the theorem proving based reliability analysis of embedded systems is to construct a formal model of the given system in higher-order-logic, while using formalized discrete and continuous random variables. The second step is to utilize the formal model of the system to express system properties as higher-order-logic goals. The prerequisite for this step is the ability to express probabilistic and statistical properties related to both discrete and continuous random variables in higher-order-logic. All probabilistic properties of discrete and continuous random variables can be expressed in terms of their Probability Mass Function (PMF) and Cumulative Distribution Function (CDF), respectively. Similarly, most of the commonly used statistical properties can be expressed in terms of the expectation and variance characteristics of the corresponding random variable. Thus, we require the formalization of PMF, CDF, expectation, and variance for both discrete and continuous random variables in order to be able to express the given system's reliability characteristics as higher-order-logic theorems. The third and the final step for conducting reliability analysis in a theorem prover is to formally verify the higher-order-logic goals developed in the previous step using a theorem prover. For this verification, it would be quite handy to have access to a library of some pre-verified theorems corresponding to some commonly used properties regarding probability distribution functions, expectation, and variance. This way, we can build upon such a library of theorems and thus speed up the verification process. The formalization details associated with the prerequisites of the above-mentioned steps are briefly described now.

Discrete Random Variables and their PMF

A random variable is called discrete if its range, i.e., the set of values that it can attain, is finite or at most countably infinite. Discrete random variables can be completely characterized by their PMFs that return the probability that a random variable X is equal to some value x, i.e., $Pr(X = x)$. Discrete random variables are quite frequently used to model randomness in reliability analysis. For example, the Bernoulli random variable is widely used to model the fault occurrence in a component and the Binomial random variable may be used to represent the number of faulty components in a lot.

Discrete random variables can be formalized in higher-order-logic as deterministic functions with access to an infinite Boolean sequence B^∞; an infinite source of random bits with data type (*natural* → *bool*) (Hurd, 2002). These deterministic functions make random choices based on the result of popping the top most bit in the infinite Boolean sequence and may pop as many random bits as they need for their computation. When the functions terminate, they return the result along with the remaining portion of the infinite Boolean sequence to be used by other functions. Thus, a random variable that takes a parameter of type α and ranges over values of type β can be represented by the function

$$F: \alpha \to B^\infty \to \beta \, x \, B^\infty$$

For example, a Bernoulli(½) random variable that returns 1 or 0 with probability ½ can be modeled as

bit = λs. (if shd s then 1 else 0, stl s)

where the variable *s* represents the infinite Boolean sequence and the functions *shd* and *stl* are the sequence equivalents of the list operations *'head'* and *'tail'*. A function of the form *λx. t(x)* represents a lambda abstraction function that maps *x* to *t(x)*. The function *bit* accepts the infinite Boolean sequence and returns a pair with the first element equal to either 0 or 1 and the second element equal to the unused portion of the infinite Boolean sequence.

The higher-order-logic formalization of the probability theory (Hurd, 2002) also consists of a probability function $\mathbb{P}$ from sets of infinite Boolean sequences to *real* numbers between 0 and 1. The domain of $\mathbb{P}$ is the set $\mathscr{E}$ of events of the probability. Both $\mathbb{P}$ and $\mathscr{E}$ are defined using the Caratheodory's Extension theorem, which ensures that $\mathscr{E}$ is a σ-algebra: closed under complements and countable unions. The formalized $\mathbb{P}$ and $\mathscr{E}$ can be used to formally verify all the basic axioms of probability. Similarly, they can also be used to prove probabilistic properties for random variables. For example, we can formally verify the following probabilistic property for the function *bit*, defined above,

$$\mathbb{P} \, \{s \mid fst \, (bit \, s) = 1\} = ½$$

where *{x|C(x)}* represents a set of all elements *x* that satisfy the condition *C*, and the function *fst* selects the first component of a pair.

The above mentioned foundations can be utilized to formalize most of the commonly used discrete random variables and verify their corresponding PMF relations. In this chapter, we will utilize the models for Bernoulli random variable formalized as higher-order-logic function *prob_bern* and verified using the following PMF relations in (Hurd, 2002).

$$\forall p. \, 0 \leq p \land p \leq 1 \Rightarrow (P \, \{s \mid fst \, (prob\_bern \, p \, s)\} = p)$$

The Geometric random variable returns the number of Bernoulli trials needed to get one success and thus cannot return 0. This is why we have *(n+1)* in Theorem 2, where *n* is a positive integer {0,1,2,3 …}. Similarly, the probability *p* in Theorem 2 represents the probability of success and thus needs to be greater than 0 for this theorem to be true as has been specified in the precondition.

Continuous Random Variables and the CDF

A random variable is called continuous if it ranges over a continuous set of numbers that contains all real numbers between two limits. Continuous random variables can be completely characterized by their CDFs that return the probability that a random variable X is exactly less than or equal to some value x, i.e., $Pr(X \leq x)$. Examples of continuous random variables include measuring T, the arrival time of a data packet at a Web server $(S_T = \{t \mid 0 \leq t < \infty\})$ and measuring V, the voltage across a resistor $(S_V = \{v \mid -\infty < v < \infty\})$.

The sampling algorithms for continuous random variables are non-terminating and hence require a different formalization approach than discrete random variables, for which the sampling algorithms are either guaranteed to terminate or satisfy probabilistic termination, meaning that the probability that the algorithm terminates is 1. One approach to address this issue is to utilize the concept of the nonuniform random number generation, which is the process of obtaining arbitrary continuous random numbers using a Standard Uniform random number generator. The main advantage of this approach is that we only need to formalize the Standard Uniform random variable from scratch and use it to model other continuous random variables by formalizing the corresponding nonuniform random number generation method.

Based on the above approach, a methodology for the formalization of all continuous random variables for which the inverse of the CDF can be represented in a closed mathematical form is presented in (Hasan, 2008). The first step in this methodology is the formalization of the Standard Uniform random variable, which can be done by using the formalization approach for discrete random variables and the formalization of the

mathematical concept of limit of a *real* sequence (Harrison, 1998). The formalization details are outlined in (Hasan, 2008).

The second step in the methodology for the formalization of continuous probability distributions is the formalization of the CDF and the verification of its classical properties. This is followed by the formal specification of the mathematical concept of the inverse function of a CDF. This definition along with the formalization of the Standard Uniform random variable and the CDF properties can be used to formally verify the correctness of the Inverse Transform Method (ITM). The ITM is a well-known nonuniform random generation technique for generating nonuniform random variables for continuous probability distributions for which the inverse of the CDF can be represented in a closed mathematical form. Formally, it can be verified for a random variable X with CDF F using the Standard Uniform random variable U as follows

$$Pr\left(F^{-1}(U) \leq x\right) = F(x)$$

The formalized Standard Uniform random variable can now be used to formally specify any continuous random variable for which the inverse of the CDF can be expressed in a closed mathematical form as $X = F^{-1}(U)$. Whereas, the CDF of this formally specified continuous random variable, X, can be verified using simple arithmetic reasoning and the formal proof of the ITM. Based on this approach, Exponential, Uniform, Rayleigh and Triangular random variables have been formalized and their CDF relations have been verified (Hasan, 2008).

Statistical Properties for Discrete Random Variables

In reliability analysis, statistical characteristics play a major role in decision making as they tend to summarize the probability distribution characteristics of a random variable in a single number.

Due to their widespread interest, the computation of statistical characteristics has now become one of the core components of every contemporary reliability analysis framework.

The expectation for a discrete random variable *X*, which attains values in the positive integers only, is formally defined as follows.

$$\forall X.\ expec\ X = suminf\ (\lambda n.\ n\ \mathbb{P}\ \{s \mid fst\ (X\ s) = n\})$$

where the mathematical notions of the probability function $\mathbb{P}$ and random variable *X* have been inherited from (Hurd, 2002), as presented in the previous section. The function *suminf* represents the HOL formalization of the infinite summation of a *real* sequence (Harrison, 1998). The function *expec* accepts the random variable *X* with data type $B^{\infty} \to natural\ x\ B^{\infty}$ and returns a *real* number. The above definition can be used to verify the average values of most of the commonly used discrete random variables (Hasan, 2008).

In order to verify the correctness of the formal definition of expectation and facilitate reasoning about expectation properties in probabilistic systems, many widely used expectation properties have been formally verified in the HOL theorem prover (Hasan, 2008). Namely being the linearity of expectation, Markov and Chebyshev's inequalities, variance and linearity of variance.

Statistical Properties for Continuous Random Variables

The expectation of a continuous random variable has been formally defined in (Hasan, 2009b) using the Lebesgue integral (Galambos, 1995) as follows:

$$\forall X.\ expec\_cont\ X = \int_{\Omega} X\ dP$$

where *X* is a random variable, defined on a probability space (Ω, σ, P). This definition is general enough to cater for both discrete and continuous random variables. The reason behind its limited

usage in the probabilistic analysis domain is the complexity of solving the Lebesgue integral, which takes its foundations from the measure theory that most engineers and computer scientists are not familiar with. This limitation has been tackled in (Hasan, 2009b) and the main idea is to verify two relatively simplified expressions for expectation by building on top of the Lebesgue integral based definition. The first expression is for the case when the given continuous random variable is bounded in the positive interval *(a,b)* and the second one is for an unbounded random variable in (Hasan, 2009b). Both of these expressions are verified using the fundamentals from measure and Lebesgue integral theories but once verified, they can be utilized to verify expectation properties of any continuous random variable without applying these complex underlying concepts. The usage of these expressions is illustrated by verifying the expectation (Hasan, 2009b) and variance (Abbasi, 2010) relations for Uniform, Triangular and Exponential random variables.

APPLICATIONS

We now illustrate the usage of the formalization, mentioned so far in this paper, for conducting reliability analysis of two embedded systems using the HOL theorem prover.

Reliability Analysis of Reconfigurable Memory Arrays

Memory is an integral part of every embedded system. To ensure reliable operation is safety-critical embedded system applications, reconfigurable memory arrays with spare rows and columns are quite frequently used as reliable data storage components. The spare memory rows and columns can be utilized to automatically replace rows or columns that are found to contain a cell fault, such as stuck-at or coupling fault. One of the biggest design challenges is to estimate, prior to the actual fabrication process, the right number of these spare rows and spare columns for meeting the reliability specifications. Since the fault occurrence in a memory cell is an unpredictable event, probabilistic techniques are utilized to estimate the number of spare rows and columns to ensure reliability. For example, it has been proposed in (Shi, 1992) that if the probability of stuck-at fault occurrence is given by

$$\frac{1}{n}\left[(a+b) + \frac{w(n)}{\sqrt{n}}\right]$$

then a *nxn* square memory array with *a.n* and *b.n* spare rows and columns, respectively, is almost always repairable, i.e., the probability of repairability tends to 1 as *n* becomes very large. Where, the real sequence *w* in the above expression tends to infinity as the value of *n* becomes very large. We now utilize the presented approach to formally verify this result using the HOL theorem prover. The first step in this regard is to develop a formal model of stuck-at faults in a square memory array, which can be done using the two recursive functions depicted in Box 1.

The function *mem_fault_model* accepts three parameters: the number of rows *r*, number of columns *c*, and the probability of fault occurrence *p*. It recursively manipulates these three parameters, with the help of the function *mem_fault_model_ helper* and returns the number of faults found in the memory array of size *rxc*. It is important to note that the fault occurrence behavior, which is the random component in this model, is represented by the formalized Bernoulli random variable function *prob_bern* (Hurd, 2002) above. The function *mem_fault_model* basically performs a Bernoulli trail, with the probability of obtaining a *True* being equal to the probability of fault occurrence, for each cell of the memory array and returns the total number of *True* outcomes obtained.

Now, in order to verify the condition of repairability, given in (Shi, 1992), we define the following special case of our general memory model. (see Box 2)

The function *mem_fault_model_repairability* accepts four parameters: the number of rows and columns of a square reconfigurable memory *n*, the fractions of spare rows and columns *a* and *b*, respectively, and the real sequence *w*. It utilizes the function *mem_fault_model* to return the number

Box 1.

$$
\begin{aligned}
&\forall p. &&mem\_fault\_model\_helper\ 0\ p = unit\ 0\ \wedge \\
&\forall c\ p. &&mem\_fault\_model\_helper\ (c+1)\ p = bind\ (mem\_fault\_model\_helper\ c\ p) \\
& && \quad (\lambda a.\ bind\ prob\_bern)\ (\lambda b.\ unit\ (if\ b\ then\ (a+1)\ else\ a)) \\
&\forall c\ p. &&mem\_fault\_model\ 0\ c\ p = unit\ 0\ \wedge \\
&\forall r\ c\ p. &&mem\_fault\_model\ 0\ c\ p = bind\ (mem\_fault\_model\ r\ c\ p) \\
& && \quad (\lambda a.\ bind\ mem\_fault\_model\_helper\ c\ p)\ (\lambda b.\ unit\ (a+b))
\end{aligned}
$$

Box 2.

$$
\begin{aligned}
&\forall n\ a\ b\ w.\ mem\_fault\_model\_repairability\ n\ a\ b\ w = \\
& \qquad mem\_fault\_model\ n\ n\ \frac{1}{n}\left[(a+b) + \frac{w(n)}{\sqrt{n}}\right]
\end{aligned}
$$

of stuck-at faults for the specific case of a square *nxn* memory array with the fault occurrence probability equal to the expression, given by (Shi, 1992). This way, by developing a formal model of our system, we are done with the first part of the formal reliability analysis.

The next step is to formally specify the average, variance of stuck-at faults properties of interest as higher-order-logic goals for our theorem prover and then verify them using the HOL theorem prover. We formally analyzed the average, variance and tail distribution bounds along with the repairability condition in this case study. For example, the average number of faults can be expressed as the goal shown in Box 3 using the formal definition of number of faults.

The first four assumptions in the above theorem ensure that the fractions *a* and *b* are in by the interval *(0,1)* as the number of spare rows and columns cannot exceed the original number of rows and columns. Whereas, the precondition *1 < n* has been used in order to ensure that the given memory array has at least more than one cell. The last assumption provides the bounds for the real sequence *w*. These bounds have been used in order to prevent the stuck-at fault occurrence probability

p from falling outside its allowed interval *(0,1)*. It is interesting to note that no such restriction on the sequence *w* was imposed in the paper-and-pencil based analysis of the repairability problem given in (Shi, 1992). This fact clearly demonstrates the strength of formal methods based analysis as it allowed us to highlight this corner case, which if ignored could lead to the invalidation of the whole repairability analysis. The conclusion of Theorem 1 presents the mathematical relation for the expected number of stuck-at faults. The formal proof of this goal involved probability and real theoretic reasoning along with some set theory principles.

In a similar way, theorems corresponding to variance and tail distribution of the stuck-at faults were verified and further details are provided in (Hasan, 2009). Building upon these results, the reparability problem can also be formally analyzed as the theorem shown in Box 4 where *lim M* represents the HOL formalization of the limit of a real sequence *M* (i.e., $\lim M = \lim_{n \to \infty} M(n)$) (Harrison, 1998). The new assumption *lim (λn. 1/w(n)) = 0)* formally represents the intrinsic characteristic of *real* sequence *w* that it tends to infinity as its argument *n* becomes very large. The theorem

Box 3.

$$\forall\ n\ a\ b\ w.\ (0 \le a) \land (a \le 1) \land (0 \le b) \land (b \le 1) \land (1 < n) \land$$
$$(\forall\ n.\ (0 < w(n)) \land (w(n) < (a+b)\sqrt{n})) \Rightarrow$$
$$(expec\ (\lambda s.\ mem\_fault\_model\_repairability\ n\ a\ b\ w\ s) = n^2(\frac{a+b}{n} - \frac{w\big(n\big)}{n\sqrt{n}})$$

Box 4.

$$\forall\ a\ b\ w.\ (0 \le a) \land (a \le 1) \land (0 \le b) \land (b \le 1) \land (1 < n) \land$$
$$(\forall\ n.\ (0 < w(n)) \land (w(n) < (a+b)\sqrt{n})) \land (lim\ (\lambda n.\ 1/w(n)) = 0) \Rightarrow$$
$$lim\ (\lambda n.\ \mathbb{P}\ \{s \mid fst\ (mem\_fault\_model\_repairability\ n\ a\ b\ w\ s) \le (a+b)\ n\}) = 1$$

proves that under these assumptions a very large square memory array is almost always repairable (with probability 1) since the probability that the number of faults is less than the number of spare rows and columns is 1. The formal verification details about this theorem can be found in (Hasan, 2009).

The above theorem leads to the accurate estimation of the number of spare rows and columns required for reliable operation against stuck-at faults of any reconfigurable memory array without any CPU time constraints. Due to the formal nature of the models, the high expressiveness of higher-order logic, and the inherent soundness of theorem proving, we have been able to verify generic properties of interest that are valid for any given memory array with 100% precision; a novelty which is not available in simulation. Similarly, we have been able to formally analyze properties that cannot be handled by model checking. The proposed approach is also superior to the paper-and-pencil proof methods (Shi, 1992) in a way as the chances of making human errors, missing critical assumptions and proving wrongful statements are almost nil since all proof steps are applied within the sound core of the HOL theorem prover. Another distinguishing feature of this analysis is its generic nature as all the theorems are verified for all sizes *nxn* of memories with any number of spare rows *a.n* or columns *b.n*. These additional benefits come at the cost of the time and effort spent, while formalizing the memory array and formally reasoning about its properties. But, the fact that we were building on top of already verified probability theory foundations helped

significantly in this regard as the memory analysis only consumed approximately 80 man-hours and 1200 lines of HOL code.

Reliability Analysis of Combinational Logic Circuits

Reliability analysis of combinational logic circuits has become imperative these days due to the extensive usage of nanotechnologies in their fabrication. Traditionally, such reliability analysis is done using simulation or paper-and-pencil proof methods. But, these techniques do not ensure accurate results and thus may lead to disastrous consequences when dealing with safety critical applications. The presented formal reliability analysis approach can be used to overcome this problem. In this section, we present a formal reliability model of a single combinational gate. This model, also referred to as the von-Neumann error model (Han, 2005) can then be utilized to analyze more complex combinational logic based digital circuits. For illustration purposes, we present the example of a comparator circuit.

The behavior of a faulty gate or component using the von-Neumann model can be formalized as the two functions shown in Box 5.

The empty list is denoted by *()* and the cons operator is denoted by *::* in HOL. The first function *rv_list* accepts a list of random variables and returns the corresponding list of the same random variables such that the outcome of each one of these random variables is independent of the outcomes of all the others. This is done by recursively using the remaining portion of the

Box 5.

$$rv\_list\ () = unit\ ()\ \wedge$$
$$\forall\ h\ t.\ rv\_list\ (h::t) = bind\ h\ (\lambda x.\ bind\ rv\_list\ t)\ (\lambda y.\ unit\ (x::y))$$

$$\forall\ f\ P\ e.\ faulty\_comp\ f\ P\ e = bind\ (prob\_bern\ e)\ (\lambda x.\ bind\ rv\_list\ P)$$
$$(\lambda y.\ unit\ (if\ x\ then\ \neg(f\ y)))$$

infinite Boolean sequence of each random variable to model its subsequent random variable in the list using the monadic functions *unit* and *bind*. The second function *faulty_comp* accepts three variables. The first one is a function *f* that represents the Boolean logic functionality of the given component. The second input to the function *faulty_comp* is a list of Boolean random variables *P*, which corresponds to the values available at the input of the component. Whereas, the third input is the probability *e* of error occurrence in the component. The function *faulty_comp* returns a Boolean value corresponding to the output of the component with parameters *f* and *e*, when its inputs are modeled by calling the random variables in the list of random variables *P* independently. It is important to note here that we have used the function *prob_bern* for the Bernoulli random variable to model the random behavior associated with the error occurrence in the component. Therefore, the function *faulty_comp* basically models the erroneous behavior of a component based on the von-Neumann model (Han, 2005) which assumes that the component flips its output with a probability e given that the input and output lines function correctly.

Next, we verify a general expression for the probability of obtaining a *True* or a logical 1 at the output of the von-Neumann model of a component, which is very closely related to the gate reliability in the *probabilistic gate model* (PGM) based approach (Han, 2005). (see Box 6)

The theorem is verified under the assumption that the error probability *e* of a component is bounded in the closed interval *[0,1]* and every member of the random variable list *P* is measurable, i.e., it belongs to the class of independent functions as discussed earlier. The right-hand-side of the theorem represents the given probability in terms of the probability of obtaining a *True* from an error-free component, which is much easier to reason about. The HOL proof of this theorem is based on the independence of the error occurrence, the PMF of the Bernoulli random variable and some basic probability axioms.

The above theorem can now be used to formally reason about the probability of obtaining a logical 1 from any logical gate that may exhibit a faulty behavior. In order to be able to automatically reason about the reliability of digital circuits, we formally verified this probability for some of the commonly used gates. For example, the functionality of an n-bit AND gate can be formally defined as:

and_gate () = True ∧
∀ *h t. and_gate (h::t) = h* ∧ *(and_gate t)*

and the theorem corresponding to the probability of obtaining a *True* from this component can be expressed as depicted in Box 7.

Box 6.

$$\forall\ e f P.\ (0 \le e) \wedge (e \le 1) \wedge (\forall\ x.\ mem\ x\ P \Rightarrow x \in indep\_fn) \Rightarrow$$
$$\mathbb{P}\ \{s \mid f\ (fst\ (faulty\_comp\ f\ P\ e)\} =$$
$$e\ (1 - (\mathbb{P}\ \{s \mid f\ (fst\ (rv\_lst\ P\ s))\}) + (1-e)\ \mathbb{P}\ \{s \mid f\ (fst\ (rv\_lst\ P\ s)\}$$

Box 7.

$$\forall\ e\ P.\ (0 \le e) \wedge (e \le 1) \wedge (\forall\ x.\ mem\ x\ P \Rightarrow x \in indep\_fn) \Rightarrow$$
$$\mathbb{P}\ \{s \mid f\ (fst\ (faulty\_comp\ and\_gate\ P\ e)\} =$$
$$e\ (1 - prob\_rv\_list\_mul\ P + (1-e)\ prob\_rv\_list\_mul\ P$$

The function *prob_rv_list_mul* recursively returns the multiplication of the probabilities of each random variable being equal to *True* in the given list of random variables. The proof of this theorem is based on the general expression for the probability of obtaining a *True* or a logical 1 at the output of the von-Neumann model of a component, presented above, and the fact that the probability of obtaining a logical 1 at the output of an error-free AND-gate is equal to the product of the probabilities of obtaining all logical 1's at its inputs. The result of the above theorem is generic and can be specialized for any AND-gate with a specific number of inputs. In a similar way, the functionality of any gate can be defined and its reliability can be verified.

In Box 8, we formally define the reliability of a gate as the probability that the gate produces the error free result (Han, 2005).

The function *rel* accepts three parameters. The variables *f* and *e* represent the Boolean logic functionality of the given component and the probability of error occurrence in the component, respectively. Whereas, the third variable *L* is a function that accepts an error probability as a *real* number and returns a list of Boolean random variables with the same type as the variable *P* in the function *faulty_comp*. The function *rel* returns the desired reliability of the component with functionality *f* and error probability *e*. The

Figure 1. Comparator circuit

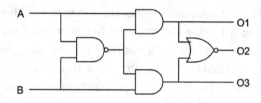

left-hand-side term in the set represents the output of the component while considering the effect of error and the right-hand-side term represents the error free output of the given component.

An alternate more convenient expression for reliability can be verified as depicted in Box 9 (Taylor, 2006).

The main advantage of the above expression is that it can be used to evaluate the reliability of a logical gate in terms of the probability of attaining a logical 1 at its output, which can be verified as has been demonstrated for the AND gate above. This expression also facilitates the reliability assessment of a combination of gates.

For illustration purposes, consider the comparator circuit of Figure 1. The reliability for its output *O1* or *O3* for an input pattern *(pA,pB)* can be formally expressed as shown in Box 10.

The assumptions ensure that probability variables, *pA*, *pB* and *e* lie within the interval *(0,1)*. The left-hand-side of the proof goal represents the reliability of the given comparator circuit, using

Box 8.

$$\forall f L e. \ rel f L e = \mathbb{P} \{s \mid (fst \ (faulty\_comp \ f \ (L \ e) \ e \ s =$$
$$(fst \ (faulty\_comp \ f \ (L \ 0) \ 0 \ (snd \ (faulty\_comp \ f \ (L \ e) \ e \ s)))))\}$$

Box 9.

$$\forall L e. \ (0 \le e) \wedge (e \le 1) \Rightarrow$$
$$rel f L e = \mathbb{P}\{s \mid (fst \ (faulty\_comp \ f \ (L \ e) \ e \ s\} \ \mathbb{P} \ \{s \mid (fst \ (faulty\_comp \ f \ (L \ 0) \ 0 \ s\} +$$
$$(1-\mathbb{P}\{s \mid (fst \ (faulty\_comp \ f \ (L \ e) \ e \ s\}) \ (1- \mathbb{P} \ \{s \mid (fst \ (faulty\_comp \ f \ (L \ 0) \ 0 \ s\})$$

Box 10.

> $\forall$ *pA pB e. (0 $\leq$ pA $\wedge$ (pA$\leq$ 1) $\wedge$ (0 $\leq$ pB $\wedge$ (pB $\leq$ 1) $\wedge$ (0 $\leq$ e) $\wedge$ (e $\leq$ 1) $\Rightarrow$*
> *rel and_gate*
>   *(λx. [prob_bern pA; (faulty_comp nand_gate [prob_bern pA; prob_bern B] x)]) e =*
>   *pA(1-e+(2e-1)pApB)+*
>   *e(1-2pA(1-e+(2e-1)pApB))) (pA(1-(pApB)))+(1-(pA(1-e+(2e-1)pApB)+*
>   *e(1-2pA(1-e+(2e-1)pApB))))(1-pA(1-(pApB))))*

the function *rel* and the right-hand-side gives the reliability in terms of the variables *pA*, *pB* and *e*. The function *and_gate* represents the AND-gate in the figure for which the reliability is required. It is a two input gate and its list of random variables, which corresponds to the inputs of the gate, contains two random variables. The first input is coming from a primary port and therefore we use the Bernoulli random variable function *prob_bern* with input probability *pA* of getting a logical 1 at this input for its input random variables list. The second input of the AND-gate is coming from a 2-input NAND-gate, for which the inputs are in turn connected to the primary ports A and B and these connections can be observed in the input random variable list for the function *nand_gate*. The distinguishing feature of the above theorem is its generic nature, i.e., it is true for all values of *e*, *pA* and *pB*. In other words, once this theorem is verified it can be readily used to evaluate the reliability of outputs *O1* or *O3* for any values of *e*, *pA* and *pB*.

The general reliability theorems and the reliability of individual gate theorems forms the main core of the proposed infrastructure for the reliability analysis of combinational logic circuits. The foundational work took around 120 man hours and is composed of approximately 2000 lines of HOL code. This formalization can be used to assess the reliability of any design and some interesting examples, including the ISCAS-85-C6288 benchmark that is composed of over 2400 gates, are given in (Hasan, 2011).

CONCLUSION

This chapter provides a brief overview of the existing capabilities of higher-order-logic theorem proving based reliability analysis of embedded systems. The main idea behind this emerging trend is to use random variables formalized in higher-order logic to capture the unpredictable phenomenon found in embedded systems in their formal models and then use these models to formally reason about corresponding probabilistic and statistical properties in a theorem prover. Because of the formal nature of the models, the analysis is 100% accurate and due to the high expressiveness of higher-order logic a wider range of systems can be analyzed. Thus, the theorem proving based analysis approach can prove to be very useful for the reliability optimization of safety critical and highly sensitive embedded system applications. The presented approach has been illustrated by providing the formal reliability analysis of two applications. The analysis results exactly matched the results obtained by paper-and-pencil proof techniques and are thus 100% precise. The successful handling of these diverse embedded system reliability issues by the higher-order-logic theorem proving approach clearly demonstrates its feasibility.

There are many open research issues in the domain of theorem proving based reliability analysis of embedded system. To name a few, first of all the capability to reason about multiple continuous random variables is not available. Secondly, some of the most commonly used random variables, like the Normal random variable, have not been formalized so far. Thirdly, very little work related to the formalization of stochastic processes and Markov Chains is available despite their wide usage in reliability analysis of embedded systems. For example, the formalization of Discrete Time Markov Chains has been reported in (Liu, 2011) and this work can be extended to formalize classified and continuous time Markov chains. Moreover, the usage of formal information theoretic analysis of embedded system designs based on the work of (Mhamdi, 2011) is also worth exploring.

REFERENCES

Abbasi, N., Hasan, O., & Tahar, S. (2010). Formal lifetime reliability analysis using continuous random variables. In *Proceedings of Logic, Language* [LNCS]. *Information and Computation*, *6188*, 84–97.

Baier, C., Haverkort, B., Hermanns, H., & Katoen, J. (2003). Model checking algorithms for continuous time Markov chains. *IEEE Transactions on Software Engineering*, *29*(4), 524–541. doi:10.1109/TSE.2003.1205180.

Baier, C., & Katoen, J. (2008). *Principles of model checking*. Boston: MIT Press.

Baier, C., & Katoen, J. P. (2008). *Principles of model checking*. Cambridge, MA: MIT Press.

Balarin, F., Hsieh, H., Jurecska, A., Lavagno, L., & Sangiovanni-Vincentelli, A. (1996). Formal verification of embedded systems based on CFSM networks. In *Proceedings of the Design Automation Conference*, (pp. 568-571). Springer.

Galambos, J. (1995). *Advanced probability theory*. New York: Marcel Dekker Inc..

Hall, A. (2007). Realizing the benefits of formal methods. *Journal of Universal Computer Science*, *13*(5), 669–678.

Han, J., Taylor, E., Gao, J., & Fortes, J. (2005). Faults, error bounds and reliability of nanoelectronic circuits. In Proceedings of Application-Specific Systems, Architecture Processors, (pp. 247–253). IEEE.

Harrison, J. (1998). *Theorem proving with the real numbers*. Berlin: Springer. doi:10.1007/978-1-4471-1591-5.

Harrison, J. (2009). *Handbook of practical logic and automated reasoning*. Cambridge, UK: Cambridge University Press. doi:10.1017/CBO9780511576430.

Hasan, O. (2008). *Formal probabilistic analysis using theorem proving*. (PhD Thesis). Concordia University, Montreal, Canada.

Hasan, O., Abbasi, N., Akbarpour, B., Tahar, S., & Akbarpour, R. (2009b). Formal reasoning about expectation properties for continuous random variables. [). Berlin: Springer.]. *Proceedings of Formal Methods*, *5850*, 435–450.

Hasan, O., Abbasi, N., & Tahar, S. (2009). Formal probabilistic analysis of stuck-at faults in reconfigurable memory arrays. [LNCS]. *Proceedings of Integrated Formal Methods*, *5423*, 277–291. doi:10.1007/978-3-642-00255-7_19.

Hasan, O., Patel, J., & Tahar, S. (2011). Formal reliability analysis of combinational circuits using theorem proving. *Journal of Applied Logic*, *9*(1), 41–60. doi:10.1016/j.jal.2011.01.002.

Hasan, O., Tahar, S., & Abbasi, N. (2010). Formal reliability analysis using theorem proving. *IEEE Transactions on Computers*, *59*(5), 579–592. doi:10.1109/TC.2009.165.

Hurd, J. (2002). *Formal verification of probabilistic algorithms*. (PhD Thesis). University of Cambridge, Cambridge, UK.

Liu, L., Hasan, O., & Tahar, S. (2011). Formalization of finite-state discrete-time Markov chains in HOL. [LNCS]. *Proceedings of Automated Technology for Verification and Analysis*, *6996*, 90–104. doi:10.1007/978-3-642-24372-1_8.

Mhamdi, T., Hasan, O., & Tahar, S. (2011). Formalization of entropy measures in HOL. In *Proceedings of Interactive Theorem Proving (ITP-11) (LNCS) (Vol. 6898*, pp. 233–248). Berlin: Springer. doi:10.1007/978-3-642-22863-6_18.

Shi, W., & Fuchs, W. K. (1992). Probabilistic analysis and algorithms for reconfiguration of memory arrays. *IEEE Transactions on Computer-Aided Design of Integrated Circuits and Systems, 11*(9), 1153–1160. doi:10.1109/43.160001.

Taylor, E., Han, J., & Fortes, J. (2006). Towards the accurate and efficient reliability modeling of nanoelectronic circuits. In *Proceedings of the Nanotechnology Conference*, (pp. 395–398). IEEE.

Ulrich, K., Daniel, G., & Rolf, D. (2006). Complete formal verification of multi core embedded systems using bounded model checking. In Proceedings of Design, Applications, Integration and Software, (pp. 147-150). IEEE.

ADDITIONAL READING

Coble, A. R. (2010). *Anonymity, information, and machine-assisted proof*. (PhD thesis). University of Cambridge, Cambridge, UK.

Daumas, M., Lester, D., Martin-Dorel, E., & Truffert, A. (2010). Improved bound for stochastic formal correctness of numerical algorithms. *Innovations in Systems and Software Engineering, 6*(3), 173–179. doi:10.1007/s11334-010-0128-x.

Elleuch, M., Hasan, O., Tahar, S., & Abid, M. (2011). Formal analysis of a scheduling algorithm for wireless sensor networks. [LNCS]. *Proceedings of Formal Engineering Methods, 6991*, 388–403. doi:10.1007/978-3-642-24559-6_27.

Hasan, O., & Tahar, S. (2007a). Formalization of continuous probability distributions. In *Proceedings of Automated Deduction (CADE-21) (LNCS) (Vol. 4603*, pp. 2–18). Berlin: Springer.

Hasan, O., & Tahar, S. (2007b). Verification of probabilistic properties in the HOL theorem prover. In *Proceedings of Integrated Formal Methods (IFM-07) (LNCS) (Vol. 4591*, pp. 333–352). Berlin: Springer. doi:10.1007/978-3-540-73210-5_18.

Hasan, O., & Tahar, S. (2007c). Formalization of the standard uniform random variable. *Theoretical Computer Science, 382*(1), 71–83. doi:10.1016/j.tcs.2007.05.009.

Hasan, O., & Tahar, S. (2008a). Using theorem proving to verify expectation and variance for discrete random variables. *Journal of Automated Reasoning, 41*(3-4), 295–323. doi:10.1007/s10817-008-9113-6.

Hasan, O., & Tahar, S. (2008b). Performance analysis of ARQ protocols using a theorem prover. In *Proceedings of the International Symposium on Performance Analysis of Systems and Software (ISPASS-08)*, (pp. 85-94). IEEE Computer Society.

Hasan, O., & Tahar, S. (2008c). Verification of expectation properties for discrete random variables in HOL. In *Proceedings of Theorem Proving in Higher-Order Logics (TPHOLs-07) (LNCS) (Vol. 4732*, pp. 119–134). Berlin: Springer. doi:10.1007/978-3-540-74591-4_10.

Hasan, O., & Tahar, S. (2009a). Probabilistic analysis of wireless systems using theorem proving. *Electronic Notes in Theoretical Computer Science, 242*(2), 43–58. doi:10.1016/j.entcs.2009.06.022.

Hasan, O., & Tahar, S. (2009b). Performance analysis and functional verification of the stop-and-wait protocol in HOL. *Journal of Automated Reasoning, 42*(1), 1–33. doi:10.1007/s10817-008-9105-6.

Hasan, O., & Tahar, S. (2009c). Formal verification of tail distribution bounds in the HOL theorem prover. *Mathematical Methods in the Applied Sciences*, *32*(4), 480–504. doi:10.1002/mma.1055.

Hasan, O., & Tahar, S. (2010a). Formally analyzing expected time complexity of algorithms using theorem proving. *Journal of Computer Science and Technology*, *25*(6), 1305–1320. doi:10.1007/s11390-010-9407-0.

Hasan, O., & Tahar, S. (2010b). Formal probabilistic analysis: A higher-order logic based approach. In *Proceedings of ASM, Alloy, B and Z (LNCS)*, (Vol. 5977, pp. 2-19). Berlin: Springer.

Hasan, O., & Tahar, S. (2011a). Reasoning about conditional probabilities using a higher-order-logic theorem prover. *Journal of Applied Logic*, *9*(1), 23–40. doi:10.1016/j.jal.2011.01.001.

Hasan, O., & Tahar, S. (2011b). Formal analysis of real-time systems. In Khalgui, M., & Hanisch, H. M. (Eds.), *Reconfigurable Embedded Control Systems: Applications for Flexibility and Agility*. Hershey, PA: IGI Global.

Hölzl, J., & Heller, A. (2011). Three chapters of measure theory in isabelle/HOL. [LNCS]. *Proceedings of Interactive Theorem Proving*, *6808*, 135–151. doi:10.1007/978-3-642-22863-6_12.

Mhamdi, T., Hasan, O., & Tahar, S. (2010). On the formalization of the lebesgue integration theory in HOL. [LNCS]. *Proceedings of the Interactive Theorem Proving*, *6172*, 387–402. doi:10.1007/978-3-642-14052-5_27.

KEY TERMS AND DEFINITIONS

Formal Methods: Formal methods are mathematical techniques, often supported by computer-based tools, for the specification and verification of software and hardware systems. The main principle behind formal analysis of a system is to construct a computer based mathematical model of the given system and formally verify, within a computer, that this model meets rigorous specifications of intended behavior.

Higher-Order Logic: Higher-order logic is a system of deduction with a precise semantics. It differs from the more commonly known predicate and first-order logics by allowing quantification over function variables. This extension substantially increases the expressiveness of the logic and thus higher-order logic can be used for the formal specification of most of the mathematical concepts and theories.

Probabilistic Analysis: Probabilistic analysis of an embedded computing system is the process of applying probability theory based reasoning to estimate the probabilities associated with interesting events associated with the given system. The main idea behind probabilistic analysis is to mathematically model the random and unpredictable elements of the given system by appropriate random variables. The probabilistic properties of these random variables are then used to judge the system's behavior.

Reliability: Reliability of an embedded computing system is usually defined as the probability that the system performs its intended function until sometime under specific conditions. Reliability analysis of an embedded system provides probabilistic information regarding parameters like, downtime, availability, number of failures, capacity, and cost.

Theorem Proving: Theorem proving is a widely used formal method. The system that needs to be analyzed is mathematically modeled in an appropriate logic and the properties of interest are verified using computer-based tools. The core of theorem provers usually consists of some well-known axioms and primitive inference rules. Soundness is assured as every new theorem must be created from these basic axioms and primitive inference rules or any other already proved theorems or inference rules.

Chapter 3
Liveness, Deadlock–Freeness, and Siphons

Kamel Barkaoui
CEDRIC-CNAM – Paris, France

ABSTRACT

This chapter deals with the structure theory of Petri nets. The authors define the class of P/T systems, namely K-systems, for which the equivalence between controlled-siphon, deadlock-freeness, and liveness properties holds. Using the new structural notions of ordered transitions and root places, they revisit the non-liveness characterization of P/T systems satisfying the cs-property and define by syntactical manner new and more expressive subclasses of K-systems where the interplay between conflict and synchronization is relaxed.

1. INTRODUCTION

Place/Transition (P/T) systems are a mathematical tool well suited for the modelling and analyzing systems exhibiting behaviour such as concurrency, conflict and causal dependency among events. The use of structural methods for the analysis of such systems presents two major advantages with respect to other approaches: the state explosion problem inherent to concurrent systems is avoided, and the investigation of the relationship between the behaviour and the structure (the graph theoretic and linear algebraic objects and properties associated with the net and initial marking) usually leads to a deep understanding of the system. Here we deal with liveness of a marking, i.e., the

fact that every transition can be enabled again and again. It is well known that this behavioural property is as important as formally hard to treat. Although some structural techniques can be applied to general nets, the most satisfactory results are obtained when the inter-play between conflicts and synchronization is limited. An important theoretical result is the controlled siphon property (Barkaoui & Peyre, 1996). Indeed this property is a condition which is necessary for liveness and sufficient for deadlock-freeness. The aim of this work is to define and recognize structurally a class of P/T systems, as large as possible, for which the equivalence between liveness and deadlock freeness holds. In order to reach such a goal, a deeper understanding of the causes of the

DOI: 10.4018/978-1-4666-3922-5.ch003

non equivalence between liveness and deadlock-freeness is required.

This chapter is organized as follows. In section 2, we recall the basic concepts and notations of P/T systems. In section 3, we define a class of P/T systems, namely K-systems first introduced in (Barkaoui, Couvreur, & Klai, 2005), for which the equivalence between controlled-siphon property (cs-property), deadlock freeness, and liveness holds. In section 4, we revisit the structural conditions for the non liveness under the cs-property hypothesis. In section 5, we define by a syntactical manner several new subclasses of K-systems where the interplay between conflict and synchronization is relaxed. Such subclasses are characterized using the new structural notions of ordered transitions and root places. In section 6, we define two other subclasses of K-systems based on T-invariants. We conclude with a summary of our results and a discussion of an open question.

2. BASIC DEFINITIONS AND NOTATIONS

This section contains the basic definitions and notations of Petri nets' theory (Reisig, 1985) which will be needed in the rest of this chapter.

2.1. Place/Transition Nets

Definition 1: *A P/T net is a weighted bipartite digraph $N = (P, T, F, V)$ where: $P \neq \varnothing$ is a finite set of node places; $T \neq \varnothing$ is a finite set of node transitions; $F \subseteq (P \times T) \cup (T \times P)$ is the flow relation; $V: F \to \mathrm{IN}^+$ is the weight function (valuation).*

Definition 2: *Let $N = (P, T, F, V)$ be a P/T net. The preset of a node $x \in (P \cup T)$ is defined as $^\bullet x = \{ y \in (P \cup T) \text{ s.t. } (y, x) \in F \}$, The postset of a node $x \in (P \cup T)$ is defined as $x^\bullet = \{ y \in (P \cup T) \text{ s.t. } (x, y) \in F \}$, the preset (resp. postset) of a set of nodes is the union of the preset (resp. postset) of its elements. The*

sub-net *induced by a sub-set of places $P' \subseteq P$ is the net $N' = (P', T', F', V')$ defined as follows: $T = {}^\bullet P \cup P^\bullet$; $F = F \cap ((P \times T) \cup (T \times P))$; V is the restriction of V on F'. The sub-net induced by a sub-set of transitions $T' \subseteq T$ is defined analogously.*

Definition 3: *Let $N = (P, T, F, V)$ be a P/T net. A shared place p ($|p^\bullet| \geq 2$) is said to be homogenous iff: $\forall t, t' \in p^\bullet$, $V(p, t) = V(p, t')$. A place $p \in P$ is said to be non-blocking iff: $p^\bullet \neq \varnothing \Rightarrow M \, in_t \in {}_{\bullet p} \{V(t, p)\} \geq M \, in_t \in {}_{p\bullet} \{V(p, t)\}$. If all shared places of P are homogenous, then the valuation V is said to be homogenous. The valuation V of a P/T net N can be extended to the application W from $(P \times T) \cup (T \times P) \to \mathrm{IN}$ defined by: $\forall u \in (P \times T) \cup (T \times P)$, $W(u) = V(u)$ if $u \in F$ and $W(u) = 0$ otherwise.*

Definition 4: *The matrix C indexed by $P \times T$ and defined by $C(p, t) = W(t, p) - W(p, t)$ is called the incidence matrix of the net. An integer vector $f \neq 0$ indexed by P ($f \in \mathbf{Z}^P$) is a P-invariant iff $f^t \cdot C = 0^t$. An integer vector $g \neq 0$ indexed by T ($g \in \mathbf{Z}^T$) is a T-invariant iff $C \cdot g = 0$. $\|f\| = \{ p \in P / f(p) = 0 \}$ (resp. $\|g\| = \{t \in t / g(t) = 0\}$) is called the support of f (resp. of g). We denote by $\|f\|^+ = \{ p \in P / f(p) > 0 \}$ and by $\|f\|^- = \{ p \in P / f(p) < 0 \}$. N is said to be conservative iff there exists a P-invariant f such that $\|f\| = \|f\|^+ = P$.*

2.2. Place/Transition Systems

Definition 5: *A marking M of a P/T net $N = (P, T, F, V)$ is a mapping $M: P \to \mathrm{IN}$ where $M(p)$ denotes the number of tokens contained in place p. The pair (N, M_0) is called a P/T system with M_0 as initial marking. A transition $t \in T$ is said to be enabled under M, in symbols $M \xrightarrow{\;t\;}$, iff $\forall p \in {}^\bullet t$: $M(p) \geq V(p, t)$. If $M \xrightarrow{\;t\;}$, the transition t may occur, resulting in a new marking M', in symbols $M \xrightarrow{\;t\;} M'$, with: $M'(p) = M(p) - W(p, t) + W(t, p)$, $\forall p \in P$. The set of all reachable markings, in symbols $R(M_0)$, is the smallest* *set such that $M_0 \in R(M_0)$ and $\forall M \in R(M_0)$, $t \in T$, $M \xrightarrow{t} M' \Rightarrow M' \in R(M_0)$. If $M_0 \xrightarrow{t_1} M_1 \xrightarrow{t_2} \dots M_{n-1} \xrightarrow{t_n}$, then $\sigma = t_1 t_2 \dots t_n$ is called an occurrence sequence.*

In the following, we recall the definition of some basic behavioural properties.

Definition 6: *Let (N, M_0) be a P/T system. A transition $t \in T$ is said to be dead for a marking $M \in R(M_0)$ iff $\nexists M^* \in R(M)$ s.t. $M^* \xrightarrow{t}$. A marking $M \in R(M_0)$ is said to be a dead marking iff $\forall t \in T$, t is dead for M. (N, M_0) is weakly live (or deadlock-free) for M_0 iff $\forall M \in R(M_0)$, $\exists t \in T$ such that $M \xrightarrow{t}$ ((N, M_0) has no dead marking). A transition $t \in T$ is said to be live for M_0 iff $M \in R(M_0)$, $\exists M' \in R(M)$ such that $M' \xrightarrow{t}$ (t is not live iff $\exists M' \in R(M_0)$ for which t is dead). (N, M_0) is live for M_0 iff $\forall t \in T$, t is live for M_0. A place $p \in P$ is said to be marked for $M \in R(M_0)$ iff $M(p) \geq M in_{t \in p \cdot}\{V(p, t)\}$. A place $p \in P$ is said to be bounded for M_0 iff $\exists k \in \mathbb{N}$ s.t. $\forall M \in R(M_0)$, $M(p) \leq k$. (N, M_0) is bounded iff $\forall p \in P$, p is bounded for M_0. If N is conservative then (N, M_0) is bounded for any initial marking M_0.*

2.3. Controlled Siphon Property

A key concept of structure theory is the siphon.

Definition 7: *Let (N, M_0) be a P/T system. A nonempty set $S \subseteq P$ is called a siphon iff $\cdot S \subseteq S \cdot$. Let S be a siphon, S is called minimal iff it contains no other siphon as a proper subset. In the following, we assume that all P/T nets have homogeneous valuation, and $V(p)$ denotes $V(p, t)$ for any $t \in p \cdot$.*

Definition 8: *A siphon S of a P/T system $N = P, T, F, V$ is said to be controlled iff: S is marked at any reachable marking i.e. $\forall M \in R(M_0)$, $\exists p \in S$ s.t. p is marked.*

Definition 9: *A P/T system (N, M_0) is said to be satisfying the controlled-siphon property (cs-property) iff each minimal siphon of (N, M_0) is controlled.*

In order to check the cs-property, two main structural conditions (*sufficient but not necessary*) permitting to determine whether a given siphon is controlled are developed in [3,9]. These conditions are recalled below.

Proposition 1: *Let (N, M_0) be a P/T system and S a siphon of (N, M_0). If one of the two following conditions holds, then S is controlled: 1) $\exists R \subseteq S$ such that $R \cdot \subseteq \cdot R$, R is marked at M_0 and places of R are non-blocking (siphon S is said to be containing a trap R). 2) $\exists$ a P-invariant $f \in \mathbb{Z}^P$ such that $S \subseteq \|f\|$ and $\forall p \in (\|f\|^- \cap S)$, $V(p) = 1$, $\|f\|^+ \subseteq S$ and $\sum_{p \in S} [f(p) . M_0(p)] > \sum_{p \in S} [f(p).(V(p)-1)]$.*

A siphon controlled by the first (resp. second) mechanism is said to be trap-controlled (resp. invariant controlled).

Now, we recall two well-known basic relations between liveness and the cs-property (Barkaoui & Peyre, 1996). The first states that the cs-property is a sufficient deadlock-freeness condition, the second states that the cs-property is a necessary liveness condition.

Proposition 2: *Let (N, M_0) be a P/T system. The following property holds: (N, M_0) satisfies the cs-property $\Rightarrow$ (N, M_0) is weakly live (deadlock-free).*

Proposition 3: *Let (N, M_0) be a P/T system. The following property holds: (N, M_0) is live $\Rightarrow$ (N, M_0) satisfies the cs-property.*

Hence, for P/T systems where the cs-property is a sufficient liveness condition, there is an equivalence between liveness and deadlock freeness. In the following section, we define such systems and propose basic notions helping for their recognition.

3. K-SYSTEMS

In this section, we start by introducing a new class of P/T systems, namely *K-systems* for which the equivalence between liveness and deadlock freeness properties holds. First, let us establish some new concepts and properties related to the causality relationship among dead transitions.

Definition 10: *Let (N, M_0) be a P/T system. A reachable marking $M^* \in R(M_0)$ is said to be stable iff $\forall t \in T$, t is either live or dead for M^*. Hence, T is partitioned into two subsets $T_D(M^*)$ and $T_L(M^*)$, and for which all transitions of $T_L(M^*)$ are live and all transitions of $T_D(M^*)$ are dead.*

Proposition 4: *Let (N, M_0) be a weakly live but not live P/T system. There exists a reachable stable marking M^* for which $T_D \neq \emptyset$ and $T_L \neq \emptyset$.*

Proof: Trivial, otherwise the net is live $(T = T_L)$ or not weakly live $(T = T_D)$.

Remark: This partition is not necessarily unique but there exists at least one. It is important to note that T_D is maximal in the sense that all transitions that do not belong to T_D, will never become dead.

Definition 11: *Let $N = (P, T, F, V)$ be a P/T net, $r \in P$, $t \in r^\bullet$. r is said to be a root place for t iff $r^\bullet \subseteq p^\bullet$, $\forall p \in {}^\bullet t$.*

An important feature of root places is highlighted in the following proposition.

Proposition 5: *Let $N = (P, T, F, V)$ be a P/T net, $r \in P$, $t \in r^\bullet$. If r is a root place for t then $\forall t' \in r^\bullet$, ${}^\bullet t \subseteq {}^\bullet t'$.*

Proof: Let t be a transition having r as a root place and let t' be a transition in $r^\bullet$. Now, let p be a place in ${}^\bullet t$ and let as show that $p \in {}^\bullet t'$:

Since r is a root place for t and $p \in {}^\bullet t$ then we have $r^\bullet \subseteq p^\bullet$ and hence $t' \in r^\bullet$ implies that $t' \in p^\bullet$, equivalently $p \in {}^\bullet t'$.

Given a transition t, $Root(t)_N$ denotes the set of its root places in N. When the net is clear from the context, this set is simply denoted by $Root(t)$.

Definition 12: *Let t be a transition of T. If $Root(t) \neq \emptyset$, t is said to be an ordered transition iff $\forall p, q \in {}^\bullet t$, $p^\bullet \subseteq q^\bullet$ or $q^\bullet \subseteq p^\bullet$.*

Remark: An ordered transition has necessarily a root but one transition admitting a root is not necessarily ordered. P/T Systems where all transitions are ordered are called ordered systems. Consider Figure 1, one can check that $Root(t_1) = \{a\}$, $Root(t_2) = \{b\}$, $Root(t_3) = \{e\}$, and $Root(t_4) = \{d\}$. Transitions t_1, t_3, and t_4 are ordered but not t_2.

Proposition 6: *Let (N, M_0) be a not live P/T system. Let r be a root of a transition t: $t \in T_D \Rightarrow r^\bullet \cap T_L = \emptyset$ (i.e. $r^\bullet \subseteq T_D$).*

Figure 1. A not ordered transition

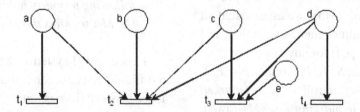

Proof: As $^\bullet t \subset ^\bullet t'$ for every t' of $r^\bullet$: t, dead for M, can never be enabled, a fortiori t' cannot be enabled.

Also, we can state the following: if all input transitions of a place are dead, then all its output transitions are dead.

Proposition 7: *Let (N, M_0) be a not live P/T system. Let p be a place of P: $^\bullet p \cap T_L = \varnothing \Rightarrow p^\bullet \cap T_L = \varnothing$.*

Proof: Suppose that the proposition is not true. In this case, there exists a place p with all input transitions in T_D ($^\bullet p \cap T_L = \varnothing$) and at least one output transition t_v in T_L ($p^\bullet \cap T_D \neq \varnothing$). Since t_v is live, after a finite number of firings, place p becomes non marked because all its input transitions are dead. So t_v becomes dead. This contradicts that $t \in T_L$ (and maximality of T_D).

Proposition 8: *Let (N, M_0) be a not live P/T system. Let p be a bounded place of P: $p^\bullet \cap T_L = \varnothing \Rightarrow ^\bullet p \cap T_L = \varnothing$.*

Definition 13: *Let (N, M_0) be a P/T system. (N, M_0) is a K-system iff for all stable markings M^*, $T_D(M^*) = T$ or $T_L = T$. The above property is called the K-property.*

Remark: According to the previous definition, one can say that the K-systems contain all the live systems and a subclass of not deadlock-free systems. One can then deduce the following theorem.

Theorem 1: *Let (N, M_0) be a P/T system. (N, M_0) is a K-system. Then the three following assertions are equivalent: (1) (N, M_0) is deadlock free, (2) (N, M_0) satisfies the cs-property, (3) (N, M_0) is live.*

Proof: $\Rightarrow$ Note first that we immediately have (3) $\Rightarrow$ (2) $\Rightarrow$ (1) using Propositions 2 and 3. The proof is then reduced to show that deadlock freeness is a sufficient liveness condition for

K-systems. Assume that the K-system (N, M_0) is not live then by definition it is not deadlock free (since $T_D(M^*) = T$ for each stable marking M^*).

$\Leftarrow$ The converse consists to prove the following implication: $((1) \Rightarrow (3)) \Rightarrow (N, M_0)$ is a K-system

Assume that (N, M_0) is not a K-system. Then, by definition, there exists a stable marking m^* for which $T_D \neq \varnothing$ and $T_L \neq \varnothing$. Hence, (N, M_0) is deadlock free but not live, which contradicts $((1) \Rightarrow (3))$.

Definition 13 of K-systems is a behavioural one. In the following part of this chapter we deal with the problem of recognizing, in a structural manner, the membership of a given P/T system in the class of K-systems.

4. STRUCTURAL NON-LIVENESS CHARACTERIZATION

In this section, we highlight some intrinsical properties of systems satisfying the cs-property but not live. Our idea is to characterize a "topological construct" making possible the simultaneous existence of dead and live transitions for such systems.

Lemma 1: *Let (N, M_0) be a P/T system satisfying the cs-property but not live. Let M^* be a reachable stable marking. There exists $t^* \in T_D$ such that: $\forall p \in ^\bullet t^*$ such that $^\bullet p \cap T_L = \varnothing$, $M(p) = M^*(p) \geq V(p, t^*)$ $\forall M \in R(M^*)$.*

Proof: Suppose that $\forall t \in T_D$, there exists $p_t \in ^\bullet t$ with $^\bullet p \cap T_L = \varnothing$ and $M^*(p_t) < V(p_t, t^*)$. Let $S = \{p_t, t \in T_D\}$. By construction, $^\bullet S \subseteq T_D$ and $T_D \subseteq S^\bullet$ (for all $p_t \in S$, $^\bullet p_t \cap T_L = \varnothing$). So S is a siphon. Since $\forall p_t \in S$, $M^*(p_t) < V(p_t, t)$, S is non-marked for M^* ($M^* \in R(M^*)$) and hence the cs-property hypothesis is denied. Using now Proposition 7, (if a place p has no live input transition then all output transitions of *p* are dead), one can deduce that the marking of such places does not change for all reachable markings from M^*.

Theorem 2: *Let (N, M_0) be a P/T system satisfying the cs-property but not live. Let M^* be a reachable stable marking. There exists a non-ordered transition $t^* \in T_D$ and $\forall M \in R(M^*)$, $\exists p \in {}^\bullet t^*$ s.t. $M(p) < V(p, t^*)$.*

Proof: Let t^* be a transition satisfying Lemma 1. Let us denote by $L_p(t^*)$ the subset of shared places included in ${}^\bullet t^*$ and defined as follows: $L_p(t^*) = \{p \in {}^\bullet(t^*)$ s.t. ${}^\bullet p \cap T_L \neq \varnothing$ and $p^\bullet \cap T_L \neq \varnothing\}$.

We first prove that $L_p(t^*) \neq \varnothing$ ($L_p(t^*) \subseteq {}^\bullet t^*$). Suppose that $L_p(t^*) = \varnothing$: any input place of t^* having a live input transition (there exists at least one otherwise t^* will be enabled at M^* using Proposition 7). As the other input places of t^* are such that their pre-conditions on t^* are satisfied at M^* and remain satisfied (Proposition 7), we can reach a marking M from M^* such that t^* would be enabled at M. This contradicts that t^* is dead for M^*. Moreover, t^* is not ordered otherwise $L_p(t^*) = \{p_1, ..., p_m\}$ ($|L_p(t^*)| = m$) can be linearly ordered. Without loss of generality we may assume that $p_1^\bullet \subseteq ... \subseteq p_m^\bullet$. Then there exists a marking M' reachable from M^* for which a transition $t \in p_1^\bullet \cap T_L$ and t^* are enabled (homogenous valuation). This contradicts that t^* is dead for M^*. Since $L_p(t^*)$ ($\subset {}^\bullet t^*$) has no root place we deduce that t^* is not ordered.

Finally, $\forall M \in R(M^*)$, $L_p(t^*)$ contains a non marked place otherwise t^* would be not dead for M^*.

From the previous theorem (Theorem 2) one can derive easily the following result.

Theorem 3: *Let (N, M_0) be an ordered P/T system. The two following statements are equivalent: (1) (N, M_0) satisfies the cs-property, (2) (N, M_0) is live.*

This last result permits us to highlight the structural and behavioural unity among the following subclasses of ordered P/T systems (not necessarily bounded): asymmetric choice systems (Barkaoui & Peyre, 1996) (AC), Join Free (JF) systems, Equal Conflict (EC) systems (Teruel & Silva, 1996), and Extended Free Choice (EFC) nets. Let us recall that, for theses subclasses, except AC nets, the cs-property is reduced to the well-known Commoner's property (Barkaoui & Minoux, 1992), (Barkaoui, Couvreur, & Dutheillet, 1995), (Desel, 1992), (Esparza & Silva, 1992) and the liveness monotonicity (Barkaoui & Peyre, 1996)) holds.

In the following, we show how to exploit this material in order to recognize structurally other subclasses of K-systems, with non-ordered transition, for which the equivalence between deadlock-freeness and liveness holds. Such structural extensions are based on the two following concepts: the notion of root places as a relaxation of the strong property of ordered transitions and the covering of non-ordered transitions by invariants.

5. DEAD-CLOSED SYSTEMS

From our better understanding of requirements which are at the heart of non-equivalence between deadlock-freeness and liveness, we shall define new sub-classes of K-systems for which membership problem is always reduced to examining the net without requiring any exploration of the behaviour.

Let t be a transition of a P/T system, we denote by $D(t)$ the set of transitions defined as follows: $D(t) = \{t' \in T$ s.t. $t \in T_D \Rightarrow t' \in T_D\}$

This set is called the *dead closure* of the transition t. In fact, $D(t)$ contains all transitions that are dead once t is assumed to be dead.

In the following, we show how one can compute structurally a subset $D_{Sub}(t)$ of $D(t)$ for any transition t.

Given a transition t_0, we set $D_{Sub}(t_0) = \{t_0\}$ and enlarge it using the three following structural rules related to Propositions 6, 7, and 8, respectively:

- $\mathbf{R_1}$: Let p be a root place of t, $t \in D_{Sub}(t_0) \Rightarrow p^\bullet \subseteq D_{Sub}(t_0)$.
- $\mathbf{R_2}$: Let p be a place of P, $^\bullet p \subseteq D_{Sub}(t_0) \Rightarrow p^\bullet \subseteq D_{Sub}(t_0)$.
- $\mathbf{R_3}$: Let p be a bounded place of P, $p^\bullet \subseteq D_{Sub}(t_0) \Rightarrow {}^\bullet p \subseteq D_{Sub}(t_0)$.

Formally, $D_{Sub}(t_0)$ is defined as the smallest subset of T containing t_0 and fulfilling rules R_i ($i = 1...3$). When the computed subsets $D_{Sub}(t)$ are all equal to T, we deduce that the system is a K-system.

Definition 14: *Let (N, M_0) be a P/T system. (N, M_0) is said to be a dead-closed system if for every transition t of N: $D_{Sub}(t) = T$.*

Algorithm 1 (Barkaoui, Couvreur, & Klai, 2005) computes the subset $D_{Sub}(t)$ for a given transition t. Its complexity is similar to classical graph traversal algorithms. An overall worst-case complexity bound is $\emptyset(|P| \times |T|)$.

Theorem 4: *Let (N, M_0) be a dead-closed system. Then (N, M_0) is a K-system.*

Proof: The proof is obvious since the computed set $D_{Sub}(t)$ for every transition t is a subset of $D(t)$.

Using theorem 1 one can deduce the following result.

Corollary 1: *Let (N, M_0) be a dead-closed system. The three following statements are equivalent: (1) (N, M_0) is deadlock free, (2) (N, M_0) satisfies the cs-property, (3) (N, M_0) is live.*

Consider the net of Figure 2, note first that it is a conservative net. One can check, by applying the algorithm computing $D(t)$, that it is a dead-closed system. It contains the four following minimal siphons: $S_1 = \{a, b, d\}$, $S_2 = \{e, c, f\}$, $S_3 = \{e,$

Algorithm 1. Computing $D_{Sub}(t)$

```
1: Input: a transition t;//t is assumed to be dead
2: Output: D_Sub(t), a set of transitions;//D(t)
3: Variable D_t marked: a set of transitions//
4: Begin
5: D_Sub(t) ← {t};
6: D_t marked ← ∅ ;
7: for (D_t marked ← ∅; (D_Sub(t) \ D_t marked) ≠ ∅; D_t marked ← D_t marked ∪{t}) do
8: get t from D_Sub(t)\D_t marked;
9: if r is root place then
10: D_Sub(t) ← D_Sub(t)∪r•;//application of R_1
11: for each (p∈t•) do
12: if (•p ⊆ D_Sub(t)) then
13: D_Sub(t) ← D_Sub(t)∪p•;//application of R_2
14: end if
15: end for
16: for for each (p∈•t) such that (p is bounded) do
17: if p•⊆D_Sub(t) then
18: D_Sub(t) ← D_Sub(t)∪•p;//application of R_3
19: end if
20: end for
21: end if
22: end for
23: End
```

$b, d\}$, and $S_4=\{a, f, d\}$. For any initial marking (e.g. $M_0=a+b+e+f$) satisfying the four following conditions: $a+b+d>0$, $e+c+f>0$, $e+b+d-f>0$, and $a+f+d-e>0$, this net satisfies the cs-property and hence is live.

5.1. Root Systems

Here, we define a subclass of dead-closed systems called *Root Systems* exploiting in particular the causality relationships among output transitions of root places. Before, we define a class of P/T nets where each transition admits a root place, such nets are called *Root nets*.

Definition 15: *Let N =(P, T, F, V) be a P/T net. N is a root net iff $\forall t \in T$, $\exists$ a place $r \in P$ which is a root for t.*

Every transition t of N has (at least) a root place, but it is not necessarily ordered. Thus, ordered nets are strictly included in root nets.

The class of *Root nets* is extremely large, we have to add some structural constraints in order to recognize structurally their membership in the class of dead-closed systems.

Figure 2. An example of K system

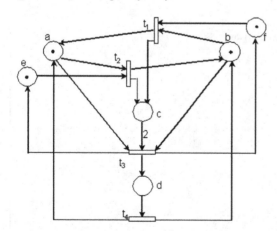

Given a root net N, we first define a particular subnet called Root component based on the set of the root places of N. The *Root component* is slightly different from the subnet induced by the root places: It contains all root places and adjacent transitions. But, a (root) place p admits an output transition t in the root subnet if and only if p is a root place for t.

Definition 16: *Let N =(P, T, F, V) be a root net and $Root_N$ be the set of its root places. The Root component of N is the net $N'^* = (Root_N, T^*, F^*, V^*)$ defined as follows: $T^*= Root_N^\bullet = T$, $F^* \subseteq (F \cap ((Root_N \times T^*) \cup (T^* \times Root_N)))$, s.t. $(p, t) \in F^*$ iff $(p, t) \in F$ and p is a root place for t, and $(t, p) \in F^*$ iff $(t, p) \in F$, V^* is the restriction of V on F^*.*

Definition 17: *Let (N, M_0) be P/T system. (N, M_0) is called a Root System iff N is a root net and its root component N^* is conservative and strongly connected.*

Theorem 5: *Let (N, M_0) be a Root-system. (N, M_0) is a dead-closed system.*

Proof: Note first that the subnet N^* contains all transitions of N (N is weakly ordered). Let us show that $D(t)=T$ for all transition $t \in T$ in N^*. Let t and t' be two transitions and suppose that t is dead. Since N^* is strongly connected, there exists a path $P_{t' \rightarrow t} = t' r_1 t_1 \ldots t_n r_n t$ leading from t' to t s.t. all the places r_i ($i \in \{1 \ldots\}$) are root places. Let us reason by recurrence on the length $|P_{t' \rightarrow t}|$ of $P_{t' \rightarrow t}$. $|P_{t' \rightarrow t}| = 1$: Obvious. Suppose that the proposition is true for each path $P_{t' \rightarrow t}$ with $|P_{t' \rightarrow t}|=n$. Let $P_{t' \rightarrow t}$ be an $n+1$-length path leading from t' to t.

Using Proposition 6 (or rule R_1), one can deduce that all output transitions of r_n are dead. Now, since r is a bounded place, we use Proposition 8 (or R_3) to deduce that all its input transition are dead and fortiori the transition t_n (the last transition before t in the path) is dead. Now the path $P_{t'} \rightarrow_{tn}$ satisfies the recurrence hypothesis. Consequently, one can deduce that t' is dead as soon as t_n is dead.

The following corollary is a direct consequence of Theorems 5, 4, and 1, respectively.

Corollary 2: *Let (N, M_0) be a Root-system. The three following assertions are equivalent: (1) (N, M_0) is deadlock free; (2) (N, M_0) satisfies the cs-property; (3) (N, M_0) is live.*

Example: The K-system (dead-closed) of Figure 2 is not a Root system. Indeed, its root component N^* (Figure 3) is not strongly connected.

However, the non-ordered system (N, M_0) of Figure 4 (t_1 is not ordered and p_{11}, p_{12} are not root places) is a Root system. In fact, the corresponding root component is conservative and strongly connected.

Let us analyze structurally the corresponding net N. One can check that N admits the eight following minimal siphons: $S_1 = \{p_5, p_6\}$, $S_2 = \{p_3, p_4\}$, $S_3 = \{p_1, p_2\}$, $S_4 = \{p_5, p_{10}, p_4, p_9\}$, $S_5 = \{p_5, p_{10}, p_7, p_2, p_8, p_9\}$, $S_6 = \{p_{12}, p_2, p_4\}$, $S_7 = \{p_3, p_7, p_2, p_8\}$, and $S_8 = \{p_5, p_{11}, p_9\}$. These siphons are invariant-controlled for any initial marking satisfying the following conditions: $p_5 + p_6 > 0$, $p_3 + p_4 > 0$, $p_1 + p_2 > 0$, $p_5 + p_{10} + p_4 + p_9 > 0$, $p_5 +$ $p_{10} + p_7 + p_2 + p_8 + p_9 > 0$, $p_{12} + p_2 + p_4 > 0$, $p_3 + p_7 + p_2 + p_8 > 0$, and $p_{11} + 2.p_9 + 2.p_5 - p_3 - p_7 > 0\}$. Such conditions hold for the chosen initial marking $M_0 = p_1 + p_3 + p_5 + p_{12}$. Consequently, (N, M_0) satisfies the cs-property i.e. live (according to Theorem 5).

Obviously, the structure of N^* is a sufficient but not a necessary condition to ensure the K-property (and its membership in the class of K-systems). However, by adding structure to the subnet induced by the Root places (considered as modules) one can provide methods for synthesis of live K-systems.

In the following section, we first prove that the class of dead-closed systems is closed by a particular synchronization through asynchronous buffers. Then, this result will be used to extend the subclass of dead-closed systems structurally analyzable.

5.2. SDCS: Synchronized Dead-Closed Systems

In this section we prove that the class of dead-closed systems admits an inter-esting feature: it is closed by a particular synchronization through asynchronous buffers. The obtained class is a modular subclass of P/T nets called *Synchronized Dead-Closed Systems* (SDCS). By *modular* we

Figure 3. An example of non-root but K system

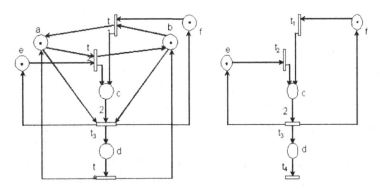

Figure 4. An example of root system

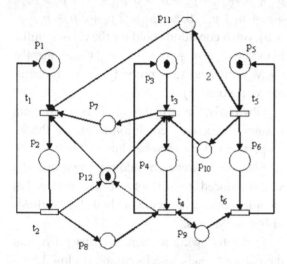

emphasize that their definition is oriented to a bottom-up modelling methodology or structured view: individual agents, or modules, in the system are identified and modelled independently by means of live (i.e. cs-property) dead-closed systems (for example root systems), and the global model is obtained by synchronizing these modules through a set of places, the *buffers*. Such building process was already be used to define the class of Deterministically Synchronized Sequential Processes (DSSP) (see Reisig, 1982; Teruel, Recalde, & Silva, 1985; Souissi, 1991) for successive generalization) where elementary modules are simply live and safe state machines and where the interplay between conflict and synchronization is limited compared to dead-closed systems.

Definition 18: *A P/T system* (N, M_0), *with* $N=(P, T, F, V)$, *is a Synchronized dead-closed System (or simply an SDCS) if and only if* P *is the disjoint union* $P_1,..., P_n$ *and B, T is the disjoint union* $T_1,..., T_n$, *and the following holds: (1) For every* $i \in \{1,..., n\}$, *let* $N_i = (P_i, T_i, F_{\lfloor ((Pi \times Ti)\cup(Ti \times Pi))}, V_{\lfloor ((Pi \times Ti)\cup(Ti \times Pi))})$. *Then* $(N_i, m_{0\lfloor Pi})$ *is a live dead-closed system. (2) For every* $i, j \in \{1,..., n\}$, *if* $i \neq j$ *then* $V_{\lfloor ((Pi \times Ti}$

$)\cup(Ti \times Pi))} =0$. *(3) For each module* N_i, $i \in \{1,..., n\}$: *(a)* $\exists$ *(a buffer)* $b \in B$ *s.t.* $b^\bullet \subseteq T_i$ *(a private output buffer), (b)* $\forall b \in B$, b *preserves the sets of root places of* N_i *(i.e.,* $\forall t \in T_i$, $Root(t)_{Ni} \subseteq Root(t)_N$). *(4) Let* $B' \subseteq B$ *denotes the set of the output private buffers of N, then there exists a subset* $B'' \subseteq B'$ *such that the subnet induced by the dead-closed systems* $(N_i, i \in \{1,..., n\})$ *and the buffers of* B'' *is conservative and strongly connected.*

Actually, we synchronize dead-closed system in such a way that we preserve the K-property (i.e. the equivalence between deadlock-freeness and liveness). Contrary to the DSSP modules, competition between those of an SDCS sys-tem is allowed, as long as the sets of root places of modules are preserved by composition (3.*b*) (but not necessarily the set of equal conflicts). After composition, a buffer can be a root place in the composed net but it cannot take the place of another one. Moreover, no restriction is imposed on the connection nature of the buffers. This allows modules to compete for resources. A second feature of SDCS class which enlarges the description power of DSSP is the fact that a given buffer does not have to be an output (destination) private as long as it exists such a buffer for each module (3.*a*).

Hence, one can easily prove that the class of SDCS represents a strict generalization of conservative and strongly connected DSSP systems. Moreover, when we compose dead-closed systems, or even root systems, the obtained system remains dead-closed.

Figure 5 illustrates an example of SDCS system. This system is composed of two modules, N_1 and N_2 (enclosed by the dashed lines) communicating through three buffers b_1, b_2, and b_3. Each module is represented by a Root system (N_1 is not a state machine). Also, each buffer is not restrained to respect internal modules conflict as long as it preserves their root places. For instance, the buffer

b_1 does not respect the conflict between transitions t_1 and t_3 of N_1 ($V(b_1, t_1)$=1 but $V(b_1, t_3)$=0) but it preserves the root place p_1 of t_1. This system is not a Root-system since its root component N^*, induced here by N_1, N_2 and the buffers b_2 and b_3, (the buffer b_1 is not a root place), is strongly connected but not conservative (the buffer b_3 is not structurally bounded). However, this system is an SDCS since, with notations of Definition 18, the subset $B'' = \{b_1, b_2\}$ allows the condition (4) of to be satisfied.

The following theorem states that the class of SDCS is a subclass of dead-closed Systems. This means that when we synchronize several dead-closed systems as described in Definition 18 we obtain a dead-closed system.

Theorem 6: *Let (N, M_0) be an SDCS system. Then (N, M_0) is a dead-closed system.*

Proof: Let t and t' be two transitions of N and suppose that t is dead. Let N_n and N_1 be the modules containing t and t', respectively. Since the subnet induced by modules and output private buffers is strongly connected, there exists an (elementary) path $\boldsymbol{P}_{N1} \rightarrow_{Nn} = N_1 b_1 ... b_{n-1} N_n$ leading from N_1 to N_n and each b_i ($i \in \{1,..., n-1\}$) is a buffer having N_{i+1} as output private. Let us reason by induction on the number of modules N_i ($i \in \{1,..., n\}$) involved in the path, Let us note $| \boldsymbol{P}_{Ni} |$ such a number.

- $| \boldsymbol{P}_{Ni} | = 0$: i.e. t and t' belong to the same module N_1. Since N_1 is a dead-closed system, one can use Theorem 4 (N_1 is also a K-system) to deduce that t' is dead.

- Suppose that the proposition is true for each path $\boldsymbol{P}_{N1} \rightarrow_{Nn}$ involving less than n modules.

- Let $\boldsymbol{P}_{N1} \rightarrow_{Nn}$ be a path leading from N_1 to N_n and passing through n modules.

- Consider b_{n-1}, the output private buffer of the module N_n. Using Theorem 5 one can deduce that all transitions in N_n are dead. Now, since b_{n-1} is a bounded place, we use Proposition 8 to deduce that all its input

Figure 5. An example of SKS system

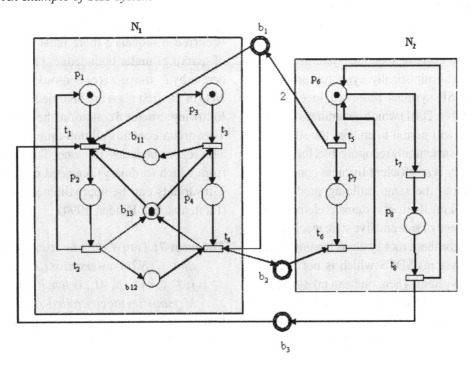

transitions are dead and fortiori those of the module N_{n-1} (the module that appears before N_n in the path) are dead. The sub-path leading from N_1 to N_{n-1} involves $n-1$ modules and hence satisfies the recurrence hypothesis. Consequently, one can deduce that t is dead as soon as an input transition of b_{n-1} (belonging to N_{n-1}) is dead.

Corollary 3: *Let (N, M_0) be an synchronized dead-closed system. The three following assertions are equivalent: (1) (N, M_0) is deadlock free, (2) (N, M_0) satisfies the cs-property, (3) (N, M_0) is live.*

The previous corollary is a direct consequence of Theorems 6, 4, and 1, respectively.

The main practical advantage of the definition of the SDCS class systems is that the equivalence between deadlock freeness and liveness can be preserved when we properly synchronize several dead-closed systems. A larger subclass based on the root nets structure can be obtained by applying the basic building process of the SDCS in a recursive way, i.e. modules can be Root systems, SDCS (or simply synchronized root systems) or more complex systems defined in this way. We are then able to revisit and extend the building process of the class of modular systems called multi-level deterministically synchronized processes (DS)*SP systems proposed in (Teruel, Recalde, & Silva, 2001) which generalizes DSSP. Such a result will permit to enlarge the subclass of K-systems, structurally recognizable, for which the cs-property is a sufficient liveness condition. One can follow the same building process of (DS)*SP by taking live root systems as elementary modules (instead of safe and live state machines). We synchronize these root systems leading to an (root-based system) SDCS which is not necessarily a Root system. Then, one can take several (root-based system based) SDCS and synchronize them in the same way. The resulting net, that is dead-closed system, can be considered as an agent

in a further interconnection with other agents, etc. Doing so, a multi-level synchronization structure is built: the obtained system is composed of several agents that are coupled through buffers; these agents may also be a set of synchronized agents, etc. This naturally corresponds to systems with different levels of coupling: low level agents are tightly coupled to form an agent in a higher level, which is coupled with other agents, and so on. The class of systems thus obtained is covered by dead-closed systems, but largely generalizes strongly connected and conservative (DS)*SP (for which the deadlock freeness is a sufficient liveness condition (Teruel, Recalde, & Silva, 2001)). From this view, the system of Figure 5 can be viewed as "multilevel" SDCS where the module N_1 is composed of two submodules (Root systems) communicating through three buffers b_{11}, b_{12}, and b_{13} (which is not output private but it preserves the set of the root places).

6. OTHER SUBCLASSES BASED ON T-INVARIANTS

Finally, we define two other subclasses of live K-systems, exploiting the fact that in every infinite occurrence sequence there must be a repetition of markings under boundedness hypothesis. We denote by T_{no} the subset of non-ordered transitions. Nets of the first class are bounded and satisfy the following structural condition: the support of each T-invariant contains all non-ordered transitions. This class includes the one T-invariants nets from which (ordinary) bounded nets covered by T-invariants can be approximated as proved in (Lautenbach & Ridder, 1994).

Theorem 7: *Let (N, M_0) be a P/T system such that: (i) N is conservative. (ii) $\forall$ T-invariant j: $T_{no} \subseteq \| j \|$. (N, M_0) is live if and only if (N, M_0) satisfies the controlled-siphon property.*

Proof: Assume that (N, M_0) satisfies the cs-property but is not live. According to

Theorem 2, $T_D \neq \varnothing$ and $T_L \neq \varnothing$. Consider the subnet induced by T_L. This subnet is live and bounded for M^*. There exists necessarily an occurrence sequence for which count-vector is a T-invariant j and $T_{no} \not\subset \| j \|$. This contradicts condition (*ii*).

Now, we define a last subclass of non-ordered systems (systems having a non-ordered transition) where the previous structural condition (*ii*) is refined as follows: for any non-ordered transition t, we cannot get a T-invariant on the subnet induced by $T \setminus D(t)$.

Theorem 8: *Let* (N, M_0) *be a non-ordered system satisfying the two following conditions: (i)* N *is conservative. (ii)* $\forall$ *T-invariant* j *and* $\forall t \in T_{no}$: $(\| j \| \cap D(t)) \neq \varnothing$. (N, M_0) *is live if and only if* (N, M_0) *satisfies the controlled-siphon property.*

Proof: Let (N, M_0) be satisfying the cs-property but not live. Consider the sub-net induced by T_L. This subnet is live and bounded. Hence, there exists a T-invariant j corresponding to an occurrence sequence in the subnet and do not cover neither the (not ordered) transition t^* nor any transition in $D(t^*)$ $((\| j \| \cap D(t^*)) = \varnothing)$. This contradicts condition (*ii*).

Remark: Note that the non-ordered system (t_3 is not ordered) of Figure 2 can also be recognized structurally as a K-system since conditions (*i*) and (*ii*) of Theorem 8 ($D(t_3) = T$) are satisfied.

CONCLUSION

The aim of this chapter was to deepen into the structure theory on P/T systems, namely K-systems, for which the equivalence between controlled-siphon property, deadlock freeness, and liveness holds. Using the new structural concepts of ordered transitions and root places, we present a refined characterization of the non-liveness condition under cs-property hypothesis. Such result permits us to revisit from a new perspective some well-known results and to structurally characterize new and more expressive subclasses of K-systems. This work poses a challenging question: What are the structural mechanisms ensuring a siphon to be controlled other than based on trap or p-invariant concept? The interest of a positive answer is a broader decision power of controlled siphon property in particular for systems where the purely algebraic methods such rank theorem (Desel, 1992) reach their limit.

REFERENCES

Barkaoui, K., Couvreur, J.-M., & Dutheillet, C. (1995). On liveness in extended non self-controlling nets. *Lecture Notes in Computer Science, 935*, 25–44. doi:10.1007/3-540-60029-9_32.

Barkaoui, K., & Minoux, M. (1992). A polynomial-time graph algorithm to decide liveness of some basic classes of bounded Petri nets. *Lecture Notes in Computer Science, 616*, 62–75. doi:10.1007/3-540-55676-1_4.

Barkaoui, K., & Peyre, J.-F.-P. (1996). On liveness and controlled siphons in Petri nets. *Lecture Notes in Computer Science, 1091*, 57–72. doi:10.1007/3-540-61363-3_4.

Barkaoui, K. J., & Couvreur, K., & Klai. (2005). On the equivalence between deadlock freeness and liveness in Petri nets. *Lecture Notes in Computer Science, 3536*, 90–111. doi:10.1007/11494744_7.

Desel, J. (1992). A proof of the rank theorem for extended free choice nets. *Lecture Notes in Computer Science, 616*, 134–153. doi:10.1007/3-540-55676-1_8.

Esparza, J., & Silva, M. (1992). A polynomial-time algorithm to decide liveness of bounded free choice nets. *Theoretical Computer Science, 102*(1), 185–205. doi:10.1016/0304-3975(92)90299-U.

Lautenbach, K., & Ridder, H. (1994). Liveness in bounded petri nets which are covered by T-invariants. In *Proceedings 15th International Conference* (LNCS), (vol. 815, pp. 358–375). Berlin: Springer.

Reisig, W. (1982). Deterministic buffer synchronization of sequential processes. *Acta Informatica*, *18*, 117–134. doi:10.1007/BF00264434.

Reisig, W. (1985). *Petri nets: An introduction.* New York: Springer-Verlag.

Souissi, Y. (1991). Deterministic systems of sequential processes: A class of structured petri nets. In *Proceedings of the 12th International Conference on Application and Theory of Petri Nets* (pp. 62–81). IEEE.

Teruel, E., Recalde, L., & Silva, M. (1985). Modeling and analysis of sequential processes that cooperate through buffers. *IEEE Transactions on Robotics and Automation*, *11*, 267–277.

Teruel, E., Recalde, L., & Silva, M. (2001). Structure theory of multi-level deterministically synchronized sequential processes. *Theoretical Computer Science*, *254*(1-2), 1–33. doi:10.1016/S0304-3975(99)00112-7.

Teruel, E., & Silva, M. (1996). Structure theory of equal conflict systems. *Theoretical Computer Science*, *153*(1&2), 271–300. doi:10.1016/0304-3975(95)00124-7.

Chapter 4
Model–Based Functional Safety Analysis and Architecture Optimisation

David Parker
University of Hull, UK

Martin Walker
University of Hull, UK

Yiannis Papadopoulos
University of Hull, UK

ABSTRACT

The scale and complexity of computer-based safety critical systems pose significant challenges in the safety analysis of such systems. In this chapter, the authors discuss two approaches that define the state of the art in this area: failure logic modelling and behavioural modelling safety analyses. They also focus on Hierarchically Performed Hazard Origin and Propagation Studies (HiP-HOPS)—one of the advanced failure logic modelling approaches—and discuss its scientific and practical contributions. These include a language for specification of inheritable and reusable component failure patterns, a temporal logic that enables assessment of sequences of faults in safety analysis as well as algorithms for top-down allocation of safety requirements to components during design, bottom-up verification via automatic synthesis of Fault Trees and Failure Modes and Effects Analyses, and dependability versus cost optimisation of systems via automatic model transformations. The authors summarise these contributions and discuss strengths and limitations in relation to the state of the art.

DOI: 10.4018/978-1-4666-3922-5.ch004

INTRODUCTION

The use of classical safety and reliability analysis and rule-based design techniques has been increasingly challenged in recent years due to the growing scale and complexity of modern engineering systems. New technologies and the subsequent introduction of complex failure modes renders classical manual analyses of safety critical systems, such as Failure Modes & Effects Analysis (FMEA) and Fault Tree Analysis (FTA), increasingly difficult and error prone.

Two distinct strands of work have emerged in an attempt to meet this challenge and enable fast, accurate analyses of modern safety critical systems. The first category includes approaches that are based on formal verification techniques and rely on formal modelling and fault simulation to provide information about the failure behaviour of systems. The second category is based on the concept of compositional component-based safety analysis, enabling analysis to take place hierarchically on the basis of failure information represented at the component level of the system model.

HiP-HOPS (Hierarchically Performed Hazard Origin and Propagation Studies) is an advanced compositional safety analysis approach with software support that has been developed to simplify aspects of the engineering and analysis process. After annotating system components with logic that specifies how those components can cause and react to failures, HiP-HOPS automatically generates and analyses both FMEAs and Fault Trees (FTs) from engineering system models. It has also been extended with many additional capabilities, including automatic architectural optimisation and the allocation of safety integrity levels.

Classical analysis methodologies typically involve not just manual analysis but also manual construction of the analysis model (e.g. an FMEA or a fault tree), requiring substantial expertise and investment even with tool support. By contrast, the manual effort required by modern techniques is generally much more limited; for example, in HiP-HOPS, the only manual effort is the initial annotation of component failure data as part of existing system design modelling. The rest of the process is fully automatic and therefore much faster, drastically reducing the time and effort required to examine the safety of a system.

This automation enables safety analysis to be conducted rapidly as part of an iterative design process and allows safety to become a full, contributing factor to new design evolutions, rather than a hurdle that must be surmounted only at the end of the design, when changes to a mature system model may be much more expensive. By identifying potential safety and reliability issues early in the design process, new ideas and design variations can be proposed and more readily evaluated, potentially leading to safer, cheaper systems. A further benefit arising from the speed and scalability of the underlying algorithms is the ability to analyse large, complex systems that would otherwise be limited to partial or fragmented manual analyses.

In the next section we first describe the classical safety analysis techniques of FMEA and FTA and then go on to discuss the field of modern safety analysis techniques by describing the two main categories of approaches in more detail. Subsequently, we focus on HiP-HOPS in particular as a prominent example of a contemporary safety analysis approach, introducing the core concepts behind its operation, its potential for extensions into new areas, and lastly discussing some of the advantages it presents to designers and analysts of safety critical systems. Finally we take a look at what the future may hold and present a summary of our conclusions.

BACKGROUND

Fault Tree Analysis and Failure Modes and Effects Analysis

FMEA was introduced towards the end of the 1940s (U.S. Military, 1949), and FTA makes its first appearance two decades later in the 1960s for use with the Minuteman missile system (Ericson, 1999; Vesely et al, 2002). Both are widely used throughout the safety critical industries, including the aerospace, nuclear, and automotive industries. They enable safety analysts to identify potential faults in a system and allow those faults to be prevented or mitigated.

FMEA is the simpler of the two techniques. It is an inductive technique, working "bottom up" by hypothesising the occurrence a certain failure event or condition and trying to infer the effects of that event on the system as a whole. A number of criteria such as severity, probability, and detectability are presented alongside these inferences in a table, allowing an analyst to quickly see the probable causes and effects of failures in the system.

By contrast, FTA is a deductive technique, working "top down" to determine what combinations of events may have caused a given system failure. Fault trees show the logical relationship between a *top event* (typically a system level failure) and one or more *basic events* (e.g. component failure modes or environmental conditions) via a combination of logical gates, such as AND and OR. FTA typically involves both a logical (qualitative) analysis, which reduces the fault tree into a set of *minimal cut sets* describing the smallest possible combinations of failures required to cause the top event, and a probabilistic (quantitative) analysis, which is subsequently performed to calculate the probability of the top event occurring given the probabilities of the basic events that cause it.

Experience from the aerospace and process industries suggests that the application of classical manual analyses, such as FTA and FMEA, is hindered by the increasing complexity of systems, quickly becoming laborious and error prone. This is because construction of fault trees and FMEA has historically been a manual process, relying on the expertise of system designers and safety experts to describe the failure behaviour of the system in question. Consequently a thorough assessment and interpretation of the results of such analyses becomes difficult to achieve within the

constraints of most projects. This is compounded by the separation of the results and the design being analysed; the effects of any changes made to the design of the system may not be apparent without a repeated analysis (also long and costly, even with tool support).

Modern Safety Analyses

The ongoing development of new computing technology has encouraged the development of modern safety analysis tools and techniques that take advantage of the computational power available to produce results of unprecedented detail and depth, even when applied to hitherto prohibitively large, complex systems. These range from supporting tools that automate only the analysis to more comprehensive modelling & analysis methodologies that automate even more of the process. Examples of the former type include the venerable SETS (Worrell and Stack, 1978) and the more modern Fault Tree+ (Isograph Software, 2002), which both provide automated fault tree analysis; however, they still require the fault tree to be constructed manually, with all the disadvantages that entails. The more comprehensive approaches aim to solve this issue by also automating the synthesis of the analysis models, such as fault trees, as well as the analysis of those models. These techniques are also generally more closely integrated with the design process, allowing existing engineering design models to be used as the basis of the analysis rather than requiring designers to produce new system models for analysis purposes. As a result of these developments, the gap in the ongoing race between system complexity and analysis capability is once again closing.

As noted in the preceding section, classical FTA and FMEA safety analysis techniques have a very distinct error model that is entirely separate from the functional system design model which informs it. The more modern approaches that are reviewed further below in this section have system and error models that exist in a spectrum that includes techniques that share the same separation weakness of the classic techniques to approaches where the system and error model are tightly integrated. These characteristics are important when considering the relative merits of the approaches, but they don't speak to the fundamental distinctions that separate the different techniques.

Lisagor *et al.* (2006) define two categories that can be used for classifying safety analysis approaches: formal verification techniques and compositional safety analysis, and typically modern safety analysis techniques will fall in to one of the two categories. The core principles of both types, together with major examples, will be described in the following section.

Compositional Safety Analysis Techniques

The first category consists of the compositional safety analysis approaches: the development of formal and semi-formal languages to enable specification, composition, and analysis of system failure behaviour based on safety information about the components that comprise the system. Although most are not fully automated, in that they depend on the manual entry of the initial component failure data, they can be usefully applied in the analysis of both hardware and software architectures in the context of a model-based design process.

FPTN (Failure Propagation and Transformation Notation) (Fenelon and McDermid, 1993) is one of the earliest developments in the area of compositional safety analysis techniques and was designed to bridge the gap between deductive FTA and inductive FMEA processes. Its goal was to describe the generation and propagation of component failures in the system by using component modules. Failures can be combined within and propagated between modules via connections between their inputs and outputs.

A drawback of the technique is that the error model and the system model are separate, and as the system model is modified and developed it can become desynchronized with the error model (Wallace, 2005) and consequently FPTN

has mostly been limited to use as a notation for describing failure specifications.

FPTC (Fault Propagation and Transformation Calculus) (Wallace, 2005) sought to overcome this weakness by linking its failure model to the architectural model such that dependencies between them can be identified and maintained. Failure expressions are specified directly in the components of the system model and describe how failures of different classes can either be propagated between the inputs and outputs of a component or mitigated by transformation into normal behaviour. The connections of the architectural system model are used to transmit failure information between the components and allows the effects of component failures on the rest of the system to be determined. Probabilistic analysis can be performed via an extension that allows probability values to be stored in the expressions (Ge *et al.*, 2009). Although FPTC overcomes the desynchronisation drawback of FPTN, it also sacrifices some deductive capabilities because it relies on injecting one failure combination at a time into the system and repeating the analysis for all combinations. This makes it highly susceptible to combinatorial explosion and makes it difficult to generate information on the effects of multiple failures, like that provided by normal FTA.

CFTs (Component Fault Trees) define the failure logic of components as a graph of interconnected fault trees building on the specification used by FPTN. A system hierarchy of CFTs can be built by composing them in larger subsystems, and because they are based on fault trees, they are less susceptible to the combinatorial explosion of inductive techniques such as FPTC (Grunske and Kaiser, 2005; Grunske and Neumann, 2002).

SEFTs (State-Event Fault Trees) (Grunske *et al.*, 2005; Kaiser *et al.*, 2007) enable analysis of dynamic systems that have transitions between different states. They achieve this by developing CFTs to distinguish between events, which occur instantaneously, and states, which hold for a period of time and are triggered by events. More complex dynamic behaviour can also be represented by sequences and histories of events, as well as the use of NOT gates to define events that have not happened yet. A downside to this more complex logic is that it is no longer possible to use traditional FTA algorithms, instead relying on a conversion to Deterministic Stochastic Petri Nets (Ciardo and Lindermann, 1993), which can then be quantitatively analysed by Petri Net tools such as Time-NET (Zimmerman *et al.*, 1999). Another weakness of SEFTs is scalability: modelling of different states can result in state-space explosion, particularly in larger models.

HiP-HOPS is another compositional safety analysis technique that synthesises and analyses fault trees using compositional component failure data; it will be described further in the next section.

Formal Verification Techniques

Formal modelling engines can simulate the normal functioning of a system design. Faults and failures can then be injected into these simulations in order to determine their effects. Where simulation data exists for the modelling domain, it can be used directly without any further need for additional annotation of the model. This is an advantage of formal verification techniques: because the required information can be extracted directly from the existing simulation components, it leads to a reduction in the overhead of model development.

Two of the best known tools and techniques in this category are FSAP-NuSMV (Bozzano and Villafiorita, 2006) and Altarica (Bieber *et al.*, 2004). The first of these is the combination of the graphical interface FSAP (Formal Safety Analysis Platform) with the NuSMV-SA model checking and safety analysis engine to provide model design and safety analysis in a single cohesive environment. It is possible to use the tool for normal model-checking processes such as property verification and counter-example generation as well as injected fault simulation. Although the tool can be used to generate fault trees, it is limited to fault trees that link directly from effects (top events) to combinations of causes

(basic events), though NOT gates can also be included. In common with other model-checking approaches, FSAP-NuSMV's main disadvantage is that it is susceptible to combinatorial explosion as the number of failure modes being considered increases.

Altarica provides a formal modelling language that can be used to describe states and events in complex hierarchical models (Griffault *et al.*, 1999). The ability to model dynamic and state-based systems enable it to generate Petri Nets in addition to standard non-dynamic fault trees. Unlike FSAP-NuSMV, it lacks a coherent design and analysis environment and the analysis of the generated failure model has to be handled by external tools. Bieber *et al.* (2004) identified a weakness in Altarica in that, where bidirectional signals or flows are modelled, it can be subject to fault propagation loops. SMV-based approaches, such as the one above, do not have this problem and can be used instead in such cases (McMillan, 1990).

Deductive Cause Consequence Analysis (DCCA) uses mathematical proofs (which can be further verified by other model checkers such as SMV) to verify whether a component failure will lead to a system failure by defining the behaviour of the system with temporal logic and finite automata and enabling a simulation of the system. (Ortmeier, 2005) It can be used to determine the minimal critical set of failure modes required to cause a system hazard. Reer and Reif (2007) combined DCCA with the industrial design tool SCADE and Güdemann *et al.* (2008) extended it with DFOA (Deductive Failure Order Analysis), enabling temporal fault trees to be automatically generated and analysed from the dynamic system model.

Model-based Deviation Analysis, or MDA (Heimdahl et al, 2002), is an extension of the earlier developed Software Deviation Analysis and takes a different approach to the other formal techniques in that it seeks to model the effects of deviations of system input data, rather than internal failures of the system itself. It uses ranges and quantifiable limits in input data, formulated in temporal logic, which are then simulated using a model checker. The results of simulating error input data can be compared with separate runs of nominal input data to detect critical deviations between them and identify the causes. The typical requirement to develop both nominal and error datasets is a downside to using the technique that adds extra effort.

In each of these techniques, the combinatorial and state-space explosion weakness can to some extent be mitigated, or at least reduced, by applying informal techniques such as FTA as an initial step to identify failures of particular interest to investigate formally.

HIP-HOPS

HiP-HOPS is a compositional safety analysis tool that consists of three main phases as illustrated in Figure 1.

- **A modelling phase:** Where the system architecture is modelled and its components annotated with local failure data.
- **A synthesis phase:** Where networks of interconnected fault trees are generated by combining the component failure annotations.
- **An analysis phase:** Where the fault trees undergo qualitative and quantitative analysis and FMEA information is synthesized.

Modelling Phase

The HiP-HOPS modelling phase begins with specifying the components of the system and the connections between them that allow the transfer of material, energy, or data; typically, a modelling tool such as Matlab Simulink (MathWorks, 2012) or SimulationX (ITI, 2012) is used to do this. The system can be sub-composed in subsystems and components to give a hierarchical description of the system. This helps to manage design complexity and also allows propagations of failures to occur 'vertically' through the hierarchy, as well

Figure 1. An overview of the HiP-HOPS phases

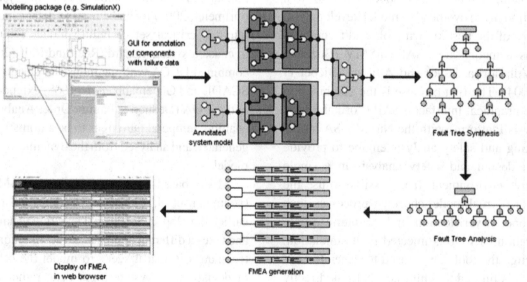

as horizontally through the connections between components.

For the purposes of safety analysis, once the topology of the system has been modelled, the components need to be annotated with local failure behaviour annotations. These describe how deviations of component output (output deviations) are caused by the logical combination of deviations propagated from the input of the component (input deviations) and internal failures of the component itself (basic events).

The failure annotations describe 'mini' fault trees where the top event of each tree is an output deviation comprising a component port and a failure class that specifies the type of failure occurring at the port. For example: Omission-OutputPort1 specifies that there is an omission of expected output occurring at OutputPort1. Failure classes are not specified by HiP-HOPS; the user can specify their own types as long as they are used consistently across the whole model. Below the top event, Boolean operators such as AND and OR can be used to describe the combination of basic events and input deviations. Input deviations are specified in the same way as output deviations with a failure class and a port definition.

For quantitative analysis to take place, basic events can be given probabilistic failure models such as constant failure and repair rates, MTTR/MTTF, Binomial and Poisson distributions etc. These can later be used to calculate probability values for system level failures.

The local failure data can be stored for later re-use in a component library as they are self-contained and have no dependencies with other components. This can reduce the time needed to annotate components in future systems.

Figure 2 shows an example failure annotation of a valve component.

The figure shows a valve component with two inputs (in and control) and one output. Below it the identified internal failure modes of the component along with expected failure and repair rates are displayed in a table. These internal failures are referenced by the output deviations such that,

for example, an omission of output can be caused by the valve being blocked or stuckClosed or by an omission of the input or a low signal from the control input.

Synthesis Phase

The modelling and annotation phase is largely manual though this effort can be reduced through the re-use of library components. The remaining phases are completely automatic beginning with the synthesis phase. When considered independently from a system, the output and input deviations of a component failure expression only represent potential failures. When the component is added to a system and, crucially, connected to other annotated components, then the unrealised input deviations can now be triggered by the output deviations of 'upstream' components. Similarly, the output deviations of this component can now trigger input deviations further downstream.

In HiP-HOPS this is achieved by working backwards through the system from the outputs (e.g. actuators) towards the inputs (e.g. data sensors) of the system. When an output deviation is encountered during the traversal it is connected to the corresponding input deviation of the same failure class. This is illustrated in Figure 3.

It should be noted that fault trees produced by this mechanical process record the propagation of failure in a very strict and methodical way with the logical structure of the tree determined only by the interconnections between the components and the local analyses of these components. Unlike the structures of many manually constructed fault trees that are defined using implicit assumptions by the designer, the structure of HiP-HOPS synthesised fault trees is easily understood.

Analysis Phase

The output of the synthesis phase is a network of interconnected fault trees that describe the global propagation of failure in the system. In the analysis phase the synthesised system fault trees undergo a

Figure 2. An example of local failure annotations for a computer controlled valve

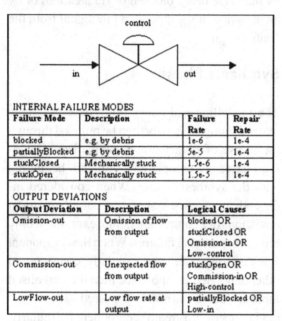

INTERNAL FAILURE MODES

Failure Mode	Description	Failure Rate	Repair Rate
blocked	e.g. by debris	1e-6	1e-4
partiallyBlocked	e.g. by debris	5e-5	1e-4
stuckClosed	Mechanically stuck	1.5e-6	1e-4
stuckOpen	Mechanically stuck	1.5e-5	1e-4

OUTPUT DEVIATIONS

Output Deviation	Description	Logical Causes
Omission-out	Omission of flow from output	blocked OR stuckClosed OR Omission-in OR Low-control
Commission-out	Unexpected flow from output	stuckOpen OR Commission-in OR High-control
LowFlow-out	Low flow rate at output	partiallyBlocked OR Low-in

qualitative analysis to determine the minimal cut sets. This process strips out any redundant logic in the fault tree using various logical reduction techniques, leaving the smallest combinations of basic event failures required to cause a system level failure.

Once the minimal cut sets have been obtained, they are quantitatively analysed—where probabilistic data was added to the basic events in the annotation phase—to calculate unavailability values for the top events of the fault trees.

During the qualitative analysis pass, in addition to generating the minimal cut sets, a multiple failure mode FMEA is also being generated. The FMEA shows the direct relationships between component failures and system failures. A classical FMEA only shows the *direct effects* of single points of failure, whereas because of the way the HiP-HOPS generates the FMEA from the fault trees, it is not restricted in this manner. Figure 4 shows how it can also determine the *further effects* of component failure, showing what effects it has when it occurs in combination with other component failures elsewhere. One particular benefit of the algorithm is that it highlights component failures (such as C5 in Figure 4) which are single point of failure for more than one system-level failure effects (e.g. C5 causes both F1 and F2). This represents an especially vulnerable point in the system and a prime candidate for parallel redundancy or substitution with a more reliable component.

Extensions to HiP-HOPS

HiP-HOPS has been extended in a number of areas to provide enhanced capabilities for safety analysis. Some of these will be discussed here.

Automatic Architectural Optimisation

The use of automated safety analysis tools as part of an iterative design process can help to identify weak points in the design early enough to remedy them, but the sheer scale of the design space often means there can be too many possible remedies to explore in detail, and designer expertise is relied upon to select a good solution. It is possible to

Figure 3. Connecting local failure data together to synthesise system fault trees

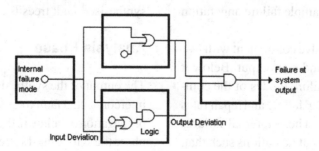

Figure 4. Converting fault trees into a multiple failure mode FMEA

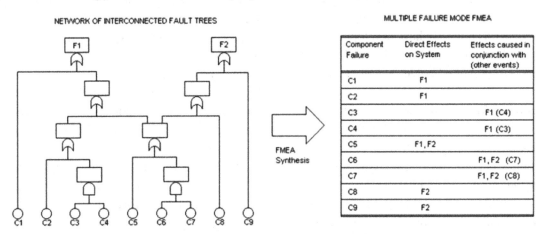

automatically explore this design space to identify optimal or near-optimal design candidates through the use of optimisation, allowing thousands of designs to be rapidly evaluated.

The speed of the analysis provided by HiP-HOPS has allowed optimisation to become a feasible choice. Through the use of genetic algorithms (Goldberg, 1989), which mimic the evolution of biological life to evaluate a population of candidates and ensure 'survival of the fittest', HiP-HOPS can automatically generate highly optimised designs based on the variability information provided by the designer. Typically the variability information takes the form of possible alternative implementations of components, each of which has different cost and reliability characteristics; for example, one implementation may be expensive but reliable, and another cheap but less reliable. Through the use of a customised version of the NSGA-II (Non-Dominated Sorting Genetic Algorithm – Deb *et al.*, 2002), HiP-HOPS performs a multi-objective optimisation, experimenting with different solutions and evaluating different, often conflicting, attributes—such as cost and unavailability—to produce the "Pareto set" of optimal solutions. The Pareto set is the set of solutions that are the best trade-offs between the different attributes being evaluated; thus one may have two optimal candidates, one of which is very cheap but unreliable, while the other is very expensive but more reliable. If a third candidate was just as reliable as the second but cheaper, then it would 'dominate' the second candidate and would replace it as part of the optimal Pareto set.

The HiP-HOPS optimisation capability is continually being improved and extended. Other forms of variability are possible, e.g. whole components can be replaced with compatible but more robust subsystems, e.g. replacing a single, series component with a parallel version. We have also been developing approaches that allow for the optimisation of allocation strategies for software tasks running on embedded hardware, e.g. to balance performance, robustness, and cost over two processors. The result is a powerful capability that offers significant advantages over a purely manual evaluation of different design options (Papadopoulos *et al.*, 2011).

Generalisable Failure Logic

As described above, the failure behaviour of components is described in HiP-HOPS using a set of logical expressions that relate output deviations to combinations of faults propagated to the inputs and internal failure modes. Such expressions are reusable and can be stored in a library of components to be used again in later models, but sometimes they need to be modified to suit the new context – for example, if new failure classes are needed, or if a component is modified with a different number of inputs and/or outputs.

To solve this issue, we have developed a more generalised version of the HiP-HOPS failure description language known as "Generalisable Failure Logic" or GFL (Wolforth *et al.*, 2010). GFL allows a form of parameterisation by defining operators such as ANY, ALL, EXCEPT, and SAME which can be applied to different elements of the failure expressions, e.g. allowing an expression to define an AND relationship across an arbitrary number of inputs, or propagating only the same failure classes from inputs to outputs. HiP-HOPS automatically expands these expressions at the synthesis stage when applied to a concrete implementation, meaning that a generalised expression from a component library can easily capture common patterns of failure (such as voting, propagation, and parallel redundancy) and be more readily reused in multiple different contexts.

Dynamic Fault Tree Analysis

One problem with traditional analysis techniques such as FTA and FMEA is that they are static in nature and cannot easily be applied to dynamic systems—those in which the system behaviour changes over time, depending on its mode of operation. Such systems are increasingly common as they display superior reliability and performance characteristics; for example, an FTA of a primary-standby system that can react to failure of its primary component by activating a dormant standby is a dynamic system. This adaptive behaviour is more complex to analyse, however, and can in some cases yield inaccurate results that do not account for the *sequence* of events.

Recently there have been attempts to improve FTA to enable it to be applied to dynamic systems. One such methodology is the Dynamic Fault Tree (DFT) approach (Dugan *et al.*, 2000),

which introduces new fault tree gates to represent functional dependencies, spare components, and sequences of failures. Quantitative analysis is achieved through the use of Markov chains, allowing the failure behaviour of dynamic systems to be more accurately captured, but qualitative analysis is neglected and although it provides important capabilities, the technique is prone to combinatorial explosion.

To provide a solution for dynamic qualitative analysis, we have developed a similar temporal fault tree analysis approach in HiP-HOPS that allows for the representation, reduction, and analysis of sequences of events: Pandora (Walker & Papadopoulos, 2009). Like DFTs, Pandora introduces new temporal gates to represent the sequential or simultaneous occurrence of events, and provides a temporal logic based on Boolean logic to allow "minimal cut sequences"—analogous to minimal cut sets—to be generated. This helps to grant analysts a more accurate and more useful understanding of how dynamic systems can fail.

Automatic Allocation of Safety Requirements

New standards of safety are continually being set, such as the new automotive safety standard, ISO 26262. ISO 26262 describes how ASILs—Automotive Safety Integrity Levels, representing a required level of safety for a component or system element and ranging from A (low safety requirement) to D (high safety requirement)—can be decomposed over parallel architectures, such that multiple components of a lower safety level (such as A or B) can combine to produce an overall architecture with a higher safety level (such as C or D) due to the redundancy it offers. This means that a system can meet a high safety requirement through the use of robust design instead of requiring all of its components to have that same high safety requirement, which could be very expensive.

However, in even simple systems, there are many possible decomposition strategies that can be employed, meaning that a manual determination of the best way to allocate ASILs (or any other form of SILs) is very difficult.

We have developed a technique that builds upon the FTA capabilities of HiP-HOPS (which concisely represents the failure dependencies between components) to automatically generate different, optimal allocations of ASILs to different parts of the system model. The technique has been applied to example systems modelled using the EAST-ADL automotive architecture description language (Walker *et al.*, 2010) with the intention of providing support for designers working with the ISO 26262 standard. By understanding how different combinations of failures cause a system failure that must meet a given ASIL, HiP-HOPS can determine what possible combinations of minimal ASILs can be allocated to individual components or failure modes while still meeting the overall safety requirement. Although still under development, this is a powerful new capability that may offer valuable insight to designers and analysts seeking to meet ISO 26262 and similar safety standards in the future.

CONCLUSION

The increasing scale and complexity of modern engineering systems, together with more stringent safety constraints and increasing pressures on design lifetimes and budgets, leads to a situation where comprehensive new analysis methodologies and automated tool support can offer significant benefits over manual use of classical safety analysis techniques.

Formal verification and compositional safety analysis techniques both have different disadvantages and advantages (Lisagor *et al.*, 2006) with respect to the level of detail and automation

provided and the scalability of the algorithms to handle combinations of multiple failures. Both can be integrated with nominal design models and tools; formal verification techniques are often fully automated as a result, taking the information they need from the system simulation model, but suffer much more from combinatorial explosion in large models. By contrast, compositional approaches typically require some additional modelling effort but are often more scalable and therefore applicable to even larger systems. However, both types of techniques are undeniably better than classical manual techniques, offering both faster and more detailed analysis capabilities. The use of such techniques—often in concert, enabling the advantages of different techniques to complement each other—allows the successful analysis of much larger, more complex systems than ever before, and leading to a more streamlined design process in which safety can play a leading role in guiding the system development, rather than being regarded more as an obstacle to be overcome.

In the future, the capabilities of these modern analysis approaches are likely to expand further, diversifying into other forms of systems analysis and engineering design support. For example, HiP-HOPS—a state-of-the-art compositional safety analysis tool—uniquely combines fast safety analysis abilities with evolutionary optimisation algorithms. This enables it to evaluate and optimise system models with multiple objectives, such as cost and dependability, as part of an integrated process. This type of combined analysis and optimisation automation potentially offers great advantages to designers of modern safety–critical systems. Another important area of expansion is support for complex dynamic or multi-state systems, and there is a significant body of research being undertaken in this direction. Finally, new safety standards—like the ISO 26262 automotive standard—are also driving innovation in this field. HiP-HOPS capabilities for automatic decomposition and allocation of safety integrity levels is an example of how existing approaches and tools can be enhanced to support these standards and keep pace with the continuing demand for safety and reliability in the increasingly complex safety-critical systems that we all rely upon every day.

REFERENCES

Bieber, P., Bougnol, C., Castel, C., Heckmann, J.-P., Kehren, C., Metge, S., et al. (2004). Safety assessment with AltaRica. In *Proceedings of IFIP Congress Topical Sessions* (pp. 505-510). IFIP.

Bozzano, M., & Villafiorita, A. (2006). *The FSAP/NuSMV-SA safety analysis platform*. Paper presented at ECAI 2006. Riva del Garda, Italy.

Ciardo, G., & Lindermann, C. (1993). Analysis of deterministic and stochastic Petri nets. In *Proceedings of the 5th International Workshop on Petri Nets and Performance Models*. Toulouse, France: PNPM.

Deb, K., Pratap, A., Agarwal, S., & Meyarivan, T. (2002). A fast and elitist multiobjective genetic algorithm: NSGA-II. *IEEE Transactions on Evolutionary Computation, 6*(2), 182–197. doi:10.1109/4235.996017.

Dugan, J. B., Sullivan, K., & Coppit, D. (2000). Developing a low-cost high-quality software tool for dynamic fault tree analysis. *IEEE Transactions on Reliability, 49*(1), 49–59. doi:10.1109/24.855536.

Ericson, C. A. (1999). Fault tree analysis - A history. In *Proceedings of the 17th International System Safety Conference*. Retrieved from www.fault-tree.net/papers/ericson-fta-history.pdf

Ge, X., Paige, R. F., & McDermid, J. A. (2009). Probabilistic failure propagation and transformation analysis. In *Proceedings of Computer Safety, Reliability and Security (LNCS)* (*Vol. 5775*, pp. 215–478). Berlin: Springer. doi:10.1007/978-3-642-04468-7_18.

Goldberg, D. E. (1989). *Genetic algorithms in search, optimisation, and machine learning*. Reading, MA: Addison-Wesley Professional.

Griffault, A., Arnold, A., Point, G., & Rauzy, A. (1999). The AltaRica formalism for describing concurrent systems. *Fundamenta Informaticae, 34*.

Grunske, L., & Kaiser, B. (2005). *An automated dependability analysis method for COTS-based systems. LNCS* (pp. 178–190). Berlin: Springer.

Grunske, L., Kaiser, B., & Papadopoulos, Y. I. (2005). Model-driven safety evaluation with state-event-vased components failure annotations. In *Proceedings of the 8th International Symposium on Component-Based Software Engineering* (pp. 33-48). IEEE.

Grunske, L., & Neumann, R. (2002). Quality improvement by integrating non-functional properties in software architecture specification. In *Proceedings of EASY'02 Second Workshop on Evaluation and Architecting System Dependability*, (pp. 23-32). San Jose, CA: EASY.

Güdemann, M., Ortmeier, F., & Reif, W. (2008). Computing ordered minimal critical sets. In *Proceedings of Formal Methods for Automation and Safety in Railway and Automotive Systems*. IEEE.

Heimdahl, M. P., Choi, Y., & Whalen, M. W. (2002). Deviation analysis through model checking. In *Proceedings of the 17th IEEE International Conference on Automated Software Engineering*. Edinburgh, UK: IEEE.

International Organization for Standardization. (2009). *ISO/DIS 26262*. Geneva, Switzerland: ISO.

Isograph Software. (2002). *Fault tree+ v11: Software tool*. Retrieved April 10, 2012 from http://www.isograph-software.com/index.htm

ITI. (2012). *SimulationX v3.5: Software tool*. Retrieved April 10, 2012 from http://www.itisim.com/

Kaiser, B., Gramlich, C., & Forster, M. (2007). State/event fault trees – A safety analysis model for software controlled systems. *Reliability Engineering & System Safety*, *92*, 1521–1537. doi:10.1016/j.ress.2006.10.010.

Lisagor, O., McDermid, J. A., & Pumfrey, D. J. (2006). Towards a practicable process for automating safety analysis. In *Proceedings of the 16th International Ship and Offshore Structures Conference (ISSC'06)*, (pp. 596-607). Albuquerque, NM: Systems Safety Society.

MathWorks. (2012). *MATLAB simulink R2012a: Software tool*. Retrieved April 10, 2012 from http://www.mathworks.co.uk/

Military, U. S. (1949). *Procedure for performing a failure modes effect and criticality analysis. United States Military Procedure MIL-P-1629*. Washington, DC: US Military.

Ortmeier, F., Reif, W., & Schellhorn, G. (2005). Deductive cause-consequence analysis (DCCA). In *Proceedings of the 16th IFAC World Congress*. IFAC.

Papadopolous, Y., Walker, M., Parker, D., Rüde, E., Hamann, R., & Uhlig, A. et al. (2011). Engineering failure analysis and design optimisation with HiP-HOPS. *Engineering Failure Analysis*, *18*, 590–608. doi:10.1016/j.engfailanal.2010.09.025.

Papadopoulos, Y., Walker, M., Reiser, M.-O., Servat, D., Abele, A., & Johansson, R. ... Weber, M. (2010). Automatic allocation of safety integrity levels. In *Proceedings of the 8th European Dependable Computing Conference - CARS Workshop*, (pp. 7-11). Valencia, Spain: ACM Press. ISBN: 978-1-60558-915-2

Reer, F., & Reif, W. (2007). Using deductive cause-consequence analysis (DCCA) with SCADE. In *Proceedings of the 26th International Conference in Computer Safety, Reliability and Security*, (pp. 465-478). IEEE.

Vesely, W. E., Stamatelatos, M., & Dugan, J. Fragola, J., Minarick, J., & Railsback, J. (2002). Fault tree handbook with aerospace applications. Washington, DC: NASA Office of Safety and Mission Assurance.

Walker, M., & Papadopoulos, Y. (2009). Qualitative temporal analysis: Towards a full implementation of the fault tree handbook. *Control Engineering Practice*, *17*(10), 1115–1125. doi:10.1016/j.conengprac.2008.10.003.

Wallace, M. (2005). Modular architectural representation and analysis of fault propagation. *Electronic Notes in Theoretical Computer Science*, *141*(3), 53–71. doi:10.1016/j.entcs.2005.02.051.

Wolforth, I. P., Walker, M. D., Grunske, L., & Papadopoulos, Y. I. (2010). Generalisable safety annotations for specification of failure patterns. *Software, Practice & Experience*, *40*(5), 453–483.

Worrell, R. B., & Stack, D. W. (1978). *A SETS user manual for the fault tree analyst. NUREG CR-04651*. Washington, DC: US Nuclear Regulatory Commission.

Zimmermann, A., German, R., Freiheit, J., & Hommel, G. (1999). *TimeNET 3.0 tool description*. Paper presented at the International Conference on Petri Nets and Performance Models. Zaragosa, Spain.

KEY TERMS AND DEFINITIONS

Failure Modes and Effects Analysis (FMEA): A typically inductive safety analysis technique that describes the systems level effects of component level failures.

Fault Tree Analysis: Deductive safety analysis technique that can reduce a fault tree to its minimal cut sets.

Generalisable Failure Logic (GFL): Generalised version of the HiP-HOPS failure description language.

Hierarchically-Performed Hazard Origin and Propagation Studies (HiP-HOPS): A state of the art compositional safety analysis and optimisation tool.

Multi-Objective Optimisation: Search space exploration algorithms, typically meta-heuristic, that use the Pareto dominance concept.

Pandora: Qualitative temporal fault tree analysis that allows the modelling and analysis of sequences of failures in HiP-HOPS.

Safety Integrity Level (SIL): Representing a required level of safety for a component or system element; also ASIL (Automotive SIL), which is a SIL applied to the automotive domain and defined in ISO 26262.

Chapter 5
Expressing and Validating OCL Constraints using Graphs

Najet Zoubeir
Institut Supérieur d'Informatique, Tunisia

Adel Khalfallah
Institut Supérieur d'Informatique, Tunisia

Samir Benahmed
Faculté des Sciences de Tunis, Tunisia

ABSTRACT

The definition of the semantics of visual languages, in particular Unified Modeling Language (UML) diagrams, using graph formalism has known a wide success, since graphs fit the multi-dimensional nature of this kind of language. However, constraints written in Object Constraint Language (OCL) and defined on these models are still not well integrated within this graph-based semantics. In this chapter, the authors propose an integrated semantics of OCL constraints within class diagrams, using graph transformation systems. Their contribution is divided into two parts. In the first part, they introduce graph constraint patterns, as the translation into graphs of a subset of OCL expressions. These patterns are validated with experimental examples using the GROOVE toolset. In the second part, the authors define the relation between OCL and UML models within their graph transformation system.

1. INTRODUCTION

The formal definition of the semantics of visual languages has been the focus of many works, in order to extend the scope of such languages to more critical domains. For example, UML diagrams have been formalized using different formalisms, such as formal specification languages (PVS [Aredo, 1999; Ledang & Souquires, 2001], CSP [Ng & Butler, 2003], Z [Dupuy, 2000; France & Bruel, 2001; France, Bruel, Larrondo-Petrie, & Grant, 1997],...). Among these formalisms, graph transformation systems have known a fair success representing the visual languages seman-

DOI: 10.4018/978-1-4666-3922-5.ch005

tics, since this formalism is formal, universal and easily understood. Many graph-based semantics were proposed for UML diagrams, such as the Dynamic Meta-Modeling approach introduced by Hausmann, which formalizes many of the UML diagrams, such as the statechart diagrams (Engels, Hausmann, Heckel, & Sauer, 2000; Hausmann, 2001), the sequence diagrams (Hausmann, Heckel, & Sauer, 2002; Hausmann, Heckel, & Sauer, 2004) and the activity diagrams (Hausmann, 2005). Other works try rather to define integrated semantics for a number of UML diagrams. For example, (Kuske, Gogolla, Kollmann, & Kreowski, 2002), and (Gogolla, Ziemann, & Skuske, 2003) propose a graph-based integrated semantics for UML class, object and statechart diagrams, and (Holscher, Ziemann, & Gogolla, 2006) works on a larger subset of UML diagrams, including further the use cases and interaction diagrams.

In this context, expressing constraints on UML diagrams, written in the Object Constraint Language (OCL) is studied in many works (Bauer, 2008; Rutle, Rossini, Lamo, & Wolter, 2012; Dang & Gogolla, 2009; Rensink & Kleppe, 2008; Bottoni, Koch, Parisi-Presicci, & Taentzer, 2002). In general, the purpose of these works is to provide a semantics of OCL constraints using graphs. The work in (Bauer, 2008) defines the notion of conditions on attributes in DMM graphs, without considering the OCL syntax, since he does not directly manipulate UML diagrams. In fact, the author considers conditions on graph nodes as an additional refinement of the matching in graph transformation rules. He uses the GROOVE toolset (Groove, 2012) for the representation and manipulation of graphs and constraints. Rutle et al. in (Rutle, Rossini, Lama, & Wolter, 2012) propose constraint aware model transformations based on the diagram predicate framework (DPF), which is a generic graph-based specification framework. The authors propose to define constraints in the transformation rules specified by a joined modeling language, used to join the source modeling language to the target modeling language. The

constraints are written in First-Order Logic (FOL), and represented in diagrams by diagrammatic signatures. Although this approach is based on the formal meta-modeling framework DPF, we consider that the proposed constraint semantics (1) is not well integrated with models, since it uses a different notation (FOL), and (2) is restricted to the meta-level, because constraints are used only to control which structure to create in the target model, and which constraints to add to the created structure.

The work of Dang et al. in (Dang & Gogolla, 2009) propose to integrate OCL constraints with Triple Graph Grammars (TGG), and realize this approach by a tool as an extension of USE (UML based Specification Environment). OCL conditions are used in meta-models in order to precisely represent well-formed models, and in models as their properties. However, OCL constraints are represented in the proposed approach in their textual form. So the integration of OCL with TGG is carried out by the tool, and not in a visual form. The work presented in (Resink & Kleppe, 2008) formally extends type graphs to be more compliant with UML. This extension includes a set of object oriented notions such as inheritance and multiplicity, and defines the notion of graph constraints. The work organizes these constraints in categories, such as bidirectionality and multiplicities on associations, and acyclicity of containments, and proposes formal definition for each category. However, the authors do not specify the details of OCL constraints since they do not aim to define a semantics for them, and just classify them as a general category. Bottoni et al. in (Bottoni, Koch, Parisi-Presicci, & Taentzer, 2002) propose an OCL constraints visualization based on collaboration diagrams, and an operational semantics based on graph transformation units. They propose to express constraints by graph transformation rules, such as a constraint satisfaction is represented by the matching between the rule and the instance graph. However, the OCL constraints are manipulated as expressions, without defining how these expressions are integrated within models. In fact, the authors use OCL invariants in their examples, but give no details about the use of the other OCL placements, such as preconditions and postconditions.

Considering the set of works previously presented, we noticed that in the definition of UML diagrams semantics using graph transformations, the semantics of OCL constraints is whether defined in a non-accurate way (Resink & Kleppe, 2008), or defined separately from UML diagrams and hence lacks of a solid integration in the graph transformation systems (Rutle, Rossini, Lamo, & Wolter, 2012; Dang & Gogolla, 2009; Bottoni, Koch, Parisi-Presicii, & Taentzer, 2002). In this chpater, we propose an integrated semantics of OCL constraints within class and object diagrams, using graph transformation systems. We propose to represent models composed by class and object diagrams and OCL constraints in an integrated form using graph transformation systems, as depicted in the Figure 1.

Our main contribution is the proposition of an integrated semantics of OCL constraints based on graph transformation systems. In a first part, we propose a number of patterns representing a set of OCL expressions using graph notations. These patterns allow translating OCL constraints to graph constraints. We relied on experimental examples using the GROOVE toolset in order to

validate our patterns. Then, in a second part, we explain how to use and interprete these graph constraints within graph transformation systems, in the same way as OCL constraints are used and interpreted within a UML model.

The remainder of this paper is organized as follows: In section 2 we will briefly present the notions of graphs and graph transformations. In section 3 we will illustrate the graph constraint patterns we propose, and section 4 will describe the use of these patterns in graphs representing class diagrams, in a way similar to the use of OCL constraints in UML models. Finally, in section 5 we will exemplify our proposal using an illustration example.

2. CONSIDERED GRAPHS

In our work, we consider the graphs defined in (Hausmann, 2005): "The graph notion (...) is a typed, attributed, node and edge labeled multigraph that allows for node inheritance in the type graph and uses special datatype nodes (DT) for the representation of attributes." So we deal with type graphs, instance graphs and rule graphs, such as the operation semantics is described by transformation rules. The following definitions are used to present the different concepts belonging to a graph transformation system (Hausmann, 2005). In these definitions, we consider a combined label alphabet Λ providing labels to nodes and edges, and containing the special label $\perp$ as defined in (Hausmann, 2005). We consider also an extension of this alphabet called $\Lambda' = \Lambda \cup \{\bullet\}$ which contains the wildcard symbol $\bullet$ which evaluates to true when compared to any other label of Λ' (Hausmann, 2005).

Definition 1 (Graph): $G = N, E, l_N$ with

- N the finite and non-empty set of nodes,

Figure 1. The integration of class and object diagrams with OCL constraints in graph transformation systems

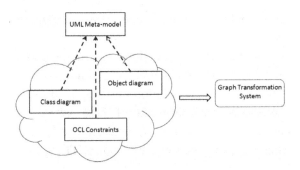

- E the finite set of directed edges, $E \subseteq N \times \Lambda' \times \Lambda' \times \Lambda' \times N$,
- $l_N : N \to \,\rangle\,'$ the labeling function for nodes.

Definition 2 (Edge-Label Preserving Graph-Morphism (elp-morphism)): An elp graph morphism is a structure and edge label preserving morphism between graphs. $m(G, H) = m_N$ with $m_N : N^G \to N^H$ the node mapping function, and $\forall a, l1, l2, l3, b \in E^G$: $m_N(a), l_1', l_2', l_3', m_N(b) \in E^H$ with $l_1 = l_1', l_2 = l_2', l_3 = l_3'$.

Definition 3 (Typed Graph): $GT = G, type$ with G a graph as defined above, $type : G \to TG$ the typing elp-morphism and TG a graph with the additional requirement that l_N^{TG} is injective.

Definition 4 (Type Graph with Inheritance): Inheritance in the type graph TG is expressed by special edges I. $GI = TG, I, A$ with TG a graph with the additional requirement that l_N^{TG} is injective $I \subseteq N^{TG} \times N^{TG}$ the set of inheritance edges which must not form a circle $A \subseteq N^{TG}$ the set of abstract nodes.

We consider graphs that were designed by (Hausmann, 2005) as DMM Type Graphs, DMM Instance Graphs and DMM Rule Graph.

Definition 5 (DMM Type Graph): $G_{DMMT} = \{N, E, l_N, I, A, DT$ with N, E, l_N, I, A a type graph with inheritance $DT \subset N$ the set of data types $l_N(N) \subseteq \Lambda \setminus \{\bot\}$ $E \subseteq \big((N \setminus DT) \times \Lambda \times \Lambda \times \Lambda \times (N \setminus DT)\big)$ $\cup \big((N \setminus DT) \times \{\bot\} \times \{\bot\} \times \Lambda \times DT\big)\}$.

Definition 6 (DMM Instance Graph): $G_{DMMI} = \{G, type$ with $type : G \to TG$ the typing elp-morphism

$TG \in G_{DMMT}$

$l_N(N^G) \subseteq \Lambda$

$l_E(E^G) \subseteq \Lambda \times \Lambda \times \Lambda$

$\forall s \in DT^{TG} : type_N^{-1}(s) \subseteq D_s\}$.

TG is the Concrete Transitive Closure defined in (Hausmann, 2005).

Definition 7 (DMM Rule Graph): $G_{DMMR} = \{G, type$ with

$type : G \to \hat{TG}$

$TG \in G_{DMMT}$

$l_N(N^G) \subseteq \Lambda'$

$l_E(E^G) \subseteq \Lambda' \times \Lambda' \times \Lambda'$

$\forall s \in DT^{TG} : type_N^{-1}(s) \subseteq D_s\}$.

$\hat{TG}$ is the Abstract Transitive Closure defined in (Hausmann, 2005).

According to these definitions, we refine Figure 1, such as a class diagram will be translated to a type graph; an object diagram to an instance graph, and the OCL expressions to a set of graph transformation rules as depicted in Figure 2. Our contribution is composed by two main parts: First we define a set of graph constraint patterns representing the translation into graphs of OCL expressions. The definition of these patterns is based on experimental examples, and validated using the Computation Tree Logic (CTL) within the toolset GROOVE. In the second part of our contribution, we describe the use of these graph constraints in other graphs, representing class and object diagrams.

3. GRAPH CONSTRAINTS PATTERNS

In our work, we are trying to represent OCL constraints within graphs representing class diagrams. In order to do that, we propose a set of graph constraints patterns. These patterns was created according to a subset of the OCL expressions abstract syntax (illustrated by the meta-model of Figure 3) and concrete syntax, both described in (OMG, n.d.). We note that we do not consider constraints figuring as adornment in UML diagrams, such as *{ordered}* and *{xor}*, but only OCL constraints defined by the Object Management Group (OMG) in (OMG, n.d.).

In order to validate our patterns, we relied on experimental examples of expressions that we verified in some cases, using CTL within the GROOVE toolset. CTL is used with the invariant constraints to check that the graph constraint expresses the exact meaning of the OCL constraint, in the full state space of the corresponding transition system generated by GROOVE (more details in section 4.1). The patterns presented in this

paper correspond to the following meta-classes from the OCL expressions meta-model: *LiteralExp, VariableExp*, and *FeatureCallExp*. Considering the facts that the meta-classes *MessageExp* and *StateExp* concern the UML statechart diagram, and the meta-class *LoopExp* (and its descendants) is a repetitive form of an OCL expression, we did not propose corresponding patterns for them. The use of a simple-graph transformation tool such as GROOVE to manipulate multi-graphs should not be a problem, since it is possible to translate typed multi-graph production systems into typed simple-graph production systems (Boneva, Hermann, Kastenberg, & Rensink, 2007).

In what follows, we will present our graph constraints patterns, using illustrations based on GROOVE notations, and eventually accompanied by descriptions and examples. In each pattern visualization, the red-colored elements are generic elements, that have to be replaced with specific values or graph elements when instantiating the pattern.

3.1. Literal Expression Pattern

A literal expression of a type T is a value of this type. Using the GROOVE notation, this is represented by a node labeled with the type followed by the literal value, as depicted in Figure 4. We

Figure 2. Refinement of the integration of class and object diagrams with OCL constraints in graph transformation systems

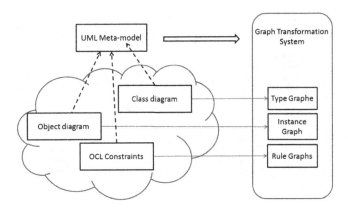

should mention that we do not deal with NULL literal and invalid literal expressions. This pattern is used for constants and valued attributes.

3.2. Variable Expression Pattern

In OCL, a variable expression is just a name that refers to a variable or self (OMG, n.d.). In our context, the keyword self will be represented by a node belonging to the instance graph, to which a graph constraint expression is linked, as it will be explained in section 3.3. So the Variable Expression Pattern is used to represent variables, as illustrated in Figure 5(a).

3.3. Feature Call Expression Patterns

In this category we propose two patterns: the Property Call Expression Pattern and the Operation Call Expression Pattern.

3.3.1. Property Call Expression Pattern

A Property Call Expression in OCL refers to an attribute of a class, and evaluates to the value of this attribute (OMG, n.d.). In the concrete syntax of this expression, the property name is marked with the keyword '@pre', which refers to the value of a feature at the start of the operation. This value will eventually be modified by the operation. In graphs, the use of '@pre' is represented by a node representing an attribute, that will be deleted, in order to be replaced by a new one containing the new value. The Property Call Expression Pattern generic structure is depicted in Figure 5(b), such as the blue color is used to represent a node that will be deleted by a graph transformation rule.

3.3.2. Operation Call Expression Patterns

This category contains four patterns: the Operators Pattern, the Universal Quantifier Pattern, the

Figure 3. OCL expressions meta-model

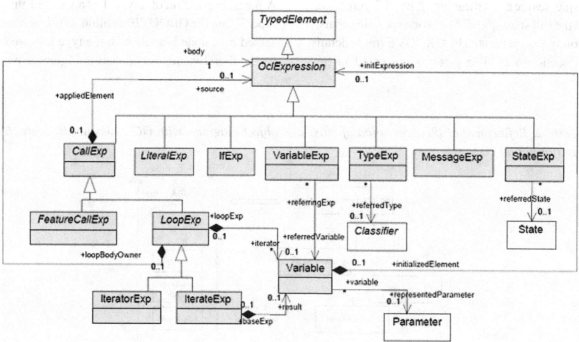

Figure 4. Literal expression pattern

Figure 5. (a) Variable expression pattern; (b) property call expression pattern

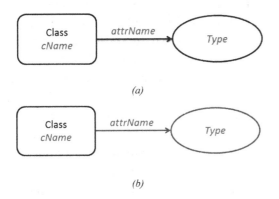

Existential Quantifier Pattern, and the Exclusion Pattern.

3.3.2.1. Unary and Binary Operator Pattern

In order to represent operators, we use the notion of product nodes defined in GROOVE (Rensink, Boneva, Kastenberg, & Staijen, 2011). Product nodes are related to their operands (which are expressions) by *Argument Edges*. These nodes are generally used in the instance level. We will use it in the pattern visualization in a generic form

with expression patterns to express Unary and binary operator Patterns. Figure 6 illustrates the Binary Operators pattern: the node P is the operator and the π_0 and π_1 edges link the operator respectively to its first and second operands, which are expressions.

The result will be visualized by a node presenting its type and value, linked to the product node with an edge labeled by the operation carried out on the arguments. The Unary Operator Pattern is similar to the Binary Operator Pattern, with only one argument π_0.

3.3.2.2. Universal and Existential Quantifier Pattern

The Universal Quantifier Pattern is used to illustrate OCL expressions with the keyword *forAll*. In order to represent these expressions with graphs, we interpreted the expression *Collection.forAll(expression)* as for all the elements in *Collection*, there exists *expression*. In GROOVE notation, we need to use an existential node nested in a universal node in order to express OCL expressions with the keyword *forAll*.

The OCL expressions with the keywords *exists* and *includes* are boolean expressions expressing whether a certain expression is or not satisfied by at least one element of the collection. In GROOVE notation, the existential node cannot be used by its own, it should be always nested in a universal node.

That is why we define a pattern for both expressions. This pattern is depicted in Figure 7. The node of type "Class" linked to the universal

Figure 6. Binary operator pattern

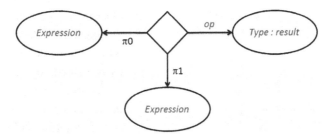

node represents the objects of the collection, and all the nodes belonging to the expression must be linked to the existential node.

4. THE USE OF GRAPH CONSTRAINTS IN GRAPHS

In the definition of the use of OCL in UML models, described in the OCL specification document (OMG, n.d.), the authors distinguish three things that need to be separated for every OCL expression occurrence: the placement, the contextual classifier, and the self instance.

4.1. Placement

The placement represents the position where the OCL expression is used in the UML model. The standard placements of OCL expressions within class diagrams are summarized by (Yang, 2004) as shown in the Figure 8.

In the Figure 8, the placements are association-ends roles associated to the class *oclExpression* that belong to the OCL meta-model. We notice that the author did not represent the class Constraint from the UML meta-model, whose role is to relate the expressions to their constrained elements. Except for the initial value of an attribute and the definition expressions, which we did not consider in this paper, all the graph constraints

Figure 7. Quantifier pattern

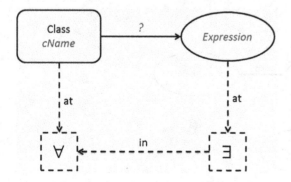

placements have to be expressed in graph transformation rules as explained below:

1. **Pre-Condition:** A pre-condition is a boolean expression associated to an operation. It defines a condition that must hold before the execution of that operation. Since an operation semantics is depicted by a graph transformation rule in our proposal, a pre-condition associated to this operation will be represented by a graph expression linked to one or more nodes in the graph transformation rule expressing the operation semantics.

2. **Post-Condition:** A post-condition is also a boolean expression associated to an operation, that corresponds to a condition that must hold after the operation executes. In the context of graphs, a post-condition can be expressed only if it concerns a new created node. The creation of nodes in a graph transformation rule corresponds to whether a modification of an attribute's value, or to the creation of a new object. So a post-condition will be represented in the graph transformation rule associated to the considered operation, by a graph expression linked to one or more new created nodes.

3. **Operation Body:** This type of expressions concerns query operations. It is simply represented by the graph transformation rule expressing the query operation semantics.

4. **Invariant:** By definition, an invariant is a boolean expression over a class (classifier in general) that must be verified by all the instances of this class. In the context of graphs, in order to define invariants, we have to ensure that all the nodes representing a class instances verify the considered invariant expression during the whole simulation, which includes also the new nodes created by transformation rules.

   We propose to represent a graph constraint invariant with an empty side-effect graph transformation rule, which contains the invariant expression, according to the graph constraint patterns already presented. This rule must be verified in the whole state space during the simulation. That is why, invariant rules have to be checked using CTL formulas. For example, let I be the following OCL invariant:

```
context Companie
inv : Companie.employe->
   forAll(e:Employe|e.age < 65)
```

And let R be the corresponding rule to I. R is depicted in Figure 9. To ensure that R is

verified for all instances, we have to check that the CTL expression 1 holds for all states. The result of this formula depends on the host graph.

$$AG \quad R \tag{1}$$

5. **Derivation:** By definition, a derived value expression is an invariant that states that the value of the attribute or association end must always be equal to the value obtained from evaluating the expression. That is why

Figure 8. Standard placements in OCL (Yang, 2004)

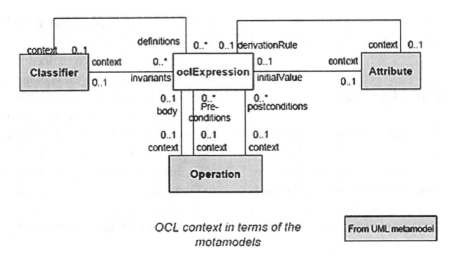

Figure 9. Example of an invariant expression

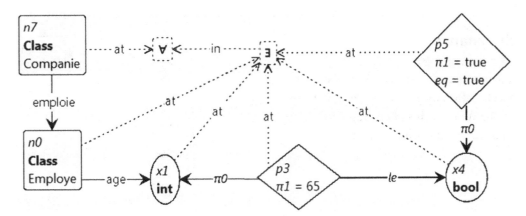

Figure 10. Circular buffer class diagram and OCL constraints: (a) circular buffer class diagram; (b) circular buffer OCL constraints

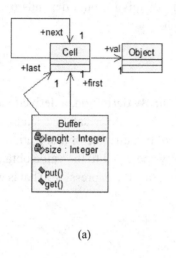

(a)

context Buffer

inv inv1 : self.lenght >= 0 **and** self.lenght <= self.**size**

context Buffer::get()

pre : self.lenght >= 1

post : self.lenght = self.lenght@**pre** - 1

context Buffer::put()

pre : self.lenght < self.**size**

post : self.lenght = self.lenght@**pre** + 1

(b)

we consider this placement equivalent to the Invariant placement.

4.2. Contextual Classifier

By definition, the contextual classifier defines the namespace in which the expression is evaluated. In the previous figure, the contextual classifiers are the classes imported from the UML meta-model, which are: Classifier, Attribute and Operation. In the translation to the graph formalism, all of these three elements are represented by nodes. So the contextual classifier will be always represented by a node, to which a graph constraint expression is linked.

4.3. Self Instance

As the self instance is always an instance of the contextual classifier, we propose to represent it by a node belonging to the instance graph, to which a graph constraint expression is linked.

5. ILLUSTRATION EXAMPLE

We devote this section to an illustration example, which illustrates how a class diagram accompanied with OCL constraints is translated to a graph transformation system, according to our proposal. Our example is the Circular Buffer, inspired from GROOVE toolset samples. The circular buffer class diagram and OCL constraints are depicted in Figure 10.

In the context of the class "Buffer," the invariant expresses the fact that the attribute length is

Figure 11. Circular buffer type graph

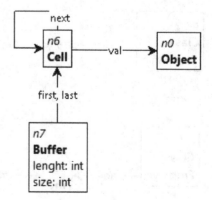

Figure 12. Graph transformation rule for the "get" operation with its pre and post conditions

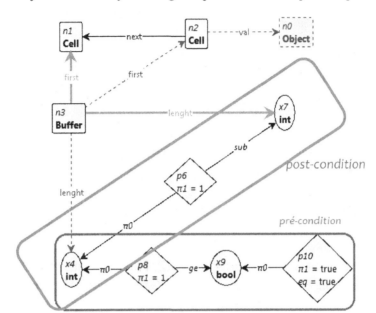

Figure 13. Graph transformation rule for the "put" operation with its pre and post conditions

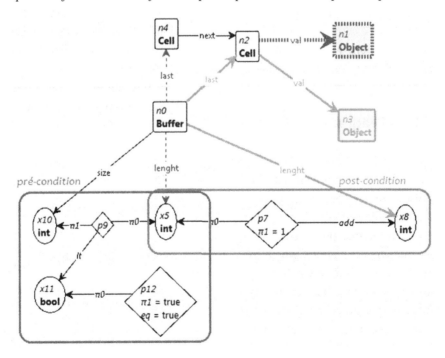

Figure 14. Graph transformation rule for invariant inv1

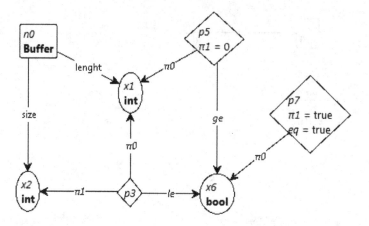

a positive value less than or equal to the buffer size. For the "get" operation, the precondition says that it should be at least one element in the buffer, and the postcondition expresses the fact that the buffer length should be reduced by 1 after a "get" operation. The "put" operation precondition requires that the buffer should not be full, and its postcondition expresses the fact that the buffer length should be increased by 1 after a "put" operation.

In the rest of this section, we will represent our graphs (type graph and rule graphs) using GROOVE.

5.1. From a Class Diagram to a Type Graph

Since the circular buffer example is inspired from the GROOVE toolset samples, the type graph corresponding to the class diagram of Figure 10(a) we propose is close to the one proposed by the toolset, with some minor modifications, which are the use of the attributes length for the number of the occupied cells and size for the buffer capacity. Figure 11 illustrates the type graph corresponding to the circular buffer class diagram of Figure 10(a).

5.2. Representing OCL Constraints in Graph Transformation Rules

5.2.1. "Get" Operation Constraints

The "get" operation has a precondition and a postcondition (cf. Figure 10b):

- The precondition constraint is an operation call expression, corresponding to a binary operator, which pattern is depicted in Figure 6;
- The postcondition constraint is composed by a property call expression, which is the

Figure 15. Considered instance graph

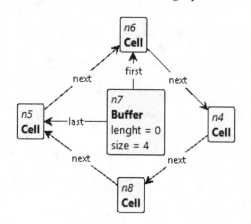

operand of an operation call expression, also corresponding to a binary operator.

According to our proposal, the "get" operation semantics is represented by a graph transformation system. In this rule should be represented the preconditions and the postconditions constraints related to the considered operation. The graph transformation rule corresponding to the "get" operation and its pre and postconditions is depicted in Figure 12.

5.2.2. "Put" Operation Constraints

Similarly to the "get" operation, the "put" operation also has a precondition and a postcondition (cf. Figure 10b), corresponding respectively to a binary operator call expression, and a property call expression, which is the operand of a binary operator call expression. The graph transformation rule corresponding to the "put" operation and its pre and postconditions is depicted in Figure 13.

5.2.3. The Invariant Constraint

The Buffer invariant, named *inv1* (cf. Figure 10b), is composed by the conjunction of two binary operator call expressions. Following our proposal, we created a graph transformation rule representing the invariant constraint, using multiple instances of the binary operator pattern, as illustrated in Figure 14. Then, we used the GROOVE model checker to verify that this rule holds for all the states, for the instance graph depicted in Figure 15. This means that the invariant graph constraint is verified for all the buffer instances generated by the application of the "get" and "put" transformation rules, applied on the considered instance graph.

6. DISCUSSION AND FURTHER WORK

In this paper, we proposed an integrated semantics of UML class and object diagrams accompanied by OCL constraints. After presenting the basic concepts, we started by the definition of a set of graph constraint patterns, used to express OCL constraints within graphs, representing class diagrams. Our patterns are validated using CTL formulas on experimental examples. Then we clarified the use of these graph constraints within graphs representing class and object diagrams, in accordance with the OCL specification document. Finally, we exemplified our proposal using an illustration example, showing the representation of a class diagram accompanied with OCL constraints by a graph transformation system.

Positioning this work within the framework of MDA four layered architecture (OMG, 2003), type graphs will represent the M1 level, and instance graphs will correspond to the M0 one. However, due to the universal character of graphs, this mapping can be generalized such as type graphs and instance graphs will correspond respectively to M_{n+1} and M_n levels, for $n \in [0..3]$. So we will be able to define and validate OCL constraints on graphs representing models and meta-models. In the future this work, we aim to validate models by studying the constraints preservation when a transformation, such as design patterns introduction, is applied on these models.

REFERENCES

Aredo. (1999). Formalizing UML class diagrams in PVS. In *Proceedings of OOPSLA'99 Workshop on Rigorous Modeling and Analysis with the UML: Challenges and Limitations*. OOPSLA.

Bauer. (2008). Enhancing the dynamic meta modeling formalism and its eclipse-based tool support with attributes. (Bachelor thesis). University of Paderborn.

Boneva, H. Kastenberg, & Rensink. (2007). Simulating multigraph transformations using simple graphs. In *Proceedings of the Sixth International Workshop on Graph Transformation and Visual Modeling Techniques, Electronic Communications of the EASST, 2007*. EASST.

Bottoni, K. Parisi-Presicci, & Taentzer. (2002). Working on OCL with graph transformations. In *Proceedings of APPLIGRAPH Workshop on Applied Graph Transformation*, (pp. 1–10). APPLIGRAPH.

Dang & Gogolla. (2009). On Integrating OCL and triple graph grammars. In *Models in Software Engineering* (pp. 124–137). Berlin: Springer-Verlag.

Dupuy. (2000). Couplage de notations semi-formelles et formelles pour la spécification des systèmes d'information. (PhD thesis). Université Joseph Fourier – Grenoble 1, Grenoble, France.

Engels, H. (1939). Heckel, & Sauer. (2000). Dynamic meta modeling: A graphical approach to the operational semantics of behavioral diagrams in UML. *Lecture Notes in Computer Science*, 323–337.

France, B. Larrondo-Petrie, & Grant. (1997). Rigorous object-oriented modeling: Integrating formal and informal notations. In *Proceedings of the 6th International AMAST Conference* (LNCS), (vol. 1349). Sydney, Australia: Springer-Verlag.

France & Bruel. (2001). *Rigorous analysis and design with the unified modeling language*. Retrieved from http://www.univ-pau.fr/bruel/Tutorials/etapsTut.html

Gogolla, Ziemann, & Kuske. (2003). Towards an integrated graph based semantics for UML. *Electronic Notes in Theoretical Computer Science, 72*(3). doi:10.1016/S1571-0661(04)80619-4.

Groove. (2012). *Graphs for object-oriented verification*. Retrieved from http://groove.cs.utwente.nl/

Hausmann, Heckel, & Sauer. (2002). Dynamic meta modeling with time: Specifying the semantics of multimedia sequence diagrams. *Electronic Notes in Theoretical Computer Science, 72*(3).

Hausmann, Heckel, & Sauer. (2004). Dynamic meta modeling with time: Specifying the semantics of multimedia sequence diagrams. *Software & Systems Modeling, 3*(3), 181–193. doi:10.1007/s10270-003-0045-7.

Hausmann. (2001). *Dynamische metamodellierung zur spezifikation einer operationalen semantik von UML*. (Masters thesis). Universitt Paderborn.

Hausmann. (2005). *Dynamic meta modeling: A semantics description technique for visual modeling languages*. (PhD thesis). University of Paderborn.

Holscher, Ziemann, & Gogolla. (2006). On translating UML models into graph transformation systems. Journal of Visual Languages and Computing Archive, 17(1).

Kuske, G. Kollmann, & Kreowski. (2002). An integrated semantics for UML class, object and state diagrams based on graph transformation. Lecture Notes in Computer Science, 11–28.

Ledang & Souquires. (2001). *Formalizing UML behavioral diagrams with B*. Paper presented in the Tenth OOPSLA Workshop on Behavioral Semantics: Back to Basics. Tampa Bay, FL.

Ng & Butler. (2003). Towards formalizing UML state diagrams in CSP. In Proceedings of the 1st IEEE International Conference on Software Engineering and Formal Methods. IEEE Computer Society.

OMG. (2003). Retrieved from http://www.omg.org

OMG. (2011). Retrieved from http://www.omg.org/spec/UML/2.4/Superstructure

OMG. (n.d.). Retrieved from http://www.omg.org/spec/OCL/2.3.1

Rensink, B. Kastenberg, & Staijen. (2011). User manual for the GROOVE tool set. Enschede, The Netherlands: Department of Computer Science, University of Twente.

Rensink & Kleppe. (2008). On a graph-based semantics for UML class and object diagrams. In *Proceedings fo ECEASST, 2008*. ECEASST.

Rutle, Rossini, Lamo, & Wolter. (2012). A formal approach to the specification and transformation of constraints in MDE. *Journal of Logic and Algebraic Programming*, *81*, 422–457. doi:10.1016/j.jlap.2012.03.006.

Yang. (2004). *OCL 2.0 and its relationship to meta-*modeling. Modelling, Simulation and Design lab (MSDL) Presentations.

KEY TERMS AND DEFINITIONS

Computational Tree Logic (CTL): CTL is a branching-time temporal logic, expression state and path formulas on the state space. CTL is a restriction of the full expressive tree logic CTL*.

Graph Transformation System (GTS): A GTS is the set of graph transformation rules with eventually type graphs and instance graphs.

GRaphs for Object-Oriented Verification (GROOVE): GROOVE is a graph transformation framework developed at the University of Twente, The Netherlands. It focuses on the use of simple graphs for the design, compilation and run of systems modeled as Graph Transformation Systems.

Model Transformation: It is the process of converting a model to another model within the same system. The input and output models should satisfy source and target meta-models.

Object Constraint Language (OCL): OCL is a formal language standardized by the Object Management Group (OMG) for the expression of constraints in UML models. Originally, this language was an IBM contribution to UML 1.1; it has become a part of the modeling standard since UML 1.3.

Unified Modeling Language (UML): UML is an object-oriented Visual Modeling Language (VML), which combines existing object-oriented VML (Booch, OMT and OOSE) and provides diagrams for modeling different aspects of systems. UML is now the most popular industry standard VML in software engineering.

Visual Language (VL): A VL is defined by its concrete and abstract syntax, besides its semantic domain and mapping. In general, the abstract syntax of VL is captured by meta-modeling.

Chapter 6

A UML–Compliant Approach for Intelligent Reconfiguration of Embedded Control Systems

Amen Ben Hadj Ali
Tunis El Manar University, Tunisia

Samir Ben Ahmed
Tunis El Manar University, Tunisia

Mohamed Khalgui
Xidian University, China

Antonio Valentini
O3neida Europe, Belgium

ABSTRACT

The chapter deals with UML-based design of Reconfigurable Embedded Control Systems (RECS). The different software architectural configurations of the control system are described as a set of inter-connected software components. A software agent is defined in order to handle dynamic reconfiguration scenarios. The agent has the ability to interact with users and to monitor the system's environment in order to apply valid reconfiguration scenarios at different levels of the system's architecture. In order to address all possible forms of reconfiguration, three architectural levels are defined. A set of UML-compliant metamodels are proposed in order to describe the knowledge about the reconfiguration agent, the system architecture, the reconfiguration scenarios, and the reconfiguration events. The validity of the reconfiguration scenarios is checked by using a UML-based environment that allows evaluation of the architectural and reconfiguration constraints. The proposed reconfiguration approach is applied to two industrial production systems, FESTO and ENAS.

INTRODUCTION

In the context of modern Embedded Control Systems (ECS), one of the most important challenges is the tradeoff between performance and rapid response to market changes and customer needs (Leitão, 2004). This tradeoff is better obtained when addressed early in the development process at design time. Indeed, modern ECS become more complex because they incorporate increasing amounts of software. In order to counter the effect of growing complexity, ECS are often designed in

DOI: 10.4018/978-1-4666-3922-5.ch006

a component-based fashion as a network of inter-connected software components using different technologies that have been proposed for this aim such as IEC61499 (IEC-Part1, 2005; Lewis, 2001). Consequently, even small changes in the system design or any failure at run-time require a cost- and time-intensive effort to adapt the system. One of the most promising directions to address these issues is the reconfiguration which refers to the process of modifying the system's structure and behavior during its execution. Being reconfigurable is important for reacting fast to sudden and unpredictable requirement changes with minimum cost and risk. Within the literature of ECS, two reconfiguration policies could be identified depending on the way of re-configuration execution: static (offline) (Angelov, Sierszecki & Marian, 2005) or dynamic (online) reconfiguration. In the last case, two sub-classes exist: manual reconfigurations to be executed by users (Rooker, Sunder, Strasser, Zoitl, Hummer & Ebenhofer, 2007) and automatic (intelligent) reconfigurations to be performed by intelligent agents (Brennan, Vrba, Tichý, Zoitl, Sünder, Strasser & Marík, 2008).

In last years, researches have been conducted on architectures and software engineering in order to enable development of reconfigurable ECS (Khalgui, 2011). The architecture of RECS can be described by different software configurations such that each one is designed by a set of inter-connected software components (controllers) and each one of these components has to control a part of the system (Khalgui & Mosbahi, 2010). The reconfiguration of ECS corresponds to the execution of reconfiguration scenarios on the software architecture of the system (Khalgui & Mosbahi, 2011). A reconfiguration scenario is an ordered sequence of reconfiguration operations that consist of adding/removing controllers, adding/removing connections between them or updating their data or code. Each operation corresponds to a transi-

tion from one configuration to another and it is triggered under particular conditions as response to reconfiguration requests. A request represents a need to improve the system's performance, or to recover and prevent hardware/software errors, or also to adapt the system's behavior to new require-ments according to the environment's evolution.

In our research work we are focusing on the design of reconfigurable agents-based ECS in a platform independent way and with flexible recon-figuration spectrum covering manual, automatic and hybrid (i.e. a combination between manual and automatic) execution. For this purpose, we propose a UML-based approach for the design and validation of such systems. The Unified Modelling Language (OMG-UML, 2010) is the general-purpose language for modeling intensive-software systems. The proposed approach is the first to our knowledge to deal with UML-based design and validation of reconfigurable agents-based ECS which is an attempt to answer three research questions: (1) how to model reconfigura-tion and system's architecture, (2) how to execute reconfigurations on systems, and (3) how to ensure that reconfiguration agent brings the system into correct and safe behaviors.

In order to answer these questions, there are two ingredients of the proposal, the specification and the validation of the solution. The specification of the solution is covered by a set of UML-com-pliant metamodels enabling to specify the RECS architectures with their constraints, the intended reconfiguration scenarios and the architecture of the reconfiguration agent. The specification of RECS is based on the central concept of control-ler components described as UML components (OMG-UML, 2010) which are self-contained units, with ports as interfaces for external com-munications. Therefore, the concept of controller component used in this paper corresponds to a platform independent software unit that can be instantiated in several specific platform languages (such as Java or C++). The reconfiguration agent has the ability to monitor the system's evolution and to apply appropriate reconfiguration scenarios under well-defined constraints at different granularity levels of the system's architecture. In order to cope with all possible reconfiguration scenarios of UML-based ECS, we define three levels of reconfigurations: architectural reconfigurations which allow to add/remove controller components, structural reconfigurations which update compositions of components and their internal implementations, and finally data reconfigurations which consist of data updating. Furthermore, we focus on typical requirements of real-time systems (such as timeliness and predictability) which were identified in (Strasser, Muller, Sunder, Hummer, & Uhrmann, 2006) as major requirements for safe and dynamic reconfigurations. Also, we assume that the reconfiguration agent can receive at the same time many reconfiguration requests from different sources. In order to guarantee a correct behavior, the agent assures the execution of these requests according to their priority values.

The exploration of different design alternatives and validation of specific configurations are required to bring the control system into safe and correct behaviors. For this purpose, the specifications of software architectures of ECS are enriched with a set of OCL (Object Constraint Language) invariants (OMG-OCL, 2010) that must hold all the time in order to preserve integrity and correctness even after reconfiguration. In addition, transitions among different configurations are determined by the reconfiguration operations which are constrained by pre- and post OCL conditions. In our work, we use a UML-based tool which is the USE tool (UML-based Specification Environment) (Gogolla, Büttner & Richters, 2007) to address the validation of models by simulating operation calls. Operations are realized by so-called command sequences which may create or delete objects or links and may modify attribute and data values. Therefore, a valid reconfiguration scenario is defined by a collection of system configurations and

configuration transitions in which all pre-defined OCL constraints are satisfied. To better highlight our contributions, we apply our reconfiguration approach to two industrial benchmark production systems FESTO (FESTO, 2008) and ENAS (ENAS, 2008).

BACKGROUND

The reconfiguration of embedded control systems is currently a very active research area where considerable progresses have been made. In the remainder of this section, we focus on recent works on dynamic reconfiguration of embedded-control systems. In (Thramboulidis, Doukas, & Frantzis, 2004; Thramboulidis 2004) Thramboulidis and all propose a new vision for reconfigurations of distributed control applications. The main aim is to bridge their works on software engineering (e.g. UML) with IEC 61499-based methodologies (IEC-Part1, 2005). More specifically, in (Thramboulidis, Doukas, & Frantzis, 2004), the authors investigate model transformations between RealTime-UML and FB-based models. The strength of this work is to get maximum benefits from the expertise of control engineers with the IEC61499 standard. The works presented in (Khalgui, Mosbahi, Zhiwu & Hanisch, 2010; Brennan, Fletcher & Norrie, 2002; Shen, Wang & Hao, 2006; Alsafi & Vyatkin, 2010; Zoitl, Lepuschitz, Merdan & Vallee, 2010) use the agent-based paradigm to deal with dynamic reconfigurations of industrial systems. In this context, an agent can represent (1) physical resources, such as machine tools, robots, and products (physical decomposition) or (2) logical objects, such as schedulers (functional decomposition) (Shen, Wang, & Hao, 2006). In (Khalgui, Mosbahi, Zhiwu & Hanisch, 2010), the authors deal with intelligent reconfigurations of FB-based control systems. The presented solution is based on an agent-based architecture that integrates local reconfigurations (at the component-level) with higher-level agents (Coordination Agents) in order to achieve coherent distributed intelligent control in the industrial automation domain. The major contribution of this work is the support of particular reconfiguration operations that were not or rarely treated in previous works. However, in this solution, real-time constraints are not considered. In (Alsafi & Vyatkin, 2010), the authors propose an ontology-based reconfiguration agent that attempts to reconfigure a manufacturing system after realizing changes in the requirements or the manufacturing environment. In conjunction with the multi-agent paradigm, the authors use Web-based technologies (namely Semantic Web) in order to simplify the representation of manufacturing environment knowledge which is essential for the reconfiguration agent. As input, the reconfiguration agent receives an ontological knowledge model of the manufacturing environment. Then, it infers useful facts from this ordered description to generate new configurations and therefore to decide whether a reconfiguration requirement can be satisfied or not. The advantage of coupling multi-agent and semantic Web technologies is the improvement of reliability and interoperability of the agent-based solution. In (Brennan, Fletcher & Norrie, 2002), the authors propose an agent-based reconfiguration approach to save the whole system when faults occur at run-time. In (Zoitl, Lepuschitz, Merdan & Vallee, 2010) the authors present a real-time reconfiguration architecture for distributed control systems. More specifically, the low-level control of physical components is depicted with real-time requirements handling. The major contribution of this work consists to define a reconfiguration application (RCA) which interacts with the application under reconfigurations through three interfaces.

In the reviewed literature, safety-related issues are implicitly considered as a part of reconfiguration services in the majority of existing works. In our work we are particularly concerned with safety-related issues within ECS. From this vision, the reconfiguration application must fulfill functional as well as safety requirements (IEC-61508, 2000). Safety requirements specify for example self-checking capabilities that determine wrong stimulus handling mechanisms that passivate invalid reconfiguration events. In addition, it is essential that the actions involved in the reconfiguration process be completed correctly, with respect to real-time requirements (such as timeliness, responsiveness and predictability (Zoitl, Sünder & Terzic, 2006) and preserve an application's integrity during periods of runtime reconfiguration. In addition, dynamic reconfigurations should allow users to make online changes and intelligent reconfiguration can assist them when making changes especially by ensuring that users don't make an unsafe change. Furthermore, human-interaction is a major requirement to simplify the maintenance and increased acceptances of reconfigurable ECS (Terzic, Zoitl, Rooker, Strasser, Vrba, & Marík, 2009).

Although the agent technology is a suitable approach for the implementation of reconfigurable ECS, further effort still to be done in order to enhance the applicability of existing approaches in the industrial domain. The reviewed works present some limitations, indeed, they support exclusively one of the reconfiguration policies (static, dynamic, automatic or manual) while an intelligent solution should support all reconfiguration forms in order to offer more flexibility and to cover more than one cause (request) of reconfiguration (i.e. to resolve hardware faults, to add new functionalities, to improve performances and to adapt to the environment changes). Within the proposed approach the reconfiguration agent is an interactive one which has the ability to execute different kinds of reconfigurations or to combine them (hybrid execution) and also to interact with the user in order to enforce a specific execution mode in particular situations. Therefore, we assume that the reconfiguration agent is multi-event (i.e. can receive more than one reconfiguration request at once). It monitors the system's evolution by using event's notifications and reacts to reconfiguration requests according to their priority values. Furthermore, existing reconfiguration approaches don't cover specific reconfiguration techniques such as data modification. The proposed reconfiguration agent allows to deal with different kinds of possible reconfigurations at different architectural levels by updating the architectural structure of the system (add/remove components and connections) as well as the internal structure of the system's components (updating code and data).

On the other hand, no structured and mature enough development methodology or tool is currently used in industrial practice for the agent-based control systems design, verification and implementation. The use of standard languages and open technologies, namely software engineering technologies, e.g. UML and model-driven development, is one of the most promising directions to answer this issue since they provide a communication platform between complex, distributed and heterogeneous systems and applications. The existing works that tackle ECS design with UML are usually aiming at facilitating the development process by using UML CASE tools and environments in further phases of development cycle such as for code generation. Nevertheless, no reconfiguration approach exists currently for UML-based architectures of ECS. Such approach should allow to define valid reconfiguration solutions for these architectures with all the needs and requirements such as safety concerns, real-time constrains and usability. Therefore, the main gaol of this chapter is to present a novel model-based approach which deals with intelligent reconfigurations of agents-based ECS at both design time and runtime.

A UML-COMPLIANT APPROACH FOR THE DESIGN OF RECONFIGURABLE ECS

The proposed approach is centred on a reconfiguration agent who applies the reconfiguration scenarios on UML-based reconfigurable embedded control system. The reconfiguration agent orchestrates the architecture's reconfigurations with respect to identified reconfiguration requests (events) as well as predefined reconfiguration scenarios. In addition it has the ability to monitor the environment's evolution and the user requirements to adapt the system thereafter by applying the reconfiguration scenarios. In order to apply safe reconfigurations, the selected reconfiguration scenario must satisfy architectural invariants defined on architecture model in addition of reconfiguration constraints. The conceptual model of the whole reconfigurable system's software architecture comprises four models to be organized into a set of packages: Architecture model, Reconfiguration model, Reconfiguration requests model and Agent model. The respective concepts of each model are given in a UML class diagram and will be detailed in the following sections.

Architecture Metamodel

The architecture metamodel is based on the UML 2.3 component concept (OMG-UML, 2010). A component can contain other components and events can be delegated from the top-level component to its subcomponents. Ports are the only external access points for components and their provided and required interfaces specify all interactions which occur at the port. An interface allows the specification of structural features such as attributes and association ends, as well as behavioral features such as operations and events. A port is a feature of a classifier that specifies a distinct interaction point between the classifier and its environment. The class Connector describes links between components that allow one component to provide the services (via provided interfaces) that another component requires (via required interfaces). The connectors are of two kinds: assembly connectors, bridge a component's required interface with the provided interface of another component, while delegation connectors allow to relate two interfaces of the same type. In addition to the basic concepts, we define the Reconfigurable Element class in order to offer more flexibility for our approach. Indeed, we assume that any part of the system can be reconfigured, especially the system should not impose any non-reconfigurable core set of components. Within the field of reconfigurable software architectures, a system (represented by the class *SystemArch*) can be implemented by a collection of configurations such that each configuration (represented by the *ArchConfiguration* class), is a network of communicating software components.

Different configurations can be optimized for different services or operating conditions. A software architecture has a default configuration corresponding to the nominal operating scenario (the *defaultConfig* attribute is set to *true*). Other configurations are loaded in response to their respective reconfiguration requests. The attribute *Operational Mode* of a given software architecture defines possible production plans of the system. Each architectural configuration can correspond to one or more operational modes. The class *Architectural constraints* represents the conditions that the system's architecture must satisfy during its evolution in order to guarantee a correct and safe behavior of the system. These constraints are expressed in OCL (Object Constraint Language) (OMG-OCL, 2010). The OCL constraints, that we present in this paper are written and validated with the tool USE (Gogolla, Büttner & Richters, 2007).

Reconfiguration Requests Metamodel

The reconfiguration might be required as a response to stimuli (*Reconfiguration Requests*) such as changes in the system's operating environment or failures of software/hardware components. Therefore, we distinguish four types of reconfiguration requests: *Problem diagnosis*, *improvement* requests, *prevention* requests and *adaption* requests. A reconfiguration request is also characterized by a source (*Source* class)

which represents the entity that generates the stimulus. The source can be *internal* to the system (the stimulus emanates from a specific architectural element within a chosen configuration) or *external* to the system, i.e. produced by the user or the operating environment. In order to guarantee a correct behavior, the reconfiguration agent assures the execution of these requests according to their priority values. The authors define two types of priorities for reconfiguration requests: Global Priority (GP) and Local Priority (LP). Global priority defines an order relation for reconfiguration requests of different kinds. Local priority attributes priority values to requests of the same kind (the authors can probably apply FIFO or LIFO to manage requests of same type). Table 1 summarizes global priorities for different types of reconfiguration requests. The authors assume that reconfiguration requests of type Problem Diagnosis have the higher priority in the order of execution. In addition, Local Priorities of requests are calculated according to predefined attributes such as severity and duration.

Reconfiguration Metamodel

The main goal of our work is to apply intelligent reconfigurations to ECS. This goal is addressed by choosing and executing appropriate reconfiguration scenarios to handle corresponding requests. The proposed reconfiguration approach is a conceptual framework which aims to address reconfiguration issue according to two views, (1) the modelling view (architectural level, related constraints, etc.), (2) and the execution view. These

Table 1. Global priority

Reconfiguration request type	Priority value
Problem Diagnosis	1
Improvement Request	2
Adaption Request	3
Prevention Request	4

views respectively correspond to answers to two research questions: how a reconfiguration scenario is modelled and how this scenario is applied to reconfigurable elements. The *Reconfiguration Metamodel* describes necessary conceptual elements to respond the first question. The second question is addressed by the *Agent Metamodel* (see section 7). Below, we detail the concepts described within the reconfiguration metamodel.

Basic Reconfiguration Operations

The main concept in the reconfiguration metamodel is the *Reconfiguration Operation*. This concept corresponds to an elementary task that the reconfiguration agent can execute when there is a need to change the architecture configuration (i.e. a *Reconfiguration Request*). An ordered sequence of such operations constitutes a *Reconfiguration Scenario*. Therefore, the class of *Reconfiguration Operation* describes reconfiguration scenarios that can be applied to a software architecture model at different architectural levels. A *Reconfiguration Operation* is a response to its cause which is a *Reconfiguration Request* notification and affects a *Reconfigurable Element* of the *Architecture model*. We assume that each reconfiguration operation is elementary (not decomposable) and concerns only one reconfigurable element at once.

Three basic operations can be applied for reconfigurable elements: addition, removal and update. These types are depicted by the attribute *typeOp* of the class *Reconfiguration Operation*. In addition, a reconfiguration operation is characterized by the architectural level at which it can be applied. This level corresponds to the granularity of the reconfigurable element concerned by the reconfiguration operation. In this work, we distinguish three architectural levels which are defined as following:

- **Architectural Reconfiguration:** This reconfiguration changes the software architecture when particular conditions are sat-

isfied. It is realized by adding or removing software components,

- **Structural Reconfiguration:** This reconfiguration changes the software structure of the application in terms of connections (addition/removals of connections), interfaces, operations or code. The reconfiguration of interfaces consists in modifying services provided by a software component through its interfaces. This is traduced either by changing the whole of provided services either by changing the signature of a service. The reconfiguration of operations consists to add or remove an operation if the component is implemented as a class. The reconfiguration of the code allows to update the internal implementation of software components,

- **Data Reconfiguration:** In this case, the reconfiguration allows to update data.

Note finally that the priority attributed to a reconfiguration operation has the same value of the corresponding reconfiguration request. Furthermore, the operation's type depends on the architectural level of the reconfiguration. Thus, an architectural reconfiguration deals only with adding or removing software components. However, at the data level we can only update data.

Reconfiguration Constraints

Each reconfiguration operation is related to three constraints: *start* and *stop conditions* corresponding respectively to necessary conditions of activation and deactivation of the reconfiguration operation. The guard condition represents an invariant that must be satisfied during the activation time of the operation. All of the constraints associated with a reconfiguration operation are expressed in OCL and are related to components from the architectural model. The *Meta Constraint* class describes constraints that are important for the correct execution of *Reconfiguration scenarios*.

For example, we describe below three *Meta-constraints*:

Constraint 1: It must be ensured that only certain reconfiguration operations are simultaneously active while executing a given reconfiguration scenario.

Constraint 2: The priorities of reconfiguration operations must be correctly handled.

Constraint 3: If a reconfiguration scenario is activated, then the involved reconfiguration operations must be activated according to their synchronization constraints. These constraints will be detailed in the following sub-section.

Execution and Synchronization

A *Reconfiguration Scenario* is an ordered sequence of three types of nodes: *start* node, *final* node and *reconfiguration* nodes. The definition of an order relation is necessary for coordinating the execution of a such scenario and thus to facilitate the task of the *Reconfiguration Agent*. The execution order is defined on reconfiguration operations by considering their *priority* values, their *Synchronization Constraints* and also their respective constraints (*startCondition*, *stopCondition* and *guard*). Therefore, at any moment of the runtime, the *Reconfiguration Agent* has information about the currently active reconfiguration operation and can consider all relevant factors that may influence the decision about which reconfiguration operation should be activated or deactivated. The synchronization constraints that can be defined among reconfiguration operations are of three kinds: *simultaneity* constraints, *exclusion* constraints and *precedence* constraints. When two (or more) reconfiguration operations are simultaneously executed, then we apply a *simultaneity* constraint among them. The simultaneity is expressed as follows:

```
context ReconfigOperation inv:
self.synchroniztionConstraint-
```

```
>forall(sc | sc.typeSynchro =
'simultaneity' and sc. reconfigOpera-
tion->forall(op | op <>
self implies (op.state='activated'
and self.state='activated')))
```

Exclusion constraints indicate that the reconfiguration operations must be executed exclusively. These constraints can be expressed as follows:

```
context ReconfigOperation inv:
self.synchroniztionConstraint-
>forall(sc | sc.typeSynchro =
'exclusion' and sc. reconfigOpera-
tion->forall(op | op <>
self implies ((op.state='activated'
and
self.state='deactivated') or (op.
state= 'deactivated' and
self.state='activated')))))
```

Precedence constraints define an execution order on reconfiguration operations. These constraints are deduced from the combination of *start* and *stop conditions* of the concerned operations. In addition, we assume that each *Reconfiguration operation* has an execution *Strategy*. By the strategy concept, we represent the mode of execution of the reconfiguration operation. In our work, we distinguish three execution strategies: *automatic*, *manual*, and *hybrid*. The first mode corresponds to a full automatic execution assured by the agent. In the second case, the execution of the operation is delegated to users. In the hybrid mode, the agent collaborates with users in order to achieve the execution of the operation.

Time Constraints

Timeliness is a critical property of real-time systems and imposes that when a reconfiguration request occurs, the reconfiguration operation must be made in time (Strasser, Muller, Sunder, Hummer & Uhrmann, 2006). Thus, we assume that reconfiguration operations introduce no unbounded delays into any scenario switching. We enrich the proposed reconfiguration model with two meta-constraints that provide a mechanism for representing delays on reconfiguration operations. The timeliness meta-constraints impose that: each reconfiguration operation is only allowed to be active for a limited time period and has a maximum reaction delay to give a response for a coming reconfiguration request. In order to express such constraints, we use a real-time extension of the OCL language (OCL/RT) (Cengarle & Knapp, 2002). Deadlines for reconfiguration operations can be represented in the following manner:

```
context ReconfigurationOperation::ac
tivate()
pre: self.state='deactivated'
post: Time.now <= Time.now@pre +
self.max_Duration
```

Where Time is a primitive data type that represents the global system time and *max_Duration* is a property of the class *Reconfiguration Operation* representing a time interval. The above constraint represents a maximum permissible execution time equal to *max_Duration* for the reconfiguration operation. Delays in reactions to reconfiguration requests can be represented in the following manner:

```
context ReconfigurationOperation::ac
tivate()
pre: self.ReconfigRequest.n_time +
self.reaction_Delay <= Time.now
post: ...
```

Where *n_time* is the notification time of the last reconfiguration request corresponding to the reconfiguration operation. The property *reaction_delay* of the class *Reconfiguration Operation* expresses a time interval. This constraint represents a maximum delay to be equal to *reaction_delay* for any reaction to the *Reconfiguration Request*.

Agent's Metamodel

The role of *Reconfiguration Agent* is to define and execute reconfiguration scenarios in response to any kind of reconfiguration request. Reconfiguration scenarios are triggered when the need for any change arises. Requests for reconfiguration result from either problem diagnosis, requests for improvements or preventions of problems.

Agent's Architecture

The *Reconfiguration Agent* can be structured into software components with clearly defined tasks and interfaces. A set of external components (*Architecture, Reconfiguration, Reconfiguration Requests models* and a component representing the system's *user*) interact with the *Reconfiguration Agent* component, providing required inputs for enacting reconfiguration scenarios. We identify three major components in the reconfiguration agent model: The *Monitor*, the *Diagnoser* and the *Reconfigurator*. Each one of these components is able to supervise and enact one phase in a three-phases reconfiguration process: *Monitor*, *Diagnose* and *Reconfigure*. The *Monitor* is in charge of receiving reconfiguration events from *Reconfiguration Requests Model* and scheduling them according to their priority values. As output, the *Monitor* generates an *ordered list* of detected reconfiguration requests. The *Diagnoser* receives ordered reconfiguration events, analyzes them within the *Events Selector* and extracts the most prior event. The *Scenario Selector* sub-component receives as inputs the selected event form the *Event Selector*, the necessary information about the operational mode from the *Architecture Model* and the reconfiguration constraints from the *Constraints Analyzer*. The output of the *Diagnoser* is a selected *Reconfiguration Scenario* that suits to the active Operational Mode and satisfies the Meta Constraints. The reconfiguration phase is carried out by the component *Reconfigurator*. This component is detailed in the next sub-section.

The reconfigurator component consists of three sub-components: (1) the *Operations Scheduler* selects a subset of reconfiguration operations according to their priority level and provides them through the interface *Scheduled list*. (2) Selected operations are then taken as inputs by the component *Reconfiguration Operation Selector* which is in charge of choosing an adequate reconfiguration operation to compensate the reconfiguration request. This component acts as a planner: given a reconfiguration request, it looks for appropriate reconfigurations, and selects one of them with the corresponding execution *strategy*. (3) The *Operation Actuator* is the component that assures the execution of selected reconfiguration operations. This component has the ability to negotiate with users in the case of a *hybrid* strategy. In a such case, the agent can allow manual executions or enforce automatic modes in order to fulfill with safety requirements

Reconfiguration Execution

We denote by N_A the number of all possible software architectural configurations implementing the system, AC_i ($1 \leq i \leq N_A$) denotes a particular architectural configuration which is represented by a structural diagram (class, object or component diagram) CD_i ($1 \leq i \leq N_A$). The possible behaviors of a given AC_i are depicted by a set of Structural Configurations (SC) which are represented by UML behavior diagrams. In this paper, we use sequence diagrams and state machines to represent the behavioral view of the system and also the reconfiguration agent. We denote by $SC_{i,j}$ each behavior diagram corresponding to a given AC_i ($1 \leq j \leq N_{i,S}$) where $N_{i,S}$ represents the number of possible structural configurations corresponding to AC_i. Finally, the system can have different combinations of data values for each $SC_{i,j}$ that may influence the system's behaviour. We denote by $DC_{i,j,k}$ ($1 \leq k \leq N_{i,j,D}$) a data configuration corresponding to a structural configuration $SC_{i,j}$ which corresponds in turn to a given architectural configuration AC_i.

The integer $N_{i,j,D}$ represents the number of possible data configurations corresponding to a given $SC_{i,j}$. In order to apply a reconfiguration scenario $_{i,j,k}$, the agent executes three steps as follows (1) the class diagram CD_i corresponding to AC_i is loaded in memory, (2) then the structural configuration $SC_{i,j}$ is chosen, and (3) finally, the data configuration $DC_{i,j,k}$ is applied.

RUNNING EXAMPLES

In order to highlight the contributions of our work, we propose to reconfigure two manufacturing systems named FESTO (FESTO, 2008) and ENAS (ENAS, 2008) which are well-documented demonstrators used by many universities for research and education purposes.

First System: FESTO

FESTO is composed of three units: *Distribution*, *Test* and *Processing* units. The Distribution unit is composed of a pneumatic *feeder* and a *converter* to forward cylindrical work pieces from a stack to the testing unit which is composed of the *detector*, the *tester* and the *elevator*. This unit performs checks on work pieces for height, material type and color. Work pieces that successfully pass this check are forwarded to the rotating disk of the processing unit, where the drilling of the work piece is performed. A hole with a given depth is drilled on the work piece at this unit. Finally a checking module is used to confirm the drilled hole.

Assumptions on System's Operation

We describe our approach to reconfigure a subpart of the FESTO system which is the *processing unit*. In the scope of this paper, we assume that the processing unit can operate with one or two drilling machines (Drill_Machine1 and Drill_Machine2). In order to perform a hole in a work piece, we assume that each Drilling Machine can perform one or several passes according to the quality of the drilling bit, the depth of the hole to be drilled (represented by the *depth* attribute of the class Drilling Machine) and the material quality of the work piece. The depth of the hole is measured in centimeter. The maximal number of passes that a drilling machine can perform is represented by the attribute *number_Passes* of type integer in the class *Drilling Machine*. The quality of the drilling bit is represented by the attribute *lifeD* which corresponds to the life duration of the bit measured in number of hours. The attribute w_Hours is an integer that represents the number of working hours effectuated by the Drilling Machine. Thus the drilling machine must be deactivated if w_Hours $\geq$ lifeD. The FESTO system can exhibit different operational modes in order to resolve hardware problems, to improve the performance or to adapt to changing requirements. The operational mode is represented in this case study by the attribute *operationMode* of the class *Processing Unit*. The required number of pieces to be produced is represented by the attribute *prodRate* (production rate) of type integer of the class *Processing Unit*. We distinguish three main configurations to represent the architecture (AC) of the processing unit. Each one of these configurations (AC_i, 1i3) is represented by an object diagram OD_i where each object represents a control object of the corresponding machine. In the first mode (mode1), the work pieces are drilled in a single pass by one of the drilling machines (DM1 or DM2) and then transferred to the checking module (CM1). In this case the depth of the hole to be drilled is also prefixed (d=a) and the production rate must be less than a given value N. In the second mode (mode2), the work pieces must be drilled in several passes (k passes where k1) and then transferred to the checking module. This scenario occurs when the quality of the piece material requires several passes. In the third possible mode (mode3), the depth of the hole is changed from an initial value

d=a to a new value d=a+b. In the second and the third mode the rate of production can be changed (*prodRate* $\geq$ N).

Reconfiguration Agent's Behavior

In the considered case study, we highlight all possible reconfiguration scenarios that can be applied to UML-based ECS. The distinguished behaviors of the system correspond to different reconfiguration scenarios that can be applied by the reconfiguration agent. In the considered example the reconfiguration request consists to change the depth of the drilled hole (d=a+b). Therefore the agent executes the reconfiguration scenario $R_{3,1,1}$ in order to respond to the given request. The execution of this scenario will be detailed in the subsequent sections.

Architectural Reconfiguration

At the architectural level, the reconfiguration agent can apply an architectural reconfiguration by adding an object that controls one of the drilling machines (DM1 or DM2) if there is a need to enhance the production rate (number of drilled pieces). In the opposite case, the reconfiguration agent can delete one of the control objects if the corresponding hardware component is broken or if there is no need to use it.

Structural Reconfiguration

At the structural level, the reconfiguration agent can for example apply a reconfiguration in order to update the code of the *drill(depth)* method of the class *DrillingMachine* so that each instance of this class can perform a given number of passes (*number_passes*1). This kind of reconfiguration can be applied to any architectural reconfiguration (AC_i, i) of the system.

The state machine represents a structural configuration ($SC_{3,1}$) corresponding to the architectural configuration AC_3 where the system operates with two drilling machines and each one can perform K passes to drill a piece. Each state represents a control task of a particular machine in the processing unit.

Data Reconfiguration

At the data level, the reconfiguration agent can only update values of data proper to each object within the loaded AC.

Second System: ENAS

The EnAS system (EnAS, 2008) is mainly composed of a belt, two Jack stations (J1 and J2) and two Gripper stations (G1 and G2). The Jack stations place new drilled pieces from FESTO and close tins with caps, whereas the Gripper stations remove charged tins from the belt into storing units. The pieces shall be placed inside tins to close with caps afterwards. Two different production strategies can be applied: we place in each tin one or two pieces according to production rates of pieces, tins and caps.

Architectural Reconfiguration

We distinguish two architectural configurations (AC_1 and AC_2) to represent the architecture of the EnAS system. Each one of these configurations is represented by an object diagram where each object represents a control object of the corresponding machine. According to production parameters, two cases are distinguished: (1) in the first production policy (first object diagram), the Jack station J1 places from the production station a new piece and closes the tin with the cap. In this case, the Gripper station G1 removes the tin from the belt into a first storing station St1. (2) in the

second policy (second object diagram), the Jack station J1 places just a piece in the tin, which is moved thereafter into the second Jack station J2 to place a second new piece. Once J2 closes the tin with a cap, the belt moves the pallet into the Gripper station G2 to remove the tin (with two pieces) into a second storing station St2. When the system operates according to the second production policy and the gripper G2 is broken, then we should change to the first policy and also the system architecture must change by loading the control component G1.

Structural Reconfiguration

When an error occurs and one of the stations J1 or G1 is broken then the system is stopped. At this level, the reconfiguration agent can apply a reconfiguration in order to update the connections between control components. For example in the second architectural configuration AC_2, if the first structural configuration $SC_{2,1}$ is active the system operates with two jack stations J1 and J2 and if J2 is broken then another structural configuration $SC_{2,2}$ is loaded in which the Jack station J1 is running alone with the gripper station G2 in order to place only one piece in the tin. Therefore the connection between the two instances J1 and J2 (instance of the *precedes* association) is deleted and replaced by a connection between J1 and G2 (instance of the *transfersTo* association). In the same way, if the configuration $SC_{2,1}$ is loaded and the Jack station J1 is broken, then we should activate the structural configuration $SC_{2,3}$, where the behavior of J2 should be changed to place a piece in the tin that should be closed.

Validation with USE Tool

In this sub-section we describe the validation of the approach applied to the two production systems FESTO and EnAS using the USE tool which allows to validate models by simulating operation calls. As a first example applied on FESTO, we consider the reconfiguration model of an architectural reconfiguration operation in the Processing Unit. The considered operation consists in adding a controller object of the second Drilling Machine when the production rate is greater than N (N=100). The preconditions of the reconfiguration model read the values before the corresponding reconfiguration operation changes the state of the architecture. The postconditions check them after the changes took place. A validation instance checks if the transition (between initial configuration and final configuration) corresponds to correct operation executions, i.e., for the applied operation the postconditions should return the boolean value True. The correct execution of the considered architectural reconfiguration operation implies the satisfaction of the pre/post conditions of the method *activate()* defined within the class *ArchitecturalReconfig* (which is a subclass of the class *Reconfiguration Operation*). The pre and post conditions correspond respectively to the conditions *start* and *stop* related to the class *ArchitecturalReconfig* of the *Reconfiguration Metamodel* (section 3). These conditions are described in the considered case as follows:

```
context ArchitecturalReconfig::activa
te(): Boolean
pre startAdd: DrillingMachine.allIn-
stances->
exists (x | x.state= 'activated') and
DrillingMachine.allInstances -> size
= 1
post stopAdd: (DrillingMachine.allIn-
stances -
DrillingMachine.allInstances@pre) ->
size = 1
and (DrillingMachine.allInstances -
DrillingMachine.allInstances@pre)->
forAll(dm|dm.oclIsNew())
```

The precondition *startAdd* of the architectural reconfiguration operation stipulates that it must exist at minimum one activated drilling machine (state = 'activated') and that the number of existing drilling machines is equal to 1 (DM1). The postcondition verifies that there is exactly one added object (DM2) of type *Drilling Machine*. The postcondition *stopAdd* uses the OCL operation oclIsNew to check for the creation of the new controller object (of type *Drilling Machine*). We use a command script to animate the model. The script simulates three operation calls for the operation *activate()* of the class *Reconfiguration Operation*. The first one is expected to succeed while the second and the third should violate the postconditions. We give below a part of the used command script that shows different results of the operation call.

```
-- Script generated by USE 2.6.2
!create ProcessUnit1: ProcessUnit
!set ProcessUnit1.operationMode:=
'model'
...
!set DM1.state:= 'activated'
--instantiation of the class Recon-
figuration
--Operation with an automatic strat-
egy
!create arop1: ArchitecturalReconfig
!set st1.typeSt:= 'automatic'
!set rq1.priority:= 1
...
-- first activate() operation call
-- pre and post conditions are satis-
fied
!openter arop1 activate()
!create DM2: DrillingMachine
!opexit true
!set DM2.state:= 'activated'
!set DM1.state ='IsBroken'
 -- second call precondition fails
because the first DM is broken
```

```
!openter arop1 activate()
!create DM2: DrillingMachine
!opexit false
 -- third call, postcondition fails
because the -- DM2 has already been
created
 --above
!openter arop1 activate()
!opexit false
```

The considered reconfiguration applied to the EnAS system is a structural reconfiguration and it consists in deleting a controller object of the first Jack Station when the production mode of EnAS is the second one (AC_2). The correct execution of the considered structural reconfiguration operation implies the satisfaction of the pre/post conditions of the method *activate()* defined within the class *StructReconfigDelete* (which is a subclass of the class *Reconfiguration Operation*). The pre and post conditions correspond respectively to the conditions *start* and *stop* related to this class.

```
context StructReconfigDelete::activat
e(js: JackStation): Boolean
pre startRemove: js.enas.operation-
Mode = 'second'
and js.enas.gripperStation -> exists
(gs | gs.range = 'second')
and js.state = 'IsBroken'
and JackStation.allInstances-> size
= 2
and JackStation.allInstances ->
exists(x | x.state= 'activated')
post stopRemove: result = JackSta-
tion.allInstances-> excludes (js)
```

The precondition *startRemove* of the structural reconfiguration operation imposes that the EnAS system operates according to the second production policy (AC_2), that the first Jack Station is broken and that the number of existing Jack Stations is equal to 2 (JS1 and JS2). The postcondition

stopRemove verifies that the controller object (of type JackStation) is deleted (JS1).

The command script used to animate the model simulates two operation calls for the operation *activate()* of the class *Reconfiguration Operation*. The first one violates the preconditions and fails while the second satisfies pre and post conditions. A part of the used command script is given below.

```
-- Script generated by USE 2.6.2
!create Enas1: Enas
!set Enas1.operationMode:= 'second'
!create JS1: JackStation
!set JS1.state:= 'activated'
!set JS1.range:= 'first'
...
!create structOp1: StructReconfigDe-
lete
!set structOp1.priority:= 1
!insert (JS1,structOp1) into opCon-
cerns
-- first call of the structural re-
configuration operation fails
-- because the first JS is not broken
and the operationMode is the second
one
!openter structOp1 activate(JS1)
!set JS1.state:= 'IsBroken'
-- second call of the structural re-
configuration operation
-- pre conditions are satisfied
-- post conditions are not satisfied
because JS1 is not yet removed
!openter structOp1 activate(JS1)
!opexit true
!openter structOp1 activate(JS1)
!delete (JS1,JS2) from precedes
!delete (JS1,GS2) from transfersTo
!destroy JS1
-- post conditions are satisfied be-
cause JS1 is removed
!opexit true
```

FUTURE RESEARCH DIRECTIONS

In this work, we focus on reconfigurations with centralized architectures. Several aspects will be addressed in future works. First of all, we plan a complete implementation of our architecture, as well as further experimentations on other case studies. We also plan to study simulations of agents-based reconfigurable ECS. Furthermore, the application of safe reconfiguration scenarios is conditioned by the correctness of the reconfiguration agent behaviour. For this reason we aim to use formal verification methods in order to validate functional and temporal properties of UML-based embedded system specifications and also to guarantee the correctness of their reconfigurations. Finally, we want to extend the proposed framework to allow reconfigurations of UML-based distributed reconfigurable software architectures.

CONCLUSION

We have proposed a novel approach for the design and validation of agents-based reconfigurable ECS. The approach is a model-based one with UML-compliant metamodels defined to specify required knowledge in reconfigurable ECS in a platform independent way. In addition, our approach is innovative since it allows to couple agent-based paradigm with UML standard in order to supervise the reconfiguration execution in ECS software architecture. The reconfiguration agent has the ability to apply reconfigurations with different execution strategies at three levels of granularity: the architectural, the structural, and the data level. The validation of the proposed approach is undertaken using the USE tool. In order to show the applicability of the approach in practice, we applied it to reconfigure two production systems which are FESTO and EnAS.

REFERENCES

Alsafi, Y., & Vyatkin, V. (2010). Ontology-based reconfiguration agent for intelligent mechatronic systems in flexible manufacturing. *Journal Robotics and Computer-Integrated Manufacturing*, *26*(4), 381–391. doi:10.1016/j.rcim.2009.12.001.

Angelov, C., Sierszecki, K., & Marian, N. (2005). Design models for reusable and reconfigurable state machines. *Lecture Notes in Computer Science*, *3824*, 152–163. doi:10.1007/11596356_18.

Bollinger, J. G., et al. (1998). Visionary manufacturing challenges for 2020. In *Proceedings of the Committee on Visionary Manufacturing Challenges, Board on Manufacturing and Engineering Design, Commission on Engineering and Technical Systems*. Washington, DC: National Research Council, National Academy Press.

Brennan, R., Fletcher, M., & Norrie, D. (2002). An agent-based approach to reconfiguration of real-time distributed control systems. *IEEE Transactions on Robotics and Automation*, *18*(4), 444–451. doi:10.1109/TRA.2002.802211.

Brennan, R., Vrba, P., Tichý, P., Zoitl, A., Sünder, C., Strasser, T., & Marík, V. (2008). Developments in dynamic and intelligent reconfiguration of industrial automation. *Computers in Industry*, *59*(6), 533–547. doi:10.1016/j.compind.2008.02.001.

Cengarle, M., & Knapp, A. (2002). Towards OCL/RT. *Lecture Notes in Computer Science*, *239*, 390–409. doi:10.1007/3-540-45614-7_22.

Description, F. E. S. T. O. (2008). *Martin Luther University, Germany*. Retrieved from http://aut.informatik.uni-halle.de/forschung/testbed/

EnAS. (2008). *Martin Luther University, Germany*. Retrieved from http://aut.informatik.uni-halle.de/forschung/enas_demo/

Gogolla, M., Büttner, F., & Richters, M. (2007). USE: A UML-based specification environment for validating UML and OCL. *Science of Computer Programming*, *69*, 27–34. doi:10.1016/j.scico.2007.01.013.

IEC. (2000). *61508 – Functional safety of electrical/electronic/programmable electronic safety-related systems*. Geneva, Switzerland: International Electrotechnical Commission.

International Electrotechnical Commission. (2005). *Function blocks: Part 1: Architecture*. Geneva, Switzerland: International Eectrotechnical Commission.

Khalgui, M. (2011). Reconfigurable multiagent embedded control systems: From modeling to implementation. In Khalgui, M., & Hanisch, H. M. (Eds.), *Reconfigurable Embedded Control Systems: Applications for Flexibility and Agility* (pp. 1–30). Academic Press. doi:10.1109/TC.2010.96.

Khalgui, M., & Mosbahi, O. (2010). Feasible distributed reconfigurable architecture for embedded IEC61499 function blocks. *International Journal of Discrete Event Control Systems*, *1*(1), 99–113.

Khalgui, M., & Mosbahi, O. (2011). Specification and verification of reconfigurable embedded architectures. *International Journal of Discrete Event Control Systems*, *1*(1), 1–18.

Khalgui, M., Mosbahi, O., Li, Z., & Hanisch, H.-M. (2010). Reconfiguration of distributed embedded-control systems. *IEEE/ASME Transactions on Mechatronics*.

Leitão, P. (2004). *An agile and adaptive holonic architecture for manufacturing control*. (PhD Thesis). University of Porto.

Lewis, R. (2001). *Modelling control systems using IEC 61499*. London: Institution of Engineering and Technology.

Object Management Group. (2010a). Object constraint language specification v2.2. *OMG Document Number: formal/2010-02-01*. Retrieved from http://www.omg.org/spec/OCL/2.0/PDF

Object Management Group. (2010b). Unified modelling language: Superstructure specification v2.3. *OMG Document Number: formal/2010-05-05*. Retrieved from http://www.omg.org/spec/UML/2.3

Randell, B., Lee, P. A., & Treleaven, P. C. (1978). Reliability issues in computing system design. *Computing Surveys*, *10*, 220–232. doi:10.1145/356725.356729.

Rooker, M.-N., Sunder, C., Strasser, T., Zoitl, A., Hummer, O., & Ebenhofer, G. (2007). Zero downtime reconfiguration of distributed automation systems: The eCEDAC approach. In *Proceedings of the Third International Conference on Industrial Applications of Holonic and Multi-Agent Systems, 2007*. Berlin: Springer-Verlag.

Shen, W., Wang, L., & Hao, Q. (2006). Agent-based distributed manufacturing process planning and scheduling: A state-of-the-art survey. *IEEE Transactions on Systems, Man and Cybernetics. Part C, Applications and Reviews*, *36*(4), 563–577. doi:10.1109/TSMCC.2006.874022.

Strasser, T., Muller, I., Sunder, C., Hummer, O., & Uhrmann, H. (2006). Modeling of reconfiguration control applications based on the IEC 61499 reference model for industrial process measurement and control systems. In *Proceedings of the IEEE Workshop on Distributed Intelligent Systems*. IEEE.

Terzic, I., Zoitl, A., Rooker, M. N., Strasser, T., Vrba, P., & Marík, V. (2009). Usability of multi-agent based control systems in industrial automation. In *Proceedings of the Holonic and Multi-Agent Systems for Manufacturing, 4th International Conference on Industrial Applications of Holonic and Multi-Agent Systems*. Linz, Austria: IEEE.

Thramboulidis, K. (2004). Using UML in control and automation: A model driven approach. In *Proceedings of the 2nd IEEE International Conference on Industrial Informatics*. Berlin, Germany: INDIN.

Thramboulidis, K., Doukas, G., & Frantzis, A. (2004). Towards an implementation model for FB-based reconfigurable distributed control applications. In *Proceedings of the 7th International Symposium on Object-oriented Real-time Distributed Computing (ISORC 04)*. Vienna, Austria: ISORC.

Zoitl, A., Lepuschitz, W., Merdan, M., & Vallee, M. (2010). A real-time reconfiguration infrastructure for distributed embedded control systems. In *Proceedings IEEE Emerging Technologies and Factory Automation*. IEEE.

KEY TERMS AND DEFINITIONS

Controller Components: Self-contained units described as UML components >with ports as the interface for communication.

Reconfiguration: The reconfiguration of ECS corresponds to the execution of reconfiguration scenarios on the software architecture of the system.

Reconfiguration Agent: A software unit that executes reconfiguration scenarios to adapt the software architecture to a given change.

Reconfiguration Operation: A transition from one configuration to another which is triggered under particular conditions as response to reconfiguration requests with respect to their priority values.

Reconfiguration Request: A notified change in the system that requires the application of reconfiguration operations by the reconfiguration agent.

Reconfiguration Scenario: An ordered sequence of reconfiguration operations.

Software Architecture: A set of inter-connected components which are platform independent software units that can be instantiated in several specific platform languages (such as Java or C++).

Chapter 7
Development of Automated Systems using Proved B Patterns

Olfa Mosbahi
University of Carthage, Tunisia

Mohamed Khalgui
University of Carthage, Tunisia

ABSTRACT

This chapter proposes an approach for reusing specification patterns for the development of automated systems composed of two components: the controller and the controlled parts. The first is a software component controlling the second one that models the physical device and its environment. Specification patterns are design patterns that are expressed in a formal specification language. Reusing a specification pattern means instantiating it and the proofs associated. This chapter shows through a case study how to define specification patterns in Event-B, how to reuse them, and also how to reuse the proofs associated with specification patterns.

1. INTRODUCTION

The idea of design patterns is not restricted to the field of computer science or object oriented software. Design patterns were actually introduced by Christopher Alexander in the field of architecture. In 1977 he spoke of patterns as, "each pattern describes a problem which occurs over and over again in our environment, and then describes the core of the solution to that problem, in such a way that you can use this solution a million times over, without ever doing it the same way twice" (Alexander, 1977). Related to Event-B, by design patterns we understand former developments that can be reused in the current development. Of course not every development is a good choice for reuse. What we are interested in are generic solutions of common problems. Although reusability is a good reason for having patterns, in Event-B, there is another important point. We

DOI: 10.4018/978-1-4666-3922-5.ch007

aspire the reuse of proofs. A substantial part of the work when developing in Event-B is proving the correctness of the models. When reusing an already proved development, why should one do the same proofs again? The goal of design patterns in Event-B is therefore: *The reuse of already proved solutions, to refine the problem at hand, without doing any proofs.*

In our research work, we are interested in the formal development of automated systems. These systems are composed of two components: the controlled (operative part) and the controller (control part). The behavior of the first is continuous and modeled by a discrete model, whereas the second is software which has discrete behavior by nature and its goal is to restrict the controlled component behavior. Controller and controlled interact to form the automated system (Figure 1) as a closed-loop control one in which control actions are dependent on its outputs. Modeling continuous processes can be performed in design patterns. Indeed, formal specifications are increasingly used in industry and it becomes interesting to use some of these specifications in new projects. Reuse a formal specification means first defines a formal specification pattern and also the way to combine these patterns in the construction of a new application. B is a powerful notation that can make it hard for the newcomer to decide how to structure and develop a B specification, and hard for a reviewer or implementer to comprehend a specification written in an unfamiliar style.

Our motivation is a desire to make B more usable by commercial non specialist developers and our reason for investigating patterns comes from experience in the industrial use of B. B textbooks introduce the mathematical bases of B, the notation, and essential elements of the use of B. However, few books provide advice on how to "do" B in practice. Illustrations clearly show how a feature was used by the author, but context and intent are implicit, and there is rarely any advice on how to reuse or adapt the B text. The work in this paper is a new presentation of the concept of pattern applied to enhance the "semantic structure" of B, thereby helping the writing; reading and presentation of B. Formalisms such as B have a role to play in general software development. So the patterns should enable:

- Writing of formal texts by generalists, because the patterns present formal solutions to common problems,
- Development of tools to support the use of formal methods by generalists, by recognizing and assisting in the application of patterns, and by breaking down the formal concepts into merchandisable or tool-supportable components.

We have chosen in this paper the B language to formally specify the notion of specification pattern for the following reasons:

- Where B is already being used, then there is no need to learn a new formalism to define and reuse specification patterns,
- B is supported by tools that validate the specification. We will use them to validate the definition of specification patterns and

Figure 1. Automated system in a closed loop

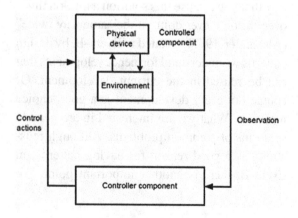

the different reuse mechanisms. A designer will thus reuse not only pieces of formal specifications but also their proofs.

This paper is organized as follows. The next section is an introduction to patterns. Section 3 presents an overview of the Event-B. Section 4 is a discussion of the reuse notion in B: B patterns. Section 5 presents our proposed approach: refinement B patterns. Section 6 presents an industrial case study which illustrates our approach. Finally, we conclude this work in the last section with our perspectives.

2. PATTERNS

Patterns, initially introduced by (Alexander, 1977) in the context of architecture, have been introduced into software engineering, to document and promote best practice, and to share expertise. A pattern provides a solution to a problem in a context. Existing patterns cover a wide range of issues, from coding standards (Beck, 1997), through program design (Gamma, 1995), to domain analysis (Fowler, 1997), and meta-concerns such as team structures and project management (Coplien, 1995). Patterns do not stand in isolation. As (Alexander, 1977) explain, a Pattern language is a collection of patterns, expressed at different levels, that can be used together to give a structure at all levels of the system under development. The names of the patterns provide a vocabulary for describing problems and design solutions.

Typically, a pattern comprises a template or algorithm and a statement of its range of applicability. A catalogue, which records pattern descriptions, is organized to facilitate pattern selection. In providing for the selection of appropriate patterns, the description of the intent of the pattern is crucial. This describes the situation for which the pattern is appropriate. The

pattern catalogue uses meaningful pattern names to guide users to appropriate patterns. It is also common to use a visual representation. For instance, (Gamma, 1995; Larman, 2001) use UML diagrams to visualize object oriented program and design patterns. A good pattern catalogue can be applied to assist all elements of construction of a description (program, design etc) in its language. Some patterns are general purpose, occurring in similar forms across many media (for example, across languages, development phases, contexts). For example, all notations require commentary which is clear, consistent, and adds meaning to the text, and all notations have common usage conventions that can be expressed as patterns.

Some patterns are specific to the language for which they are written. For example, (Gamma, 1995) note that some patterns provided for Smalltalk programming are built-in features of other object oriented programming languages. In the formal language context, some Z patterns for identifying proof obligations would be irrelevant in the tool-supported B Method, in which the corresponding proof obligations are automatically generated. Equally, if a Z practitioner is using an architectural pattern other than Delta/Xi, then most of the patterns written for use with the Delta/Xi pattern (promotion, change part of the state etc) are irrelevant.

3. OVERVIEW OF THE EVENT-B METHOD

The Event-B method (Abrial, 1996) is based on the B notation (Abrial, 1996). It extends the methodological scope of basic concepts such as set-theoretical notations and generalized substitutions in order to take into account the idea of *formal models*. Roughly speaking, a formal model is characterized by a (finite) list x of *state variables* possibly modified by a (finite) list of *events*; an invariant $I(x)$ states some properties that must always be satisfied by the variables x and maintained by the activation of the events. Generalized substitutions provide a way to express the transformations of the values of the state variables of a formal model. An event consists of two parts: a *guard* (denoted *grd*) and an action. A guard is a predicate built from the state variables, and an *action* is a generalized substitution (denoted *GS*).

An event can take one of the forms shown in the table below. Let *BA(x,x')* be the before-after predicate associated with each event shape. This predicate describes the event as a logical predicate expressing the relationship linking the values of the state variables just before (x) and just after (x') the event "execution". In the table below, x denotes a vector build on the set of state variables of the model. In the general substitution $x: p(x_0;x)$, x denotes the *new value* of the vector, whereas x_0 denotes its *old value* and t represents a vector of distinct local variables (see Figure 2).

Proof obligations are associated to events and state that the invariant condition $I(x)$ is preserved. We next give the general rule to be proved. It follows immediately from the very definition of the before-after predicate, $BA(x;x')$ of each event: $I(x) \land BA(x;x') \Rightarrow I(x')$.

The B model has the following form:

```
MODEL                   name
SETS                         sets
CONSTANTS            constants
PROPERTIES         properties of
sets and constants
VARIABLES            variables x
INVARIANT            invariants
```

```
I(x)
ASSERTIONS                A(x)
INITIALISATION      initialization of
variables
EVENTS                      events
END
```

An abstract B model has a name; the clause SETS contains definitions of sets; the clause CONSTANTS allows one to introduce information related to the mathematical structure to solve and the clause PROPERTIES contains the effective definitions of constants. The clause ASSERTIONS contains the list of theorems to be discharged by the proof engine. The clause VARIABLES contains a (finite) list of state variables possibly modified by a (finite) list of events; the clause INVARIANT states some properties that must always be satisfied by the variables and maintained by the activation of the events. The clause EVENTS contains all the system events which preserve the invariants. Construction by refinement (Back, 1998; Back, 1989) is a technique suitable for the development of complex systems. The refinement of a formal model allows us to enrich a model in a step by step approach. It is used to transform an abstract model into a more concrete version by modifying the state description. This is essentially done by extending the list of state variables, by refining each abstract event into a corresponding concrete version, and by adding new events. The abstract state variables, and the concrete ones, are linked together by means of a gluing invariant. A number of proof obligations ensure that (1) each abstract event is correctly refined by its corresponding concrete version, (2) each new event refines skip,

Figure 2. Event forms

Event	Before-after Predicate BA(x, x')	Guard
BEGIN x : P(x₀,x) END	$P(x,x')$	TRUE
SELECT G(x) THEN x : Q(x₀,x)	$G(x) \land Q(x,x')$	$G(x)$
ANY t WHERE G(t,x)		
THEN x : R(x₀,x,t) END	$\exists t.(G(t,x) \land R(x,x',t))$	$\exists t.G(t,x)$

(3) no new event takes control forever, and (4) relative deadlock-freeness is preserved.

Click_n_Prove tool (Abrial, 2007) is the new proactive interface of the interactive prover of Atelier B (ClearSy, 2002) and its free version B4free (ClearSy, 2004) and it has been developed by Jean-Raymond Abrial and Dominique Cansell. The tool generates the proof obligations associated with a model or a refinement and it also provides automatic and interactive proof procedures to discharge these proof obligations. ProB (Leuschel et al., 2003) is a model checker used in order to make partial verifications and to find counter- examples on B models. It provides a convenient way to discover invariants and to test them before the proof.

4. B REFINEMENT PATTERNS: AN APPROACH FOR REUSING PATTERNS IN B

The aim of this section is to investigate the ability of B to specify patterns and the different reuse mechanisms. We have chosen to consider the Event-B language as it is. This means that we want to define the reuse mechanisms only with the different B mechanisms such as refinement, and so on. Thus, the proofs generated during the reuse process are only those generated by the corresponding B mechanisms.

4.1. B Patterns

Designing models of a complex system using refinement and proofs are very hard and often not very well used. This proof-based modelling technique is not automatically done, since we need to extract some knowledge from the system in an incremental and clever way. The Event-B allows one such development and many case studies have been developed, including sequential algorithms (Abrial, 2003), distributed algorithms (Abrial et

al.', 2003; Cansell et al., 2006), parallel algorithms (Abrial, 2005) or embedded systems for controlling train like METEOR (Behm, 1999) or Roissy Val (Badeau et al., 2005). The last example was developed faster because previous models were reused and a specific automatic refining tool (EDITB). EditB provides automatic refinement from an abstract B model, which can be proved more quickly and automatically using or adding specific rules in the B prover; EditB is a "private" tool and only Siemens uses it to develop systems. The interesting thing is that the engineer activity (typing model) is very much simplified. This tool seems to apply a similar technique to those used in design patterns. It is the application of well-engineered patterns for a specific domain.

Five years ago Jean-Raymond Abrial, D. Cansell and D. Méry worked on using genericity in Event-B (Abrial, 2003). When a designer develops a generic development (a list of models related by refinement) both modelling and proof are easily done. Models are more abstract and consequently the set of proof obligations can be discharged more automatically or in an interactive way (it is less noisy for the prover). The generic development can be reused by instantiation of the carrier sets and constants of the development (list of models). We obtain a new development (list of models) which is correct, if all instantiated sets and constants satisfy properties of the generic development. An interesting point is that we do not prove the proof obligation of the instantiated development. This technique is well known by mathematicians who prove abstract theorems and reuse these on specific cases reproving the instantiated axioms of the theorem to obtain (for free or without proof) the instantiated goal of the theorem.

Recently, Jean-Raymond Abrial has presented (Abrial, 2006) patterns for the action-reaction paradigm to systematically develop the mechanical press controller. These contributions follow the same direction leading to reuse previous proof based developments, to give guidelines for mechanical refinement in daily software development. In our opinion, a B pattern is an Event-B development which is proved, sufficiently generic and can be partially reused in another specific B development to produce automatically new refinement models: proofs are (partly) inherited from the B pattern.

4.2. B Refinement Patterns

A B refinement pattern consists on a set of constants, properties related to these constants, variables, events, and invariants stating some properties that must always be satisfied by variables and maintained by activation of the events. These model elements will be directly inserted in the system model under construction, after instantiation of the pattern elements (variables, invariants, constants, properties, and events).

A B pattern is proved when events described in the model satisfy invariant properties. Therefore, any correct instantiation of the design pattern will lead to the production of correct model elements. A pattern can be applied once or several times, producing new modeling elements.

As a response to the controller command, the action of the controlled component evolves by either:

- Changing the state which can be considered instantaneous according to the granularity of time (closing a relay, ignition a flame ...). The action here is with *"immediate execution,"*
- Activating a *continuous process* which is continuously activated until reaching

an expected state (threshold temperature reached, level of filling reached...). We need in this case to stop the process when the system reaches the final state. The action here is with *"deferred execution."*

These actions can be modeled by events. At abstract level, there is no need to distinguish between the two types of events (*immediate* and *deferred execution*) since we need to reach a state: closed relay in one side and reached threshold temperature in the other one. At concrete level, there is no need to refine the first type of event but the second abstract event is refined into an event that activates the process, an event that observes the progression process, an event that observes the reaching of the desired state and an event that observes the completion state of the process.

This kind of refinement consists on leading a transition at abstract level into a continuous process at concrete level which will be activated in the begin state of the transition and stopped when the goal is reached.

Although what we call refinement pattern can be classified among design patterns, we preferred this term which makes better account of our intention. This is to refine one or more abstract events by concrete ones to perform an operation (eg a manufacturing operation). In contrast to design patterns, we do not use invariants but we associate with our refinement pattern a variant which captures the fact that the process progresses to achieve the transition purpose.

The transition associated to an abstract event can be realized in concrete level by a process that must start, maintain active until the final state is

Figure 3. Transition diagram corresponding to the pattern application

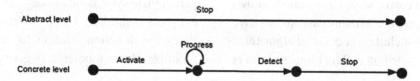

reached and then stop it. The abstract event is refined into the following four events:

- Activation of the process,
- Progression (discrete simulation of the process progression),
- Detection of the desired state,
- Stopping the process.

This pattern associates to an abstract event the concrete ones which refine it and a *loop variant* which decreases at each execution of the progression event. To prove the refinement pattern, we have to prove that all generated proof obligations are verified, in particular, that the desired state is reached when the *loop variant* has reached its lower bound. The behavior generated by the refinement pattern is represented in Figure 3.

This refinement pattern defined by the generic *loop variant* and the four events *Activate*, *Progress*, *Detect* and *Stop* can be described as a "*meta-pattern*". The action of the event *Progress* decreases the *loop variant*. It is necessary to instantiate this pattern that can be verified by the Click_n_prove tool.

4.3. Applying B Refinement Pattern

We propose below an example of a refinement proved pattern. It was developed under a manufacturing system (Mixer-Weigher process) and it is a simple pattern that models a tank filling by some liquid q (continuous process). At abstract level, the event is defined as follows (see Figure 4):

```
Filled_tank = SELECT
content = 0
```

THEN
```
content:= q
END;
```

The variable *content* models the quantity of liquid presented in the tank.

At concrete level, the refinement pattern is defined by the following four events:

- **Init_filling:** The event activating the filling process by the liquid q. It allows also the opening of the valve;
- **Let_filling:** The event observing the progression filling process (variable *volume*) by the liquid q;
- **Detect_level:** The event corresponding to the observation of the reached goal (*detect*:= TRUE);
- **Filled_tank:** The event disabling the process by closing the valve.

Figure 5 shows a transition diagram describing the precedence relationship between events.

These events are described as follows:

```
Init_filling =
SELECT
volume = 0 ∧
valve = closed
THEN
valve:= open
END;
Let_filling =
SELECT
valve = open ∧
volume < q
THEN
```

Figure 4. Abstract filled_tank event

Figure 5. Transition diagram corresponding to the filling tank pattern

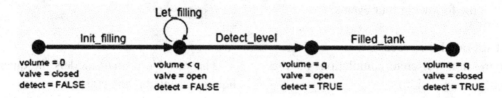

```
volume:= volume+1
END;
Detect_level =
SELECT
volume = q ∧
valve = open
THEN
detect:= TRUE
END;
Filled_tank =
SELECT
detect = TRUE ∧
valve = open
THEN
valve:= closed
END;
```

The refinement pattern is always defined by the following invariants:

```
pat1: valve ∈ {closed, open}
pat2: volume ∈ (0..q)
pat3: detect ∈ BOOL
```

The variables *valve* and *volume* model respectively the valve and the filling volume. The variable *volume* refines the *content* one.

Concerning the event *Let_filling*:

• It is, of course, the discretization of a continuous process;

• It is not an operation to perform as an opening or closing a valve but it helps to take into account the passage of time and reason about temporal properties (liveness),i.e, once the process starts, we eventually reach a state where the tank is full;

• Finally, this approach highlights the multiform concept of time, one of the foundations of synchronous languages like Esterel where every physical phenomenon is an observation of time elapsing. We studied this point in (Mosbahi et al., 2004) where different physical processes correspond to different observations of the time passage.

The event *Let_filling* models the process progression and decreases the *loop variant (q-volume)* while running the action *volume:= volume+1*. At abstract level, the event *Let_filling* is modeled as follows where *volume$0* models the initial value of volume:

```
Let_Filling = BEGIN
volume:| (volume ∈ NATURAL ∧ (q-vol-
ume) < (qvolume$0))
END;
```

The gluing invariant connecting the abstract variable (*content*) and the concrete ones (*valve, volume, detect*) is defined as follows:

```
(0 ≤ volume < q ⇒ content = 0) ∧
(volume = q ∧ detect = TRUE ∧ valve
= open ⇒ content = 0) ∧
(volume = q ∧ detect = TRUE ∧ valve
= closed ⇒ content = q)
```

Concerning the reuse of proofs, it is not automatically taken into account by the tools Click_n_prove (Abrial, 2007) or Rodin (Rodin, 2007). What we mean by reuse of proofs when applying a refinement pattern is that we define all constants, properties on constants, variables, invariants, gluing invariants and events. During refinement, the refinement proof obligations generated, are verified in the same way when we apply a refinement pattern, because we instantiate the variables and the event names.

5. INDUSTRIAL CASE STUDY: THE MIXER-WEIGHER PROCESS

We present in this section a case study which is a manufacturing system to illustrate the use of the B refinement patterns.

5.1. Description of the System

The automated system presented in Figure 6 allows producing a mixing product for a certain time *tm*, a quantity of a solid (bricks) with a mixture of two liquids (A and B). Products A and B, which were previously weighed on a weighing unit C, and soluble bricks brought one by one on a belt motor T are fed into a tripper mixer N. A cycle starts with push button and causes a sequential weighing and bringing of the bricks as follows:

- Weighing product A up to mark *"ma"* of the weighing unit (level indication *WA* in the tank A), next dosing product B up to mark *"mb"* of the weighing unit (level in-

dication *WB* in the tank B), followed by emptying the contents of the weighing unit C into the mixer.
- Bringing two bricks.

The batch cycle ends with the mixer operating and tipping. The products A and B are contained in two tanks. Each one is fitted with a valve (*VA* and *VB*). The weighing unit C also fitted with a value *VC* to empty its content in a bowl mixer.

The individual plant objects operate as follows:

- When valves *va* or *vb* are open, the liquid level of container C rises respectively at the rate of *WA* or *WB*. When the valve *vc* is open, the liquid level in container C decreases at the rate *WC*.
- Two successive bricks enter the mixer after the elapse of the average time belt time, when the belt is operating.
- The total mixing time should be *tm*. Upon the tipping initiation, the mixer tips in *tt* and it can return to the upright position in *tu*.

5.2. Modeling of the System

In this section, we propose to build a control-command program to operate the installation (the opening-closing valves, starting-stopping

Figure 6. Mixer-weigher process

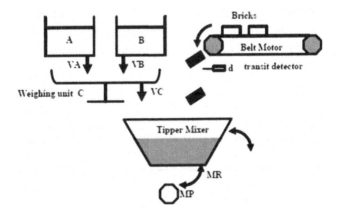

engines). One of the problem difficulties is to find the right abstraction. Two possibilities are presented:

- **To model the different states of the installation during the production in a manufacturing cycle:** Starting-stopping engines, opening-closing valves.
- **To model the product in its various production steps with abstraction of the installation elements:** A mixture of liquids, a mixture of liquid and solid... In this case, the order of intermediate states is imposed by the manufacture process.

5.2.1. Abstract Model

The initial model of the mixer problem consists of a cycle "manufacturing-delivery" of a product where manufacturing specifications are given during refinements. The manufacturing consists on mixing, for a time *tm*, *ma* quantity of liquid *A*, *mb* quantity of liquid *B* and *n* solid bricks.

During manufacturing, a product is represented by a quadruplet $(qa \rightarrow qb \rightarrow nb \rightarrow ts)$ that gives information on its composition and mixing time where:

- *qa* designs the quantity of liquid *A*,
- *qb* designs the quantity of liquid *B*,
- *nb* designs the number of fell bricks,
- *ts* designs the mixing time.

Figure 7 presents the abstract model of the production system. The event *Start* begins the manufacturing process and resets the product to $(qa \mapsto qb \mapsto nb \mapsto ts)$. The event *Manufacture* transforms the product from $(0 \mapsto 0 \mapsto 0 \mapsto 0)$ to

$(ma \mapsto mb \mapsto n \mapsto tm)$ corresponding to the final product. The event *Deliver* updates the location of the product to *out*. The event *Stop* stops the production process once the product is delivered. The location of the product during manufacturing process is modeled by the variable *loc_product*. If the product corresponds to $(0 \mapsto 0 \mapsto 0 \mapsto 0)$, its location is undefined (value *no_where*). If it is during manufacture, its location is inside the system (value *in*) and once manufactured its location is outside (value *out*).

Simulation of the B model with ProB: We have used ProB in (Leuschel et al., 2003), which is a simulator and model checker for the (B/Event-B) method. It allows fully automatic animation of many B specifications, and can be used to systematically check a specification for errors. ProB's animation facilities allow users to gain confidence in their specifications, and unlike the animator provided by the B-Toolkit, the user does not have to guess the right values for the operation arguments or choice variables.

The model is valid and all generated proof obligations are verified in an automatic way with the B click_n_prove tool.

5.2.2. Concrete Model

In the first refinement, we model the product in its various stages of production in Box 1.

This refinement reflects this sequence of manufacture. To get the product $(ma \mapsto mb \mapsto n \mapsto 0)$, we must add *n* bricks to $(ma \mapsto mb \mapsto 0 \mapsto 0)$ to the mixer.

To get the product $(ma \mapsto mb \mapsto n \mapsto tm)$, it is necessary to operate the mixer containing the product $(ma \mapsto mb \mapsto n \mapsto 0)$ during *tm* time units.

Box 1.

Figure 7. Mixer abstract mode

```
MODEL          M₀
SETS           LOCATION = {no_where, in, out, mixer, tank}
CONSTANTS      ma, mb, n, tm
PROPERTIES
    ma : NATURAL1 ∧ mb ∈ NATURAL1 ∧
    n ∈ NATURAL1 ∧ tm ∈ NATURAL1
VARIABLES      product, running, loc_product
INVARIANT
    running ∈ BOOL ∧ loc_produit ∈ LOCATION ∧
    product ∈ (0..ma)* (0..mb)*(0..n)*(0..tm)
INITIALISATION
    product := (0↦0↦0↦0) || running := FALSE || loc_product := no_where
EVENTS
Start = SELECT running = FALSE
        THEN running := TRUE || loc_product := no_where || product := (0↦0↦0↦0)
        END;
Manufacture = SELECT running = TRUE ∧ loc_product = no_where
        THEN product := (ma↦mb↦n↦tm) || loc_product := in
        END;
Deliver = SELECT loc_product = in   THEN loc_product := out
        END;
Stop = SELECT loc_product = out ∧ running = TRUE
        THEN running := FALSE
        END
END
```

In the second refinement, we refine the location of the product during its production and we add the new locations *tank* and *mixer*.

In the third refinement, we describe in detail each step in the manufacturing process. The idea introduced here is that an atomic event with *deferred execution* is refined at an abstract level into a set of events at concrete level modeling the action of the process taking place in time. Indeed, time can be represented in different ways according to the performing process. Time can be represented by the filling or emptying a tank, by bricks that move on the conveyor to reach the fall point, by a bowl mixer that switches between vertical and horizontal positions so we use design patterns to model and refine events with *deferred execution* actions.

For the tank filling process with liquid *A*, the event *Getting_VA* is refined by the following events:

- **Open_VA:** Allows the opening of the valve *VA*,
- **Filling_tankAC:** Observes the progress of the tank filling (*content(tank)*) by *A*,
- **Detect_WA:** Corresponds to the observation of the reached goal (*WA:= TRUE*),
- **Getting_VA:** Disables the process by closing the valve *VA*.

The refinement pattern is defined by the invariants in Box 3.

The event *Filling_tankAC* decreases the *loop variant* (ma-x). We cannot express the *variant* in the Event-B (this option will be provided in the RODIN project), we have recourse to a stratagem that is to introduce in the abstract level, the new event which decreases explicitly the *variant*. This new event is modeled in Box 4 (where $x\$0$ models the initial value of x).

The gluing invariant connecting the abstract variable (*product*) and the concrete ones (*VA, content(tank), WA*) is defined in Box 5.

In the same way and for the filling tank process with liquid *B*, the event *Getting_VB* is refined by the events: *Open_VB, Filling_tankBC, Detect_WB* and *Getting_VB*.

The refinement pattern presented in Section 4.2 is applied to this production system to create new modeling elements (variables, events) and enrich invariance properties. It is instantiated with new variables and events described above. The pattern parameters are: event names (*Init_filling, Let_filling, Detect_level* and *Filled_tank*), and variables names (*valve, volume, detect* and *q*) (see Box 6).

This pattern is applied two times, first in the filling process of the tank with liquid *A* and second with liquid *B*. The event *Getting_bricks* is

Box 2.

```
Open_VA =   SELECT
            VA = close ∧ content(tank) = (0↦0↦0↦0)
            THEN VA := open
            END;
Filling_tankAC = ANY x WHERE
            x ∈ 0..ma-1 ∧ content(tank) = (x↦0↦0↦0) ∧ VA = open
            THEN content(tank) := (x+1↦0↦0↦0)
            END;
Detect_WA = SELECT   content(tank) = (ma↦0↦0↦0)
            THEN WA := TRUE
            END;
Getting_VA = SELECT   WA = TRUE ∧ VA = open
            THEN VA := closed
            END;
```

Box 3.

```
pat1 : VA ∈ {closed, open}
pat2 : content ∈ LIEUX ⇸ (0..ma)*(0..mb)*(0..n)*(0..tm)
pat3 : WA ∈ BOOL
```

Box 4.

```
Filling_tankAC = BEGIN
                 x:|(x ∈ NATURAL ∧ (ma-x) < (ma-x$0))
                 END;
```

Box 5.

```
((0↦0↦0↦0) ≤ content(tank) < (ma↦0↦0↦0) ⇒ product = (0↦0↦0↦0)) ∧
(content(tank) = (ma↦0↦0↦0) ∧ WA = TRUE ∧ VA = open ⇒ product = (0↦0↦0↦0)) ∧
(content(tank) = (ma↦0↦0↦0) ∧ WA = TRUE ∧ VA = closed ⇒ product = (ma↦0↦0↦0))
```

Box 6.

Init_filling ⤳ Open_VA		Init_filling ⤳ Open_VB	
Let_filling ⤳ Filling_tankAC		Let_filling ⤳ Filling_tankBC	
Detect_level ⤳ Detect_WA		Detect_level ⤳ Detect_WB	
Filled_tank ⤳ Getting_VA		Filled_tank ⤳ Getting_VB	
content ⤳ product		content ⤳ product	
volume ⤳ content(tank)		volume ⤳ content(tank)	
valve ⤳ VA		valve ⤳ VB	
detect ⤳ WA		detect ⤳ WB	
q ⤳ (ma ↦ 0 ↦ 0 ↦ 0)		q ⤳ (ma ↦ mb ↦ 0 ↦ 0)	

refined also by the following events in the same way:

- **Init_convoyer:** Activates the falling process of bricks by starting the belt motor (variable *belt_motor*),
- **Let_falling_bricks:** Observes the process progression of falling bricks,
- **Detect_bricks:** Observes that the number of bricks is reached (*WN:=TRUE*),

- **Getting_bricks:** Disables the process by stopping the belt motor.

The event *Let_falling_bricks* decreases the *loop variant* (*n-x*). At abstract level, this new event is modeled in Box 8.

The event *Mixing* is also refined by the following events in the same way:

- **Init_mix:** Activates the motor of the mixing process (*mixer_motor*),

Box 7.

```
Init_convoyer = SELECT
                 belt_motor = off ∧ VC = close
            THEN   belt_motor := on
            END;
Let_falling_bricks = ANY x WHERE
                 x : 0..n-1 ∧ belt_motor = on ∧ content(mixer) = (ma↦mb↦x↦0)
            THEN   content(mixer) := (ma↦mb↦x+1↦0)
            END;
Detect_bricks = SELECT content(mixer) = (ma↦mb↦n↦0)
            THEN   WN := TRUE
            END;
Getting_bricks = SELECT belt_motor = on ∧ WN = TRUE
            THEN   belt_motor := off
            END;
```

Box 8.

```
Let_falling_bricks = BEGIN
                 x:|(x ∈ NATURAL ∧ (n-x) < (n-x$0))
            END;
```

Box 9.

```
Init_mix =       SELECT
                 mixer_motor = off ∧ VC = close
            THEN   mixer_motor := on
            END;
Let_mixing =     ANY t WHERE
                 t ∈ 0..ts-1 ∧ mixer_motor = on ∧ content(mixer) = (ma↦mb↦n↦t)
            THEN   content(mixer) := (ma↦mb↦n↦t+1)
            END;
Detect_time =    SELECT   content(mixer) = (ma↦mb↦n↦tm)
            THEN   WT := TRUE
            END;
Manufacture = SELECT   mixer_motor = on ∧ WT = TRUE
            THEN   mixer_motor := off
            END;
```

- **Let_mixing:** Observes the progression of the mixing process,
- **Detect_time:** Observes that the mixing time is reached($WT:=TRUE$),
- **Manufacture:** Stops the motor of the mixing process.

The event *Let_mixing* decreases the *loop variant* (*tm-t*). At abstract level, this new event is modeled in Box 10.

5.3. Verification by Proof and Model Checking

For us, the primary way of verification is done by mechanical proof. But we also have used model-checking with ProB (Leuschel et al., 2003) in order to make partial verifications and to find counter-examples. In order to have a finite number of transitions with our models, we cannot let some variable time increase indefinitely. Therefore, we define another version for the event which deals with these variables for model-checking. In any case, model-checking provides a convenient way to discover invariants and to test them before the proof.

With the B prover the proof is cut into small "Proof Obligations" (PO). Some of those PO are automatically discharged and some need user interactions. All proofs of the first model are done automatically; for the first refinement 19 PO are interactive; for the second refinement 54; and for the last refinement 89. Of course all the proofs are done with the tool of the B method.

The procedure of proof, with an invariant, leads to the discovery of an invariant strong enough to be inductive. We can always start with a small invariant containing types of variables and some requirements for the refinements of data or events. If we start to do the proof with an invariant that is too weak then the proof will fail with an impossible interactive proof. With this failure we see the missing piece of information about the system state: we add it to the invariant and retry to prove.

CONCLUSION AND PERSPECTIVES

In this paper, we have proposed a concept of reusing models and proofs in Event-B in the form of design patterns for the development of automated systems. We have studied the reuse of patterns by using Event-B mechanisms which are formally defined and we can benefit from the advantages of the Event-B, especially the "reuse" of proofs and the tool.

The following necessary step will be the development of a tool to assist the designer during the specification of an application by pattern reuse. The example presented in this paper is rather simple. A more complex example just involves more patterns but the method presented in the paper is still applicable, provided that a tool is available. The aim is to define the notion of proof linked to a model and to specify the reuse of proofs with the Event-B. This perspective is new, since the reuse of proofs is not possible with a formal method like Event-B. However, such a possibility requires several works on new examples in order to analyze the consequences on the proof obligations.

At the moment, there are only the few design patterns that were developed for the case studies.

Box 10.

```
Let_mixing = BEGIN
          t:|(t ∈ NATURAL ∧ (tm-t) < (tm-t$0))
          END;
```

It is desirable to have a library of patterns for common problems. Furthermore, we want to have also patterns in other areas than in business protocols.

REFERENCES

Abrial, Cansell, & Mery. (2003a). Formal derivation of spanning trees algorithms. *Lecture Notes in Computer Science, 2651*, 457–476. doi:10.1007/3-540-44880-2_27.

Abrial, Cansell, & Mery. (2003b). A mechanically proved and incremental development of IEEE 1394 tree identify protocol. *Formal Aspects of Computing, 14*(3), 215–227. doi:10.1007/s001650300002.

Abrial & Cansell. (2005). *Formal construction of a nonblocking concurrent queue algorithm (a case study in atomicity)*.

Abrial & Cansell. (2007). *Click'n'prove within set theory*.

Abrial. (1996a). *The B-book: Assigning programs to meanings*. Cambridge, UK: Cambridge University Press.

Abrial. (1996b). Extending B without changing it (for developing distributed systems). In H. Habrias (Ed.), *Proceedings of the 1st Conference on the B method*, (pp. 169–191). Academic Press.

Abrial. (2003). Toward a synthesis between Z and B. *Lecture Notes in Computer Science, 2651*, 168–177.

Abrial. (2006). *Using design patterns in formal development - Example: A mechanical press controler*.

Alexander. (1977). *A pattern language: Towns, buildings, construction*. Oxford, UK: Oxford University Press.

Back & Sere. (1989). Stepwise refinement of action systems. In *Mathematics of Program Construction* (pp. 115–138). Berlin: Springer.

Back & Wright. (1998). *Refinement calculus: A systematic introduction*. Berlin: Springer-Verlag.

Badeau & Amelot. (2005). Using B as a high level programming language in an industrial project: Roissy VAL. *Lecture Notes in Computer Science, 3455*, 334–354. doi:10.1007/11415787_20.

Beck. (1997). *Smalltalk best practice patterns*. Upper Saddle River, NJ: Prentice-Hall.

Behm, B. Faivre, & Meynadier. (1999). METEOR: A successful application of B in a large project. In J. M. Wing, J. Woodcock, & J. Davies (Eds.), *Proceedings of FM'99: World Congress on Formal Methods* (LNCS), (pp. 369-387). Berlin: Springer-Verlag.

Cansell & Mery. (2006). Formal and incremental construction of distributed algorithms: On the distributed reference counting algorithm. *Theoretical Computer Science, 364*.

Coplien. (1995). A generative development - Process pattern language. In J. Coplien & D. Schmidt (Eds.), *Pattern Languages of Program Design*, (pp. 183–237). Reading, MA: Addison-Wesley.

Fowler. (1997). *Analysis patterns: Reusable object models*. Reading, MA: Addison-Wesley Publishing Company.

Gamma, H. Johnson, & Vlissides. (1995). Design patterns. Reading, MA: Addison-Wesley.

Larman. (2001). *Applying UML and patterns* (2nd ed). Upper Saddle River, NJ: Prentice Hall.

Leuschel & Butler. (2003). ProB: A model checker for B. In *Proceedings of FME 2003: Formal Methods* (LNCS), (vol. 2805, pp. 855–874). Berlin: Springer-Verlag.

Mosbahi & Jaray. (2004). *Représentation du temps en B événementiel pour la modélisation des systèmes temps réel. Rapport interne*. LORIA.

Chapter 8
Emerging Real-Time Methodologies

Giorgio C. Buttazzo
Scuola Superiore Sant'Anna, Italy

ABSTRACT

The number of computer-controlled systems has increased dramatically in our daily life. Processors and microcontrollers are embedded in most of the devices we use every day, such as mobile phones, cameras, media players, navigators, washing machines, biomedical devices, and cars. The complexity of such systems is increasing exponentially, pushed by the demand of new products with extra functionality, higher performance requirements, and low energy consumption. To cope with such a complex scenario, many embedded systems are adopting more powerful and highly integrated hardware components, such as multi-core systems, network-on-chip architectures, inertial subsystems, and special purpose co-processors. However, developing, analyzing, and testing the application software on these architectures is not easy, and new methodologies are being investigated in the research community to guarantee high predictability and efficiency in next generation embedded devices. This chapter presents some recent approaches proposed within the real-time research community aimed at achieving predictability, high modularity, efficiency, and adaptability in modern embedded computing systems.

1. INTRODUCTION

Complex embedded systems, like cell phones and multimedia devices, share a number of features that determine a set of design requirements:

- **Limited resources:** Small portable devices are designed under space, weight, and energy constraints. Often they also have cost constraints related with mass production and strong industrial competition. As a consequence, embedded applications typically run on small processing units with limited memory and computational power. To make these devices cost-effective, it is mandatory to make a very efficient use of the computational resources, both at the application and the operating system level.

- **High concurrency and resource sharing:** Typically, several functions are simultane-

DOI: 10.4018/978-1-4666-3922-5.ch008

ously active, often sharing the same set of resources. For instance, in a cell phone, different tasks can be performed at the same time, such as browsing, downloading, playing music, and receiving a call. Most of them need the same resources to run, as processor, memory, display, and sound codec. As a consequence, tasks can experience variable blocking delays due to the interference generated by the synchronization mechanisms required to access shared resources. To reduce inter-task interference and make tasks execution more predictable, proper scheduling algorithms have to be adopted at the operating systems level to isolate the timing behavior of concurrent tasks.

- **Interaction with the environment:** Most embedded devices interact with the environment and have demanding quality specifications, whose satisfaction requires the system to timely react to external events and execute computational activities within precise timing constraints. The operating system is responsible for ensuring a predictable execution behavior of the application to allow an off-line guarantee of the required performance.

- **Dynamic behavior:** In embedded systems characterized by several concurrent tasks, the overall computational load is not constant, but can have high variations, depending on the tasks activated by the user and the resources needed by the activities, which in turn may depend on the actual data. If not properly handled, overload conditions may cause undesired effects, from a transient performance degradation to a complete system crash. A certain degree of adaptivity in the resource management policies is essential to reallocate resources during peak load situations.

The combination of real-time features in tasks with dynamic behavior, together with cost and resource constraints, creates new problems to be addressed in the design of such systems, at different architecture levels. The classical worst-case design approach, typically adopted in hard real-time systems to guarantee timely responses in all possible scenarios, is no longer acceptable in highly dynamic environments, because it would waste the resources and prohibitively increase the cost.

Instead of allocating resources for the worst case, smarter techniques are needed to sense the current state of the environment and react as a consequence. This means that, to cope with dynamic environments, a real-time system must be *adaptive*; that is, it must be able to adjust its internal strategies in response to a change in the environment to keep the system performance at a desired level or, if this is not possible, degrade it in a controlled fashion.

Implementing adaptive embedded systems requires specific support at different levels of the software architecture. The most important component affecting adaptivity is the kernel, but some flexibility can also be introduced above the operating system, in a software layer denoted as the *middleware*. Some adaptation can also be done at the application level; however, it potentially incurs in low efficiency due to the higher overhead normally introduced by the application level services. Normally, for efficiency reasons, adaptation should be handled at the lower layers of the system architecture, as close as possible to the system resources. For those embedded systems that are distributed among several computing nodes, special network methodologies are needed to achieve adaptive behavior and predictable response.

The rest of this document presents several techniques to make next generation embedded systems more predictable and adaptive to environmental changes. In particular, Section 1 summarizes the most relevant results on real-time scheduling; Section 2 illustrates how to achieve modularity and isolate the temporal behavior of independent tasks; Section 3 presents different feedback schemes to adapt an embedded system to variable workload conditions; and finally, the last section concludes the chapter and states some perspectives.

2. PREDICTABLE SCHEDULING

The most important property for a real-time computing system is not high speed, but predictability. A predictable system should enable the user to determine in advance the temporal behavior of the application, and in particular the response time of each computational activity in the system. The deterministic behavior of a system typically depends on several factors, ranging from the hardware architecture to the operating system. Architectural features that have major influence on task execution include interrupts, DMA, cache, and pre-fetching mechanisms. Although such features improve the average performance of the processor, they introduce a non-deterministic behavior in process execution, prolonging the worst-case response times.

The operating system mechanism that mostly affects predictability is the scheduling algorithm, which is responsible for selecting the running task among a set of tasks ready to execute. A particular execution sequence of tasks on a processor is called a *schedule*. A schedule is said to be *feasible* if all the executed tasks are able to complete within a set of specified constraints.

2.1. Periodic Task Scheduling

Periodic tasks represent the major computational activities in an embedded system, involving sensory acquisition, filtering, data processing, control, and actuation. A periodic task τ_i is characterized by an initial activation time (or phase) Φ_i, a worst-case computation time C_i, a period T_i, and a relative deadline D_i. The ratio $U_i = C_i/T_i$ is referred to as

the task utilization and represents the fraction of the processor utilized by task τ_i. In a system consisting of n periodic tasks, the quantity

$$U = \sum_{i=1}^{n} U_i$$

is referred to as the total processor utilization and represents a measure of the computational load of the task set.

A periodic tasks is cyclically executed several times on different data, thus generating several execution instances, called jobs, denoted as $\tau_{i,k}$ ($k = 1, 2, \ldots$). Each job is characterized by an activation time $r_{i,k}$, a computation time $C_{i,k}$, and an absolute deadline $d_{i,k} = r_{i,k} + D_i$. The first job $\tau_{i,1}$ is activated at time $r_{i,1} = \Phi_i$, while the others jobs are exactly separated by a period T_i; thus, the generic activation time of job $\tau_{i,k}$ occurs at time

$$r_{i,k} = \Phi_i + (k - 1)T_i. \tag{1}$$

Two basic approaches are used today to schedule periodic real-time tasks on a uniprocessor system: one consists in assigning each task a fixed priority and then executing the corresponding active jobs in a priority order; the second method executes active jobs according to their absolute deadline. Both scheduling algorithms are typically executed in a preemptive fashion, meaning that the execution of the current job can be interrupted at any time in favor of a new job with higher priority (or earlier absolute deadline), and resumed later.

2.1.1. Fixed Priority Scheduling

One of the most common method for assigning fixed priorities to a periodic task set is the Rate-Monotonic (RM) algorithm, proposed and analyzed in 1973 by Liu and Layland (1973). According to RM, each task is assigned a fixed priority directly proportional to its activation frequency, so that tasks with shorter period have higher priority. Liu and Layland showed that RM is optimal among all static scheduling algorithms, meaning that RM can always find a feasible schedule for a task set Γ, if there exists one using a fixed priority assignment. They also proved that a set Γ of n periodic tasks is schedulable by RM if the total task set utilization is less than a given bound; that is, if

$$\sum_{i=1}^{n} U_i \leq U_{\text{lub}}(n) \tag{2}$$

where $U_{lub}(n)$, referred to as the *utilization least upper bound*, is a decreasing function of n:

$$U_{\text{lub}}(n) = n(2^{1/n} - 1). \tag{3}$$

For n tending to infinity, function $U_{lub}(n)$ tends to $\ln(2) \cong 0.69$, meaning that, for systems consisting of a large number of tasks, RM can guarantee a feasible schedule only if the total computational load is no greater than 69 percent.

Note that the schedulability test expressed by Equation (2) only gives a sufficient condition for guaranteeing a feasible schedule under RM. This means that a task set can be schedulable by RM even though the feasibility test is not satisfied. On the other hand, it is also possible to claim that a periodic task set cannot be feasibly scheduled by any algorithm if $U > 1$.

A tighter schedulability test, called the Hyperbolic Bound (Bini, 2003), allows checking the feasibility of a task set under RM if

$$\prod_{i=1}^{n} (U_i + 1) \leq 2. \tag{4}$$

With respect to the Liu and Layland test, the Hyperbolic Bound provides a tighter condition, since it is able to guarantee more feasible task sets.

A necessary and sufficient test to verify the schedulability of a periodic task set has been proposed by Audsley et al. (1993) and consists in checking whether, for each task τ_i, its worst-case response time R_i is less than its relative deadline D_i. The worst-case response time R_i of a task is computed according to the following recurrent relation:

$$R_i = C_i + \sum_{k \in hp(i)} \left\lceil \frac{R_i}{T_k} \right\rceil C_k. \tag{5}$$

where $hp(i)$ denotes the set of tasks having priority higher than that of task τ_i and $\lceil x \rceil$ denotes the ceiling of a rational number, i.e., the smaller integer greater than or equal to x. The equation above can be solved by an iterative approach, starting with $R_i(0) = C_i$ and terminating when $R_i(s) = R_i(s-1)$. If $R_i(s) > D_i$ for some task, then the task set cannot be feasibly scheduled.

Note that the response time test can be performed also for tasks with relative deadlines less than periods. In this case, it can be shown that RM is not optimal, while optimality can be achieved by the Deadline Monotonic (DM) algorithm, proposed by Leung and Whitehead (1982), according to which priorities are inversely proportional to relative deadlines.

2.1.2. Earliest Deadline First

The Earliest Deadline First (EDF) algorithm is a dynamic scheduling rule that selects jobs according to their absolute deadlines. Specifically, a job with a shorter absolute deadline will be executed before a job with a longer absolute deadline.

Dertouzos (1974) showed that EDF is optimal among all possible scheduling algorithms, meaning that EDF can always find a feasible schedule for a task set Γ, if there exists one. Liu and Layland (1973) proved that a set Γ of n periodic tasks is schedulable by EDF if and only if

$$\sum_{i=1}^{n} U_i \leq 1. \tag{6}$$

Note that the dynamic priority assignment rule allows EDF to exploit the full processor capacity, scheduling task sets with utilization up to 1.

In general, compared with fixed-priority schemes, EDF is superior in many aspects, generating a lower number of context switches and allowing a better exploitation of the remaining idle time for the execution of aperiodic activities (Buttazzo, 2005).

Under EDF, the schedulability analysis of periodic task sets with deadlines no greater than periods can be performed using the Processor Demand Criterion (Baruah, 1990). According to this method, a task set is schedulable by EDF if and only if, in every interval of length L, the overall computational demand is no greater than the available processing time, that is, if and only if $U < 1$ and

$$\forall L > 0 \sum_{i=1}^{n} \left\lfloor \frac{L + T_i - D_i}{T_i} \right\rfloor C_i \leq L \tag{7}$$

where $\lfloor x \rfloor$ denotes the floor of a rational number, i.e., the highest integer less than or equal to x. Notice that, in practice, the number of points in which the test has to be performed can be limited to the set of absolute deadlines not exceeding $L_{max} = \min\{L^*, H\}$, where $H = \text{lcm}(T_1, ..., T_n)$ is the *hyperperiod* and

$$L^* = \max\left\{ D_1, ..., D_n, \frac{\sum_{i=1}^{n}(T_i - D_i)U_i}{1 - U} \right\}. \tag{8}$$

2.1.3. Limited Preemptive Scheduling

Most of real-time scheduling algorithms are used in a *preemptive* fashion, meaning that the running task can be interrupted at any time in favor of an incoming task with higher priority. However, arbitrary preemptions introduce a significant runtime overhead and may cause high fluctuations in task execution times, so degrading system predictability.

A non-preemptive scheduler better preserves program locality and produces more predictable execution times. Moreover, it naturally guarantees the exclusive access to shared resources without using special concurrency control protocols that introduce additional overhead and complexity. Finally, non-preemptive scheduling allows reducing the input-output delay and jitter in control applications (Buttazzo, 2007) and permits the use of stack sharing techniques (Baker, 1991) to save memory space in small embedded systems with stringent memory constraints.

The price that must paid when using non-preemptive schedulers is a higher blocking delay on high priority tasks, which cannot immediately preempt a lower priority task. In the presence of low priority tasks with long execution times, such extra blocking delays may drastically reduce schedulability to an unacceptable level. However, if preemption is reduced, rather than totally forbidden, the schedulability level can be preserved and even improved, especially in fixed priority systems.

Recently, three limited preemptive approaches have been proposed in the literature to reduce preemption while preserving the schedulability of the task set. Each method uses a different criterion to postpone preemption: priority, time, and position.

- **Preemption Thresholds:** This approach, proposed by Wang and Saksena (1999), allows a task to disable preemption up to a specified priority level, called *preemption threshold*. Each task is assigned a regular priority and a preemption threshold, and the preemption is allowed to take place only when the priority of the arriving task is strictly higher than the threshold of the running task.

- **Deferred Preemptions:** According to this method, first introduced by Baruah (2005) under EDF, each task τ_i specifies the longest interval q_i that can be executed non-preemptively. In this model, non-preemptive regions are triggered by the arrival of a higher priority task and programmed by a timer to last exactly for q_i units of time (unless the task finishes earlier), after which preemption is enabled. Once a timer is set at time t, additional activations arriving before the timeout $(t + q_i)$ do not postpone the preemption any further. Once a preemption takes place, a new high-priority arrival can trigger another non-preemptive region.

- **Fixed Preemption Points:** According to this approach, a task implicitly executes in non-preemptive mode and preemption is allowed only at predefined locations inside the task code, called *preemption points*. In this way, a task is divided into a number of non-preemptive chunks (also called subjobs). If a higher priority task arrives between two preemption points of the running task, preemption is postponed until the next preemption point. This approach, proposed by Burns (1994), is also referred to as *Cooperative scheduling*, because tasks cooperate to offer suitable preemption points to improve schedulability.

The previous approaches have been recently compared and analyzed by Buttazzo, Bertogna, and Yao (2012). The most relevant result that clearly emerges from several simulation experiments is that, under fixed priority scheduling, any of the considered algorithms dominates both fully preemptive and non-preemptive scheduling, even when preemption cost is neglected.

Each specific algorithm for limiting preemptions has advantages and disadvantages. The preemption threshold mechanism has a simple and intuitive interface and can be implemented by introducing a low runtime overhead; however, preemption cost cannot be easily estimated, since the position of each preemption, as well as the overall number of preemptions for each task, cannot be determined off-line. Using deferred preemptions, the number of preemptions for each task can be better estimated, but still the position of each preemption cannot be determined off-line. The method based on fixed preemption points represents the most predictable solution for estimating preemption costs, since both the number of preemptions and their positions are fixed and known from the task code. Moreover, simulation experiments clearly show that this approach is the one generating less preemptions and higher schedulability ratios for any task set parameter configuration. However, it requires adding explicit preemption points in the program; hence, achieving portability of legacy code is still a challenge for future works.

3. ACHIEVING TEMPORAL ISOLATION

When multiple computations concurrently execute on the same processor, tasks are subject to a reciprocal interference that can degrade the performance of the entire application. For a given real-time scheduling algorithm, the worst-case interference on task τ_i is taken into account in the schedulability analysis by estimating the preemption delay introduced by high priority jobs. However, if some jobs execute more than expected (overrun), the exceeding executions can introduce extra delays in lower priority tasks, possibly jeopardizing the schedulability of the task set.

To prevent sporadic overruns from affecting the schedulability of other tasks, each task should be assigned a fraction of the processor and should be executed in isolation, within a protected environment, where it cannot steal the time reserved to other tasks. Such a temporal protection mechanisms can be implemented inside an operating system using a *resource reservation* approach (Abeni, 2004), described in the following section.

3.1. Resource Reservation

Resource reservation is a scheduling technique for bounding the effects of task overruns in systems with variable computational load. According to this method, the processor bandwidth is partitioned into fractions, each dedicated to single tasks or task groups. The operating system must then guarantee (through a proper enforcement mechanism) that the tasks executing within a given partition do not interfere with other tasks running in different partitions, so isolating their execution behavior. In this way, a task receiving a fraction α_i of the total processor bandwidth behaves as it were executing alone on a slower processor with a speed equal to α_i times the full speed. The advantage of this approach is that each task can be guaranteed in isolation, independently of the behavior of the other tasks.

Figures 1 and 2 provide an intuitive explanation of the different execution behavior of three tasks executed in a priority-based kernel and in a reservation-based kernel, respectively. In the example, the processor is partitioned into three reservations of bandwidth 0.5, 0.3, and 0.2, assigned to tasks τ_1, τ_2, and τ_3, respectively. In both figures, the computational demand of each task is illustrated as a variable flow that changes over time.

In a priority-based kernel, when the computational demand of a high-priority task exceeds its expected value, the exceeding computation time is stolen from the lower priority tasks (Figure 1). As a result, high-priority tasks execute as much as they need, whereas lower priority tasks can be delayed beyond their deadlines. As an extreme case, if the highest priority task misbehaves entering an infinite loop, all the other tasks will never run; thus, a single task failure can propagate to the entire application. On the contrary, in a reservation-based kernel, when a task τ_i exceeds its expected computational demand, only τ_i is delayed (Figure 2). Hence, the misbehavior of a task does not propagate to other tasks.

A resource reservation technique for fixed priority scheduling was first presented by Mercer, Savage and Tokuda (1994a). According to this method, a reservation is implemented through a server mechanism that enables the associated task to execute for Q_s units of time every P_s units. The ratio $U_s = Q_s/P_s$ is referred to as the reservation bandwidth. When the task consumes its reserved budget Q_s, it is suspended until the next period, if the reservation is hard, or it is scheduled in background as a non real-time task, if the reservation is soft. If the task is not finished, another time budget Q_s is assigned at the beginning of the next period, and so on. In this way, the execution of a task running within a reservation is *reshaped* to be more uniform along the timeline, so avoiding long intervals of time in which the task holds the processor.

Under EDF scheduling, resource reservation can be efficiently implemented through the

Figure 1. A set of tasks executed in a priority-based kernel

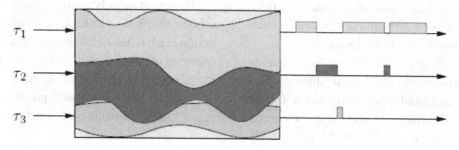

Figure 2. A set of tasks executed in a reservation-based kernel

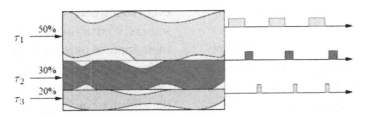

Constant Bandwidth Server (CBS) (Abeni, 1998, 2004), which is a service mechanism also controlled by two parameters, (Q_s, P_s), where Q_s is the maximum *server budget* and P_s is the *server period*. The ratio $U_s = Q_s/P_s$ is also referred to as the reservation bandwidth. At each instant, two state variables are maintained: the current server deadline d_s and the current server budget q_s. Each job handled by a CBS is scheduled using the current server deadline and whenever the server executes a job, the budget q_s is decreased by the same amount. At the beginning, $d_s = q_s = 0$. Since a job is not activated while the previous one is active, the CBS algorithm can be formally defined as follows:

1. When a job $\tau_{i,j}$ arrives, if $q_s \geq (d_s - r_{i,j})U_s$, it is assigned a server deadline $d_s = r_{i,j} + P_s$ and q_s is recharged at the maximum value Q_s, otherwise the job is served with the current deadline using the current budget.
2. When $q_s = 0$, the server budget is recharged at the maximum value Q_s and the server deadline is postponed at $d_s = d_s + P_s$. Note that there are no finite intervals of time in which the budget is equal to zero.

The CBS version presented above is meant for handling soft reservations. In fact, when the budget is exhausted, it is always replenished at its full value and the server deadline is postponed (i.e., the server is always active). As a consequence, a served task can execute more than Q_s in each period P_s, if there are no other tasks in the system. However, the CBS can be easily modified

to enforce hard reservations just by postponing the budget replenishment to the server deadline.

3.2. Schedulability Analysis

In a system consisting of n reservations, each implemented by a periodic server with bandwidth U_i, the feasibility of the schedule can be guaranteed as shown in Section 2. In particular, if reservations are scheduled by RM, the schedulability of the system can be verified by Equation (2) or Equation (4); if they are scheduled by EDF, schedulability can be verified by Equation (6).

The feasibility analysis of a real-time task within a reservation is more complex and requires the precise knowledge of how time is made available by the server. Although a reservation is typically implemented using a periodic server characterized by a budget Q_s and a period P_s, there are cases in which temporal isolation can be achieved by executing tasks in a static partition of disjoint time slots.

To characterize a reservation independently on the specific implementation, Mok et al. (2001) introduced the concept of *bounded delay partition* that describes a reservation R_k by two parameters: a bandwidth α_k and a delay Δ_k. The bandwidth α_k measures the fraction of resource that is assigned to the served tasks, whereas the delay Δ_k represents the longest interval of time in which the resource is not available. In general, the minimum service provided by a resource can be precisely described by its *supply function* (Lipari, 2003; Shin, 2003), representing the minimum amount of processing time the resource can provide in a given time interval.

Definition 1: *Given a reservation, the* supply function $Z_k(t)$ *is the minimum amount of time provided by the reservation in every time interval of length $t \geq 0$.*

In the particular case in which a reservation is implemented by a periodic server with unspecified priority that allocates a budget Q_k every period P_k, then the supply function is the one illustrated in Figure 3, where

$$\begin{cases} \alpha_k = Q_k / P_k \\ \Delta_k = 2(P_k - Q_k). \end{cases} \qquad (9)$$

Once the bandwidth and the delay are computed, the supply function of a resource reservation can be lower bounded by the following *supply bound function*:

$$sbf_k(t) \overset{def}{=} \max \left\{ 0, \alpha_k(t - \Delta_k) \right\}. \qquad (10)$$

The supply bound function provides a nice abstraction for modeling a processor reservation R_k, because it is independent of the specific implementation and it allows characterizing the resource availability by only two parameters: the bandwidth α_k, which represents the fraction of the allocated resource, and the delay Δ_k, which represents the worst-case delay for using the resource. Figure 4 presents an alternative view of a processor consisting of two reservations dedicated to two tasks, τ_1 and τ_2.

The (α_k, Δ_k) parameters of each reservation can be computed off-line to satisfy the computational demand of the served tasks, as presented by Buttazzo, Bini, and Wu (2011b).

It is worth observing that reservations with smaller delays are able to serve tasks with shorter deadlines, providing better responsiveness. However, small delays can only be achieved with servers with a small period, which introduce more runtime overhead due to preemptions. If σ is the runtime overhead due to a context switch (subtracted from the budget every period), then the effective bandwidth of reservation R_k is

$$\alpha_k^{eff} = \frac{Q_h - \sigma}{P_k} = \alpha_k \left(1 - \frac{\sigma}{Q_k} \right).$$

Expressing Q_k and P_k as a function of α_k and Δ_k we have

$$Q_k = \frac{\alpha_k \Delta_k}{2(1 - \alpha_k)}$$

$$P_k = \frac{\Delta_k}{2(1 - \alpha_k)}$$

Hence,

$$\alpha_k^{eff} = \alpha_k + \frac{2\sigma(1 - \alpha_k)}{\Delta_k}. \qquad (11)$$

Within a reservation, the schedulability analysis of a task set under fixed priorities can be performed through the following Theorem (Bini, et al., 2009):

Theorem (Bini et al., 2009): *A set of preemptive periodic tasks with relative deadlines less than or equal to periods can be scheduled by a fixed priority algorithm, under a reservation characterized by a supply function $Z_k(t)$, if and only if*

$$\forall\, i = 1, ..., n \,\exists\, t \in (0, D_i]: W_i(t) \leq Z_k(t). \qquad (12)$$

where $W_i(t)$ represents the Level-i workload, computed as follows:

Figure 3. A reservation implemented by a periodic server

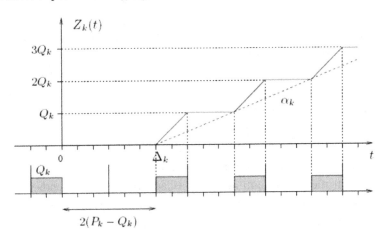

Figure 4. An example of two reservations characterized by given bandwidth and delay parameters

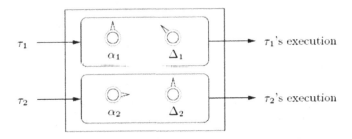

$$W_i(t) = C_i + \sum_{h:P_h > P_i} \left\lceil \frac{t}{T_h} \right\rceil C_h. \qquad (13)$$

$$dbf(t) \stackrel{def}{=} \sum_{i=1}^{n} \left\lfloor \frac{t + T_i - D_i}{T_i} \right\rfloor C_i. \qquad (15)$$

Similarly, the schedulability analysis of a task set under EDF can be performed using the following theorem (Bini, et al., 2009):

Theorem (Bini et al., 2009): *A set of preemptive periodic tasks with utilization U_p and relative deadlines less than or equal to periods can be scheduled by EDF, under a reservation characterized by a supply function $Z_k(t)$, if and only if $U_p < \alpha_k$ and*

$$\forall\, t > 0 \,\, dbf(t) \leq Z_k(t). \qquad (14)$$

where dbf(t) is the Demand Bound Function (Baruah, 1990) defined as

Note that, if $Z_k(t)$ is lower bounded by the supply bound function, the test becomes only sufficient.

4. ADAPTING TO DYNAMIC LOADS

Although resource reservation is essential for achieving predictability in the presence of tasks with variable execution times, the overall system performance becomes quite dependent on a correct bandwidth allocation. In fact, if the processor bandwidth reserved to a task is much less than its average computational demand, the task may slow down too much, degrading the system's performance. On the other hand, if the allocated bandwidth is much greater than the actual needs, the system will run with low efficiency, wasting the available resources.

Unfortunately, a precise off-line evaluation of the reservation parameters is not always possible for different reasons. From one hand, the estimation of the computational requirements of a task is data dependent and is affected by several architecture features, such as cache, prefetch mechanism, and device access policies. On the other hand, a task may enter different operational modes at runtime, so the amount of resource reserved for a mode may not be suitable in another mode. To cope with such a dynamic behavior, whenever the reserved bandwidth does not match the actual computational demand, the system should be able to adapt the reservation parameters to better satisfy the application needs. The adaptation policies proposed in the literature can be distinguished into three main categories:

- **Resources reclaiming:** This approach consists in recycling the amount of reserved bandwidth unused by some tasks to other more demanding tasks. Such an adaptation is performed at the kernel level and it is transparent to the application.
- **Local adaptation:** This approach consists in modifying the computational demand of the served task to better meet the available resource bandwidth. Such an adaptation is performed at the application level by the task experiencing a quality degradation.
- **Global adaptation:** This approach consists in modifying the reservation parameters to better satisfy the application demand, while ensuring the schedulability of the system. Such an adaptation is performed at the system level by a global resource manager that controls all reservation parameters.

4.1. Resource Reclaiming

A typical approach adopted to reclaim the bandwidth unused in a reservation makes use of a capacity sharing mechanism that allows a task to use the residual budget left in other reservations.

Capacity sharing algorithms have been developed both under fixed priority servers (Bernat, 2002, 2004) and dynamic priority servers (Caccamo, 2003). For example, the CASH algorithm (Caccamo, 2005) extends CBS to include a slack reclamation. When a server becomes idle with residual budget, the slack is inserted in a queue of spare budgets (CASH queue) ordered by server deadlines. Whenever a new server is scheduled for execution, it first uses any CASH budget whose deadline is less than or equal to its own.

The Bandwidth Inheritance (BWI) algorithm (Lamastra, 2001) applies the idea of priority inheritance to CPU resources in CBS, allowing a blocking low-priority process to steal resources from a blocked higher priority process. IRIS (Marzario, 2004) enhances CBS with fairer slack reclaiming, so slack is not reclaimed until all current jobs have been serviced and the processor is idle. BACKSLASH (Lin, 2005) is another algorithm that enhances the efficiency of the reclaiming mechanism under EDF.

All the mechanisms described above need to be implemented at a kernel level and are completely transparent to the application, which can be executed without any change in the code.

4.2. Local Adaptation

Local adaptation requires application tasks to monitor their performance and reduce their resource demand if a degradation is detected. Detecting the performance degradation typically requires some kernel probes to measure the progress of computation. For instance, in a video player the quality of display can be measured by the number of frames processed per second. When a quality degradation is detected, the task is responsible to reduce its computational demand to better meet the available amount of resource. Depending on the specific application, different actions can be taken:

- **Service adaptation:** This action consists of switching to another operational mode characterized by different computational demand. In this way, the utilization is reduced by decreasing the computation time C_i.

- **Job skipping:** This action consists of skipping some job of a periodic task. The skip is controlled by a factor S_i expressing the minimum number of jobs between two consecutive skips. In this way, the utilization is reduced by decreasing the skip factor S_i.

- **Period adaptation:** This action consists of varying the task period. In this way, the utilization is reduced by increasing the period T_i.

Figure 5 illustrates the typical feedback loop implemented by a task that applies a local adaptation policy. Depending on the specific application, each task may decide to apply a specific strategy (service adaptation, job skipping, or period adaptation) to modify its utilization. The three strategies are described in the following sections.

4.2.1. Service Adaptation

To apply this approach a task must be specifically designed to provide the required service according to different algorithms, each having different computation time and quality. For instance, a video player could switch to a mode with lower resolution, whereas an approximate computation algorithm could decide to stop earlier and provide a result with a reduced precision.

If task τ_i wants to decrease its utilization by ΔU_i, its new computation time C_i^{new} should be such that

$$\frac{C_i^{new}}{T_i} = U_i - \Delta U_i$$

that is,

$$C_i^{new} = C_i - T_i \Delta U_i.$$

This means that the new mode selected by the task should have a computation time no greater than C_i^{new}.

The concept of imprecise and approximate computation has emerged as a new approach to increasing flexibility in dynamic scheduling by trading computation accuracy with timing requirements. If the available processing time is not enough to produce high-quality results within the deadline, there could be enough time for producing approximate results with a lower quality. This method has been formalized by many authors (Liu, 1987; Shi, 1991; Liu, 1994; Nat, 1995) and specific techniques have been developed for designing programs that can produce partial results.

In this model, a task τ_i is decomposed into a *mandatory* subtask, with computation time M_i,

Figure 5. Feedback scheme adopted in a local adaptation strategy

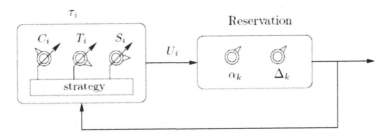

and an *optional* subtask, with computation time O_i. The mandatory subtask is the portion of the computation that must be done to produce a result of acceptable quality, whereas the optional subtask refines this result (Shi, 1989). Both subtasks have the same arrival time and the same deadline as the original task τ_i; however, the optional subtask becomes ready for execution when the mandatory part is completed. To guarantee a minimum level of performance, the mandatory part must be completed within its deadline, whereas the optional subtask can be left incomplete, if necessary, at the expense of the quality of the result produced by the task.

In systems that support imprecise computation, the *error* ε_i of a task τ_i is defined as the length of the optional computation discarded in the schedule. An error $\varepsilon_i > 0$ means that a portion of the optional part of τ_i has been discarded in the schedule at the expense of the quality of the result produced by task τ_i, but for the benefit of other tasks that can provide outputs with higher precision.

For a set of periodic tasks, the problem of deciding the best level of quality compatible with a given load condition can be solved by associating each optional part of a task a reward function $\rho_i(\sigma_i)$, which indicates the reward accrued by the task when it receives σ_i units of service beyond its mandatory portion. This problem has been addressed by Aydin et al. (2001), who presented an optimal algorithm that maximizes the weighted average of the rewards over the task set.

4.2.2. Job Skipping

Another way to reduce the computational load of a periodic task is to sporadically abort the execution of some job. This approach is suitable for real-time applications characterized by soft or firm deadlines, such as those typically found in multimedia systems, where skipping a video frame once in a while is better than processing it with a long delay. Sporadic skips can be tolerated also in some control applications, where the controlled system is characterized by a high inertia.

According to such a task model, originally proposed by Koren and Shasha (1995), each periodic task τ_i is characterized by an additional parameter S_i, expressing the minimum number of jobs between two consecutive skips (hence, $S_i \geq 2$). For example, $S_i = 5$ means that task τ_i can skip one instance every five. If $S_i = \infty$, then no skips are allowed and τ_i is equivalent to a hard periodic task. In this model, each job is denoted as *red* or *blue*: a red job must be executed within its deadline, whereas a blue job can be aborted at any time. To meet the constraint imposed by the skip parameter S_i, each scheduling algorithm must have the following characteristics: if a blue job is skipped, then the next $S_i - 1$ jobs must be red; if a blue job is completed successfully, the next job is also blue.

Koren and Shasha showed that the worst case for a periodic skippable task set occurs when all tasks are synchronously activated and the first $S_i - 1$ jobs of every task τ_i are red (*deeply-red condition*). This means that if a task set is schedulable under the deeply-red condition, it is also schedulable in any other situation.

A sufficient feasibility test for a set of tasks with skips can be derived using the Processor Demand Criterion (Bar, 1990) described in Section 2, under the deeply-red condition and assuming that in the worst case all blue jobs are aborted. In this worst-case scenario, the processor demand of τ_i due to the red jobs in an interval $[0, L]$ can be obtained as the difference between the demand of all the jobs and the demand of the blue jobs:

$$g_i^{skip}(0, L) = \left(\left\lfloor \frac{L}{T_i} \right\rfloor - \left\lfloor \frac{L}{T_i S_i} \right\rfloor \right) C_i. \qquad (16)$$

A necessary condition can be easily derived by observing that a schedule is certainly infeasible if the utilization factor due to the red jobs is greater than one. That is, if

$$\sum_{i=1}^{n} \frac{C_i(S_i - 1)}{T_i S_i} > 1. \qquad (17)$$

Note that, if a task is managed by a periodic reservation server with parameters $Q_s = (S_i - 1)C_i$ and $P_s = S_i T_i$, the bandwidth required by the task is

$$U_s = \frac{S_i - 1}{S_i} U_i = U_i - \frac{U_i}{S_i}$$

meaning that a skip factor S_i produces a bandwidth saving $\Delta U_i = U_i / S_i$.

4.2.3. Period Adaptation

The computational demand of a task τ_i can also be reduced by decreasing its activation frequency, that is, by increasing its period T_i. In particular, if the period is increased by ΔT_i, the task utilization reduces by ΔU_i such that

$$\frac{C_i}{T_i + \Delta T_i} = U_i - \Delta U_i.$$

Hence, to reduce the utilization of ΔU_i, the task period has to be increased by

$$\Delta T_i = T_i \frac{\Delta U_i}{U_i - \Delta U_i}.$$

This solution can be applied in several real-time applications where timing constraints are not rigid, but depend on the system state. For example, in a flight control system, the sampling rate of the altimeters is a function of the current altitude of the aircraft: the lower the altitude, the higher the sampling frequency. A similar need arises in mobile robots operating in unknown environments, where trajectories are planned based on the current sensory information. If a robot is equipped with proximity sensors, to maintain a desired perfor-

mance, the acquisition rate of the sensors must increase whenever the robot is approaching an obstacle. Finally, in most control applications, the control performance is a function of the sampling rate \cite (But, 2007b), thus task utilization can be traded with control performance.

4.3. Global Adaptation

Global adaptation is performed at system level by a global resource manager, which can modify reservation parameters to better satisfy the application demand, while ensuring the schedulability of the system. Reservation parameters can be changed upon specific requests coming from the served tasks, or directly by the manager itself, which can periodically monitor the performance of the application and reallocate the resources to better meet the actual computational demand. Figure 6 shows a typical example of a global adaptation scheme, where a resource manager receives the actual resource consumption as a feedback from the kernel and tunes the reservation parameters to match the actual demand.

Providing the actual resource consumption of each task τ_i requires the operating system to have a specific monitoring mechanism to keep track of the actual execution time $e_{i,k}$ of each task instance $\tau_{i,k}$. Given these measurements, the actual computation time $\hat{C}_i$ of a task τ_i can be estimated in a moving window containing a history of the last M measurements $e_{i,k}, e_{i,k-1}, \dots e_{i,k-M+1}$, where k denotes the current job index. This value can be used to evaluate the bandwidth currently needed by the task, as

$$\hat{U}_i = \hat{C}_i / T_i.$$

Then, $\hat{U}_i$ can be used as a reference value in a feedback loop to adapt the reservation bandwidth allocated to the task according to the actual needs. Note that, whenever a reservation is adapted online, the resource manager must also guarantee

Figure 6. An example of two adaptive reservations controlled by a global resource manager

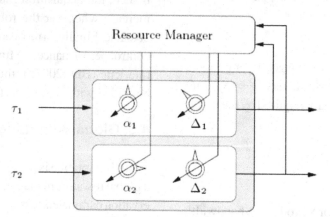

the schedulability of each reservation by ensuring that the overall allocated bandwidth does not exceed the maximum utilization bound of the adopted scheduling algorithm. If the sum of all reservation bandwidths exceeds the maximum utilization bound, then the resource manager must apply a compression algorithm to bring the overall allocated bandwidth below such a bound.

4.3.1. Elastic Compression

A simple ad efficient method for compressing a set of utilizations up to a given desired value has been proposed by Buttazzo et al. (1998), and later extended by the same authors to deal with shared resources (Buttazzo, 2002). The idea is to consider each task as flexible as a spring with a given elasticity, whose utilization can be modified by changing the period within a specified range. Each task is characterized by four parameters: a computation time C_i, a minimum period T_i^{min}, a maximum period T_i^{max}, and an elastic coefficient $E_i \geq 0$, which specifies the flexibility of the task to vary its utilization for adapting the system to a new feasible rate configuration. The greater E_i, the more elastic the task.

In the following, T_i denotes the actual period of task τ_i, which is constrained to be in the range $[T_i^{min}, T_i^{max}]$. Any task can vary its period according to its

needs within the specified range. Any variation, however, is subject to an *elastic guarantee* and is accepted only if there is a feasible schedule in which all the other periods are within their range.

Under the elastic model, given a set of n periodic tasks with utilization $U > 1$, the objective of the elastic guarantee is to compress task utilizations to reach a new desired utilization $U_d \leq 1$ such that all the periods are within their ranges. The following definitions are also used:

$$U_i^{min} = C_i / T_i^{max};$$

$$U_{min} = \sum_{i=1}^{n} U_i^{min};$$

$$U_i^{max} = C_i / T_i^{min};$$

$$U_{max} = \sum_{i=1}^{n} U_i^{max}.$$

Note that, if $U_{min} \leq U_d$, a feasible solution can always be found; hence, this condition has to be verified a priori.

In the special case in which $U_i^{min} = 0$ (that is, $T_i^{max} = \infty$) for all tasks, the compressed task utilizations can be derived by solving a set of n spring linear equations, under the constraint that $\sum_{i=1}^{n} U_i = U_d$. The resulting compressed values are:

$$\forall i \quad U_i = U_i^{\max} - (U_{\max} - U_d)\frac{E_i}{E_s}. \qquad (18)$$

where $E_s = \sum_{i=1}^{n} E_i$.

If each task has a finite maximum period, so that its utilization cannot be less than a minimum value U_i^{min}, the problem of finding the values U_i requires an iterative solution. In fact, if during compression one or more periods reach their maximum value, the additional compression can only vary the remaining tasks. Thus, at each instant, the task set Γ can be divided into two subsets: a set Γ_f of fixed tasks having maximum period, and a set Γ_v of variable tasks that can still be compressed. If U_v^{max} is the sum of the maximum utilizations of tasks in Γ_v, and U_f is the total utilization factor of tasks in Γ_f, then, to achieve a desired utilization $U_d \le 1$, each task has to be compressed up to the following utilization:

$$\forall \tau_i \in \Gamma_v \quad U_i = U_i^{\max} - (U_v^{\max} - U_d + U_f)\frac{E_i}{E_v} \quad (19)$$

where

$$U_v^{\max} = \sum_{\tau_i \in \Gamma_v} U_i^{\max} \qquad (20)$$

$$U_f = \sum_{\tau_i \in \Gamma_f} U_i^{\min} \qquad (21)$$

$$E_v = \sum_{\tau_i \in \Gamma_v} E_i. \qquad (22)$$

If there are tasks for which $U_i < U_i^{min}$, then the period of those tasks has to be fixed at its maximum value T_i^{max} (so that $U_i = U_i^{min}$), sets Γ_f and Γ_v must be updated (hence, U_f and E_v recomputed), and Equation (19) applied again to the tasks in Γ_v. If there is a feasible solution, that is, if $U_{min} \le U_d$, the iterative process ends when each value

U_i computed by Equation (19) is greater than or equal to its corresponding minimum U_i^{min}.

4.3.2. Examples of Adaptive Real-Time Systems

Several adaptive reservation schemes have been proposed in the research literature. Abeni and Buttazzo (1999) originally proposed a feedback scheduling mechanism, implemented in the HARTIK real-time kernel (Lam, 1997), for tuning reservations for multimedia activities. Another feedback scheme has been proposed by Abeni et al. (2005), who implemented adaptive reservations in the Linux kernel to manage the quality of service of time sensitive applications.

An adaptive resource reservation mechanism has been implemented in the Linux kernel (Fag, 2009) to efficiently handle concurrent multimedia applications on a multiprocessor platform (Bin, 2011). Here, a resource manager assigns a fraction of the platform capacity to each application, which runs as if it were executing alone on a less-performing virtual platform, independently of the other applications' behavior. In this sense, each application's temporal behavior is not affected by the others and can be analyzed in isolation.

The elastic compression algorithm has been effectively used in a global feedback scheme to automatically adapt task utilization to fully utilize the processor when worst-case computation times are not available off-line, but can be estimated online by a monitoring mechanism (But, 2002b). Elastic scheduling has been also used in combination with dynamic voltage scaling to reduce energy consumption in processors with discrete voltage/frequency modes (Mar, 2007).

Finally, note that local and global adaptation strategies can also be integrated so that, while a global resource manager controls the reservation bandwidths, each task can vary its computational requirements if the amount of reserved resources is not sufficient to accomplish the goal within a specified service level. A hierarchical scheme integrating local and global adaptation has been presented by Abeni and Buttazzo (2001). The inner feedback loop controls the reserved bandwidth, while the outer loop controls the computational demand requested by the application. To avoid instability, the local adaptation is performed at a slower rate than the global one, so that the task adapts only when the global control is not effective.

CONCLUSION AND PERSPECTIVES

The current trend in embedded systems shows that hardware is evolving more rapidly than software, causing a strong need for methodologies able to achieve portability, modularity, and scalability of performance. Surprisingly, such a growth in hardware complexity was not balanced by a corresponding evolution of the control software for a predictable an efficient management of the computational resources. As a consequence, most of today's embedded systems are still implemented on top of fixed priority kernels or by adopting ad hoc techniques to exploit new hardware features.

This chapter presented some new software methodologies proposed within the real-time research community to simultaneously address multiple objectives, such as predictability, efficiency, modularity, portability, and adaptability.

Predictability and efficiency is achieved through the use of proper real-time scheduling algorithms (like Rate Monotonic and Earliest Deadline First), which optimally utilize the processor and can be efficiently analyzed to estimate the worst-case response time of each task.

Modularity and portability is obtained through the use of resource reservation mechanisms, which allow implementing a temporal protection environment, where a task can be executed in isolation as it were executing alone on a dedicated virtual processor with reduced bandwidth. In this way, a task can be analyzed independently of the behavior of the other tasks, but only as a function of its computational requirements and the allocated bandwidth.

Finally, adaptability is achieved through the use of proper feedback schemes that can be implemented both at the application level (local adaptation) or at the system level (global adaptation). Local adaptation is aimed at reducing the computational requirement of a task through the most appropriate strategy, for instance by switching to another operation mode, by decreasing the activation rate, or by sporadically skipping some of its instances. Global adaptation is aimed at adjusting the reservation parameters to better match the actual task requirements.

All the presented methodologies have been successfully implemented and tested in a research environment by several authors on different operating systems and platforms. However, the real challenge for the future is to transfer such techniques to the industry to make next generation embedded systems more predictable and efficient, as well as portable to different computing platforms, and adaptable to dynamic load conditions. An effective way to achieve such a transition is through an intensive dissemination of research results in high-level courses, and through the development of specific tools that facilitate system designers to use the new methodologies in real-world applications.

REFERENCES

Abeni, L., & Buttazzo, G. C. (1998). Integrating multimedia applications in hard real-time systems. In *Proceedings of the 19th IEEE Real-Time Systems Symposium (RTSS'98)*. Madrid, Spain: IEEE.

Abeni, L., & Buttazzo, G. C. (1999). Adaptive bandwidth reservation for multimedia computing. In *Proceedings of the 6th IEEE International Conference on Real-Time Computing Systems and Applications* (pp. 70–77). Hong Kong, China: IEEE.

Abeni, L., & Buttazzo, G. C. (2001). Hierarchical qos management for time sensitive applications. In *Proceedings of the IEEE Real-Time Technology and Applications Symposium*. Taipei, Taiwan: IEEE.

Abeni, L., & Buttazzo, G. C. (2004). Resource reservations in dynamic real-time systems. *Real-Time Systems, 27*(2), 123–165. doi:10.1023/B:TIME.0000027934.77900.22.

Abeni, L., Cucinotta, T., Lipari, G., Marzario, L., & Palopoli, L. (2005). QoS management through adaptive reservations. *Real-Time Systems, 29*(2-3), 131–155. doi:10.1007/s11241-005-6882-0.

Audsley, N., Burns, A., Richardson, M., Tindell, K., & Wellings, A. (1993). Applying new scheduling theory to static priority pre-emptive scheduling. *Software Engineering Journal, 8*(5), 284–292. doi:10.1049/sej.1993.0034.

Aydin, H., Melhem, R., Mossé, D., & Alvarez, P. M. (2001). Optimal reward-based scheduling for periodic real-time tasks. *IEEE Transactions on Computers, 50*(2), 111–130. doi:10.1109/12.908988.

Baker, T. P. (1991). Stack-based scheduling of realtime processes. *Journal of Real-Time Systems, 3*(1), 67–99. doi:10.1007/BF00365393.

Baruah, S. (2005). The limited-preemption uniprocessor scheduling of sporadic task systems. In *Proceedings of the 17th Euromicro Conference on Real-Time Systems* (pp. 137–144). Palma de Mallorca, Spain: Euromicro.

Baruah, S., Rosier, L., & Howell, R. (1990). Algorithms and complexity concerning the preemptive scheduling of periodic, real-time tasks on one processor. *Journal of Real-Time Systems, 2*(4), 301–324. doi:10.1007/BF01995675.

Bernat, G., Broster, I., & Burns, A. (2004). Rewriting history to exploit gain time. In *Proceedings of the 25th IEEE Real-Time Systems Symposium*. Lisbon, Portugal: IEEE.

Bernat, G., & Burns, A. (2002). Multiple servers and capacity sharing for implementing flexible scheduling. *Real-Time Systems, 22*(1-2), 49–75. doi:10.1023/A:1013481420080.

Bini, E., Buttazzo, G. C., & Buttazzo, G. M. (2003). Rate monotonic scheduling: The hyperbolic bound. *IEEE Transactions on Computers, 52*(7), 933–942. doi:10.1109/TC.2003.1214341.

Bini, E., Buttazzo, G. C., Eker, J., Schorr, S., Guerra, R., & Fohler, G. et al. (2011). Resource management on multicore systems: The ACTORS approach. *IEEE Micro, 31*(3), 72–81. doi:10.1109/MM.2011.1.

Bini, E., Buttazzo, G. C., & Lipari, G. (2009). Minimizing CPU energy in real-time systems with discrete speed management. *ACM Transactions on Embedded Computing Systems, 8*(4), 31:1–31:23.

Burns, A. (1994). Preemptive priority based scheduling: An appropriate engineering approach. In Advances in Real-Time Systems (pp. 225–248).

Buttazzo, G. C. (2005). Rate monotonic vs. EDF: Judgment day. *Real-Time Systems, 29*(1), 5–26. doi:10.1023/B:TIME.0000048932.30002.d9.

Buttazzo, G. C., & Abeni, L. (2002). Adaptive workload management through elastic scheduling. *Real-Time Systems, 23*(1), 7–24. doi:10.1023/A:1015342318358.

Buttazzo, G. C., Abeni, L., & Lipari, G. (1998). Elastic task model for adaptive rate control. In *Proceedings of the IEEE Real Time System Symposium*. Madrid, Spain: IEEE.

Buttazzo, G. C., Bertogna, M., & Yao, G. (2012). Limited preemptive scheduling for real-time systems: A survey. *IEEE Transitions on Industrial Informatics*.

Buttazzo, G. C., Bini, E., & Wu, Y. (2011). Partitioning parallel applications on multiprocessor reservations. *IEEE Transitions on Industrial Informatics, 7*(2), 302–315. doi:10.1109/TII.2011.2123902.

Buttazzo, G. C., & Cervin, A. (2007). Comparative assessment and evaluation of jitter control methods. In *Proceedings of the 15th International Conference on Real-Time and Network Systems* (pp. 137–144). Nancy, France: IEEE.

Buttazzo, G. C., Lipari, G., Caccamo, M., & Abeni, L. (2002). Elastic scheduling for flexible workload management. *IEEE Transactions on Computers, 51*(3), 289–302. doi:10.1109/12.990127.

Buttazzo, G. C., Marti, P., & Velasco, M. (2007). Quality-of-control management in overloaded real-time systems. *IEEE Transactions on Computers, 56*(2), 253–266. doi:10.1109/TC.2007.34.

Caccamo, M., Buttazzo, G. C., & Sha, L. (2000). Capacity sharing for overrun control. In *Proceedings of the IEEE Real-Time Systems Symposium.* Orlando, FL: IEEE.

Caccamo, M., Buttazzo, G. C., & Thomas, D. (2005). Efficient reclaiming in reservation-based real-time systems with variable execution times. *IEEE Transactions on Computers, 54*(2), 198–213. doi:10.1109/TC.2005.25.

Dertouzos, M. (1974). Control robotics: The procedural control of physical processes. *Information Processing, 74*, 807–813.

Faggioli, D., Trimarchi, M., Checconi, F., & Scordino, C. (2009). An EDF scheduling class for the linux kernel. In *Proceedings of the 11th Real-Time Linux Workshop* (pp. 197–204). Dresden, Germany: IEEE.

Koren, G., & Shasha, D. (1995). Skip-over: Algorithms and complexity for overloaded systems that allow skips. In *Proceedings of the IEEE Real-Time Systems Symposium.* Pisa, Italy: IEEE.

Lamastra, G., Lipari, G., & Abeni, L. (2001). A bandwidth inheritance algorithm for real-time task synchronization in open systems. In *IEEE Proceedings of the 22nd Real-Time Systems Symposium.* London, UK: IEEE.

Lamastra, G., Lipari, G., Buttazzo, G. C., Casile, A., & Conticelli, F. (1997). HARTIK 3.0: A portable system for developing real-time applications. In *Proceedings of the 4th IEEE International Conference on Real-Time Computing Systems and Applications* (pp. 43–50). Taipei, Taiwan: IEEE.

Leung, J., & Whitehead, J. (1982). On the complexity of fixed-priority scheduling of periodic real-time tasks. *Performance Evaluation, 2*(4), 237–250. doi:10.1016/0166-5316(82)90024-4.

Lin, C., & Brandt, S. A. (2005). Improving soft real-time performance through better slack management. In *Proceedings of the IEEE Real-Time Systems Symposium.* Miami, FL: IEEE.

Lipari, G., & Bini, E. (2003). Resource partitioning among real-time applications. In *Proceedings of the 15th Euromicro Conference on Real-Time Systems* (pp. 151–158). Porto, Portugal: Euromicro.

Liu, C., & Layland, J. (1973). Scheduling algorithms for multiprogramming in a hard-real-time environment. *Journal of the Association for Computing Machinery, 20*(1), 46–61. doi:10.1145/321738.321743.

Liu, J., Lin, K., & Natarajan, S. (1987). Scheduling real-time, periodic jobs using imprecise results. In *Proceedings of the IEEE Real-Time System Symposium* (pp. 210-217). San Jose, CA: IEEE.

Liu, J., Shih, W. K., Lin, K. J., Bettati, R., & Chung, J. Y. (1994). Imprecise computations. *Proceedings of the IEEE, 82*(1), 83–94. doi:10.1109/5.259428.

Marinoni, M., & Buttazzo, G. C. (2007). Elastic DVS management in processors with discrete voltage/frequency modes. *IEEE Transactions on Industrial Informatics, 3*(1), 51–62. doi:10.1109/TII.2006.890494.

Marzario, L., Lipari, G., Balbastre, P., & Crespo, A. (2004). IRIS: A new reclaiming algorithm for server-based real-time systems. In *Proceedings of the IEEE Real-Time and Embedded Technology and Applications Symposium*. Toronto, Canada: IEEE.

Mercer, C. W., Savage, S., & Tokuda, H. (1994). Processor capacity reserves for multimedia operating systems. In *Proceedings of IEEE International Conference on Multimedia Computing and Systems*. Boston, MA: IEEE.

Mok, A. K., Feng, X., & Chen, D. (2001). Resource partition for real-time systems. In *Proceedings of the 7th IEEE Real-Time Technology and Applications Symposium* (pp. 75–84). Taipei, Taiwan: IEEE.

Natarajan, S. (Ed.). (1995). *Imprecise and approximate computation*. Dordrecht, The Netherlands: Kluwer Academic Publishers. doi:10.1007/b102247.

Shih, W., Liu, W., & Chung, J. (1991). Algorithms for scheduling imprecise computations with timing constraints. *SIAM Journal on Computing, 20*(3), 537–552. doi:10.1137/0220035.

Shih, W., Liu, W., Chung, J., & Gillies, D. (1989). Scheduling tasks with ready times and deadlines to minimize average error. *Operating System Review, 23*(3), 14–28. doi:10.1145/71021.71022.

Shin, I., & Lee, I. (2003). Periodic resource model for compositional real-time guarantees. In *Proceedings of the 24th Real-Time Systems Symposium* (pp. 2–13). Cancun, Mexico: IEEE.

Wang, Y., & Saksena, M. (1999). Scheduling fixed priority tasks with preemption threshold. In *Proceedings of the 6th IEEE International Conference on Real-Time Computing Systems and Applications* (pp. 328–335). Hong Kong, China: IEEE.

Chapter 9
Merging and Splitting Petri Net Models within Distributed Embedded Controller Design

Luis Gomes
Universidade Nova de Lisboa, Portugal
& UNINOVA-CTS, Portugal

João Paulo Barros
Instituto Politécnico de Beja, Portugal
& UNINOVA-CTS, Portugal

Anikó Costa
Universidade Nova de Lisboa, Portugal
& UNINOVA-CTS, Portugal

Filipe Moutinho
Universidade Nova de Lisboa, Portugal
& UNINOVA-CTS, Portugal

Fernando Pereira
Instituto Politécnico de Lisboa, Portugal
& UNINOVA-CTS, Portugal

ABSTRACT

Design of distributed embedded controllers can benefit from the adoption of a model-based development attitude, where Petri nets modeling can provide support for a comprehensive specification and documentation of the system together with verification capabilities and automatic deployment into implementation platforms. This chapter presents a Petri nets-based development flow based on composition and decomposition of Petri net models, using Input-Output Place-Transition Petri nets (IOPT nets) as the underlying formalism, allowing reusability of models in new situations through a net addition operation, as well as partitioning of the model into components using a net splitting operation. Distributed embedded controllers are addressed adding the concept of time domains to IOPT nets. Finally, a tool chain framework is presented supporting the whole development process, from specification to implementation, including property verification, simulation, and automatic code generation for deployment into implementation platforms (considering hardware-based implementation and VHDL coding or software-oriented implementation and C coding).

DOI: 10.4018/978-1-4666-3922-5.ch009

1. INTRODUCTION

According to what is usually referred as Moore's law, stated in 1965, on-chip density (and resources) roughly doubles every 18 months. Unfortunately, this sustained increase of resources available at chip level has not been followed with identical increase of designer's productivity. The lack of methods and tools that adequately support designer's productivity led to what is normally called the *productivity gap*. Several attempts have been carried on by different communities, companies, and consortiums to provide designers with adequate methodologies and engineering tools to reduce this gap. Also, the increase on resources availability allows the development of more complex system, and as the complexity of the design increases, the lack of methods and tools to verify and to assure specific system's properties becomes more visible, leading to what is sometimes called the *verification gap*.

Having an adequate set of selected formalisms and computation models, complemented by a set of the "right" tools, are key aspects to fight against those *productivity and verification gaps*.

In this sense, along the last decades, the role of Model-Based Development has increased its importance within system design methodologies, as far as it can adequately support designer's needs to integrate the reusability of already available components in the development flow and the use of design automation tools. This should be amenable to support automatic code generation and deployment into implementation platforms and an easy mapping to new or updated platforms.

Complementing the referred concerns, as far as the complexity of the system increases, new challenges for distributed embedded controller design have arrived. These challenges have led to face the need to decompose the system into different components, which could be physically distributed, as well to consider the use of embedded system co-design techniques allowing the concurrent design of hardware and software parts for some components.

Overall, the balanced usage of the referred attitudes have been contributing for improving several metrics on distributed embedded controller design, namely cost-performance relation, time-to-market, system robustness, and power consumption, among others.

Figure 1 summarizes a model-based development flow for distributed embedded controllers, where composition and decomposition of models play a central role. The system model is obtained from the composition of partial models and can adequately support splitting into components to be deployed into implementation platforms, as different as System-on-Chip solutions (including or not network-on-chip communication support), networks of distributed industrial controllers (including multi-bus architectures), or solutions

Figure 1. From partial models to deployment into implementation platforms (adapted from Gomes & Costa, 2006)

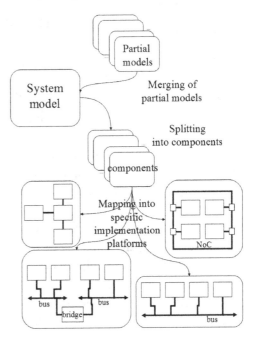

161

based on direct interconnection of the generated components.

Several modeling formalisms already proved their adequacy for embedded controllers' design and fully support model-based development flow strategies, as illustrated in Figure 1. State-based operational modeling formalisms are the most common selected formalisms to be used. Those formalisms include state diagrams, hierarchical and concurrent state diagrams, statecharts, and Petri nets.

Petri nets are in a very good position to be used as reference modeling formalism of the development flow, either when used directly by the designer to express the behavior of some part of the system, or as an underlying model to be used by engineering tools (whenever the entry modeling formalism is a different one, which will be translated into a behavioral equivalent Petri net model). In this chapter, a class of Petri nets is used as the central modeling formalism. This class is named Input-Output Place-Transition Petri nets (IOPT nets). It extends Place-Transition nets with signals and events dependencies, in order to properly model the physical dependencies of the control system with the environment.

A tool chain framework around IOPT nets is ready to be used and interoperate with other engineering development frameworks, thus contributing to shorten the scarcity of Petri nets tools currently available addressing distributed embedded controllers design. The tool chain framework covers all the development phases, from editing to automatic code generation, thus fighting the the scarcity of Petri net tools allowing code generation, which has been an obstacle to the effective use of Petri nets for this type of systems.

The chapter follows with section 2 devoted to co-relate and compare some aspects of the development methodology with other works from the literature, while section 3 gives a brief description of IOPT nets, covering syntax and semantics. Section 4 addresses the development flow of distributed embedded controllers, while section 5 is devoted to a brief presentation of the tool chain framework. Finally, section 6 identifies some current challenges and future development while the last section concludes.

2. BACKGROUND AND RELATED WORKS

To improve the development of systems using Petri nets, several operations on nets, such as merging and splitting methods have been proposed. Merging methods (also known as adding or composition methods) support bottom-up approaches to generate large models using a set of sub-models, which are easier to develop, or are available from previous projects (allowing its reuse). Splitting methods (also known as decomposition or partitioning methods) are used to improve model readability, analysis, verification, and implementation. Splitting methods can also be used to split parts of available models, which can then be merged with other sub-models, in a bottom-up approach.

The majority of the proposed merging methods use node fusion or token-based folding to merge sub-models (Gomes & Barros, 2005). The merging can be done in three ways: (1) only by place fusion (asynchronous composition), such as in (Jensen, 1992); (2) just by transition fusion (synchronous composition), such as in (Notomi & Murata, 1994); (3) or even using both fusions, such as in (Berthelot, 1987; Christensen & Petrucci, 2000). The token-based folding is done merging structural symmetries and obtaining more compact models, through high-level Petri net classes (Genrich, 1987; Jensen, 1992).

When considering non-autonomous Petri nets models, as those relevant for controller modeling, NCES (Net Condition/Event System) models were proposed (Rausch & Hanisch 1995). NCES can be seen as an extension of Petri nets that was motivated by the need for modular modeling and the support for the composition of modules.

Timed NCES (TNCES) have been used to model service oriented manufacturing systems, as in (Popescu, Soto, & Lastra 2012), as well as for IEC 61499 function blocks representation for distributed control and automation used within PLC (Programmable Logic Controller) application area (Vyatkin & Hanisch 1999) (Vyatkin 2006).

Although splitting methods are mostly used to improve models readability and to simplify its analysis and verification, they are also used to support systems implementation. Splitting methods are often based in the duplication of nodes, such as in (Berthelot, 1987), which is the inverse operation of node fusion. In several papers, such as in (Berthelot, 1987; Ciardo & Trivedi, 1991; Haddad, Ilie, & Klai, 2002), decomposition methods are used to analyze systems properties, avoiding the construction of the global state space. In (Mennicke, Oanea, & Wolf, 2009) a decomposition method is used to simplify the analysis and to obtain Web services from business processes modeled by Petri nets. Decomposition methods are proposed in several works, such as in (Vogler & Wollowski, 2002), to simplify the synthesis of asynchronous circuits. In (Nascimento, Maciel, Lima, Sant'ana, & Filho, 2004) Petri net models (specifying hardware processes) are partitioned into a set of sub-models to allow its implementation in a smaller FPGA. In (Bruno, Agarwal, Castella, & Pescarmona, 1995; Tacken, Rust, & Kleinjohann, 1999) two decomposition methods for high-level Petri nets were proposed to support the distributed implementation of systems. To support the implementation of a synchronous system as a Globally Asynchronous Locally Synchronous (GALS) system, a desynchronisation technique was proposed in (Dasgupta & Yakovlev, 2009).

Although Petri nets are widely used to develop embedded controllers, as in (Rust & Kleinjohann, 2001; Gomes & Fernandes 2010), there is a lack of net methods to properly support their distributed implementation. Having a distributed implementation may be a system requirement or a system optimization, allowing, for example, the reduction

of power consumption, electromagnetic interference, and development time and costs (through the reuse of previously developed components). In order to adequately support distributed implementations, a full specification of each component and the interaction between components are required.

In order to fill the mentioned lack a net splitting method was proposed in (Costa & Gomes, 2009), allowing the partitioning of Petri net models into a set of concurrent components, which was complemented by a Petri net extension proposal (Moutinho & Gomes, 2012) to support the distribution of concurrent components, providing the specification of distributed embedded controllers as GALS systems. The main advantages of this net splitting method compared with the remaining ones are its high flexibility and the suitable specification of the interaction between components. This method will be described in detail throughout this chapter.

3. IOPT NETS

3.1. Brief Overview of IOPT Nets

IOPT nets (Gomes et al., 2007) extend the class of place-transition Petri nets (e.g. Reisig, 1985) with constructs that allow the interaction between the net, which models the controller, and the environment. When constructing the net model, the environment is seen as a set of input and output events and signals that are associated, by net annotations, to some places and transitions. These non-autonomous annotations impose some restrictions upon the net model behavior: the net becomes non-autonomous, as in interpreted and synchronized nets of David and Alla, and Silva (David & Alla 1992; Silva, 1985).

The non-autonomous annotations allow the association of input signals and events to places and transitions. Output events can be associated to transitions and output signals to places. More specifically, output signals are made dependent on conditions associated to places. Moreover, it is also possible to define output signals activation associated with transition firing and output events. Input signals are associated to transitions as Boolean conditions. IOPT nets have a maximal step semantics, i.e., in each step all *ready* and *enabled* transitions will fire. Conflicts should be resolved by the use of priorities in transitions or a-priori by addition of specific arbiters. By *ready* we mean a transition allowed to fire by the non-autonomous annotations (signals and events). An *enabled* transition is allowed to fire in the usual semantics for autonomous nets where each input place must have enough tokens to be removed by the respective transition input arcs. Finally, IOPT nets also support test arcs and weights in normal and test arcs, a bound attribute for places, input events, explicit specification for the sets of conflicting transitions (conflict sets), and an explicit specification for sets of synchronous transitions (synchrony sets), slightly different to the high-level ones proposed in (Christensen & Hansen, 1992), as identified later in the chapter. These synchrony sets specify transition fusions.

Regarding test arcs, besides the usual advantage of allowing tests without token consumption (different from the use of one input and one symmetrical output arc), test arcs also allow the construction and usage of fair arbiters (e.g. Gomes, 2005).

The bound attribute for places is used to feed automatic code generation tools with relevant information for implementation. In fact, this attribute is filled with the maximum reachable marking only after verification of properties using state space generation. The objective is to minimize memory consumption in the generated code. Hence, this attribute has no influence in the model behavior.

We also allow the modeler to distinguish between two types for signal values: integer ranges or Boolean values. Next, the semantics for IOPT nets is presented.

3.2. Formal Semantics and Syntax

This section presents the syntax and semantics of IOPT nets as in (Gomes et al., 2007). To formally define IOPT nets, we start be characterizing the fundamental characteristics of the controller to be modeled. This is characterized through two main components:

1. Description of the physical interaction with the controlled system (the interface of the controller);
2. Description of the behavioral model, which is expressed through an IOPT model.

As already stated, from the net modeler point of view, the controller is a set of active input and output signals and events.

Definition 1: System interface (Gomes et al., 2007): The interface of the controlled system with an IOPT net is a tuple ICS = (IS, IE, OS, OE) satisfying the following requirements:

1. IS is a finite set of input signals.
2. IE is a finite set of input events.
3. OS is a finite set of output signals.
4. OE is a finite set of output events.
5. $IS \cap IE \cap OS \cap OE = \emptyset$.

At implementation level, a stub code allows input events to be seen as another kind of input signal. Next, we define a system state, as seen by the controller, i.e. the net.

Definition 2: System input state (Gomes et al., 2007): Given an interface ICS=(IS, IE, OS, OE) with a controlled system (Def. 1), a system input state is defined by a pair SIS=(ISB,IEB) satisfying the following requirements:

1. ISB is a finite set of input signal bindings: $ISB \subseteq IS \times \mathbf{N}_0$.

2. IEB is a finite set of input event bindings: IEB $\subseteq$ IE $\times$ **B**.

IOPT nets use an inscription language allowing the specification of algebraic expressions, variables, and functions for the specification of transition guards and conditions in output actions associated to places. Preferably, the inscription language should be a programming language targeted for code generation. Currently, C and VHDL are being used for software and hardware centric implementations, respectively. Next, we present the semantics of IOPT nets; the set of Boolean expressions is named BE and Var(E) returns the set of variables in a given expression E.

Definition 3: IOPT net (Gomes et al., 2007): Given a controller with an interface ICS=(IS, IE, OS, OE), an IOPT net is a tuple N=(P, T, A, TA, M, weight, weightTest, priority, isg, ie, oe, osc) satisfying the following requirements:

1. P is a finite set of places.
2. T is a finite set of transitions (disjoint from P).
3. A is a set of arcs, such that A $\subseteq$ ((P $\times$ T) $\cup$ (T $\times$ P)).
4. TA is a set of test arcs, such that TA $\subseteq$ (P $\times$ T).
5. M is the marking function: M: P $\rightarrow$ N_0.
6. **weight:** A $\rightarrow$ N_0.
7. **weightTest:** TA $\rightarrow$ N_0.
8. Priority is a partial function applying transitions to non-negative integers: priority: T $\rightarrow$ N_0.
9. isg, is an *input signal guard* partial function applying transitions to boolean expressions (where all variables are input signals): isg: T $\rightarrow$ BE, where $\forall$eb $\in$ isg(T), Var(eb) $\subseteq$ IS.
10. ie is an input event partial function applying transitions to input events: ee: T $\rightarrow$ IE.
11. oe is an output event partial function applying transitions to output events: ee: T $\rightarrow$ OE.

12. osc is an output signal condition function from places into sets of rules: osc: P $\rightarrow$ P(RULES), where RULES $\subseteq$ (BES $\times$ OS $\times$ N_0), BES $\subseteq$ BE and $\forall$e $\in$ BES, Var(e) $\subseteq$ ML with ML the set of identifiers for each place marking after a given execution step: each place marking has an associated identifier, which is used when executing the generated code.

Transitions have associated priorities, as well as input and output events. They can also have guards, which are functions of external input signals. Output signals can be changed by output events associated to transition firing, or at the end of each execution step, applying rules dependent on place markings.

The IOPT nets have maximal step semantics: whenever a transition is enabled, and the associated external conditions are true (the input event and the input signal guard) the transition is fired. The synchronized paradigm also implies that net evolution is only possible at specific instants in time named *tics* that are defined by an external global clock. An execution step is the period between two *tics*.

In the following definitions we use M(p) to denote the marking of place p in a net with marking M, and •t and •S to denote the input places of a given transition t or of a given set of transitions S, respectively: •t = {p | (p, t) $\in$ A}; •S = {p | (p, t) $\in$ A $\wedge$ t $\in$ S}, $\Diamond$t = {p | (p, t) $\in$ TA }; $\Diamond$S = {p | (p, t) $\in$ TA $\wedge$ t $\in$ S}.

Definition 4: Enable condition - (Gomes et al., 2007): Given a net N = (P, T, A, TA, M, weight, weightTest, priority, isg, ie, oe, osc) and a system interface ICS=(IS, IE, OS, OE) between N and a system input state SIS = (ISB, IEB), a transition t, with no structural conflicts, is enabled to fire, at a given *tic*, iff the following conditions are satisfied:

1. $\forall$p $\in$ •t, M(p) $\geq$ weight(p, t)

2. $\forall p \in \Diamond t, M(p) \geq weightTest(p, t)$
3. The transition t input signal guard evaluates to true for the given input signal binding: $isg(t)<ISB>$
4. $(ie(t), true) \in IEB$

Additionally, a transition t in a structural conflict with other transitions is only enabled if it has the maximum priority among the transitions in the respective conflict set CS:

$$\forall t' \in CS, t' \neq t \Rightarrow priority(t') \leq priority(t)$$

Definition 5: IOPT net step (Gomes et al., 2007): Let N = (P, T, A, TA, M, weight, weightTest, priority, isg, ie, oe, osc) be a net and ICS=(IS, IE, OS, OE) a system interface between N and a system with input state SIS = (ISB, IEB). Let also ET $\subseteq$ T be the set of all enabled transitions as defined in Def. 4. Then, Y is a step in N iff the following condition is satisfied:

$$Y \subseteq ET \wedge \forall t_1 \in (ET \setminus Y), \exists SY \subseteq Y, (\bullet t_1 \cap \bullet SY) \neq \emptyset \wedge \exists p \in (\bullet t_1 \cap \bullet SY),$$

$$(weight(p, t_1) + \Sigma_{t \in SY} weight(p, t) > M(p))$$

An IOPT net step is maximum. This means that no additional transition can be fired without becoming in effective conflict with some transition in the chosen maximal step. Finally, we define an IOPT net step occurrence and the respective successor marking.

Definition 6: Step occurrence and successor marking (from (Gomes et al., 2007)): Given a net N = (P, T, A, TA, M, weight, weightTest, priority, isg, ie, oe, osc) and a system interface ICS = (IS, IE, OS, OE) between N and a system with input state SIS = (ISB, IEB), the occurrence of a step Y in net N returns the net N' = (P, T, A, TA, M', weight, weightTest, priority, isg, ie, oe, osc), equal to

the net N except for the successor marking M' which is given by the following expression:

$$M' = \{ (p, m - \Sigma_{t \in Y \wedge (p, t) \in A} weight(p, t) + \Sigma_{t \in Y \wedge (t,p) \in A} weight(t,p)) \in (P \times \mathbf{N}_0) \mid (p,m) \in M \}$$

Figure 2 presents a simple IOPT net modeling the controller of a parking lot controller. The control of the entrance area is associated with the sub-model at the left hand side, having three places associated with entrance free (place entryP1), car present and waiting for gate opening (place entryP2), and car entering with gate opened (place entryP3). Initial marking reflects entrance free situation, while all transitions can have external events associated to impose evolution of the model synchronized with external inputs coming from the environment under control; places can also have actions to be active when the place is marked (namely to open the gate). A similar sub-model is used for exit area, and the central sub-model is responsible for modeling the number of free and occupied parking places. Transitions entryT2_parkT1 and parkT2_exitT2 model synchronization between those three areas.

This section ends with two definitions about the semantics of two newer extensions to nets, which were introduced to support decomposition of nets and distributed execution: synchronous sets (relying on Directed Synchronous Channels) and asynchronous sets (supported by Asynchronous Channels). In the following sections, those concepts will be explored.

Definition 7: Synchrony set. A synchrony set is a set of transitions. Each transition within a synchrony set has a label master (t_m) or a label slave (t_s). One synchrony set can contain several slave transitions t_s, but only one master transition t_m. Transitions within a synchrony set are linked through a directed synchronous channel, where the master transition initiates the communication when

Figure 2. A simple IOPT net example of a parking lot controller

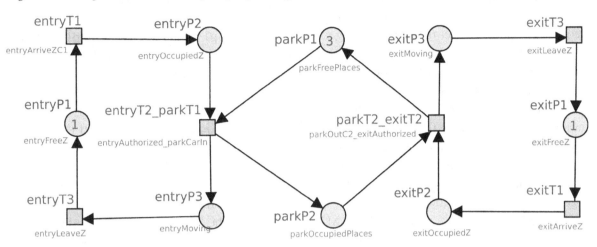

enabled and ready and all transitions of the synchrony set fire at the same execution step.

Definition 8: Time-Domains (TDs) and simple asynchronous-channels (ACs). The IOPT net class was extended in (Moutinho & Gomes, 2012) with time-domains (TDs) and simple asynchronous-channels (ACs) to allow the specification of GALS systems. An extended IOPT net is a tuple IOPT2GALS = (N, ACs, TDs), where ACs defined by ACs $\subseteq$ (T×T) is the set of all simple asynchronous-channels, and TDs is the set of all time-domains, which includes the time-domains of all nodes (places and transitions) and asynchronous-channels, such as TDs = TDs$_p$ $\cup$ TDs$_T$ $\cup$ TDs$_{AC}$, where TDs$_p$: P $\rightarrow$ **N**, TDs$_T$: T $\rightarrow$ **N**, TDs$_{AC}$: ACs $\rightarrow$ **N**. Each simple AC connects two transitions and is defined by AC $\subseteq$ (t$_m$ × t$_s$), where t$_m$ is a master transition, and t$_s$ is a slave transition, such as t$_m$ $\in$ T, t$_s$ $\in$ T, and t$_m$ $\neq$ t$_s$.

In a directed synchronous channel, each time the master transition fires, an event is sent to the slave transitions in the same execution step (zero time delay), whereas in an asynchronous-channel each time the master transition fires, an event is sent to the slave transition with a time delay, different

from zero, which depends of the associated TD. This way, asynchronous-channels are suitable to specify the interaction between components with distinct time domains and interconnected through communication channels. To obtain the specification of components with specific time-domains, their sub-models nodes are associated with specific TDs. This way, is possible to specify globally-asynchronous locally-synchronous systems.

3.3. Net Composition

IOPT nets, as low level Petri nets, have severe limitations when dealing with larger models. In fact, a few tens of nodes can already originate a huge readability and even a construction problem if one tries to avoid crossing lines. Modularity is also fundamental for reusability and maintainability. Consequently, numerous model composition techniques and languages introducing higher levels of abstraction have been proposed in literature (e.g. Gomes & Barros, 2005). For IOPT nets, the used composition approach, named *net addition*, is horizontal, hence non-hierarchical, and based upon place fusion and transition fusion. Yet, differently from other proposals, the information for node fusion is not embedded or even part of the composed modules. Instead, the node fusions, either place or transition fusions, are not specified in the composed models: for a given composition, the modeler specifies a set of models (acting as modules) to be composed and also, and separately, a set of node fusions between the nodes in those modules. It is important to note that each model is seen and can be used as a template for the generation of modules that are then composed. Due to the separation between model specification and the eventual composition specifications, any model instance (a module) can become part of a larger one, trough net addition.

For example, if we have models M1 and M2 and want to generate a new module (named Composed) through the composition of one instance of M1 with two instances of M2, we could use the following specification:

Composed:= (M1 + M2[1...2]) (M1.p1/M2[1]. p2 -> pa, M1.t1/M2[2].tx -> ta).

Basically, the specification lists the several modules (instances of models) and several node fusions. For each node fusion the nodes to be fused are listed, as well the resulting node. In the above example, the resulting module (Composed) is generated in two steps:

1. The three modules (M1, M2[1], and M[2]) are put side by side;
2. Place p1 in module M1 (M1.p1) is fused with place p2 in module M2[1] (M2[1].p2). The resulting node is node pa. This becomes part of module Composed. Similarly, transition t1 in module M1 (M1.t1) is fused with transition tx in module M2[2] (M2[2].tx). The resulting node is node ta that becomes part of module Composed.

Considering sub-models of Figure 3, where model on the left hand side models the parking area, and the model on the right hand side can model both entry and exit areas, it is possible to obtain the model of Figure 2 through the following composition specification:

Parking1in1out:= (entry + park + exit)

(entry.T2/park.T1 -> entryT2_parkT1, park.T2/ exit.T2 -> parkT2_exitT2)

Figure 3. Sub-models to be composed

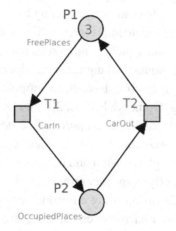
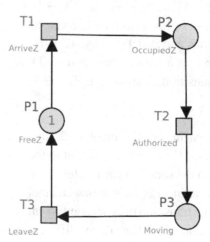

4. DISTRIBUTED EMBEDDED CONTROLLERS DEVELOPMENT FLOW

This section presents the different steps of the development flow for distributed embedded controllers, adopting a model-based development attitude where Petri nets play the role of central modeling formalism. It starts with a presentation of the underlying methodology and continues with presentation of strategies to decompose the model into sub-models using the net splitting operation. Latter, these are associated with components amenable to be deployed within a distributed platform.

4.1. Underlying Methodology

The different phases of the underlying overall system development methodology for distributed embedded controllers are presented in Figure 4. A model-based development attitude is adopted, where Petri nets are used as the central formalism allowing taking advantage of their characteristics. As proposed, Petri nets support the different phases of the system development, including the construction of the system model and the decomposition into sub-models, which will be associated with distributed components of the system, and where integration of hardware-software co-design techniques could be exercised. As a benefit from its strong execution semantics, it is possible to integrate design automation tools, allowing automatic code generation and deployment into implementation platforms.

The first step of the methodology is responsible for the construction of partial sub-models, which are obtained from the analysis of the system functionalities, initially expressed using UML (Unified Modeling Language) use cases. The designer needs to start defining the intended functionalities for the controller and use cases have proved to be an adequate form to express them. In this sense, capture of complex and/or primitive functionalities of the controller are

obtained constructing a set of use cases, allowing validation by users at the very beginning of the design process. Each use case will be (manually) translated into a model.

The set of operational modeling formalisms considered to support this task include several state-based behavioral notations, namely state diagrams, hierarchical and concurrent state diagrams, state charts, Petri nets, and sequence diagrams, as presented in Figure 5.

The common characteristic of those modeling formalisms is that they can be translated into a behaviorally equivalent Petri net model, which in turn could be composed with additional partial models obtained from the translation of the different use cases.

Composability of the obtained Petri net models can be adequately supported using the net addition operation (Barros & Gomes, 2003, 2004).

In this sense, the main result of the construction phase is a system model representing the behavior of the controller. This model can be used to support analysis of system properties, anticipating some

Figure 4. Development flow for distributed embedded systems

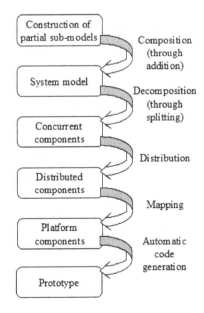

Figure 5. Construction of partial sub-models phase

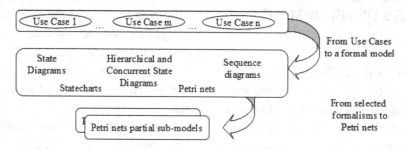

ill-formed properties and allow their correction (namely deadlock avoidance), or enforcing some desirable property (as maximum number of specific resources). Whenever the need for a change is identified, it should be propagated to previous steps, as adequate.

The following steps of the methodology address the decomposition of the model, allowing identification of a set of concurrent sub-models, which can be seen as concurrent components (which will be executed considering a synchronous semantics). After, we need to abandon the synchronous semantics paradigm and consider a set of distributed components having different time domains associated with their execution, which are associated with concurrent components produced in the previous step. As a final step before generation of code, the mapping of distributed components into specific platforms is produced.

The set of criteria to be used for the decomposition operation is highly dependent on the specific application, and it should come as no surprise to have some degree of matching between the concurrent components we get after decomposition and (some of) the sub-models initially obtained from each use case analysis and translation. Anyway, the process of model composition and further splitting into components will automatically generate the communication mechanisms among components, necessary to obtain systems' functionalities that were not present when considering initial partial sub-models.

When considering the mapping phase, specific decisions related with the support for com-

munication mechanisms among components need to be adopted. The list of solutions include point-to-point connections (direct connection or asynchronous connection considering different time domains for sender and receiver, leading to Globally-Asynchronous-Locally-Synchronous [GALS] systems), as well as support from dedicated networks (as Network-on-Chip [NoC], industrial automation or building automation networks), or even general-purpose networks (as those based on TCP-IP protocol). Independently of the chosen solution, the communication infrastructure among components will lead to the addition of some specific components into the final solution, while keeping communication and computation separated in different components, as usual for good practice.

Considering final deployment into implementation distributed platform, each of these platform components (generated from distributed components sub-models with the addition of communication components) will be used to feed automatic code generation processes for each of the distributed controllers' platforms.

For this automatic code generation phase, several specific tools can be considered allowing generation of VHDL code for hardware-based implementation, as well C/C++ code (or other type of specific programming language) for software-centered implementations. At this point, hardware-software co-design techniques can be used to optimize final implementation taking into account specific metrics, namely performance, power consumption, cost, and so on. If at this point of the development, some changes/corrections are identified to support specific improvements, returning to a previous phase of the development flow can be considered.

It is important to note that at the different phases of the methodology referred in Figure 4, properties' verification need to be performed in order to identify ill-behaviors or to enforce specific behavioral features. Again, if changes/corrections need to be introduced, returning to a previous phase of the development flow can be adequate or necessary to fix the problem.

As far as non-autonomous Petri nets models are considered, to accommodate dependencies on external signals and events, main verification technique need to rely on the construction of the state space associated with the system model, as the system model needs to accommodate sub-models for the controller parts, as well as sub-models for the communication infrastructure.

4.2. From Global Model to Concurrent Components: Splitting the Model

Having distributed execution in mind is imperative to decompose the global system model into several sub-models. It is common to find several proposals for model decomposition, where the communication between the sub-models is modeled through places.

Taking advantages of the IOPT Petri net class, which was defined having embedded system modeling in mind and where characteristics such as events and external signal modeling are included, a net decomposition method was proposed, named *net splitting*. There, the communication between sub-models is modeled through a set of transitions. The communication transitions belong to a directed communication channel. Each channel can contain several transitions that belong to different sub-models. One of those transitions is named *master* transition. It initiates the communication by generating an output event. All

the other transitions are named *slave* transition. They can read the generated output event as an associated input event.

The *net splitting* operation is based on the definition of a valid cutting set and three cutting rules. Those rules define how the graph structure of a Petri net is modified. In this sense, let us consider the graph of a Petri net $N = \{P, T, F\}$ and the cutting set $CTS = \{P_{CTS}, T_{CTS}\}$, where $P_{CTS} \subset P$ and $T_{CTS} \subset T$. Splitting the net N by CTS will result in a set of disconnected subnets N_i: $N:l:CTS = \cup_{i=1}^{n} N_i$.

Definition 9: Valid Cutting Set CTS: Is a set of nodes satisfying the following characteristics:

- There are no arc between any two nodes of the cutting set: if $x,y \in CTS$ then $\bullet x \neq y$ and $\bullet y \neq x$.
- When removing the nodes from the global Petri net model N, at least two disconnected subnets are obtained.
- All structural conflict situations have to be solved locally; this means that transitions which are involved in a conflict situation have to belong to the same subnet.

In the following paragraphs, the splitting rules are briefly presented. The dashed arrows on the figures represent the communication channel between the subnets. A detailed definition of the net splitting operation rules can be found at (Costa, 2010).

Splitting rule #1 defines the cutting rule when the cutting node is a place. To be considered as a valid cutting node the place should not be involved in a conflict situation, or, if it is, then all transitions involved in the conflict have to remain in the same subnet. As the results of the splitting operation, the pre-set transitions of the place that will belong to a different subnet will be duplicated (in order to duplicate the locality associated with the node and assure a coherent evolution in the different subnets). Those transitions will belong to a directed synchronous channel, where the transition that was duplicated is the master transition. This transition will generate an output event and its duplicated transition will be the slave transition that will read the generated output event and will belong to the subnet where the cutting place belongs.

Definition 10: Splitting Rule #1: Let $p \in CTS$. If $p \bullet \in N_i \rightarrow p \in N_i$. If $\exists \bullet p \in N_j \rightarrow \exists (\bullet p)\_copy \in N_i$ where $i \neq j$. $\bullet p$ and $(\bullet p)\_copy$ are elements of a directed synchronous channel, where $\bullet p$ has the attribute *master* and $(\bullet p)\_copy$ has the attribute slave.

The Figure 6 illustrates this rule.

Rule #2 and Rule #3 are associated to the situations where the cutting node is a transition. Situations where the pre-set places of the cutting transition belong to only one subnet (Rule #2) is distinguished from others belonging to more than one subnet (Rule #3).

In this case the cutting transition is duplicated in the subnets where its pos-set places belong, but not in the pre-set places. As in the previous case, those transitions belong to a directed synchronous channel, where the duplicated transitions are the slave transitions that read the generated output event by the cutting transition.

Definition 11 - Splitting Rule #2: Let $t \in CTS$. If $t \in N_i$ and $\forall \bullet t \in N_i$ and $\exists t \bullet \in N_j$ where $i \neq j$ $\rightarrow \exists t\_copy \in N_j$. t and t_copy are elements of a directed synchronous channel, where t has the attribute *master* and t_copy has the attribute slave.

This rule #2 is illustrated on the Figure 7.

Rule #3 define the situation when the pre-set places of a cutting transition belong to different subnet. In that case, it is not enough to simply duplicate the cutting transition and create a directed synchronous channel between them, but is also necessary to replicate the original firing condition for the cutting transition. Hence, it is also necessary to duplicate the pre-set places with their pre-set transitions that belong to a different subnet as the cutting transition.

Definition 12: Splitting Rule #3: Let $t \in CTS$. If $t \in N_i$ and $\exists \bullet t \in N_j$ where $i \neq j \rightarrow \exists t\_copy \in N_j$. t and t_copy are elements of a Directed Synchronous Communication Channel, where t has the attribute *master* and t_copy has the attribute slave. More over in this case is necessary to replicate the initial firing condition of t by duplicating its pre-set places with their pre-set transitions if $\bullet t \in N_j$ and $t \in N_i$ where $i \neq j \rightarrow \exists \bullet t\_copy$ and $\bullet (\bullet t)\_copy \in N_i$.

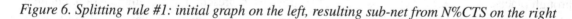

Figure 6. Splitting rule #1: initial graph on the left, resulting sub-net from N%CTS on the right

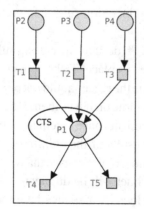
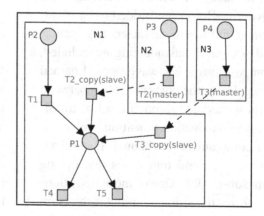

Figure 7. Splitting rule #2: initial graph on the left, resulting sub-net from N%CTS on the right

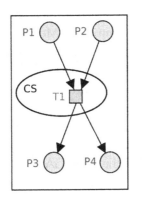
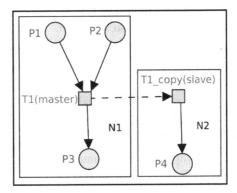

Figure 8. Splitting rule #3: initial graph on the left, resulting sub-net from N%CTS on the right

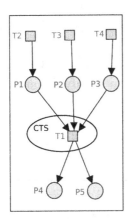
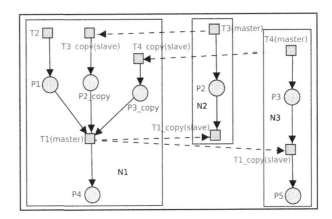

Figure 9. Concurrent components sub-models for the parking lot controller

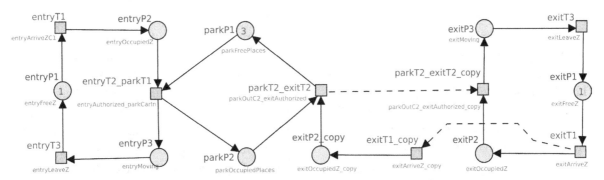

Once again ●(●t) and ●(●t)_copy belong to a directed synchronous channels between those transitions. Figure 8 illustrates this rule.

Coming back to our running example of the parking lot controller, modeled in Figure 2, considering a cutting set composed by transition parkT2_exitT2 (CTS={parkT2_exitT2}), allowing producing of a specific sub-model associated with the exit area, applying the net splitting operation to the model of Figure 2, the model of Figure 9 is obtained.

4.3. From Concurrent Components into Distributed Embedded Controllers

In spite of all the known disadvantages of synchronous systems when compared to asynchronous system, such as lower performance, higher power consumption, and electromagnetic interference, most embedded controllers are synchronous systems. In fact, synchronous systems are easier to specify, test/verify, and implement (synthesize), and their development is better supported by commercial design tools.

Although the majority of Petri net classes have asynchronous execution semantics, the IOPT-net class, which was defined to support the development of automation and embedded controller systems, has synchronous execution semantics. Additionally, IOPT-nets have maximal-step execution semantics, making them suitable to specify hardware and software systems with deterministic behavior.

To obtain a set of concurrent components of a controller specified by an IOPT-net model, the net splitting operation (Costa & Gomes, 2009) was proposed, as referred in previous section. This operation provides a set of interacting sub-models specifying concurrent components. The execution semantics of the resulting interacting components is globally synchronous.

The globally synchronous execution semantics is adequate for centralized controllers but not for distributed controllers. Most of the times it is not possible or appropriate to synchronize distributed components, either due to platform constraints, or due to optimization purposes. Having components being executed at distinct frequencies can decrease power consumption or electromagnetic interference. Such a system is a Globally-Asynchronous-Locally-Synchronous (GALS) system, where each component is synchronous with a specific clock frequency, distinct from clock frequencies from the other components, making the global system asynchronous.

To support the specification, verification, and implementation of GALS systems using IOPT-nets, the IOPT-net class was extended in (Moutinho & Gomes, 2012) with time-domains and asynchronous-channels. Time-domains are used to identify system components (sub-models) with different clock signals, and asynchronous-channels are used to specify the interaction between components (sub-models).

Inserting time-domains in the sub-models resulting from the net splitting operation, and replacing the synchronous-channels (introduced by the same operation) by asynchronous-channels, a distributed and GALS specification is obtained. This specification together with the tool chain framework presented in the next section, support the behavior verification and the implementation of GALS systems using IOPT net models.

An asynchronous-channel (like a synchronous channel) carries events from the master transition to slave transitions, but whereas in a synchronous channel events are sent in zero time delay, in an asynchronous-channel, the time delay from master to slaves is different from zero (it is dependent on AC time-domain).

Figure 10 presents the distributed specification of the car parking controller model that was previously split into two concurrent components (as presented in Figure 9), one to control the entrance of the park and the number of free/occupied places, and the other to control the parking exit. This distributed specification, which has GALS execution semantics, was obtained introducing time-domains to Petri net nodes (places and transitions), and replacing synchronous-channels by asynchronous-channels. The distributed specification is also composed by two components, each one with a specific time-domain (*td:1* and *td:2*), which means that each one is synchronous with a specific clock frequency, independent from the clock frequency of the other component. The two components interact through two asynchronous-channels, one connects transition *parkT2_exitT2* with transition *parkT2_exitT2_copy*, and the other connects transition *exitT1* with transition *exitT1_copy*. Each asynchronous-channel has a specific time-domain, which means that the time spent by an event from *parkT2_exitT2* to *parkT2_exitT2_copy* is independent from the time spent by an event from *exitT1* to *exitT1_copy*.

Although the change in the execution semantics from globally synchronous to GALS may introduce some behavioral changes, those deviations usually do not compromise the required properties. To verify if the desired behavioral properties of the initial model remain in the GALS model, the model checking tool presented in the next section is used.

This model checking tool also obtains and adds to the extended IOPT-net model from Figure 10 (specifying the distributed controller of the car parking lot as a GALS system) required

information to implement each component of the GALS system and the communication channels. Then, platform specific information is introduced, which includes the mapping of the connections between components inputs/output and platform pins or variables, the specification of how the communication channels will be implemented, and the specification of the network topology for the communication channels. Finally, code generation tools for software and hardware platforms are then used to automatically generate the implementation code of the distributed controller.

5. TOOLS FRAMEWORK

The IOPT Petri net class (Gomes, Barros, Costa, & Nunes, 2007) was designed to support the development of embedded system controllers, and was extended with synchronous channels to support decomposition (Costa & Gomes, 2009), and with asynchronous channels to support distributed execution, as proposed in (Moutinho & Gomes, 2012), accommodating the development of GALS systems. To fulfill these goals, an integrated tool framework was created around the IOPT class, initially developed within the FORDESIGN project (Gomes, Barros, Costa, Pais, & Moutinho, 2005), including Petri net model editors (Nunes, Gomes, & Barros, 2007), debug and simulation tools (Gomes & Lourenço, 2010), model checking and state-space generation (Pereira, Moutinho, &

Figure 10. Distributed components sub-models for the parking lot controller

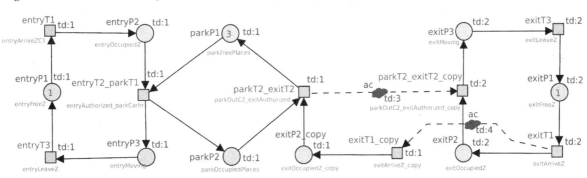

Gomes, 2012), automatic code generation tools (for C as in (Gomes, Rebelo, Barros, Costa, & Pais, 2010) and for VHDL as in (Gomes, Costa, Barros, & Lima, 2007)) and other tools to support higher level model operations (namely net addition [Barros & Gomes, 2003, 2004] and net splitting [Costa & Gomes, 2009]). An animator tool (Gomes & Lourenço, 2010) permits the design of animated synoptic user interfaces, used both to execute animated simulations on personal computers and also to implement graphical user interfaces for the embedded systems. The tools from the IOPT tool-chain can be used separately, as individual applications, or through a Web user interface, available online at the authors' research group Web page.

Design of embedded system controllers usually starts with the definition of the desired system behavior and the specification of a set of signals and events that establish the communication between the controller and controlled system. This task can be systematically performed using standard modeling techniques, for example, with the definition of a set of UML use-cases (Gomes & Costa, 2006) representing the interactions of the controller with the controlled system and the user interface. After all use-cases are defined, they are converted into IOPT Petri net sub-models, and edited using an IOPT editor, as the Snoopy-IOPT Editor (Nunes, Gomes, & Barros 2007) or the IOPT Editor offered by the Web user interface (as in Figure 11), which has been tested with some of the most common browser (as Mozilla Firefox, Google Chrome, and Opera). Using these sub-models and a net addition operation (currently supported by the Snoopy-IOPT Editor), the global specification of the controller is obtained.

Beside the usual functionality available in other Petri net editors, the IOPT editors contain additional tools to manipulate non-autonomous characteristics, including the definition of input and output signals and events. The signals correspond to Boolean or integer range variables, used by the controller to communicate with the

Figure 11. Web-based IOPT nets editor snapshot

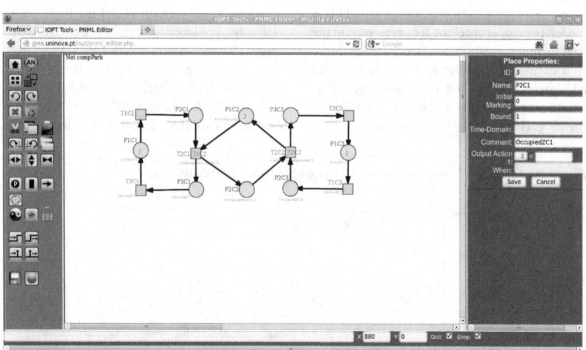

external world and the events correspond to instantaneous changes in signal values, where predefined thresholds are crossed in a specific direction. The user can subsequently associate the input events to transitions and define Boolean guard functions that use input signals to inhibit transition firing. In the same way, transitions can also be associated with output events that are triggered when the transition fires and output signal values can be associated with places.

To validate the resulting controller model, the model-checking tools, comprehending a state-space generator tool and a query system (Pereira, Moutinho, & Gomes, 2012), can be used to automatically check if the model implements the correct behavior and satisfies a set of system requirements. The state-space generator automatically verifies important system properties and common model mistakes, as the occurrence of deadlock states that prevent future evolution of the system and conflicts between concurrent transitions that can lead to non-deterministic execution. It also collects statistics, including the place minimal and maximal bounds, used to calculate the capacity of the memory elements required to implement each net place. Figure 12 presents the state space automatically generated by the tool; whenever the number of states is too

large to be adequately graphically presented, a file will be produced with the results, supporting off-line analysis.

The query system is used to test design requirements and check if the designed controller operates according to the desired specifications. Design requirements are often specified as a set of rules describing conditions that should happen or must be avoided. Each of these rules can be converted into a query that is applied to all states present in the state-space graph. For example, a car parking entrance gate should never open when the parking lot is already full. This rule can be converted into a state-space query that checks for states where the entrance gate is open and the car parking capacity is full. In the same way, an automatic vending machine should not deliver products before successful payment. This rule corresponds to a state-space query checking if a product is being picked up from the shelf and payment is not present. On other side, most controllers must operate in a reversible way, ensuring that the system can always return to the home state. For example, a car parking lot controller must return to the original state after all cars leave and the lot is empty. The presence of states in the state-space graph from where the system cannot reach the

Figure 12. State space associated with an IOPT net model

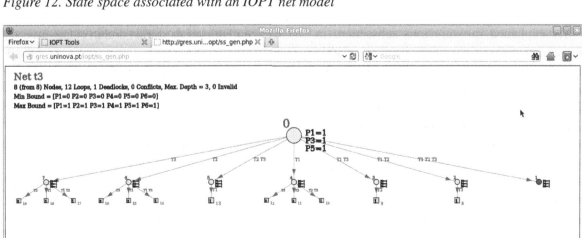

original state, potentially indicate a model containing errors.

Queries are specified using a query language that enables the definition of Boolean expressions applied to every state calculated during state-space generation. Each query expression can use the values of place marking, output signals influenced by output events, the transitions fired to produce each state, literal constant, plus arithmetic, comparative and Boolean operators. The reachability of individual states is performed using a "REACH(state)" function.

Whenever a design error is detected, controller models must be corrected and rechecked using the model-checking tools. To automate this process, the system stores a query database that is automatically executed each time the state-space is generated. This way the query system works as an automatic regression test system, able to detect the reappearance of old errors each time a model is changed.

When an embedded system controller has to be implemented in distributed environments, with several components spread by different physical locations or by different platforms, the initial specification has to be decomposed. A net splitting tool (Costa & Gomes, 2009) is available in the Snoopy-IOPT Editor to support the partition of models into several interacting concurrent components (sub-models), ensuring the preservation of the system behavior and the conservation of relevant system properties.

As explained in a previous subsection, in distributed implementations may not be possible or adequate to perform a globally synchronous implementation (all components of the distributed controller synchronized by the same clock signal). GALS implementations of distributed controllers emerge as the natural solution. To obtain the GALS specification, time-domains and asynchronous-channels proposed in (Moutinho & Gomes, 2012), are introduced in the interacting sub-models that result from net splitting operation. Changing the

execution semantic from globally synchronous to GALS may introduce some minor changes in the system behavior, which require a new verification, using the IOPT model checking tool extended for GALS systems (Moutinho & Gomes, 2011b). The verification of this GALS specification is a simple task, because it is used the same verification approach and the queries previously defined to verify the centralized specification. If the result of any query is changed, the designer must change the centralized specification, in order to guarantee that then changing the execution semantics from globally synchronous to GALS, the intended behavior properties are preserved.

When implementing the final controllers, a Configurator tool (Costa, Gomes, Barros, Oliveira, & Reis, 2008) enables the mapping of the signals and events present on the IOPT model to the physical IO pins available on the target device. A new version of the Configurator tool is currently under development, which also automatically generate several types of communication channels (such as asynchronous wrappers or serial communication architectures) to interconnect hardware and software components using different network topologies (such as ring and mesh topologies). After the mapping, the automatic code generation tools, IOPT2C (Gomes, Rebelo, Barros, Costa, & Pais, 2010) and IOPT2VHDL (Gomes, Costa, Barros, & Lima, 2007), that respectively generate software C code and synthesize VHDL hardware implementations, are used. The software code can run both on the target architectures used to implement the final controllers and also to perform simulations on personal computers.

Simulation and debugging can be performed with an Animator tool (Gomes & Lourenço, 2010), used to build animated synoptic screens that represent the system state in real time. Synoptic screens are designed using a background image and a set of rules, composed by logical conditions relating the system state and input signals. Whenever the current system state verifies these rules, specific images are presented at certain screen locations. The images can be icons, buttons, or just bitmap images used to implement "SCADA-like" presentations. Animation programs use the code automatically generated by the IOPT2C tool to implement the controller behavior and code produced by the Animator to implement the animation rules, plus user-interface code to simulate changes in input and output signals. Finally, the IOPT2Anim4Debug tool automatically creates debug Animation screens depicting the IOPT Petri net model and a set of rules to display the system state in real time, including signals, place marking and transition firing.

Another tool, GUIGen4FPGA (Moutinho, Pereira, & Gomes, 2011) translates Animator screens into VHDL hardware descriptions, enabling the automatic generation of interactive embedded system graphical user interfaces with support for pointing devices and touch screens.

The entire tool-chain covers all tasks starting from the model definition, edition and partition, to model-checking, debug and simulation, to the final controller implementations using automatic code generators and automatic user interface code creation. Based on a user-friendly Web user interface and automatic code generators, the IOPT-tools enable the design of embedded controllers and distributed embedded controllers without the need to write low level code. The model-checking and simulation tools help in the detection of model flaws during the early design stages, greatly reducing development time and cost.

6. DISCUSSION ON FUTURE TRENDS

Challenges of different types and magnitudes are present when considering distributed embedded controllers design. Hence, that is also true for the presented development methodology. It is impossible to exhaust the topic. Anyway, three major

future directions need to be referred considering the presented methodology and associated tool chain:

1. Extend IOPT nets with high-level Petri nets features (in line with Colored Petri nets) in order to accommodate data processing capabilities, as well as to support more compact modeling, which is very important as the system complexity increases;
2. Extend modeling capabilities integrating hierarchical and structuring mechanisms, also to cope with model complexity;
3. Keeping abreast the challenge of an updated tool chain widely used and accepted by academicians and engineering practitioners in the area of distributed embedded controllers design.

The first two go in the direction of having a more powerful framework allowing the handling of more complex models, while the last one identifies a major challenge for all "academic tools": to be seen as an "engineering tool" and not as a "toy prototype." For that end, extension of the tool chain framework to specific areas of application is of major importance; as one example, industrial control area can be referred, where integrating direct support for standards is also a major challenge (namely IEC-61499 for distributed automation systems).

CONCLUSION

Petri nets have been widely used for modeling and design of embedded controllers. This chapter presented a development methodology flow allowing Petri nets usage covering the whole development cycle for distributed embedded controllers, including modeling, verification, simulation, and implementation of distributed controllers specified with IOPT net models.

Both composition and decomposition of IOPT net models were addressed along the chapter. Composition of models supports their reusability in new situations and can be accomplished through net addition operation and fusion of sets of nodes. On the other hand, decomposition of a model into a set of models is the basis to support distributed implementations. A net splitting operation based on the definition of a cutting set allows the production of concurrent sub-models. These can be the basis to obtain distributed components to be executed in parallel considering different time domains associated with their executions. In this sense, specification, verification, and implementation of distributed controllers systems, considered as Globally-Asynchronous-Locally-Synchronous (GALS) systems, are addressed adding the concept of time domains to IOPT nets models. An integrated tool chain was also presented. This offers support for the whole development process from specification to implementation, including automatic code generation and deployment into heterogeneous implementation platforms, ranging from hardware-based platforms (synchronous or asynchronous) to software-centric solutions (stand-alone applications, processes, general purpose computer, dedicated computing platforms), and including hardware-software integrated platforms (reconfigurable computing platforms and FPGAs).

ACKNOWLEDGMENT

This work was partially financed by Portuguese Agency "FCT - Fundação para a Ciência e a Tecnologia" in the framework of project PEst-OE/EEI/UI0066/2011. Filipe Moutinho was supported by a FCT grant, ref. SFRH/BD/62171/2009.

REFERENCES

Barros, J. P., & Gomes, L. (2003). Modifying Petri net models by means of crosscutting operations. In *Proceedings of ACSD'2003 - Third International Conference on Application of Concurrency to System Design*. ACSD. ISBN 0-7695-1887-7

Barros, J. P., & Gomes, L. (2004). Net model composition and modification by net operations: a Pragmatic approach. In *Proceedings of IN-DIN'2004 – 2nd IEEE International Conference on Industrial Informatics*. Berlin, Germany: IEEE.

Berthelot, G. (1987). In Brauer, W., Reisig, W., & Rozenberg, G. (Eds.), *Transformations and decompositions of nets* (Vol. 254, pp. 359–376). Lecture Notes in Computer Science Berlin, Germany: Springer-Verlag.

Bruno, G., Agarwal, R., Castella, A., & Pescarmona, M. P. (1995). In De Michelis, G., & Diaz, M. (Eds.), *CAB: An environment for developing concurrent applications* (Vol. 935, pp. 141–160). Lecture Notes in Computer Science Berlin, Germany: Springer-Verlag. doi:10.1007/3-540-60029-9_38.

Christensen, S., & Hansen, N. D. (1994). In Valette, R. (Ed.). Lecture Notes in Computer Science: *Vol. 815. Coloured Petri nets extended with channels for synchronous communication*. Zaragoza, Spain: Springer-Verlag. doi:10.1007/3-540-58152-9_10.

Christensen, S., & Petrucci, L. (2000). Modular analysis of Petri nets. *Computer*, *43*(3), 224–242. doi:10.1093/comjnl/43.3.224.

Ciardo, G., & Trivedi, K. S. (1991). A decomposition approach for stochastic Petri net models. In *Proceedings of the Fourth International Workshop on Petri Nets and Performance Models* (pp. 74-83). Melbourne, Australia: IEEE. doi: 10.1109/PNPM.1991.238780

Costa, A. (2010). *Petri net model decomposition - A model based approach supporting distributed execution*. (PhD thesis). Universidade Nova de Lisboa, Lisbon, Portugal.

Costa, A., & Gomes, L. (2009). Petri net partitioning using net splitting operation. In *Proceedings of the 7th IEEE International Conference on Industrial Informatics* (pp. 204-209). Cardiff, UK: IEEE. doi: 10.1109/INDIN.2009.5195804

Costa, A., Gomes, L., Barros, J. P., Oliveira, J., & Reis, T. (2008). Petri nets tools framework supporting FPGA-based controller implementations. In *Proceedings of the 34th Annual Conference of the IEEE Industrial Electronics Society (IECON'08)*. Orlando, FL: IECON. doi: 10.1109/IECON.2008.4758345

Dasgupta, S., & Yakovlev, A. (2009). Desynchronisation technique using Petri nets. *Electronic Notes in Theoretical Computer Science*, *245*, 51–67. doi:10.1016/j.entcs.2009.07.028.

David, R., & Alla, H. (1992). *Petri nets & grafcet, tools for modelling discrete event systems*. London, UK: Prentice-Hall International Ltd..

Genrich, H. J. (1987). In Brauer, W., Reisig, W., & Rozenberg, G. (Eds.), *Predicate/transition nets* (*Vol. 254*, pp. 207–247). Lecture Notes in Computer Science Berlin, Germany: Springer-Verlag.

Gomes, L. (2005). On conflict resolution in Petri nets models through model structuring and composition. In *Proceedings of 2005 3rd IEEE International Conference on Industrial Informatics* (pp. 489-494). IEEE.

Gomes, L., & Barros, J. P. (2005). Structuring and composability issues in Petri nets modeling. *IEEE Transactions on Industrial Informatics*, *1*(2), 112–123. doi:10.1109/TII.2005.844433.

Gomes, L., Barros, J. P., Costa, A., & Nunes, R. (2007). The input-output place-transition Petri net class and associated tools. In *Proceedings of the 5th IEEE International Conference on Industrial Informatics (INDIN'07)*. Vienna, Austria: IEEE.

Gomes, L., Barros, J. P., Costa, A., Pais, R., & Moutinho, F. (2005). Formal methods for embedded systems co-design: The FORDESIGN project. In *Proceedings of ReCoSoC'05 - Reconfigurable Communication-Centric Systems-on-Chip*. ReCoSoC.

Gomes, L., & Costa, A. (2006). Petri nets as supporting formalism within embedded systems co-design. In *Proceedings of the International Symposium on Industrial Embedded Systems (IES'06)*. IES. doi: 10.1109/IES.2006.357468

Gomes, L., Costa, A., Barros, J. P., & Lima, P. (2007). From Petri net models to VHDL implementation of digital controllers. In *Proceedings of 33rd Annual Conference of the IEEE Industrial Electronics Society (IECON'07)*. Taipei, Taiwan: IEEE.

Gomes, L., & Fernandes, J. M. (Eds.). (2010). *Behavioral modeling for embedded systems and technologies: Applications for design and implementation*. Hershey, PA: IGI Global.

Gomes, L., & Lourenco, J. P. (2010). Rapid prototyping of graphical user interfaces for Petri-net-based controllers. *IEEE Transactions on Industrial Electronics*, *57*, 1806–1813. doi:10.1109/TIE.2009.2031188.

Gomes, L., Rebelo, R., Barros, J. P., Costa, A., & Pais, R. (2012). From Petri net models to C implementation of digital controllers. In *Proceedings of IEEE International Symposium on Industrial Electronics (ISIE'10)*. Bari, Italy: IEEE.

Haddad, S., Ilie, J. M., & Klai, K. (2002). An incremental verification technique using decomposition of Petri nets. In *Proceedings of IEEE International Conference on Systems, Man and Cybernetics*, (Vol. 2, pp. 381- 386). IEEE. doi: 10.1109/ICSMC.2002.1173442

Jensen, K. (1992). *Coloured Petri nets: Basic concepts, analysis methods and practical use.* Berlin, Germany: Springer-Verlag.

Mennicke, S., Oanea, O., & Wolf, K. (2009). Decomposition into open nets. In T. Freytag & A. Eckleder (Eds.), *16th German Workshop on Algorithms and Tools for Petri Nets*, (Vol. 501, pp. 29-34). Karlsruhe, Germany: CEUR-WS.org.

Moutinho, F., & Gomes, L. (2011). State space generation algorithm for GALS systems modeled by IOPT Petri nets. In *Proceedings of the 37th Annual Conference on IEEE Industrial Electronics Society* (pp. 2839-2844). Melbourne, Australia: IEEE. doi: 10.1109/IECON.2011.6119762

Moutinho, F., & Gomes, L. (2012). Asynchronous-channels and time-domains extending Petri nets for GALS systems. In Camarinha-Matos, L., Shahamatnia, E., & Nunes, G. (Eds.), *IFIP AICT* (*Vol. 372*, pp. 143–150). Boston: Springer. doi:10.1007/978-3-642-28255-3_16.

Moutinho, F., Pereira, F., & Gomes, L. (2011). Automatic generation of VHDL for controllers with graphical user interfaces. In *Proceedings of the 20th IEEE International Symposium of Industrial Electronics (ISIE'11)*. Gdansk, Poland: IEEE.

Nascimento, P. S. B., Maciel, P. R. M., Lima, M. E., Sant'ana, R. E., & Filho, A. G. S. (2004). A partial reconfigurable architecture for controllers based on Petri nets. In *Proceedings of the 17th Symposium on Integrated Circuits and Systems Design* (pp. 16-21). IEEE. doi: 10.1109/SBCCI.2004.240918

Notomi, M., & Murata, T. (1994). Hierarchical reachability graph of bounded Petri nets for concurrent-software analysis. *IEEE Transactions on Software Engineering, 20*(5), 325–336. doi:10.1109/32.286423.

Nunes, R., Gomes, L., & Barros, J. P. (2007). A graphical editor for the input-output place-transition Petri net class. In *Proceedings of IEEE Conference on Emerging Technologies and Factory Automation, (ETFA'07)*. IEEE. doi: 10.1109/EFTA.2007.4416858

Pereira, F., Moutinho, F., & Gomes, L. (2012). A state-space based model-checking framework for embedded system controllers specified using IOPT Petri nets. In Camarinha-Matos, L., Shahamatnia, E., & Nunes, G. (Eds.), *IFIP AICT* (*Vol. 372*, pp. 123–132). Boston: Springer. doi:10.1007/978-3-642-28255-3_14.

Popescu, C., Soto, M. C., & Lastra, J. L. M. (2012). A Petri net-based approach to incremental modelling of flow and resources in service oriented manufacturing systems. *International Journal of Production Research, 50*(2), 325–343. doi:10.10 80/00207543.2011.561371.

Rausch, M., & Hanisch, H.-M. (1995). Net condition/event systems with multiple condition outputs. In *Proceedings of ETFA'95 - 1995 INRIA/IEEE Symposium on Emerging Technologies and Factory Automation*, (vol. 1, pp. 592-600). Paris: IEEE.

Reisig, W. (1985). *Petri nets: An introduction.* New York, NY: Springer-Verlag.

Rust, C., & Kleinjohann, B. (2001). *Modeling intelligent embedded real-time systems using high-level Petri nets.* Paper presented at the Forum on Specification & Design Languages - FDL. Lyon, France.

Silva, M. (1985). *Las redes de Petri: En la automática y la informática.* Madrid, Spain: Editorial AC.

Tacken, J., Rust, C., & Kleinjohann, B. (1999). A method for prepartitioning of Petri net models for parallel embedded real-time systems. In *Proceedings of the 6th Annual Australasian Conference on Parallel And RealTime Systems* (pp. 168-178). Melbourne, Australia: Springer-Verlag.

Vogler, W., & Wollowski, R. (2002). In Agrawal, M., & Seth, A. (Eds.), *Decomposition in asynchronous circuit design* (*Vol. 2556*, pp. 336–347). Lecture Notes in Computer Science Berlin: Springer.

Vyatkin, V. (2006). Execution semantic of function blocks based on the model of net condition/event systems. In *Proceedings of the 4th IEEE International Conference on Industrial Informatics,* (pp. 874–879). IEEE.

Vyatkin, V., & Hanisch, H.-M. (1999). A modeling approach for verification of IEC1499 function blocks using net condition/event systems. In *Proceedings of ETFA '99 - 1999 7th IEEE International Conference on Emerging Technologies and Factory Automation*, (pp. 261–270). IEEE.

Chapter 10
Safety Reconfiguration of Embedded Control Systems

Atef Gharbi
University of Carthage, Tunisia

Antonio Valentini
O3neida Europe, Belgium

Hamza Gharsellaoui
University of Carthage, Tunisia

Mohamed Khalgui
University of Carthage, Tunisia & CNR Research Council, Italy & Xidian University, China

ABSTRACT

The authors study the safety reconfiguration of embedded control systems following component-based approaches from the functional level to the operational level. At the functional level, a Control Component is defined as an event-triggered software unit characterized by an interface that supports interactions with the environment (the plant or other Control Components). They define the architecture of the Reconfiguration Agent, which is modelled by nested state machines to apply local reconfigurations. The authors propose technical solutions to implement the agent-based architecture by defining UML meta-models for both Control Components and also agents. At the operational level, a task is assumed to be a set of components having some properties independently from any real-time operating system. To guarantee safety reconfigurations of tasks at run-time, the authors define service and reconfiguration processes for tasks and use the semaphore concept to ensure safety mutual exclusions. They apply the priority ceiling protocol as a method to ensure the scheduling between periodic tasks with precedence and mutual exclusion constraints.

INTRODUCTION

Embedded Control Systems have become useful in our daily lives such as automotive application, industrial management, control avionics, ... To reduce their cost of development, these systems must be reusable. The component-based programming seems the best solution for the development of such systems.

Several component technologies are proposed such as JavaBeans (related to Sun society) (Jubin, 2000), Component Object Model (related to Microsoft society) (COM, 2010), Corba Component

DOI: 10.4018/978-1-4666-3922-5.ch010

Model (provided by the Object Management Group [OMG]) (Pérez, 2002).

However, there are few kinds of component technologies (such as Koala [Jonge, 2009], PBO [Stewart, 1997], PECOS [Wuyts, 2005], ...) used in the development of embedded system due to extra-functional properties to be verified (for example quality of service, timeliness, ...) (Artist, 2003).

Anyway, each component technology has its benefits and its drawbacks.

As in our work, we want to be independent of any component technology, we propose a new concept of component named "Control Component" which is considered as a software part having interaction with other Control Components and ensuring control of the plant through data provided from (resp. to) sensors (resp. actuator).

A Control System is assumed to be a composition of Control Components with precedence constraints to control the plant according to well-defined execution orders.

The proposed method to ensure Functional Safety of the interconnected Control Component is an agent-oriented software. On the one hand, we study the Functional Safety in a central system i.e. a single agent supervising the whole system.

This agent reacts as soon as an error occurs in the plant. The decision taken may vary from changing the set of Control Components that constitute the system, modifying the connection between different Control Components, substituting the behavior of some Control Component by another behavior or even modifying data. According to these functionalities, it is possible to define the architecture of the agent as based on four levels.

We propose useful meta-models for Control Components and also for intelligent agents. These meta-models are used to implement adaptive embedded control systems.

As we choose to apply dynamic scenarios, the system should run even during automatic recon-

figurations, while preserving correct executions of functional tasks.

Given that Control Components are defined in general to run sequentially, this feature is inconvenient for real-time applications which typically handle several inputs and outputs in a too short time constraint.

To meet performance and timing requirements, a real-time must be designed for concurrency.

To do so, we define at the operational level some sequential program units called real-time tasks.

Thus, we define a real-time task as a set of Control Components having some real-time constraints. We characterize a task by a set of properties independently from any Real Time Operating System (RTOS).

We define service processes as software processes for tasks to provide system's functionalities, and define reconfiguration processes as tasks to apply reconfiguration scenarios at run-time. In fact, service processes are functional tasks of components to be reconfigured by reconfiguration processes.

To guarantee a correct and safety behavior of the system, we use semaphores to ensure the synchronization between processes. We apply the famous algorithm of synchronization between reader and writer processes such that executing a service is considered as a reader and reconfiguring a component is assumed to be a writer process. The proposed algorithm ensures that many service processes can be simultaneously executed, whereas reconfiguration processes must have exclusive access.

We study in particular the scheduling of tasks through a Real Time Operating System. We apply the priority ceiling protocol proposed by (Sha, 1990) to avoid the problem of priority inversion as well as the deadlock between the different tasks. The priority ceiling protocol supposes that each semaphore is assigned a priority ceiling which is equal to the highest priority task using this semaphore. Any task is only allowed to enter its critical section if its assigned priority is higher than the priority ceilings of all semaphores currently locked by other tasks. Finally, we implement a real-time task through the use of RTLinux as an example of RTOS.

The contributions of this research work have been applied on the benchmarking production system: FESTO system (used as running example) allowing us to validate our results.

The main contributions of this paper are the following: (1) a complete study of Safety Reconfigurable Embedded Control Systems from the functional level (i.e. dynamic reconfiguration system) to the operational level (i.e. decomposition of the system into a set of tasks with time constraints); (2) a global definition of real-time task with its necessary parameters independently from any real-time operating system; (3) the scheduling of these real-time tasks considered as periodic tasks with precedence and mutual exclusion constraints; (4) implementation of a real-time task within RTLinux as a RTOS.

To our best of knowledge, there is no research works which deal with these different points together.

We present in the next section the state of art. The section 3 presents the FESTO system considered as a benchmark production system. We present in section 4 the conceptual meta-model for a Control Component. The section 5 deals with the architecture of Reconfiguration agent. We introduce in section 6 the real-time task model and study the safety of its dynamic reconfiguration as well as the scheduling between the different tasks. We finally conclude the paper in the last section.

STATE OF ART

In this section, we present related works to prove the originality of the current chapter.

Component-Based Technology for Embedded System

There are several component-based technologies as found in the literature to develop embedded systems. We can by no means describe them all. This survey describes some of the component-based technologies which seem to be more relevant.

Koala Component

The Koala (C[K]omponent Organizer and Linking Assistant) component technology is designed and used by Philips for development of software in consumer electronics (Jonge, 2009).

The Koala Component consists of Architecture Description Language (ADL) to define the architecture and the interaction between components and a set of tools to compile and to generate the component. The Koala component presents a set of provided and required interfaces (each one is defined by Interface Description Language). The components are written in C language, the compiler generates automatically the C header file. For more information on Koala compiler, we refer to (KoalaTool, 2010).

Although the main interest in using Koala component, this component suffers from many drawbacks such as (Akerholm, 2004): (1) Koala is considered as a proprietary technology not as an industrial standard; (2) Koala does not have tools to analyze run-time properties; (3) Tools for testing and debugging is lacking too, but they use source code components, and a simple interaction model; (4) The Koala use is restricted to a specific operating system.

PBO Component

The PBO (Port Based Object) component (Stewart, 1997) is a generic component used to implement dynamically reconfigurable real-time system. The algebraic model of a port automaton is combined with the software abstraction of an object to define a Port Based Object. The PBO model is considered simple. In fact, the functionality of PBO is defined as methods in a classical object, the input and output ports are defined as port-automaton theory and configuration constants are useful to reconfigure components.

Although the main interest in using PBO component, this component has certain deficiencies such as (Stewart, 1997): (1) It is not possible to define a composite component; (2) There is no way to verify non-functional properties (for example memory consumption or schedulability); (3) Independent tasks are not allowed to communicate with other components (which requires loosely).

PECOS Component

A PECOS (PErvasive COmponent System) component is characterized by a name, a set of property bundles (used to store meta information about component such as worst-case execution time, schedulability), a set of ports and a behavior (Wuyts, 2005).

A Pecos component can be passive, active or event component depending on how its action is executed.

Passive Component: It is executed by the component that contains it (i.e. it does not have its own thread control).

Active Component: Which is related to a thread periodically executed (having its own thread control).

Event Component: Is like active component but its action is executed once a specific event occurs. This kind of component is very convenient to represent the sensors as well as the actuators.

The port in a Pecos component has a name, a type of data, and a direction (input, output, or input/output). Only ports having the same type are enabled to be connected together.

The CoCo language is used as ADL to specify the components, the devices and the whole architecture. Besides, it is possible to generate executable from CoCo sepcification.

Despite its proven success, the PECOS component is not highly suited for larger systems, due to its lack of expressing more complicated systems (Akerholm, 2004). In fact, it is very efficient for small resource constrained embedded systems.

Function Block

A Function Block is defined in this technology as an event triggered software component composed of an interface and an implementation. The interface contains data/event inputs/outputs to support interactions with the environment, whereas the implementation contains algorithms to be executed when corresponding input events occur.

There are many standards related to Function Block such as IEC 61508 and IEC 61499.

The IEC61508 standard is considered as international safety standard because it is not related to any particular industrial sector such as railway applications (EN50126, EN50128, EN50129) or the nuclear power plant (IEC61513).

The standard defines approach to classify risk and presents how to avoid, detect and control design fault.

As it is cited in (Faller, 2004), the main drawbacks of IEC 61508 standard are:

1. IEC 61508 and derived standards are voluminous and quite difficult to read and understand;
2. It is difficult to apply for smaller projects and makes Management of Functional Safety expensive for Small and Medium Enterprises.

The IEC 61499 standard is built on IEC 61131-1 standard for Programmable Logic Controller (PLC) language.

This standard provides a framework to design a distributed and embedded controlled system.

However the IEC 61499 presents some drawbacks such as (Olsen, 2005):

1. The standard does not indicate low-level communication requirements;
2. The standard does not precise how the function blocks are scheduled on resources.

Synthesis

In Crnkovic (2003), the authors study several component models applied in embedded systems with respect to industrial requirements. The industrial requirements may be technical requirement (such as analysis, tests, portability, resource constraints, component model and computation model) or development requirement (like reusability, maintainability and understandability). They conclude that there is not a specific technology that satisfies all the industrial requirements.

BENCHMARK PRODUCTION SYSTEM: FESTO

We present the Benchmark Production System (Detailed descriptions are available in the Website: http://aut.informatik.uni-halle.de): FESTO available in the research laboratory at the Martin Luther University in Germany.

The FESTO Benchmark Production System is a well-documented demonstrator used by many universities for research and education purposes, and it is used as a running example in the context of this paper. FESTO is composed of three units: Distribution, Test and Processing units. The Distribution unit is composed of a pneumatic feeder and a converter to forward cylindrical work pieces from a stack to the testing unit which is composed of the detector, the tester and the elevator. This unit performs checks on work pieces for height, material type and color. Work pieces that successfully pass this check are forwarded to the rotating disk of the Processing unit, where the drilling of the work piece is performed. We assume in this research work two drilling machines *Drill_machine1* and *Drill_machine2* to drill pieces. The result of the drilling operation is next checked by the checking machine and the work piece is forwarded to another mechanical unit. In this research paper, three production modes of FESTO are considered according to the rate of input pieces denoted by *number_pieces* into the system (i.e. ejected by the feeder).

Case 1: High production. If *number_pieces* $\geq$ *Constant1*, then the two drilling machines are used at the same time in order to accelerate the production. In this case, the Distribution and the Testing units have to forward two successive pieces to the rotating disc before starting the drilling with *Drill_machine1* and *Drill_machine2*. For this production mode, the periodicity of input pieces is $p = 11$ *seconds*.

Case 2: Medium production. If *Constant2* $\leq$ *number_pieces* < *Constant1*, then we use *Drill_machine1 or Drill_machine2* to drill work pieces. For this production mode, the periodicity of input pieces is $p = 30$ *seconds*.

Case 3: Light production. If *number_pieces* < *Constant2*, then only the drilling machine *Drill_machine1* is used. For this production mode, the periodicity of input pieces is $p = 50$ *seconds* (Figure 1).

On the other hand, if one of the drilling machines is broken at run-time, then we have to only use the other one. In this case, we reduce the periodicity of input pieces to $p = 40$ *seconds*. The system is completely stopped in the worst case if the two drilling machines are broken.

SOFTWARE CONTROL COMPONENTS

To be independent of any language or industrial technology, we propose the concept of Control Components in (Gharbi, 2009) as software units of adaptive embedded control systems. A component is classically defined as "a coherent package of software that can be independently developed and delivered, and that offers interfaces to be connected, unchanged, with other components in order to compose a larger system" (Souza, 1998).

In the following paragraphs, we extend our previous published papers by proposing conceptual meta-models for Control Components.

Conceptual Meta-Model for Control Components

An embedded control system is assumed to be a set of control components with precedence constraints, to allow controls of devices by reading and interpreting data from sensors, before reacting and activating corresponding actuators. Three concepts have to be defined to compose a system: Control Components, interfaces and connectors.

A "Control Component" is defined as an event-triggered software unit owning data to execute system's functionalities.

An interface has a main role to define "components access points" (Szyperski, 2002).

By believing that internal designs and implementations of components are hidden, the corresponding interfaces allow their external interactions.

An interface specifies all signatures of operations to be provided or required by a component. Therefore, remote components have accesses through its interfaces.

A Control Component may have different interfaces such that each one defines offered services.

Furthermore, the interface of a component is independent of the corresponding implementation. Consequently, it is easy to modify the latter without changing the interface and vice-versa. The connector is used to ensure connections between provided and required interfaces of components (for example data transmission). A principal characteristic of connectors is to link interfaces with complementary roles. In the current paper, we are interested in the original design and implementation of components.

Figure 1. The normal execution case

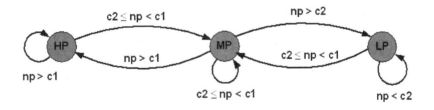

Key
HP: High Production
MP: Medium Production
LP: Light Production
np: number of pieces
c1: constant1
c2: constant2

Figure 2. The composition meta-model of a control component

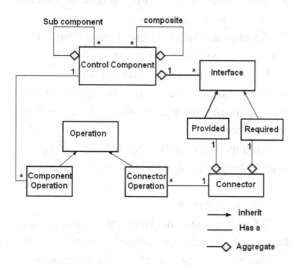

As a new contribution in the current paper, we propose the conceptual meta-model of Control Components in Figure 2 where the classes *Control Component*, *Interface* and *Connector* are distinguished. Note that an object *Control Component* may be composed of several sub-components. Moreover, it may have one or many *Interface* objects. Note also that an *Interface* object may be a *Provided* or *Required* interface.

A *Provided* interface presents services for external components, whereas a *Required* interface defines the need of a service from remote components.

An object of type *Connector* is a link between *Provided* and *Required* objects. A connector is especially deployed when it links distributed components on different devices. Finally, the classes *Control Component* and *Interface* provide some operations which may be represented by *Operation* class in general (or more specific with *Component Operation* and *Interface Operation* classes). *Component Operations* are for example creating or destroying Control Components, whereas *Interface Operations* are connecting and disconnecting between two interfaces.

Running Example: We show in Figure 3 a static view describing possible instances that are created from different classes.

The *Test* object, which is an instance of *Control Component* class, has as operation *TestOp* object (instance of *Component Operation* class).

The *TestDone* object, which is an instance of *Interface Provided* class, represents data to be sent to the required interface of succ(*Test*), for which we associate the connector object *c2*. The *MoveDone* object, which is an instance of *Interface Required* class, represents data to be received from the provided interface of pred(*Test*), for which we associate the connector object *c1*.

Conceptual Model of Component-Based Embedded Control Systems

We define in this chapter a new implementation of component-based embedded control systems. We propose according to the well-known UML language the concepts of sensors, actuators, Control Components, Execution Traces, Execution Trace Networks and Systems (Figure 4).

- **Sensor:** Is defined by the following information: (1) Name: the identifier of the sensor, (2) Min: the minimum value to be pro-

Figure 3. The object diagram of put piece control component

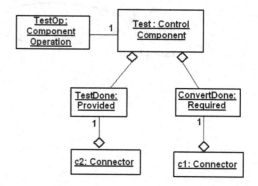

Figure 4. The general conception of an application based on control components

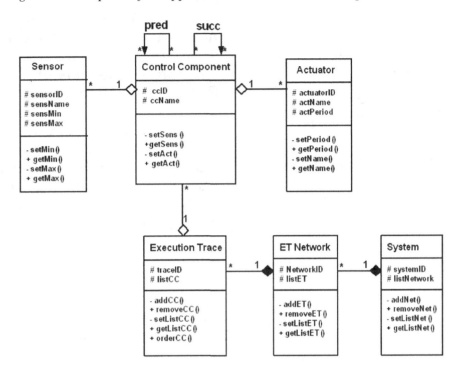

vided by the sensor, and (3) Max: the maximum value to be provided by the sensor,

- **Actuator:** Each actuator is characterized by the following data: (1) Name: the identifier of the actuator, and (2) Period: the execution period,

- **Control Component:** Is represented as follows: (1) Name: the name of the control component, (2) Min: the minimum value accepted by the control component, (3) Max: the maximum value accepted by the control component, (4) List of sensors: the list of sensors related to the control component, and (5) Actuator: the actuator associated to the control component,

- **Execution Trace:** Represents the solution to be applied. The Execution Trace is represented as follows: (1) Name: the name of the execution trace, and (2) listCC: the list of Control Components,

- **Execution Trace Network:** Represents different reconfigurations that can be applied for a given policy. The Execution Trace Network is represented as follows: (1) Name: the name of the execution trace network, and (2) listET: the list of execution traces,

- **System:** Is represented by different policies that can be applied. The System is represented as follows: (1) Name: the name of the execution trace network, and (2) listNetwork: the list of execution trace networks.

Running Example: We present in Figure 5 a static view where we show the *FESTO* object which is an instance of *System* class, and which is

Figure 5. The object diagram of FESTO system

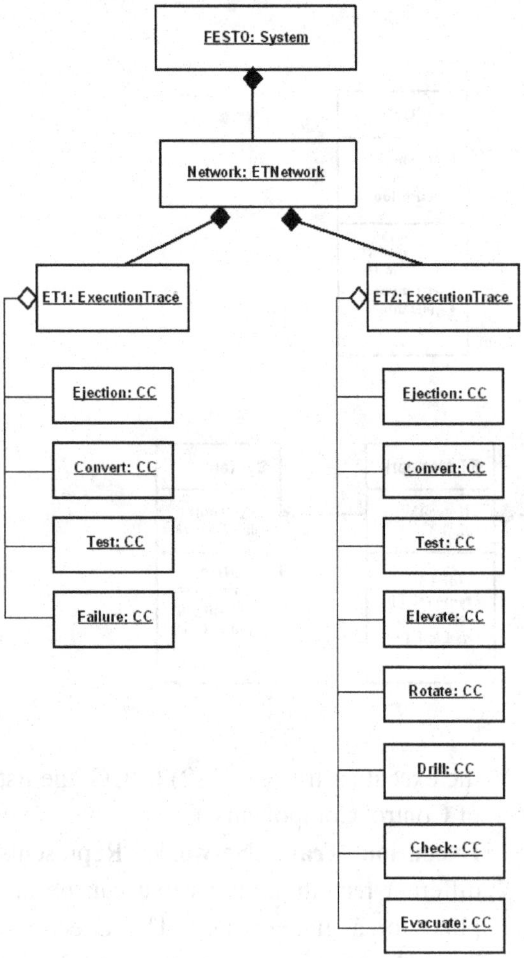

event occurs. This agent is described with nested state machine. We define also the Reconfiguration Agent especially its generic behavior.

Software Architecture of Reconfiguration Agent

We propose an agent-based architecture to control embedded systems at run-time. The agent checks the environment's evolution and reacts when new events occur by adding, removing or updating Control Components of the system. To describe the dynamic behavior of an intelligent agent that dynamically controls the plant, we use nested state machines in which states correspond to finite state machines.

A finite state machine can be defined as a state machine whose states, inputs and outputs are enumerated. The nested state machine is represented as the following:

$$NSM = (SM_1, SM_2, ..., SM_n)$$

Each state machine (SM_i) is a graph of states and transitions. A state machine treats the several events that may occur by detecting them and responding to each one appropriately.

We define a state machine as the following:

$$SM_i = (S_i, S_{i0}, I_i, O_i, \text{Pre-cond}_i, \text{Post-cond}_i, t_i)$$

$S_i = \{s_{i1}, .., s_{ip}\}$: the states;

S_{i0} = the initial state;

$I_i = \{I_{i1}, .., I_{im}\}$: the input events;

$O_i = \{O_{i1}, .., O_{ik}\}$: the ouput events;

Pre-cond$_i$ = the set of conditions to be verified before the activation of a state;

Post-cond$_i$ = the set of conditions to be verified once a state is activated;

$t_i = S_i \times I_i \rightarrow S_i$: the transition function.

constituted by only one *Network* object (instance of *ETNetwork* class).

The Execution Trace Network is composed of two execution traces: The first execution trace (*ET1*) is composed of the following objects: *Ejection, Convert, Test*, and *Failure*. The second execution trace (*ET2*) contains the following objects: *Ejection, Convert, Test, Elevate, Rotate, Drill, Check* and *Evacuate*.

RECONFIGURATION AGENT

In this section, we present the Conceptual Architecture For Reconfiguration Agent checking the environment's evolution and reacting when any

Figure 6. The meta-model nested state machine

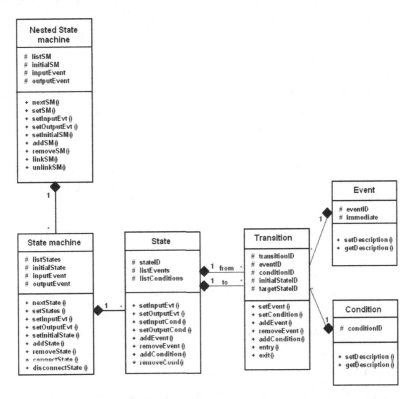

We propose a conceptual model for a nested state machine in Figure 6 where we define the classes *Nested State Machine*, *State machine*, *State*, *Transition*, *Event* and *Condition*.

The *Nested State Machine* class contains a certain number of *State machine* classes. This relation is represented by a composition. The *Transition* class is double linked to the *State* class because a transition is considered as an association between two states. Each transition has an event that is considered as a trigger to fire it and a set of conditions to be verified. This association between the *Transition* class and *Event* and *Condition* classes exists and is modeled by the aggregation relation.

We define for each device of the execution environment a unique agent that checks the environment evolution and takes into account user requirements to apply automatic reconfiguration scenarios.

We define the following units that belong to four hierarchical levels of the agent architecture:

First level: Architecture Unit this unit checks the plant evolution and changes the system software architecture (adds/removes Control Components) when particular conditions are satisfied,

Second level: Control Unit for a particular loaded software architecture, this unit checks the plant evolution and reconfigures compositions of corresponding Control Components,

Third level: Implementation Unit for a particular composition of Control Components, this unit reconfigures their implementations,

Fourth level: Data Unit this unit updates data if particular conditions are satisfied.

We design the agent by nested state machines where the Architecture Unit is specified by an Architecture State Machine (denoted by ASM) in which each state corresponds to a particular software architecture of *execution(Sys)*. Therefore, each transition of the ASM corresponds to the load (or unload) of Control Components into (or from) the memory. We construct for each state *S1* of the ASM a particular Control State Machine (denoted by CSM) in the Control Unit. This state machine specifies all compositions of Control Components when the system software architecture corresponding to the state *S1* is loaded. Each transition of any CSM has to be fired if particular conditions are satisfied. For each state *S2* of a state machine CSM, we define in the Implementation Unit a particular Implementation State Machine (denoted by ISM) in which each state defines particular implementations of Control Components that we compose in the state *S2*.

Finally, the Data Unit is specified also by Data State Machines (denoted by DSMs) that define all possible values of data in the system.

Running Example: We present in Figure 7 the nested state machines of our FESTO agent. The first level is specified by ASM where each state defines a particular software architecture of the system (i.e. a particular composition of blocks to load in the memory).

The *ASM* state machine is composed of two states *ASM1* and *ASM2* corresponding to the first

Figure 7. Specification of the FESTO agent by nested state machines

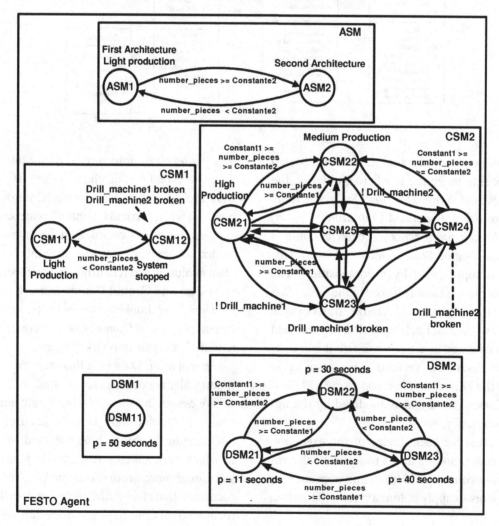

(i.e. the Light Production Mode) and the second (the High and Medium modes) architectures.

We associate for each one of these states a CSM state machine in the Control Unit. The state machines *CSM1* and *CSM2* correspond to the states *ASM1* and *ASM2*. In *CSM2* state machine, the states *CSM21* and *CSM22* correspond respectively to the High and the Medium production modes (where the second architecture is loaded). To fire a transition from *CSM21* to *CSM22*, the value of *number_pieces* should be in [*Constant2*, *Constant1*[. We note that the states *CSM12* and *CSM25* correspond to the blocking problem where the two drilling machines are broken. Finally, the Data Unit is specified by a DSM state machine defining the values. The state machines *DSM1* and *DSM2* correspond to the state machines *CSM1* and *CSM2*. In particular, the state *DSM21* encodes the production periodicity when we apply the High production mode (i.e. the state *CSM21* of *CSM2*), and the state *DSM22* encodes the production periodicity when we apply the Medium mode (i.e. *CSM22* of *CSM2*). Finally, the state DSM23 corresponds to *CSM23* and *CSM24* and encodes the production periodicity when one of the drilling machines is broken.

Notation: We denote in the following by,

- n_{ASM} the number of states in the ASM state machine (i.e. the number of possible software architectures implementing the system). ASM_a ($a \in [1, n_{ASM}]$) denotes a state of ASM to encode a particular architecture (i.e. particular subset of *execution(Sys)*). This state corresponds to a particular CSM state machine that we denote by CSM_a ($a \in [1, n_{ASM}]$),

- n_{CSM_a} the number of states in CSM_a and let $CSM_{a,b}$ ($b \in [1, n_{CSM_a}]$) be a state of CSM_a. This state corresponds to a particular ISM state machine that we denote by $ISM_{a,b}$,

- $n_{ISM_{a,b}}$ the number of states in $ISM_{a,b}$ and let $ISM_{a,b,c}$ ($c \in [1, n_{ISM_{a,b}}]$) be a state of $ISM_{a,b}$,

- n_{DSM} the number of Data State Machines corresponding to all possible reconfiguration scenarios of the system. This number is not depending on the Implementation state machine,

- n_{DSM_d} the number of states in DSM_d. $DSM_{d,e}$ ($e \in [1, n_{DSM_d}]$) denotes a state of the state machine DSM_d which can correspond to one of the following cases:
  ◦ One or more states of ISM or CSM state machines,
  ◦ All the ASM state machines.

The agent automatically applies at run-time different reconfiguration scenarios if hardware errors occur at run-time. Each scenario denoted by Reconfiguration$_{a,b,c,d,e}$ corresponds to a particular

Figure 8. The internal agent behavior

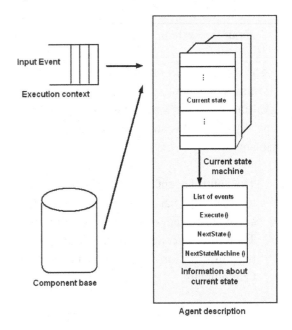

composition of Control Components Comp$_{a,b,c,d,e}$ as follows:

1. The software architecture ASM$_a$ is loaded in the memory,
2. The control policy is fixed in the state CSM$_{a,b}$,
3. The implementation is fixed in the state ISM$_{a,b,c}$,
4. The data configuration corresponding to the state DSM$_{d,e}$ is applied.

Conceptual Architecture for Reconfiguration Agents

We propose a generic architecture for reconfiguration agents depicted in Figure 8.

This architecture consists of the following parts:

1. The Event Queue to save different input events that may take place in the system,
2. The reconfiguration software agent that reads an input event from the Event Queue and reacts as soon as possible,
3. The set of state machines such that each one is composed of a set of states,
4. Each state represents a specific information about the system.

The agent, based on nested state machines, determines the new system's state to execute according to event inputs and also conditions to be satisfied. This solution has the following characteristics:

1. The control agent design is general enough to cope with various kinds of embedded-software-based component application. Therefore, the agent is uncoupled from the application and from its Control Components.

2. The agent is independent of nested state machines: it permits to change the structure of nested state machines (add state machines, change connections, change input events, and so on) without having to change the implementation of the agent. This ensures that the agent continues to work correctly even in case of modification of state machines.

3. The agent is not supposed to know components that it has to add or remove in a reconfiguration case.

In the following algorithm, the symbol Q is an event queue which holds incoming event instances, ev refers to an event input, S_i represents a State Machine, and $s_{i,j}$ a state related to a State Machine S_i. The internal behavior of the agent is defined as follow:

1. The agent reads the first event ev from the queue Q;

Algorithm 1. GenericBehavior

```
begin
while (Q.length() > 0) do
ev ← Q.Head()
For each state machine SM_i do
s_{i,j} ← currentState_i
If ev ∈ I(s_{i,j}) then
For each state s_{i,k} ∈ next(s_{i,j})
such that s_{i,k} related to S_i do
If execute(s_{i,k}) then
currentState_i ← s_{i,k}
break
end if
end for
For each state s_{l,k} ∈ next(s_{l,j})
such that s_{l,k} related to S_l do
If execute(s_{l,k}) then
currentState_l ← s_{l,k}
break
end if
end for
end if
end for
end while
end.
```

2. Searches from the top to the bottom in the different state machines;

3. Within the state machine SM_i, the agent verifies if *ev* is considered as an event input to the current state $s_{i,j}$ (i.e. $ev \in I$ related to $s_{i,j}$).

In this case, the agent searches the states considered as successor for the state $s_{i,j}$ (states in the same state machine SM_i or in another state machine SM_l);

4. The agent executes the operations related to the different states;

5. Repeats the same steps (1-4) until no more event exists in the queue to be treated.

First of all, the agent evaluates the pre-condition of the state $s_{i,j}$. If it is false, then the agent exits, Else the agent determines the list of Control Components concerned by this reconfiguration, before applies the required reconfiguration for each one. Finally, it evaluates the post-condition of the state $s_{i,j}$ and generates errors whenever it is false.

```
Function execute(s_{i,j}) : boolean
begin
If ¬ s_{i,j}.PreCondition then
return false
else
listCC ← getInfo(s_{i,j}.info)
 For each CC ∈ listCC do
CC.reconfigure()
end for
If ¬ s_{i,j}.PostCondition then
Generate error
end if
return true
end if
end.
```

REAL-TIME TASK: DEFINITION, DYNAMIC RECONFIGURATION, SCHEDULING, AND IMPLEMENTATION

In this section, we present a Real-Time Task as a general concept independently from any real-time operating system, its dynamic reconfiguration, the scheduling between several tasks and the implementation in a specific real-time operating system (which is RTLinux).

Real Time Task Definition

A real time task is considered as a process (or a thread depending on the Operating System) having its own data (such as registers, stack, …) which is in competition with other tasks to have the processor execution.

A task is handled by a Real-Time Operating System (RTOS) which is a system satisfying explicitly response-time constraints by supporting a scheduling method that guarantees response time especially to critical tasks.

In this paragraph, we aim to present a real-time task as a general concept independently from any real-time operating system.

Nowadays, there are many real time operating systems (for example RTLinux, Windows CE, eCos, QNX, …) offering the basic functions for instance multitasking, real-time responses and so on. However, there is some difference in the ease of use, performance and debugging facilities. To be independent from any Real-Time Operating System and to be related to our research work, we define a task Γ_i as a sequence of Control Components, where a Control Component is ready when its preceding Control Component completes its execution. $\Gamma_{i,j}$ denotes the j-th Control Component of Γ_i (Figure 9).

Figure 9. Real time task

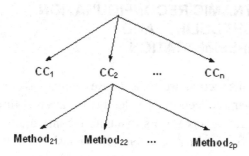

Thus, our application consists of a set of periodic tasks $\Gamma = (\Gamma_1, \Gamma_2, ..., \Gamma_n)$.

All the tasks are considered as periodic this is not a limitation since non-periodic task can be handled by introducing a periodic server.

Running Example: In the FESTO Benchmark Production System, the tasks Γ_1 to Γ_9 execute the following functions:

- (Γ_1) Feeder pushes out cylinder and moves backward/back;
- (Γ_2) Converter pneumatic sucker moves right/left;
- (Γ_3) Detection Module detects workpiece, height, color and material;
- (Γ_4) Shift out cylinder moves backward/ forward;
- (Γ_5) Elevator elevating cylinder moves down/up;
- (Γ_6) Rotating disc workpiece present in position and rotary indexing table has finished a 90 rotation;
- (Γ_7) Driller 1 machine drills workpiece;
- (Γ_8) Driller 2 machine drills workpiece;
- (Γ_9) WarehouseCylinder removes piece from table.

In the following paragraphs, we introduce the meta-model of a task. We study also the dynamic reconfiguration of tasks. After that, we introduce the task scheduling. Finally, we present the task implementation within RTLinux as a Real-Time Operating System.

A Meta-Model Task

In this article, we extend the work presented in (Pedreiras, 2007) by studying both a task and a scheduler in a general real-time operating system where each task is characterized by:

- **Identifer:** Each task Γ_i has a name and an identifier.
- **Temporal properties:** Each task Γ_i is described by a deadline D_i (which corresponds to the maximal delay allowed between the release and the completion of any instance of the task), a period T_i, a worst-case execution time C_i. It is released every T_i seconds and must be able to consume at most C_i seconds of CPU time before reaching its deadline D_i seconds after release ($C_i \leq D_i \leq T_i$). We assume that these attributes are known, and given as constants (see Table 1).
- **Constraints:** Resources specification ρ_i, precedence constraints and/or QoS properties to be verified.
- **State:** A Real-Time Operating System implements a finite state machine for each task and ensures its transition. The state of a task may be in one of the following possible states Ready, Running, Blocked or Terminated. Every task is in one of a few different states at any given time:
  - **Ready:** The task is ready to run but waits for allocation of the processor. The scheduler decides which ready task will be executed next based on priority criterion (i.e. the task having the highest priority will be assigned to the processor).

Table 1. A task set example

Task	Comp. Time C_i	Period T_i	Deadline D_i
Γ_1	20	70	50
Γ_2	20	80	80
Γ_3	35	200	100
Γ_4	62	90	81

- ○ **Blocked:** A task cannot continue execution because it has to wait (there are many reasons such that waiting for event, waiting on semaphore or a simple delay).
- ○ **Running:** In the running state, the processor is assigned to the task, so that its instructions can be executed. Only one task can be in this state at any time, while all the other tasks can be simultaneously in other states.
- ○ **Terminated:** When a task terminates its execution, the task allocator deletes it and releases the resources taken by this task (Figure 10).

- **Priority:** Each task is assigned a priority value which may be used in the scheduling.

$$\Gamma_i = (D_i; C_i; T_i; I_i; O_i; \rho_i; (CC_i^1, ..., CC_i^{ni}));$$

- A deadline D_i;
- An execution time C_i;
- A period T_i;
- A set of inputs I_i;
- A set of outputs O_i;
- A set of constraints ρ_i;
- A set of n_i Control Components ($n_i \geq 1$) such that the task Γ_i is constituted by CC_i^1, ..., CC_i^{ni}.

One of the core components of an RTOS is the task scheduler which aims to determine which of the ready tasks should be executing. If there are no ready tasks at a given time, then no task can be executed, and the system remains idle until a task becomes ready (Figure 11).

Running Example: In the FESTO Benchmark Production System, when the task Γ_1 is created, it is automatically marked as Ready task. At the instant *t1*, it is executed by the processor (i.e. it is in the Running state). When the task Γ_1 needs a resource at the instant *t2*, it becomes blocked.

Figure 10. Task states

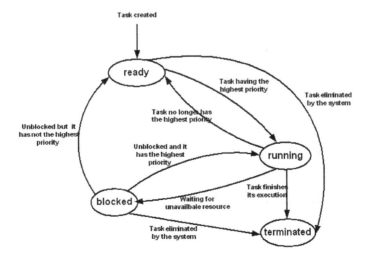

Figure 11. Scheduling task

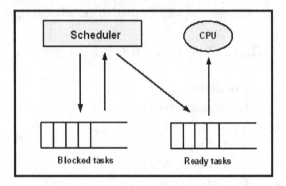

Whenever the resource is available at the instant *t3*, the task Γ_1 is transformed into ready state. Finally, it is executed again since the time *t4*. It is terminated at the instant *t5* (Figure 12).

A scheduler related to a real-time operating system is characterized by (Figure 13):

- **readyTask:** A queue maintaining the set of tasks in ready state.
- **executingTask:** A queue maintaining the set of tasks in executing state.
- **minPriority:** The minimum priority assigned to a task.
- **maxPriority:** The maximum priority assigned to a task.

- **timeSlice:** The threshold of preempting a task (the quantity of time assigned to a task before its preemption).

Several tasks may be in the ready or blocked states. The system therefore maintains a queue of blocked tasks and another queue for ready tasks. The latter is maintained in a priority order, keeping the task with the highest priority at the top of the list. When a task that has been in the ready state is allocated the processor, it makes a state transition from ready state to running state. This assignment of the processor is called dispatching and it is executed by the dispatcher which is a part of the scheduler.

Running Example: In the FESTO Benchmark Production System, we consider three tasks Γ_1, Γ_2 and Γ_3 having as priority p1, p2 and p3 such that p1 < p2 < p3. We suppose that the task Γ_1 is running when the task Γ_2 is created at the instant *t1*. As a consequence, there is a context switch so that the task Γ_1 stays in a ready state and the other task Γ_2 begins its execution as it has higher priority. At the instant *t2*, the task Γ_3 which was already blocked waiting a resource, gets the resource. As the task Γ_3 is the highest priority, the task Γ_2 turns into ready state and Γ_3 executes

Figure 12. The variation of states related to the task Γ_1

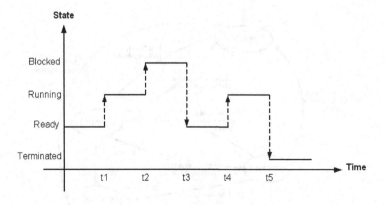

Figure 13. The real time operating system

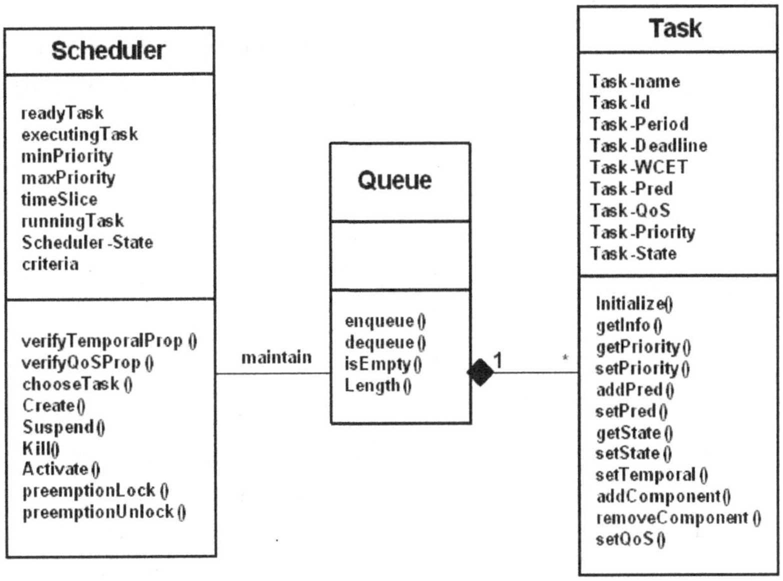

Scheduler
readyTask
executingTask
minPriority
maxPriority
timeSlice
runningTask
Scheduler-State
criteria
verifyTemporalProp ()
verifyQoSProp ()
chooseTask ()
Create()
Suspend()
Kill()
Activate()
preemptionLock ()
preemptionUnlock ()
maintain
Queue
enqueue ()
dequeue ()
isEmpty()
Length()
1
*
Task
Task-name
Task-Id
Task-Period
Task-Deadline
Task-WCET
Task-Pred
Task-QoS
Task-Priority
Task-State
Initialize()
getInfo ()
getPriority()
setPriority()
addPred ()
setPred ()
getState ()
setState ()
setTemporal ()
addComponent()
removeComponent ()
setQoS ()

its routine. The task Γ_3 continues processing until it has completed, the scheduler enables Γ_2 to become running (Figure 14).

Feasible and Safety Dynamic Reconfiguration of Tasks

We want to study the system's safety during reconfiguration scenarios. In fact, we want to keep tasks running while dynamically reconfiguring them. We assume for such system's task several software processes which provide functional services, and assume also reconfiguration processes that apply required modifications such as adapting connections, data or internal behaviors of the component. The execution of these different tasks is usually critical and can lead to incorrect behaviors of the whole system. In this case, we should schedule which process should be firstly activated to avoid any conflict between processes.

Consequently, we propose in this section to synchronize processes for coherent dynamic reconfigurations applied to several tasks.

Reconfiguration and Service Processes

We want in this section to synchronize service and reconfiguration processes of a task according to the following constraints: (1) whenever a reconfiguration process is running, any new service process must wait until its termination; (2) a reconfiguration process must wait until the termination of all service processes before it begins its execution; (3) it is not possible to execute many reconfiguration

Figure 14. The context switch between tasks

Priority
Context switch
Context switch
Context switch
Task 3
Task 2
Task 2
Task 1
Time
t1
t2
t3

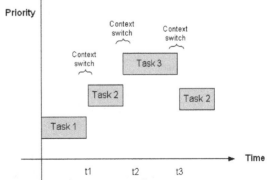

Algorithm 2. Execute a service related to a task

```
begin service
P(serv)
Nb ← NB + 1
if (NB = 1) then
P(reconfig)
end if
V(serv)
execute the service
P(serv)
Nb ← NB - 1
if (NB = 0) then
V(reconfig)
end if
V(serv)
end service
```

processes in parallel; (4) several service processes can be executed at the same time.

To do that, we use semaphores and also the famous synchronization algorithm between readers and writer processes such that executing a service plays the role of a reader process and reconfiguring a task plays the role of a writer process.

In the following algorithm, we define *serv* and *reconfig* as semaphores to be initialized to 1.

The shared variable Nb represents the number of current service processes associated to a specific task. Before the execution of a service related to a task, the service process increments the number Nb (which represents the number of service processes). It tests if it is the first process (i.e. Nb is equal to one).

In this case, the operation P(reconfig) ensures that it is not possible to begin the execution if there is a reconfiguration process.

```
P(serv)
Nb ← NB + 1
if (NB = 1) then
P(reconfig)
end if
V(serv)
```

After the execution of a service related to a task, the corresponding process decrements the

number Nb and tests if there is no service process (i.e. Nb is equal to zero).

In this case, the operation V(reconfig) authorizes the execution of a reconfiguration process.

```
P(serv)
Nb ← NB - 1
if (NB = 0) then
V(reconfig)
end if
V(serv)
```

Consequently, each service process related to a task does the following instructions:

Running Example: Let us take as a running example the task *Test* related to the FESTO system. To test a piece before elevating it, this component permits to launch the *Test Service Process*. Figure 15 displays the interaction between the objects *Test Service Process*, *Service semaphore* and *Reconfiguration semaphore*.

The flow of events from the point of view of *Test Service Process* is the following:

1. The operation P(serv) leads to enter in critical section for *Service semaphore*;
2. The number of services is incremented by one;
3. If it is the first service, then the operation P(reconfig) permits to enter in critical section for *Reconfiguration semaphore*;
4. The operation V(serv) leads to exit from critical section for *Service semaphore*;
5. The *Test Service Process* executes the corresponding service;
6. Before modifying the number of service, the operation P(serv) leads to enter in critical section for *Service semaphore*;
7. The number of services is decremented by one;
8. If there is no service processes, then the operation V(reconfig) permits to exit from critical section for *Reconfiguration semaphore*;

Figure 15. The service process scenario

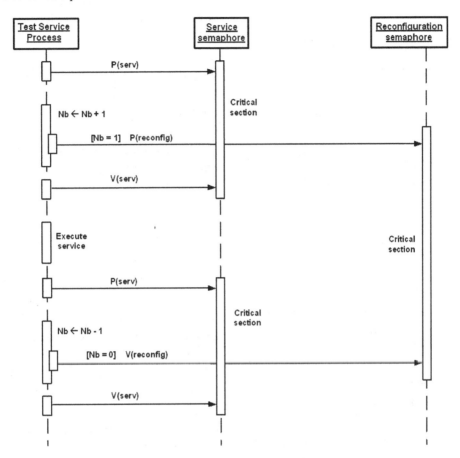

9. The operation V(serv) leads to liberate *Service semaphore* from its critical section.

With the operation P(reconfig), a reconfiguration process verifies that there is no reconfiguration processes nor service processes which are running at the same time. After that, the reconfiguration process executes the necessary steps and runs

Algorithm 3. Reconfigure a task

```
begin reconfiguration
P(reconfig)
execute the reconfiguration
V(reconfig)
end reconfiguration
```

the operation V(reconfig) in order to push other processes to begin their execution.

Each reconfiguration process specific to a task realizes the following instructions:

Running Example: Let us take as example the task *Elevate* related to FESTO system. The agent needs to reconfigure this task which permits to launch the *Elevate Reconfiguration Process.*

The Figure 16 displays the interaction between the following objects *Elevate Reconfiguration Process* and *Reconfiguration semaphore.*

The flow of events from the point of view of *Elevate Reconfiguration Process* is the following:

1. The operation P(reconfig) leads to enter in critical section for *Reconfiguration semaphore*;

Figure 16. The reconfiguration process scenario

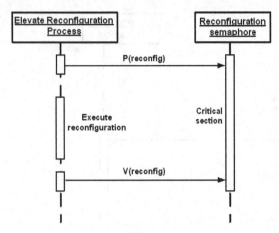

2. The *Elevate Reconfiguration Process* executes the corresponding reconfiguration;
3. The operation V(reconfig) leads to liberate *Reconfiguration semaphore* from its critical section.

Verification of Safety of the Synchronization

To verify the safety of the synchronization, we should verify if the different constraints mentioned above are respected.

First property: Whenever a reconfiguration process is running, any service processes must wait until the termination of the reconfiguration.

Let us suppose that there is a reconfiguration process (so the integer *reconfig* is equal to zero and the number of current services is zero).

When a service related to this component is called, the number of current services is incremented (i.e. it is equal to 1) therefore the operation P(reconfig) leads the process to be in a blocked state (as the integer *reconfig* is equal to zero).

When the reconfiguration process terminates the reconfiguration, the operation V(reconfig) permits to liberate the first process waiting in the semaphore queue.

In conclusion, this property is validated.

Second property: Whenever a service process is running, any reconfiguration processes must wait until the termination of the service.

Let us suppose that there is a service process related to a component (so the number of services is greater or equal to one which means that the operation P(reconfig) is executed and *reconfig* is equal to zero).

When a reconfiguration is applied, the operation P(reconfig) leads this process to be in a blocked state (as the *reconfig* is equal to zero).

Whenever the number of service processes becomes equal to zero, the operation *V(reconfig)* allows to liberate the first reconfiguration process waiting in the semaphore queue.

As a conclusion, this property is verified.

Third property: Whenever a reconfiguration process is running, it is not possible to apply a new reconfiguration process until the termination of the first one.

Let us suppose that a reconfiguration process is running (so *reconfig* is equal to zero).

Whenever, a new reconfiguration process tries to execute, the operation P(reconfig) puts it into a waiting state.

After the reconfiguration process which is running is terminated, the operation V(reconfig) allows to liberate the first reconfiguration waiting process. Consequently, this property is respected.

Fourth property: Whenever a service process is running, it is possible to apply another process service.

Let us suppose that a service process *P1* is running. Whenever, a new service process *P2* tries to begin the execution, the state of *P2* (activated or blocked) depends basically on the process *P1*:

- If *P1* is testing the shared data *Nb*, then the operation P(serv) by the process *P2* leads it to a blocking state. When the process *P1* terminates the test of the shared data *Nb*, the operation V(serv) allows to launch the process waiting in the semaphore's queue.

- If *P1* is executing its service, then the operation P(serv) by the process *P2* allows to execute normally.

Thus, this property is validated.

Task Scheduling with Priority Ceiling Protocol

How to schedule periodic tasks with precedence and mutual exclusion constraints is considered as important as how to represent a task in a general real-time operating system. In our context, we choose the priority-driven preemptive scheduling used in the most real-time operating systems. The semaphore solution can lead to the problem of priority inversion which consists that a high priority task can be blocked by a lower priority task. To avoid such problem, we propose to apply the priority inheritance protocol proposed by (Sha, 1990).

The priority inheritance protocol can be used to schedule a set of periodic tasks having exclusive access to common resources protected by semaphores. To do so, each semaphore is assigned a priority ceiling which is equal to the highest priority task using this semaphore. A task Γ_i is allowed to enter its critical section only if its assigned priority is higher than the priority ceilings of all semaphores currently locked by tasks other than Γ_i.

Schedulability test for the priority ceiling protocol: a set of n periodic tasks using the priority ceiling protocol can be scheduled by the rate-monotonic algorithm if the following inequalities hold,

$$\forall \ i, 1 \leq i \leq n, C_1/T_1 + C_2/T_2 + \dots + C_i/T_i + B_i/T_i \leq i(2^{1/i}-1)$$

where B_i denotes the worst-case blocking time of a task Γ_i by lower priority tasks.

Running Example: In the FESTO Benchmark Production System, we consider three tasks *R1* (a reconfiguration task), *S1* and *S2* (service tasks) having as priority *p1*, *p2* and *p3* such that *p1* > *p2* > *p3*.

The sequence of processing steps for each task is as defined in the section previous paragraph where S (resp. R) denotes the service (resp. reconfiguration) semaphore:

R1 = { ... P(R) execute reconfiguration V(R) ... }

S1 = { ... P(S) ... P(R) ... V(S) execute service P(S) ... V(R) ... V(S) ... }

Figure 17. The priority ceiling protocol applied to three tasks R1, S1, and S2

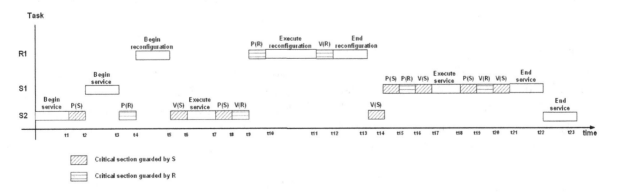

Table 2. The event and its corresponding action in the Figure 17

Event	Action
t0	S2 begins execution.
t1	S2 locks S. The task S2 inherits the priority of S.
t2	The task S1 is created. As it has more priority than S2, it begins its execution.
t3	The task S1 fails to lock S as its priority is not higher than the priority ceiling of the locked S. The task S2 resumes the execution with the inherited priority of S.
t4	The task S2 locks R. The task S2 inherits the priority of R. The task R1 is created and preempts the (execution of S2 as it has the highest priority).
t5	The task R1 fails to lock R as its priority is not higher than the priority ceiling of the locked R. The task S2 resumes the execution of the critical section.
t6	The task S2 unlocks S.
t7	The task S2 executes a service.
t8	The task S2 locks S.
t9	The task S2 unlocks R and therefore has as priority the same as S. The task R1 becomes having the highest priority. As it has more priority than S2, it resumes its execution.
t10	The task R1 locks R.
t11	The task R1 executes the reconfiguration.
t12	The task R1 unlocks R.
t13	The task R1 terminates its execution.
t14	The task S2 unlocks S (thus S2 becomes having the lowest priority). Therefore, the task S1 resumes its execution.
t15	The task S1 locks S.
t16	The task S1 locks R.
t17	The task S1 unlocks S.
t18	The task S1 executes its service.
t19	The task S1 locks S.
t20	The task S1 unlocks R.
t21	The task S1 unlocks S.
t22	The task S1 achieves its execution.
t23	The task S2 resumes the execution and terminates its service.

S2 = { … P(S) … P(R) … V(S) execute service P(S) … V(R) … V(S) … }

Therefore, the priority ceiling of the semaphore *R* is equal to the task *R1* (because the semaphore *R* is used by the tasks *R1*, *S1* and *S2* and we know that the task *R1* is the highest priority) and the priority ceiling of the semaphore *S* is equal to the task *S1* (because the semaphore *S* is used by the tasks *S1* and *S2* and the priority task of *S1* is higher).

We suppose that the task *S2* is running when the task *S1* is created at the instant t3. We suppose also that the task *R1* is created at the instant t5.

In the Figure 17, a line in a high level indicates that the task is executing, a line in a low level indicates that the the task is blocked or preempted by another task.

Figure 18. Definition of a task in the RTLinux

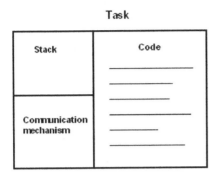

The following Table 2 explains more in details the example.

Task Implementation within RTLinux

We have presented the notion of a task as a purely conceptual design model. In this section, we present the task more concretely using RTLinux as a real-time operating system.

In the RTLinux, as it is indicated in (Cottet, 2002), a realtime program is not created as a standalone but rather as a module which is loaded in the Linux kernel space.

The module consists of the following elements:

1. A code to execute the task's function;
2. A stack to save the task's context;
3. A communication mechanism in order to communicate with other tasks. In fact, Real-time tasks communicate with the processor using particular queues called RT-FIFO ensuring that a real-time task cannot be blocked if it is using a RT-FIFO to read or write data (Figure 18).

This module has two main functions which are: int init_module() and void cleanup_module(). The init_module function is called when the module is first loaded into the kernel. However, the cleanup module is called when the module is unloaded. A realtime application is constituted by several threads. To create a new realtime thread, we use the pthread_create() function. This function is only called from the Linux kernel thread (which means using init_module()):

```
#include <pthread.h>
int pthread_create(pthread_t *
thread, pthread_attr_t * attr, void
*(*start_routine)(void *), void *
arg);
```

Figure 19. The interaction between two real tasks in the FESTO system

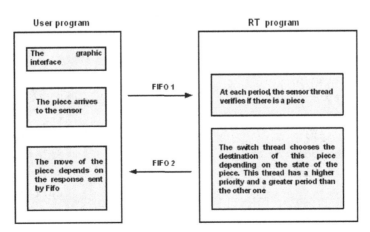

Thread priority can be modified at thread creation time by using: pthread_attr_setschedparam().

Running Example: As it is presented at the beginning of this article, FESTO is composed of three units: Distribution, Test and Processing units. We are interested here into the testing unit which is composed of the detector, the tester and the elevator. This unit performs checks on work pieces for height, material type and color. Work pieces that successfully pass this check are forwarded to the rotating disk of the Processing unit, where the drilling of the work piece is performed.

We present here an example of two periodic real-time tasks using RTLinux which are sensor_thread to detect the presence of piece and switch_thread to decide the piece destination depending on the state of the piece (Figure 19).

```
#include <rtl.h>
#include <time.h>
#include <pthread.h>
#include <rtl_fifo.h>
#include "pieces.h"
pthread_t sensor_thread;//detect and
determine the nature of piece
pthread_t switch_thread;//take deci-
sion
int current_status = 0;//detect the
current piece
struct pieces piece;
void * sensor_routine(void *t)
{
    int fifo=(int) t;
    char buf;
    struct sched_param p;
    p.sched_priority = 1;
    pthread_setschedparam (pthread_
self(), SCHED_FIFO, &p);
    pthread_make_periodic_np
(pthread_self(), gethrtime(),
4000000);
    while (1)
    {
        pthread_wait_np ();
        if (!rtf_isempty(fifo))
        {
            rtf_get(fifo,&buf,1);
            rtl_printf("launch
routine %c ", buf);
            piece.type=buf;
            piece.xcord=0;
            current_status=0;
        }
    }
    return 0;
}
void * switch_routine(void *t)
{
    int fifo=(int) t;
    char buf;
    int C;
    struct sched_param p;
    p.sched_priority = 3;
    pthread_setschedparam (pthread_
self(), SCHED_FIFO, &p);
    pthread_make_periodic_np
(pthread_self(), gethrtime(),
100000);
    while (1)
    {
        pthread_wait_np ();
        if (current_status==0)
        {
            C=rtf_
flush(fifo);
            buf=piece.type;
            rtf_
put(fifo,&buf,1);
            rtl_
printf("sensor le type est: %c
",buf);
        }
        current_status ++;
    }
```

```
      return 0;
}
int init_module(void)
{
      int c[2];
      rtf_destroy(1);
      rtf_destroy(2);
      c[0]=rtf_create(1,100);
      c[1]=rtf_create(2,100);
      pthread_create (&sensor_thread,
NULL, sensor_routine, (void *)1);
      pthread_create (&switch_thread,
NULL, switch_routine, (void *)2);
      return 0;
}
void cleanup_module(void) {
      pthread_delete_np (sensor_
thread);
      pthread_delete_np (switch_
thread);
      rtf_destroy(1);
      rtf_destroy(2);
}
```

CONCLUSION

Safety Reconfiguration of Embedded Control Systems is studied from the functional to the operational level. In the functional level, we propose Control Component for many reasons: (1) the separation of concerns which means that each Control Component can be defined alone after that all the system can be reproduced; (2) the modification of Control component is very simple (such as modification of data, algorithm, connection, …); (3) the reuse of Control Component (it is not specific for only one application).

The need for an intelligent software agent having the ability to reconfigure the system (i.e. to change its architecture, the connection between the components or to substitute a component with another) is well justified.

We define the architecture of the agent where a Reconfiguration Agent is affected to each device of the execution environment to handle local automatic reconfigurations.

In the operational level, we define the concept of real-time task in general to deploy a Control Component in a Real-Time Operating System. The dynamic reconfiguration of tasks is ensured through a synchronization between service and reconfiguration processes to be applied. We propose to use the semaphore concept for this synchronization such that we consider service processes as readers and reconfiguration processes as writers. We propose to use the priority ceiling protocol as a method to ensure the scheduling between periodic tasks with precedence and mutual exclusion constraints.

REFERENCES

Akerholm & Fredriksson. (2004). *A sample of component technologies for embedded systems*.

Brinksma., et al. (2003). *ROADMAP: Component-based design and integration platforms*. Retrieved from http://www.artist-embedded.org

Cottet, D. Kaiser, & Mammeri. (2002). Scheduling in real-time systems. New York: John Wiley & Sons Ltd.

Crnkovic & Larsson. (2002). *Building reliable component-based software systems*. Boston: Artech House.

Crnkovic. (2003). *Component-based approach for embedded systems*.

D'Souza & Wills. (1998). *Objects, components and frameworks: The catalysis approach*. Reading, MA: Addison-Wesley.

de Jonge. (2009). Developing product lines with third-party components. *Electronic Notes in Theoretical Computer Science*, 63–80.

EN50126. (1999). *Railway applications – The specification and demonstration of dependability, reliability, availability, maintainability and safety (RAMS).* Comite Europeen de Nomalisation Electrotechnique.

EN50128. (2002). *Railway applications – Software for railway control and protection systems.* Comite Europeen de Nomalisation Electrotechnique.

EN50129. (2002). *Railway applications – Safety related electronic systems for signalling.* Comite Europeen de Nomalisation Electrotechnique.

Faller. (2004). Project experience with IEC 61508 and its consequences. *Safety Science,* (42), 405-422.

Genssler et al. (2002). *PECOS in a nutshell.*

Genßler, N. (n.d.). [Components for embedded software the PECOS approach.]. *Schonhage..*

Gharbi, Khalgui, & Hanisch. (2009). Functional safety of component-based embedded control systems. In *Proceedings of the 2nd IFAC Workshop on Dependable Control of Discrete Systems.* IFAC.

IEC61513. (2002). *Nuclear power plants – Instrumentation and control for systems important to safety – General requirements for systems.* Geneva, Switzerland: International Electrotechnical Commission.

IEC 61508. (1992). *Functional safety of electrical/electronic programmable electronic systems: Generic aspects: Part 1: General requirements.* Geneva, Switzerland: International Electrotechnical Commission.

Jubin & Friedrichs. (2000). *Enterprise javabeans by example.* Upper Saddle River, NJ: Prentice Hall.

Microsoft. (n.d.). *COM specification.* Retrieved from http://www.microsoft.com/com

Olsen, Wang, Ramirez-Serrano, & Brennan. (2005). Contingencies-based reconfiguration of distributed factory automation. *Robotics and Computer-integrated Manufacturing,* 379–390. doi:10.1016/j.rcim.2004.11.011.

Pedreiras & Almeida. (2007). *Task management for soft real-time applications based on general purpose operating system.*

Pérez, Priol, & Ribes. (2002). *A parallel CORBA component model.* Research report N 4552.

Sha, Rajkumar, & Lehoczky. (1990). Priority inheritence protocols: An approach to real-time synchronization. *IEEE Transactions on Computers, 39*(9), 1175–1185. doi:10.1109/12.57058.

Stewart, Volpe, & Khosla. (1997). Design of dynamically reconfigurable real-time software using port-based objects. *IEEE Transactions on Software Engineering,* (23): 592–600.

Szyperski, Gruntz, & Murer. (2002). *Component software beyond object-oriented programming.* Reading, MA: Addison-Wesley.

Transformation. (n.d.). Retrieved from http://www.program-Transformation.org/Tools/KoalaCompiler

van Ommering, van der Linden, Kramer, & Magee. (2000). The koala component model for consumer electronics software. *IEEE Computer,* 78-85.

Wuyts, Ducasse, & Nierstrasz. (2005). A data-centric approach to composing embedded, real-time software components. *Journal of Systems and Software,* (74): 25–34. doi:10.1016/j.jss.2003.05.004.

Chapter 11
Task Scheduling under Uncertain Timing Constraints in Real–Time Embedded Systems

Pranab K. Muhuri
South Asian University, India

K. K. Shukla
Banaras Hindu University, India

ABSTRACT

In real-time embedded systems, timeliness of task completion is a very important factor. In such systems, correctness of the output depends on the timely production of results in addition to the logical outcome of computation. Thus, tasks have explicit timing constraints besides other characteristics of general systems, and task scheduling aims towards devising a feasible schedule of the tasks such that timing constraints, resource constraints, precedence constraints, etc. are complied. In real-time embedded systems, the most important timing constraint of a task is the deadline, as tasks must be completed within this time. The next important timing constraint is the processing time, because a task occupies a processor only for this duration of time. However, in the early phase of real-time embedded systems design only an approximate idea of the tasks and their characteristics are known. As a result, uncertainty or impreciseness is associated with the task deadlines and processing times; hence, it is appropriate to use fuzzy numbers to model deadlines and processing times in real-time embedded systems. The chapter introduces a new method using mixed cubic-exponential Hermite interpolation technique for intuitively defining smooth Membership Functions (MFs) for fuzzy deadlines and processing times. The effect of changes in parameterized MFs on the task schedulability and task priorities are explained. Examples are given to demonstrate the significant features and better performance of the new technique.

DOI: 10.4018/978-1-4666-3922-5.ch011

1. INTRODUCTION

Real-time systems are those systems for which a timely response to the external stimuli within a specified time frame is a must (Krishna & Shin, 1997). In other words, computing systems where catastrophe may occur or results may become useless if task completion takes more than some specified time are known as real-time systems (Ramamritham & Stankovic, 1994). Communication Systems, Defense Systems, Aircraft Flight Control Systems, Air Traffic Control, Space Stations, Nuclear Power Plants etc. depend solely on real-time computing and are examples of Real-Time Systems. Real-Time Systems draw attention to various issues especially in scheduling, resource allocation, and communication between components and subsystems etc. Three main measures that count the merits of real-time systems are: predictably very rapid response to urgent events, high degree of schedulability (i.e. surety of feasible schedule) and stability during transient overload (Sha, 1994).

Computing applications of real-time systems, i.e. time critical systems, require satisfying explicit timing constraints of the tasks and hence these timing constraints play the most important role for the purposeful and safe operation of real-time systems. These timing constraints may be hard or soft. Therefore, real-time systems can be classified into hard real-time systems and soft real-time systems. Computing systems with hard timing constraints are known as hard real-time systems, whereas those with soft timing constraints are known as soft real-time systems. The timing constraints of a particular set of tasks in a real-time system comprises of task arrival or release times, relative task deadlines, absolute task deadlines, processing times, intervals between subsequent invocations of tasks i.e. period etc as defined below:

- The *release time* of task is the time before which it cannot start execution.

- The time within which a task must be completed after it is released is known as the *relative deadline* of that particular task.
- Release time plus the relative deadline gives the *absolute deadline* of a task.
- The time required by the processor to execute a particular task is known as the *processing time or execution time*.
- Tasks may be periodic, aperiodic, or sporadic.
- When tasks are released periodically they are *periodic tasks*.
- An invocation of *sporadic tasks* happens in irregular intervals rather than periodically. An upper bound on the invocation rate characterizes the sporadic tasks.
- *Aperiodic tasks* are not periodic nor carry any bound on invocation rate.

Task scheduling plays a crucial role in real-time systems. It works to devise a feasible schedule subject to a given set of tasks and task characteristics, timing constraints, resource constraints, precedence constraints etc. There are some remarkable differences between real-time scheduling problems and those of operations research. In operations research scheduling, usually the objective is to find optimal static schedule when some specific service characteristics of a fixed system is given. However, Real-time task scheduling may be *Static or Dynamic* (Sha, et al., 2004). Static scheduling is at the centre of many classical scheduling problems. In this case, the scheduling algorithms have complete knowledge of the tasks characteristics and their timing parameters. The scheduling is done in advance of actual operation. At the time of devising a schedule, the static scheduling algorithms must have the prior knowledge of all the future release times. As an example, let us consider a process control application, where a fixed set of sensors and actuators works in a well-defined environment and processing requirements. Here, the static scheduling algorithms produce a single schedule which is fixed for ever. In the case of dynamic scheduling, tasks are scheduled once they arrive in the system. Dynamic scheduling algorithms schedule the ready tasks in the systems, for which all the required information is available. However, they are completely unaware of the nature and characteristics of the new task arrivals. Therefore, from time to time task schedule changes in this type of systems. Robot teams cleaning chemical leakage, army command and critical control applications are good examples of systems, where dynamic scheduling strategies are essential.

A real-time system may be considered to have a general model as per following:

$T = \{T_i \mid i = 1, 2, 3, \ldots\ldots\ldots\ldots n\}$ are a set of n tasks such that:

- Estimated worst case processing time/execution time of task T_i is c_i.
- Period of task T_i is P_i.
- Relative deadline of task T_i is d_i.
- Absolute deadline of task T_i is D_i.
- Release time of task T_i is r_i.
- At the j-th invocation, the release time and absolute deadline of the task T_i are respectively r_{ij} and D_{ij}. That is, period of the j − th invocation of task T_i begins at time $r_{ij} = r_i + (j-1)P_i$ and completes by $D_{ij} = d_i + r_{ij} = d_i + I_i + (j-1)P_i$, $j = 1, 2, \ldots\ldots$
- At the j − th invocation, the completion time for task T_i is C_{ij}.

Most of the real-time scheduling algorithms follow *Priority-Driven Scheduling,* where, each task is assigned a priority based on some criteria. This approach never leaves the systems idle if there are any tasks waiting in the ready queue. Priority-driven scheduling is also known as event-driven, as scheduling decisions are made only when tasks

are released or complete execution. As this approach lists the tasks in the ready queue according to the assigned priority, priority-driven scheduling is also known as list scheduling. Priority-driven scheduling policy is greedy in nature, because it tries to make scheduling decisions which are locally optimal. Most of the scheduling algorithms used for non real-time systems, e.g. First In First Out (FIFO), Last In First Out (LIFO), Shortest Execution Time First (SETF), Longest Execution Time First (LETF) etc. are priority-driven (Liu, 2001). Among them, the first two assign priorities according to release times, while the later two assign priorities according to the execution times. Since the tasks priorities can also be changed dynamically in the case of round-robin scheduling approach, to some extent this may also be termed as priority-driven.

Liu and Layland in their seminal paper (Liu & Layland, 1973) assumed that priority-driven scheduling in a single processor real-time system shall have a number of features viz. tasks are periodic, tasks are released at the beginning of the period, deadlines are equal to the periods, tasks are independent of any resource or precedence constraints, all tasks have fixed worst case processing time (upper bound) less than or equal to the period, self-suspension of tasks are not allowed, preemption is allowed, negligible context switching overhead compared to task processing time, number of priority levels are unlimited. Priority-driven algorithms differ from each other based on how priorities are assigned to the tasks. Therefore, the priority-driven approach of the real-time scheduling theory may further be subdivided into two very important areas: *Fixed Priority Scheduling and Dynamic Priority Scheduling.* Fixed priority scheduling policies generally work at task-level. Priority of each periodic task is fixed with respect to other tasks in a real-time task set. That is, different invocations of a particular task have the same priority (Liu, 2001). In dynamic priority scheduling different priorities are assigned to different invocations of each task. Therefore the priorities of tasks changes with respect to that of other tasks as and when task invocations are released and complete execution. This is the reason why they are called dynamic priority scheduling algorithms. There are a number of remarkable works on priority-driven scheduling for real-time systems. Among, the fixed priority scheduling algorithms are the famous Rate Monotonic (RM) and Deadline Monotonic (DM) scheduling policies. Among the dynamic priority scheduling policies the Earliest Deadline First (EDF) scheduling algorithm and Least Laxity First (LLF) scheduling algorithm are most popular. We shall now discuss EDF and RM scheduling schemes with appropriate numerical examples.

RM Scheduling

The Rate Monotonic (RM) scheduling policy is the most widely used and studied real-time scheduling algorithm (Krishna & Shin, 1997). In this algorithm, priority assignment is based on the task periods. The shorter the period of a task, the higher is its priority. As the frequency of task invocation is the inverse of its period, in other words we can say that the higher the frequency of task invocation the higher is the task priority (Liu, 2001). RM is an optimal static priority scheduling algorithm. That is, for a task set, if RM algorithm cannot produce a feasible schedule, then no other static priority scheduling algorithm can produce a feasible schedule. For a set of n independent preemptable tasks, rate monotonic

Table 1. Task characteristics

Task (T$_i$)	Release Time (r$_i$)	Execution Time (e$_i$)	Relative Deadline (d$_i$)	Period (P$_i$)
T$_1$	0	2	6	6
T$_2$	2	4	12	12
T$_3$	4	6	22	22

algorithm always produces a feasible schedule, that is ensures the meeting of all task deadline, if $\sum_{i=1}^{n} \frac{e_i}{P_i} \leq n(2^{1/n} - 1)$. The quantity $\sum_{i=1}^{n} \frac{e_i}{P_i}$ is known as the processor utilization factor.

Example 1

We consider a real-time task set with task characteristics as noted in the Table 1.

The RM schedule of the task set, which is generated by Cheddar Real-Time Simulator (Singhoff, Plantec, Dissaux, & Legrand, 2009) is shown in the Figure 1. Here, $P_1 < P_2 < P_3$; therefore, according to RM scheduling policy, task T_1 has the highest priority, then comes task T_2 and in the last it is the task T_3. Whenever an invocation of T_1 is released, it preempts other running tasks. Similarly, task T_2 may also preempt task T_3. It is observed at time 12 (Figure 1) when task T_3 is preempted due to the arrival of the second invocation of task T_1. The preemption continues for task T_2 also, since before the second invocation of task T_1 completes execution, second invocation of next high priority tasks T_2 arrives.

EDF Scheduling

The EDF scheduling policy assigns priorities according to absolute deadline of tasks. The earlier the absolute deadline of a task, the higher is the priority (Krishna & Shin, 1997; Liu, 2001). EDF is a task level dynamic priority-scheduling algorithm and invocation–level fixed priority scheduling algorithm. This is because once any particular invocation of a task is placed in the ready queue as per the assigned EDF priority relative to the invocations of other tasks, its order in the queue remains fixed. Let us consider one example of classical EDF scheduling for periodic preemptable tasks with relative deadline equal to the period. There are no shared resources and precedence constraints. If for a task set the processor utiliza-

Figure 1. RM schedule generated by cheddar (Singhoff, Plantec, Dissaux, & Legrand, 2009)

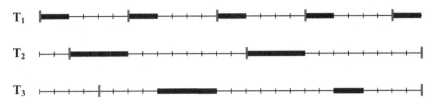

tion is less than equal to 1, then EDF scheduling algorithm can provide feasible schedule for the task set on a single processor real-time system. When the relative deadlines are not equal to the task periods, a set of real-time tasks is not schedulable (Krishna & Shin, 1997) by the EDF scheduling policy if,

- $u_i > 1$
- There exists

$$t < \min\left\{P + d_{\max}, \frac{u_i}{1 - u_i} \max_{1 \le i \le n}\left\{P_i - d_i\right\}\right\}$$

such that $h_T(t) > t$

Here, $u_i = \sum_{i=1}^{n} \frac{e_i}{P_i}$, $d_{\max} = \max_{1 \le i \le n}\left\{d_i\right\}$, P is the hyperperiod (or lcm, least common multiple) of the task periods and $h_T(t)$ is the sum of the execution time of all tasks in the task set for which the absolute deadline is less than t. The following example explains the general EDF scheduling algorithm discussed above.

Example 2

We consider a task set with four tasks in the task set having characteristics are shown in Table 2. The EDF schedule of the tasks, generated by Cheddar (Singhoff, Plantec, Dissaux, & Legrand, 2009) is shown in Figure 2. As soon as T_1 arrives it starts execution since it is the only task in the waiting queue. At time 1, when task T_3 arrives, task T_1 gets preempted by task T_3 as it is of higher priority (D_3 is less than D_1). Before task

T_3 finishes execution at time 4 task T_2 arrives. However, since $D_2 > D_3$, T_2 is of low priority than T_3, therefore cannot preempt task T_3. Therefore, T_3 continues execution until completion at time 4. However, since $D_2 < D_1$, hence T_2 is of higher priority than T_1. So, task T_2 starts execution after the completion of task T_3 at time 4. T_2 completes execution at time 9. After that, the processor goes to the preempted task T_1. When the second invocation of task T_3 arrives at time 11, it preempts task T_1 again and occupies the processor until its completion at time 14. Thereafter, the processor again goes to task T_1. At time 17, second invocation of task T_2 arrives. However, its absolute deadline is 32 (2+15+15), which is higher than D_1. Therefore it cannot preempt task T_1 and goes to the waiting queue. The same happens to the third invocation of task T_3. Task T_1 completes execution at time 22 and by that time both task T_2 (second invocation) and T_3 (third invocation) arrives in the waiting queue. Thus the processor goes to task T_3 at time 22. After the third invocation of task T_3 completes execution at time 25, the processor goes to T_2 for the execution of its second invocation. Dertouzos (1974) showed that EDF is optimal among all preemptive scheduling algorithms. For preemptable tasks without any resource contention in single processor real-time systems, EDF is an optimal scheduling policy. This means that for such systems, if EDF cannot provide a feasible schedule for a task set, then no other scheduling algorithm can do so.

In real-time embedded systems, time is a very important factor. This is because, in such systems, correctness of the result depends on the timely

Table 2. Task characteristics

Task (T_i)	Release Time (r_i)	Execution Time (e_i)	Relative Deadline (d_i)	Absolute Deadline (D_i)	Period (P_i)
T1	0	11	30	30	30
T_2	2	5	15	17	15
T_3	1	3	10	11	10

production of results as well as on the logical outcome of computation (Ramamritham & Stankovic, 1994). Therefore, in this type of systems task must have explicit timing constraints besides other characteristics of general systems. The most important timing constraint of a real-time task is deadline; because, execution of a real-time task must be completed within this time. Another important timing constraint is the processing time. Because when a task is under execution, the processor remains busy for this duration of time. However, in the early phase of real-time system design only an approximate idea of the tasks and their characteristics are known. Therefore, uncertainty or impreciseness is associated with the task deadlines and processing times. Ishii, Tada, and Masuda (1992) considered fuzzy due dates for the time for a general scheduling problem. Terrier & Chen (1994) applied fuzzy calculus to real-time task scheduling problem and considered fuzzy execution time for the first time. Lee, Tiao, and Yen (1994) proposed a model for fuzzy rule based scheduler. Murata, Ishibuchi, and Gen (1997) formulated multi–objective fuzzy scheduling problem considering the importance of individual jobs with OWA (ordered weighted averaging) operator. Very significant works on fuzzy real-time scheduling were carried out by Litoiu and Tadei (2001, 1997) and Muhuri, Pranab, and Shukla (2008, 2009). They have used a cost function called 'satisfaction of schedulability', introduced earlier by Ishii, Tada, and Masuda (1992) and investigated the task scheduling in real-time systems by modeling task deadlines and processing times with triangular type (Litoiu & Tadei (1997), trapezoidal type (Muhuri, Pranab, & Shukla, 2008), semi-elliptical type (Muhuri, Pranab, & Shukla, 2008) and other fuzzy membership functions (Muhuri, Pranab, & Shukla, 2009). Therefore, fuzzy numbers (Zimmermann, 1996; Klir, Clair, & Bo, 1997; Slany, 1996) are considered to model task deadlines and processing times in real-time systems as fuzzy deadlines and fuzzy processing times represent real-time systems better. This is because, classical real-time scheduling models, which consider real-time tasks with crisp timing parameters, suffer from the following limitations (Litoiu & Tadei, 2001):

Modeling Shortcomings: Although separate models and solutions exist for hard real-time sys-

Figure 2. Cheddar (Singhoff, Plantec, Dissaux, & Legrand, 2009) generated EDF schedule

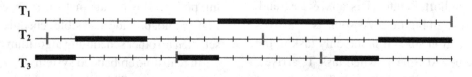

tems and soft real-time systems, excellent models that may be utilized for both hard and soft real-time systems are not available. On the other hand, all decisions about real-time systems have to be made during design time; when, even the source code and the tasks timing constraints are not known. Therefore, task deadlines and processing times etc. are all designer approximations. As crisp numbers appear as special cases of fuzzy numbers, therefore fuzzy numbers comes as a beautiful tool to model both hard and soft real-time tasks indifferently. This justifies the use of fuzzy numbers for timing parameters of real-time tasks.

Design Limitations: Deterministic models for real-time systems are always over constrained. Designs are accepted if they ensure meeting the deadlines. If deadlines are missing then the designs are rejected. This happens at the time of solving the models and truly no information is provided regarding, for how much the deadlines are actually missed. However, considerations of fuzzy numbers to model processing times and deadlines provide the designers wider options and sufficient information to take decisions on the model design.

2. REAL-TIME SCHEDULING WITH DEADLINES AND PROCESSING TIMES AS TRIANGULAR FUZZY MF

To model the existing uncertainties in the timing constraints of real-time tasks we have considered fuzzy set theory since it allows expert help for task modeling and it provides more flexibility in modeling because without any significant addition in complexity we can choose from a wide variety of fuzzy membership types (Zimmermann, 1996; Klir, Clair, & Bo, 1997; Slany, 1996) for a particular timing parameter. The scheduling of real-time tasks having fuzzy constraints can be termed as fuzzy real-time scheduling. In this section, we explain the fuzzy real-time scheduling model Litoiu

and Tadei (2001, 1997) and Muhuri, Pranab, and Shukla (2008, 2009) for triangular membership functions. The effects of the choice of different types of membership functions and their fuzzy parameters are studied and simulation results are given (Muhuri, Pranab, & Shukla, 2008). When the width of the trapezoid is zero, Litoiu's model (Litoiu & Tadei, 2001) for triangular membership function, which we are discussing below, appears as a special case of the trapezoidal model given in Muhuri, Pranab, and Shukla (2008).

Let us consider the relative deadline d_i of task T_i as the trapezoidal (or triangular) type fuzzy number such that $[a_i, b_i]$ is its 0-cut, then

$$d_i = \left(a_i, a_i', b_i', b_i \right) \text{ (for triangular case,}$$
$$a_i' = b_i') \tag{2.1}$$

Therefore, the absolute deadline of the task T_{ij} (j-th invocation of the i-th task) can be expressed as Equation (2.2) in Box 1.

Now, considering μ as the membership function for the fuzzy deadline D_{ij} and C_{ij} as the crisp execution time, the following cost function viz., satisfaction of schedulability

(S_D) is introduced to see the compliance of the deadlines over all the periods (see Equation (2.3) in Box 2).

In Equation (2.3), the completion time C_{ij} is the sum of deterministic execution times and hence deterministic in nature. If we consider a general bell shaped membership function with $[a_{ij}, b_{ij}]$ as it is 0-cut then, as shown in the Figure 3, we can

see that The quantity $\dfrac{\displaystyle\int_{a_{ij}}^{C_{ij}} \mu(D_{ij})d(D_{ij})}{\displaystyle\int_{a_{ij}}^{b_{ij}} \mu(D_{ij})d(D_{ij})}$ is actu-

ally the measure of dissatisfaction, how far the task completion time is missing the deadline. Here, the denominator is the total area under the curve, whereas the numerator is the shaded area.

Box 1.

$$D_{ij} = \left(a_i + I_i + (j-1)P_i, \; a_i' + I_i + (j-1)P_i, \; b_i' + I_i + (j-1)P_i, \; b_i + I_i + (j-1)P_i \right) = \left(a_{ij}, a_{ij}', b_{ij}', b_{ij} \right)$$

(2.2)

Box 2.

$$S_{D_i}(C_{ij}) = \begin{cases} 1 & \\ 1 - \dfrac{\displaystyle\int_{a_{ij}}^{C_{ij}} \mu(D_{ij})d(D_{ij})}{\displaystyle\int_{a_{ij}}^{b_{ij}} \mu(D_{ij})d(D_{ij})} & if \; a_{ij} \le C_{ij} \le b_{ij} \\ 0 & if \; C_{ij} > b_{ij} \end{cases}$$

(2.3)

The satisfaction function (S_D), as a function of crisp completion time C_{ij}, is continuous and strictly decreasing; the greater the completion time, the less is the satisfaction. Therefore if P is the hyperperiod (least common multiple of the task periods) of the task set, the problem of scheduling a set of task T_i with fuzzy deadlines D_{ij} and crisp completion time C_{ij} at the j-th invocation may be summarized as:

Maximize $S_D = \min_{i,j} S_{D_i}(C_{ij})$, (2.4)

finding an optimal assignment of priorities. Here, the schedulability should be examined over P time units. Therefore in the above Equation (2.4), $i = 1, \ldots, n$ and $j = 1, \ldots, P / P_i$. Next we consider the processing times are fuzzy trapezoidal (or triangular) numbers and D_{ij} as crisp. Then, the completion times are also trapezoidal (or triangular) fuzzy numbers. This is because, the completion time, as the sum of processing times, will be a fuzzy number when processing times are fuzzy. Therefore, we consider the fuzzy completion time C_{ij} of the j-th invocation of the i-th task to be a fuzzy trapezoidal number with $[e_{ij}, f_{ij}]$ as 0-cut as expressed below:

$$C_{ij} = \left(e_{ij}, e_{ij}', f_{ij}', f_{ij} \right)$$ (2.5)

Thus, to measure schedulability over the whole task set and every task invocation, the cost function satisfaction of schedulability $S_{C_i}(D_{ij})$, is introduced. For the task Ti in its j-th invocation, $S_{C_i}(D_{ij})$ is defined by Equation (2.6) in Box 3.

The integral exists for obvious reasons and in the interval $[e_{ij}, f_{ij}]$ the function S_{Ci} is strictly increasing and continuous. Therefore the problem is summarized as:

Maximize $S_C = \min_{i,j} S_{C_i}(D_{ij})$, $i = 1, \ldots, n$

and $j = 1, \ldots, P / P_i$ (2.7)

Figure 3. General fuzzy deadline

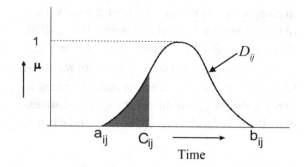

Box 3.

$$S_{C_i}(D_{ij}) = \begin{cases} 1 & if \ D_{ij} < e_{ij} \\ \dfrac{\displaystyle\int_{e_{ij}}^{D_{ij}} \mu(C_{ij})d(C_{ij})}{\displaystyle\int_{e_{ij}}^{f_{ij}} \mu(C_{ij})d(C_{ij})} & if \ e_{ij} \leq D_{ij} \leq f_{ij} \\ 0 & if \ D_{ij} > f_{ij} \end{cases} \qquad (2.6)$$

finding an optimal assignment of priorities.

Now considering both the deadlines and processing times as fuzzy trapezoidal numbers the scheduling problem for the task set, the problem may be summarized as:

Maximize $S = \min_{i,j} \max_{C_{ij}, D_{ij}}$
$\min\left(S_{C_i}(D_{ij}), S_{D_i}(C_{ij})\right), i = 1, \dots, n,$
$j = 1, \dots, P / P_i$ \hfill (2.8)

finding an optimal assignment of priorities.

Let us now consider, $\min_{i,j} S_{D_i}(C_{ij}) = t$ (2.9)

Then, $S_{D_i}(C_{ij}) \geq t \quad \forall i = 1, \dots, n$ and $j = 1, \dots, P / P_i$. (2.10)

From the continuity of the satisfaction S_d and it's inverse function, we may write:

$C_{ij} \leq I_i + (j-1)P_i + d_i'(t), i = 1, \dots, n$ and $j = 1, \dots, P / P_i$ \hfill (2.11)

In Equation (2.11) the quantity $d_i'(t)$ is a crisp quantity. It is termed as modified deadlines and it will depend on the minimum satisfaction, t. The optimal priority assignment of the real-time tasks are according to the increasing order of $d_i'(t)$. Now, our interest is to find those values of t $(0 \leq t \leq 1)$ for which modified deadlines of two tasks become equal i.e. those t_{ij} that satisfy Equation (2.12) in Box 4.

Since the modified deadline of different tasks changes at these t_{ij}, so the priorities of the tasks also changes at these points. Thus, we check the priorities of the tasks over various intervals $\left[t_m, t_{m+1}\right]$ obtained by sequentially placing the

Box 4.

$$\{t_{ij} \mid d_i'(t) = d_j'(t), j = 1, \dots, n, i = 1, \dots, n, 0 \leq t_{ij} \leq 1\} \qquad (2.12)$$

Table 3. Results for the example 3

Satisfaction Crossover Points (t_{ij})	Satisfaction Intervals	Tasks Priority within the Intervals	Interval of Highest Satisfaction	Satisfaction of Tasks	Satisfaction of Schedulability	Optimal Task Priority
$t_{12} = 0.5000$ $t_{13} = 0.2813$ $t_{23} = 0.2222$	[0.0000, 0.2222]	[T_3, T_2, T_1]	[0.5000, 1.0000]	T_1: 1.0000 T_2: 1.0000 T_3: 0.9990	0.9990	T_1: 1 T_2: 2 T_3: 3
	[0.2222, 0.2813]	[T_2, T_3, T_1]				
	[0.2813, 0.5000]	[T_2, T_1, T_3]				
	[0.5000, 1.0000]	[T_1, T_2, T_3]				

quantities t_{ij} in the increasing order. In a particular interval $\left[t_m, t_{m+1} \right]$, the order of the task deadlines and hence the task priorities remain same. Thus we apply successive search technique to identify the interval in which satisfaction is maximum. The priorities of the tasks in this interval give us the best priority assignment. After finding the highest satisfaction interval and its associated task priority the satisfaction of schedulability for the task set over that interval is calculated. For this purpose, the fuzzy completion times of the tasks needs to be computed. Then, the satisfaction of the schedulability is determined for the worst fuzzy completion time $W_i(C_i)$. The worst fuzzy completion time $W_i(C_i)$ may be calculated using the equation:

$$W_i(C_i) = \sum_{j=1}^{i} e_j \left\lceil C_i / P_j \right\rceil + B_{L_i} \qquad (2.13)$$

Here, B_{L_i} is the time for which a high priority task is blocked by a low priority one. Considering the worst case situation, when the processor is also requested by all other tasks, to calculate C_i / P_j, the latest extremity of C_i i.e. f_i is taken. In doing this, the fuzzy division is transformed into ordinary arithmetic division. Now, a triangular fuzzy number (*TFN*) is specified by three

parameters $\left(a_{ij}, a'_{ij} (= b'_{ij}), b_{ij} \right)$ as shown in Figure 4.

The membership function (μ) of a triangular fuzzy number may be expressed as Equation (2.14) in Box 5.

We consider task deadlines D_{ij} to be represented by $TFN\left(x; a_{ij}, b'_{ij}, b_{ij} \right)$. Then, the satisfaction function S_{D_i} can be expressed as Equation (2.15) in Box 6.

The modified deadlines of the task set T_i can be calculated using the following equations:

$$d'_i = \begin{cases} a_i + \sqrt{(1-t)X_i} & if\ t > L_i \\ b_i - \sqrt{(tY_i)} & if\ t \le L_i \end{cases} \qquad (2.16)$$

Here,

$$L_i = (b_i - b'_i)/(b_i - a_i);$$
$$X_i = (b_i - a_i)(b'_i - a_i);$$
$$Y_i = (b_i - a_i)(b_i - b'_i).$$

Following expressions are used to calculate K_1, K_2, K_3 and K_4, from the union $(K_1 \cup K_2 \cup K_3 \cup K_4)$ of which the quantities t_{ij} can be found. Here, $Z_{ij} = (b_j - a_i)^2$ and $Q_{ij} = (b_i - a_j)^2$.

Table 4. Results for the example 4

Satisfaction Crossover Points (t_{ij})	Satisfaction Intervals	Tasks Priority in the Interval	Interval of Highest Satisfaction	Satisfaction of Tasks	Satisfaction of Schedulability	Optimal Task Priority
$t_{12} = 0.5000$ $t_{23} = 0.9339$	[0.0000, 0.5000]	[T_2, T_1, T_3]	[0.9339, 1.0000]	T_1: 1.0000 T_2: 0.9800 T_3: 1.0000	0.9800	T_1: 1 T_2: 3 T_3: 2
	[0.5000, 0.9339]	[T_1, T_2, T_3]				
	[0.9339, 1.0000]	[T_1, T_3, T_2]				

Figure 4. Triangular fuzzy membership function

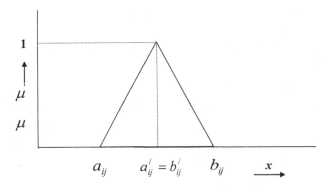

Table 5. Fuzzy deadlines in parametric representation

Task Deadline Sr. No. ⟹	D_1 (Deadline for Task T_1 in Parametric Form)	D_2 (Deadline for Task T_2 in Parametric Form)
A	(2, 1, 3, 1, 3, -1, 4, -1)	(2, 1, 3, -1, 3, 1, 4, -1)
B	(2, 1, 3, 1, 3, -1, 4, -1)	(2, 0.5, 3, 1, 3, -0.5, 4, -1)
C	(2, 0.5, 3, -12, 3, 12, 4, -0.5)	(2, 1, 3, 1, 3, -1, 4, -1)
D	(2, 1, 3, -15, 3, 15, 4, -0.8)	(2, 0.8, 3, -15, 3, 15, 4, -1)
E	(2, 1, 3, -15, 3, 15, 4, -1)	(2, 0.5, 3, -15, 3, 15, 4, -0.5)
F	(2, 1, 3, -1, 3, 1, 4, -1)	(2, 0.8, 3, 0.2, 3, -0.2, 4, .8)

Box 5.

$$TFN\left(x; a_{ij}, b_{ij}^{/}, b_{ij}\right) = \begin{cases} 0 \left(\dfrac{x - a_{ij}}{b_{ij}^{/} - a_{ij}}\right) & if \ x < a_{ij} \\ & if \ a_{ij} \leq x \leq b_{ij}^{/} \\ \left(\dfrac{b_{ij} - x}{b_{ij} - b_{ij}^{/}}\right) & if \ b_{ij}^{/} \leq x \leq b_{ij} \\ 0 & if \ x \geq b_{ij} \end{cases}$$

(2.14)

Box 6.

$$S_{d_i}(C_{ij}) = \begin{cases} 1 & if \ C_{ij} < a_{ij} \\ 1 - \dfrac{(C_{ij} - a_{ij})^2}{(b_{ij} - a_{ij})(b_{ij}^{/} - a_{ij})} & if \ a_{ij} \leq C_{ij} \leq b_{ij}^{/} \\ \dfrac{(b_{ij} - C_{ij})^2}{(b_{ij} - a_{ij})(b_{ij} - b_{ij}^{/})} & if \ b_{ij}^{/} \leq C_{ij} \leq b_{ij} \\ 0 & if \ C_{ij} > b_{ij} \end{cases}$$

(2.15)

3. REAL-TIME SCHEDULING WITH TASK DEADLINES AND PROCESSING TIMES AS PARAMETRIC FUZZY NUMBERS

For task scheduling in real-time embedded systems with fuzzy deadlines and execution times, there is a need to specify the memberships conveniently by the schedule designer. Simple MFs like Triangular, as explained in the previous section, have been used earlier by several researchers Litoiu and Tadei (2001, 1997), Muhuri, Pranab, and Shukla (2008, 2009). Although these MFs are simple to understand and analyze, yet, they contain discontinuities and restrict the designer in specifying task characteristics. We therefore introduce a novel method for intuitively defining smooth MFs for deadlines and execution times, using mixed cubic-exponential Hermite interpolation technique (Guerra & Stefanini, 2005). This method is very versatile and can model all kind of symmetric and asymmetric MFs, where Triangular and Trapezoidal MFs appear as special cases. Thus, the fuzzy real-time scheduling model is extended here for general fuzzy numbers in parametric representation. This gives a wider choice to the designers (Muhuri, Pranab, & Shukla, 2009). Mathematical models for this are developed and used in several test cases using the Cheddar real-time simulator (Singhoff, Plantec, Dissaux, & Legrand, 2009). First, the definition of a fuzzy number in the $\alpha - cut$ setting and the expressions for the addition and subtraction of fuzzy numbers in this setting are given here for ready reference. Thereafter, the parametric representation of fuzzy numbers based on monotonic interpolation is introduced for task scheduling in real-time systems. Finally, we shall discuss the approximated membership function for the parametric fuzzy numbers using the mixed cubic Hermite interpolation technique (Guerra & Stefanini, 2005).

A continuous fuzzy number/interval (say, u) is defined (Guerra & Stefanini, 2005) as any pair (u^-, u^+), where:

1. (u^-, u^+) are functions given by $u^\pm : [0, 1] \rightarrow R$

Box 7.

$$K_1 = \left\{ t_{ij} \mid t_{ij} = \left(\frac{a_i - a_j}{\sqrt{X_i} - \sqrt{X_j}} \right)^2 \right\} \text{ for } t_{ij} > L_i, \ t_{ij} > L_j$$

$$K_2 = \left\{ t_{ij} \mid t_{ij} = \left(\frac{b_i - b_j}{\sqrt{Y_i} - \sqrt{Y_j}} \right)^2 \right\} \text{ for } t_{ij} \leq L_i, \ t_{ij} \leq L_j$$

$$K_3 = \left\{ t_{ij} \mid t_{ij} = \frac{2X_i Y_j - (X_i - Y_j)(Z_{ij} - X_i) \pm 2\sqrt{Z_{ij} X_i Y_j (X_i + Y_j - Z_{ij})}}{(X_i + Y_j)^2} \right\} \text{ for } t_{ij} > L_i, t_{ij} \leq L_j$$

$$K_4 = \left\{ t_{ij} \mid t_{ij} = \frac{2X_j Y_i - (X_j - Y_i)(Q_{ij} - X_j) \pm 2\sqrt{Q_{ij} X_j Y_i (X_j + Y_i - Q_{ij})}}{(X_j + Y_i)^2} \right\} \text{ for } t_{ij} > L_i, t_{ij} \leq L_j$$

2. $u^- : \alpha \rightarrow u_\alpha^- \in R$ is a function which is bounded and monotonically increasing (non-decreasing) $\forall \alpha \in [0, 1]$

3. $u^+ : \alpha \rightarrow u_\alpha^+ \in R$ is a function which is bounded and monotonically decreasing (non-increasing) $\forall \alpha \in [0, 1]$

4. $u_\alpha^- \leq u_\alpha^+ \ \forall \alpha \in [0, 1]$

In the case of fuzzy intervals, $u_1^- < u_1^+$ and for fuzzy numbers, $u_1^- = u_1^+$. The $\alpha - cut$ of the fuzzy number u can be expressed as $u_\alpha = [u_\alpha^-, u_\alpha^+]$. Conveniently u^- and u^+ can be referred as the left and right branches of the fuzzy number u. Figure 5 shows the $\alpha - cut$ representation of a general fuzzy interval. If u and v are two fuzzy numbers such that $u = (u^-, \ u^+)$ and $v = (v^-, \ v^+)$, then the addition and subtraction operations among them in terms of $\alpha - cuts$ for $\alpha \in [0, 1]$ can be given by:

1. **Addition:** $(u + v)_\alpha = (u_\alpha^- + v_\alpha^-, \ u_\alpha^+ + v_\alpha^+)$

$\quad$ (3.1)

2. **Subtraction:**

$\quad (u - v)_\alpha = (u_\alpha^- - v_\alpha^+, \ u_\alpha^+ - v_\alpha^-)$ (3.2)

Now, using the mixed cubic-exponential Hermite interpolation technique we get a parametric representation of the fuzzy number in terms of $\alpha - cuts$ with four pairs of components, as given below:

$$u = (u_0^-, u_0'^-, u_1^-, u_1'^-, u_0^+, u_0'^+, u_1^+, u_1'^+) \quad (3.3)$$

Here, we assumed that within a sub-interval $[\alpha_{i-1}, \alpha_i]$ the values of $u^\pm(\alpha_{i-1}) = u_{i-1}^\pm$ and $u^\pm(\alpha_i) = u_i^\pm$ and their first derivates $u'^\pm(\alpha_{i-1}) = u_{i-1}'^\pm$ and $u'^\pm(\alpha_i) = u_i'^\pm$ are known. If u and v are two fuzzy numbers such that $u = (u_0^-, u_0'^-, u_1^-, u_1'^-, u_0^+, u_0'^+, u_1^+, u_1'^+)$ and $v = (v_0^-, v_0'^-, v_1^-, v_1'^-, v_0^+, v_0'^+, v_1^+, v_1'^+)$ then the addition and subtraction of u and v can respectively be given by Equations (3.4) and (3.5) in Box 8.

We are giving only the expressions for addition and subtraction operations as they are needed for calculating the fuzzy completion time, fuzzy lateness etc. in the real-time scheduling problem. Now by inverting the $\alpha - cut$ functions of u_α^- and u_α^+, following expression for the approximated fuzzy membership function $\mu_x, x \in R$, can be obtained:

Figure 5. General fuzzy interval in its $\alpha - cut$ representation (for fuzzy interval, $u_1^- = u_1^+$)

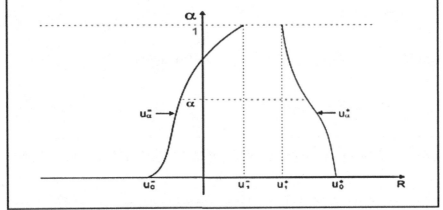

$$\mu_x = \begin{cases} 0 & if \ x \leq x_m^- \\ \mu_x^- & if \ x \in [x_m^-, x_M^-] \\ 1 & if \ x \in [x_M^-, x_m^+] \\ \mu_x^+ & if \ x \in [x_m^+, x_M^+] \\ 0 & if \ x \geq x_m^- \end{cases}$$

where,

1. $x_m^- = u_0^-$ and $x_M^+ = u_0^+$ are the corresponding points to the support of the fuzzy number. The points $x_M^- = u_1^-$ and $x_m^+ = u_1^+$ gives the interval (number if $x_M^- = x_m^+$) on the x-axis with membership value 1.

2. μ_x^- are increasing (non-decreasing) functions such that $\mu_{x_m^-}^- = 0$ and $\mu_{x_M^-}^- = 1$. And μ_x^+ are decreasing (non-increasing) functions such that $\mu_{x_m^+}^+ = 1$ and $\mu_{x_M^+}^+ = 0$.

The following relationships exist between μ_x^- and μ_α^- and between μ_x^+ and μ_α^+ :

1. $\mu_x^- = \alpha \leftrightarrow u_\alpha^- = x, \forall \alpha \in [0,1], \forall x \in [x_m^-, x_M^-]$ (3.7)

2. $\mu_x^+ = \alpha \leftrightarrow u_\alpha^+ = x, \forall \alpha \in [0,1], \forall x \in [x_m^+, x_M^+]$ (3.8)

Also, at the end points of the interval the derivatives of μ_x^- and μ_x^+ can be given by

1. $\left(\mu_x^-\right)' = \dfrac{1}{u_0^{'-}}$ at $x = x_m^-$ and $\left(\mu_x^-\right)' = \dfrac{1}{u_1^{'-}}$ at $x = x_M^-$ (3.9)

2. $\left(\mu_x^+\right)' = \dfrac{1}{u_1^{'+}}$ at $x = x_m^+$ and $\left(\mu_x^+\right)' = \dfrac{1}{u_0^{'+}}$ at $x = x_M^+$ (3.10)

The membership function is $\mu = (x_m^-, \mu_m^{'-}, x_M^-, \mu_M^{'-}, x_m^+, \mu_m^{'+}, x_M^+, \mu_M^{'+})$ (3.11) where, the monotonic components of μ_x^- and μ_x^+ are approximated, using the mixed cubic-exponential Hermite interpolation, as given by Equations (3.12) and (3.13) in Box 9.

We shall now use the parametric representation of fuzzy numbers to model task deadlines and processing times to investigate the real-time scheduling problem for tasks with fuzzy deadlines and processing times in parametric form. Various shapes of MFs obtained by changing the derivatives at the points $u_0^-, u_1^-, u_1^+, u_0^+$ are shown in Figure 6. So, the designer has a wider variety of MFs to choose according to different requirements and nature of the associated uncertainties in task characteristics. Now, we consider the deadline d as the fuzzy number such that $[u_0^-, u_0^+]$ is its 0-cut. Then, we can write,

$$d = (u_0^-, u_0^{'-}, u_1^-, u_1^{'-}, u_0^+, u_0^{'+}, u_1^+, u_1^{'+}).$$

Thus, the relative deadline (d_i) of the task T_i can be expressed by

$$d_i = (u_{0i}^-, u_{0i}^{'-}, u_{1i}^-, u_{1i}^{'-}, u_{0i}^+, u_{0i}^{'+}, u_{1i}^+, u_{1i}^{'+}) \quad (3.14)$$

Hence, the absolute deadline of the task T_i at its j-th invocation can be expressed as Equation (3.15) in Box 10.

Box 8.

1. $u + v = (u_0^- + v_0^-, u_0^{'-} + v_0^{'-}, u_1^- + v_1^-, u_1^{'-} + v_1^{'-}, u_0^+ + v_0^+, u_0^{'+} + v_0^{'+}, u_1^+ + v_1^+, u_1^{'+} + v_1^{'+})$ (3.4)
2. $u - v = (u_0^- - v_0^+, u_0^{'-} - v_0^{'+}, u_1^- - v_1^+, u_1^{'-} - v_1^{'+}, u_0^+ - v_0^-, u_0^{'+} - v_0^{'-}, u_1^+ - v_1^-, u_1^{'+} - v_1^{'-})$ (3.5)

Box 9.

$$\mu_x^- = \mu_m^- + \frac{\mu_m'^-}{1+w^-} + t^2(3-2t)\left[\mu_M^- - \mu_m^- - \frac{\mu_m'^- + \mu_M'^-}{1+w^-}\right] + \frac{\mu_M'^- t^{1+w^-} - \mu_m'^-(1-t)^{1+w^-}}{1+w^-} \qquad (3.12)$$

$$\mu_x^+ = \mu_m^+ + \frac{\mu_m'^+}{1+w^+} + t^2(3-2t)\left[\mu_M^+ - \mu_m^+ - \frac{\mu_m'^+ + \mu_M'^+}{1+w^+}\right] + \frac{\mu_M'^+ t^{1+w^+} - \mu_m'^+(1-t)^{1+w^+}}{1+w^+} \qquad (3.13)$$

Here, $\mu_m^- = 0, \mu_M^- = 1, \mu_m^+ = 1, \mu_M^+ = 0, \mu_m'^- = \dfrac{x_M^- - x_m^-}{u_0'^-}, \mu_M'^- = \dfrac{x_M^- - x_m^-}{u_1'^-}, \mu_m'^+ = \dfrac{x_M^+ - x_m^+}{u_1'^+},$

$\mu_M'^+ = \dfrac{x_M^+ - x_m^+}{u_0'^+}, \quad t^\pm = \dfrac{x - x_m^\pm}{x_M^\pm - x_m^\pm}$ and $w^\pm = \dfrac{\mu_m'^\pm - \mu_M'^\pm}{\mu_M^\pm - \mu_m^\pm}.$

Similarly considering the processing times as fuzzy numbers in parametric form, we get the fuzzy completion time in parametric form. Then the completion time of the task T_i in parametric representation, with its 0-cut as $[v_{0i}^-, v_{0i}^|]$, can be expressed as:

$$C_i = (v_{0i}^-, v_{0i}'^-, v_{1i}^-, v_{1i}'^-, v_{0i}^+, v_{0i}'^+, v_{1i}^+, v_{1i}'^+) \qquad (3.16)$$

Now, using Equation (3.6) for the MFs and Equations (3.12) and (3.13) respectively for the left and right branches of the fuzzy deadlines, the satisfaction function is given as Equation (3.17) in Box 11.

As a special case, for triangular fuzzy numbers, if in the Expression (3.15) we consider $u_{0ij}'^- = u_{1ij}^- - u_{0ij}^-,$ $u_{1ij}'^- = u_{1ij}^- - u_{0ij}^-,$

$u_{0ij}'^+ = u_{1ij}^+ - u_{0ij}^+$ and $u_{1ij}'^+ = u_{1ij}^+ - u_{0ij}^+$, then we get $\mu_m'^- = 1, \mu_M'^- = 1, \mu_m'^+ = -1$ and $\mu_m'^+ = -1$. This reduces the Equation (3.17) to Equation (3.18) (see Box 12).

We now consider the processing times as fuzzy numbers in parametric form and deadline as crisp number. Let us take $B_{ij} = L(v_{1ij}^-) - L(v_{0ij}^-) + (v_{1ij}^+ - v_{1ij}^-) + R(v_{0ij}^+) - R(v_{1ij}^+)$ with $L(v_{0ij}^-)$ and $L(v_{1ij}^-)$ as the value of $L(x)$ at the points v_{0ij}^- and v_{0ij}^+ respectively, while $R(v_{0ij}^+)$ and $R(v_{1ij}^+)$ as value of $R(x)$ at v_{0ij}^+ and v_{1ij}^+. Then the satisfaction of schedulability, $S_{C_i}(D_{ij})$ for the task T_i can be expressed as Equation (3.19) in Box 13.

Box 10.

$$D_{ij} = (u_{0i}^- + I_i + (j-1)P_i, u_{0i}'^-, u_{1i}^- + I_i + (j-1)P_i, u_{1i}'^-,$$
$$u_{0i}^+ + I_i + (j-1)P_i, u_{0i}'^+, \ u_{1i}^+ + I_i + (j-1)P_i, u_{1i}'^+)$$
$$= (u_{0ij}^-, u_{0ij}'^-, u_{1ij}^-, u_{1ij}'^-, u_{0ij}^+, u_{0ij}'^+, u_{1ij}^+, u_{1ij}'^+) \qquad (3.15)$$

Figure 6. Various membership function shapes model

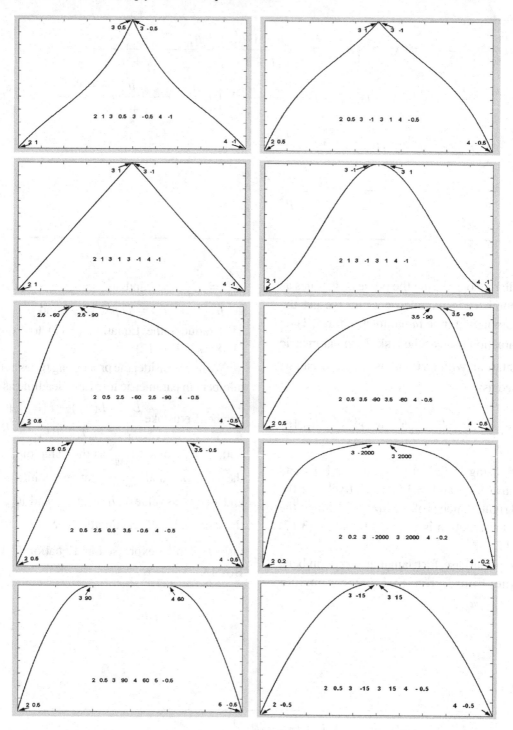

(On respective diagrams the parameters $u = (u_0^-, u_0'^-, u_1^-, u_1'^-, u_0^+, u_0'^+, u_1^+, u_1'^+)$ are shown)

Box 11.

$$S_{D_i}(C_{ij}) = \begin{cases} 1 & \\ 1 - \dfrac{L(C_{ij}) - L(u_{0ij}^-)}{A_{ij}} & if \quad C_{ij} < u_{0ij}^- \\ 1 - \dfrac{L(u_{1ij}^-) - L(u_{0ij}^-) + (C_{ij} - u_{1ij}^-)}{A_{ij}} & if \quad u_{0ij}^- \le C_{ij} < u_{1ij}^- \\ & if \quad u_{1ij}^- \le C_{ij} < u_{1ij}^+ \\ 1 - \dfrac{L(u_{1ij}^-) - L(u_{0ij}^-) + (u_{1ij}^+ - u_{0ij}^-) + R(C_{ij}) - R(u_{1ij}^+)}{A_{ij}} & if \quad u_{1ij}^+ \le C_{ij} \le u_{0ij}^+ \\ 0 & if \quad C_{ij} > u_{0ij}^+ \end{cases}$$

where, $A_{ij} = L(u_{1ij}^-) - L(u_{0ij}^-) + (u_{1ij}^+ - u_{1ij}^-) + R(u_{0ij}^+) - R(u_{1ij}^+)$. And $L(u_{0ij}^-)$, $L(u_{1ij}^-)$, are respectively the value of $L(x)$ at the points u_{0ij}^- and u_{0ij}^+, while $R(u_{0ij}^+)$, $R(u_{1ij}^+)$ are the same of $R(x)$ at the points u_{0ij}^+ and u_{1ij}^+ with (1)

$$L(x) = $$

$$\frac{1}{N}\left[\mu_m'^- + \left(\frac{u_{0ij}^-}{\Delta u_{ij}^-}\right)^2\left(3 + \frac{2u_{0ij}^-}{\Delta u_{ij}^-}\right)\right]x - \frac{3u_{0ij}^-}{N\left(\Delta u_{ij}^-\right)^2}\left(1 + \frac{u_{0ij}^-}{\Delta u_{ij}^-}\right)x^2 + \frac{1}{N\left(\Delta u_{ij}^-\right)^2}\left(1 + \frac{2u_{0ij}^-}{\Delta u_{ij}^-}\right)x^3 \qquad (2)$$

$$- \frac{x^4}{2N\left(\Delta u_{ij}^-\right)^3} + \frac{\Delta u_{ij}^-}{N(1+N)}\left[\mu_M'^-\left(\frac{x - u_{0ij}^-}{\Delta u_{ij}^-}\right)^{1+N} + \mu_m'^-\left(1 - \frac{x - u_{0ij}^-}{\Delta u_{ij}^-}\right)^{1+N}\right]$$

$$R(x) = $$

$$\left(1 + \frac{1}{M}\left[\mu_m'^+ - \left(\frac{u_{1ij}^+}{\Delta u_{ij}^+}\right)^2\left(3 + \frac{2u_{1ij}^+}{\Delta u_{ij}^+}\right)\right]\right)x + \frac{3u_{1ij}^+}{M\left(\Delta u_{ij}^+\right)^2}\left(1 + \frac{u_{1ij}^+}{\Delta u_{ij}^+}\right)x^2 - \frac{1}{M\left(\Delta u_{ij}^+\right)^2}\left(1 + \frac{2u_{1ij}^+}{\Delta u_{ij}^+}\right)x^3$$

$$+ \frac{x^4}{2M\left(\Delta u_{ij}^+\right)^3} + \frac{\Delta u_{ij}^+}{M(1+M)}\left[\mu_M'^+\left(\frac{x - u_{1ij}^+}{\Delta u_{ij}^+}\right)^{1+M} + \mu_m'^+\left(1 - \frac{x - u_{1ij}^+}{\Delta u_{ij}^{+-}}\right)^{1+M}\right]$$

$$(3)$$

$$N = 1 + \mu_m'^- + \mu_M'^-, \ \Delta u_{ij}^- = u_{1ij}^- - u_{0ij}^-, \ M = 1 - \mu_m'^+ - \mu_M'^+ \ and \ \Delta u_{ij}^+ = u_{0ij}^+ - u_{1ij}^+.$$

Box 12.

$$S_{D_i}(C_{ij}) = \begin{cases} 1 & if \ C_{ij} < u_{0ij}^- \\ 1 - \dfrac{(C_{ij} - u_{0ij}^-)^2}{(u_{0ij}^+ - u_{0ij}^-)(u_{1ij}^- - u_{0ij}^-)} & if \ u_{0ij}^- \le C_{ij} \le u_{1ij}^- \\ \dfrac{(u_{0ij}^+ - C_{ij})^2}{(u_{0ij}^+ - u_{0ij}^-)(u_{0ij}^+ - u_{1ij}^+)} & if \ u_{1ij}^+ \le C_{ij} \le u_{0ij}^+ \\ 0 & if \ C_{ij} > u_{0ij}^+ \end{cases}$$

4. SIMULATION RESULTS

To assess the relative performance of fuzzy real-time scheduling using different membership functions to model fuzzy uncertainty in execution times and deadlines, we conducted several simulation experiments using our own C software for computing the modified deadlines and then using it to run Cheddar real-time simulator (Singhoff, Plantec, Dissaux, & Legrand, 2009). A number of simulation experiments were conducted by changing the fuzziness (Zimmermann, 1996) of the deadlines and we got some interesting results. Measure of Fuzziness (F) is used to represent the *degree of fuzziness* of a fuzzy set $\tilde{A} = \left\{ x, \mu_{\tilde{A}}(x) \right\}$. We used the following measure of fuzziness given by Yager (1979):

$$F_p(\tilde{A}) = 1 - \frac{D_p(\tilde{A}, \cancel{C}\tilde{A})}{\left\| Supp(\tilde{A}) \right\|} \qquad (29)$$

where,

$$D_p(\tilde{A}, \cancel{C}\tilde{A}) = \left[\int_a^b \left| \mu_{\tilde{A}}(x_i) - \mu_{\cancel{C}\tilde{A}}(x_i) \right|^p dx \right]^{1/p},$$

$Supp(\tilde{A})$ is the support of $\tilde{A}$, $\cancel{C}\tilde{A}$ is the complement of $\tilde{A}$ and [a, b] is the 0-cut of the membership function for $\tilde{A}$. We have taken here $p = 2$, i.e., L_2 norm to measure the set difference. From the numerous experiments we conducted, the following cases are given to demonstrate various results we obtained for fuzzy real-time scheduling problem with different membership functions.

Example 3

We took a three task system T= {T_1, T_2, T_3} with the following characteristics (see Figures 7-9):

$T_1 : e_1 = (30, 40, 50),\ P_1 = 170,\ r_1 = 0,\ d_1 = (154, 160, 166),\ F_1 = 0.83$

$T_2 : e_2 = (65, 70, 75),\ P_2 = 170,\ r_2 = 0,\ d_2 = (155, 160, 165),\ F_2 = 0.82$

$T_3 : e_3 = (25, 30, 35),\ P_3 = 170,\ r_3 = 0,\ d_3 = (159, 161, 163),\ F_3 = 0.71$

The membership function shapes for the task set are shown in the Figure 3. The plots of the satisfaction function, S_D for the task set are shown in the Figure 4. In the Table 3, given above, the results are summarized. Here, we get three satisfaction crossover points, viz. $t_{12} = 0.5000$, $t_{13} = 0.2813$ and $t_{23} = 0.2222$ at which respective task priorities are changed. Thus four satisfaction intervals are obtained; which are O_1: [0, 0.2222], O_2: [0.2222, 0.2803], O_3: [0.2803, 0.5000] and

Box 13.

$$S_{C_i}(D_{ij}) = \begin{cases} 0 & \\ \dfrac{L(D_{ij}) - L(v_{0ij}^-)}{B_{ij}} & if \quad D_{ij} < v_{0ij}^- \\ \dfrac{L(v_{1ij}^-) - L(v_{0ij}^-) + (D_{ij} - v_{1ij}^-)}{B_{ij}} & if \quad v_{0ij}^- \le D_{ij} < v_{1ij}^- \\ & if \quad v_{1ij}^- \le D_{ij} < v_{1ij}^+ \\ 1 - \dfrac{R(v_{0ij}^+) - R(D_{ij})}{B_{ij}} & if \quad v_{1ij}^+ \le D_{ij} \le v_{0ij}^+ \end{cases} \qquad (3.19)$$

Figure 7. Membership function shapes for example 3

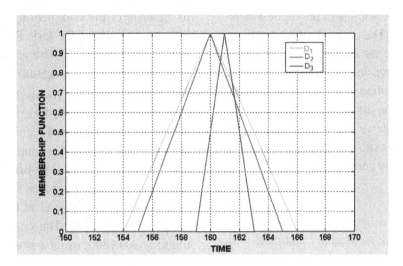

Figure 8. Plots of satisfaction function (S_D) for the tasks of example 4

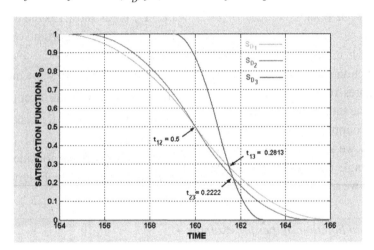

Figure 9. Timing diagram of the optimal task schedule for example 3

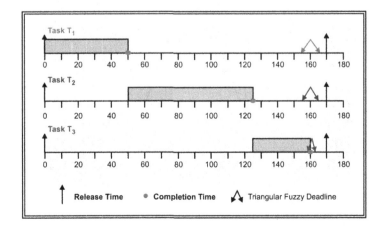

O_4: [0.5000, 1]. The satisfaction of schedulability is 0.9990, which belongs to the highest satisfaction interval O_4. The optimal schedule, determined according to the task priorities in O_4, is $[T_1, T_2, T_3]$ as shown in timing diagram in the Figure 9. The convention followed throughout the chapter is that in the timing diagrams wherever the completion time is fuzzy, the symbol (•) represents the right extremity of the membership function of the fuzzy completion time.

Example 4

We consider the task set used in Example 3 with modified characteristics for task T_3 as given below:

$T_3 : e_3 = (25, 30, 35)$, $P_3 = 170$, $r_3 = 0$, $d_3 = (154.5, 161, 167.5)$, $F_3 = 0.84$

Here, the fuzziness in its deadline is increased. The membership function shapes for the task set are shown in the Figures 10-11 and Table 4.

From the plots of the satisfaction function (S_D) for Example 3 and Example 4, given in Figures 8 and 10 respectively we see that change in the fuzziness of only a single task effects the whole task set. In Example 3 we see that tasks may loose

priority on slightest change in satisfaction (due to changes in the completion times). However, here the priority of the task T_1 is always higher than that of task T_3. There are two satisfaction crossover points, $t_{12} = 0.5000$ and $t_{23} = 0.9339$. So, three satisfaction crossover intervals viz. O_1: [0, 0.5000], O_2: [0.5000, 0.9339] and O_3: [0.9339, 1] are possible. Figure 12 gives the plot of the completion time, deadline and satisfaction functions S_D and S_C for the least priority task T_2. The satisfaction of schedulability (S) for the task set is mentioned on Figure 11 at the intersection of the plots of S_D and S_C. The satisfaction of schedulability is 0.9800, which belongs to the satisfaction interval O_3. Hence, the optimal priority assignments are according to the task priority within this interval. The optimal task schedule is $[T_1, T_3, T_2]$ as shown as the timing diagram in the Figure 3. One important observation from the results of the Example 3 and 4 is that when the fuzzy deadlines have same mode, then for $t > L_i$ the task priorities are according to earliest a_i. However, when $t \leq L_i$, task with earlier b_i is of higher priority.

In Example 3, we considered triangular membership function. For Example 4, we have con-

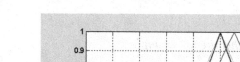

Figure 10. Membership function shapes for example 4

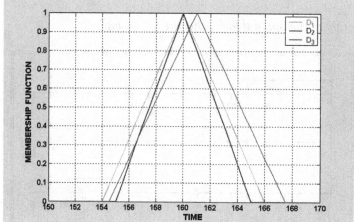

Figure 11. Plots of satisfaction function, S_D for example 4

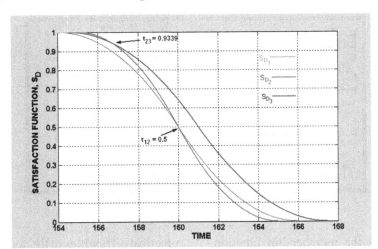

Figure 12. Plot of completion time, deadline, S_D, and S_C for the least priority task T_2

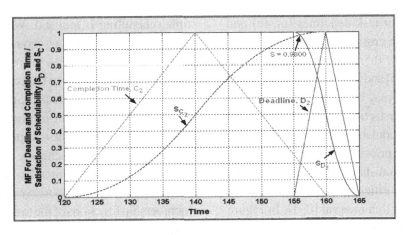

(The Satisfaction of Schedulability (S) of the task set is mentioned)

sidered little changes in the fuzziness of the task T_3 considered in Example 3. Here we got different results for satisfaction crossover points, satisfaction intervals and satisfaction of schedulability. Therefore, the designer needs to give extra care in choosing fuzziness for the timing parameters of real-time tasks. Thus, we see that by formulating the real-time scheduling model in the fuzzy setting the designers get lots of flexibility in making the model close to the real situation.

Next, we have included one simulation experiment for parameterized membership based fuzzy RTS. It will be clear from these example

that the parameterized method gives considerable flexibility to the schedule designer for choosing membership function shapes. Designers can then model various task deadlines and processing times in a realistic manner and observe the effect of his choices on satisfaction of schedulability.

Example 5

In this example, we consider two tasks with deadlines represented by different combinations of parametric fuzzy numbers as specified in the following Table 5.

Figure 13. Timing diagram of the optimal task schedule for example 4

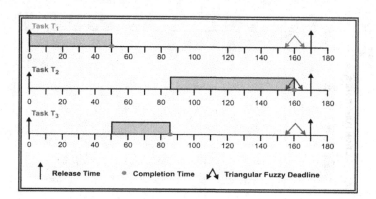

Figure 14 shows the membership function shapes and the variations of the satisfaction functions for different task sets considered in the Example 5. From the Figure 14 we observe that for combinations of task deadlines (a), (c) and (e) one satisfaction crossover point exists at the satisfaction value of 0.5. Hence, two satisfaction intervals viz. [0, 0.5] and [0.5, 1] exist. Thus, these task combinations may be assigned priorities on the basis of the satisfaction interval to which the satisfaction of schedulability belongs. However, for calculating task priorities for combinations (b) and (d) there are no satisfaction crossover intervals and hence task priorities do not change as there is only one satisfaction interval [0, 1]. In Figure 14, the case (f) is unusual one. Although due to several crossover points between the satisfaction function plots one may get the impression that the scheduler will have difficulty in prioritizing the tasks, however in reality the priority inversion takes place only once.

CONCLUSION AND FUTURE DIRECTIONS

Task scheduling in real-time embedded systems is an active research area. A number of researchers are actively engaged in contributing with a number of approaches for solutions to the task scheduling problem in real-time embedded systems. Due to practical difficulties in the accurate estimation of task execution times and specification of deadlines in early phases of software design, the importance of fuzzy modeling of timing constraints in real-time scheduling is realized. We have presented the real-time scheduling model for tasks with triangular fuzzy deadlines and processing times in the Section 2. Contrary to the conclusive remarks of Litoiu et. al. that small changes in the fuzzy numbers do not affect the priority assignment, we have observed that if the completion time varies then the optimal tasks schedule changes at different points for various membership functions of the deadlines. We have observed that for different membership functions of the tasks deadlines there may be different satisfaction crossover points, where modified deadlines (hence priority) of the tasks changes. Asymmetry in the membership functions captures the importance of various tasks and the priorities can be modified naturally based on the importance of the tasks. Again it is found that for the same worst case completion time, different membership functions for the task deadlines may generate different feasible schedule for a task set. Thus, we see that by formulating the real-time scheduling model in the fuzzy setting the designers get lots of flexibility in making the model close to the real situation.

In fuzzy real-time scheduling, Membership Functions (MFs) are used to represent deadline and execution times. Although simple MFs like

Figure 14. Plot of MFs and satisfaction functions (S_D) for example 5

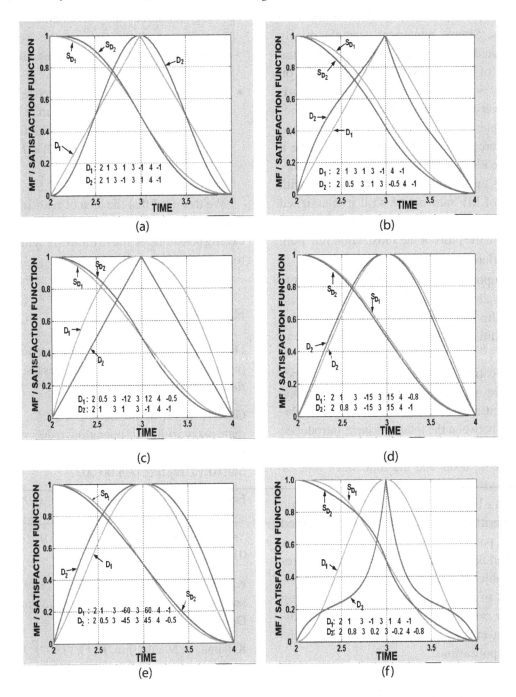

Triangular, Trapezoidal etc. have the advantage of simpler understanding and analysis, they contain discontinuities and designer gets restricted choice in specifying task characteristics. Thus in the second part of the chapter (Section 3) we have presented a novel approach, where task deadlines and processing times are represented by parameterized fuzzy numbers. The parametric method presented in Section 3 is very versatile and has the ability to model a wide variety of symmetric and asymmetric MFs as it allows intuitive specification of smooth MFs for deadlines and execution times. Simple numerical examples nicely demonstrated the usefulness of the method and the effect of changes in parameterized MFs on the satisfaction of schedulability and task priorities. It is very likely that different task deadlines (and completion times) may have to be modeled using different MFs. Although this will make it difficult to identify the task with minimum satisfaction, as task with minimum satisfaction with one type of MF may not be so if it is assigned another MF for its deadline. This effect can be observed in the plots of the satisfaction function, S_D for different MFs (Figure 14).

The importance of realistic modeling of the real-time scheduling problem cannot be under estimated. This area offers rich research opportunity in several directions. Few of these are given below:

- Allocation of slack times to the non-periodic real-time or non real-time tasks. Specifically one may try to find some relation between the total fuzziness introduced in the timing constraints of the real-time periodic tasks and the total slack time of the system.
- Using Evolutionary programming/Genetic Algorithms (GAs) along with fuzzified task parameters to obtain an optimal task schedule. GAs can optimize a multi-criteria objective function incorporating timeliness of tasks, energy consumption during their execution, as well as any other additional criteria to be optimized for a particular application.
- Performance of the real-time systems with soft computing techniques mentioned above may be studied under transient overload conditions, where some aperiodic tasks arrive to make the problem more challenging for the scheduler.

- Soft computing based real-time scheduling techniques may be extended to multiprocessor cases, where the scheduling problem is known to be computationally intractable.
- Last but not the least, a theoretical analysis of schedulability conditions may be developed for real-time task sets with fuzzy timing parameters using Zadeh's Extension Principle.

We thus find that the area of real-time scheduling using soft computing techniques is full of exiting possibilities and in future the author hopes to continue research in this area.

REFERENCES

Dertouzos, M. L. (1974). Control robotics: The procedural control of physical processes. *Information Processing, 74*.

Guerra, M. L., & Stefanini, L. (2005). Approximate fuzzy arithmetic operations using monotonic interpolations. *Fuzzy Sets and Systems, 150*, 5–33. doi:10.1016/j.fss.2004.06.007.

Ishii, H., Tada, M., & Masuda, T. (1992). Two scheduling problems with fuzzy due dates. *Fuzzy Sets and Systems, 46*, 339–347. doi:10.1016/0165-0114(92)90372-B.

Klir, G. J., St. Clair, U., & Bo, Y. (1997). *Fuzzy set theory- foundations and applications*. New Delhi: PHI Publishers.

Krishna, C. M., & Shin, K. G. (1997). *Real-time systems*. Singapore: McGraw-Hill.

Lee, J., Tiao, A., & Yen, J. (1994). A fuzzy rule-based approach to real-time scheduling. In *Proceedings of the FUZZ-IEEE*, (pp. 1394 – 1399). IEEE.

Litoiu, M., & Tadei, R. (1997). Real-time task scheduling allowing fuzzy due dates. *European Journal of Operational Research, 100*, 475–481. doi:10.1016/S0377-2217(96)00094-X.

Litoiu, M., & Tadei, R. (2001). Fuzzy scheduling with application to real-time systems. *Fuzzy Sets and Systems, 121*, 523–535. doi:10.1016/S0165-0114(99)00176-1.

Litoiu, M., & Tadei, R. (2001). Real-time task scheduling with fuzzy deadlines and processing times. *Fuzzy Sets and Systems, 117*, 35–45. doi:10.1016/S0165-0114(98)00283-8.

Liu, C. L., & Layland, J. V. (1973). Scheduling algorithms for multiprogramming in hard real-time systems. *Journal of the ACM, 20*, 46–61. doi:10.1145/321738.321743.

Liu, J. W. S. (2001). *Real-time systems*. New Delhi: Pearson Education Asia.

Muhuri, Pranab, K., & Shukla, K. K. (2008a). Real-time task scheduling with fuzzy uncertainty in processing times and deadlines. *Applied Soft Computing, 8*(1), 1–13. doi:10.1016/j.asoc.2006.06.006.

Muhuri, P. K., & Shukla, K. K. (2008b). Designing optimal task schedule by membership functions choice in fuzzy real-time scheduling. In *Proceedings of the 2nd National Conference on Mathematical Techniques: Emerging Paradigms for Electronics and IT Industries (MATEIT-2008)*. MATEIT.

Muhuri, Pranab, K., & Shukla, K. K. (2009). Real-time scheduling of periodic tasks with processing times and deadlines as parametric fuzzy numbers. *Applied Soft Computing, 9*(3), 936–946. doi:10.1016/j.asoc.2008.11.004.

Murata, T., Ishibuchi, H., & Gen, M. (1997). Multi-objective fuzzy scheduling with the OWA operator for handling different scheduling criteria and different job importance. *Proceedings of the FUZZ-IEEE, 2*, 773–778.

Ramamritham, K., & Stankovic, J. A. (1994). Scheduling algorithms and operating systems support for real-time systems. *Proceedings of the IEEE, 82*(1), 55–67. doi:10.1109/5.259426.

Sha, L. (1994). Generalized rate-monotonic scheduling theory: A framework for developing real-time systems. *Proceedings of the IEEE, 82*(1), 68–82. doi:10.1109/5.259427.

Sha, L. et al. (2004). Real-time scheduling theory: A historical perspective. *Real-Time Systems, 28*, 101–155. doi:10.1023/B:TIME.0000045315.61234.1e.

Singhoff, F., Plantec, A., Dissaux, P., & Legrand, J. (2009). Investigating the usability of real-time scheduling theory with the cheddar project. *Real-Time Systems, 43*(3), 259–295. doi:10.1007/s11241-009-9072-y.

Slany, W. (1996). Scheduling as a fuzzy multiple criteria optimization problem. *Fuzzy Sets and Systems, 78*, 192–222. doi:10.1016/0165-0114(95)00168-9.

Terrier, F., & Chen, Z. (1994). Fuzzy calculus applied to real-time scheduling. In *Proceedings of the FUZZ-IEEE*, (pp. 1905 –1910). IEEE.

Yager, R. R. (1979). On the measure of fuzziness and negation part I: Membership in the unit interval. *International Journal of General Systems, 5*, 221–229. doi:10.1080/03081077908547452.

Zimmermann, H. J. (1996). *Fuzzy set theory and its applications*. New Delhi: Allied Publishers Limited. doi:10.1007/978-94-015-8702-0.

Chapter 12
New Optimal Solutions for Real–Time Reconfigurable Periodic Asynchronous OS Tasks with Minimizations of Response Times

Hamza Gharsellaoui
University of Carthage, Tunisia

Atef Gharbi
University of Carthage, Tunisia

Olfa Mosbahi
University of Carthage, Tunisia & CNR Research Council, Italy & Xidian University, China

Mohamed Khalgui
University of Carthage, Tunisia & CNR Research Council, Italy & Xidian University, China

Antonio Valentini
O3neida Europe, Belgium

ABSTRACT

This chapter deals with Reconfigurable Uniprocessor embedded Real-Time Systems to be classically implemented by different OS tasks that we suppose independent, asynchronous, and periodic in order to meet functional and temporal properties described in user requirements. The authors define a schedulability algorithm for preemptable, asynchronous, and periodic reconfigurable task systems with arbitrary relative deadlines, scheduled on a uniprocessor by an optimal scheduling algorithm based on the EDF principles and on the dynamic reconfiguration. Two forms of automatic reconfigurations are assumed to be applied at run-time: Addition-Remove of tasks and just modifications of their temporal parameters: WCET and/or Periods. Nevertheless, when such a scenario is applied to save the system at the occurrence of hardware-software faults, or to improve its performance, some real-time properties can be violated. The authors define a new semantic of the reconfiguration where a crucial criterion to consider is the automatic improvement of the system's feasibility at run-time by using an Intelligent Agent that automatically checks the system's feasibility after any reconfiguration scenario to verify if all tasks meet

DOI: 10.4018/978-1-4666-3922-5.ch012

the required deadlines. Indeed, if a reconfiguration scenario is applied at run-time, then the Intelligent Agent dynamically provides otherwise precious technical solutions for users to remove some tasks according to predefined heuristic (based on soft or hard task), or by modifying the Worst Case Execution Times (WCETs), periods, and/or deadlines of tasks that violate corresponding constraints by new ones, in order to meet deadlines and to minimize their response time. To handle all possible reconfiguration solutions, they propose an agent-based architecture that applies automatic reconfigurations in order to re-obtain the system's feasibility and to satisfy user requirements. Therefore, the authors developed the tool RT-Reconfiguration to support these contributions that they apply to a Blackberry Bold 9700 and to a Volvo system as running example systems and we apply the Real-Time Simulator Cheddar to check the whole system behavior and to evaluate the performance of the algorithm (detailed descriptions are available at the Website: http://beru.univ-brest.fr/~singhoff/cheddar). The authors present simulations of this architecture where they evaluate the agent that they implemented. In addition, the authors present and discuss the results of experiments that compare the accuracy and the performance of their algorithm with others.

INTRODUCTION

Real-Time systems are playing a crucial role in our society, and in the last two decades, there has been an explosive growth in the number of real-time systems being used in our daily lives and in industry production. Systems such as chemical and nuclear plant control, space missions, flight control systems, military systems, telecommunications, multimedia systems, and so on all make use of real-time technologies. The most important attribute of real-time systems is that the correctness of such systems depends on not only the computed results but also on the time at which results are produced. In other words, real-time systems have timing requirements that must be guaranteed. Scheduling and schedulability analysis enables these guarantees to be provided. Common denominators for these embedded systems are real-time constraints. These systems are often safety critical and must react to the environment instantly on an event. Imagine for example the airbag of a car not going off instantly as a crash occurs; reaction time delay would be disastrous (Gharsellaoui et al., 2011). Several interesting academic and industrial research works have been made last years to develop reconfigurable systems. We distinguish in these works two reconfiguration policies: static and dynamic reconfigurations where static reconfigurations are applied off-line to apply changes before the system cold start (Angelov et al., 2005) whereas dynamic reconfigurations are applied dynamically at run-time. Two cases exist in the last policy: manual reconfigurations applied by user (Rooker et al., 2007) and automatic reconfigurations applied by Intelligent Agents (Khalgui, 2010; Al-Safi & Vyatkin, 2007).

Also, today in academy and manufacturing industry, many research works have been made dealing with real-time scheduling of embedded control systems. The new generations of these systems are addressing today new criteria as flexibility and agility. For this reason many reconfigurable embedded control systems have been developed in recent years.

In this book chapter, we are interested in the automatic reconfiguration of embedded real time Systems.

We define at first time a new semantic of this type of reconfiguration where a crucial criterion to consider is the automatic improvement of the system's feasibility at run-time. We propose thereafter an Agent-based architecture to handle all possible reconfiguration scenarios. Therefore, nowadays in industry, new generations of embedded real time systems are addressing new criteria as flexibility and agility. A disturbance is defined in this current book chapter as any internal or external event allowing the addition or removal of tasks to adapt the system's behavior. A reconfiguration scenario means the addition, removal, or update of tasks in order to save the whole system on the occurrence of hardware/software faults, or also to improve its performance when disturbances happen at run time. To reduce their cost, these systems have to be changed and adapted to their environment without any disturbance. It might therefore be interesting to study the temporal robustness of real-time system in the case of a reconfiguration where the reconfiguration results in a change in the value of tasks parameters: WCET, deadline and period. This new reconfiguration semantic is considered in our work and we will present its benefits. We are interested in this work in automatic reconfigurations of real-time embedded systems that should meet deadlines defined in user requirements (Baruah & Goossens, 2004). A task is synchronous if its release time is equal to 0. Otherwise, it is asynchronous. These systems are implemented by sets of tasks that we assume independent, periodic and asynchronous (e.g. they are activated at any t time units). According to (Liu & Layland, 1973) we characterize each task, τ_i by a period to be denoted by T_i, by a deadline denoted by D_i, by an initial offset S_i (a release time), and by a Worst Case Execution Time (WCET) denoted by C_i. We assume that the relative deadline of each task can be different from its corresponding period. We assume also that the whole system is scheduled by the earliest Deadline First (EDF) scheduling policy (Liu & Layland, 1973). In single processor system, the Earliest Deadline First (EDF) scheduling algorithm is optimal (Dertouzos, 1974), in the sense that if a task set is feasible, then it is

schedulable by EDF. Therefore, the feasibility problem on single processor systems can be reduced to the problem of testing the schedulability with EDF. For this reason, the usage of Earliest Deadline First (EDF) scheduling policy is starting to catch the attention of industrial environments, given its benefits in terms of increased resource usage. EDF is now present at different layers of a real-time application such as programming languages, operating systems, or even communication networks. So, it is available in real-time languages like Ada 2005 (Tucker S. & al., 2006) or RTSJ (http://www.rtsj.org/), and in real-time operating systems such as SHaRK (http://shark.sssup.it/). It has been also implemented at the application level in OSEK/VDX embedded operating systems, and there are real-time networks using EDF for scheduling messages too; for instance in general purpose networks, or in the CAN Bus (Pedreiras & Almeida, 2002). A feasible schedule is a schedule in which all tasks meet their deadlines. The feasibility problem for a set of independent periodic tasks to be scheduled on a single processor has been proven to be co-NP-complete in the strong sense (Leung & Merril, 1980; Baruah et al., 1990). Leung and Merril (Leung & Merril, 1980) proved that it is necessary to analyze all deadlines in the hp $= [0, 2 * \text{LCM} + \max_k (A_{k,1})]$, whereLCM is the well-known Least Common Multiple of all task periods and $(A_{k,1})$ is the earliest offset (starting time) of each task τ_k. Baruah et al. (1990) proved that, when the system utilization U is strictly less than 1, the Leung and Merrils condition is also sufficient. Reconfiguration policies are classically distinguished into two strategies: static and dynamic reconfigurations. Static reconfigurations are applied offline to modify the assumed system before any system cold start (Angelov et al., 2005), whereas dynamic reconfigurations can be divided into two cases: manual reconfigurations applied by users (Rooker et al., 2007) and automatic reconfigurations applied by intelligent agents (Khalgui et al., 2011; Al-Safi & Vyatkin, 2007). This chapter focuses on the dynamic reconfigurations of assumed asynchronous real-time embedded control systems that should meet deadlines defined according to user requirements (Baruah & Goossens, 2004). This work is a complete generalization of (www. loria.fr/nnavet/cours/DEA2004-2005/slide1.pdf; www.loria.fr/navet/cours/DEA2004-2005/slide2. pdf) work where the special case, of synchronous real-time OS tasks with EDF algorithm has been studied. Here, we define the dynamic reconfiguration as any change in software to lead the whole embedded system into a better safe state at run time. We define a new semantics of reconfigurations that allow automatic improvements of system performances at run-time even if there are no hardware faults (Khalgui, 2010). The general goal of this paper is to be reassured that any reconfiguration scenario changing the implementation of the embedded system does not violate real-time constraints: i.e. the system is feasible and meets real-time constraints even if we change its implementation and to correctly allow the minimization of the response time of this system after any reconfiguration scenario. We define an automatic reconfiguration as any operation allowing additions-removes or updates of tasks at run-time. Therefore the system's implementation is dynamically changed and should meet all considered deadlines of the current combination of tasks. Nevertheless, when a reconfiguration is applied, the deadlines of new and old can be violated. We define an agent-based architecture that checks the system's evolution and defines useful solutions when deadlines are not satisfied after each reconfiguration scenario and the Intelligent Agent handles the system resources in such way that, meeting deadlines is guaranteed. Three cases of suggestions are possible to be provided by the agent: remove of some tasks from the new list, modification of periods or/and deadlines, and modification of worst case execution times of

tasks. For this reason and in this original work, we propose a new algorithm for optimization of response time of this system. To obtain this optimization, we propose an intelligent agent-based architecture in which a software agent is deployed to dynamically adapt the system to its environment by applying reconfiguration scenarios. Before any reconfiguration scenario, the initial real-time embedded control system is assumed to be feasible. The problem is that when a scenario is applied and new tasks are added, the processor utilization U will be increased and/or some deadlines can be violated. We propose an agent that applies new configurations to change the periodicity, WCET of tasks or also to remove some of them as a worst case solution. The users should choose the minimum of these solutions to re-obtain the system's feasibility and to guarantee the optimality. The problem is to find which solution proposed by the agent that reduce the response time. To obtain these results, the intelligent agent calculates the processor utilization U before and after each addition scenario and calculates the minimum of those proposed solutions in order to obtain R_k optimal noted R_k^{opt}, where R_k^{opt} is the minimum of the response time of the current system under study given by the following equation:

$$R_k^{opt} = \min \left(R_{k,1}, R_{k,2}, R_{k,3} \right).$$

To calculate these previous values $R_{k,1}$, $R_{k,2}$ and $R_{k,3}$, we proposed a new theoretical concepts S (t, d), $\hat{S}(t,d)$ and W (t, d) for the case of real-time periodic asynchronous OS tasks. Where S(t, d) is the new function of job arrival with deadline at t time, $\hat{S}(t,d)$ is the new function of major job arrival with deadline at t time and W(t, d) is the amount of workload in wait of treatment of which the execution must be ended before the deadline d at t time. A tool named RT-Reconfiguration is developed in our research laboratory at INSAT University to support all the services offered by the agent. The simulator Cheddar (Singhoff & Legrand, 2004) is used to verify and to prove the schedulability analysis of the considered tasks given by our tool. We give in the following section a useful background before we detail thereafter the book chapter problems and we present our contributions.

BACKGROUND

The study of real-time embedded systems is growing at an exponential rate. Widespread deployment and complexity Software is becoming an important component of embedded systems, even the training manpower on the design and implementation of embedded software is becoming increasingly important. This section provides a review of the research related to our work. Users of this technology face a set of challenges: the need for fast, predictable, and bounded responses to events such as interrupts and messages, and also the ability to manage system resources to meet processing deadlines. However, the Real-time and Embedded Systems Forum intends to plug this gap by bringing together system developers and users to build upon existing standards where they exist, evolve Product Standards that address market requirements, and develop Testing and Certification Programs that deliver products meeting these requirements. Ultimately the vision of the Forum is to grow the marketplace through the development of standardized systems based on real software solutions. Industry sectors that will benefit from the Forum include aerospace/defense, telecommunications, manufacturing, automotive, and medical/scientific research. This will advance standards development based on real software solutions. It will also establish test tools for suppliers to use to establish Confidence that their products conform. Consequently, the impact

of software on the customer and, hence, on market shares and competition will be enormous. So, we can conclude that software is established as a key technology in the domain of real-time embedded systems (Gharsellaoui et al., 2011).

Real-Time Scheduling

The Definition of "Real-Time"

We consider a computing system or operating system to be a *real-time* one to the extent that: time-physical or logical, absolute or relative- is part of the system's logic and in particular, the completion time constraints of the applications' computations are explicitly used to manage the resources, whether statically or dynamically.

Time constraints, such as deadlines, are introduced primarily by natural laws- e.g., physical, chemical, biological -which govern an application's behavior and establish acceptable execution completion times for the associated real-time computations.

Real-time scheduling theory provides a formal framework for checking the schedulability of a tasks configuration and finding feasible, as well as optimal, scheduling. The aim of this section is to give a brief overview of this framework, and afterwards to introduce the notion of functional determinism. Real-time scheduling has been extensively studied in the last thirty years (Baruah & Goossens, 2004). Several Feasibility Conditions (FC) for the dimensioning of a real-time system are defined to enable a designer to grant that timeliness constraints associated to an application are always met for all possible configurations. Different classes of scheduling algorithm are followed nowadays: (1) Clock-driven: primarily used for hard real-time systems where all properties of all jobs are known at design time. (2) Weighted round-robin: primarily used for scheduling a real-time traffic in high-speed. (3) Priority-driven: primarily used for more dynamic real-time systems with a mixture of time-based and event-based activities. Among all priority driven policies, Earliest Deadline First (EDF) or Least Time to Go is a dynamic scheduling algorithm used in real-time operating systems. It places processes in a priority queue. Whenever a scheduling event occurs (task finishes, new task released, etc.) the queue will be searched for the process closest to its deadline. This process is the next to be scheduled for execution. EDF is an optimal scheduling algorithm on preemptive uniprocessor in the following sense: if a collection of independent periodic jobs characterized by arrival times equal to zero and by deadlines equal to corresponding periods, can be scheduled by a particular algorithm such that all deadlines are satisfied, then EDF is able to schedule this collection of jobs.

Reconfigurable Scheduling

The nature of real-time systems presents us with the job of scheduling tasks that have to be invoked repeatedly. These tasks however may range from simple aperiodic tasks with fixed execution times to dynamically changing periodic tasks that have variable execution times.

Periodic tasks are commonly found in applications such as avionics and process control requiring data sampling on a continual basis. On the other hand, sporadic tasks are associated with event driven processing such as user response and non-periodic devices. Given a real-time system the goal of a good scheduler is to schedule the system's tasks on a processor, so that every task is completed before the expiration of the task deadline. These and some of the other issues like stability and feasibility are examined here.

Scheduling Policies

A scheduling strategy consists in organizing the execution of a tasks set under constraints. Usually, scheduling strategies are classified as preemptive versus non-preemptive, and off-line versus on-line policies. In non-preemptive case, each task instance, when started, completes its execution without interruptions. Conversely, in preemptive case, the scheduling unit can suspend a running task instance if a higher priority task asks for the processor. Off-line scheduling is based on a schedule which is computed before run-time and stored in a table executed by a dispatcher. One of the most popular off-line scheduling strategies is cyclic executive approach. With this method, tasks are executed in a predefined order, stored in a cyclic frame whose length is the least common multiple of the tasks periods. Each task can then be executed several times in the frame according to its period.

In the Round Robin scheduling algorithm at each instant, a scheduling policy chooses among the set of all active instances exactly one instance for being executed on the processing unit. In a uniprocessor system there will never be more than one running process. If there are more processes, the rest will have to wait until the CPU is free and can be rescheduled. At any one time, a process can only be in one state and will continue to change states until it terminates. Figure 1 shows a state diagram of a process. In Figure 1 the scheduler uses the Round-Robin scheduling algorithm that is designed especially for time-sharing systems. To implement the Round-Robin scheduling, we keep the ready queue as a FIFO (First In First Out) queue of processes. New processes are added to the tail of the ready queue. The CPU scheduler picks the first process from the ready queue, sets a timer to interrupt after 1 time quantum, and dispatches the process.

Conversely, the idea of on-line scheduling is that scheduling decisions are taken at run-time whenever a running task instance terminates or a new task instance asks for the processor. The three most popular on-line scheduling strategies are Rate Monotonic (RM), Deadline Monotonic (DM) and Earliest Deadline First (EDF) (Liu & Layland, 1973). RM is an on-line preemptive static priority scheduling strategy for periodic and independent tasks assuming that T = D (period equals deadline) for each task t. The idea is to determine fixed priorities by task frequencies: tasks with higher rates (shorter periods) are assigned higher priority. DM is a generalization of RM with tasks such that $T_t = D_t$. In that case, tasks with shorter deadlines are assigned higher priority. EDF is a more powerful strategy. It is an on-line preemptive dynamic priority scheduling approach for periodic or aperiodic tasks. The idea is that, at any instant, the priority of a given task instance waiting for the processor depends on the time left until its deadline expires. Lower is this time, higher is the priority.

Earliest Deadline First (EDF) Policy

Earliest Deadline First (EDF) or Least Time to Go is a dynamic scheduling algorithm used in real-time operating systems. It places processes in a priority queue. Whenever a scheduling event occurs (task finishes, new task released, etc.) the queue will be searched for the process closest to its deadline. This process is the next to be scheduled for execution. EDF is an optimal scheduling algorithm on preemptive uniprocessors, in the following sense: if a collection of independent *jobs,* each characterized by an arrival time, an execution requirement, and a deadline, can be scheduled (by any algorithm) such that all the

jobs complete by their deadlines, the EDF will schedule this collection of jobs such that they all complete by their deadlines. In other hand, if a set of tasks is not schedulable under EDF, then no other scheduling algorithm can feasibly schedule this task set. So, compared to fixed priority scheduling techniques like rate-monotonic scheduling, EDF can guarantee all the deadlines in the system at higher loading. With scheduling periodic processes that have deadlines equal to their periods, EDF has a utilization bound of 100%. The necessary and sufficient condition for the schedulability of the tasks follows that for a given set of n tasks, $\tau_1, \tau_2 \ldots \tau_n$ with time periods $T_1, T_2 \ldots T_n$, and computation times of $C_1, C_2 \ldots C_n$, the deadline driven schedule algorithm is feasible if and only if

$$\sum_{i=1}^{n} \frac{C_i}{T_i} \leq 1, EXP1$$

where U is the CPU utilization, C_i is the worst-case computation-times of the *n* processes (Tasks) and the T_i is their respective inter-arrival periods (assumed to be equal to the relative deadlines), (Liu & Layland, 1973).

We assumed that the period of each task is the same as its deadline. However, in practical problems the period of a task may at times be different

Figure 1. Scheduling of the system described in Table 2 by EDF

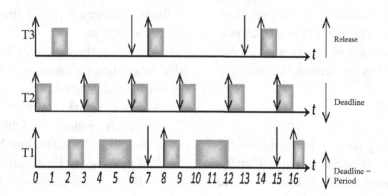

from its deadline. In such cases, the schedulability test needs to be changed. If $T_i > D_i$, then each task needs C_i amount of computing time every $min\ (T_i, D_i)$ duration of time. Therefore, we can rewrite $EXP1$ as:

$$\sum_{i=1}^{n} \frac{C_i}{min(T_i, D_i)} \leq 1, EXP2$$

However, if $p_i < d_i$, it is possible that a set of tasks is EDF schedulable, even when the task set fails to meet the $EXP2$. Therefore, $EXP2$ is conservative when $T_i < D_i$, and is not a necessary condition, but only a sufficient condition for a given task set to be EDF schedulable.

Example

Consider 3 periodic Tasks scheduled using EDF, the following acceptance test shows that all deadlines will be met (see Table 1).

The utilization will be:

$$\frac{1}{8} + \frac{2}{5} + \frac{4}{10} = 0.925 = 92.5\%$$

The theoretical limit for any number of processes is 100% and so the system is schedulable.

Consider now 3 periodic Tasks scheduled using EDF, Figure 2 shows that all deadlines will be met (see Table 2).

However, when the system is overloaded, the set of processes that will miss deadlines is large-

Table 1. A first task set example

Tasks	Execution Time = C	Period = T=D
T1	1	8
T 2	2	5
T 3	4	10

Table 2. A second task set example

Tasks	Execution Time = C	Period = T	Deadline = D
T1	3	8	7
T2	1	3	3
T 3	1	7	6

ly unpredictable (it will be a function of the exact deadlines and time at which the overload occurs). This is a considerable disadvantage to a real time systems designer. The algorithm is also difficult to implement in hardware and there is a tricky issue of representing deadlines in different ranges (deadlines must be rounded to finite amounts, typically a few bytes at most). Also, the limitation of the EDF is that we cannot tell which tasks will fail during a transient overload. Even though the average case CPU utilization is less than 100%, it is possible for the worst-case utilization to go beyond and thereby the possibility of a task or two being aborted. It is desirable to have a control over which tasks fail and which does not; however, this is not possible in EDF. Therefore EDF is not commonly found in industrial real-time computer systems. The situation is

Figure 2. Scheduling of the system described in Table 3 by RM

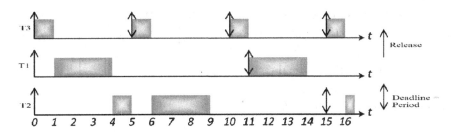

somewhat better in RM because it is the low priority tasks that are preempted.

Rate Monotonic Algorithm (RM Policy)

This is a fixed priority algorithm and follows the philosophy that higher priority is given to tasks with the higher frequencies. Likewise, the lower priority is assigned to tasks with the lower frequencies. The scheduler at any time always chooses the highest priority task for execution. By approximating to a reliable degree the execution times and the time that it takes for system handling functions, the behavior of the system can be determined before. The rate monotonic algorithm can successfully schedule tasks in a static priority environment but it has bound of less that 100% efficiency. The CPU utilization of tasks τ_i where $1 \leq i \leq n$, is computed as the ratio of worst case computing time C_i to the time period T_i. The total utilization of the CPU is computed as follows:

$$Un = \sum_{i=1}^{n} \frac{C_i}{T_i} \qquad (1)$$

Here the frequency of the task is the reciprocal of the time period of the particular task. For the RM algorithm the worst-case schedulable time bound W_n for a set of n tasks was shown to be:

$$Wn = n^*(2^{1/n} - 1) \text{ (Liu \& Layland, 1973) } (2)$$

From (2), we can observe that $W_1 = 100\%$, $W_2 = 83\%$, $W_3 = 78\%$ and as the task set grow in size, $W_n = 69\%$ (ln2). Thus for a set of tasks for which the total CPU utilization is less than 69% means that all the deadlines will be met. The tasks are guaranteed to meet their deadlines if $U_n \leq W_n$. If $U_n > W_n$, then only a subset of the original task set can be guaranteed to meet the deadline which forms the upper echelon of the priority ordering.

This set of tasks will be the critical set (Liu & Layland, 1973). Another problem that exists is the inability for RM to support dynamic changes in periods, which is a regular feature of dynamically configurable systems. For example, consider a task set of three τ_1, τ_2, and τ_3, with time periods $T_1 = 30$ ms, $T_2 = 50$ ms and $T_3 = 100$ ms respectively. The priorities assigned are according to the frequency of occurrence of these tasks and so τ_1 is the highest priority task. If the period for the first task changes to $T_1 = 75$ms, we would then under RM require that the priority orderings be changed to, τ_2, τ_1, and τ_3. This change is detrimental to the completion of the scheduled jobs, which have to finish before their deadlines expire. The problem with RM encouraged the use of dynamic priority algorithms (see Table 3).

Example

See Table 3 and Figure 2.

Deadline Monotonic Algorithm (DM Policy)

The priority of a task under RM is proportional to the rate at which jobs in the task are released while the priority of a task under DM is inversely proportional to the relative deadline of the task. Also, priorities may also be assigned dynamically: One of the problems with RM is that many systems will need job deadlines shorter than the job's period which violates the assumption mentioned

Table 3. A task set example

Tasks	Execution Time = C	Period = T	Deadline = D
T1	3	11	11
T2	4	15	15
T 3	1	5	5

earlier. A solution to this problem arrived in 1982 with the introduction of the Deadline Monotonic (DM) algorithm (Leung & Merril, 1980). With DM, a job's priority is inversely proportional to its relative deadline. That is to say, the shorter the relative deadline, the higher the priority. RM can be seen as a special case of DM where each job's relative deadline is equal to the period. However, the similarities end there. The "69%" feasibility test which we saw earlier doesn't work with DM. The DM feasibility test involves calculating how long it takes a job to go from the start of its period to the point where it finishes execution. We will call this length of time the response time and denote it with R. After calculating R we then compare it with the job's relative deadline. If it is shorter then this job passes the test, otherwise it fails because a deadline can be missed. We have to check the feasibility of every job we define. New schedulability tests have been developed by the authors for the deadline monotonic approach. These tests are founded upon the concept of *critical instants* (Liu L. and Layland J., 1973). These represent the times that all processes (Tasks) are released simultaneously. When such an event occurs, we have the worst-case processor demand. Implicitly, if all processes can meet their deadlines for executions beginning at a critical instant, then they will always meet their deadlines. Thus, we have formed the basis for a schedulability test: check the executions of all processes for a single execution assuming that all processes are released simultaneously (Gharsellaoui et al., 2011) (see Figure 3 and Table 4).

Example

See Table 4 and Figure 3.

Least Laxity First (LLF) Algorithm

Least Laxity First algorithm (LLF) assigns priority bases upon the slack time of a task. The laxity time is temporal difference between the deadline, the remaining processing time and the run time. LLF always schedules first an available task with the smallest laxity. The laxity of a task indicates how much the task will be scheduled without being delayed. LLF is a dynamic scheduling algorithm and optimal to use an exclusive resource. LLF is commonly used in embedded systems. Since the run time is not defined, laxity changes continuously. The advantage of allowing high utilization is accompanied by a high computational effort at schedule time and poor overload performance (Gharsellaoui et al., 2011) (see Figure 4 and Table 5).

Example

See Table 5 and Figure 4.

Table 4. A task set example

Tasks	Execution Time = C	Period = T	Deadline = D
T1	3	12	10
T2	2	15	8
T 3	1	5	5

Table 5. A task set example

Tasks	Execution Time = C	Period = T	Deadline = D
T1	4	8	8
T2	2	6	6

Figure 3. Scheduling of the system described in Table 4 by DM

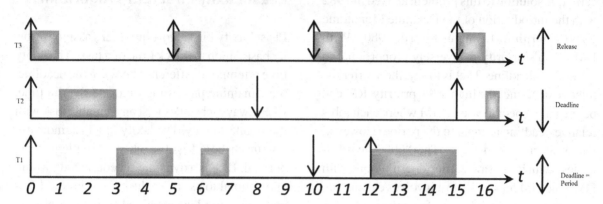

Figure 4. Scheduling of the system described in Table 5 by LLF

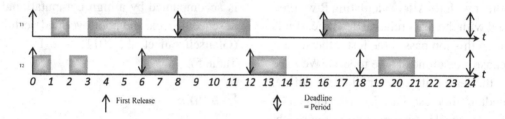

Round Robin (RR) Algorithm

Round Robin (RR) is one of the simplest scheduling algorithms for processes in an operating system, which assigns time slices to each process in equal portions and in circular order, handling all processes without priority. Round Robin scheduling is both simple and easy to implement. Effectiveness and efficiency of RR are arising from its low scheduling overhead of (1), which means scheduling the next task takes a constant time. In Round Robin Scheduling, the time quantum is fixed and then processes are scheduled such that no process get CPU time more than one time quantum in one go. If time quantum is too large, the response time of the processes is too much which may not be tolerated in interactive environment. If time quantum is too small, it causes unnecessarily frequent context switch leading to more overheads resulting in less throughput (Gharsellaoui et al., 2011) (see Figure 5).

Example

See Table 6 and Figure 5.

STATE OF THE ART ON RECONFIGURABLE EMBEDDED SYSTEMS

A task is an executable program implementing one and only one functional module. A task may be periodic, sporadic, or aperiodic. In most cases, especially in the context of critical systems, tasks

Table 6. A task set example

Tasks	Execution Time = C	Period = T	Deadline = D
T1	6	14	14
T2	3	14	14
T 3	4	14	14

Figure 5. Scheduling of the system described in Table 6 by RR

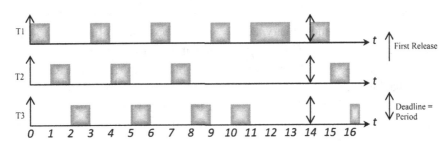

are supposed to be periodic. In the following, we only consider periodic tasks. According to (Liu & Layland, 1973), periodic task may be characterized by static parameters (T, r, D, B, W) where T is the task period, r is the release date (first activation), D is the (relative) deadline, and (B and W) are the best and worst case execution time (BCET and WCET). B and W depend on multiple elements: the processor, the compiler, the Memories. Estimation of these parameters is a wide research area which is considered in the scope of this work. Few results have been proposed to deal with deadline assignment problem. In (Baruah et al., 1999), the authors propose to modify the deadlines of a task set to minimize the output, seen as secondary criteria of this work.

In (George & Courbin, 2011), the deadlines are modified to guarantee close-loop stability of a real-time control system. In (Marinca et al., 2004), a focus is done on the deadline assignment problem in the distributed for multimedia flows. The deadline assignment problem is formalized in term of a linear programming problem. The scheduling considered on every node is non-preemptive EDF or FIFO with a jitter cancelation applied on every node. A performance evaluation of several deadline assignment schemes is proposed. In (George & Courbin, 2011), Balbastre and Crespo propose an optimal deadline assignment algorithm for periodic tasks scheduled with preemptive EDF in the case of deadline less than or equal to periods. The goal is to find the minimum deadline reduction factor still meeting all the deadlines of the tasks.

In the case of a variable speed processor, reducing the frequency can create overloads that can result in deadline miss. We identify several approaches to deal with overloads conditions:

- Remove some tasks to come back to a normal load.
- Adapt the task parameters to come back to a normal load
  - Modification of periods (or deadlines),
  - Modification of worst case execution times of tasks.

In the first case, several solutions from the state of the art have been proposed:

- Stop the faulty task or put it in background. This is the solution used by most industrial systems. Probably not the best.
- Use a heuristic to remove some tasks. In (George & Courbin, 2011; Lock, 1986) proposes to remove the task with the lowest importance. The importance is characterized by a Time Value Function (TVF) providing a statistical overload management with no guarantee to solve the overload problem.
- Applied for EDF scheduling, REDF (robust earliest deadline first) described in (Stankovic et al., 1993), where a partitioning of critical real-time tasks and non-critical real-time tasks is proposed. The critical

tasks should always meet their deadlines. The non critical tasks are removed if necessary according to their value density. A task τ_i has a value v_i and a value density v_i / C_i. With this mechanism, for an identical value, the task having a long duration will be removed first.

- Applied for EDF scheduling, D-OVER proposed in (George & Courbin, 2011), where the authors assigns a Time Value Function (TVF) to every task. A value equal to 0 is equivalent to a deadline miss. The goal is to obtain the maximum value among all the tasks. They prove that their algorithm is optimal in the sense that is achieves the maximum possible benefit for an on-line algorithm (1/4 of an omniscient algorithm).

In the second case, the task parameters must be adapted on-line to cope with the overload. The idea is to adapt the periods of the tasks when needed to reduce the processor utilization. This approach has been proposed in the case of equally important tasks by gracefully adjusting the task periods. In this paper, they introduce a novel scheduling framework to propose a flexible workload management a run time. They present the concept of elastic scheduling (introduced in George & Courbin, 2011). The idea behind the elastic model is to consider the flexibility of a task as a spring able to increase or decrease its length according to workload conditions. The length of a spring is associated to the current processor utilization of its tasks. For a periodic task τ_i, the period T_i is the actual period and is supposed to range from $T_i^{\min}$ to $T_i^{\max}$. The processor utilization of τ_i is C_i/T_i. The period adaptation is done with a new parameter: E_i defining an elastic coefficient. The greater E_i, the more elastic the task. Decreasing processor utilization result is applying a compression force on the spring that

results in a period decrease. This model is well adapted to the case of deadlines equal to periods as it is possible in this case to derive sufficient feasibility for Fixed Priority (FP) with Rate Monotonic algorithm (Liu & Layland, 1973); and necessary and sufficient feasibility conditions for EDF (Liu & Layland, 1973) based on the processor utilization U. In this case, determining if a task set is still schedulable after a task period change is not complex and can be done at run time. In (Buttazzo, 2006), the author proposes to use also the elastic model to adapt the period of the tasks to reach high processor utilization in the case of discrete voltage levels in variable speed processors. In soft real-time systems, another approach has been proposed, to bound the number of deadline miss. The (m, k)-firm approach introduced by Hamdaoui and Ramanathan in (George & Courbin, 2011), can be used to specify that a task should have at least m consecutives instances over k meeting their deadlines. This algorithm, first conceived in the context of message transmission, is a best effort algorithm. In (George & Courbin, 2011), Bernat et al. propose to extend the *(m, k)-firm* model with the *Weakly-hard* model, considering non consecutives deadline miss.

Balbastre and Ripoll show how much a task can increase its computation time still meeting the system feasibility when tasks are scheduled EDF. They consider the case of only one task increasing its WCET (George & Courbin, 2011).

Theorem 6 (George & Courbin, 2011): *Let τ^C be the task set where every WCET is multiplied by a scaling factor α. Let τ^T be the task set where every Task period is divided by α. The task set τ^C is schedulable if and only if the task set τ^T is schedulable.*

Laurent George and Pierre Courbin considered in their works the benefits of sensitivity analysis for the reconfiguration of sporadic tasks when only one task parameter can evolve (WCET, Period, or Deadline). In the case where applications are defined by several modes of execution, a reconfiguration consists of a mode change. A mode is defined its task set. Changing the mode of an application changes the task set run by the system. The problem of mode change is to study if it is possible end a mode and start a new one still preserving all the timeliness constraints associated to all the tasks in both modes. Mode change is a current active research area and has been considered for sensitivity analysis could be used to determine if a mode change results in acceptable WCET, period or deadline changes. Finally, we believe in the limitation of all these related works in particular cases and we note that all these related works consider the reconfiguration of only one task parameter which can evolve (WCET, Period or Deadline) (George & Courbin, 2011).

The only research work dealing with multi-parameters reconfiguration is that we propose in the current book chapter in which we give solutions to the user for all these problems presented by the tool RT-*Reconfiguration*.

PROBLEMS

Embedded systems architecture is classically decomposed into three main parts. The control software is often designed by a set of communicating functional modules, also called tasks, usually encoded with a high level programming language (e.g. synchronous language) or a low level one (e.g. Ada or C). Each functional module is characterized by real-time attributes (e.g. period, deadline) and a set of precedence constraints. The material architecture organizes hardware resources such as processors or devices. The scheduler decides in which order functional modules will be executed so that both precedence and deadline constraints

are satisfied. Behavioral correctness is proved as the result of the logical correctness, demonstrated with the use of formal verification techniques (e.g. theorem proving or model checking) on the functional part, and the real-time correctness which ensures that all the computations in the system complete within their deadlines. This is a non trivial problem due both to precedence constraints between tasks, and to resource sharing constraints. This problem is addressed by the real-time scheduling theory which proposes a set of dynamic scheduling policies and methods for guaranteeing/proving that a tasks configuration is schedulable. However, in spite of their mutual dependencies, these two items (functional verification and schedulability) are seldom addressed at the same time: schedulability methods take into account only partial information on functional aspects, and conversely the verification problem of real-time preemptive modules has been shown undecidable. To overcome this difficulty, a third property is often required on critical systems, especially for systems under certification: determinism, i.e. all computations produce the same results and actions when dealing with the same environment input. The benefit of this property, if ensured, is to limit the combinatorial explosion, allowing an easier abstraction of real-time attributes in the functional view. For instance, preemptive modules may be abstracted by non preemptive ones characterized by fixed beginning and end dates. The interesting consequence is to allow separated functional and real-time analyses. For ensuring determinism, two ways can be followed: either to force it, or to prove it. Several approaches were proposed in order to guarantee determinism. One of the simplest manners is to remove all direct communications between tasks. This seems quite non realistic but it can be achieved by developing an adequate architecture, for instance, current computed data are stored in a different memory while consumed input are the ones produced in a precedent cycle. The execution order between tasks within each cycle does not impact the produced values. However, the main disadvantage is to lengthen the response time of the system. This solution is then not suitable for systems requiring short response time.

A second approach is based on off-line non preemptive strategies, such as cyclic scheduling. Provided that functional modules are deterministic, the global scheduled behavior will also be deterministic. This solution is frequently followed by aircraft manufacturer for implementing critical systems such as a flight control system. However this strategy has two main several drawbacks. Firstly this scheduling leads to a low use of resources because tasks are supposed to use their whole Worst Case Execution Time (WCET). To overcome this first problem, tasks are required to be as small as possible. Secondly, off-line scheduling strategies often need for over-dimensioning the system in order to guarantee acceptable response times to external events. For that purpose, tasks periods are often to be reduced (typically divided by 2) compared to the worse period of the polled external events. The guaranty that WCET and BCET (resp. worst and best case execution times) coincide provides a third interesting context. Any off-line scheduling is then deterministic and it is possible to modify the task model to produce a deterministic on-line scheduling. Unfortunately, warranting that BCET is equal to WCET is hardly possible. This can limit the programming task (no use of conditional instruction or on the contrary use of dead code to enforce equality). Other more recent approaches are based on formal synchronous programming languages. Systems are specified as deterministic synchronous communicating processes, and are implemented either by a sequential low-level code which enforces a static execution order, or by a set of tasks associated with static or dynamic scheduling policies. Implementation is correct-by-construction, i.e., it preserves the functional semantics (and then determinism). These approaches are interesting, for they allow to by-pass the determinism verification problem. Previous solutions are not suitable for highly dynamic non-synchronous systems with high Workload.

On-line preemptive scheduling strategies are often optimal, easy to implement, but deeply non-deterministic when associated to asynchronous communication models. Problematic reconfiguration appears when there are temporal indeterminism on execution time and preemption. Consequently, if on-line preemptive scheduling policies are needed (for performance reasons for instance), it is the necessary to verify determinism. The aim of this book chapter is to answer the question is a scheduling deterministic for a particular multi-periodic tasks model and a given policy? The result is that the determinism problem is decidable even in case of preemptive on-line scheduling policies. So, Due to the increasing complexity of the developed systems it is necessary to model correctly and to implement the chosen design in a correct manner. In the rest of this Book Chapter, we only consider single-processor systems.

CONTRIBUTIONS

In addition, before the main contributions are explained in this book chapter, we are interested in automatic reconfigurations of real-time embedded systems that should meet deadlines defined in user requirements. These systems are implemented sets of tasks that we assume independent, periodic and synchronous (e.g. they are simultaneously activated at time t = 0 time units). We assume also that the deadline of each task is equal to the corresponding period. We define an agent-based architecture that checks the system's evolution and defines useful solutions when deadlines are not satisfied after each reconfiguration scenario and the Intelligent Agent handles the system resources in such way that, meeting deadlines is guaranteed. The resulting contributions of this Book Chapter can be divided into five cases of suggestions are possible to be provided by the agent:

- Remove of some tasks from the new list,
- Modification of periods and/or deadlines,
- Modification of worst case execution times of tasks.

The general problem of our project is to be reassured that any reconfiguration scenario changing the implementation of the embedded system does not violate real-time constraints: i.e. the system is feasible and meets real-time constraints even if we change its implementation.

Formalization of Reconfigurable Real-Time Embedded Systems

Nowadays, manual and automatic reconfigurations are often useful technical solutions to change the system's behavior at occurrences of software/ hardware faults or also to improve the performance. Let *Sys* be such system to be classically composed of a set of real-time tasks that support all different functionalities. We mean by a dynamic reconfiguration any operation allowing addition, removal or also update tasks at run-time. Let *Sys* be the set of all possible tasks that can implement the system, and let us denote by $Current_{Sys}(t)$ the current set of tasks implementing the system *Sys* at t time units. These tasks should meet all required deadlines defined in user requirements. In this case, we note that $Feasibility(Current_{Sys}(t)) \equiv True$.

Example

Let us suppose a real-time embedded system (*Volvo system*) to be initially implemented by 5 characterized tasks (Table 7). These tasks are feasible because the processor utilization factor U = 0.87 < 1. These tasks should meet all required deadlines defined in user requirements and we have $Feasibility (Current_{V\,olvo}(t)) \equiv True$.

We suppose that a reconfiguration scenario is applied at t1 time units to add 3 new tasks C; G; H.

The new processor utilization becomes U = 1.454 > 1 time units. Therefore, the system is unfeasible.

$Feasibility (Current_{V\,olvo}(t)) \equiv False$.

Table 7. The Volvo case study

Task	T_i	C_i	D_i	U^{100}	U_{asy}	U_{OPT}
A	10	2	10	20%	20%	4.7%
B	20	2	5	10%	40%	4%
D	50	6	50	12%	12%	1.6%
E	100	8	100	8%	8%	5.6%
F	2000	7	100	7%	7%	9%
C	50	1	2	2%	50%	1%
G	2000	8	100	8%	8%	18.6%
H	2000	8	2000	8%	0.4%	18.6%

Agent-Based Architecture for Reconfigurable Embedded Control Systems

We define in this section an agent-based architecture for reconfigurable real-time embedded systems that should classically meet different deadlines defined in user requirements. The agent controls all the system's evolution and provides useful solutions for users when deadlines are violated after any dynamic (manual or automatic) reconfiguration scenario.

Running Example

In our real-time embedded system *Volvo* to be initially implemented by 5 characterized tasks which are feasible because the processor utilization factor $U = 0.87 < 1$. We suppose that a reconfiguration scenario is applied at t1 time units to add 3 new tasks C; G; H. The new processor utilization becomes $U = 1.454 > 1$ time units. Therefore the system is unfeasible. Feasibility $(Current_{V olvo}(t)) \equiv False$.

To check the whole system behavior of this system *Volvo*, we present simulations given by the real-time simulator Cheddar in Figure 6.

CONTRIBUTION 1: NEW THEORETICAL PRELIMINARIES

This section aims to define a new theoretical preliminaries for a set of asynchronous real time tasks scheduling under EDF based on the concepts defined in (www.loria.fr/nnavet/cours/DEA2004-2005/slide1.pdf; www.loria.fr/navet/cours/DEA2004-2005/slide2.pdf), which compute a feasible schedule for a set of synchronous real time tasks scheduling under EDF. These new theoretical preliminaries will be used in the following two contributions. Our main contribution is the optimal schedulability algorithm of uniprocessor periodic real-time tasks implementing reconfigurable systems. By applying a preemptive scheduling, the assumed system is characterized by periodic tasks such that each one is defined by a tuple $(S_i; C_i; D_i; T_i)$. A system is called asynchro-

Figure 6. Simulations of the Volvo case study with cheddar

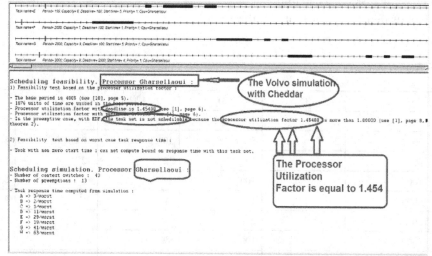

nous, if its tasks have offsets and are not simultaneously ready. Note that in synchronous systems, all offsets are zero and all tasks are released at time t = 0. In this work, when a hardware problem occurs in the studied system, a reconfiguration scenario is automatically applied in this system which has to react by changing its implementation from a subset of tasks to a second one. A reconfiguration scenario corresponds therefore to the addition, the removal or the update of real-time tasks. The general problem of our project is to be reassured that any reconfiguration scenario changing the implementation of the system does not violate real-time constraints: i.e. the system is feasible and meets real-time constraints even if we change its implementation. In this work also, we analyze the feasibility of real-time systems with a single processor by using preemptive Earliest Deadline First (EDF) scheduling algorithm. EDF is an optimal scheduling algorithm on preemptive uniprocessors in the following sense: if a collection of independent periodic (synchronous and asynchronous) jobs can be scheduled by a particular algorithm such that all deadlines are satisfied, then EDF is able to schedule this collection of jobs (instances) (Dertouzos, 1974).

We propose in this paper an agent-based architecture that checks the system's evolution and defines useful solutions for users when deadlines are violated. Therefore, for every set of OS tasks, we check its on-line feasibility by executing it when the corresponding reconfiguration scenario is automatically applied by the agent at run-time.

We apply these different solutions on the *Volvo* Benchmark (Industrial Case Study) that we consider as running example.

Formalization

By considering asynchronous real-time tasks, the schedulability analysis should be done in the Hyper-Period hp = [0, 2*LCM + $\max_k(A_{k,1})$], where LCM is the well-known Least Common Multiple and $(A_{k,1})$ is the earliest start time (arrival

time) of each task τ_k (Leung & Merril, 1980). The reconfiguration of the system Current (t) means the modification of its implementation that will be as follows at t time units:

$$\text{Current}_\Gamma(t) = \xi\_new \cup \xi\_old$$

where ξ_old is a subset of n1 old periodic tasks which are asynchronous and not affected by the reconfiguration scenario (e.g. they implement the system before the time t), and ξ_new is a subset of n2 new asynchronous tasks in the system. We assume that an updated task is considered as a new one at t time units. By considering a feasible System *Sys* before the application of the reconfiguration scenario, each task of ξ_old is feasible, e.g. the execution of each instance is finished before the corresponding deadline: Let n1 and n2 be the number of tasks respectively in ξ_old and ξ_new such that n1 + n2 = n (the number of a mixed workload with periodic asynchronous tasks in Current$_\Gamma$(t)). To estimate the amount of work more priority than a certain under EDF, it is inevitably necessary to us to take into account deadlines because the more priority work is the work which has the earliest deadline. In particular, we propose one function of job arrival with deadline, one function of workload with deadline and finally, we propose the function of major job arrival with deadline for periodic asynchronous tasks.

For example, In the *Volvo* case study, we have the first subset ξ_old composed of the following five initial tasks

$$\xi\_old = \{A;\ B;\ D;\ E;\ F\}\big(n1\ =\ 5\big),$$

this system is feasible and U = 0.87. We suppose that a reconfiguration scenario is applied at t time units to add a second subset composed of three new tasks $\{C;\ G;\ H\} = \xi\_new\big(n2\ =\ 3\big)$.

Therefore, the system Current$_\Gamma$(t) is composed of eight tasks (n = 8 = 3 + 5) as shown in

Table 7 and it's unfeasible. Feasibility(Current $_\Gamma$ (t)) ≡ False.

By applying the well-known scheduling real-time simulator Cheddar, the EDF scheduling result is shown in Figure 6. The processor utilization factor (U) becomes equal to 1.454 after adding the 3 new tasks and the task set seems to be not schedulable.

New Function of Job Arrival with Deadline

We propose new functions of job arrival which integrate the deadlines by the following levels:

In the Instance Level

$S_{k,n}(t1,t2,d) = C_{k,n} * \prod_{[t1 \le Ak,n<t2]} * \prod_{[Dk,n\le d]} = S_{k,n}(t1,t2) * \prod_{[Dk,n\le d]}$ Where $S_{k,n}(t1,t2,d)$ is the amount of job with lower deadline or equal to d brought by the instance $\tau_{k,n}$ meanwhile of time [t1,t2[, and $\prod [\alpha] = 1$ if the predicat α = true.

In the Task Level We Propose

$$S_k\left(t1, t2, d\right) = \sum_{n \in \aleph} C_{k,n} * \prod_{[t1 \le Ak,n<t2]} * \prod_{[Dk,n\le d]},$$

where $S_k(t1,t2,d)$ is the amount of job with lower deadline or equal to d brought by all the instances of τ_k meanwhile of time [t1,t2[.

For a Set of Tasks Γ We Propose

$$S_{\text{Current }\Gamma(t)}\left(t1, t2, d\right) = \sum_{i \mapsto \tau_i in\text{Current}\Gamma(t)} S_i\left(t1, t2, d\right),$$

where $S_{\text{Current }\Gamma(t)}$ (t1, t2, d) is the amount of job with lower deadline or equal to d brought by all the instances of tasks that composed Current $_\Gamma$(t) meanwhile of time [t1, t2].

New Function of Workload with Deadline

In the study of the EDF policy, it is necessary to us to know at the certain moments the workload in wait of treatment of which the execution must be ended before a certain deadline. So, we propose one function of workload with deadline:

In the Instance Level

$$W_{k,n}\left(t,d\right) = S_{k,n}\left(A_{k,1},t,d\right) - \int_{A_{k,1}}^{t} \prod_{k,n}(u,d)du$$

$$(a)$$

where $\prod_{k,n}(t,d) = \prod_{k,n}(t)^* \prod_{[Dk,n\le d]}$. $W_{k,n}(t,d)$ is the amount of job with lower deadline to d brought by the instance $\tau_{k,n}$ which again is to be executed at the moment t. If $A_{k,1} = 0$, we restraint to the case of synchronous tasks.

In the Task Level

$$W_k(t,d) = S_k(A_{k,1},t,d) - \int_{A_{k,1}}^{t} \prod_k (u,d)du = \sum_{n \in \aleph} W_{k,n}\left(t,d\right)$$

where W_k (t,d) is the amount of job with lower deadline to d brought by all the instances of τ_k which gain is to be executed at the moment t.

For a Set of Tasks Γ

For the Current $_\Gamma\left(t\right) = \xi\_new \cup \xi\_old$, we propose:

$$W_{\text{Current }\Gamma(t)}(t,d) = \sum_{i \mapsto \tau_i in\text{Current}\Gamma(t)} W_i\left(t,d\right) = S_{\text{Current }\Gamma(t)}(A_{k,1},t,d) - \int_{A_{k,1}}^{t} \prod_\Gamma (u,d)du,$$

where $W_{Current \, \Gamma \, (t)}$ (t,d) is the amount of job with lower deadline to d brought by all the instances of tasks that composed Current $_\Gamma$ (t) which again is to be executed at the moment t.

CONTRIBUTION 2: AGENT-BASED REAL-TIME RECONFIGURABLE MODEL

This section aims to propose an intelligent Agent-based architecture which is able to propose technical solutions for users after any dynamic reconfiguration scenario.

Agent's Principal

Let Γ be the set of all possible tasks that can implement the system, and let us denote by Current $_\Gamma$ (t) the current set of periodic asynchronous tasks implementing the system at t time units. These tasks should meet all required deadlines defined in user requirements. By considering a feasible System Γ before the application of the reconfiguration scenario, each one of the tasks of ξ_old is feasible, e.g. the execution of each instance is finished before the corresponding deadline. In this case, we note that Feasibility (Current $_\Gamma$ (t)) $\equiv$ True.

An embedded system can be dynamically reconfigured at run-time by changing its implementation to delete old or to add new real-time tasks. We denote in this research by ξ_new a list of new asynchronous tasks to be added to Current $_\Gamma$ (t) after a particular reconfiguration scenario. In this case, the intelligent agent should check the system's feasibility that can be affected when tasks violate corresponding deadlines, and should be able to propose technical solutions for users.

Let us return now, to the Equation (a), we can notice that for d < $D_{k,n}$, we have $W_{k,n}$(t,d) = 0 for any value of t and the $W_{k,n}$(t,$D_{k,n}$) > 0 for t > $D_{k,n}$ which involves that $\tau_{k,n}$ cannot meet its deadline,

(it can violates it). Consequently, the task τ_k can violates also its relative (corresponding) deadline and all the system Current $_\Gamma$ (t) will be unfeasible at t time units. In this case the following formula is satisfied:

$$\sum_{i=1}^{n} \frac{C_i}{\min(T_i, D_i)} > 1,$$

Now, we apply at time t a dynamic reconfiguration scenario in order to adapt the system's behavior and to guarantee the system's feasibility which depends of two major goals of the reconfiguration:

- The first major goal to control the problem's complexity is to minimize response time of asynchronous periodic tasks of Current $_\Gamma \big(t \big)$ = $\xi\_new \cup \xi\_old$, then the agent will not modify the ξ_old tasks and should provide different solutions for users by reconfigure only ξ_new which is composed by n_2 asynchronous periodic tasks in order to satisfy functional requirements,
- The second major goal of obtaining the system's feasibility is to meet deadlines of asynchronous periodic tasks, then, the agent should react by updating of the global system Current $_\Gamma \big(t \big)$ = $\xi\_new \cup \xi\_old$, which is composed by n_1 and n_2 asynchronous periodic tasks in order to re-obtain the system's feasibility and provides different solutions for users.

First Case: Minimizing the Response Time of Periodic Tasks

In this case, the objective is to reduce the periodic response times as much as possible, still guaranteeing that all periodic tasks complete within their deadlines.

Solution 1: Removal of Tasks (1)

We define in this solution a perfect admission controller as a new heuristic, which is defined as an admission control scheme in which we always admit a task if and only if it can be scheduled. Such a control policy can be implemented as follows. Whenever a task arrives, the agent computes the processor utilization $C_i/\min(T_i, D_i)$ of each task τ_i and generates the feasible superset $\Omega_{feasible}$ which defines the different feasible subsets of tasks in achieving good periodic responsiveness where $U(t) = \sum_{i=1}^{n} \dfrac{C_i}{\min(T_i, D_i)} \leq 1$, is enforced.

$\Omega_{feasible} = \{\tau_. \subseteq \text{Current}_r/\text{Feasibility}(\tau) \equiv \text{True}\}$

Each subset τ corresponds to a possible implementation of the system such that:

$\tau = \xi\_new \cup \xi\_old$

$\sum_{\tau_i \in Asynchronous\_Tasks} \dfrac{C_i}{\min(T_i, D_i)} \leq 1$ (Stankovic J., & al. 1998).

In this case we remove all tasks of ξ_new, we stock them in a list and we begin by using an acceptance test, e.g., periodic tasks ξ_new that would cause U (t) to exceed this bound are not accepted for processing. In other words, when a task arrives at the system, it is tentatively added to the set of tasks in the system. The admission controller then tests whether the new task set is schedulable. The new task is admitted if the task set is schedulable, e.g., would not cause U (t) to exceed the bound (U (t) $= \sum_{i=1}^{n_1+j} \dfrac{C_i}{\min(T_i, D_i)} \leq 1$ is enforced where $j \in [0; n_2]$). Otherwise, there are two possible cases:

- **First case:** If the arrival task is hard, then it will be accepted and we will randomly remove another soft task from the [1... n1 + j −1] previous tasks to be rejected and still guaranteeing a feasible system,
- **Second case:** If the arrival task is soft, it will be dropped (rejected) immediately.

The agent computes the processor utilization $C_i/\min(T_i, D_i)$ of each task τ_i and generates the feasible superset $\Omega_{feasible}$ which defines the different feasible subsets of tasks.

The agent suggests all possible combinations of tasks for users who have the ability to choose

Figure 7. The Volvo case study simulation

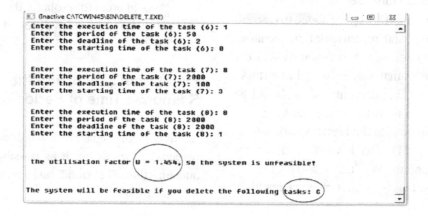

the best combination that satisfies functional requirements.

Running Example

The agent should react to propose useful solutions for users in order to re-obtain the system's feasibility. In our *Volvo* system, we present in Figure 7 the results described by the developed tool RT - Configuration. These results are the possibilities of the considered tasks which can be removed from the subset. The user can choose one of these solutions to have a feasible system.

In Figure 7, the agent proposes the task C to be removed to re-obtain the system's feasibility.

By applying the well-known scheduling real-time simulator Cheddar, the EDF scheduling result is shown in Figure 8.

The processor utilization factor (U) becomes equal to 0.954 after removing the task C, and the task set becomes schedulable (feasible).

Second Case: Meeting Deadlines of Periodic Tasks

Solution 1: Modification of Periods (2)

The agent proceeds as a second solution to change the periods of tasks of ξ_new and ξ_old. To obtain a feasible system, the formula in Box 1 should be satisfied.

Running Example

The agent should react to propose useful solutions for users in order to re-obtain the system's feasibility. In our *Volvo* system, we present in Figure 9 the results described by the developed tool RT - Configuration. These results are the new temporal parameters of the considered tasks. The user can choose one of these solutions to have a feasible system. We note that: $\xi\_new = \{C; G; H\}$ and $\xi\_old = \{A; B; D; E; F\}$.

The agent computes the constant values $\beta_j (j \in [0; 5])$ corresponding respectively as follows:

Figure 8. The Volvo case study simulation with cheddar

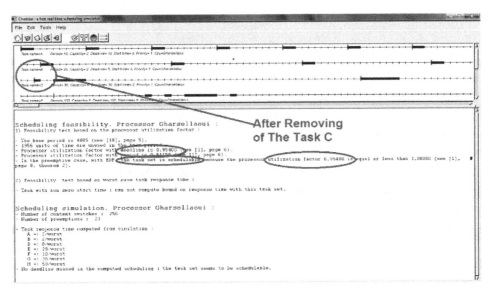

Box 1.

$$\sum_{i=1}^{n_1-j} \frac{Ci}{\min(T_i, D_i)} + \sum_{i=n_1-j+1}^{n_1+n2} \frac{Ci}{\min(T_i, D_i) + \theta i} = 1, \text{ where } j \in [0; n_1].$$

$$\rightarrow \sum_{i=n_1-j+1}^{n_1+n2} \frac{Ci}{\min(T_i, D_i) + \theta i} = 1 - \sum_{i=1}^{n_1-j} \frac{Ci}{\min(T_i, D_i)}, \text{ Let } \beta_j \text{ be } (\min(T_i, D_i) + \theta i)$$

$$\rightarrow \frac{1}{\beta_j} \sum_{i=n_1-j+1}^{n_1+n2} Ci = 1 - \sum_{i=1}^{n_1-j} \frac{Ci}{\min(T_i, D_i)}$$

$$\rightarrow \beta_j = \left[\frac{\displaystyle\sum_{i=n_1-j+1}^{n_1+n2} Ci}{1 - \displaystyle\sum_{i=1}^{n_1-j} \frac{Ci}{\min(T_i, D_i)}} \right] = \text{constant, the new period of } \Gamma \text{ tasks is therefore deduced from } \beta_j.$$

Figure 9. The Volvo case study simulation

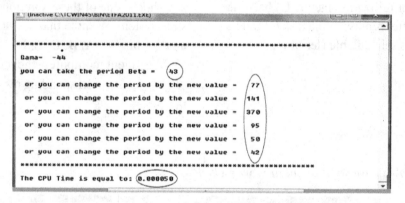

$\beta_0 = 43$, $\beta_1 = 77$, until $\beta_5 = 42$ time units where $\xi\_old\varnothing$ and $\xi\_new = \{A; B; D; E; F; C; G; H\}$

By applying the well-known scheduling real-time simulator Cheddar, the EDF scheduling result is shown in Figure 10.

The processor utilization factor (U) becomes equal to 0.942 after updating the tasks C, G and H by the new value of period equal to 43 and the task set becomes schedulable (feasible).

Solution 2: Modification of Worst Case Execution Times (3)

The agent proceeds now as a third solution to modify the Worst case Execution Times (WCET) of tasks of ξ_new and ξ_old. To obtain a feasible system, the formula in Box 2 should be satisfied.

Running Example

The agent should react to propose useful solutions for users in order to re-obtain the system's feasibility. In our *Volvo* system, we present in Figure 11 the results described by the developed tool RT-reconfiguration. These results are the new

Figure 10. The Volvo case study simulation with cheddar

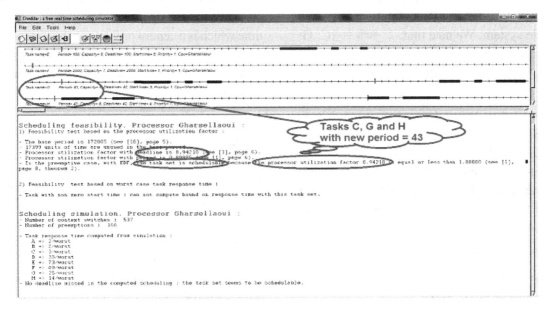

Box 2.

$$\sum_{i=1}^{n_1-j} \frac{Ci}{\min(T_i, D_i)} + \sum_{i=n_1-j+1}^{n_1+n2} \frac{Ci+\alpha i}{\min(T_i, D_i)} = 1$$

$$\rightarrow \sum_{i=n_1-j+1}^{n_1+n2} \frac{Ci+\alpha i}{\min(T_i, D_i)} = 1 - \sum_{i=1}^{n_1-j} \frac{Ci}{\min(T_i, D_i)}$$

$$\rightarrow \sum_{i=n_1-j+1}^{n_1+n2} \frac{\alpha i}{\min(T_i, D_i)} = 1 - \sum_{i=1}^{n_1-j} \frac{Ci}{\min(T_i, D_i)} - \sum_{i=n_1-j+1}^{n_1+n2} \frac{Ci}{\min(T_i, D_i)}$$

$$\rightarrow \sum_{i=n_1-j+1}^{n_1+n2} \frac{\alpha i}{\min(T_i, D_i)} = 1 - \sum_{i=1}^{n_1+n2} \frac{Ci}{\min(T_i, D_i)}$$

Let γ_j be the following constant: $\gamma_j = \alpha i =$ Constant,

$$\rightarrow \gamma_j = \left| \frac{1 - \sum_{i=1}^{n_1+n2} \frac{Ci}{\min(T_i, D_i)}}{\sum_{i=n_1-j+1}^{n_1+n2} \frac{1}{\min(T_i, D_i)}} \right|$$

The new WCET of Γ tasks is therefore deduced from γ_j.

temporal parameters of the considered tasks. The user can choose one of these solutions to have a feasible system. We note that: $\xi\_new = \{C; G; H\}$ and $\xi\_old = \{A; B; D; E; F\}$

The agent computes the constant values γ_j, ($j \in [0; 5]$) corresponding respectively to the new values of the Worst Case Execution Times (WCET). Here $\gamma = -44$, and the minimum value of WCET in the *Volvo* system is equal to 1, so $\gamma = -44 + ($Minimum WCET $= 1) = -43 \leq 0$. Therefore, the agent deduces that modifications of Worst Case Execution Times (WCET) cannot solve the problem.

CONTRIBUTION 3: OPTIMIZATION OF RESPONSE TIME

This section aims to present the principle of response time minimization. Indeed, in this paper, we are interested in an automatic reconfiguration of Operating System's (OS) functional tasks. All the tasks are supposed to be independent, periodic, and synchronous/asynchronous. We assume also that the whole system is scheduled by the Earliest Deadline First (EDF) scheduling policy. So, we shall deduct from this schedulability certain basic properties of the system, and then we shall

become attached to finer characterizations with in particular the determination of borders on response time which is a central problem in the conception of the real-time systems. For this reason, we present the function of major job arrival with deadline in the following paragraph.

New Function of Major Job Arrival with Deadline

In the Background, we defined the function of job arrival with deadline. Now and in order to analyze the feasibility, we shall have to quantify, the maximal amount of job of term less than or equal to one certain date was engendered on an interval of time, it is the function of major job arrival with deadline. This function applied to the task τ_k, noted $\hat{S}_k(.)$, limits the function of major job arrival with deadline of the task τ_k, on everything interval of time of duration Δt: $S_k(A_{k,j}, A_{k,j} + \Delta t, A_{k,j} + d) \leq \hat{S}_k(\Delta t, d)$, $\forall A_{k,j}$ (the beginning of the interval in which the function is estimated) ≥ 0, $\forall \Delta t \geq 0$, $\forall d \geq 0$.

We assume now the case where $D_{k,n} = A_{k,n} + \bar{D}_k$, $\forall k,n$. We consider an interval of time $[A_{k,j}, A_{k,j} + \Delta t[$, Which is the maximum amount of job which can be engendered for one periodic tasks with deadline on this interval? We know that most

Figure 11. The Volvo case study simulation

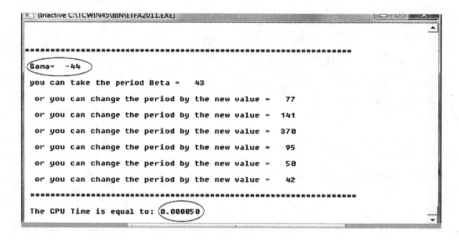

high time of execution of an instance is C_k. Let us determine the maximum number of instances in an interval of time of the type $[A_{k,j}, A_{k,j} + \Delta t]$. We note $A_{k,n0}$ the first instance of τ_k, after $A_{k,j}$ and $A_{k,n1}$ the last one before $A_{k,j} + \Delta t$ with $n = n_1 - n_0 + 1$ the number of instances in this interval $[A_{k,j}, A_{k,j} + \Delta t[$.

There are two conditions so that the job of an instance $\tau_{k,i}$ is counted, it is necessary that:

1. $A_{k,i} < A_{k,j} + \Delta t$: the maximum number of instances is most big n which verifies:
    $A_{k,n0} + (n - 1)*T_k < A_{k,j} + \Delta t$. Where $A_{k,n0}$ $[A_{k,j}, A_{k,j} + T_k[$. If $A_{k,n0} = A_{k,j}$, we have n maximum and we obtain the following expression: $n < \Delta t / T_k + 1$. (b)

The biggest integer n which satisfies (b) is

$$n = \left\lceil \frac{\Delta t}{T_k} \right\rceil$$

2. $D_{k,i} < A_{k,j} + d$: the respect for this condition involves that the deadline of $\tau_{k,n1}$ will have to verify:
    $D_{k,n1} = A_{k,n1} + \bar{D}_k \leq A_{k,j} + d$.

As $A_{k,n1} \geq A_{k,n0} + (n - 1)*T_k$, we have $A_{k,n0} + (n - 1)*T_k + \bar{D}_k \leq A_{k,j} + d$. Where $A_{k,n0}$ $[A_{k,j}, A_{k,j} + T_k[$. If $A_{k,n0} = A_{k,j}$, we have n maximum and we obtain the following expression:

$$n \leq (d - \bar{D}_k) / T_k + 1. \tag{c}$$

The biggest integer n which satisfies (c) is

$$n = \left\lceil \frac{d - \bar{D}_k}{T_k} \right\rceil + 1 \tag{d}$$

An implicit condition is that $n \geq 0$, notice in (d) that as $\bar{D}_k$ can be arbitrarily big, n can be negative. The biggest n which verifies three conditions (b, c and d) is finally:

$$n = \min\left(\left\lceil \frac{\Delta t}{T_k} \right\rceil, \left\lceil \frac{d - \bar{D}_k}{T_k} \right\rceil^+ + 1 \right).$$

where $(a)^+ = \max(0, a)$. We obtain finally the function of major job arrival with following deadline for τ_k:

$$\hat{S}_k(\Delta t, d) = \min\left(\left\lceil \frac{\Delta t}{T_k} \right\rceil, \left\lceil \frac{d - \bar{D}_k}{T_k} \right\rceil^+ + 1 \right) * C_k$$

$$\tag{e}$$

Interference Period with Deadline d under EDF

The end of execution of an instance $\tau_{k,n1}$, with a deadline $D_{k,n}$, is the end of one period of activity of the processor in which all the executed instances have a deadline less or equal to $D_{k,n}$. So, we define the period of interference with a deadline d as:

Definition: A period of interference with a deadline d is an interval of time $[B_j, Ej[$ such as: $W_{1..m}(B_j, d) = W_{1..m}(E_j, d) = 0$ and $B_j < t < E_j \rightarrow W_{1..m}(t, d) > 0$. On the same trajectory, we can have several periods of interferences there with deadlines d and we shall note $B_j(d)$ and $E_j(d)$ the beginning and the end of the ith period of interference. So, the end of the period of interference with deadline d satisfies:

$$E_j(d) = \min\{t > B_j(d) / W_{1..m}(t, d) = 0\}. \tag{f}$$

Inside the period of interference, the workload with deadline less than or equal to d evolves in time according to the Equation (a)

$$W_{1..m}(t,d) = S_{1..m}(B_j(d),t,d) - \int_{B_j(d)}^{t} \prod_{1..m}(u,d)du$$

As the function $\prod_{1..m}(t,d)$ is always equal to 1 inside the period of interference, we have:

$$W_{1..m}(t,d) = S_{1..m}(B_j(d),t,d) - (t - B_j(d)).$$

By injecting this relation in the Equation (f) and after a change of variable ($t = B_j(d) + \Delta t$), we obtain this characterization of $E_j(d)$ that we shall use to determine the response time borders:

$$E_j(d) = \min \{\Delta t > 0 / S_{1..m}(B_j(d), B_j(d) + \Delta t, d)) = \Delta t \}$$

Significant Activation Dates under EDF

We note $E_0(d)$ the end of the first period of interference with deadline d which follows the simultaneous activation of all the tasks except of the task τ_k under study. An instance $\tau_{k,n}$ ends its execution (in later) in $E_0(d)$ if d is the deadline of $\tau_{k,n}$ ($d = D_{k,n}$), that is for $A_{k,n} = d - \bar{D}_k$. If we calculate the response time of $\tau_{k,n}$ for all the possible values of d for the first period of interference of the major activation scenario, we shall find inevitably one border at the response time of any instances of τ_k on any trajectory:

$$\hat{R}_k = MAX_{d \in} (E_0(d) - (d - \bar{D}_k)).$$

The biggest size of this first period of interference is noted L. So that an instance $\tau_{k,n}$ belongs to this first period of interference, it is necessary that $A_{k,n} + C_k \leq L$, where from $d \leq L + \bar{D}_k - C_k$.

Furthermore, the first possible deadline date is d $= \bar{D}_k$ who corresponds to $A_{k,n} = 0$.

We have then, $\hat{R}_k = MAX_{d \in, d \geq} \bar{D}_k$, $d \leq L + \bar{D}_k - Ck (E_0(d) - (d - \bar{D}_k))$. As $d \in \mathbb{R}$, it is not possible to make the calculation for all possible values but we can limit ourselves to significant values of d, that is values of d which correspond to $A_{i,1}$ ($i \in [1..m]$). Let us build orderly sequence of the deadlines of all the instances of all tasks. The only values of d for which it is necessary to calculate $E_0(d)$ are values such as d is a deadline date included between $\bar{D}_k$ and $L + \bar{D}_k - C_k$. The set D_k of all the values of d to examine is thus:

$$D_k = \{d = n*T_i + \bar{D}_i / d \geq \bar{D}_k, d \leq L + \bar{D}_k - C_k, n \in _N, i \in [1..m]\}. \tag{g}$$

Calculation of Response Time Borders under EDF

The value of the biggest possible period of interference of the system noted L is common to all the tasks. This maximal period occurs after the simultaneous provision of an instance of all the tasks:

$$L = \min \{\Delta t > 0/ \hat{S}_{1..m}(0, \Delta t) = \Delta t\} \tag{h}$$

with $\hat{S}_{1..m}(0,t) = \hat{S}_{1..m}(0,t,+\infty)$ is the function of major job arrival who adds the job of all the instances whatever are their deadlines. In the case of periodic tasks, as it was studied before, we have:

$$\hat{S}_{1..m}(\Delta t) = \sum_{i=1}^{m_1} \left\lceil \frac{\Delta t}{T_i} \right\rceil * C_i$$

Now, according to the previous three solutions calculated by the Intelligent Agent (Solution 1, Solution 2, and Solution 3), we define:

- L_1 according to Solution 1, by the following expression:

$$L_1 = \min \{ \Delta t > 0 / \hat{S}_{1..m_1} \left(0, \Delta t \right) = \Delta t \},$$

where $\hat{S}_{1..m_1} \left(0, \Delta t \right) = \sum_{i=1}^{m_1} \left\lceil \dfrac{\Delta t}{T_i} \right\rceil * C_i$ and $m1 \leq$ m resulting from the removal tasks generated by the first solution (Solution 1).

- L_2 according to Solution 2, by the following expression:

$$L_2 = \min \{ \Delta t > 0 / \hat{S}_{1..m} \left(0, \Delta t \right) = \Delta t \},$$

where $\hat{S}_{1..m} \left(\Delta t \right) = \sum_{i=1}^{m} \left\lceil \dfrac{\Delta t}{\beta_i} \right\rceil * C_i$ and β_i resulting from the new periods generated by the second solution (Solution 2).

- L_3 according to Solution 3, by the following expression:

$$L_3 = \min \{ \Delta t > 0 / \hat{S}_{1..m} \left(0, \Delta t \right) = \Delta t \},$$

where $\hat{S}_{1..m} \left(\Delta t \right) = \sum_{i=1}^{m} \left\lceil \dfrac{\Delta t}{T_i} \right\rceil * \gamma_i$ and γ_i resulting from the new worst case execution times generated by the third solution (Solution 3).

L_1 is thus (respectively L_2 and L_3), the limit when n aims towards the infinity, of the suite:

$$L_1^0 = \sum_{i=1}^{m_1} C_i, \; L_1^n = \sum_{i=1}^{m_1} \left\lceil \dfrac{L_1^{n-1}}{T_i} \right\rceil * C_i \; \text{(respectively}$$

$$L_2^0 = \sum_{i=1}^{m} C_i, \; L_2^n = \sum_{i=1}^{m} \left\lceil \dfrac{L_2^{n-1}}{\beta_i} \right\rceil * C_i$$

and

$$L_3^0 = \sum_{i=1}^{m} \gamma_i, \; L_3^n = \sum_{i=1}^{m} \left\lceil \dfrac{L_3^{n-1}}{T_i} \right\rceil * \gamma_i) \tag{i}$$

The obtaining of L_1 (respectively L_2 and L_3), allows us to build the set D_k^1 (respectively D_k^2 and D_k^3) defined by (g). For every value of $d \in D_k^1$ (respectively D_k^2 and D_k^3), it is now necessary to calculate the end of the corresponding period of interference $E_{0,1}(d)$ (respectively $E_{0,2}(d)$ and $E_{0,3}(d)$).

According to (h) and (e): $E_{0,1}(d)$ is the limit when n aims towards the infinity of the suite:

$$E_{0,1}^0(d) = \varepsilon,$$

$$E_{0,1}^n(d) = \sum_{i=1}^{m_1} (\min (\left\lceil \dfrac{E_{0,1}^{n-1}}{T_i} \right\rceil, \left\lfloor \dfrac{d - \bar{D}_i}{T_i} \right\rfloor + 1))^+ \; * C_i,$$

$E_{0,2}(d)$ is the limit when n aims towards the infinity of the suite:

$$E_{0,2}^0(d) = \varepsilon,$$

$$E_{0,2}^n(d) = \sum_{i=1}^{m} (\min (\left\lceil \dfrac{E_{0,2}^{n-1}}{\beta_i} \right\rceil, \left\lfloor \dfrac{d - \bar{D}_i}{\beta_i} \right\rfloor + 1))^+ \; * C_i,$$

and $E_{0,3}(d)$ is the limit when n aims towards the infinity of the suite:

$$E_{0,3}^0(d) = \varepsilon,$$

$$E_{0,3}^n(d) = \sum_{i=1}^m (\min(\left\lceil \frac{E_{0,3}^{n-1}}{T_i} \right\rceil, \left\lfloor \frac{d-\bar{D}_i}{T_i} \right\rfloor +1)) * \gamma_i.$$

where ε is a positive and unimportant but necessary real value to affect the convergence. For every value of d $\in D_k^1$ (respectively D_k^2 and D_k^3), the corresponding response time is:

- $R_{k,1} = (E_{0,1}(d) - (d - \bar{D}_k))$, The biggest value is the border of the response time (R $_{\{k,1\}}$max).

- $R_{k,2} = (E_{0,2}(d) - (d - \bar{D}_k))$, The biggest value is the border of the response time (R $_{\{k,2\}}$max).

- $R_{k,3} = (E_{0,3}(d) - (d - \bar{D}_k))$, The biggest value is the border of the response time (R $_{\{k,3\}}$max).

We define now, R_k optimal noted R_k^{opt} according to the previous three solutions calculated by the intelligent Agent (Solution 1, Solution 2, and Solution 3) by the following expression:

$R_k^{opt} = \min (R_{k,1}, R_{k,2}, R_{k,3})$ (the minimum of the three values)   (j).

So, the calculation of R_k^{opt} allows us to obtain and to calculate the minimizations of response times values and to get the optimum of these values.

Final Conclusion

This research work dealing with multi-parameters reconfiguration is that we propose in the current paper in which, we give solutions to the user for all these problems presented by the tool RT-Re-

configuration. This work also, concentrates on the context of systems containing a set of tasks which is not feasible. The reconfiguration was applied in order not only to obtain the systems feasibility, but also to get the performance of the system by reducing the response time of the processes to be tolerated in interactive environment in order to obtain the optimization of the response time of the studied reconfigurable system.

Algorithm

Given a set of periodic, independent tasks to be scheduled by EDF on a single processor, Spuri (1996) proposed an algorithm for computing an upper bound on the worst-case response time of a task. His algorithm, however, does not consider task offsets. This means that the analysis proposed by Spuri is still valid even in the case of tasks with offsets (asynchronous case), but the results may be pessimistic. A first approach to the problem of computation of worst-case relative response times would be to apply Spuri's method, considering each task to be independent from other tasks of the same set of tasks. However, this approach is extremely pessimistic. Palencia and Gonzalez (Palencia & Gonzalez, 2003) introduced a new method that is much less pessimistic than Spuri's one by taking into consideration the offsets among tasks of the same set of tasks.

The following algorithm is our original contribution to the problem, which is able to provide both a response time minimization and a feasibility of the studied system.

We now introduce this algorithm, our original contribution to the problem, by these different codes to be supported by the agent for a feasible reconfiguration of an embedded system.

Intuitively, we expect that our algorithm performs better than the Spuri's, the Palencia and Gonzlez ones. We show the results of our proposed algorithm by means of experimental result's evaluation.

Box 3. Begin Algorithm

Code1 Removal-Tasks () $U \leftarrow 0$;

– For each partition $\beta \subseteq \tau_{new} \cup \tau_{old}$

– i = 1;

$$- \ U + \ = \ \frac{C_i}{\min(T_i, Di)};$$

– **If** $U \leq 1$

– Then display (β);

Save (m$_1$);

Else display i+1;

Code2 Modify Periods_Deadlines_WCET()

– Compute (β_i);

– Compute (γ_i);

– For $\min(T_i, Di) \in \xi \_ new \cup \xi \_ old$

– Display parameters ();

Code3 Generate_parameters (m$_1$, β_i, γ_i);

– Compute (R$_{k,1}$);

– Compute (R$_{k,2}$);

– Compute (R$_{k,3}$);

– Generate (R_k^{opt});

End Algorithm

Complexity

The EDF-schedulability in the case of periodic synchronous tasks (with deadline equal to period) is decidable in polynomial time. In the case of asynchronous tasks, i.e. each task has an offset S_i, such that jobs are released at $k*T_i + S_i$ ($k \in \mathbb{N}$), then testing the feasibility is strongly coNP-hard (Leung & Merril, 1980). This complexity was decreased in our approach to O(nlog(n)) because the proposed algorithm is recursive, and the Earliest Deadline First algorithm also, would be maintaining all tasks that are ready for execution in a queue. Any freshly arriving task would be inserted at the end of queue. Each task insertion will be achieved in O(1) or constant time, but task selection (to run next) and its deletion would require O (n) time, where n is the number of tasks in the queue. EDF simply maintaining all ready tasks in a sorted priority queue that will be used a heap data structure. When a task arrives, a record

for it can be inserted into the heap in O(log (n)) time where n is the total number of tasks in the priority queue. Therefore, the time complexity of Earliest Deadline First is equal to that of a typical sorting algorithm which is O (n log (n)). So O(nlog (n)) time is required. In other hand, the busy period, which is computed for every analyzed task set and has a pseudo-polynomial complexity for U ≤ 1 (Spuri M., 1996) is decreased also by the optimization of the response time. The most important results are presented in our work. So, we can deduce that using our proposed approach under such conditions may be advantageous.

Theorem

We assume a preemptive, asynchronous and periodic task system Γ to be composed of n periodic reconfigurable tasks, where each task is described by a period T_i, an arbitrary relative deadline D_i, a Worst Case Execution time (WCET) C_i and a release offset S_i.

If Γ is unfeasible and we apply a reconfiguration scenario based on EDF algorithm using the three previous solutions described in (1), (2) and (3) then, these tasks are scheduled with minimum response time. The system Γ is feasible and more over, we obtain an optimal response time for this system in the hyper-period $hp = [0, 2*LCM+\max_k(A_{k,1})]. (4)$

Proof

We prove the above theorem by proving the contrapositive, i.e., by showing that if Γ is not schedulable by EDF, then (4) is false.

Let t_b be the first instant at which a job of some task τ_i misses its deadline under EDF. Since τ_i misses its deadline at t_b, then all the system will be unfeasible, then the hyper-period $hp = [0, 2*LCM + \max_k(A_{k,1})]$ is not bounded and it diverge.

Or, initially we supposed that the hyper-period $hp = [0, 2*LCM + \max_k(A_{k,1})]$ is bounded and converge. Thus, (4) is false as claimed.

We now want to prove the property of optimality addressed above, in the previous proposed theorem. That is the response time of the asynchronous periodic requests under the EDF algorithm are the best achievable. This is exactly what is stated by the following lemma.

Lemma: Let A be any on-line preemptive algorithm, Γ a periodic task set, and τ an asynchronous periodic task. If $R^A_{\Gamma\cup\tau}(\tau)$ is the response time of τ when $\Gamma \cup \tau$ is scheduled by A, then $R^{EDF}_{\Gamma\cup\tau}(\tau) \leq R^A_{\Gamma\cup\tau}(\tau)$

Proof: According to the Equation (a), we can notice that for $d < D_{k,n}$, we have $W_{k,n}(t,d) = 0$ for any value of t. Where $W_k(t,d)$ is the amount of job with lower deadline to d brought by all the n instances of τ_k. $D_{k,n}$ is the relative deadline of the n_{th} instance of the task τ. So, for each instant t' that, $t' \geq t$ and $t' = d$, we have:

$$W^{EDF}_{k,n}(t,t') = 0.$$

It follows that:

$$W^{EDF}_{\text{Current}_\Gamma}(t,t') = 0$$

and

$$W^{EDF}_{\text{Current}_\Gamma}(t,t') \leq W^A_{\text{Current}_\Gamma}(t,t'),$$

it follows that:

$$R^{EDF}_{\Gamma\cup\tau}(\tau) \leq R^A_{\Gamma\cup\tau}(\tau)$$

That is, under the EDF algorithm, τ is never completed later than under A. By end, the optimality property was proved.

EXPERIMENTAL ANALYSIS AND DISCUSSION

In this section, in order to check the suggested configurations of tasks allowing the system's feasibility and the response time minimization, we simulate the agent's behavior on a Blackberry Bold 9700 presented by Xi Wang (2011) and on a *Volvo* system presented by (Volvo Construction Equipment, http://www.volvoce.com). This simulation presents some results by virtually applying real-time reconfigurations in the operating system of Blackberry Bold 9700 and in the operating system of a Volvo system. The Blackberry Bold 9700 is assumed to be initially composed of 50 tasks and dynamically reconfigured at run-time to add 30 new ones in which a task can be a missed call, a received message, or a Skype call. According to Wang (2011), the implemented Blackberry Bold 9700 is characterized as follows:

- **Mobile type:** 3G (WCDMA), GSM, and WCDMA,
- **Support band:** GSM 850/900/1800/1900,
- **Data transmission:** GPRS, EDGE, and HSDPA,
- **Producer:** RIM, Canada,
- **Commerce available:** November, 2009,
- **OS:** Blackberry OS 5.0,
- **Battery:** Lithium battery, 1500 mAh,
- **CPU:** Marvell PXA930, 624MHz,
- **Storage:** Micro-SD 32GB, and
- **Memory:** 256MB ROM and 256MB RAM.

The *Volvo* system as shown in Table 1 is assumed to be initially composed of 5 tasks and dynamically reconfigured at run-time to add 3 new ones. In this paper, any real-time reconfiguration and response time minimization is based on the real-time embedded control system reconfiguration. Moreover, in order to meet all real-time constraints, both initial WCETs C_i, the relative deadline D_i and also periods T_i of each task are reconfigured by the intelligent agent RT-Reconfiguration.

In this case, we are interested in the reconfiguration of these task's parameters, however we just present S_i, C_i and T_i of each task, and we assume that periods are equal to deadlines. The goal is to minimize the response time of the whole system and to meet their relative deadlines.

By applying the well known scheduling real-time simulator Cheddar (Singhoff & Legrand, 2004) the EDF scheduling result is shown in Figure 12.

The developed intelligent agent RT-Reconfiguration can configure all the parameters and evaluate the processor utilization factor

$$U = \sum_{i=1}^{n} \frac{Ci}{\min(T_i, D_i)}. \text{ (see Figure 13)}.$$

The previous tests were performed on an Intel(R) Core(TM) 2 Duo CPU (2.00 GHz, 3GHz RAM) on MS Windows 7. By considering asynchronous real-time tasks, the schedulability analysis should be done in the Hyper-Period HP $= [0, 2*LCM + \max_k(A_{k,1})]$, where LCM is the well-known Least Common Multiple. Let n be

Figure 12. The Blackberry Bold 9700 simulation with cheddar

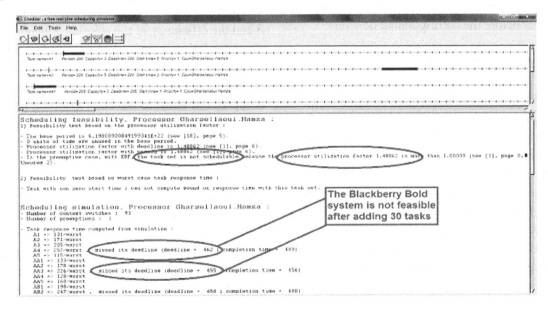

Figure 13. The Blackberry Bold 9700 simulation with RT-reconfiguration

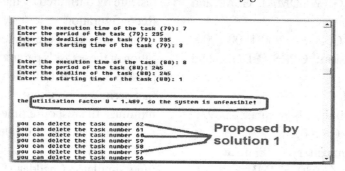

the number of tasks in Current $_\Gamma$ (t). The reconfiguration of the system Γ means the modification of its implementation that will be as follows at t time units:

$$Current_\Gamma\left(t\right)= \xi\_new \cup \xi\_old,$$

where ξ_old is a subset of old tasks which are not affected by the reconfiguration scenario (e.g. they implement the system before the time t), and ξ_new a subset of new tasks in the system. We assume that an updated task is considered as a new one at t time units. By considering a feasible System Γ before the application of the reconfiguration scenario, each one of the tasks of ξ_old is feasible, e.g. the execution of each instance is finished before the corresponding deadline.

Analysis of Results

In order to evaluate the proposed approach and to determine their advantages we consider the systems Blackberry Bold 9700 and *Volvo* defined in the running examples.

As shown in Figures 14 and 15, the X axis (abscissa axis) represents the number of removal tasks. If the removal rate is equal to 5, implying that we remove 5 tasks at each reconfiguration scenario. Then, more than 50 tasks, we can't remove another ones because the studied system will be disastrous.

As shown in Figure 16, the X axis (abscissa axis) represents the number of reconfigured tasks. If the reconfiguration rate is equal to 10, implying that we modify 10 task's parameters (Deadlines/Periods or WCETs) at each reconfiguration scenario. The running time for the Blackberry Bold 9700 system ranges from 0 to 550 microseconds using the first solution. The utilization factor (U) decreases from 1.489 to 0.389 microseconds using the first solution, from 1.489 to 0.709 microseconds using the second solution and it decreases from 1.489 to 0.478 microseconds using the third solution.

As the results show (Figure 16), we can observe, especially from the second half of the curve, and demonstrate the importance and efficiency of the solution 1 against the solution 2 and the solution 3 and the efficiency of the solution 3 against the second solution in term of utilization factor (U) decreasing.

Based on these observed results, we can compare our work to the corresponding papers in the state of the art which cannot reach these results and why, we can confirm that this method is very advantageous given the fast response time and the performance of the schedulability of such studied system.

As shown in Figure 17, the X axis (abscissa axis) represents the number of reconfigured tasks. If the reconfiguration rate is equal to 1, implying that we modify 1 task's parameters (Deadlines/Periods or WCETs) at each reconfiguration

Figure 14. The utilization factor evolution of the Blackberry Bold system (solution 1)

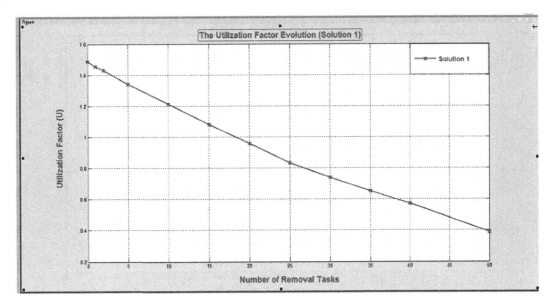

Figure 15. The response time evolution of the Blackberry Bold system (solution 1)

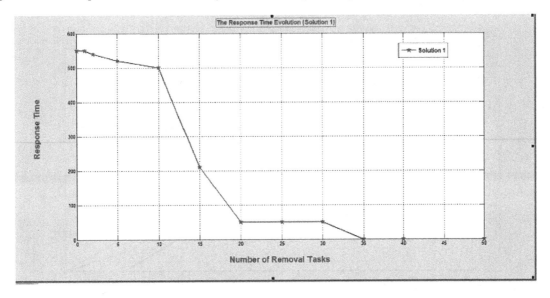

scenario. The running time for the *Volvo* system ranges from 0 to 40 microseconds using the first solution, it ranges from 0 to 50 microseconds using the second one and it ranges from 0 to 60 microseconds using the third solution.

As the results show (Figure 17), we can observe, especially from the second half of the curve, and demonstrate the importance and efficiency of the solution 1 against the solution 2 and the solution 3, and the efficiency of the solution 3 against the second solution in term of response time speed.

The second important observation was obtained by the comparison of our proposed approach

Figure 16. The comparison between the 3 solutions (the Blackberry Bold system)

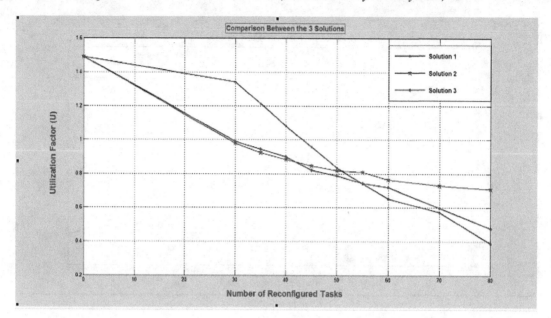

Figure 17. The comparison between the 3 solutions (the Volvo system)

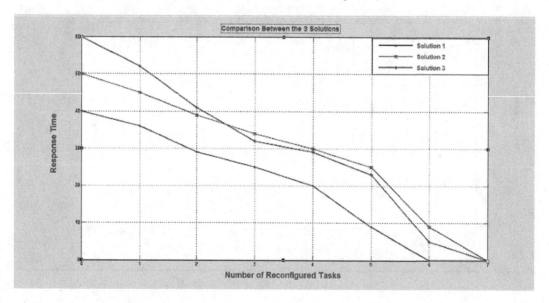

against the others from the literature about the current values. We tested the feasibility of the same task sets Blackberry Bold 9700, and *Volvo* by other algorithms, so that we can compare the results directly. We carried out several test runs and examined them under different aspects. The

total utilization of the static schedule is 75%, the classic one is 145.4% and the other proposed by our method is 63.1%.

Discussion and Evaluation

The test greatly reduces the processor utilization factor $U = \sum_{i=1}^{n} \dfrac{Ci}{\min(T_i, D_i)}$ in comparison to the original processor utilization factor, so the combination of both three solutions in order to obtain the optimization of the response time by calculating L_{opt} leads to an improved algorithm for the analysis of asynchronous systems.

So, we can therefore confirm that this method is nowadays very advantageous given the fast response time and the performance of the RT-Reconfiguration tool.

By applying the three solutions of this tool RT-Reconfiguration, we conclude that our approach can allow more reactive and also more efficient feasible systems. This advantage can be important in many cases where critical control tasks should be intensively executed in small periods of time. This work also, concentrates on the context of systems containing a set of tasks which is not feasible; the reconfiguration was applied in order not only to obtain the system's feasibility but also to get the performance of the system by reducing the response time of the processes to be tolerated in interactive environment and by avoiding unnecessarily frequent context switch leading to more overheads resulting in less throughput. This advantage was increased and proved clearly with the Blackberry Bold 9700 system proposed by (Wang, 2011) and on a *Volvo* case study proposed by (Volvo Construction Equipment, http://www.volvoce.com).

Both, the Figures 10, 14, 15, and 16 illustrate this advantage. Moreover, with the revolution of semiconductors technology and the development of efficient reconfiguration tools, the use of our method and the RT-Reconfiguration tool will becomes increasingly important, and very advantageous for rapid and efficient response time of the periodic reconfigurable OS tasks, especially when the user has no other choice than to choose the previous proposed solutions and to decide the proper values of each reconfigured task's parameters in order to obtain the system's feasibility and to minimize the response time of the studied systems.

FUTURE RESEARCH DIRECTIONS

We plan in future works to resolve several problems for the Reconfigurable real-time embedded systems.

Another problem that has to be resolved in the future deals with the study of each reconfiguration scenario of sporadic and aperiodic tasks to be released in different times and the minimization of their response time. We plan also to study the reconfigurations of dependent and distributed real-time tasks. Finally, our important future work is the generalization of our contributions for the Reconfigurable real-time embedded systems.

CONCLUSION

The book chapter deals with reconfigurable systems to be implemented by different tasks that should meet real time constraints. In this paper, we propose a new theory for the minimization of the response time of periodic asynchronous constrained deadline real-time tasks with EDF algorithm that can be applied to uniprocessor systems and proved it correct. We showed that this theory was capable to reconfigure the whole system by calculating worst case response times for a simple example using EDF scheduler. Previous work in this area has been described, and several different solution techniques have been suggested. These solutions techniques are primarily intended to reduce the processor demand and the response time by adapting the scheduling parameters (WCET, Period or Deadline) in a uniprocessor system by removing some tasks, changing the periods/deadlines or by reducing the worst case execution time of each task set independent of the number of tasks.

A tool is developed and tested to support all these services. This approach is applied to a Blackberry Bold 9700 and to a *Volvo* system. To satisfy user requirements, we apply the Real-Time Simulator, cheddar to check the whole system behavior.

REFERENCES

Al-Safi, Y., & Vyatkin, V. (2007). An ontology based reconfiguration agent for intelligent mechatronic systems. In *Proceedings of the 4th International Conference of Holistic Multi-Agent Systems Manufacturing* (LNCS), (vol. 4659, pp. 114-126). Regensburg, Germany: Springer.

Angelov, C., Sierszecki, K., & Marian, N. (2005). Design models for reusable and reconfigurable state machines. In Yang, L. T. et al. (Eds.), *Proceedings of Embedded Ubiquitous Computing* (pp. 152–163). IEEE. doi:10.1007/11596356_18.

Arcticus Systems. (n.d.). *Web-page*. Retrieved from http://www.arcticus.se

Baruah, S., & Goossens, J. (2004). Scheduling real-time tasks: Algorithms and complexity. In Leung, J. Y.-T. (Ed.), *Handbook of Scheduling: Algorithms, Models, and Performance Analysis*. Academic Press.

Baruah, S., Rosier, L., & Howell, R. (1990). Algorithms and complexity concerning the preemptive scheduling of periodic real-time tasks on one processor. *The Journal of Real-Time Systems, 2*.

Burns, A., & Baxter, G. (2006). Time bands in systems structure. In *Structure for Dependability: Computer-Based Systems from an Interdisciplinary Perspective*. London: Springer. doi:10.1007/1-84628-111-3_4.

Davis, R. I., Zabos, A., & Burns, A. (2008). Efficient exact schedulability tests for fixed priority real-time systems. *IEEE Transactions on Computers, 57*(9), 1261–1276. doi:10.1109/TC.2008.66.

Dertouzos, M. L. (1974). *Control robotics: The procedural control of physical processes*. Information Processing.

George, L., & Courbin, P. (2011). Reconfiguration of uniprocessor sporadic real-time systems: The sensitivity approach. In *Knowledge on Reconfigurable Embedded Control Systems: Applications for Flexibility and Agility*. Hershey, PA: IGI Global.

Gharsellaoui, H., Gharbi, A., Khalgui, M., & Ben Ahmed, S. (2011). Feasible automatic reconfigurations of real-time OS tasks. In *Handbook of Research on Industrial Informatics and Manufacturing Intelligence: Innovations and Solutions*. Academic Press.

Ha, S. R.K. (Soft Hard Real-Time Kernel). (n.d.). *Home page*. Retrieved from http://shark.sssup.it/

Hnninen, K., & Riutta, T. (2003). *Optimal design*. (Masters thesis). Mlardalens Hgskola, Dept of Computer Science and Engineering.

Khalgui, M. (2008). A deployment methodology of real-time industrial control applications in distributed controllers. *Computers in Industry Journal, 59*(5), 450–462. doi:10.1016/j.compind.2007.12.008.

Khalgui, M. (2010). NCES-based modeling and CTL-based verification of reconfigurable embedded control systems. *Computers in Industry Journal, 61*(3), 198–212. doi:10.1016/j.compind.2009.09.004.

Khalgui, M., Mosbahi, O., Li, Z. W., & Hanisch, H.-M. (2011). Reconfigurable multi-agent embedded control systems: From modeling to implementation. *IEEE Transactions on Computers, 60*(4), 538–551. doi:10.1109/TC.2010.96.

Leung, J.-T., & Merril, M. (1980). A note on preemptive scheduling of periodic real-time tasks. *Information Processing Letters*, *3*(11), 115–118. doi:10.1016/0020-0190(80)90123-4.

Liu, C., & Layland, J. (1973). Scheduling algorithms for multi-programming in a hard-real-time environment. *Journal of the ACM*, *20*(1), 46–61. doi:10.1145/321738.321743.

Liu, J. W. (2000). *Real-time systems*. Upper Saddle River, NJ: Prentice Hall.

Loria. (2005a). Retrieved from www.loria.fr/nnavet/cours/DEA2004-2005/slide1.pdf

Loria. (2005b). Retrieved from www.loria.fr/nnavet/cours/DEA2004-2005/slide2.pdf

Mki-Turja, J., & Nolin, M. (2004). Tighter response-times for tasks with offsets. In *Proceedings of the of the 10th International Conference on Real-Time Computing Systems and Applications (RTCSA04)*. RTCSA.

Palencia, J. M. G. (2003). Harbour, offset-based response time analysis of distributed systems scheduled under EDF. In *Proceedings of the 15th Euromicro Conference on Real-Time Systems*. Porto, Portugal: Euromicro.

Pedreiras, P., & Almeida, L. (2002). EDF message scheduling on controller area network. *Computing & Control Engineering Journal*, *13*(4), 163–170. doi:10.1049/cce:20020402.

Rooker, M. N., Sunder, C., Strasser, T., Zoitl, A., Hummer, O., & Ebenhofer, G. (2007). Zero downtime reconfiguration of distributed automation systems: The CEDAC approach. In *Proceedings of the 3rd International Conference of Industrial Applied Holonic Multi-Agent Systems*, (pp. 326-337). IEEE.

RTSJ (Real-Time Specification for Java). (n.d.). *Home page*. Retrieved from http://www.rtsj.org/

Singhoff, L. N. L. M. F., & Legrand, J. (2004). Cheddar: A flexible real time scheduling framework. *ACM SIGAda Ada Letters*, *24*(4), 1–8. doi:10.1145/1046191.1032298.

Spuri, M. (1996). *Analysis of deadline scheduled real-time systems (Technical Report -2772)*. Institut National de Recherche en Informatique et en Automatique.

Stankovic, J., Spuri, M., Ramamritham, K., & Buttazzo, C. (1998). *Deadline scheduling for real-time systems*. Norwell, MA: Kluwer Academic Publishers. doi:10.1007/978-1-4615-5535-3.

Tucker, S., Taft, R. A., Duff, R. L., & Brukardt, E. Ploedereder, & Leroy. (Eds.), Ada 2005 reference manual: Language and standard libraries. Lecture Notes in Computer Science, 4348.

Volvo. (n.d.). *Construction equipment*. Retrieved from http://www.volvoce.com

Wang, X., Khalgui, M., & Li, Z. W. (2011). Dynamic low power reconfigurations of real-time embedded systems. In *Proceedings of the 1st Pervasive and Embedded Computing Systems*. Algarve, Portugal: IEEE.

KEY TERMS AND DEFINITIONS

Dynamic Reconfiguration: The dynamic reconfiguration means qualitative changes on-line (at run time) in the structures, functionalities and algorithms of the "Control System" as a response to qualitative changes of control goals, of the controlled "physical system," or of the environment the control system behaves within.

Embedded Systems: An embedded system is a computer system designed to perform one or a few dedicated functions often with real-time computing constraints. It is *embedded* as part of a complete device often including hardware and mechanical parts. By contrast, a general-purpose computer, such as a Personal Computer (PC), is designed to be flexible and to meet a wide range of end-user needs. Embedded systems control many devices in common use today.

Intelligent Agent: On the Internet, an intelligent agent (or simply an *agent*) is a program that gathers information or performs some other service without your immediate presence and on some regular schedule. Typically, an agent program, using parameters you have provided, searches all or some part of the Internet, gathers information you are interested in, and presents it to you on a daily or other periodic basis. An agent is sometimes called a bot (short for robot).

Processor Utilization Factor: Given a set of n periodic tasks, processor utilization factor U is the fraction of processor time spent in the execution of the task set.

Real-Time Constraints: Execution of real-time tasks must satisfy three types of constraints. Timing constraints enforce each task instance to complete its execution before D after the date the task is released (D is a relative deadline); precedence constraints force partially task instance order and the read of current data values; resource constraints represent the exclusive access to shared resources.

Real-Time OS Tasks: Smallest identifiable and essential piece of a job that serves as a unit of work, and as a means of differentiating between the various components of a project. Often used as an alternative term for activity.

Response Time of an Instance: Is the time (measured from the release time) at which the instance is terminated.

Run-Time Environment: Stands for "Runtime Environment." As soon as a software program is executed, it is in a runtime state. In this state, the program can send instructions to the computer's processor and access the computer's memory (RAM) and other system resources. When software developers write programs, they need to test them in the runtime environment.

Chapter 13
Task Migration in Embedded Systems:
Design and Performance

Abderrazak Jemai
University of Tunis El Manar, Tunisia & University of Carthage, Tunisia

Kamel Smiri
University of Tunis El Manar, Tunisia & University of Kairouan, Tunisia

Habib Smei
ISET de Rades, Tunisia

ABSTRACT

Task migration has a great consideration is MPSoC design and implementation of embedded systems in order to improve performance related to optimizing execution time or reducing energy consumption. Multi-Processor Systems-on-Chip (MPSoC) are now the leading hardware platform featured in embedded systems. This chapter deals with the impact of task migration as an alternative to meet performance constraints in the design flow. The authors explain the different levels of the design process and propose a methodology to master the migration process at transaction level. This methodology uses some open source tools like SDF3 modified to provide performance estimation at transaction level. These results help the designer to choose the best hardware model in replacement of the previous software implementation of the task object of migration. Using the SDF3 tool, the authors model a multimedia application using SDF graphs. Secondly, they target an MPSoC platform. The authors take a performance constraint to achieve 25 frames per second.

DOI: 10.4018/978-1-4666-3922-5.ch013

INTRODUCTION

Currently, multimedia applications have important computation needs, and induce high transfers of data. They will do much more than just playback pre-recorded audio and video; they will employ sophisticated image processing techniques and integrate complex computer graphics, all delivered with high interactivity and real-time response. Furthermore, multimedia applications are composed of several independent tasks that can run in an autonomous way as soon as they have the appropriate input data at their input points.

To fulfill the need for computation, while ensuring correct performances, designers often have resort to software-to-hardware tasks migration. But when implementing applications on MPSoC systems, migrating software tasks to hardware tasks is a costly process. One of the ways to avoid such expenses is performance estimation at different design levels.

The general problematic needed to be answered is how to help a designer to estimate the performances of an application which have to be executed on an MPSoC platform, at design level. This chapter specifically targets performance estimation of software-to-hardware migration on MPSoC systems with SDF graphs. The first section of this chapter presents the state of the art on performance estimation of MPSoC systems. The second section describes an approach for performance estimation of MPSoC systems with SDF graphs. The experimentations are presented in details in the third section, through the case study of a MPJEG decoder. The chapter ends with a conclusion and a glimpse of the work perspectives.

1. STATE ART OF PERFORMANCE ESTIMATION IN MPSOC DESIGN

Several research projects already tackle the subject of performance estimation of migration on MPSoC systems. Indeed, recently, research is more and more concerned with the use of the Synchronous Data Flow (SDF) graph in the MPSoC design. Jerraya (2008) points out that NoC-MPSoC design is the subject of more than 60 research projects over the world.

For their part, Kumar and al. (Kumar, Mesman, Theelen, Corporaal, & Ha, 2008) have proposed a solution to analyze applications that are modeled by SDF graphs and executed on MPSoC platform through the use of Resource Manager (RM). RM is a task which controls and directs the use of resources. It is responsible for resources access (critical or not), and optimization of their usage. The designer reserves for the RM a whole execution node (CPU, memory, bus ...) which increases the cost of the total MPSoC system.

Lahiri and all (Lahiri, Raghunathan, & Dey, 2000) presented methodologies and algorithms to design communication architectures in order to achieve the desired performance on MPSoC systems. They developed a tool named Communication Analysis Graph (CAG), which relies on SDF graphs for MPSoC performance analysis and constraint satisfaction.

Wiggers and all (Wiggers, Kavaldjiev, Smit, & Jansen, 2005) proposed a solution that consists in mapping purely software tasks and their communication channels on the target processors. They exploited the SDF graphs to compare the throughput obtained with the target throughput of the application. Finally, S. Stuijk (2007) proposed a design flow for mapping multimedia applications on NoC-MPSoC platforms.

2. AN APPROACH FOR PERFORMANCE ESTIMATION OF MPSOC SYSTEMS WITH SDF GRAPHS

We propose in this chapter a methodology for performance estimation of MPSoC systems with SDF graphs, which is called the methodology for software-to-hardware migration performance estimation (Smiri & Jemai, 2009; Eindhoven University of Technology, 2009). It targets performance estimation multimedia applications on NoC-MPSoC systems.

The methodology consists in three steps. Its starting point is the KPN model of an application. In the first step, we annotate the KPN model with the execution times of the tasks, and the sizes of the data transferred between tasks. The second step consists in formalizing both functional and non-functional constraints. The functional constraint is the performance constraints, which equals 25 frames per second. Non-functional constraints concern the types of the platform, the processors, the memory architecture, etc. The third step is a conclusion on the feasibility of the functional (performance) constraint, given the non-functional constraints.

The SDF3 tool has been developed by Stuijk, Geilen and Basten, from the Eindhoven University of Technology (Stuijk, Geilen, & Basten, 2006). It is an open-source tool and can thus be downloaded for free[1] (Eindhoven University of Technology, 2009). In our context, the main purpose of SDF3 is performance estimation of applications on NoC-MPSoC systems, through static analysis of SDF graphs. However, SDF3 is initially designed for best resource mapping at system level.

The tool is written in C++. It can be used through both an API and a set of commands. Two of these commands have been used during this work. The first is the sdf3analysis command, which allows, among others, throughput, connectivity and deadlocking analysis of SDF graphs. The second is the sdf3flow command, which executes a design flow called the predictable design flow (Stuijk, 2007). The input and output formats of the sdf3flow command is the XML format.

The predictable design flow contains four phases.

- Phase 1 aims at determining the memory that will be allocated for each actor and channel of the application graph on the tiles of the target platform.
- Phase 2 computes the minimal bandwidth needed by the application and the maximal latency on the NoC.
- Phase 3 binds the actors and channels of the application graph to the tiles of the NoC-MPSoC target platform. The arbitration is based on TDMA wheels for each processor.
- Phase 4 schedules the communications on the NoC, given the actors and channels mappings.

The output of the predictable design flow is a NoC-MPSoC configuration that satisfies the throughput constraint. The configuration contains a mapping of the actors and channels of the SDF graph to the nodes (called tiles) and connections of the NoC-MPSoC destination platform. The mapping is modeled by applying transformations to the application graph, in order to model the binding of actors and channels to tiles and connections.

3. CASE STUDY: THE MJPEG DECODER

The MJPEG codec processes video sequences that are composed of separate JPEG images. These images are 128x128 pixels high, and split in 8x8 pixels macroblocks. The succession of the tasks done by MJPEG decoder is represented on Figure 1. The first task is the Huffman decoding. It is followed by a reverse zigzag ordering, and a reverse quantization. Then comes the reverse discrete cosine transform. The two final tasks are color conversion from the YUV color space to the RGB color space, and the reordering of the pixels in order to adapt them to the output device. These two tasks are not JPEG tasks but are needed for output purposes.

Figure 1. MJPEG decoder process flow

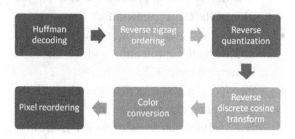

Table 1. MJPEG decoder simulation results

Migration scenario	Performance (fps)
None	12,07
IDCT	11,49
IDCT and VLD	24,07

Simulations

As a comparison element, we run a set of simulations of the application's execution on 2, 3 and 4 processor NoC-MPSoC. These simulations give an idea of the application's realizable performances. The results of these simulations are presented in Table 1. When we analyze results shown in Table 1, we note that IDCT and VLD modules should be implemented in hardware to achieve the required performance. This action is called software-to-hardware task migration of IDCT and VLD modules.

MJPEG Decoder SDF Model

The abstract functional model of MJPEG decoder is shown in Figure 2. This model, also called application graph, is represented using SDF graph.

Table 2 presents the task done by each actor of the application graph.

Gathering Required Data

Before running the sdf3flow command, some information needs to be collected.

Actors Execution Times

The first information needed to be collected is the individual execution times for actors, expressed in abstract time units. The sdf3flow command uses an abstract time-unit. The designer is hence free to map that abstract unit to any "manly" unit. The time unit used in this work is the processor cycle. There are two methods for obtaining actor execution times in cycles. The first is the use of WCET tools, which process worst-case execution times for pieces of source code, or binaries. The second is simulation, which was used in this work. Table 3 presents the individual execution times for the actors of the application graph.

Token Sizes

The command needs the sizes of the tokens that are transferred from one actor to another. In the worst case possible, the decoder has to process JPEG images with a 4:4:4 resolution, which means that no sub-sampling is used. Therefore, the luminance Y is coded with the same resolution as the blue and red chrominances. For each 8x8 pixels macroblock, the decoder will then have to process 192 samples (64 x 3). In the frequency domain, samples are coded on 2 octets because their interval is [-1024 ; 1024]. In the spatial domain, samples

Figure 2. MJPEG decoder SDF model

Table 2. Actor/task mapping

Actor	Task
VLD	Huffman decoding
IZZ	Inverse zigzag reordering
IQ	Inverse quantization
IDCT	Inverse discrete cosine transform
LIBU	Pixel reorganization and adapting to the output device

Table 3. Actors' execution times

Actor	Cycles per image	Cycles per macroblock
VLD	1.140.800	-
IZZ	446.400	1743
IQ	644.800	2518
IDCT	2.281.600	8912
LIBU	248.000	-

Table 4. Token sizes for the application graph

Channel	d2	d3	d4	d5
Size in bits (per MB)	3072	3072	3072	1536

are coded on one single octet because their interval is [0 ; 255]. The token sizes for each channel of the application graph are presented in Table 4.

Throughput Constraint

The throughput constraint has to be expressed in iterations2 per time-unit. If the target performance is n fps, and the processors of the target platform have a frequency of 50 MHz, which implies a cycle time of 20 ns per cycle, then the constraint is as follows:

Constraint = n\times * 20\times * 10^{-9}
iterations/time-unit

Communication Protocols Modeling with SDF Graphs

When a software task becomes a hardware task, the communication protocol it uses to transfer data to and from the other tasks changes. The first approach adopted was to model these changes by transforming the application graph. We established a list of protocols regarding communication between software and hardware tasks. The list contains three classes of protocols have been identified: the HS class, which stands for hardware to software communication, the SH class (software to hardware communication), and the HH class (hardware to hardware communication). Each class contains three different protocols. Those protocols are not implemented by the SDF3 tool, because the latter treats all tasks as software tasks. The protocols retained by the laboratory are the SH1 and HS1 protocols.

The SH1 Communication Protocol

Let A and B be two actors from a given SDF application graph (Figure 3). A and B are connected by a channel d.

If A is migrated to a hardware task, the communication between A and B becomes a hardware-to-software communication. In the application graph, the SH1 communication protocol is modeled by the sub-graph represented in Figure 4. The ac actor models the time necessary to send all the tokens from the actor A to the actor B. The aρ actor models the maximal latency of the NoC. The as actor models the unavailability of the B actor. Indeed, in the worst-case scenario, the B actor has consumed all the TDMA slices allocated for it, so it has to wait for its processor's TDMA wheel to complete its current turn.

The HS1 Communication Protocol

Let us assume the same starting situation as in the previous case. If B is migrated to a hardware

Figure 3. Initial subgraph

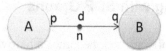

task, the communication between A and B becomes a software-to-hardware communication. It is modeled by the SDF subgraph in Figure 5. The hardware task, A, writes its results in its local memory. The B actor has to access that memory as a remote memory. It is split into two actors B1 and B2. B1 models the time necessary to send a request to the remote memory. The B2 actor models the initial B actor. The m1 actor models the time needed to access the remote memory and send the required data over the NoC.

Performance Estimation by Transformation of the Application Graph

Matching the Performances of the Simulation

As a first experiment, we are going to try to match the performance measured by the simulation in the migration-less scenario. The application graph is the one in Figure 6. The platform graph models a two processor NoC-MPSoC with the following parameters:

- **Local memory size:** 4 MB
- **Input/output tile bitrate:** 96 bits/time-unit
- **NoC packet (flit) size:** 96 bits
- **NoC packet header size:** 32 bits
- **NoC topology:** torus

Note that in the SDF3 tool, the processor frequency is not modeled as a parameter of the target platform. It is rather taken into account in the cycle time parameter that appears in the constraint's formula. Given that the simulation gave a 12 fps performance in the migration-less scenario, we calculated the following throughput constraint using that same formula:

Constraint $= 2$ x 12 x $10^{-8} = 2.4$ x 10^{-7} iterations/time-unit

After writing the correct XML descriptions for the application graph, the platform graph and the throughput constraint, we execute the sdf3flow command, which succeeds in finding a configuration of the application graph on the platform graph that satisfies that throughput constraint.

Migration of IDCT

Figure 6 represents the application graph which was applied the required transformations to model the SH1communication protocol between the IQ and IDCT actors, and the HS1 communication between the IDCT and LIBU actors.

Figure 4. Subgraph after SH1 modelling

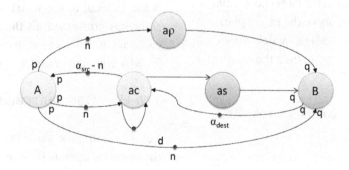

Figure 5. Subgraph after HS1 modelling

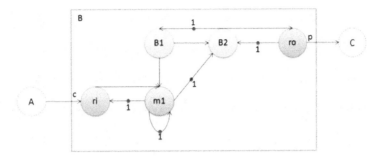

Figure 6. Application graph after modelling the IDCT migration

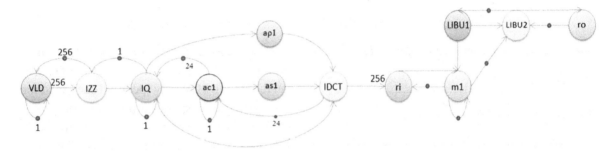

At this point, running the sdf3flow command is useless, because the command would consider the migration actors - i.e. the actors added to model the migration- as "normal" actors. Therefore, it would model communication protocols once more, which is absurd. The solution is to use the sdf3analysis command and its throughput computing option. The result is a performance gain of 0.5 fps.

Migration of VLD

Figure 7 represents the application graph which was applied the required transformation to model the HS1 communication between the VLD and IZZ actors. Using the same method as the previous case, we observe a performance gain of 2.5 fps.

Migration of VLD and IDCT

The application graph needs to be applied the required transformation to model the SH1 com-

munication between the IQ and IDCT actors, and the HS1 communication between the VLD and IZZ actors and the IDCT and LIBU actors. For readability purposes, it is not represented. The performance gain observed was of 3.5 fps.

Results

The experimentations included performance estimations for the migrations of VLD, IDCT, and VLD + IDCT tasks. After applying the appropriate transformations to the applications graph, the latter is analyzed using the sdf3analysis command to compute its throughput. Table 5 summarizes the results obtained.

Performance Estimation using Processor Specialization

The first approach models the communication protocols properly, but it doesn't guarantee the

Figure 7. Application graph after modelling of the VLD migration

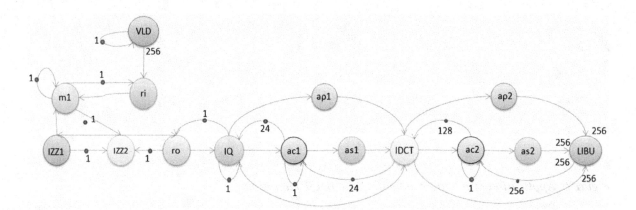

Table 5. Performances and gains of the migration scenarios

Migration scenario	Performance	Gain
No migration	12.5 fps	-
IDCT	13 fps	0.5 fps
VLD	15 fps	2.5 fps
VLD and IDCT	16 fps	3.5 fps

feasibility of the communications between the tasks. Indeed, the predictable design flow is interrupted after phase 3, which corresponds to the binding of actors and channels to the tiles of the target platform. The communication scheduling phase is not executed. We put forward a second solution, which consist in keeping the initial application graph (without any transformation). The target platform's description added a new, specialized processor for each of the hardware tasks. The type of the new processor has to be different from the other generic processors. Each actor chosen to be migrated will be specified only one execution time that corresponds to the type of the specialized processor which it is supposed to be executed on.

For instance, if an actor T is migrated, the target platform will be added a new processor of type T, and the actor will be only specified one execution time, which corresponds a processor of type T. The sdf3flow command will then automatically bind the T actor to the T-type processor. The other actors of the application graph will be bound to the other, generic processors of the platform.

Migration of IDCT

In the scenario of the IDCT migration, the target platform is that shown in Figure 8. With this platform, the sdf3flow command cannot find a configuration that satisfies a throughput constraint of 25 fps (see Figure 8).

Migration of VLD

In the scenario of the VLD migration, the target platform is that shown in Figure 9. With this platform, the sdf3flow command cannot find a configuration that satisfies throughput constraints of 25 fps. The obtained performance is less than 20 fps (see Figure 9).

Figure 8. Target platform for the IDCT migration

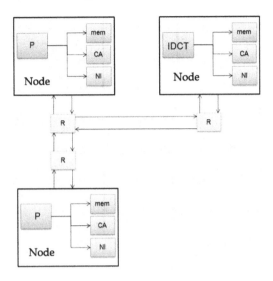

Figure 9. Target platform for the VLD migration

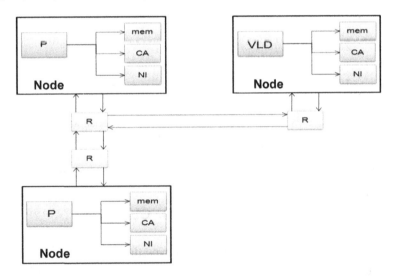

Migration of VLD and IDCT

In the scenario of a double IDCT and VLD migration, the target platform is shown in Figure 10).

The sdf3flow command cannot find a configuration that satisfies a 25 fps throughput constraint, but it can find one that satisfies a 24 fps constraint. Provided that the acceptability interval for performances is ± 1 fps, we accept the configuration.

Results Comparison

Figure 11 is a comparison of the performance gains obtains using the three methods: simulation, graph transformation, and processor specialization. In the migration-less scenario, the three methods gave equal results, which is normal provided we simply tried to match the simulation performance using the two other methods.

Figure 10. Target platform for the double IDCT and VLD migration

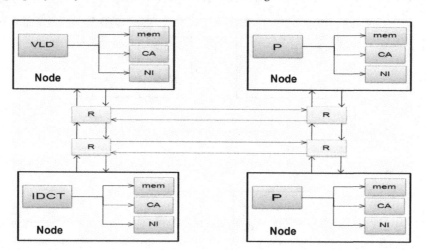

Figure 11. Comparison of the three migration modelling methods

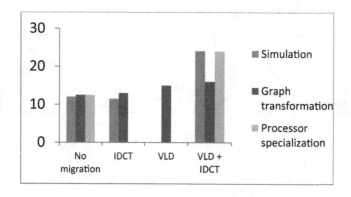

In the IDCT migration case, graph transformation and simulation performances matched one another, but the third method didn't. The only method that gave results in the VLD migration case is the graph transformation method. Indeed, no simulation involving a VLD migration was run. Finally, in the double IDCT and VLD migration scenario, we can see that the graph transformation method offers very little gain (3.5 fps), whereas the processor specialization method did actually match the performances obtained by simulation (24 fps).

CONCLUSION

During this work, we experimented two ways of modeling software-to-hardware migration and estimating its performances. The first approach did not guarantee the feasibility of the communications between the tasks, and offered very little performance gains. The second approach can guarantee that feasibility, but did not model the HS1 protocol, rather replacing it by the standard, default software-to-software communication protocol implemented in the SDF3 tool. Nonetheless, the estimated performance gains did actually meet the performances that were measured during the simulations. We can therefore validate our methodology for software-to-hardware migration performance estimation through the case study of the MJPEG decoder.

As a future improvement, the SDF3 tool being open source, it can be modified to model the HS1 communication protocol. Such modifications would include adding a "nature" attribute to the actors, which would allow differentiating between hardware and software tasks, and thus applying the suitable transformations to model the appropriate communication protocol on the application graph.

REFERENCES

Eindhoven University of Technology. (2009). *SDF3 official website*. Retrieved from http://www.es.ele.tue.nl/sdf3/

Jerraya, A. (2008). System compilation for MPSoC based on NoC. In *Proceedings of MPSoC '08, 8th International Forum on Application-Specific Multi-Processor SoC*. MPSoC.

Kumar, B., Mesman, B., Theelen, H., & Corporaal, Y. (2008). Analyzing composability of applications on MPSoC platforms. *Journal of Systems Architecture*. doi:10.1016/j.sysarc.2007.10.002.

Lahiri, K., Raghunathan, & Dey. (2000). Efficient exploration of the SoC communication architecture design space. *IEEE Computer Aided Design*.

Smiri, K., & Jemai. (2009). Migration methodology in MPSoC based on performance analysis via SDF graph. *Advances in Computational Sciences and Technology*, 149-166.

Stuijk, S. Geilen, & Basten. (2006). SDF3: SDF for free. In *Proceedings of ACSD 2006*, (pp. 276-278). ACSD.

Stuijk, S. (2007). *Predictable mapping of streaming applications on multiprocessors*. (PhD thesis). Eindhoven University of Technology.

Wiggers, M. H., Kavaldjiev, Smit, & Jansen. (2005). Architecture design space exploration for streaming applications through timing analysis. *Communicating Process Architectures*.

Zrida, H. K., Abid, M., Ammari, A. C., & Jemai, A. (2009). A YAPI system level optimized parallel model of a H.264/AVC video encoder. In *Proceedings of ACS/IEEE International Conference on Computer Systems and Applications (AICCSA'09)*. IEEE.

ENDNOTES

[1] http://www.es.ele.tue.nl/sdf3/download.php

[2] An iteration of an SDF graph is a set of executions where each actor a is executed $\gamma(a)$ times, where γ is the repetition vector of the graph.

Chapter 14

Wireless IEEE 802.11–Based Networking Approaches for Industrial Networked Systems

Ricardo Moraes
Universidade Federal de Santa Catarina, Brazil

Francisco Vasques
Universidade do Porto, Portugal

ABSTRACT

During the last few years, the demand for Real-Time (RT) communication has been steadily increasing due to a wide range of new applications. Remarkable examples are VoIP (Voice over IP) and Networked Control Systems (NCS). For such RT applications, the support of timely communication services is one of the major requirements. The purpose of this chapter is to survey the state-of-the-art on RT communication in CSMA-based networks and to identify the most suitable approaches to deal with the requirements imposed by next generation communication systems. This chapter focuses on one of the most relevant solutions that operate in shared broadcast environments, according to the CSMA medium access protocol, the IEEE 802.11 standard. From this survey, it becomes clear that traditional CSMA-based networks are not able to deal with the requirements imposed by next generation communication systems. More specifically, they are not able to handle uncontrolled traffic sources sharing the same broadcast environment.

1. INTRODUCTION

This chapter surveys the state-of-the-art on Real-Time (RT) communication in wireless CSMA-based networks. One of the main objectives is to show that traditional RT communication approaches for CSMA-based networks are not able to deal with the requirements imposed by next generation communication systems. More specifically, they are not able to handle uncontrolled traffic sources sharing the same broadcast environment. Similar conclusions could be drawn for other CSMA-based protocols, such as IEEE 802.15.4 (one of the most widespread PAN protocols) or CAN (commonly

DOI: 10.4018/978-1-4666-3922-5.ch014

used in automotive and industrial applications). However, such protocols are out of the scope of this chapter, as we are focusing on CSMA-based wireless LAN protocols.

Another purpose of this chapter is to identify the main design guidelines that will enable the support of RT communication services in CSMA-based networks, even when the communication environment is shared with uncontrolled traffic sources. As an outcome of this RT communication survey, a RT communication framework is defined, which fulfills the requirements imposed by typical RT applications. It is traditionally considered that RT communication services can be classified according to the degree of RT guarantees into hard and soft RT groups. Hard RT applications require communication services with predictable and bounded response times, and violations of these response times may have severe consequences. Instead, soft RT applications can tolerate some losses of temporal deadlines. For instance, a RT control application can tolerate occasional losses of the control law updates, especially if the control law has been modified to account for those lost updates (Ramanathan, 1999). However, this type of applications is usually less resilient against jitter on the control law updates. In the case of a NCS, it is of utmost importance to have a nearly constant average communication delay and low jitter, whatever the behavior of the communication environment.

The major challenge concerning the design of protocol architectures for CSMA-based networks is that the channel is a shared resource. Therefore, there is the need to prioritize RT data messages, when the communication infrastructure is shared with external traffic sources (Sauter & Vasques, 2006). Thus, the access to this shared resource needs to be coordinated either centrally or in a distributed manner (Tavli & Heinzelman, 2006). According to the ISO/OSI model, this coordina-

tion task is performed by Medium Access Control (MAC) protocols. Actually, the MAC protocol is the key issue in any broadcast random access network. This chapter surveys one of the most relevant random access protocol in wireless environments: the IEEE 802.11 standard protocol[1]. A relevant characteristic of this protocol is the use of the Carrier Sense Multiple Access (CSMA) mechanism to manage the medium access. Its main drawback is the non-determinism of the probabilistic contention resolution algorithm.

The demand for high performance industrial wireless networking will increase significantly in the next few years. This is a consequence of recent technology developments that demand wireless access in office environments, in public hot-spots and in domestic environments. Presently, significant efforts are being made to move from wired to wireless networks (Jonsson & Kunert, 2009; Willig, Matheus, & Wolisz, 2005). Therefore, it is reasonable to expect that in the near future, the widespread availability of wireless solutions will generate a similar de facto standard for industrial wireless communications. Within this context, the IEEE 802.11 family of protocols is one of the main contenders to become a de facto standard for industrial wireless communications (Sauter, 2010). Nevertheless, it has received only limited coverage in this research community (Willig, 2008). On the one hand, this family of protocols reveals shortcomings in the prioritization of real-time data messages. On the other hand, it is easily able to replace industrial Ethernet solutions in a transparent way, implementing the two lowest layers of the ISO/OSI model, providing all the required functionalities to enable the support of the Internet Protocol (IP) that is virtually the basis for every application over Ethernet networks. Within this context, the IEEE 802.11 family of protocols is one of the main contenders to become a *de facto* standard for industrial wireless communications

(Sauter, 2010). Nevertheless, it has received only limited coverage in this research community (Willig, 2008). On the one hand, this family of protocols reveals shortcomings in the prioritization of real-time data messages. On the other hand, it is easily able to replace industrial Ethernet solutions in a transparent way, implementing the two lowest layers of the ISO/OSI model, providing all the required functionalities to enable the support of the Internet Protocol (IP) that is virtually the basis for every application over Ethernet networks.

Traditionally, the RT communication behavior in wired CSMA environments has been guaranteed through the tight control of every communicating device (Decotignie, 2005). The coexistence of RT controlled stations with timing unconstrained stations has been made possible by constraining the traffic behavior of the latter. For instance, using traffic smoothers (Kweon & Shin, 2003; Lo Bello, Kaczynski, & Mirabella, 2005). Unfortunately, when moving from wired to wireless networks, the traffic smoothing paradigm is no longer adequate, since it is not possible to impose traffic smoothing strategies upon stations that are out of the sphere-of-control2 of the RT architecture. Therefore, there is the need to consider the presence of uncontrolled stations when dealing with wireless

communications, as the wireless communication medium act as open communication environment (Figure 1). That is, any new participant can try to access the communication medium at any instant (according to the MAC rules) and establish its own communication channels. As a consequence, the system load cannot be predicted at system setup time, nor can be effectively controlled during the system run-time.

It is foreseeable that RT communication networks will be challenged for moving from *closed* to *open* communication environments, and also for partially moving from a wired to a wireless network infrastructure. Thus a *new paradigm* for RT communications will need to emerge, as traditional RT communication paradigms are still based on closed and controlled environments. Throughout this chapter, it will become clear that the use of WLANs in RT communication domains will challenge the referred paradigm. More accurately, it will be shown that the most promising solutions to support RT communication in CSMA-based networks will be those that allow the coexistence of both RT and non-RT stations in the same communication domain. That is, solutions able to prioritize RT traffic without the need to control non-RT communicating devices.

Figure 1. Example of open communication environments

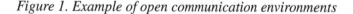

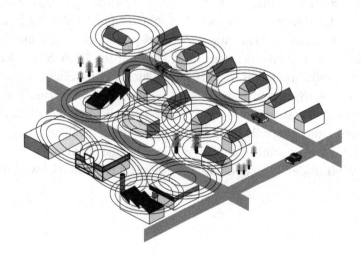

1.1. Classification Framework

The state-of-the-art on RT CSMA communications is reviewed in this chapter using a classification framework structured in two classification axes (Figure 2). The first axis is related to *how collisions are dealt with*, in order to provide a RT communication service. Traditional RT communication approaches follow an *avoiding collision* strategy to guarantee a RT communication service to supported applications. Another possibility is to replace the traditional probabilistic collision resolution algorithm, in order to deterministically solve the collisions. Finally, it is also possible to enforce the *reduction of the number of occurring collisions*, through the use of adequate loosely-coupled distributed algorithms. These are the three main classes of the first classification axis.

The second classification axis is related to the *compatibility degree* with IEEE standard devices. Specifically, this axis highlights how RT communication approaches keep or alter the compatibility with IEEE 802.11 compliant devices. Three different compatibility levels have been defined. The *level 1* subclass gets together RT communication approaches that require the compliance of *all* communicating devices with the enhanced (RT) devices. This compliance requirement impairs the use of level 1 devices in open communication environments, as it is unable to handle messages sent by external (uncontrolled) devices. On the other hand, *level 2* and *level 3* subclasses comprise RT communication approaches able to offer RT guarantees to a subset of RT devices in the presence of default (non-modified) communicating devices. The main difference between these two subclasses is related to the level of modifications required to implement an enhanced (RT) device. The implementation of a level 2 device requires the use of specific hardware, impairing the use of COTS (Commercial Off-the-Shelf) hardware. Conversely, a level 3 device can be implemented upon COTS hardware, requiring just modifications at the firmware/software level of the RT communicating devices. This is an important distinction, as the possibility of using COTS hardware is a relevant advantage when setting-up a RT communication infrastructure.

The remainder of this chapter is organized as follows. Section 2 describes the basics of the IEEE 802.11 Medium Access Mechanism, and section 3 presents the most relevant state-of-the-art approaches to support RT communication in IEEE 802.11 wireless networks. Afterwards, in Section 4 a synthesis of the state-of-the-art is done, where the described RT communication approaches are classified according to the above proposed classification axes. One of the main purposes of Section 5 is to identify the most promising RT CSMA-based approaches able to deal with the requirements imposed by next generation communication systems. Specifically, the requirements imposed by a communication environment shared with uncontrolled traffic sources. Finally, in the last section, some conclusions are drawn.

Figure 2. Classification framework

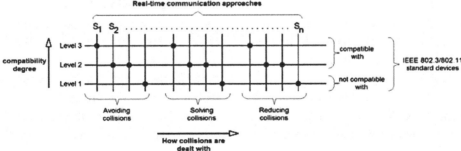

2. IEEE 802.11 MEDIUM ACCESS MECHANISMS

The IEEE 802.11 family of protocols is one of the most used sets of Wireless Local Area Networks (WLANs). It was standardized in 1999 by the IEEE as the 802.11 standard, which was later revised in 2007 ("IEEE Standard for Information Technology - Wireless LAN Medium Access Control (MAC) and Physical Layer (PHY) Specifications," 2007), incorporating the IEEE 802.11e amendment ("IEEE Standard for Information Technology - Wireless LAN Medium Access Control (MAC) and Physical Layer (PHY) Specifications Amendment 8: Medium Access Control (MAC) Quality of Service Enhancements," 2005) to the original standard. This amendment is intended to provide differentiated levels of Quality of Service (QoS) to the supported applications, including the transport of voice and video over WLANs. The wireless IEEE 802.11 networks use the CSMA (Carrier Sense Multiple Access) algorithm to manage the medium access, where stations contending for the access to a shared medium must listen before transmitting. Basically, this family of protocols has the following behavior:

1. When a station wants to transmit, it listens to the transmission medium.
2. If the medium is idle, the station will start the transmission (either immediately, or after a defined interval, depending on the specific protocol).
3. If the medium is busy, i.e., another station is transmitting, the station will defer its transmission to a later time instant that depends on the specific protocol.
4. A collision will occur whenever two (or more) stations sense the medium idle and decide to simultaneously transmit.

The CSMA medium access mechanisms that are implemented by different communication protocols differ on how the waiting time intervals before transmitting are evaluated, either after sensing the idle medium, or before re-transmitting after a collision. In the IEEE 802.11 standard ("IEEE Standard for Information Technology - Wireless LAN Medium Access Control (MAC) and Physical Layer (PHY) Specifications," 2007) it is used the CSMA with Collision Avoidance (CSMA/CA), also called Distributed Coordination Function (DCF). More accurately, the IEEE 802.11 MAC sublayer introduces two medium access coordination functions, the mandatory DCF and the optional Point Coordination Function (PCF). DCF[3] is the basic IEEE 802.11 mechanism, where stations perform a so-called *backoff procedure* before initiating a transmission. That is, when a station wants to transmit, it first senses the medium (carrier sensing); if the medium remains idle during a specific time interval called DIFS (Distributed Interframe Space) it immediately starts the transmission. Otherwise, the station selects a random time called *backoff time*. The duration of this random interval is a multiple of the Slot Time (ST), which is a system parameter that depends on the characteristics of the physical layer (PHY). The number of slots is an integer in the range of [0, CW], where CW (contention window) is initially assigned as aCW_{min}. A *backoff counter* is used to maintain the current value of the backoff time. In this case, stations keep sensing the medium (listening) for this additional random time, after detecting the medium as idle for a DIFS interval. If the medium gets busy due to interference or other transmissions while a station is down-counting its backoff counter, the station stops down-counting and defers the medium access until the medium becomes idle for a DIFS interval again. A new independent random backoff value is selected for each new transmission attempt, where the CW value is increased by (*oldCW×2 +1*), with an upper bound given by aCW_{max}. As soon as the backoff counter reaches zero, the station can retry its transmission (Figure 3).

The DCF access method imposes an idle interval between consecutive frames, which is called

Figure 3. Interframe spaces in the DCF and EDCA mechanisms

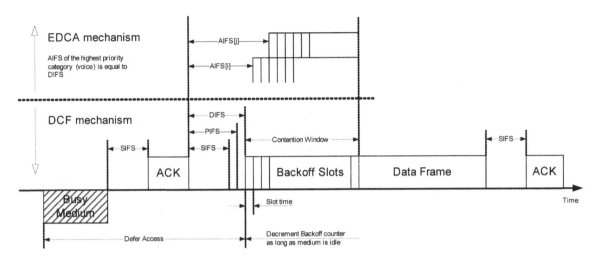

the Interframe Space (IFS). Different IFSs are defined in order to impose different priorities to multiple frame types as following: SIFS (Short Interframe Space), PIFS (PCF Interframe Space), DIFS (Distributed Interframe Space) and EIFS (Extended Interframe Space). SIFS is the shortest of the interframe spaces and it is used for ACK frames. Only stations operating under the Point Coordination Function (PCF) will use PIFS. DIFS is used by stations operating under the DCF mechanism to transmit data frames and management frames. EIFS is used in communication-error conditions.

The IEEE 802.11e amendment incorporated into the original standard an additional coordination function called Hybrid Coordination Function (HCF) that is only used in QoS network configurations (Figure 4). The HCF mechanism schedules the access to the channel by allocating transmission opportunities (TXOP) to each of the stations. Each TXOP interval is defined by a starting time and a maximum duration, i.e. the time interval during which the station keeps the medium access control. Consequently, multiple frames may be transmitted within an acquired TXOP. It may be allocated through one of two access mechanisms specified by the HCF: the *Enhanced Distributed Channel Access* (EDCA)

and the HCF *Controlled Channel Access* (HCCA) ("IEEE Standard for Information Technology - Wireless LAN Medium Access Control (MAC) and Physical Layer (PHY) Specifications," 2007).

The EDCA mechanism was designed to enhance DCF providing differentiated transmission services with four access categories (AC). Each frame arriving at the MAC layer with a defined priority will be mapped into one of the four ACs. These ACs are based on the eight priority levels of IEEE 802.1D standard, as follows: priorities 1 and 2 for background traffic (BK); priorities 0 and 3 for best effort traffic (BE); priorities 4 and 5 for video traffic (VI); and, finally, priorities 6 and 7 are mapped for voice traffic (VO) that is the highest priority level. Different levels of service are provided to each of the ACs, based on three independent mechanisms: the Arbitration Interframe Space (AIFS), the Transmission Opportunity time interval (TXOP) and the Contention Window (CW) size. For a station operating under EDCA, each frame will wait that the medium remains idle during an *AIFS[AC]* interval. The duration of the *AIFS[AC]* interval is given by:

$$AIFS = AIFSN\left[AC\right] \times aSlotTime + aSIFSTime$$

Figure 4. IEEE 802.11e MAC architecture

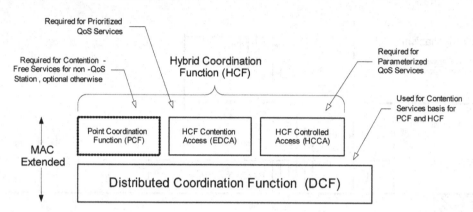

where the *AIFSN[AC]* is a positive integer that must be greater than or equal to 2 for all stations, except for the QoS Access Points (QAPs), where it shall be greater than or equal to 1. The default parameters defined for the EDCA mechanism are presented in Table 1. The aCW_{min} and aCW_{max} parameters depends on the characteristics of the physical (PHY) layer, e.g. in the IEEE 802.11a PHY mode $aCW_{min}=15$ and $aCW_{max}=1023$. Figure 3 shows the relationships between the multiple *AIFSs* in the DCF and EDCA mechanisms. It is worth mentioning that default AIFSN value for the voice category is 2. Thus, AIFS[VO] = AIFS[VI] = DIFS.

3. RT COMMUNICATION IN IEEE 802.11 WIRELESS NETWORKS

In the following subsections, a number of relevant solutions to support Real-Time (RT) communication in IEEE 802.11 wireless networks are described, according to the classification framework presented in subsection 1.1.

3.1. Avoiding Collisions

The Point Coordination Function (PCF) is one of the main solutions intended to *avoid collisions* in IEEE 802.11 wireless networks. It has been proposed in the original IEEE 802.11 standard as an optional access mechanism. It implements a centralized polling scheme to support synchronous data transmissions, where the Point Coordinator (PC) performs the role of polling master. When the PCF scheme is used, the time scale is divided in two super-frames: the Contention Period (CP), used by DCF and the Contention Free Period (CFP) used by PCF. The HCCA mechanism was proposed, in the IEEE 802.11e amendment ("IEEE Standard for Information Technology - Wireless LAN Medium Access Control (MAC) and Physical Layer (PHY) Specifications Amendment 8: Medium Access Control (MAC) Quality of Service Enhancements," 2005), to improve the PCF scheme. It is intended to guarantee bounded delay requirements, based on a Round Robin scheme. In contrast to PCF, the HCCA operates during both the CFP and CP periods (Figure 5).

The HC acquires control of the wireless medium by waiting a shorter time between transmissions than the stations using the EDCA or DCF procedures. The HC may include a CF (Contention Free) parameter set element in the Beacon frame, in order that all stations set their NAVs (Network Allocation Vectors) to the end of the controlled phase. During the CFP, the HC controls the access to the channel by polling all the stations in the polling list. To each polled station is granted a transmission opportunity (TXOP). On

Table 1. Default DCF and EDCA parameter set

Parameters		CWmin	CWmax	DIFS/AIFSN
DCF		aCWmin	aCWmax	2
EDCA	AC_BK	aCWmin	aCWmax	7
	AC_BE	aCWmin	aCWmax	3
	AC_VI	(aCWmin+1)/2-1	aCWmin	2
	AC_VO	(aCWmin+1)/4-1	(aCWmin+1)/2-1	2

the other hand, it is also allowed that the HC starts a TXOP during the CP. Similarly to the PCF scheme, the HC also polls *all* the stations in the polling list, even though some stations may have no messages to transmit. When the HC polls a station that has no packets to transfer, the station will transmit a null frame, after the QoS CF-poll. As a consequence, the polling overhead is roughly equal to the time interval from sending the polling frame till the end of the ACK frame (Son, Lee, Yoo, & Park, 2005).

A number of improvements has been proposed to reduce the HCCA polling overhead. For instance, (Gao, Cai, & Chen, 2008) proposed a new admission control framework to replace the traditional mechanism that use the mean data rate and the mean packet size to calculate the resource needed by a flow. Then, this new mechanism is adequate specially when dealing with variable bit rate (VBR) traffic over HCCA. (Rashid, Hossain, & Bhargava, 2008) have pointed out the perfor-

mance deficiencies of the HCCA scheduler and, they proposed a new scheduling scheme, namely, the prediction and optimization-based HCCA (PRO-HCCA), which use a prediction mechanism to account for the dynamic intensity of VBR traffic. This mechanism try to find an optimal allocation of available transmission time among the competing traffic streams.

(Hantrakoon & Phonphoem, 2010) proposed a simple queue management and admission control called PHCCA. The queue management modify the HCCA mechanism dividing the queue into 3 different classes, that can be organized by type or by user relevance. Furthermore, a starvation protection for the lower priority queue is implemented. Complementary to this scheme, the admission control provides a *bandwidth borrowing algorithm*, enabling a high priority queue to borrow bandwidth from lower priority queues to transmit the stored messages. (Son et al., 2005) proposed a polling scheme where the HC punishes

Figure 5. Example of CFP repetition interval

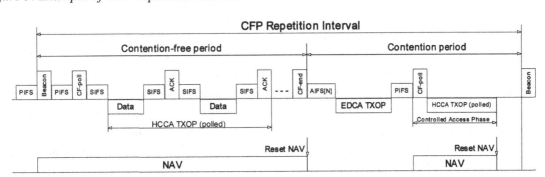

the stations that have no packets to transmit. When a station transmits a null frame, this station will not be polled again during a period of time.

In (Skyrianoglou, Passas, & Salkintzis, 2006), it is proposed a scheduling algorithm referred as ARROW (Adaptive Resource Reservation Over WLANs) that allocates the available bandwidth based on the actual amount of data awaiting transmission in every station. ARROW exploits the Queue Size field, introduced by IEEE 802.11e as part of the new QoS Data frames. This field can be used by the QoS stations to indicate the amount of buffered traffic for their traffic specifications. Therefore, the proposed scheduler utilizes this information to allocate TXOPs to QOS stations in such a way that it satisfies these transmission requirements, as long as they comply with the traffic specifications. This is done in contrast to other proposals, which perform channel allocations based on the estimated buffered data in every station.

(Lo, Lee, & Chen, 2003) designed a multipolling mechanism called *Contention Period Multipoll* (CP-Multipoll), which incorporates the DCF access scheme into the polling scheme. It uses different backoff values for the multiple message streams in the polling group, where each station executes the backoff procedure after receiving the CP-Multipoll frame. The contending order of these stations is the same as the ascending order of the assigned backoff values. The first station in the polling list initializes its transmission immediately after receiving the CP-Multipoll frame. This action avoids the interference from other stations performing the backoff procedures in the DCF mode. Moreover, in order to avoid the repeated collisions between stations that are operating on the same channel, the values assigned in the CP-Multipoll among neighboring BSSs must be different. (Lee, Ha, Park, & Lee, 2005) proposed a polling scheme based on a master slave solution. A virtual polling list (VPL) contains the MAC address of the wireless slaves to be polled, and a virtual polling period (VPP) defines the duration of the polling cycle. When a slave receives a poll

frame from the master, it can transmit a response frame back to the master, or directly to another slave. Furthermore, after polling all the slaves registered in the VPL, the master invites other slaves into the network through the broadcast of an entry claim frame. In (Willig, 1997), it is presented the FTDMA (Flexible TDMA) MAC protocol. FTDMA is based on a polling scheme, where a base station polls all registered RT stations in every frame. A frame is logically subdivided into phases: SYNC, Polling, Reservation, Register, Current Scheduler and Data Transfer. The main advantage of the FTDMA over traditional TDMA solutions is that unused slots can be used by other stations.

Solutions based on token passing mechanisms have also been proposed. In (Ergen, Lee, Sengupta, & Varaiya, 2004), it is proposed the WTRP (Wireless Token Ring Protocol), which is a MAC protocol that exchanges special tokens and uses multiple timers to maintain the nodes synchronized. The token is rotated around the ring. Each station transmits during a specified time and if enough time is left, the station invites nodes outside the ring to join it. (Cheng, Wang, Liao, & Yang, 2006) presents a wireless token-passing protocol, named *Ripple*. Basically, Ripple modifies the data transmission procedure of 802.11 DCF and employs request-to-send (RTS) and ready-to-receive (RTR) frames as tokens. A node that has the right to send a data frame will send a RTS frame, and a node which has the right to receive a data frame will send a RTR frame to the sender if the expected RTS frame has not been received. Summing up, a station can only send a DATA frame if it holds the token.

In (De Pellegrini, Miorandi, Vitturi, & Zanella, 2006), it is proposed a solution based on a Master-Slave architecture on top of IEEE 802.11. In that proposal, cyclic packets are exchanged by means of periodic queries sent by the master to the slaves. Three different techniques were proposed to handle acyclic traffic: the first technique queries the slaves that signaled the presence of acyclic data, at the end of the current polling cycle. The second technique allows a slave, when polled, to send directly acyclic data to the master. The third one exploits the decentralized nature of the IEEE 802.11 MAC protocol. When acyclic data is generated, it allows a slave to immediately try to send data to the master.

3.2. Deterministic Collision Resolution

Another approach to support Qos guarantees are those based on forcing the collision resolution schemes in favor of the RT stations. A relevant proposal has been made by (Sobrinho & Krishnakumar, 1999), who adapted the EQuB mechanism (black burst) (Sobrinho & Krishnakumar, 1998) to ad hoc CSMA wireless networks. This scheme requires the shutdown of the standard retransmission scheme. Real-time stations implementing the EQuB approach contend for the channel access after a medium interframe spacing t_{med}, rather than after the long interframe spacing t_{long}, used by standard stations. Thus, RT stations have priority over standard stations. When a RT station wants to transmit, it sorts its access rights by jamming the channel with Black Bursts (BBs), i.e., energy pulses immediately after an idle period with duration t_{med}. The length of the BB transmitted by a RT node is an increasing function of the contention delay experienced by the node. A similar scheme is presented in (Hwang & Cho, 2005), where voice nodes (RT stations) use Energy-Burst (EB) (that are similar to BB) periods to prioritize RT packets over data packets. The AP (Access Point) can transmit a VoIP packet after PIFS without backoff or contention. On the other hand, each voice station has its own address (ID), referred as VID (virtual identification). The VID can be assigned during the Traffic Stream (TS) setup procedure. The VID is expressed as a binary value, which is determined by the voice packet resolution period (VPRP). The station with the highest VID wins the contention. In (Sheu, Liu, Wu, & Tseng, 2004), it is presented a priority MAC protocol based on Sobrinho's approach, complemented by a binary

tree referred as contention tree. Basically, the black-burst scheme is adopted to distinguish the priorities of stations. Stations with the same priority send messages in a round robin manner. The basic idea is that a station can obtain an unique ID number, which depends on its position in the contention tree.

(Bartolomeu, Ferreira, & Fonseca, 2009) designed the WFTT (Wireless Flexible Time Triggered). This model combines the *bandjacking* mechanism, where data transmission is preceded by a black-burst (BB) that jams all existing communications in the channel, and the efficiency of the FTT paradigm to support RT communications. The Master controls both the transmission of noise signals and the permission of a Slave station to start a transmission.

In (Moraes, Vasques, Portugal, & Fonseca, 2007), a RT-communication approach (VTP-CSMA) has been proposed based on a traffic separation mechanism. Such mechanisms are able to prioritize RT-traffic over other traffic, without directly controlling the latter. The proposed architecture is based on a Virtual Token Passing procedure that circulates a virtual token among a number of RT devices. This virtual token is complemented by an underlying traffic separation mechanism that prioritizes the RT traffic over the non-RT traffic. The underlying traffic separation mechanism has a similar behavior to both the SVP protocol ("SpectraLink Voice Priority - Quality of Service for voice traffic in wireless LANs,") and the mechanism proposed by (Hwang & Cho, 2004). The SVP protocol specifies a backoff value of zero for stations or classes with the highest priority level. A shortcoming of this mechanism is that if multiple SVP stations attempt to transmit at the same time, consecutive collisions will occur and a failure will be reported. The mechanism proposed in (Hwang & Cho, 2004) consists in allowing the transmission of voice packets (highest priority) in the first empty slot after the first retransmission. When the first retransmission fails, the second retransmission performs the original backoff procedure. Therefore, these approaches are not able by themselves to provide RT guarantees to the supported applications.

A new isochronous medium access control (IsoMAC), based on a TDMA scheme and in combination with a wireless clock synchronization, has been proposed by (Trsek & Jasperneite, 2011). The IsoMAC approach requires the use of resource reservation techniques along with admission control, and scheduling mechanisms. It provides mechanisms to dynamically allocate bandwidth, reschedule the communication in the planned phase and to distribute the new schedule to all involved nodes. This proposal takes into account the external traffic interferences, the traffic scheduler always ensures that at least one data frame with a maximal sized payload of 2304 Byte can be transmitted within the Contention Period (CP). The evaluation results show that this mechanism is superior to standardized MAC protocols as specified in 802.11, especially in terms of communication jitter. Whenever the channel quality decreases and retransmissions occur, the flexible retransmission handling is able to retransmit the erroneous frames as fast as possible within the same superframe.

3.3. Reducing the Number of Occurring Collisions

The EDCA mechanism available in the IEEE 802.11e standard is specifically intended to reduce the number of occurring collisions. Its underlying idea was previously proposed by (Deng & Chang, 1999). It defines a set of priority classes, where the higher priority class uses the window $[0, 2^{j+1}-1]$ and the lower priority class uses the window $[2^{j+1}, 2^{j+2}-1]$, where j is the backoff stage. The EDCA function implements a CSMA/CA mechanism for the channel access under the control of the HCF coordination function. It enhances the DCF scheme, as each frame arriving to the MAC layer with a defined priority will be mapped into one of the four access categories (AC). Different

levels of service are provided to each of the AC traffics, based on three independent mechanisms: (1) the Arbitration Interframe Space (AIFS); (2) the TXOP time interval; and (3) the Contention Window size (CW). Firstly, for a station operating under EDCA, a frame will be transferred only if the channel remains idle during an *AIFS[AC]* interval. This means that the duration of the interframe space is related to the access category. Figure 3 shows the relationships between the multiple *AIFSs* in the EDCA scheme. This mechanism also introduced the TXOP concept that is the time interval during which the station keeps the medium access control. Consequently, multiple frames may be transmitted within an acquired TXOP, if there is more than one frame pending to be transferred in the AC for which the channel has been acquired. Finally, if a station wants to transmit a frame while the channel is busy, or becomes busy before the expiration of the *AIFS[AC]*, the backoff procedure is invoked (third traffic differentiation mechanism). The contention window is defined by the $aCW_{min}[AC]$ and $aCW_{max}[AC]$ attributes, in contrast to the legacy DCF where the initial values were randomly selected among the $[0,CW]$ interval defined by the physical layer. In the EDCA mechanism, the backoff procedure selects a random number, in the range $[0, CW]$, where the CW size is initialized at $aCW_{min}[AC]$. When a transmission fails, CW is increased by $[(oldCW[AC]+1)*PF - 1]$ upper bounded by $aCW_{max}[AC]$, where PF is the persistence factor (its default value is $PF=2$). On the other hand, the backoff counter decreases the backoff interval whenever the medium is detected to be idle for $AIFS[AC]$. As the EDCA mechanism provides 4 access categories, it would be expectable that the highest access category (*voice*) would be adequate to transfer RT messages. In a previous research work (Moraes, Portugal, & Vasques, 2006), we have assessed the behavior of this category when used to transfer periodic small sized packets in an open communication environment. Both the number of packet losses and the average size of the MAC queues forecast an unacceptable number of deadlines losses for RT message streams, even for intermediate load cases. Therefore, additional mechanisms must be provided in order to adequately support RT communication.

Recently, (Cena, Seno, Valenzano, & Zunino, 2010) evaluated the improvement of the EDCA mechanism combining EDCA and TDMA schemes. The reported results show that the adoption of a scheme combining both EDCA QoS and a TDMA mechanism could achieve noticeable improvements when sending urgent frames, being largely independent of the shape of the interfering traffic pattern. In (Wu, Chiu, & Sheu, 2008), it is also proposed a modified EDCA mechanism, where soft real-time guarantees constraints are guaranteed by dynamically adjusting the priority level of a traffic flow based on the estimated per-hop delay, and generating a non-uniformly distributed backoff timer for retransmitting frames according to their individual end-to-end delay requirements. In (Vaidya, Dugar, Gupta, & Bahl, 2005), it was proposed a distributed algorithm intended to provide fair scheduling in a wireless LAN, referred as DFS (Distributed Fair Scheduling). The DFS protocol behaves quite similarly to IEEE 802.11 DCF, except in what concerns the backoff interval that is initially calculated. The fundamental difference is that each station maintains a local virtual clock and, the backoff interval is selected proportionally to the finish tag of the packet to be transmitted. The finish tag is calculated similarly to the SCFQ (Self-Clocked Fair Queueing) algorithm (Golestani, 1994). In (Kwon, Fang, & Latchman, 2004), the authors modify the distributed SCFQ algorithm combined with the prioritization schemes proposed in the EDCA mechanism and specify the RT-FCR (real-time fast collision resolution), where priorities are implemented by assigning different backoff ranges based on the type of traffic. In (Lopez-Aguilera, Casademont, Cotrina, & Rojas, 2005), it was evaluated the performance of the IEEE 802.11e EDCA when its working procedure is unsynchronized. The authors proposed the use of AIFS values that are separated by values that are not multiple of the slot time. As a consequence, it would become possible to avoid collisions between frames from different access categories.

Based on the EDCA mechanism, (Villallón, Cuenca, Orozco-Barbosa, & Garrido, 2008) designed the B-EDCA mechanism that intends to provide QoS support to multimedia communication, and is able to coexist with legacy DCF-based stations. Basically, it changes the AIFS value of the highest AC to $SIFS+aSlotTime$ when stations are in the Backoff state. Moreover, in order to keep the compatibility with the HCCA mechanism, a station implementing the B-EDCA mechanism must wait for an additional SIFS time when the backoff counter reaches zero, i.e. $2 \times SIFS + aSlotTime$. Therefore, it is adequate when operating in the IEEE 802.11b PHY mode, as the waiting time will be larger than the one used by the HCCA mechanism and smaller than the time used by standard EDCA stations. (Ulusoy, Gurbuz, & Onat, 2011) proposed and implementated the Wireless Model-Based Predictive Networked Control System (W-MBPNCS) based on modifications of the MAC parameters. It uses a smaller CW_{max} value in order to limit the packet latency variance in case of collisions and smaller DIFS and CW_{min} values for higher medium access priority and lower packet latencies and; involving the faithful implementation of the COMAC (Cooperative MAC) protocol (Gokturk & Gurbuz, 2008), this protocol makes use of the neighbors of a node as a set of distributed antennas so that multiple nodes each with a single antenna function as a single multi-antenna system. Then, a source always performs cooperation with a relay node.

(Lo Bello, Kaczynski, & Mirabella, 2006) proposed a Wireless Traffic Smoother (WTS) to support soft RT traffic over IEEE 802.11 WLANs. The presented solution is similar to the traffic smoother scheme previously proposed for Ethernet networks (Lo Bello et al., 2005). However, its main drawback is that it requires the smoothing strategy to be implemented in all the communicating devices. More recently, (Toscano & Lo Bello, 2011) proposed a middleware that implements an EDF scheduler at the user-level on top of EDCA. It combines a polling-based schedule used to avoid collisions between soft real-time packets with an adaptive mechanism that exploits some feedback information about the Packet Error Rate to change the number of retransmissions according to the varying link quality.

(Hamidian & Korner, 2006) presented an interesting solution that allows stations with higher priority traffic to reserve contention-free time intervals. Basically, it proposes the transfer of the HCCA admission control from the HCCA controller to the contending stations. It uses the traffic specification (TSPEC) as defined in the draft version of the IEEE 802.11e HCCA standard ("IEEE P802.11e/D10.0, Wireless LAN Medium Access Control (MAC) and Physical Layer (PHY) Specifications Amendment 7: Medium Access Control (MAC) Quality of Service Enhancements," 2005). The TSPEC is an element sent through a management frame that contains information about the characteristics and QoS expectation of a traffic stream. For instance, the maximum service interval specifies the maximum time interval between the start of two consecutive service periods. The scheduling and the admission control of a new traffic stream is locally imposed at each station.

(Wang, Li, & Li, 2004) designed a new collision resolution mechanism, referred as gentle *DCF* or GDCF. The difference between GDCF and DCF is that GDCF takes a more conservative measure by halving the CW (Contention Window) value only if there are c consecutive successful transmissions. Conversely, DCF reset its CW to the minimum value once there is a successful transmission. (Yang & Vaidya, 2006) proposed the Busy Tone Priority Scheduling (BTPS) pro-

tocol. BTPS works similarly to the IEEE 802.11 DCF, with the difference that high priority and low priority behave differently during *IFS* and *backoff* stages. The BTPS protocol uses DIFS as the IFS for high priority stations. However, during DIFS and backoff stages, the high priority stations with queued packets send a BT1 (busy tone) pulse every M slots, where M is a constant. Between two consecutive busy tone pulse transmissions, there should be at least one empty SlotTime interval as the station must have a chance to listen to the data channel. Therefore, M could be any value larger than or equal to 2 and, the IFS of low priority stations should be larger than M slots, in order to enable sensing the busy tone signal.

In (Cena, Valenzano, & Vitturi, 2008), the authors address hybrid wired/wireless architectures for RT communication, where real-time (industrial) Ethernet networks can be extended with wireless subnetworks that rely on popular technologies, such as IEEE 802.11 and 802.15.4. (Seno, Vitturi, & Zunino, 2009) propose the use of wireless IEEE 802.11 extensions for Ethernet Powerlink, a very popular Real-Time Ethernet network,. The traditional Ethernet Powerlink data link layer specifies a channel access based on a time-division multiple access (TDMA) technique. A specific unique station, namely, the managing node (MN), is responsible for polling a set of controlled nodes (CNs). The wireless extension of Ethernet Powerlink addresses two distinct configurations based on bridge and gateway devices. In (Kjellsson, Vallestad, Steigmann, & Dzung, 2009), it is considered the integration for the case of PROFINET IO.

4. RT IEEE 802.11 SOLUTIONS CLASSIFICATION

In the previous sections, some of the most relevant CSMA-based real-time (RT) communication proposals have been presented according to how collisions are dealt with. In this section, those RT communication proposals are now classified according to a compatibility degree axis. This second classification axis highlights how such proposals keep or alter the compatibility with IEEE 802.11 compliant devices. Figure 6 classifies the reported RT communication proposals according to the classification axes illustrated in Figure 1. When dealing with next generation communication systems, it is of utmost importance the coexistence between RT stations and third stations (stations that are out of the sphere-of-control of the RT architecture). Therefore, approaches with compatibility degree level 1 are not adequate, as they are not able to handle messages sent by external (uncontrolled) devices. As a consequence, the ability to support next generation communication systems will strongly rely upon technical solutions with compatibility degree level 2, being desirable that solutions of level 3 arise.

Most part of the RT solutions that follow the avoiding collisions strategy are based on TDMA, Token-Passing, Master-Slave or Polling techniques. A common characteristic of these RT solutions is that a enhanced (RT) station is not able to support RT communication in the presence of default (non-modified) IEEE 802.11 stations (unless these default stations do not initiate any communication). That is, the majority of the avoiding collision solutions have a compatibility degree level 1. Relevant exceptions are: the im-

provements included in the HCF (PCF and HCCA) mechanism of the IEEE 802.11e amendment. However, most part of the WLAN network cards never actually implemented the PCF scheme, due to complexity reasons (Miorandi & Vitturi, 2004). Therefore, the PCF mechanism has not been a solution to support RT communication, due to the unavailability of WLAN network cards. The HCCA mechanism ("IEEE Standard for Information Technology - Wireless LAN Medium Access Control (MAC) and Physical Layer (PHY) Specifications Amendment 8: Medium Access Control (MAC) Quality of Service Enhancements," 2005) has been proposed as an improvement to the PCF mechanism. However, some studies (Gao et al., 2008; Rashid et al., 2008) have already shown that the HCCA mechanism may not be suitable to guarantee the special requirements of RT applications. A significant number of improvements have been proposed to overcome some of the drawbacks of the HCCA mechanism, as mentioned in subsection 3.1. But, it is still not clear whether the HCCA mechanism will be implemented in the next generation WLAN network cards, overcoming the unavailability problem of the PCF mechanism. Besides these approaches, all other avoiding collision approaches require the strict control of every communicating entity. Otherwise, they are not able to work properly, as

Figure 6. Supporting RT communication in IEEE 802.11

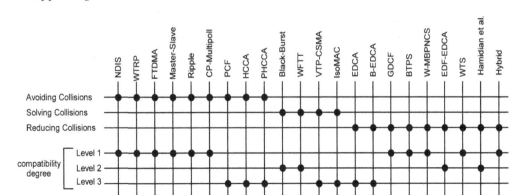

they are not able to handle messages sent by external (uncontrolled) stations.

Concerning the second sub-class (solving collisions), several Level 2 and Level 3 techniques are based on the black-burst scheme (BB), the Virtual Token approach (VTP-CSMA), the WFTT and the IsoMAC protocol. These kind of solutions implement the paradigm of forcing the collision resolution in favor of the RT stations. To our best knowledge, this type of medium access technique is the only one that allows the coexistence of RT stations with external uncontrolled traffic sources, being able to prioritize the RT communication. There are some adaptations of the black-burst scheme for forcing the collision resolution in favor of RT station, e.g. the WFTT proposal. The VTP-CSMA architecture may be compared with the black-burst scheme. The main disadvantage of the BB scheme is that it compels the modification of the MAC layer and possibly also of parts of the PHY layer (e.g. radio, ICs), which impairs the use

of COTS hardware. Although the VTP-CSMA mechanism also needs to modify parts of the MAC layer, it could be implemented in COTS hardware (e.g. FPGA) upon standard 802.11 hardware.

Finally, concerning the last subclass (reducing collisions), it is still worthwhile to mention solutions that constrain the generated traffic in a fair way, without imposing further modifications to the MAC protocol. Solutions like (Villallón et al., 2008) increases the network access fairness and reduce the number of collisions based on some priority criterion.

5. REAL-TIME FRAMEWORK FOR CSMA-BASED NETWORKS

We entirely agree with (Bianchi, Tinnirello, & Scalia, 2005) that in wireless architectures, the service differentiation mechanism must be compulsory introduced as a medium access control

Figure 7. A 2-tier architecture to support real-time communication in wireless networks

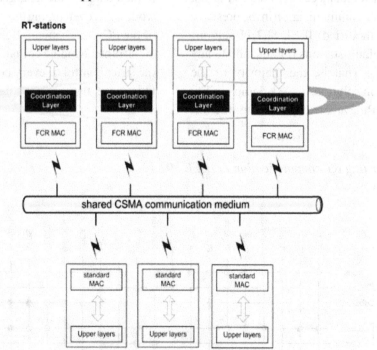

(MAC) extension. Analyzing the state-of-the-art approaches described in this paper, we may conclude that the most promising solutions to prioritize RT communication in CSMA-based networks are those that force the collision resolution in favor of the RT stations, compelling all the other contending stations to postpone the medium access. That is, all those solutions based on the "Forcing Collision Resolution" (FCR) paradigm. Unfortunately, most part of FCR-based approaches are just able to prioritize the RT traffic. This means that, whenever two or more RT stations simultaneously contend for the medium access, the FCR MAC will not be able to serialize the contending stations. Therefore, there is also the need to coordinate the medium access among the multiple RT stations.

Within this context, we consider that a 2-tier architecture (Figure 7) will be the adequate architecture to support RT communication in CSMA-based shared communication systems. This architecture encompasses: (a) in the lower layer (MAC layer), a Forcing Collision Resolution (FCR) mechanism that enforces a high priority level access to the subset of RT stations; (b) in the upper layer, a coordination mechanism that ensures a collision-free access among the subset of RT stations. This coordination mechanism can be based on, for instance, a token passing scheme or a time division multiple access (TDMA) mechanism. It must serialize the medium access of just the RT stations, as the underlying FCR layer ensures that non-RT stations will always loose the medium contention when contending with a RT-station.

CONCLUSION

WiFi networking is a well-known and extensively used network technology. However, one of its main disadvantages is the inherent non-determinism of its probabilistic contention resolution mechanism. This probabilistic behavior impairs the provision of a Real-Time (RT) communication service to the supported applications, unless additional functionalities are introduced.

On the other hand, there is a trend for the implementation of RT communication systems on top of wireless networks, and, specifically, on top of WLAN (Jonsson & Kunert, 2009; Moyne & Tilbury, 2007; Willig et al., 2005). A fundamental assumption that must be considered is that the wireless communication medium is an open communication environment, i.e., any new participant can try to access the communication medium at any instant and establish its own communication channels. Therefore, traditional RT communication approaches that guarantee RT behavior through the tight control of every communicating device (compatibility level 1) are no longer applicable.

Summing up, the coexistence of default (non-modified) devices together with modified (real-time) devices is a hard task. Specially in the case of wireless networks due to the open characteristics of the communication medium. Therefore, the underlying communication protocols must be able to guarantee the timing constraints of the RT traffic in a communication medium that is potentially being shared with external (uncontrolled) traffic sources. Thus, state-of-the-art approaches that do not allow the coexistence of both RT and non-RT stations will not be able to handle next generation communication scenarios. As a consequence, whatever the RT communication solution, it is mandatory to define a lower communication layer that enables the separation of the RT and the non-RT traffic in any shared communication environment.

REFERENCES

Bartolomeu, P., Ferreira, J., & Fonseca, J. (2009). *Enforcing flexibility in real-time wireless communications: A bandjacking enabled protocol.* Paper presented at the Emerging Technologies & Factory Automation, 2009. New York, NY.

Bianchi, G., Tinnirello, I., & Scalia, L. (2005). Understanding 802.11e contention-based prioritization mechanisms and their coexistence with legacy 802.11 Stations. *IEEE Network*, *19*(4), 28–34. doi:10.1109/MNET.2005.1470680.

Cena, G., Seno, L., Valenzano, A., & Zunino, C. (2010). On the performance of IEEE 802.11e wireless infrastructures for soft-real-time industrial applications. *IEEE Transactions on Industrial Informatics*, *6*(3), 425–437. doi:10.1109/TII.2010.2052058.

Cena, G., Valenzano, A., & Vitturi, S. (2008). Hybrid wired/wireless networks for real-time communications. *IEEE Industrial Electronics Magazine*, *2*(1), 8–20. doi:10.1109/MIE.2008.917155.

Cheng, R.-G., Wang, C.-Y., Liao, L.-H., & Yang, J.-S. (2006). Ripple: A wireless token-passing protocol for multi-hop wireless mesh networks. *IEEE Communications Letters*, *10*(2), 123–125. doi:10.1109/LCOMM.2006.02005.

De Pellegrini, F., Miorandi, D., Vitturi, S., & Zanella, A. (2006). On the use of wireless networks at low level of factory automation systems. *IEEE Transactions on Industrial Informatics*, *2*(2), 129–143. doi:10.1109/TII.2006.872960.

Decotignie, J.-D. (2005). Ethernet-based real-time and industrial communications. *Proceedings of the IEEE*, *93*(6), 1102–1117. doi:10.1109/JPROC.2005.849721.

Deng, J., & Chang, R. S. (1999). A priority scheme for IEEE 802.11 DCF access method. *IEICE Transactions on Communications. E (Norwalk, Conn.)*, *82-B*(1), 96–102.

Ergen, M., Lee, D., Sengupta, R., & Varaiya, P. (2004). WTRP-wireless token ring protocol. *IEEE Transactions on Vehicular Technology*, *53*(6), 1863–1881. doi:10.1109/TVT.2004.836928.

Gao, D., Cai, J., & Chen, C. W. (2008). Admission control based on rate-variance envelop for VBR traffic over IEEE 802.11e HCCA WLANs. *IEEE Transactions on Vehicular Technology*, *57*(3), 1778–1788. doi:10.1109/TVT.2007.909286.

Gokturk, M. S., & Gurbuz, O. (2008). *Cooperation in wireless sensor networks: Design and performance analysis of a MAC protocol.* Paper presented at the Communications, 2008. New York, NY.

Golestani, S. J. (1994). A self-clocked fair queueing scheme for broadband applications. In *Proceedings IEEE INFOCOM '94: The Conference on Computer Communications. Networking for Global Communications,* (vol. 2, pp. 636 - 646). IEEE.

Hamidian, A., & Korner, U. (2006). An enhancement to the IEEE 802.11e EDCA providing QoS guarantees. *Telecommunication Systems*, *31*(2-3), 195–212. doi:10.1007/s11235-006-6520-z.

Hantrakoon, S., & Phonphoem, A. (2010). *Priority based HCCA for IEEE 802.11e.* Paper presented at the Communications and Mobile Computing (CMC). New York, NY.

Hwang, G.-H., & Cho, D.-H. (2004). Fast retransmission mechanism for VoIP in IEEE 802.11e wireless LANs. In *Proceedings of the IEEE 60th Vehicular Technology Conference (VTC2004-Fall),* (vol. 7, pp. 4996 - 5000). IEEE.

Hwang, G.-H., & Cho, D.-H. (2005). New access scheme for VoIP packets in IEEE 802.11e wireless LANs. *IEEE Communications Letters*, *9*(7), 667–669. doi:10.1109/LCOMM.2005.1461699.

IEEE. (2005). *Standard for information technology - Wireless LAN medium access control (MAC) and physical layer (PHY) specifications amendment 8: Medium access control (MAC) quality of service enhancements. IEEE Std 802.11e-2005.* IEEE.

IEEE. (2007). Standard for information technology - Wireless LAN medium access control (MAC) and physical layer (PHY) specifications. ANSI/IEEE Std 802.11, 1999 Ed. (R2007). IEEE.

IEEE P802.11e/D10.0. (2005). *Wireless LAN medium access control (MAC) and physical layer (PHY) specifications amendment 7: Medium access control (MAC) quality of service enhancements*. IEEE.

Jonsson, M., & Kunert, K. (2009). Towards reliable wireless industrial communication with real-time guarantees. *IEEE Transactions on Industrial Informatics*, *5*(4), 429–442. doi:10.1109/TII.2009.2031921.

Kjellsson, J., Vallestad, A. E., Steigmann, R., & Dzung, D. (2009). Integration of a wireless I/O interface for PROFIBUS and PROFINET for factory automation. *IEEE Transactions on Industrial Electronics*, *56*(10), 4279–4287. doi:10.1109/TIE.2009.2017098.

Kopetz, H. (1998). Time-triggered model of computation. In *Proceedings of the Real-Time Systems Symposium*, (pp. 168 - 177). IEEE.

Kweon, S.-K., & Shin, K. G. (2003). Statistical real-time communication over ethernet. *IEEE Transactions on Parallel and Distributed Systems*, *14*(3), 322–335. doi:10.1109/TPDS.2003.1189588.

Kwon, Y., Fang, Y., & Latchman, H. (2004). Design of MAC protocols with fast collision resolution for wireless local area networks. *IEEE Transactions on Wireless Communications*, *3*(3), 793–807. doi:10.1109/TWC.2004.827731.

Lee, S., Ha, K. N., Park, J. H., & Lee, K. C. (2005). NDIS-based virtual polling algorithm of IEEE 802.11b for guaranteeing the real-time requirements. In *Proceedings of IECON*, (pp. 2427 - 2432). IECON.

Lo, S. C., Lee, G., & Chen, W. T. (2003). An efficient multipolling mechanism for IEEE 802.11 wireless LANs. *IEEE Transactions on Computers*, *52*(6), 764–768. doi:10.1109/TC.2003.1204832.

Lo Bello, L., Kaczynski, F. S., & Mirabella, O. (2006). A wireless traffic smoother for soft real-time communications over IEEE 802.11 industrial networks. In *Proceedings of the 11th IEEE International Conference on Emerging Technologies and Factory Automation (ETFA)*, (pp. 1073-1079). IEEE.

Lo Bello, L., Kaczynski, G. A., & Mirabella, O. (2005). Improving the real-time behavior of ethernet networks using traffic smoothing. *IEEE Transactions on Industrial Informatics*, *1*(3), 151–161. doi:10.1109/TII.2005.852071.

Lopez-Aguilera, E., Casademont, J., Cotrina, J., & Rojas, A. (2005). Enhancement proposal for WLAN IEEE 802.11e: Desynchronization of its working procedure. In *Proceedings of the 14th IEEE Workshop on Local and Metropolitan Area Networks LANMAN*, (pp. 1-6). IEEE.

Miorandi, D., & Vitturi, S. (2004). Analysis of master-slave protocols for real-time industrial communications over IEEE 802.11 WLANs. In *Proceedings of the 2nd IEEE International Conference on Industrial Informatics*, (pp. 143 - 148). IEEE.

Moraes, R., Portugal, P., & Vasques, F. (2006). Simulation analysis of the IEEE 802.11e EDCA protocol for an industrially-relevant real-time communication scenario. In *Proceedings of the 11th IEEE International Conference on Emerging Technologies and Factory Automation (ETFA)*, (pp. 202 - 209). IEEE.

Moraes, R., Vasques, F., Portugal, P., & Fonseca, J. A. (2007). VTP-CSMA: A virtual token passing approach for real-time communication in IEEE 802.11 wireless networks. *IEEE Transactions on Industrial Informatics*, 3(3), 215–224. doi:10.1109/TII.2007.903224.

Moyne, J. R., & Tilbury, D. M. (2007). The emergence of industrial control networks for manufacturing control, diagnostics, and safety data. *Proceedings of the IEEE*, 95(1), 29–47. doi:10.1109/JPROC.2006.887325.

Ramanathan, P. (1999). Overload management in real-time control applications using (m, k)-firm guarantee. *IEEE Transactions on Parallel and Distributed Systems*, 10(6), 549–559. doi:10.1109/71.774906.

Rashid, M. M., Hossain, E., & Bhargava, V. K. (2008). Controlled channel access scheduling for guaranteed QoS in 802.11e-based WLANs. *IEEE Transactions on Wireless Communications*, 7(4), 1287–1297. doi:10.1109/TWC.2008.060861.

Sauter, T. (2010). The three generations of field-level networks&#x2014, evolution and compatibility issues. *IEEE Transactions on Industrial Electronics*, 57(11), 3585–3595. doi:10.1109/TIE.2010.2062473.

Sauter, T., & Vasques, F. (2006). Editorial: Special section on communication in automation. *IEEE Transactions on Industrial Informatics*, 2(2), 73–77. doi:10.1109/TII.2006.875801.

Seno, L., Vitturi, S., & Zunino, C. (2009). Analysis of ethernet powerlink wireless extensions based on the IEEE 802.11 WLAN. *IEEE Transactions on Industrial Informatics*, 5(2), 86–98. doi:10.1109/TII.2009.2019727.

Sheu, J.-P., Liu, C.-H., Wu, S.-L., & Tseng, Y.-C. (2004). A priority MAC protocol to support real-time traffic in ad hoc networks. *Wireless Networks*, 10(1), 61–69. doi:10.1023/A:1026292830673.

Skyrianoglou, D., Passas, N., & Salkintzis, A. K. (2006). ARROW: An efficient traffic scheduling algorithm for IEEE 802.11e HCCA. *IEEE Transactions on Wireless Communications*, 5(12), 3558–3567. doi:10.1109/TWC.2006.256978.

Sobrinho, J. L., & Krishnakumar, A. S. (1998). EQuB - Ethernet quality of service using black bursts. In *Proceedings of the Conference on Local Computer Networks*, (pp. 286 - 296). IEEE.

Sobrinho, J. L., & Krishnakumar, A. S. (1999). Quality-of-service in ad hoc carrier sense multiple access wireless networks. *IEEE Journal on Selected Areas in Communications*, 17(8), 1353–1368. doi:10.1109/49.779919.

Son, J., Lee, I.-G., Yoo, H.-J., & Park, S.-C. (2005). An effective polling scheme for IEEE 802.11e. *IEICE Transactions on Communications. E (Norwalk, Conn.)*, 88-B(12), 4690–4693.

Tavli, B., & Heinzelman, W. (2006). *Mobile Ad hoc networks*. Dordrecht, The Netherlands: Springer. doi:10.1007/1-4020-4633-2.

Toscano, E., & Lo Bello, L. (2011). *A middleware for reliable soft real-time communication over IEEE 802.11 WLANs*. Paper presented at the Industrial Embedded Systems (SIES), 2011. New York, NY.

Trsek, H., & Jasperneite, J. (2011). *An isochronous medium access for real-time wireless communications in industrial automation systems - A use case for wireless clock synchronization*. Paper presented at the Precision Clock Synchronization for Measurement Control and Communication (ISPCS). New York, NY.

Ulusoy, A., Gurbuz, O., & Onat, A. (2011). Wireless model-based predictive networked control system over cooperative wireless network. *IEEE Transactions on Industrial Informatics*, 7(1), 41–51. doi:10.1109/TII.2010.2089059.

Vaidya, N., Dugar, A., Gupta, S., & Bahl, P. (2005). Distributed fair scheduling in a wireless LAN. *IEEE Transactions on Mobile Computing, 4*(6), 616–629. doi:10.1109/TMC.2005.87.

Villallón, N. J., Cuenca, P., Orozco-Barbosa, L., & Garrido, A. (2008). B-EDCA: A QoS mechanism for multimedia communications over heterogeneous 802.11/802.11e WLANs. *Computer Communications, 31*(17), 3905–3921. doi:10.1016/j.comcom.2008.07.012.

Wang, C., Li, B., & Li, L. (2004). A new collision resolution mechanism to enhance the performance of IEEE 802.11 DCF. *IEEE Transactions on Vehicular Technology, 53*(4), 1235–1246. doi:10.1109/TVT.2004.830951.

Willig, A. (1997). A MAC protocol and a scheduling approach as elements of a lower layers architecture in wireless industrial LANs. In *Proceedings of the IEEE International Workshop on Factory Communication Systems (WFCS'97)*, (pp. 139 - 148). IEEE.

Willig, A. (2008). Recent and emerging topics in wireless industrial communications: A selection. *IEEE Transactions on Industrial Informatics, 4*(2), 102–124. doi:10.1109/TII.2008.923194.

Willig, A., Matheus, K., & Wolisz, A. (2005). Wireless technology in industrial networks. *Proceedings of the IEEE, 93*(6), 1130–1151. doi:10.1109/JPROC.2005.849717.

Wu, Y.-J., Chiu, J.-H., & Sheu, T.-L. (2008). A modified EDCA with dynamic contention control for real-time traffic in multi-hop ad hoc networks. *Journal of Information Science and Engineering, 24*(4), 1065–1079.

Yang, X., & Vaidya, N. (2006). Priority scheduling in wireless ad hoc networks. *Wireless Networks, 12*(3), 273–286. doi:10.1007/s11276-005-5274-y.

ENDNOTES

1. The protocol defined by this standard is also known as WiFi protocol.
2. The concept "inside/outside" sphere-of-control was defined by Kopetz (1998). Whenever a RT entity is in the sphere-of-control of a subsystem, it belongs to a subsystem that has the authority to change all the value of this RT entity. Outside its sphere-of-control, the value of the entity can be observed, but cannot be modified.
3. An additional mechanism, RTS/CTS, is defined in the IEEE 802.11 standard to solve the hidden terminal problem and to adequately handle the transmission of long messages.

Chapter 15
Hardware/Software Implementation for Wireless Sensor Network Applications

Mohamed Wassim Jmal
University of Sfax, Tunisia

Olfa Gaddour
University of Sfax, Tunisia

Oussema Ghorbel
University of Sfax, Tunisia

Mohamed Abid
University of Sfax, Tunisia

ABSTRACT

Wireless Sensor Networks (WSNs) are currently attracting great interest and the number of its application domains is varying and increasing. However, some of these applications are very sensitive to the execution time and require huge memory and computation resources, which contrast to the nature of sensor motes with limited capabilities. There have been a lot of software solutions that aim to optimize the memory consumption and to reduce the execution time of WSN applications, but few previous research efforts considered a hardware/software optimization of the sensor mote resources. The limitation of studies on hardware optimization on WSN motivated the authors to write this chapter, with the objective to design a new HW architecture with FPGA technology that allows extending the sensor mote capabilities. An optimal routing protocol to efficiently route messages between motes was chosen. It enables the reduction of different communication problems such as message unreachability, long paths, and traffic congestion. The authors first study one of WSN applications that require great resources, image processing. They demonstrate how the memory and processing capabilities of classical sensor motes are not sufficient for the treatment of this application, and the point-to-point routing cannot be applied in such applications. The authors then survey the most important routing protocols for WSNs in order to select the best routing algorithm. They finally propose a reconfigurable HW/SW architecture based on FPGA for critical WSN applications. Results show that the proposed solution outperforms the performance of the classical sensor motes, and is extensible for application to other WSN applications.

DOI: 10.4018/978-1-4666-3922-5.ch015

INTRODUCTION

During the last few years, the use of embedded systems and System on Chip (SoC) has massively grown. Hence, time and cost are key factors in the success of these products in the competitive electronics marketplace.

Wireless Sensor Networks which integrate a SoC are becoming a necessity in our daily life reminding its different covered areas. Sensor Networks have been deployed for a variety of applications, including environment monitoring, health-care monitoring, transportation systems, home automation, etc. (Mainwaring *et al.*, 2002). The evolution of applications provided by these systems has spawned related problems like complexity and sensitivity.

The Discrete Wavelet Transforms (DWT) have been extensively used in many digital signal processing applications.

The design of a SoC, which integrates this kind of application, causes a lot of constraints like minimizing the time to market, the cost and energy consumption. Therefore, designers had to reduce the development time, to validate the designed system and to ensure its efficient functioning (Janapsatya, Ignjatovi, & Parameswaran, 2006).

Choosing the appropriate embedded processor, which will be integrated in the SoC to implement DWT, is an essential step. The advantage of using embedded softcores processor is their higher flexibility and easier configuration than hardcores.

In this work, a softcore embedded processor has been adopted in order to adapt its architecture as required by DWT using the Algorithm Architecture Adequacy (AAA) approach (Liu, Tanougast, & Weber, 2006)

The objective of this study is to integrate DWT on a chip using an embedded processor while increasing processing speed and minimizing costs. The Implementation of DWT in WSN is presented in Figure 1.

Virtual prototyping is an interesting designing method which allows the designer to validate the design before Hardware implantation. Modelsim software was used to simulate the program running and to determine its execution time. A hardware/Software implementation on FPGA was also done and performance was measured. A literature review of the existing routing protocols for WSNs was provided (Chakeresa & Klein-Berndtb, 2002; Perkins & Belding-Royer& Das, 2003; Erge, 2004; Kim & Montenegro, 2007). After then, they are compared in terms of energy consumption and memory overhead in order to choose the best routing protocol for the proposed solution.

The remainder of this chapter is organized as follows. First, First, the background and the related work in WSN, DWT, and SOC process cores are discussed in Section 1. Section 2 deals with problems of DWT implementation in WSNs. Section 3 presents HW/SW implementation of DWT using an embedded processor core. Section 4 describes the choice of the routing protocol for the proposed system. Finally, we conclude and give some perspectives in Section 5.

BACKGROUND

WSN and DWT

WSN is a network composed of many nodes communicating among themselves and applied in a wide range of areas, such as military applications, public safety, medical applications, surveillance domain, environmental monitoring, commercial applications, habitat and tracking (Naumowicz & Freeman, 2008; Marcelloni & Vecchio, 2009; Akyildiz & Melodia, 2007).

Recently, Wireless Sensor Network has been an active area of research and a wide range of applications have been developed (Kimura & Latifi,

Figure 1. Implementation of DWT in WSN

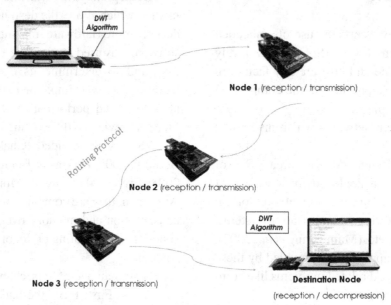

2005). Sensor nodes are mainly characterized by their scarce resources and limited energy.

In the literature, most current research related to image compression in wireless sensor networks are limited to the evaluation by simulation (Chew, Ang, & Seng, 2008; Li, Peng, Pang, & Liu, 2010). The authors have used several methods in the compression CWHN as LBT, SPIHT (Duran-Faundez, 2009), ISEC (Makkaoui, Lecuire, & Moureaux, 2010) tested by simulation and tested on a real platform on Mica2. For instance, ISEC makes a compression method at the source, which uses a coding block of 2x2 pixels and removes one pixel from the 4 to minimize the compression rate and then finds the missing pixel using three present pixels.

In (Caben & Gent, 2008), there is a comparison between two models of selecting zonal coefficient of the DCT, one using a square shaped area and the other a triangular area.

In this work, a considerable effort has been given to experimentally test one of the techniques for image compression to ensure whether they are effective for image transmission through a wireless sensor network. The selected technique is: Discrete Wavelet Transforms (DWT).

The aims of this paper are the following: First, we present a method of compressing images which is the Discrete Wavelet Transform (DWT), and we test its capability on Wireless Sensor Networks (WSNs). Second, we implement these methods on a real WSNs platform with a TelosB sensor type. Third, we execute performance evaluation in terms of image quality, execution time and memory usage.

Discrete Wavelet Transform is a mathematical transform that separates the data signal into fine-scale information known as detail coefficients, and rough-scale information known as approximate coefficients. Its major advantage is the multi-resolution representation and time-frequency localization property for signals. DWT has the capability to encode the finer resolution of the original time series with its hierarchical coefficients. Furthermore, DWT can be computed efficiently in linear time, which is important while dealing with large datasets (Antonini, Barlaud, Mathieu, Daubechies, 1992). Since image is typically a two-dimensional signal, a 2-D equivalent of the DWT is performed. This is achieved by first applying the L and H filters to the lines of samples, row-by-row, and then re-filtering the output to the columns by the same filters. As a result, the image is divided into 4 subbands, LL, LH, HL, and HH, as depicted in Figure 1 (1 Level). The LL subbands contain the low-pass information and the others contain high-pass information of horizontal, vertical, and diagonal orientation. The LL subbands provides a half-sized version of the input image which can be transformed again to have more levels of resolution. Figure 2 (2 Level) shows an image decomposed into two resolution levels.

Due to its excellent spatio-frequency localization properties, the DWT is very suitable to identify the areas in the host image. In particular, this property allows the exploitation of the masking effect of the human visual system such that if a DWT coefficient is modified, only the region corresponding to that coefficient will be modified. In general, most of the image energy is concentrated at the lower frequency sub-bands LLx and therefore these sub-bands may degrade the image significantly. On the other hand, the high frequency sub-bands HHx include the edges and textures of the image and the human eye is not generally sensitive to changes in such sub-bands. So, data could be compressed to reduce the global amount of data to send.

Several technologies and architectures are used to implement this kind of application. In the next paragraph, processor cores in Soc are presented.

Processor Cores in SoC

The design of a SoC is more often based on processor cores that are optimized and specialized to take into account the constraints of using the system.

The compilation of such processors is to produce, for a particular application, both the architecture and compiler to achieve the performance required by the application.

Indeed, for the realization of systems dedicated to image processing and telecommunications, there must be an optimized executable code and architecture with good computing time and throughput.

In the fields of telecommunications and image processing, especially at low level, encoding, decoding the compression and decompression are treatments that require a huge amount of computation.

The use of embedded software by processor cores, implanted on programmable devices integrated into a single chip, is an inevitable trend. These devices or processor cores can be of three types:

- The general purpose processors: they are based on a powerful processor core which could be RISC (Reduced Instruction Set

Figure 2. DWT applied one time (1 level) or two times (2 level)

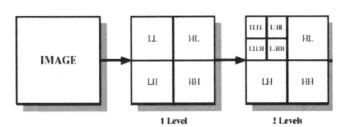

Computer) such as LEON (Gaisler, 2001) and ARM (Arm, 2001) or VLIW (Very Long Instruction Word) as the TRIMEDIA processor of Philips (Vissers, 1999). These types of processors are used for the design of embedded systems or SoC (System on Chip). Instances of general purpose processors are now available as basic components in the libraries of system designers.

- The domain-specific processors are of two types: there are two types of this kind of processors; those used for signal processing known as DSP (Digital Signal Processing) and those oriented towards the video processing known as VSP (Video Signal Processing). An example of the DSP is TMS320Cxx of Texas Instrument. The VSP are the result of changes in the DSP to address the problems of video processing but they are not usually dedicated to a particular application. For this case processor, the designer can control some parameters of architecture as the number of registers, the width of the bus, the presence of functional units and he can select the most appropriate configuration for the implementation. Although existing processor cores (general purpose or configurable) allow to rapidly prototype a system, they generally do not satisfy the constraints imposed by the applications in terms of execution time, silicon area, consumption, etc. The use of ASIP is very often necessary.

- ASIPs (Application Specific Processors) are processors incorporating functional units and a specific set of instructions to a particular application. The design of ASIPs needs very efficient compilers. The definition of an ASIP architecture and programming (code generation requires compilation tools tailored to the architecture) require design methods and tools for organizing an architecture with relevance (choice of functional units, storage units, the register structure, interconnections, the type of control, etc.). The main problem of ASIPs is the lack of software tools such as compilers and instruction set simulators.

These types of processors can be classified according to various criteria (Table 1). The target architecture can be chosen based on four criteria: real-time, system flexibility, time to market and low cost.

Soft processor cores can be used to implement WSN applications since they are easily configured and they allow good performance and smaller execution time than the conventional sensor nodes. In the next section, the implementation of DWT is presented. Performances were measured and the use of processor core technologies was justified.

PROBLEMS OF DWT IMPLEMENTATION IN WSN

The DWT have been extensively used in many digital signal processing applications. In this section, we introduce this transforms briefly, and

Table 1. Processor cores classification

	real-time	system flexibility	Time to market.	Low Coast
The general purpose processors	-	-	+++	+++
The domain-specific processors	+	+	+	++
Application-specific processors (Hardcore)	++	-	+	+
Application-specific processors (Softcore)	+++	++	+	+

outline this relevance to the implementation of compression algorithm.

This work is evaluated on the real platform in terms of space complexity, time complexity and amount of information. The evaluation will be very detailed depending on the results obtained through the execution time and memory used. In elaborated experiments, we evaluate one compression technique in image processing applications. We focus on the following question: Is this technique valid for the context of WSNs? For this, we follow the steps of scenarios, measurement parameters and materials used that allow us to do the assessment.

The variants used in the scenarios are the case for which we used only two sensors that are used one node from source to one from destination without any obstacles are: the execution time and memory used. We used TelosB motes with the TinyOS operating system to validate and measure the performance of our proposal. The characteristics of TelosB are described in Table 2.

The implementation of DWT in Telosb Node is described in the next paragraph.

The Process of Algorithm Implementation using DWT

The compression of an image at the sensor node includes several steps. First, the image is transformed into a suitable format to a compressed image. Second, the filters divide the input image into four non-overlapping multi-resolution sub-bands LL, LH, HL, and HH on the first level. The sub-band LL represents the coarse-scale DWT coefficients while the sub-bands LH, HL, and HH represent the fine-scale of DWT coefficients. Third, each

subband contains the low-pass information and the others contain high-pass information of horizontal, vertical, and diagonal orientation. The next step is quantification and coding of subbands used to reduce the number of bits needed to represent the image. The quantification method used in DWT affects the image quality. But it is better than other techniques such as the DCT affecting much the image quality (loss in number and value of pixels). The quality will depend on the value of the quantization used. The bit plane coding and subbands provide various coding modes; the compressed image can indeed be represented by increasing resolution or by increasing quality. The next step is arithmetic coding. It is a variable length coding. Unlike other encodings, it encodes the source message fully and represents a single number. Finally data packets are created for suitable transmission over the wireless sensor network.

Applied Scenario

We have used two TelosB motes to do this scenario (Figure 3). Compression and decompression are performed respectively at the source and destination nodes. The implementation is based on 802.15.4 PHY and MAC layers for radio communication which is a standard protocol for low-rate wireless personal area networks (LR-WPANs).

For experimentation, different images are being used, we choose for example Lena to do the different scenarios (Figure 4).

Performance measurements of the implementation of DWT in TelosB node were presented in the next paragraph.

Table 2. Characteristics of sensors nodes

Manufacturer	Processor	Program Memory	RAM
Crossbow	IT MSP430	48 KB	10 KB

Clock	Radio Unit	Band/Data rate	Max Consumption
8MHz	Chipcon CC2420	2.4 GHz / 250 kbps	1.8 mA

Figure 3. From the source to destination nodes using radio communication

Figure 4. Original image

Evaluation of Execution Time

The RunTime interface will be used to evaluate the duration of execution time for compression method. This interface is provided by the TinyOS platform for measuring the elapsed time between events and calculates the execution time of all the program of each processing or separate module. Using the tools described above for different image formats (16x16 and 32x32 and 64x64), we obtained the results presented in Figure 5.

Memory Usage

The memory used in this application is the memory allocated to install the program and doing in parallel the intermediate computation. These measures in Figure 6 are obtained by varying the image size.

HW/SW IMPLEMENTATION OF DWT

Software Implantation of DWT on Classical Sensor Nodes (TelosB) which includes Micro controller and a little memory space showed that this kind of applications needs more efficient hardware architecture to reduce execution time. In fact, these applications are very sensitive to the execution time and require huge memory and computation resources, which contrast to the nature of sensor motes with limited capabilities.

We describe in this Section the HW/SW implementation of DWT. For that, we present an architecture development to be used in a wireless sensor network. The architecture is dedicated to be the core of the node platform based in the use of the open hard and soft sources. Algorithm Architecture Adequacy (AAA) approach was used. A Hardware/Software implantation of DWT on

Figure 5. Evolution of execution time according to the image resolution

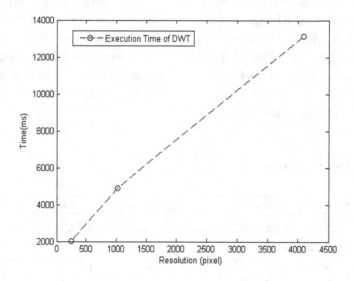

Figure 6. Memory space used by DWT algorithm

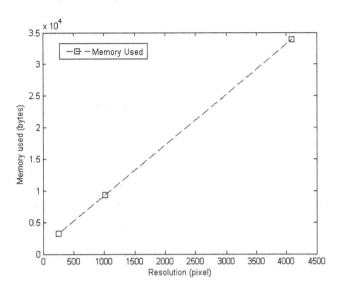

FPGA using the designed ASIP will be presented. Performance evaluation in terms of execution time and memory usage will be compared with the Software implantation on TelosB.

Open Soft Core Processor

In this part, we present the design of an architecture based on open sources for wireless sensor networks. The hardware development of the architecture is based on the use of soft core processor. To make the soft core processor suitable for wireless sensor network, changes are made in its open VHDL packages. The enhanced architecture for WSN based on Soft core is shown in Figure 7.

In this Case study, LEON processor (Gaisler, 2001) was used to implement DWT in FPGA. The LEON processor is an open source, soft core processor developed and supported by Gaisler Research. It is implemented as a high level VHDL model, fully synthesizable with common synthesis tools. The model is extensively configurable through a (graphical) configuration package, allowing options such as cache size and organization,

Figure 7. The enhanced architecture for WSN based on soft core

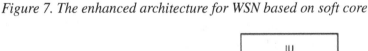

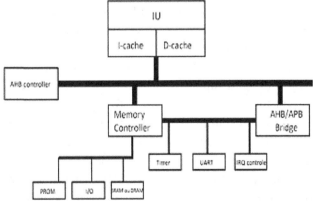

arithmetic operation implementation, I/O modules and other IP cores to be selected.

LEON3 came with the following features:

- Separate instruction and data caches (Harvard architecture)
- Interrupt controller
- On chip debugging support
- 2 24 bit timers
- Watchdog timer
- 2 UARTS
- Ethernet MAC and PCI interface
- Co-processor support

LEON3 is distributed with a large GPLed library with, among others, IP cores for a CAN controller, CCSDS telemetry and wireless control functions.

To minimize energy consumption and to meet the needs of the system we have tailored the LEON3 processor.

The first step in the design process is the configuration of the LEON3 by using a graphical configuration tool provided with the LEON3 model from Gaisler Research.

This tool is built upon the TCL/TK software, providing some menus that allow the designer to configure the system on chip.

Second, we simulate the model by running a test bench provided with LEON VHDL model. The simulation is done by a simulation tool like Modelsim from Mentor, NCSIM from Cadence2, VSS from Synopsys or GHDL from GNU.

The test program previously mentioned has to be compiled with BCC: Bare-C Cross Compiler, is a C/C++cross compiler for the LEON3 processor based on the GNU tool chain, the binutils and the standard Newlib library, with full math support and simple I/O operations (non-files).

The result of compilation is the executable file by LEON3. To ensure that the program is working before hardware implementation we used TSIM2 a complete LEON3 instruction-level simulator. TSIM can run in standalone mode or connected through a network socket to the GDB debugger, acting like a remote target using a common debugging protocol. TSIM is a commercial application but it's also available as an evaluation version for non-commercial uses.

Design Validation on FPGA

FPGAs (Field Programmable Gate Arrays or "programmable logic devices") are made of a network of logic identical cells, placed in an infrastructure of interconnection lines. The user can program the function of each cell, as well as interconnections between the cells and with the input/output circuit. The advantage of FPGAs is local configuration, without sending the circuit to the manufacturer. They can be used few minutes after their designs.

FPGAs can be configured in microseconds. Moreover, the increasing density of current programmable circuits, including FPGAs, enables rapid prototyping of complex digital circuits.

It is possible to quickly test the validity of new architectural designs: the complete implementation of a processor on FPGAs is now within this reach, allowing more opportunities than those offered by evaluation of software simulators.

Also the reprogramming of some FPGAs has opened new research areas: design methodologies for reconfigurable systems, able to evolve or adapt to variable environments and constraints.

Currently, FPGAs are used to control hard drives, but one of the important applications of FPGAs is the pattern recognition (handwriting, identifying faces, target recognition, etc..). On the other hand, improvements in performance of the FPGA architecture allow the implementation of processor cores with hardware accelerators

To validate the designed architecture on a real hardware target, we have chosen the cycloneIII starter board from Altera for the implementation. This board embeds an EP3C25F324 FPGA and a USB Blaster. It also offers 1Mbyte of SSRAM and 50 MHz oscillator.

The first step is the synthesis. From the HDL files previously configured and with a synthesis tool like simplify from synopsis or Quartus provided by Altera.

The result of synthesis was the use of 9167 logic elements.

The FPGA programming file is generated by Quartus program after pins assignment. This file is downloaded to the FPGA via USB cable provided with the development board.

The Software environment of LEON processor allowed us to generate different types of binary files (*. Exe, *. Dat, *. Rec ...) from a program written in C or assembler SPARC V8. Part of this fileset was used to validate the implementation of the SoC in cycloneIII.

The software adopted environment is based on LECCS cross-compiler. This cross-compiler generates executable code on a SPARC from a code written in C language, C + + or Ada.

We have compiled the program DWT.C for the SPARC architecture LEON processor. To get the test program running on LEON3 we used a tool provided by Gaisler research named GRMON. GRMON is a debug monitor for LEON processors. It communicates with the LEON debug support unit (DSU) and allows non-intrusive debugging of the complete target system. To be able to use this tool we had to include the debug support unit in the LEON3 architecture to provide a link for the communication with GRMON.

The implementation of DWT in LEON using FPGA allows evaluating the execution time according to the image resolution (Figure 8).

This execution time is very promising. The energy consumption is about 57mJ but because it's measured on FPGA it is not accurate. However it can give us an overview on system energy consumption. In the next section, Routing Protocols are studied to optimise the designed system.

CHOICE OF THE ROUTING PROTOCOL FOR THE PROPOSED SYSTEM

In this section, we first provide a literature review of the existing routing protocols that were proposed for WSNs. We then compare them in terms of energy consumption and memory overhead in order to choose the best routing protocol for proposed solution.

Figure 8. Evolution of execution time in FPGA according to the image resolution

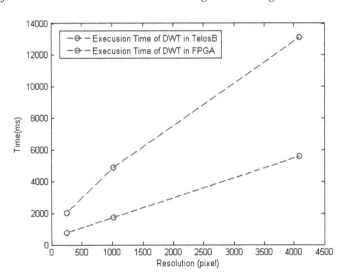

Overview on Routing Protocols in WSNs

The features of these routing protocols are populated in Table 3. The Table presents an overview on how different routing protocols fit under different categories and also compares their characteristics. In what follows we summarize the details of these routing protocols.

AODV (Perkins & Belding-Royer& Das, 2003) is a reactive routing protocol based on the broadcast of RREQ messages for the route discovery. The Backward or forward routing entries between the source and the destination are created with RREQ and RREP messages. Route entries in AODV expire after a specified time if the route becomes inactive. AODV supports sequence numbers, broascast of hello messages, local repair and route error (RERR) messages.

AODVjr (Chakeresa & Klein-Berndtb, 2002) is a simplified version from AODV as it removes many features from AODV such as sequence Numbers, Gratuitous RREP, Hop Count and Hello Messages. Only destination nodes respond to messages with RREQ and the intermediate nodes cannot send these messages. Thus, AODVjr requires low memory and energy consumption. To perform route maintenance, route lifetimes are only updated by the reception of packets and not by the sending of packets. This requires the destination to occasionally send a packet to the source.

In 2005, and before the birth of 6LoWPAN, ZigBee standard protocol was considered as the most prominent technology for LLNs. It has been characterized by its famous Cluster- Tree protocol (Erge, 2004) as a hierarchical routing protocol that uses link-state packets to form a two-tier cluster-based network, where each cluster is governed by one Cluster Head (CH). The ZigBee Cluster-

Table 3. Comparison of existing routing protocols

	Topology	Type	Algorithm	Hello messages	Local Repair	Mobility	Scalability	Memory Usage	Energy Usage	Supported Traffic	IPv6 Support
AODV	Flat	On demand	Distance vector	Use	Use	Mobile	Medium	High	High	P2P	No
AODVjr	Flat	On demand	Distance vector	No use	No use	Mobile	Low	Low	Low	P2P	No
ZigBee Cluster Tree	Hierarchical	Proactive	Link state	No use	No use	Static	High	High	High	MP2P P2MP	No
TinyAODV	Flat	On demand	Distance vector	No use	No use	Mobile	Low	Low	Low	P2P	Yes
Hilow	Hierarchical	On demand	Tree based	No use	No use	Static Mobile	Low	Low	Low	MP2P P2MP	Yes
Load	Flat	On demand	Distance vector	No use	No use	Static Mobile	Low	Low	Low	P2P	Yes
Dymo Low	Flat	On demand		No use	No use	Static Mobile	High	High	High	P2P	Yes
CTP	Hierarchical	Proactive	Source Routing	Use	Use	Mobile	Low	Low	Low	MP2P P2MP	No
Hydro	Hierarchical Flat	On Demand	Source Routing	No use	No use	Static	High	Medium	High	P2P MP2P P2MP	Yes
RPL	Hierarchical Flat	Proactive	Source Routing Distance vector	No use	Use	Static Mobile	High	Low	Low	P2P MP2P P2MP	Yes

Tree network is self-organized and it supports fault-tolerance and self-repair mechanisms. The cluster-tree is formed by several parent-to-child associations between ZigBee Routers until a certain depth. Clusters are supposed to operate in exclusive time slots to avoid interference between them.

In 2007, with the emergence of ZigBee Pro 2007, the cluster-tree routing was no longer supported for complexity of maintenance issues, and the standard has adopted flat and mesh routing based on AODV.

TinyAODV (TinyAODV, 2009) was designed to implement AODV using a small footprint. It provides for communication between any two nodes in the network. Route Response (RREP) messages are only generated by the destination node. The only routing metric employed is the hop count. Route errors are generated and locally broadcasted when a data message can no longer be sent over a given path. The packet which initiates the route discovery process is discarded. There are no messages to maintain routes because routes never expire.

With the emergence of IPv6-based networks for LLNs, a new wave of routing protocols has emerged. Several Internet drafts have been proposed (Kim & Yoo, 2005; Kim & Park, 2007; Kim & Montenegro, 2007).

Hilow (Kim & Yoo, 2005) is one of the first routing protocols proposed as an Internet draft for 6LoWPAN networks that mainly addresses scalability issues. HiLow is a hierarchical and on-demand routing protocol that takes advantage of the 6LoWPAN capabilities in terms of dynamic assignment of 16-bit short addresses. The use of 16-bit short addressing scheme allows for employing hierarchical routing which is very scalable. HiLow relies on parent to child relationship to construct the network tree. Once a 6LoWPAN node wants to join the network, it either associates with an existing neighbor parent router, which assigns it a 16-bit short address, or initiates a

new 6LoWPAN network if no other neighbor 6LoWPAN device is found. Like in any other tree routing, any router just needs to determine whether the destination of the packet should be forwarded to parent (ascendant) or child (descendant) node based on the address, which is expressed as $Adrr = PA*MCN + N$ where PA is the parent address, MCN is the maximum number of child routers of each the parent node is allowed to associate with, and N is the index of the Nth child node. This addressing mechanism is very similar to ZigBee Cluster-Tree addressing scheme.

Later, LOAD was proposed in (Kim & Montenegro, 2007) as another Internet draft and represents a flat on-demand routing protocol designed for 6LoWPAN network. It is based on AODV and supports mesh network topologies. However, LOAD does not use the destination sequence number used in AODV. For ensuring loop freedom, only the destination of a route should generate a Route Reply (RREP). LOAD uses LQI (Link Quality Indicator) and the number of hops as routing metrics for route selection. In case of a link failure, the upstream node of the broken link initiates a local route by using the route discovery mechanism. LOAD uses the link layer acknowledgements instead of Hello messages to save energy while keeping track of route connectivity.

In the same trend, Kim et al. proposed DYMO-low in (Kim & Park, 2007) as a flat routing protocol. DYMO-low operates on the link layer to create a mesh network topology of 6LoWPAN devices. It performs route discovery and maintenance. Dymo-Low does not use local repair and uses Hello messages instead. It uses sequence numbers to ensure loop freedom.

On the other side, Hydro is the default routing protocol that was proposed in the 6LoWPAN Berkeley implementation known as BLIP. This routing protocol represents a hybrid mechanism that provides both centralized control and local agility. Hydro uses a distributed algorithm to form a DAG for routing data from router nodes to border routers. Nodes report topologies periodically to the border router, allowing it to maintain a global view on the topology. All the nodes forward packets to the border router which forwards them to the appropriate destinations.

RPL (Tavakoli, 2009) is a routing protocol specifically designed for Low power and Lossy Networks (LLN). RPL is the main candidate for acting as the standard routing protocol for 6LoW-PAN networks. RPL is a Distance-Vector (DV) and a source routing protocol that is designed to operate on top of IEEE 802.15.4 PHY and MAC layers. The basic topological component in RPL is the DODAG, a Destination Oriented Directed Acyclic Graph, rooted in a special node called DODAG root. A RPL network typically consists of several DODAGs, which form together an RPL instance. A network may run multiple RPL instances concurrently; but these instances are logically independent.

Comparison of Routing Protocols for WSNs

Table 3 presents the well-known routing protocols proposed for Wireless Sensor Networks and related to standard protocols. The features of these routing protocols are populated in this Table for comparative purpose with RPL. The Table presents an overview on how different routing protocols fit under different categories and also compares their characteristics.

It can be noted from this table that the completeness of RPL makes it promising routing protocol. In fact, one reason behind the success of RPL routing protocol in comparison with the other protocols is that it provides comprehensive features including support of various types of traffic (MP2P, P2MP and P2P) and its ability to directly connect to Internet nodes with global IPv6 addresses. This turns RPL very flexible and can be easily tuned for different applications' requirements. Furthermore, RPL constructs the topology proactively and thus discards the need to broadcast RREQ messages, which is used in several AODV-based protocols. In addition, it provides the benefits of both mesh and tree routing protocols as it supports both hierarchical and flat topologies. In addition, RPL combines the distance-vector and the source routing paradigms, and supports local and global repair, which make it suitable for fault-tolerant applications. In addition, the notion of Objective Function in RPL offers a great flexibility for supporting various application requirements and enables QoS-award routing.

FUTURE RESEARCH DIRECTIONS

Wireless sensor networks are composed of sensor nodes spread over an area for the purpose

Figure 9. Designed architecture for WSN based on NIOS processor

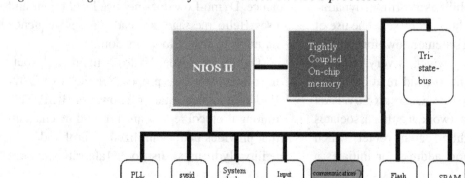

of observation and data collection. Each sensor node consists of a microprocessor coupled with a wireless communication technology and a sensor, whose ranges define the limits of detection and communication for a node. A sensor node may be responsible for detecting, processing and transmitting using specialized algorithms.

The increasing demand for more efficiency in sensor networks has forced designers to explore more solutions like use of FPGAs.

Wireless Sensor Networks and FPGAs are two popular research topics but also disjointed. The combination of these two areas can lead to very satisfactory results (Valverde *et al.*, 2012).

Currently, the design of a sensor node using FPGA technology is being studied. The chosen board is Nios Linux development kit including Stratix EP1S40F780C5. Nios II processor will be used for treatments in this system. The architecture is designed as shown in Figure 9.

This architecture can be enhanced to include other IP (IP used for display, calculation, conversion ...).

The IP communication with the sensor node can be:

- An UART (Universal Asynchronous Receiver Transmitter)

To communicate, the two connected entities must share the same transmission parameters. To establish the connection between the UART and the node a USB-Serial Conversion interface had to be designed. The core of the interface is the circuit FT232RL of FTDI CHIP that will ensure the conversion.

- One or more PIO

This IP, provided with SOPC Builder can be configured as output only, input only or bidirectional.

In our case we use two PIO IP blocks. One with 8 I/O configured in bidirectional mode (for

the parallel transfer of data 8-bits). The other IP block will be reserved for control bits. The main interface component is the FT245RL whose role is to convert the data from D + and D in 8-bit parallel data. After establishing the connection in hardware, the next step is the implementation of the communication protocol in software on NIOS II.

- A USB controller

This solution is similar to the previous solution since it uses the FT245RL for conversion. The only difference is that the USB controller becomes responsible for managing the connection.

After choosing the connection type and the corresponding architecture, it will be realized with SOPC Builder and the FPGA will be programmed.

To ensure the connection between the node and NIOS II they must be configured to work in correspondence. The sensor node that will be used is the telosB that incorporates MSP430 microcontroller of Texas Instrument.

Having completed the above steps, the designed system will be tested using a program called Blink. nC. The designed sensor node based on FPGA allows implementing several WSN applications.

CONCLUSION

The DWT used in specific WSN application need important resources of calculation, memory and energy. The majority of existing WSN platform does not satisfy these needs because they are based on microcontrollers. Therefore it is necessary to build a new platform around a microprocessor able to handle the complexity of the algorithms. The development of such a platform must take into consideration system cost, time to market and easiness of adaptation in the case of changing application. Wireless Sensor Networks which integrate a SoC are becoming a necessity in our daily life reflecting its different covered areas. The evolution of applications provided by these systems has spawned related problems like complexity and sensitivity.

Open source IP cores could be considered as solutions for SoC application development due to the maturity of some of them, in the case of the LEON processor and the presence of a huge amount of support. This could reduce the development cost and reduce total cost of ownership and providing the opportunity to break free from the shackles of proprietary systems and expensive upgrades.

This research's aim consists in designing a SoC including a softcore processor and improving the time performances of the implemented DWT program. Indeed, DWT was implemented in TelosB sensor node and execution time had been measured. The memory and processing capabilities of this classical sensor mote are not sufficient for the processing of this application. A reconfigurable HW/SW architecture based on FPGA for critical DWT was proposed. Results of implementation showed that proposed solution outperforms the performance of the classical sensor motes, and is extensible to other WSN applications.

Finally, the most important routing protocols for WSNs were surveyed and the best routing algorithm had been selected.

In future, we will study the prototyping of a configurable sensor node which combines both FPGA technology and classical sensor mote. This allows implementing several WSN applications like complex security algorithms and distributed compression approaches.

REFERENCES

Akyildiz, I. F., & Melodia, T. (2007). A survey on wireless multimedia sensor networks. *Journal Computer Networks, 51*(4).

Antonini, M., Barlaud, M., Mathieu, P., & Daubechies, I. (1992). Image coding using wavelet transform. *IEEE Transactions on Image Processing, 1*(2), 205–220. doi:10.1109/83.136597 PMID:18296155.

Arm. (2001). Retrieved December 19, 2001, from www.arm.com

Caben, K., & Gent, P. (2008). *Image compression and the discreet cosine transform.* Paper presented at International Conference on Machine Learning and Cybernetics. New York, NY.

Chakeresa, I. D., & Klein-Berndtb, L. (2002). AODVjr, AODV simplified. *Mobile Computing and Communications Review, 6*(3).

Chew, L. W., Ang, L. M., & Seng, K. P. (2008). Survey of image compression algorithms in wireless sensor networks. In *Proceedings of International Symposium on Information Technology (ITSim 2008)*. ITSim.

Duran-Faundez, C. (2009). *Transmission d'images sur les réseaux de capteurs sans fils sous la contrainte de l'énergie.* (Unpublished doctoral dissertation). Nancy University. Nancy, France.

Erge, S. C. (2004). *ZigBee/IEEE 802.15.4 summary.* Retrieved July 29, 2009, from http://staff.ustc.edu.cn/ustcsse/papers/SR10.ZigBee.pdf

Gaisler, J. (2001). *The LEON processor user's manual, version 2.4.0.* Retrieved December 19, 2001, from www.gaisler.com

Janapsatya, A., Ignjatovi, A., & Parameswaran, S. (2006). Finding optimal L1 cache configuration for embedded systems. In *Proceedings of the Asia and South Pacific Design Automation Conference*. IEEE.

Kim, K., & Montenegro, G. (2007). *6LoWPAN ad hoc on-demand distance vector routing (LOAD). IETF Internet Draft: draft-daniel-6lowpan-load-adhoc-routing-03*. IETF.

Kim, K., & Park, S. (2007). *Dynamic MANET on-demand for 6LoWPAN (DYMO-low) routing. Internet Draft: draft-montenegro-6lowpan-dymolow-routing-03*. IETF.

Kim, K., & Yoo, S. (2005). *Hierarchical routing over 6LoWPAN (HiLow). IETF: Internet Draft: draft-deniel-6lowpan-hilow-hierarchicalrouting-00.txt*. IETF.

Kimura, N., & Latifi, S. (2005). A survey on data compression in wireless sensor networks. In *Proceedings of the International Conference on Information Technology: Coding and Computing (ITCC 2005)*, (vol. 2, pp. 8-13). ITCC.

Li, W., Peng Pang, Z. Z., & Liu, J. (2010). *SPIHT algorithm combined with Huffman encoding*. Paper presented at the Third International Symposium on Intelligent Information Technology and Security Informatics. New York, NY.

Liu, T., Tanougast, C., & Weber, S. (2006). *Toward a methodology for optimizing algorithm-architecture adequacy for implementation reconfigurable system*. Paper presented at the 13th IEEE International Conference on Electronics, Circuits and Systems ICECS '06. New York, NY.

Mainwaring, J., Polastre, J., Szeczyk, R., Culler, D., & Anderson, J. (2002). *Wireless sensor networks for habitat monitoring*. Paper presented in International Workshop on Wireless Sensor Networks and Applications. New York, NY.

Makkaoui, L., Lecuire, V., & Moureaux, J. (2010). *Fast zonal DCT-based image compression for wireless camera sensor networks*. Paper presented at 2nd International Conference on Image Processing Theory, Tools and Applications, IPTA 2010. Paris, France.

Marcelloni, F., & Vecchio, M. (2009). An efficient lossless compression algorithm for tiny nodes of monitoring wireless sensor networks. *The Computer Journal, 52*(8), 969–987. doi:10.1093/comjnl/bxp035.

Naumowicz, T., & Freeman, R. (2008). Autonomous monitoring of vulnerable habitats using a wireless sensor network. In *Proceedings of the Workshop on Real-World Wireless Sensor Networks, REALWSN'08*. Glasgow, UK: REALWSN.

Perkins, C., Belding-Royer, E., & Das, S. (2003). *Ad hoc on demand distance vector routing (AODV). RFC 3561*. IETF.

Tavakoli, A. (2009). *HYDRO: A hybrid routing protocol for lossy and low power networks. IETF Internet Draft: draft-tavakoli-hydro-01*. IETF.

TinyAODV. (2009). *TinyAODV implementation under TinyOS-1.x source code*. Retrieved July 29, 2009, from tinyos-1.x/contrib/hsn/apps/TraceRouteTestAODV

Valverde, J., Rosello, V., Mujica, G., Portilla, J., Uriarte, A., & Riesgo, T. (2012). Wireless sensor network for environmental monitoring: Application in a coffee factory. *International Journal of Distributed Sensor Networks*. doi:10.1155/2012/638067.

Vissers, K. (1999). *The trimedia CPU64 VLIW media processor*. Paper presented at Session Invite ICCD'99. New York, NY.

ADDITIONAL READING

Akyildiz, I. F., & Kaushik, R. (2007). A survey on wireless multimedia sensor networks. *Computer Networks, 51*(4), 921–960. doi:10.1016/j.comnet.2006.10.002.

Akyildiz, I. F., Su, W., Sankarasubramaniam, Y., & Cayirci, E. (2002). Wireless sensor networks: A survey. *Computer Networks, 38*(4), 393–422. doi:10.1016/S1389-1286(01)00302-4.

Cao, Z. Y., Ji, Z., & Hu, M. (2005). An image sensor node for wireless sensor networks. In *Proceedings of the International Conference on Information Technology: Coding and Computing (ITCC'05)*, (Vol. 2, pp. 740–745). ITCC.

Chow, K., King-Shan, L., & Lam, E. Y. (2006). Balancing image quality and energy consumption in visual sensor networks. In *Proceedings of the International Symposium on Wireless Pervasive Computing (ISWPC'06)*. Phuket, Thailand: ISWPC.

Delaunay, X., Thiebaut, C., & Moin, G. (2008). Lossy compression by post-transforms in the wavelet domain. In *Proceedings of OBPDC'08*. Noordwijk, The Netherlands: ESA/ESTEC.

Ferrigno, L., Marano, S., Paciello, V., & Pietrosanto, A. (2005). Balancing computational and transmission power consumption in wireless image sensor networks. In *Proceedings of the IEEE International Conference on Virtual Environments, Human-Computer Interfaces, and Measures Systems (VECIMS 2005)*. Giardini Naxos, Italy: IEEE.

Fornaciari, W., Sciuto, D., Silvano, C., & Zaccaria, V. (2001). A design framework to efficiently explore energy delay trade ofs. [CODES.]. *Proceedings of CODES, 01*, 260–265. doi:10.1145/371636.371752.

Gauger, M., Minder, D., Marron, P. J., Wacker, A., & Lachenmann, A. (2008). Prototyping sensor-actuator networks for home automation. In *Proceedings of the Workshop on Real-World Wireless Sensor Networks, REALWSN'08*. ACM.

Jmal, M. W., Guidara, H., & Abid, M. (2010). A cryptographic processor design for WSN based on open sources. In *Proceedings of the 11th International Conference on Sciences and Techniques of Automatic Control & Computer Engineering (STA)*. Monastir, Tunisia: STA.

Jmal, M. W., Guidara, H., & Abid, M. (2012). Key management of wireless sensor networks - Design and implementation on FPGA. *International Journal on Sciences and Techniques of Automatic Control & Computer Engineering*. ISSN 1737-7749

Jmal, M. W., Kaaniche, W., & Abid, M. (2011). Memory cache optimization for a digital signature program: Case study. In *Proceedings of the 8th International Multi-Conference on Systems, Signals and (IEEE SSD'2011)*. Monastir, Tunisia: IEEE.

Jun, H. B., & Suh, H. W. (2009). Decision on the memory size of embedded information systems in an ubiquitous maintenance environment. *Computers & Industrial Engineering, 56*, 444–445. doi:10.1016/j.cie.2008.07.006.

Kaaniche, W., & Masmoudi, M. (2008). A signing message architecture development for smart card chip based on open sources. *The Open Electrical and Electronic Engineering Journal, 2*, 66–71. doi:10.2174/1874129000802010066.

Kimura, N., & Shahram, L. (2005). A survey on data compression in wireless sensor networks. In *Proceedings of the International Conference on Information Technology: Coding and Computing (ITCC 2005)*, (Vol. 2, pp. 8–13). ITCC.

Lu, Q., Luo, W., Wanga, J., & Chen, B. (2008). Low-complexity and energy efficient image compression scheme for wireless sensor networks. *Computer Networks, 52*, 2594–2603. doi:10.1016/j.comnet.2008.05.006.

Moussaoui, O. (2007). Efficient saving in wireless sensor networks through hierarchical-based clustering. In *Proceedings of the International IEEE Global Information Infrastructure Symposium*. Marrakeche, Morocco: IEEE.

Naumowicz, T., Freeman, R., & Schiller, J. (2008). Autonomous monitoring of vulnerable habitats using a wireless sensor network. In *Proceedings of the Workshop on Real-World Wireless Sensor Networks, REALWSN'08*. Glasgow, UK: REALWSN.

Chapter 16
Hybrid FlexRay/CAN Automotive Networks

Rodrigo Lange
Federal University of Santa Catarina, Brazil

Rômulo Silva de Oliveira
Federal University of Santa Catarina, Brazil

ABSTRACT

In recent years, the automotive industry has witnessed an exponential growth in the number of vehicular embedded applications, leading to the adoption of distributed implementations for systems in the powertrain and chassis domains. The Controller Area Network (CAN) protocol has been a de facto standard for intra-vehicular communications, while the FlexRay Communication System is being promoted as the future de facto standard for network interconnections of applications related to X-by-wire systems. Due to the characteristics of CAN and FlexRay, the coexistence of both protocols in the same vehicle is expected, leading to the use of gateways to manage the information exchange between electronic control units connected to different network segments. This chapter describes the main characteristics of CAN and FlexRay protocols, surveying the literature addressing schedulability and time analysis in both FlexRay and CAN protocols. The chapter also outlines the state-of-the-art in research about gateways for intra-vehicular communication networks.

1. INTRODUCTION

In recent years, the automotive industry has witnessed an exponential growth in the number of vehicular embedded applications, leading to the adoption of distributed implementations for electronic systems in the various vehicular domains.

Among other factors, this growth is stimulated by new requirements for safety and performance defined by several countries in the last years, by the evolution of systems related to the user comfort and experience, and by the crescent adoption of X-by-wire systems (Navet & Simonot-Lion, 2008; Zurawski, 2005).

DOI: 10.4018/978-1-4666-3922-5.ch016

The diversification of performance, cost and dependability requirements for automotive systems has resulted in the development of different communication protocols to be used throughout the car. These protocols can be as simple as communication systems for the interconnection of sensors and actuators at low speed rate such as LIN (LIN Consortium, 2012). They can also be sophisticated high-speed networks oriented for multimedia or safety critical applications such as MOST (MOST Cooperation, 2011) or FlexRay (FlexRay, 2011).

For network communications within powertrain and chassis domains, the Controller Area Network (CAN) (ISO11898-1, 2003), a network protocol developed by Robert Bosch GmbH, is today the *de facto* protocol standard. But according to several authors, CAN is not suitable for the projected demands for performance, hard real-time and dependability constraints in systems such as those related to X-by-wire applications. Due to this fact, an alliance of manufacturers including BMW, Bosch and DaimlerChrysler has developed the FlexRay protocol to meet the expected requirements. FlexRay has been heavily promoted as the future *de facto* standard for in-vehicular communications.

However, since CAN is still suitable for several applications and has a relatively low cost, in the near future it is expected the coexistence of CAN and FlexRay in the same car. In this scheme, FlexRay may be used in new high-speed functionalities and/or as a high-speed backbone between network segments that use different network protocols. It is easy to see that this kind of network architecture imposes the existence of gateways to allow the communication between ECUs connected to different network segments (Figure 1).

Although the work in (Steinbach, Korf, & Schmidt, 2010) suggests that time triggered Ethernet (TTEthernet) (TTTech Computertechnik AG, 2011) is a suitable replacement for FlexRay,

in (Lo Bello, 2011) it is stated that FlexRay will likely to continue being used in the powertrain and vehicle dynamics management. Therefore, FlexRay/CAN gateways have a key role in future in-vehicular network systems, and its design must consider the characteristics of both FlexRay and CAN protocols (Alkan, 2010; Lorenz, 2008) (Lorenz 2008; Alkan 2010). There are gateway-related commercial products (for instance, Vector's Network Design toolset (Vector, 2012)), but despite the number of researches addressing CAN and FlexRay protocols, just a few works in the literature deal with the design and timing analysis of FlexRay/CAN gateways.

The objective of this work is to survey the literature related to the design and implementation of FlexRay/CAN gateways. To a better understanding of the problems related to the design of FlexRay and CAN networks, we will first present the main characteristics of FlexRay and CAN, also surveying the existing works about scheduling and timing analysis of both protocols.

The remaining of this chapter is organized as follows. In Section 2 we present the basics of the FlexRay Communication System, including a survey of works related to scheduling and timing analysis of this protocol. Similarly, in Section 3 are presented the basics of CAN protocol. In Section 3 are also summarized works related to CAN's scheduling and timing analysis. Section

Figure 1. Example of car network with gateways (based on Navet & Simonot-Lion, 2008)

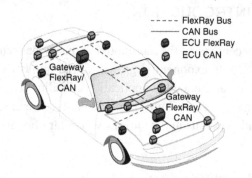

4 discusses FlexRay/CAN gateways. Finally, section 5 presents the conclusions and final remarks of this chapter.

2. FLEXRAY COMMUNICATION SYSTEM

The FlexRay Communication System is a two-channel digital serial bus for automotive applications designed to meet the demands of bandwidth, reliability, determinism and synchronization in vehicular systems with hard real-time constraints as, for example, X-by-wire systems. In order to meet these goals, FlexRay employs two communication channels with transmission rates up to 10 Mbit/s, and combines static and dynamic approaches for message transmission, incorporating the advantages of synchronous and asynchronous protocols (Nicolas Navet, Song, Simonot Lion, & Wilwert, 2005; Zurawski, 2005).

FlexRay was developed by the FlexRay Consortium, a cooperation of leading companies in the automotive industry, from the year 2000 to the year 2010. The FlexRay Consortium has concluded its work with the finalization and release of the FlexRay Communication System specification Version 3.0.1 that includes specifications for the protocol, the Electrical Physical Layer, Data Link Layer Conformance Test and Node-Local and Central Bus Guardian (FlexRay, 2011). In this section, we will present the basics of the FlexRay Communication System.

2.1. Main Characteristics of FlexRay Communication System

A FlexRay cluster consists of at least two Electronic Control Units (ECUs) with integrated Communication Controllers (CCs) interconnected by one or two communication channels.

The two FlexRay communication channels make it possible to configure a FlexRay cluster as a single-channel or dual-channel bus network, a single-channel or dual-channel star network, or in various hybrid combinations of bus and star topologies. Figure 2 shows some of the possible configurations of a FlexRay Cluster (FlexRay, 2011).

2.1.1. Frame Format

A FlexRay frame consists of three segments: the header, the payload, and the trailer. A FlexRay frame is illustrated in Figure 3.

The header consists of 5 bytes divided in 9 fields: a bit reserved for future use, a payload preamble indicator indicating if an optional vector for network management lies or not in the first bytes of the payload segment; a null frame indicator that indicates whether or not the frame contains useful data; a sync frame field indicating whether or not the frame is utilized for system synchronization; a frame indicator field indicating whether the frame is involved in the startup pro-

Figure 2. Examples of FlexRay topologies (based on FlexRay, 2011)

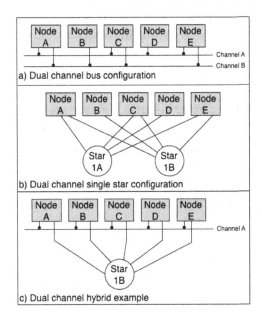

Figure 3. FlexRay frame (FlexRay, 2011)

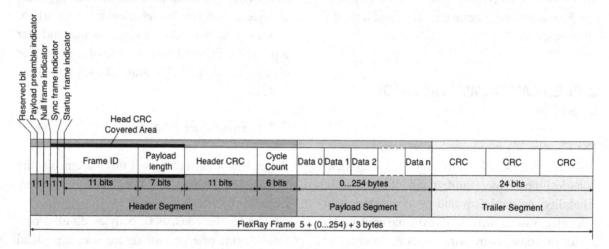

cedure or not; a frame ID field defining the slot in which the frame should be transmitted; a field indicating the size of the payload segment (payload length field); a header CRC containing a cyclic redundancy check code (CRC) and a cycle count field contains the node's view of the cycle counter *vCycleCounter* at the moment of the frame transmission (FlexRay, 2011; Navet & Simonot-Lion, 2008).

The payload segment of a FlexRay frame contains from 0 to 254 bytes of data divided into 0 to 127 two-byte words. The length of the payload segment may vary depending on whether the frame is sent in the static segment or in the dynamic segment of a communication cycle:

- If the frame is sent in the static segment, its payload length shall be fixed and identical for all frames, independent of the communication cycle or communication channel.
- If the frame is sent in the dynamic segment, its payload length may vary among different frames in the same communication cycle, among frames with a specific frame ID in different communication cycles and also among frames with a specific frame ID in different communication channels.

A FlexRay frame trailer segment contains a 24-bit CRC computed over the header and the payload segments. For more information on how to compute the CRC values please refer to (FlexRay 2011).

2.1.2. Timing and Clock Synchronization in FlexRay

Time in FlexRay is based on three timing entities: *microticks*, *macroticks* and *cycles*. An integer number of microticks forms a macrotick, and similarly, an integer number of macroticks forms a cycle.

Microticks are controller specific time units, and they are derived directly from the communication controller's oscillator clock tick. This means that microticks may have different durations in different controllers.

Macrotick is a time unit synchronized on a cluster basis and, within tolerances, its duration is the same for all nodes in the same cluster. The macrotick is composed by an integer number of microticks, but this number may differ from macrotick to macrotick in the same node due to the clock synchronization mechanism. The size of the macrotick (in μs) is given by the cluster wide constant *gdMacrotick*.

Finally, an integer number of macroticks forms a cycle, the static slots, and the minislots. The cycle is the basic element of the FlexRay media access control mechanism and will be addressed in Section 2.2.

A basic assumption for a TDMA-based system like FlexRay is that every cluster's node has approximately the same view of the global time. Due to environmental factors and/or production tolerances of the nodes timing sources, the internal time base can deviate from node to node, even if all the internal time bases are initially synchronized.

To ensure cluster synchronization, the FlexRay protocol uses a distributed synchronization mechanism in which each network node individually synchronizes itself to the cluster based on the timing of the transmitted sync frames from other nodes. This mechanism uses a combination of offset correction and rate correction. Offset correction is used to reduce the current local clock deviation and may shorten or extend the duration of a cycle. Rate correction is used to anticipate the clock's drift rate, and its value is added to the number of microticks per macrotick. A specific algorithm calculates offset and rate correction values in every odd cycle. If the correction values are within certain bounds, they are applied at the end of the cycle, during the NIT segment. Detailed information about the FlexRay Communication System can be found in (FlexRay, 2011).

2.2. FlexRay Media Access Control

The FlexRay Media Access Control (MAC) is based on a Time-Division Multiple access (TDMA) scheme, being the basic element of the FlexRay MAC the *communication cycle* (often referred as FlexRay Cycle, FC). The FC has duration in μs defined by the cluster wide constant *gdCycle*, and it is periodically executed from the beginning to the shutdown of the network. Each FC has a number that is controlled by the vari-

able *vCycleCounter*. This variable is incremented by one at the beginning of each communication cycle and ranges from 0 to *cCycleCountMax*. *cCycleCountMax* is a system constant whose maximum value is 63. When *cCycleCountMax* is reached, *vCycleCounter* is set to zero in the next communication cycle instead of being incremented (Zurawski, 2005).

Each FC is structured as a sequence of four segments: a *Static Segment*, a *Dynamic Segment* and two control segments, the *Symbol Window* (SW) and the *Network Idle Time (NIT)*. The FC is illustrated in Figure 4.

The FlexRay static segment (ST) is based on TDMA, and it is composed of an integer number *gNumberOfStaticSlots* of static slots that are incrementally counted from the beginning of each FC. Each static slot has the same duration, defined by *gdStaticSlot*. In a FlexRay cluster *gdStaticSlot* is a global value defined in the design phase. The ST arbitration is performed by assigning frame identifiers (*FrameIDs*) to each network node. In each FC, only the node that posses the *FrameID* that matches with the current slot number is allowed to transmit a message to the network. The FlexRay specification allows cycle multiplexing, which means that a node can use the same *FrameID* to transmit messages from different message streams, provided that the FCs are different. The ST provides a deterministic communication time, since we know exactly when a frame is transmitted in a given channel, thus providing a guarantee

Figure 4. FlexRay cycle (based on FlexRay, 2011)

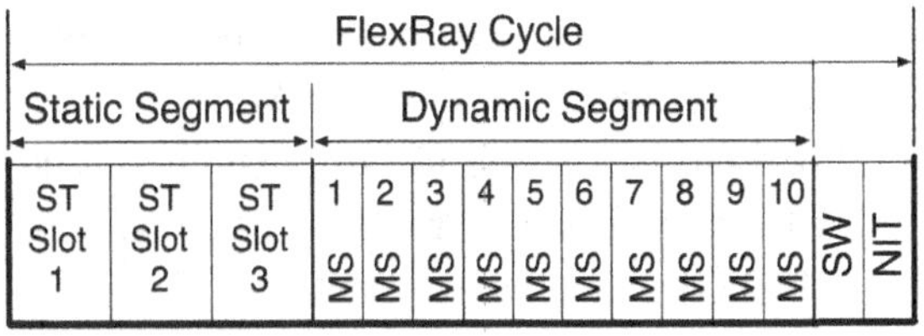

FlexRay Cycle															
Static Segment			Dynamic Segment												
ST Slot 1	ST Slot 2	ST Slot 3	1	2	3	4	5	6	7	8	9	10	SW	NIT	
			MS	MS	MS	MS	MS	MS	MS	MS	MS	MS			

of latency. It is mandatory to have each node connected to a FlexRay bus associated with at least one static slot (FlexRay, 2011; Zurawski, 2005)

In the FlexRay dynamic segment (DN), the transmission coordination uses a more flexible method, called Flexible-TDMA (FTDMA). In this method, the segment is composed of an integer number *gNumberOfMinislots* of so-called *minislots* (MS). Minislots have equal size *gdMinislot*, and frames are transmitted within dynamic slots that are superimposed on the minislots. As in the ST, each frame has its own identifier *FrameID*.

For each communication channel a node maintains a dynamic slot counter *vSlotCounter* and a MS counter *zMinislot*. The counter *vSlotCounter* is updated after the end of each dynamic slot and captures the *FrameID* of the current dynamic slot. The counter *zMinislot* stores the value of the current MS and it is updated simultaneously for both channels.

Each FlexRay node has a parameter *pLatestTx*, which represents the latest transmission instant in which the node can transmit in the DS. The value for *pLatestTx* is given by

pLatestTx=gNumberOfMinislots-aMinislotPerDynamicFrame+1

being *aMinislotPerDynamicFrame* the number of MS needed for the node's longest message (Schmidt, Alkan, Schmidt, Yuruklu, & Karakaya, 2010). When a node is allowed to transmit in a certain dynamic slot one of the following situations may occur:

- If there is no frame to transmit, and *zMinislot* haven't reached *gdNumberOfMinislots* (i.e., the end of DN), the dynamic slot has the size of only one MS.
- If there is a frame to be transmitted, and *zMinislot* has not reached *pLatestTx* of the node, the dynamic slot uses a number of MS large enough to accommodate the transmission.

- If there is a frame to be transmitted, *zMinislot* haven't reached *gdNumberOfMinislots*, but *zMinislot* has reached *pLatestTx*, the dynamic slot uses only one MS.

In the next two sections, the state-of-the-art in schedulability and timing analysis for both FlexRay segments will be surveyed.

2.3. FlexRay ST: Review of Relevant Work

This section presents relevant work addressing the scheduling and timing analysis of the FlexRay static segment.

The work presented in (Grenier, Havet, & Navet, 2008) deals with the problem of packing signals into frames that will be transmitted in the FlexRay static segment. The work considers the case where the tasks producing the signals are not synchronized with the FlexRay communication cycle. It also considers that signals are transmitted and received through AUTOSAR architecture. The work presents two algorithms to pack signals into frames. Both algorithms consider that the size and the number of allocated static slots are parameters to be minimized in order to save bandwidth. That work assumes that the length of the FlexRay cycle and the length of the static segment are known *a priori* and that they are not subject to optimization.

In (Ding, Tomiyama, & Takada, 2008) it is proposed an approach that uses genetic algorithms to find a feasible scheduling for the FlexRay static segment. That work considers that the period of the tasks and message streams in the system are integer multiples of the FlexRay cycle.

In (Lukasiewycz, Glafl, Teich, & Milbredt, 2009) it is addressed the problem of scheduling the FlexRay static segment in compliance with the AUTOSAR standard. That work proposes the use of a greedy heuristic to transform the scheduling problem into a special two-dimensional Bin-Packing Problem (BPP). The BPP is solved through an ILP formulation whose goal is to minimize the number of allocated static slots. The work considers that the lengths of the FlexRay cycle and the length of each segment are predefined.

An approach to define the schedule of the FlexRay static segment is presented in (Schmidt & Schmidt, 2009). Initially, it presents a discussion about the definition of the size of a FlexRay cycle. According to that work, all signals in a system must be scheduled in multiples of the size of the FlexRay cycle. In the paper it is demonstrated that it is favorable to choose *gdCycle* as the Greatest Common Divisor (GCD) of signal periods or an integer divisor of that value. The paper divides the problem of scheduling the ST in two subproblems. The first subproblem is the packing of periodic signals into frames to be transmitted in static slots. The second subproblem is the definition of a schedule for the static segment that minimizes the jitter and the number of allocated identifiers. For the first subproblem, it presents an ILP formulation whose goal is to maximize the allocation of the periodic signals from a given set into messages. This formulation considers, among other restrictions, that only signals with the same period can be packed in a message. For the second subproblem, it presents two ILP formulations, one for the case of a schedule without jitter and one for the case of a schedule with minimized jitter.

The work presented in (Schmidt & Schmidt, 2010a) is an extension of (Schmidt & Schmidt, 2009). The extended work proposes the use of the *FC repetition* as a parameter to capture the trade-off between the number of allocated static identifiers and the jitter. The work is based on the fact that FlexRay allows slot multiplexing, which means that messages generated by the same message stream do not need to be scheduled in every FC, but only in predetermined FCs that are identified by the value of *vCycleCounter*. Since *vCycleCounter* periodically counts from 0 to 63, only assignments that repeat every 1,2,3...64 FCs can be realized. The authors describe cycle multiplexing as *repetition*, and employ the term *offset* to denote the first FC among the possible

64 where the respective assignment starts. The repetition, offset and FrameID utilization are used in an ILP formulation whose goal is to assign an appropriate repetition for each message while achieving the joint minimization of the jitter and of the FrameIDs utilization. The work considers that the sizes of the FC, ST, DN and *gdStaticSlot* are given. It also considers that the packing of the signals into messages is defined *a priori*.

In (Haibo, Di Natale, Ghosal, & Sangiovanni-Vincentelli, 2011) it is presented a Mixed Integer Linear Programming (MILP) based framework to define signal to frame packing, frame to slot assignment, task schedule and the synchronization between signals and tasks in an AUTOSAR environment. The minimization of the allocated static slots and the maximization of the minimum laxity are the metrics for the MILP formulation. The proposed approach also assumes that the sizes of the FC, ST, DN and *gdStaticSlot* are given. That paper also presents a discussion about the two possible synchronization patterns between tasks and signals (synchronous and asynchronous) and their relation with AUTOSAR. Similarly, the paper makes several considerations about the choices that are possible when defining a FlexRay system, and the relationship between these choices and AUTOSAR.

In (Hanzálek, Benes, & Waraus, 2011) it is proposed a set of heuristic approaches to solve the problems of frame packing and scheduling for the FlexRay static segment in respect to AUTOSAR. The approach considers that the packing of signals into frames is made in an specific AUTOSAR module, not at the application level, as is done in (Grenier et al., 2008).

Common aspects in the above reported works can be highlighted. Some of the existing work considers that periods of signals or message streams are integer multiples of the FlexRay cycle (Ding et al., 2008; Schmidt & Schmidt, 2009, 2010a). Similarly, some of the proposed approaches assume that sizes of the FC, ST, DN and *gdStaticSlot* are provided, and therefore cannot be subject to further optimization (Grenier et al., 2008; Haibo et al., 2011; Lukasiewycz et al., 2009).

There is work assuming a strong synchronization between tasks, signals or message streams and the FlexRay cycle (Grenier et al., 2008; Haibo et al., 2011; Schmidt & Schmidt, 2009, 2010a). However, a solution addressing asynchronous scheduling could be of practical interest when considering the remapping of existing CAN message streams into FlexRay ones (Haibo et al., 2011).

Several of the above reported works employ an optimization technique (NIP, ILP or MILP) to define optimal sets of parameters (optimal in the sense that the resulting parameters are optimal for the given message stream set) (Haibo et al., 2011; Lukasiewycz et al., 2009; Schmidt & Schmidt, 2009, 2010a). But according to (Pop, Pop, Eles, Peng, & Andrei, 2008), optimization techniques are known to be computationally expensive, and can be unacceptable in practice due to their long computation times.

Finally, there is a common characteristic of all the reported works: signals or message streams are statically associated with unique static slots and unique FC repetition cycles, without any further optimization.

2.4. FlexRay DN: Review of Relevant Work

This section presents and discusses relevant works that address the timing analysis and the scheduling of the FlexRay dynamic segment.

In (Cena & Valenzano, 2006), the main properties of the Flexible-TDMA are analyzed. One of the main conclusions is the fact that FTDMA exchanges efficiency for flexibility, and this issue is even worst in FlexRay due to the maximum number of slots identifiers allowed in the dynamic segment.

The first attempt to model the FlexRay dynamic segment for the purpose of timing analysis is presented in (Pop et al., 2008). The authors show that to determine the worst-case transmission time of a dynamic message is a combinatorial problem that is similar to determine the number of "filled" boxes in the Bin Packing Problem (BPP). The authors consider that, in the case of FlexRay, the dynamic messages and the MS in a cycle are the items, one dynamic segment is equal to a box, *pLatestTx* is the minimum number of itens required to "fill" a box and there is a number of cycles (boxes) that are necessary to accommodate all items. The paper proposes two methods to solve the problem of calculating the *wcrt*, one that employs an ILP formulation, and another that is a heuristic that assumes a simplification in the MAC, to make it possible to solve the problem using existing approaches for the BPP problem. However, the work assumes that *pLatestTx* is defined for each dynamic message, instead of being defined for each node as stated in the FlexRay specification. This assumption can lead to optimistic results for the *wcrt* of the messages.

In (Hagiescu et al., 2007) it is proposed an approach to obtain upper bounds for the *wcrt* of messages transmitted in the dynamic segment of a FlexRay bus using Real-Time Calculus (RTC). According to that work, the commonly used RTC models for an offered service cannot be applied to the FlexRay DN due to the restrictions in the arbitration of this segment. The work presents a new model in which the lower service curve is algorithmically transformed to reflect the restrictions of the DN. The resulting lower service curve captures the minimum service provided by the dynamic segment and can be used with a component that computes the timing properties of a message.

In (Kim & Park, 2009), it is proposed a probabilistic delay model of message transmission in the DN, considering messages with variable lengths that share a same *FrameID*.

The work in (Hagiescu et al., 2007) is directly questioned in (Chokshi & Bhaduri, 2010) where it is shown that, due to simplifications in the method used to calculate the lower service curve, the previous proposal may lead to optimistic results. So, the work presents a new model to analyze the response time of data messages transmitted in the DN, also using RTC. This new model is based on the fact that the response time of a message consists of a waiting time and a communication time. That work also describes algorithmic transformations that must be performed on the service curves to allow them to be used in the proposed method.

In (Park & Sunwoo, 2010), it is proposed an optimization method to obtain optimal values for the lengths of the static slot and the communication cycle. The *wcrt* of DN frames are used as a criterion for the design of the FC. It is used a simulation algorithm that implements the principles of FTDMA to analyze the *wcrt* of the DN frames. However, the proposed algorithm does not implement key characteristics of DN, like the restriction imposed by *pLatestTx*.

The work described in (Schmidt & Schmidt, 2010b) questions the previous work presented in (Pop et al., 2008). The research presents a new ILP formulation that addresses the limitations of the previous work. According to this work, the method proposed in (Pop et al., 2008): 1) considers a fixed worst-case time interval for the analysis that has to be chosen properly, 2) requires a large number of variables, resulting in a complex ILP, and 3) does not enforce that consecutive FC have to be filled with higher-priority messages, which can lead to optimistic results for the *wcrt* of a DN message under analysis. The new formulation proposed in the paper deals with these issues. The paper also presents a scheduling algorithm to determine a feasible priority assignment for the messages of the DN, using the new ILP formulation. The proposed method considers that the set of dynamic messages is given.

To the best of our knowledge, to this date the above described papers represent the most important research addressing the scheduling and time analysis for FlexRay DN. None of them presents a universally accepted approach. It also can be noted that, due the complexity of the problem of dealing with asynchronous message streams in the context of the DN, all existing research relies on heuristics or in some optimization-based approach that use, for instance, ILP or MILP.

3. CONTROLLER AREA NETWORK (CAN)

The Controller Area Network (CAN) is a network bus designed to provide simple, robust and efficient communication for intra-vehicular communications. Since its introduction at the beginning of the 1980s, CAN became a *de facto* standard for automotive communications. Even though it was conceived for vehicular applications, through the years CAN began to be adopted in different application fields, being estimated that currently more than 400 million CAN nodes are sold every year (N Navet & Simonot-Lion, 2008).

CAN popularity, coupled with limitations of the original protocol, led to the development of new CAN-based protocols, such as the Time-Triggered CAN (TT-CAN) (Leen & Heffernan, 2002) or the Flexible Time-Triggered CAN (FTT-CAN) (Almeida, Fonseca, & Fonseca, 1999). This popularity is also reflected in the number of related work: a simple search using the term "Controller Area Network" in an index mechanism like the IEEE Xplore (IEEE - Institute of Electrical and Electronics Engineers, 2012) results in more than 3.000 entries pointing to papers related to CAN.

In this chapter, we will restrict ourselves to the CAN Specification Version 2.0. We also selected four papers that are considered relevant to the subject of this document, two related to the fixed priority scheduling of CAN messages and two related to the dynamic scheduling of CAN messages.

In the remaining of this section, we first present the CAN protocol basics, by describing the frame format and the MAC mechanism. Then selected works that address the scheduling and time analysis of the CAN protocol are presented and discussed.

3.1. CAN Protocol Basics

The Controller Area Network is an asynchronous multi-master serial digital bus with transmission rates up to 1Mb/s that uses Carrier Sense Multiple Access/Collision Resolution CSMA/CR to determine access to the bus. It is defined by the CAN Specification Version 2.0 (Bosch GmbH, 1991) and by the ISO 11898-1 (ISO11898-1, 2003).

The CAN specification defines two frame formats (the standard format and the extended format) and four kinds of frames (*data*, *remote*, *error* and *overload*). The layout of a standard data frame is shown in Figure 5, and each field of this frame will be described in the sequence. Due to the similarity between the four kinds of CAN frames, only the standard data frame will be described.

The first bit of a CAN frame is the *Start-of-Frame* (SOF), which indicates the beginning of a CAN data frame. This bit is also used to synchronize the receiving nodes. The SOF is followed by the *arbitration fields* that are the *identifier field* and by the *Remote Transmission Request* (RTR)

bit. The identifier field is a unique numeric identifier whose value determines the priority of the frame. It may be 11-bit in the standard format or 29-bit in the extended format. The RTR bit is used to discriminate between data and remote frames. The *control field* is a field that differs between the standard and the extended frame format. In the standard format, it includes the *Identifier Extension* (IDE) bit, which discriminates between standard and extended frames. Next to the IDE is the reserved bit r0. After the reserved bit comes the *Data Length Code* (DLC) which specifies the length in bytes of the data field. The *data field* is used to store the effective payload of the frame, and can contain up to 8 bytes of data. After the data field there are the CRC and acknowledge fields, and at the end of the frame comes the *End-of-Frame* (EOF) field that notifies all the nodes of the end of an error-free transmission.

The CAN media access control protocol employs a technique in which the physical characteristics of the medium are used to support a non-destructive bit-wise arbitration called Carrier Sense Multiple Access/Collision Resolution (CSMA/CR). In this arbitration scheme, nodes wait for the detection of a bus idle period before attempting to transmit. If two or more nodes start to transmit at the same time, by monitoring each bit on the bus a node can determine if it is transmitting the highest priority message and should continue, or if it should stop transmitting and wait for the next bus idle period before compete for the bus again.

Figure 5. CAN frame (based on Bosch GmbH, 1991)

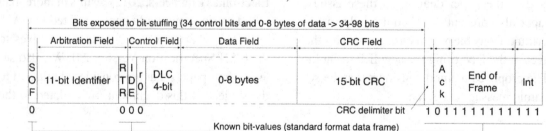

In order to provide a satisfactory degree of synchronization among the nodes, CAN rely on the so-called *bit stuffing* technique. In this technique, whenever five consecutive bits with the same logical level appear in a transmitted bit stream, the transmitting node inserts one additional stuff bit with the complementary value. The receiving nodes remove the stuff bits. The stuff bits increase the maximum transmission time of CAN messages and must be considering when calculating the worst-case response time of a CAN message (Davis, Burns, Bril, & Lukkien, 2007).

For detailed information about CAN and its characteristics please refer to (Bosch GmbH, 1991; ISO11898-1, 2003).

3.2. Scheduling and Time Analysis of CAN

As stated in the introduction of this section, there is a huge number of different approaches dealing with the problem of scheduling and time analysis of CAN. Due to this fact, in the remaining of this section we will resume four works that we considered most relevant to the subject.

It is considered that the schedulability and time analysis for CAN has started with the seminal work presented in (Tindell, Burns, & Wellings, 1995). That work showed that the worst-case transmission times of CAN messages could be calculated, allowing the industry to design CAN systems with higher network utilizations. But although the work has been cited by more than 400 subsequent papers, it was later found that the original schedulability analysis was flawed, and a new method was proposed in (Davis et al., 2007). The new work presents a set of equations for calculating the *wcrt* of CAN messages, and it is based on the equations for non-preemptive static priority scheduling (George, Rivierre, & Spuri, 1996) and on the concept of *busy period* introduced by (Lehoczky, 1990).

A priority assignment algorithm that assigns priorities to processes in a set is given in (Burns & Wellings, 2001). In that algorithm a procedure based in some *wcrt* technique tests if a process is feasible at a certain priority. The algorithm can be extended to assign priorities to CAN messages in a set with the use of the equations presented, for instance, with the method proposed in (Davis et al., 2007).

In the work presented in (Andersson & Tovar, 2009) the authors state that, since CAN's MAC implements non-preemptive fixed-priority scheduling, efficient real-time scheduling techniques such as Rate-Monotonic (RM) can be used when scheduling a CAN network. Based on this assumption, the authors use a set of equations for non-preemptive static scheduling to show that, under a RM scheduling, the maximum utilization bound for a CAN network that employs standard frame format is approximately 25%. For the extended frame format, it is approximately 29%.

Although CAN MAC is based on a non-preemptive fixed-priority scheduling scheme, some authors claim that the use of FPS to schedule the transmission of CAN messages will result in low bus utilization (Andersson & Tovar, 2009; Di Natale, 2000). Due to this fact, there are works in the literature proposing the use of dynamic scheduling schemes such as Earliest Deadline First (EDF) to obtain higher network utilization. But usually the authors agree that there are two major drawbacks that prevent the use of EDF with CAN in real environments:

- When using an EDF scheme, the priorities of the messages change dynamically, and it is necessary to continually update the ID field of each message to reflect these priorities, an action that can be infeasible in practice due to the processor overhead (Zuberi & Shin, 1995).

- EDF scheduling requires too many bits for the deadline representation in the ID field. Even if relative deadlines could be computed at each round, map the potential wide range of these relative deadlines to the small number of priority bits in the CAN ID field is not an easy task (Di Natale, 2000).

A method to deal with these drawbacks is presented in (Zuberi & Shin, 1995). In this paper, the authors propose to divide the message set in high-speed and low-speed messages, the first set to be scheduled using their *Mixed Traffic Scheduler* (MTS), a method that implements an approximation to EDF using time epoch, and the later set being scheduled using DM. Through simulations, the authors show that MTS performs better than DM and at the same level as EDF. However, in the simulations it is assumed an unrealistic workload model with a 10Mb/s physical medium, while the maximum allowed by the CAN specification is 1Mb/s (ISO11898-1, 2003).

In the work published in (Di Natale, 2000), the authors argue that the crescent computational power of the newest chips allows the implementation of true EDF to schedule the transmission of CAN messages, being the actual problems to be solved 1) the encoding of a possibly wide range of deadlines into a limited number of priority levels, and 2) the minimization of priority inversions. The work proposes the encoding of relative deadlines with a logarithmic scale, also presenting an algorithm to perform this encoding. The paper concludes by presenting a discussion on the proposed method regarding the processor overhead that is necessary to implement the dynamic encoding of message priorities at each contention round.

4. AUTOMOTIVE GATEWAYS

(Decotignie, 2005) and (Cena, Valenzano, & Vitturi, 2008) define the term gateway as a generic expression to describe a device for interconnection of hybrid networks that operates in the network layer or above. The networks interconnected by gateways can employ different communication protocols. Since the protocols often have different characteristics, a gateway often must deal with these differences.

According to (Lorenz, 2008), gateways for vehicular networks can be grouped into two categories: *hardware* gateways and *software* gateways. In this section, we give a description of existing architectures for automotive gateways. The first subsection describes architectures for gateways based primarily on software components, and the second subsection presents works with proposed architectures based mainly on hardware components.

4.1. Software Gateways

For a long time, there was not a standard for vehicular gateways. Many different vendors had their own implementations, usually incompatible with implementations from other vendors. In recent years there was an effort to standardize software architectures for automotive use. These efforts were motivated by the increasing complexity of automotive systems, and aim to improve the flexibility, scalability, quality and reliability of electrical/electronic (E/E) architectures.

Nowadays, there are several proposals of software architectures for automotive systems. However, to this date the best known architectures are the OSEK/VDX (Continental Automotive GmbH, 2012) and the Automotive Open System Architecture (AUTOSAR) (AUTOSAR, 2012; Lorenz, 2008).

OSEK/VDX is a real-time operating system (RTOS) that is a *de facto* standard for automotive ECUs. A consortium of German and French automotive industries has developed OSEK/VDX, and currently it is standardized by the ISO Standard 17356 (Lemieux, 2001). OSEK/VDX comprises standards for operating system (OSEK OS and OSEK/VDX Time-Triggered Operating System), communication (OSEK COM and OSEK/VDX Fault Tolerant Communication), network management (OSEK NM), implementation language

(OSEK OIL) and real-time interface (ORTI). But since OSEK/VDX is not designed for use on top of FlexRay, and since AUTOSAR includes a significant part of the OSEK/VDX specification, we will not extend the discussion about this standard. For further information about OSEK/VDX, please refer to (Continental Automotive GmbH, 2012; Lorenz, 2008; N Navet & Simonot-Lion, 2008).

4.1.1. Automotive Open System Architecture (AUTOSAR)

The Automotive Open System Architecture (AUTOSAR) has been proposed by a partnership of automotive manufactures and suppliers. This partnership works to develop and establish a *de-facto* open industry standard for automotive architectures (AUTOSAR, 2012).

In AUTOSAR, an application is modeled as a composition of interconnected components. A communication mechanism called "Virtual Functional Bus" (VFB) allows the interaction between components (upper half of Figure 6). During the design phase, components are mapped on specific system resources (ECUs). The virtual connections among these components are mapped onto local connections (within a single ECU) or upon network-technology specific communication mechanism, such as FlexRay frames (Figure 6, bottom half).

AUTOSAR uses a layered architecture that ensures the decoupling between the functionality and the supporting hardware or software services. For a single ECU, AUTOSAR defines an architecture with three layers: Application Layer, which is composed by "Software Components" (SW-Cs)

Figure 6. VFB view (based on Consortium, 2012)

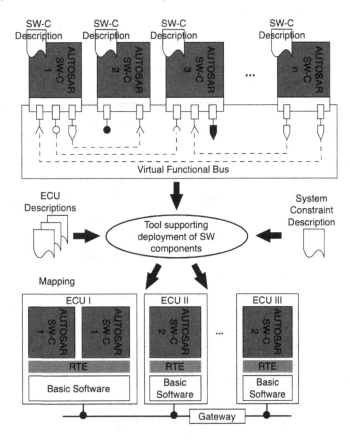

that encapsulate complete or partial automotive functionality; Real-Time Environment (RTE), which is the concrete interface between the SW-Cs and the remainder of the ECU system; and Basic Software Layer, which is standardized software that does not have any specific functionality, but offers hardware-dependent and hardware-independent services to the layer above (RTE).

The Basic Software Layer is composed by the Services Layer, the ECU Abstraction Layer, by the Complex Drivers, and by the Microcontroller Abstraction Layer.

The Services Layer offers operating system functionality, network communication and management services, memory services, diagnostic services and ECU state management. The ECU Abstraction Layer interfaces the drivers of the Microcontroller Abstraction Layer. Its parts are the *Onboard Device Abstraction*, *Memory Hardware Abstraction*, *Communication Hardware Abstraction* and *I/O Hardware Abstraction*. Complex Drivers implements complex sensor and actuator control with direct access to the microcontroller using specific interrupts and/or complex microcontroller peripherals. Finally, the Microcontroller Abstraction Layer is the lowest software layer in the Basic Software. The Microcontroller Abstractions contains the internal drivers, and it is composed by Microcontroller Drivers, Memory Drivers, Communication Drivers and I/O Drivers.

The Basic Software Layers are further divided into functional groups. An example of a functional group is Communication Services.

The communication within AUTOSAR is based on Protocol Data Units (PDUs). A PDU receives a prefix that varies according to the AUTOSAR layer. A message generated in a SW-C at the application layer is packed into an ISignalIPdu. An ISignalIPdu is packed into an Interaction Layer PDU (I-PDU) by the AUTOSAR COM module. If an I-PDU passes through the TP module, it is packed into a Network Layer PDU (N-PDU). The protocol interface sends Data Link Layer PDUs (L-PDUs) to the protocol driver. The protocol

driver sends the FlexRay frames to the bus. The full naming convention for PDUs can be found in (AUTOSAR, 2012). The path of a PDU through the VFB is defined during the design phase and cannot be changed during system execution. This means that the relationship between a PDU of one layer with a PDU of another layer cannot be modified during run time.

The Communication Hardware Abstraction (Comm HW Abstraction) is a group of modules that provide equal mechanisms to access a bus channel regardless of its location (on-chip/on-board). Comm HW Abstraction contains the FlexRay Interface (FrIf), which provides standardized mechanisms to access a FlexRay bus channel via a FlexRay Communication Controller. Comm HW Abstraction also contains the *CanIf*, which is the interface module for CAN protocol.

Communication Services groups the modules related to the in-vehicle network communication. They are interfaced with the communication drivers via the communication driver interface. AUTOSAR Specification 4.0 defines modules for FlexRay, CAN, LIN and Ethernet. Communication Services contain, among other modules, the *COM*, which provides routing of individual signals or groups of signals between different I-PDUs, the *FlexRay Transport Protocol* (FlexRay TP), which is responsible for the segmentation and reassembly of messages (I-PDUs) that do not fit in one FlexRay frame and the *CAN Transport Layer* (CanTp) which is the module between the PDU Router and the CAN Interface module.

Communication Services contains the PDU Router module, whose function is to route I-PDUs between different abstract communication controllers and upper layers. The PDU Router can perform gateway operations receiving I-PDUs from an interface module and transmitting them via the same or other interface module. Similarly, the PDU Router can receive I-PDUs from a transport protocol module and transmit them via the same or other transport protocol module. However, an I-PDU cannot be gatewayed between communication interface modules and TP modules. For example, an I-PDU cannot be received from CanIf and gatewayed to FlexRay TP. The PDU Router only route or gateway I-PDUs according to static routing paths defined during the design phase, and it is not possible to use dynamic routing.

4.2. Hardware Gateways

Implementing the gateway functionality in software has clear advantages, like standardization and high flexibility. However, software gateways usually have large memory and processor requirements, which is a disadvantage of the approach. For this reason, several authors present gateway solutions based mostly on hardware implementations (Lorenz, 2008). The proposed solutions take advantage of processors for automotive applications that have emerged in recent years. An example of these processors is the Freescale MPC5567 which have embedded communication controllers for FlexRay and CAN (Freescale, 2012). In the following, we will summarize the literature related to hardware-based FlexRay/CAN gateways.

The work in (Seo, Moon, et al., 2008) briefly describes a simple implementation of a gateway between FlexRay, CAN and LIN. However, the paper does not detail the gateway itself, nor explains how a message is converted from one protocol to another. It does not address important aspects such as global scheduling.

The work in (Seo, Kim, Moon, et al., 2008) describes a reliable gateway for in-vehicle networks that supports FlexRay, CAN and LIN protocols. The proposed gateway is based on the OSEK/VDX standard, and it uses information provided by the OSEK network management to obtain the status of destination nodes, automatically searching for alternative paths in the case of network faults. In the proposal, two mechanisms are used to determine a message transmission path: direct forwarding and routing. However, there isn't information in the papere on how the routing table

is constructed or how the mappings of messages are defined, and it doesn't deal with the timing or scheduling analysis of the system. The proposed architecture relies on Freescales's microcontrollers for automotive systems.

In (Seo et al., 2008), it is described an architecture for a fault-tolerant vehicular gateway. The work uses two Freescale microcontrollers to improve the reliability and fault-tolerance in the proposed architecture. A networked controller periodically checks the primary controller. The main focus of the paper is the description of the fault-tolerant hardware, and few details on network design are given.

A thesis about in-vehicular gateways is presented in (Lorenz, 2008). That work questions the feasibility of using software gateways like AUTOSAR in complex systems and proposes an architecture where the functionality of a gateway is partially or completely implemented in hardware. In the proposed architecture, the main functionalities of the gateway are implemented in hardware, but there is an interface to the gateway's software layer to allow its integration to existing software projects. In order to demonstrate the feasibility of the proposed architecture, the work describes the implementation in a FPGA micro-controller. The firmware of the micro-controller is generated considering network definitions described using configuration data formats. As in previous works, the focus of (Lorenz, 2008) is on the gateway hardware/software, and it does not address the overall design of in-vehicular networks that use different protocols.

The main focus of (E. G. Schmidt et al., 2010) is the study of the performance of FlexRay/CAN networks interconnected by a gateway. The paper considers the case of networks where nodes connected to a CAN segment use a gateway to exchange signals with other nodes that are connected to a FlexRay segment. Two tasks were implemented to realize the necessary protocol conversions, and it is proposed a method to map CAN signals to the payload of FlexRay messages, and vice-versa. Two performance metrics are investigated. The first is the basic operation of the gateway, which includes the correct protocol conversion, and the gateway processing delay that comprises the execution time of the related tasks. The second is the overall *wcrt* of a signal in the network. The paper also investigates the scheduling of the network, proposing a strategy in which firstly it is applied an appropriate scheduling method for the CAN segment and, if a feasible schedule is found, it is applied a scheduling method for the FlexRay segment considering the delay introduced by the gateway. Finally, the work evaluates the proposed method on a test bed composed by a gateway and several CAN and FlexRay nodes. This work, however, heavily relies on the previous methods proposed in (K. Schmidt & Schmidt, 2010a, 2010b).

Finally, the master thesis presented by (Alkan, 2010) describes a FlexRay/CAN gateway architecture mainly based on hardware. It reports how the test bed used in (E. G. Schmidt et al., 2010) was implemented.

4.3. Open Issues in the Design of Automotive Gateways

FlexRay and CAN are conceptually very different protocols. Among other differences, we can cite differences in the maximum payload length, in the bit rate and in the arbitration methods (Alkan, 2010). The project of an automotive gateway must deal with these differences, while considering that it is important to keep the end-to-end delay of a message (i.e. the time elapsed between the generation of the message and its receiving in the destination ECU) low. Due to the tendency of standardization of components in vehicular systems, it is important that a gateway is designed considering automotive standards like AUTOSAR.

Despite the number of existing proposals, to this date most of the proposed solutions for FlexRay/CAN gateways are implementations based on dedicated software, and to the best of our knowledge the only work that considers temporal requirements of messages is that described in (Alkan, 2010; E. G. Schmidt et al., 2010).

Based on the survey presented in this chapter, we can point some open issues regarding the design of FlexRay/CAN gateways:

- What is the impact of the constraints imposed by AUTOSAR when designing a gateway that respects the temporal restrictions of the signals of the system (deadline and periods)?
- Is it possible to use existing techniques for scheduling and time analysis proposed for both FlexRay and CAN in the design of gateways? The scheduling of streams proposed in (E. G. Schmidt et al., 2010) heavily relies on optimization techniques, but is it possible to use some heuristic method instead?
- What is the impact of the use of both FlexRay channels? To the best of our knowledge, existing papers consider only the use of one of the channels.
- Is it feasible to construct gateways with interfaces for more than one network segment (for instance, one FlexRay segment, one high-speed CAN segment and one low-speed CAN segment).

SUMMARY

The automotive industry has witnessed an exponential growth in the number of vehicular embedded applications. Due to the characteristics of those applications, there is an increasing adoption of distributed software architectures for the related systems, leading to the development and adoption of different network protocols.

Although there are protocols that are best suited to each vehicular functional domain, the CAN protocol is currently the *de facto* standard for network communications within the powertrain and chassis domain. But an expected increase in the demand for performance and reliability in automotive systems has led to the development of the FlexRay protocol, a digital serial bus for automotive applications heavily promoted as the future *de facto* standard for in-vehicular communications.

Since CAN is still suitable for several applications and has a relatively low cost, it is expected the coexistence of CAN and FlexRay in the same car for many years to come, resulting in a possible scenario where FlexRay will be used in new high-speed functionalities and/or as a backbone between network segments that use different network protocols. This kind of network architecture imposes the existence of gateways to allow the inter-communication between ECUs connected to different network segments.

In this work, we have surveyed the literature related to the design and implementation of FlexRay/CAN gateways, also presenting the main characteristics of FlexRay and CAN protocols with special interest in the scheduling and timing analysis of both protocols. We close the chapter presenting some open issues regarding the design of FlexRay/CAN gateways that can be investigated in the future.

REFERENCES

Alkan, M. (2010). *Interconnected FlexRay and CAN networks for invehicle communication: gateway implementation and end-to-end performance study*. Ankara, Turkey: Middle East Technical University.

Almeida, L., Fonseca, J. A., & Fonseca, P. (1999). Flexible time triggered communication system based on the controller area network: Experimental results. In *Proceedings of the Fieldbus Technology International Conference (FeT'99)*, (Vol. 99, pp. 24-31). FeT.

Andersson, B., & Tovar, E. (2009). The utilization bound of non-preemptive rate-monotonic scheduling in controller area network is 25%. In *Proceedings of the International Symposium on Industrial Embedded Systems (SIES)*, (pp. 11-18). IEEE.

AUTOSAR. (2012). *AUTOSAR specification release 4.0 rev. 3.0*. Retrieved from http://www.autosar.org/

Bosch GmbH. (1991). *Controller area network specification v2.0*.

Burns, A., & Wellings, A. J. (2001). *Real-time systems and programming languages: Ada 95, Real-time java, and real-time POSIX* (3rd ed.). Reading, MA: Addison Wesley.

Cena, G., & Valenzano, A. (2006). On the properties of the flexible time division multiple access technique. *IEEE Transactions on Industrial Informatics*, 2(2), 86–94. doi:10.1109/TII.2006.875510.

Cena, G., Valenzano, A., & Vitturi, S. (2008). Hybrid wired/wireless networks for real-time communications. *IEEE Industrial Electronics Magazine*, 2(1), 8–20. doi:10.1109/MIE.2008.917155.

Chokshi, D. B., & Bhaduri, P. (2010). Performance analysis of FlexRay-based systems using real-time calculus, revisited. In *Proceedings of the Symposium on Applied Computing*. IEEE.

Consortium, L. I. N. (2012). *LIN - Local interconnect network*. Retrieved from http://www.lin-subbus.org/

Continental Automotive Gmb, H. (2012). *OSEK/VDX portal*. Retrieved from http://portal.osek-vdx.org/

Cooperation, M. O. S. T. (2011). *Media oriented systems transport*. Retrieved from http://www.mostcooperation.com/

Davis, R. I., Burns, A., Bril, R. J., & Lukkien, J. J. (2007). Controller area network (CAN) schedulability analysis: Refuted, revisited and revised. *Real-Time Systems*. doi:10.1007/s11241-007-9012-7.

Decotignie, J. D. (2005). Ethernet-based real-time and industrial communications. *Proceedings of the IEEE*, *93*(6), 1102–1117. doi:10.1109/JPROC.2005.849721.

Di Natale, M. (2000). Scheduling the CAN bus with earliest deadline techniques. In *Proceedings of the 21st IEEE Real-Time Systems Symposium* (pp. 259-268). IEEE.

Ding, S., Tomiyama, H., & Takada, H. (2008). An effective GA-based scheduling algorithm for FlexRay systems. *IEICE Transactions on Information and Systems*. doi:10.1093/ietisy/e91-d.8.2115.

FlexRay. (2011). *FlexRay communications system protocol specification version 3.0.1*. Retrieved from http://www.flexray.com/

Freescale. (2012). *MPC5567: Qorivva 32-bit MCU for powertrain applications*. Retrieved from http://www.freescale.com/Webapp/sps/site/prod_summary.jsp?code=MPC5567

George, L., Rivierre, N., & Spuri, M. (1996). *Preemptive and non-preemptive real-time uniprocessor scheduling. Technical Report, INRIA*. INRIA.

Grenier, M., Havet, L., & Navet, N. (2008). Configuring the communication on FlexRay - The case of the static segment. In *Proceedings of the 4th European Congress Embedded Real Time Software (ERTS)*. ERTS.

Hagiescu, A., Bordoloi, U. D., Chakraborty, S., Sampath, P., Ganesan, P. V. V., & Ramesh, S. (2007). Performance analysis of FlexRay-based ECU networks. In *Proceedings of The Design Automation Conference (DAC)*, (pp. 284-289). ACM Press.

Haibo, Z., Di Natale, M., Ghosal, A., & Sangiovanni-Vincentelli, A. (2011). Schedule optimization of time-triggered systems communicating over the FlexRay static segment. *IEEE Transactions on Industrial Informatics*, *7*(1), 1–17. doi:10.1109/TII.2010.2089465.

Hanzálek, Z., Benes, D., & Waraus, D. (2011). Time constrained FlexRay static segment scheduling. In *Proceedings of The 10th International Workshop on Real-Time Networks*. IEEE.

IEEE. (2012). *IEEE Xplore digital library*. Retrieved from http://ieeexplore.ieee.org/

ISO11898-1. (2003). *ISO 11898-1: Road vehicles—Interchange of digital information—Controller area network (CAN) for high-speed communication*. International Organization for Standardization.

Kim, B., & Park, K. (2009). Probabilistic delay model of dynamic message frame in FlexRay protocol. *IEEE Transactions on Consumer Electronics*. doi:10.1109/TCE.2009.4814417.

Leen, G., & Heffernan, D. (2002). TTCAN: A new time-triggered controller area network. *Microprocessors and Microsystems*, *26*(2), 77–94. doi:10.1016/S0141-9331(01)00148-X.

Lehoczky, J. P. (1990). Fixed priority scheduling of periodic task sets with arbitrary deadlines. In *Proceedings of the 11th Real-Time Systems Symposium*, (pp. 201-209). IEEE.

Lemieux, J. (2001). *Programming in the OSEK/VDX environment*. CMP.

Lo Bello, L. (2011). The case for ethernet in automotive communications. *Tenth International Workshop on Real-Time Networks*, *8*(4), 7-15.

Lorenz, T. (2008). *Advanced gateways in automotive applications: Elektrotechnik und informatik der technische universität berlin*. Technische Universität Berlin.

Lukasiewycz, M., Glafl, M., Teich, J., & Milbredt, P. (2009). Flexray schedule optimization of the static segment. In *Proceedings of the International Conference on Hardware/Software Codesign and System Synthesis (CODES+ISSS)*. Citeseer.

Navet, N., & Simonot-Lion, F. (2008). *Automotive embedded systems handbook*. Boca Raton, FL: CRC Press. doi:10.1201/9780849380273.

Navet, N., Song, Y., Simonot-Lion, F., & Wilwert, C. (2005). Trends in automotive communication systems. *Proceedings of the IEEE*, *93*(6), 1204–1223. doi:10.1109/JPROC.2005.849725.

Park, I., & Sunwoo, M. (2010). FlexRay network parameter optimization method for automotive applications. *IEEE Transactions on Industrial Electronics*, *99*(1).

Pop, T., Pop, P., Eles, P., Peng, Z., & Andrei, A. (2008). Timing analysis of the FlexRay communication protocol. *Real-Time Systems*. doi:10.1007/s11241-007-9040-3.

Schmidt, E. G., Alkan, M., Schmidt, K., Yuruklu, E., & Karakaya, U. (2010). Performance evaluation of FlexRay/CAN networks interconnected by a gateway. In *Proceedings of the International Symposium on Industrial Embedded Systems (SIES)*, (pp. 209-212). IEEE.

Schmidt, K., & Schmidt, E. G. (2009). Message scheduling for the FlexRay protocol: The static segment. *IEEE Transactions on Vehicular Technology*, *58*(5).

Schmidt, K., & Schmidt, E. G. (2010a). Optimal message scheduling for the static segment of FlexRay. In *Proceedings of the Vehicular Technology Conference Fall (VTC 2010-Fall)*. Ottawa, Canada: IEEE.

Schmidt, K., & Schmidt, E. G. (2010b). Schedulability analysis and message schedule computation for the dynamic segment of FlexRay. In *Proceedings of the Vehicular Technology Conference Fall (VTC 2010-Fall)*. Ottawa, Canada: IEEE.

Seo, S. H., Kim, J. H., Moon, T. Y., Hwang, S. H., Kwon, K. H., & Jeon, J. W. (2008). A reliable gateway for in-vehicle networks. In *Proceedings of the 17th World Congress The International Federation of Automatic Control*. IEEE.

Seo, S. H., Moon, T. Y., Kim, J. H., Kim, S. H., Son, C. W., Jeon, J. W., & Hwang, S. H. (2008). A gateway system for an automotive system: LIN, CAN, and FlexRay. In *Proceedings of the 6th IEEE International Conference on Industrial Informatics INDIN*. IEEE.

Seo, S. H., Moon, T. Y., Kim, J. H., Kwon, K. H., Jeon, J. W., & Hwang, S. H. (2008). A fault-tolerant gateway for in-vehicle networks. In *Proceedings of the 6th IEEE International Conference on Industrial Informatics INDIN* (pp. 1144-1148). IEEE.

Steinbach, T., Korf, F., & Schmidt, T. C. (2010). Comparing time-triggered ethernet with FlexRay: An evaluation of competing approaches to real-time for in-vehicle networks. In *Proceedings of the IEEE International Workshop on Factory Communication Systems (WFCS)* (pp. 199-202). IEEE.

Tindell, K., Burns, A., & Wellings, A. J. (1995). Calculating controller area network (CAN) message response times. *Control Engineering Practice*, *3*(8), 1163–1169. doi:10.1016/0967-0661(95)00112-8.

TTTech Computertechnik AG. (2011). *TTEthernet specification*. Retrieved from http://www.ttagroup.org

Vector. (2012). *Vector informatik GmbH*. Retrieved from http://www.vector.com/

Zuberi, K. M., & Shin, K. G. (1995). Nonpreemptive scheduling of messages on controller area network for real-time control applications. In *Proceedings of Real-Time Technology and Applications Symposium* (pp. 240-249). IEEE.

Zurawski, R. (2005). *The industrial communication technology handbook*. Boca Raton: CRC Press. doi:10.1201/9781420037821.

KEY TERMS AND DEFINITIONS

Automotive Open System Architecture (AUTOSAR): A standard architecture for embedded vehicular systems.

Controller Area Network (CAN): A network protocol that is a de facto standard adopted by the automotive industry.

Dynamic Segment: A component of the FlexRay cycle that uses the Flexible-Time Division Multiple Access to coordenate network transmission.

FlexRay: A network protocol for automotive systems specifically developed to meet the performance demands expected by x-by-wire systems.

Gateway: A network device capable of joining together two networks that use different base protocols.

Hybrid Network: A data network composed by segments that use different base protocols.

Static Segment: A component of the FlexRay cycle that uses the Time Division Multiple Access to coordinate network transmission.

Timing Analysis: Method of computing the expected timing of a software and/or hardware system.

Chapter 17
Emerging Technologies for Industrial Wireless Sensor Networks

Ivanovitch Silva
Federal University of Rio Grande do Norte, Brazil

Luiz Affonso Guedes
Federal University of Rio Grande do Norte, Brazil

Paulo Portugal
University of Porto, Portugal

ABSTRACT

The evolution of industrial networks can be summarized as a constant battle to define the universal technology that integrates field devices and applications. Since the Fieldbus wars in the 1980s, diverse wired solutions have been proposed. However, this scenario has been changing due to the introduction of industrial wireless sensor networks. In the last 10 years, the development of deterministic scheduling techniques, redundant routing algorithms, and energy saving issues has brought wireless sensor networks into the industrial domain. This new communication paradigm is governed by a de facto standard, the IEEE 802.15.4, and more recently also by the IEEE 802.15.5. However, there are signs of a new battle on the horizon with the new publicly available specifications of WirelessHART, ISA100.11a, and IEC 62601. In this chapter, to the authors analyze the advantages and drawbacks of these emerging technologies for industrial wireless sensor networks.

INTRODUCTION

In an automated system, the activities related to process control can be structured using a hierarchical model characterized by vertical and horizontal information flows. The former flows occur between entities in adjacent levels, while the latter occur between entities on the same level. These activities are closely related with the communications infrastructure that supports them, and therefore it seems natural to adopt a similar model for factory communications too.

DOI: 10.4018/978-1-4666-3922-5.ch017

Although the number of levels used to characterize the control structure can range from four to six, being usually dependent on the type of industry (e.g. manufacturing, process), it is usual to employ only three levels to characterize the communication architecture: factory, cell, and field. Each level employs different types of networks, whose characteristics result from the application requirements that operate at each level.

Factory networks cover the needs of higher levels. The main activities found at this level are related to production, process and materials planning, engineering, finance, and commercial applications. Descending flows are related to manufacturing orders and also to their scheduling. Upwards flows concern the status of manufacturing orders, production quality, and requests for acquisition of materials/resources. Information flows within this level are characterized by high volumes of data, but without critical time requirements.

Cell networks cover the needs of intermediate levels. A cell comprises a set of equipments which cooperate for the execution of a given task. The main activities found at this level are scheduling, sequencing, and execution of tasks. Other activities are related to data collection concerning the performance or status of product quality equipment. Information flows for the lower levels include execution orders or control programs. Information flows from these levels concerns the status and results of executed operations and are characterized by medium or low volumes of data with demanding timing requirements, which in many cases may be critical.

Field networks meet the needs of the lowest levels. The main activities found at this level are linked with the direct control of the process, particularly with the execution of control algorithms. The interface with the process is performed by means of sensors and actuators, many of them already fitted with complex processing capabilities (smart sensors). Information flows within this level

are characterized by small volumes of data with time critical requirements. Field level networks have specific requirements that result from the nature of the applications that operate at this level. These requirements include the support of periodic and sporadic data with real-time constrains, fault tolerance regarding equipments and data transmission, high reliability, and safety aspects.

The main differences between cell/field networks and office networks result from the limitations of the technologies and the application requirements. However, technological progress has led networks that were originally designed to be used in offices (e.g. Ethernet, WiFi) to industrial domains. To better understand this context it is necessary to consider the evolution of industrial networks, from the earlier technologies to the most recent ones.

WIRELESS COMMUNICATIONS IN INDUSTRIAL ENVIRONMENTS

The emergence of technologies for industrial wireless networks was a natural evolution of the legacy industrial communication technologies. The proposal to eliminate field wiring and use a new paradigm for data transmission in industrial environments is not recent. Lessard *et al.*(1988) developed one of the first works in this area in an attempt communicating industrial devices for infrared. According to colpo and mols (2011), the use of wireless equipment can reduce installation costs by 50–90% compared to scenarios where wired devices are used. Despite eliminating costs, industrial wireless networks still face many challenges. Some open issues are related to addressing, routing, managing devices with limited physical capabilities (energy, processing, memory, etc.), security and privacy, dealing with heterogeneous technologies, safety, and standardization. Other relevant issues to be analyzed are dependability requirements (reliability and availability), as faults may lead to system failures, which can result in financial losses, environmental damage, or putting people in danger.

The use of wireless technologies in industrial environments has always been viewed with great skepticism by plant managers. These concerns were created primarily by the unreliable nature of the communication channel. This was aggravated by the fact that equipments are installed in areas subject to the influence of external agents (noise, interference, adverse weather, natural obstacles), which can lead to higher error rates than when using wired technologies (Bai & Atiquzzaman, 2003). Other errors in the communication channel are due to signal attenuation (mainly caused by the loss of power due to the distance between the transmitter and receiver) and the problem of multiple paths (due to reflection, diffraction, and scattering of the transmitted signal, multiple copies of the data can interfere with one another constructively or destructively at the reception). In general, errors in wireless communications are transient; that is, the communication channel is bad for a time and then returns to normal. In an opposite way, communication errors in wired channels are usually permanent due to faults in cables, connectors, or other components.

Security is always an issue to consider when using wireless communications. As the communication signal is transmitted through the air, any device within range can receive the signal and eventually decode it. This could lead to problems of unauthorized access to sensitive information. In the end, unauthorized persons can take advantage of the absence of security measures to inject packets into the network in order to perform attacks or to steal information. Thus, it is essential to consider the use of security measures to avoid these problems (Chang & Chen, 2012).

Another challenge is related to the coexistence of different wireless technologies in the same area. Since the transmission medium is open, there may be situations where different technologies share the same frequency range. Thus, it is important that even when they coexist in the same environment, different technologies can operate without interferences.

Despite all these challenges, with the evolution of communication technologies, new mechanisms have been developed to ensure the reliability of wireless networks (modulation and coding schemes, deterministic scheduling, jumping frequencies, and redundant topologies), making them suitable for applications in industrial environments (Gungor & Hancke, 2009; Han, Zhu, Chen, Mok, & Nixon, 2011).

Based on the characteristics described previously, the remainder of this chapter concerns a description of the main wireless communication technologies for industrial environments, such as IEEE 802.15.4, IEEE 802.15.4, WirelessHART, ISA100.11a, and WIA-PA. It is important to stress the existence of other wireless technologies such as IEEE 802.11, WISA, and IEEE 802.15.4e. Because IEEE 802.11 is not a protocol focused on industrial processes it will not be described in this survey. Even though WISA has applicability to industrial environments, it is not considered a *de facto* solution. Actually, it is a proprietary solution, and for this reason it is not considered in this survey. Finally, the IEEE task group TG4e is developing a new standard specifically for industrial environments, the IEEE 802.15.4e. However it is under evaluation. It is expected that the standardization will be approved in late 2012.

IEEE 802.15.4

The Low Rate Wireless Personal Area Networks (LR-WPANs) were designed to support devices with limited physical features (low energy consumption, a communication range of a few meters, low power processing, and reduced memory), enabling the development of pervasive applications in diverse areas (forest fire and landslide detection, greenhouse and industrial monitoring, passive localization and tracking, etc.). When a LR-WPAN is designed for an industrial environment, it is called an industrial wireless sensor network.

The LR-WPANs are standardized by IEEE 802.15.4, which specifies the physical and data link layers. The IEEE 802.15.4 standard was initially approved in 2003; however, its more recent version was approved in 2006 (IEEE-802.15.4, 2006). It is considered a *de facto* standard for the wireless sensor networks.

Physical Layer

The IEEE 802.15.4 physical layer can operate in three distinct frequency bands: the 2450 MHz ISM band (worldwide) with 16 channels, the 915 MHz band (in the US only) with 10 channels, and the 868 MHz band with only one channel (European and Japanese standards). All of them use the Direct Sequence Spread Spectrum (DSSS) access mode. Signaling in the 2450 MHz band is based on Orthogonal Quadrature Phase Shift Keying (O-QPSK) while the 868/915 MHz bands rely on Binary Phase Shift Keying (BPSK). The throughputs of the bands are 250 kbps, 40 kbps, and 20 kbps, respectively. Besides, management of the physical layer, services include the activation and deactivation of the radio transceiver, Energy Detection (ED) within the current channel, Link Quality Indication (LQI) for received packets, Clear Channel Assessment (CCA) for carrier sense multiple access with collision avoidance (CSMA-CA), channel frequency selection, and data transmission and reception. The main features present in the IEEE 802.15.4 physical layer are summarized in Table 1.

Although the physical layer can support three frequency bands, the 2450 MHz ISM band is by far the most frequently used. The use of this band generates a coexistence problem in the sense that other wireless technologies also employ the same frequency band (e.g. IEEE 802.11 and Bluetooth). In relation to coexistence with the IEEE 802.11 devices, it is possible to carry out configuration until there are four non-overlapping IEEE 802.15.4 channels. Obviously, as only four channels are available in this scenario, it is expected that the transmissions have a higher probability of suffering interference than a scenario where 16 channels are available (Angrisani, Bertocco, Fortin, & Sona, 2008). On the other hand, a minor impact is expected when coexistence with Bluetooth devices is considered, because in the Bluetooth standard the frequency band is modified 1600 times per second. Thus, it is more likely that the interferences occur in the first transmission attempts. However, an efficient retransmission mechanism can be implemented in the IEEE 802.15.4 to mitigate this interference (Young, Seong, Choi, & Hyun, 2007).

Data Link Layer

The data link layer provides medium access control to the IEEE 802.15.4 devices. In this protocol, the network was designed to operate in a centralized way where a special device, the PAN (Personal Area Network) coordinator, controls all the communication mechanisms, including the medium access control.

A device can access the medium, listening for beacon messages sent by the network coordinator. After receiving a beacon message, the device transmits data using a superframe structure. The superframe structure is divided into two parts:

Table 1. Main features present in the IEEE 802.15.4 physical layer

Features	IEEE 802.15.4 Physical Layer
Frequency bands	868 MHz (1 channel)
	915 MHz (10 channels)
	2450 MHz (16 channels)
Channel width	2 MHz
Throughput	250 kbps, 40 kbps, and 20 kbps
Modulation	O-QPSK, BPSK and ASK
Communication range	100 m to 200 m
Transmission power	0 dBm

the active and inactive periods. During the active period, the medium can be accessed with or without contention. Devices that wish to communicate during the Contention Access Period (CAP) must compete with other devices using a slotted CSMA-CA mechanism. On the other hand, a Contention Free Period (CFP) can be used for applications with restrictive requirements. Due to protocol limitations, the CFP has support for only seven time slots. Finally, the inactive period of the superframe can be used by the devices to configure an operation mode with low energy consumption and consequently increase the network lifetime (assuming that the devices are battery powered).

Another means of medium access is to use the unslotted CSMA-CA. In this mechanism, beacon messages are not used. Thus, a lower energy consumption is expected. However, as the devices are not synchronized the amount of packet collisions must increase.

Beyond the medium access control, the data link layer is also concerned with defining the types of devices and the network topology. In this way, it defines two types of devices: Reduced-Function Devices (RFDs) and Full-Function Devices (FFDs). An RFD has limited capabilities and its communications are restricted to an FFD. On the other hand, an FFD has a complete implementation of IEEE 802.15.4, enabling communication with other FFDs or an RFD. The network coordinator, for example, is an FFD. Based on these types of devices, the data link layer can organize the network as a star topology or a peer-to-peer topology.

Table 2 summarizes the main features present in the IEEE 802.15.4 data link layer.

IEEE 802.15.5

The IEEE 802.15.5 standard was created to provide resilient mesh topologies for the WPANs (IEEE-802.15.5, 2009). The resilient mesh topologies are implemented in the network layer whereas the physical and data link layers are based on IEEE 802.15.4.

The adoption of a mesh topology can improve the network reliability in the sense that redundant paths between the field devices and the network coordinator are configured. If the primary path fails, a redundant path can be used to guarantee the delivery of messages. Another advantage of the use of mesh topology is related to the expansion of the network. Devices can be placed as far as possible of network coordinator such multiple hops can be used. Thus, the devices are not limited to being configured as neighbors of the network coordinator.

For the services provided by the IEEE 802.15.5 standard, it is important to emphasize unicast and multicast communications, which are procedures to configure groups of devices and operation modes with low energy consumption. In the following, each service will be described in detail.

Unicast Communication

Communication between two single devices is known as unicast. According to the IEEE 802.15.5 standard, the basis for unicast communication is the mapping of a hierarchical tree structure. When the first device joins the network, it is considered the root of the tree. Then, when a new device is joined in the network, it will be subordinate to the root device. After the joining process, the new device is configured as a branch and it is possible

Table 2. Main features present in the IEEE 802.15.4 data link layer

Features	IEEE 802.15.4 Data Link Layer
Medium access control	Slotted CSMA-CA
	Unslotted CSMA-CA
	Contention free period
QoS	Limited to 7 time slots
Packet (payload)	127 bytes
Network topology	Star or peer-to-peer
Superframe duration	15.36ms to 251s

to receive new join requests, generating the whole structure of the tree.

After the network formation problem has been completed, the root device (network coordinator) will execute the address assignment. This mechanism is based on the demand of each branch. Devices can be configured to operate as a root of a branch. Thus, the address demand of each branch can be known *a priori*. Foreseeing the expansion of the network, the root device provides an address block beyond the demand of each branch. This procedure avoids the transmission of flooding messages to address assignment.

Beyond the information related to the hierarchical tree structure, each network device keeps a two-hop neighbor list composed of devices which are up to two hops away from it. The neighbor list is updated during the address assignment upon receiving a HELLO message. The presence of the neighbor list is essential to generate resilient paths in the mesh-tree topology.

Multicast Communication

Multicast communication is used when a message is sent to a group of devices simultaneously in a single transmission. The IEEE 802.15.5 standard relies on the logical tree structure used in unicast communication to generate multicast communication. Therefore, a multicast tree structure can be generated without flooding the network with join requests (Lee et al., 2010).

The multicast protocol is managed by five entities whose functions are described below:

- **Mesh Coordinator (MC):** The root device (network coordinator). It is responsible for keeping all information about the multicast groups in the network (coordinators of groups and members);
- **Group Member (GM):** An active device that is participating in a multicast group. A GM should relay any message whose destination is its multicast group. It is pos-

sible to configure a GM to participate in multiple groups;
- **Router (RT):** A device used to relay multicast messages. An RT is not a GM;
- **Multicast Agent (MA):** A special device used to provide multicast functionalities for resource-constrained devices;
- **Group Coordinator (GC):** A device that controls a multicast group.

When a device wishes to join a multicast group it must firstly check its neighbor list and verify whether there is any configured GM. The device must choose the closest GM. If no GM is configured in its neighbor list then a request must be sent to the GC. If the GC is unknown, the request is relayed to the MC, which will forward the request to a respective GC. The GC is responsible for replying to the request. Only after receiving a reply from the GC does the device become a GM.

Messages of a multicast group are forwarded depending on the status of devices. If a device is a GM or RT of a multicast group then it relays messages by broadcasting; otherwise it drops all of them. In the low energy consumption mode, some constrained devices can only join or leave a multicast group. Forwarding messages is forbidden for these devices.

Low Energy Consumption Mode

To increase the battery lifetime of devices, an efficient energy consumption mode must be adopted. The IEEE 802.15.5 standard provides two energy saving modes: Asynchronous Energy Saving (ASES) and Synchronous Energy Saving (SES). Both modes are designed to operate in non-beacon mode (IEEE 802.15.4), where the active period and the inactive period can be configured for flexible mesh communications.

In the ASES mode, the devices are configured (similarly to beacon mode in IEEE 802.15.4) with a time structure composed of an active and an inactive period. However, the active period of devices is not synchronized. Wakeup notification (WN) messages are sent at the beginning of the active period to signal the activation of the device. After receive a WN message, pending data can be transmitted to the source of the WN message. On the other hand, in the SES mode all devices should be synchronized network-wide. Additionally, the SES mode defines two communication operations. In the former, the devices are configured to switch to the sleep mode during the inactive period, whereas in the latter the devices can also use the inactive period for transmissions.

WIRELESSHART

WirelessHART is an industrial wireless communication standard developed by the Hart Communication Foundation (HCF) with the goal of transmitting hart messages without the legacy transmission means (4-20ma or rs484). A WirelessHART device implements the same command structure as a Hart device. Thus, a WirelessHART network is limited to the applications supported by a traditional Hart network. In September 2008, the WirelessHART standard (Hart 7.1) was approved by the International Electrotechnical Commission (IEC) as a publicly available specification (IEC 62591). WirelessHART was the first industrial wireless communication technology to attain this level of international recognition. The final version of the WirelessHART standard was approved at the beginning of 2010 (IEC-62591, 2010).

WirelessHART defines eight types of devices: network manager, network security, gateway, access point, field device, adapter, router, and handheld device. All devices that are connected to the wireless network implement basic mechanisms to support network formation, maintenance, routing, security, and reliability.

Field devices are the most basic WirelessHART devices. They are directly connected to the process and plant equipments. Field devices can transmit measurement data and receive and forward packets to and from any device. Usually they can be line, loop, or battery powered. Compatibility with legacy HART devices is guaranteed through the use of adapter devices. The adapter devices are not directly connected to the plant equipment; however, they have to support the same functionalities as field devices. On the other hand, handheld devices are used during the network's installation, configuration, and maintenance phases. They do not support routing mechanisms.

Router devices are used for routing purposes, that is, forwarding packets from one device to another. They are not directly connected to the industrial process, and thus they can be installed anywhere in the plant. Their use is not really necessary since field devices have internal routing capabilities. However, router devices can provide redundant paths to the gateway, and they can also minimize energy consumption in field devices. The gateway works as a sink point for all wireless traffic and provides the connection between the plant automation network and the wireless network. The logical communication between the gateway and the wireless network occurs through access points installed in the gateway. The amount of access points can be configured to increase redundancy and to improve the effective network throughput.

The security manager is the entity responsible for ensuring the security over the network. It provides services such as joining and network and session keys for all devices. These keys are used to authenticate and encrypt data. The storage and management of keys are also under the responsibility of the security manager. The core of the WirelessHART is the network manager. It is logically connected to the gateway and manages the entire network. The communication between the network manager and the network devices occurs through the application layer protocol. The main duties of the network manager are related to scheduling, management of the device list, routing (redundant paths), collecting information about performance, failure detection, and network formation.

The WirelessHART standard uses an architecture based on a limited version of the OSI model, where only five layers are defined. In the next sections, the main features of each layer of its architecture will be described in more detail.

Physical Layer

The physical layer defined in the WirelessHART standard is based on IEEE 802.15.4. Thus, a WirelessHART radio has the same transmission rates, modulations, and communication ranges as an IEEE 802.15.4 radio. The exceptions occur in the number of channels available and the assessment of the carrier. Due to regulatory restrictions in some countries only 15 channels (11 to 25) are supported (channel 26 is no longer supported). In relation to assessment of the carrier, although IEEE 802.15.4 supports three modes of CCA (Clear Channel Assessment), in the WirelessHART standard only CCA mode 2 is used. This means that a device only identifies a busy channel if the sensed signal has the same properties as an IEEE 802.15.4 signal.

Data Link Layer

The WirelessHART data link layer provides important mechanisms for the operation of the network, for example scheduling, QoS (Quality of Service), and information about the network topology.

The Medium Access Control (MAC) is based on a TDMA (Time Division Multiple Access) communication mechanism that uses superframes. Superframes are composed of slots, and the amount of slots indicates its periodicity. To support multiple schedule requirements, a WirelessHART network can use multiple superframes with different numbers of slots. Each slot has a fixed duration of 10 ms, which is enough time to transmit a packet and receive an acknowledgment (the maximum packet size is 133 bytes, including headers). Slots can be dedicated or shared. In general, the dedicated slot approach is used. Shared slots are basically used to transmit retries and advertising indication during the joining procedure. A slot supports up to 15 channels; thus, theoretically 15 devices can transmit simultaneously in the same time slot. Unlike IEEE 802.15.4, the WirelessHART standard uses a mechanism of frequency hopping and a channel blacklist to minimize the influence of noise/interference in the network operation and consequently to increase the communication reliability. Note that the scheduling is configured by the network manager during the joining process of a device. Eventually, the scheduling can be updated if a device fails, leaves the network, or changes the transmission interval. Thus, each device is configured with tables indicating the time and the operation (transmission or reception) to be conducted.

Regarding QoS issues, the data link layer defines four priority levels according to the type of packet: command, data, normal, and alarm. The lowest priority is assigned to the alarms to avoid flooding messages over the network. On the other hand, command messages have the highest priority to guarantee operations in critical situations.

Finally, the data link layer is also responsible for updating the network layer about the structure of the network. Each device periodically sends information to the gateway about neighbors, number of messages successfully transmitted, link quality indication, battery level, and other statistical data.

Network and Transport Layers

The network layer defined in the WirelessHART standard is the convergence point with the HART standard. The main duties of this layer are related with routing, address assignment, and end-to-end security. On the other hand, the transport layer performs only a few functions, of which the main one is related to the end-to-end reliability.

One of the most important features supported by the WirelessHART standard is the resilient mesh topology. The main advantage of this type of topology is that it offers the possibility of using redundant paths between the field devices and the gateway. In this sense, the WirelessHART standard defines two routing protocols: source routing and graph routing. The former relies on a static path configured in the current packet whereas the latter uses a graph data structure to create primary and secondary paths (more resilient). Both approaches are configured by the network manager. There are two more routing approaches, superframe and proxy routing; however, they are particular cases of graph routing.

Application Layer

Traditionally, as an OSI application layer, this layer in the WirelessHART standard provides a high level interface for users to access the network information. Additionally, it provides a mechanism for the fragmentation/reassembly of data beyond that inherent in the features of legacy technology (HART), where all the procedures are command-oriented. According to the WirelessHART standard, the commands are classified as follows:

- **Universal Commands:** Defined by the IEC and must be compatible with all WirelessHART and hart devices;
- **Common Practices Commands:** Created to maintain interoperability between different manufacturers;
- **Private Commands:** Used only during the manufacturing process;
- **Device Families Commands:** Depending on the type of sensor used;
- **Device-Specific Commands:** Defined by manufacturers specifically for each type of device. These commands are outside of the hart standard; however, they must conform to the requirements of devices.

ISA100.11A

In 2009, the International Society of Automation (ISA) approved a wireless mesh networking standard known as ISA100.11a. In 2011, the International Electrotechnical Commission (IEC) created a task force to approve ISA100.11a as a publicly available specification. Currently, the ISA100.11a standard is named in the draft version as IEC/PAS 62734 (IEC-62734, 2012).

Differently from the WirelessHART standard, whose development was based on a specific technology (HART), the ISA100.11a standard was designed based on the user application requirements. The main goals of the ISA100.11a standard are related to guaranteeing the deterministic communication latency while increasing the communication reliability. It focuses on process control and monitoring applications, with latency requirements of around 100 ms. ISA 100.11a can coexist with other wireless technologies such as cell phones, IEEE 802.11, IEEE 802.15, and IEEE 802.16, and can provide tunneling for legacy protocols (HART, Foundation Fieldbus, Profibus, Modbus).

A typical ISA100.11a network may be composed of seven types of devices: gateway, system manager, security manager, router, backbone router, Input/Output (IO) devices, and portable devices. Each device has a specific role definition that controls its functions.

The IO device is responsible for monitoring the environment and it has no routing function. This limitation was configured to minimize the energy consumption. An IO device can also be portable, and in this case, its operation is limited to testing, management, and configuration of other devices.

The routing mechanism is conducted by two devices: the router and the backbone router. The former works as a proxy, forwarding the network data towards the gateway, whereas the latter is responsible for high level routing only between the gateway and the backbone routers. All traffic between the backbone routers is based on 6LoW-PAN (IPV6 over low power wireless personal area networks) (Neves & Rodrigues, 2010). Additionally, the backbone routers can segregate the network into subnets.

Similarly, to the WirelessHART network, an ISA100.11a network is centralized to three devices: the gateway, security manager, and system manager. The gateway device provides a connection between the wireless sensor network and the plant automation network. It is also responsible for guaranteeing the tunneling with the legacy technologies. Due to its importance, there is support for redundant gateways. The most important tasks are performed by the security manager and the system manager. The system security management function is controlled by the security manager whereas the system manager governs all the network, devices, and communications.

The ISA100.11a standard uses an architecture based on a limited version of the OSI model where only five layers are defined. In the next sections, the main features of each layer of the ISA100.11a architecture will be described in more detail.

Physical Layer

The physical layer defined in ISA100.11a is based on IEEE 802.15.4 and consequently it is very similar to the WirelessHART physical layer. Additionally, there is support for 16 channels (11-26); however, the utilization of channel 26 is optional. Differently from the WirelessHART standard, the ISA100.11a physical layer uses all the carrier sense modes.

Data Link Layer

The ISA100.11a data link layer has as its main feature the ability to define the Medium Access Control (MAC) mechanism. This is a basic feature present in all the data link layers based on the OSI model. However, the ISA100.11a standard differs from classical network architectures because it defines routing in the data link layer.

From the viewpoint of the data link layer, all the devices are organized using at least one subnet. In each subnet, synchronized devices communicate with each other using time slots, superframes, links, and graphs. The system manager is responsible for configuring each network device with

the structures necessary (tables) to perform the communications.

In relation to the MAC mechanism, the approach adopted uses a TDMA configured with a frequency hopping technique. Differently from the WirelessHART standard, where only one frequency hopping profile is used, in the ISA100.11a three frequency hopping profiles (slotted, slow, hybrid) are supported. In the slotted profile, each communication occurs in a different frequency following five patterns defined previously. The sequence used to choose the channels was defined to minimize the problem of coexistence with other wireless technologies (IEEE 802.11 and Bluetooth). On the other hand, in the slow frequency hopping the change of channels occurs only in specific periods (100 ms to 400 ms). This hopping profile is used by unsynchronized devices and commissioned devices. Finally, both features presented in the two previous approaches can be used to create a hybrid hopping profile. This technique is used to optimize the transmission of alarms and retries, for example.

Independent of the adopted frequency hopping profile, the communication between two devices occurs inside a time slot with a duration of 10 ms or 12 ms. An extended time slot (12 ms) was added in ISA100.11a to support the reception of multiple acknowledgment messages in sequence (duocast communication) and the prioritization of messages. Similarly to the WirelessHART standard, the time slots are classified as dedicated and shared. The former are used for unicast and duocast communications whereas the latter are used for broadcast communications. Additionally, the medium access control in the shared time slots is performed based on CSMA-CA.

As described previously, the data link layer is also responsible for routing. However, the routing between the field devices and the backbone routers is limited. The routing between the backbone routers and the gateway is performed by the network layer. The routing protocols used in the data link layer are based on graph and source approaches.

These techniques are the same as those used in the WirelessHART network layer. The unique difference is in the fact that an ISA100.11a network can organize the devices into subnets.

Network and Transport Layers

The network layer has the main responsibility for providing the routing mechanism to backbone routers. In the data link level, the routing is limited to subnets. On the other hand, when a message reaches a backbone router the routing from that point is conducted by the network layer.

Another function performed by this layer is the address assignment. Each device in the network layer has an address of 128 bits (6LoWPAN). The mapping between the 16-bit address (data link layer) and the 128-bit address is also performed by this layer.

Finally, in case a message has a payload higher than 127 bytes, the network layer is configured to fragment the message into smaller parts. The reassembly of the message is also performed in the network layer.

Regarding the transport layer, the main function that it supports is connectionless end-to-end communication. This service is an extension of UPD over 6LoWPAN (Petersen & Carlsen, 2011).

Application Layer

The ISA100.11a application layer is object-oriented. In this paradigm a device is designed to software objects. The application layer is responsible for the inter-object communication and the interoperability between legacy technologies (e.g. HART, Foundation Fieldbus, Profibus).

Basically, the application layer creates a "contract" with all the devices to provide scheduling, limited latency, and transmission of messages. In general, the exchange of messages between the field devices and the application layer follows a publisher/subscriber model or a client/server model.

IEC/PAS 62601: WIA-PA

In 2007, the Chinese Industrial Wireless Alliance (CIWA), under the urgent requirements of process automation, approved a new wireless communication standard, the WIA-PA (Wireless Network for Industrial Automation – Process Automation). In 2008, the International Electrotechnical Commission (IEC) approved the WIA-PA standard as a publicly available specification named IEC/PAS 62601 (IEC-62601, 2011).

A typical WIA-PA network defines five types of devices. The host application is used to provide high-level access to operators. The physical access between the plant automation network and the wireless network is conducted by the gateway. In relation to intra-network communication, routers are responsible for forwarding the messages towards the gateway. The field devices and the handheld devices are considered the most basic devices. The former are responsible for the monitoring of process variables whereas the latter are used during the commissioning of network devices. Additionally, a WIA-PA network supports redundant gateways and redundant routers. This mechanism allows the reliability of the network to be improved.

The WIA-PA standard supports three types of topologies: star, mesh, and mesh-star. The communication between routers follows a mesh approach whereas the communication between a router and field devices follows a star approach, similar to a cluster topology. Thus, from a high level viewpoint, a field device communicates with the gateway through a mesh-star network.

All communication over the network is centralized by two rules generally implemented inside the gateway. The first rule is called the security manager. Its duties are concentrated on all issues related to security (storage of keys, validation of messages, authentication, etc.). On the other hand, the rule called the network manager is considered the core of the WIA-PA network. This rule is responsible for controlling all the communications over the network, from the scheduling tables to the choice of communication channels.

Similarly to WirelessHART and ISA100.11a standards, the protocol stack defined in the WIA-PA standard is based on the OSI model. However, only four layers are defined. In the next sections, the main features of each layer of its architecture will be described in more detail. As the physical layer is totally based on IEEE 802.15.4, the description of this layer will be omitted.

Data Link Layer

The data link layer defined in the WIA-PA standard was designed to provide real time, secure, and reliable communications. It is based on the IEEE 802.15.4 data link layer with the improvement of some properties (frequency hopping, retransmission, TDMA, and CSMA).

The communication unit is the time slot. The duration of the time slot is configured according to the limits imposed by IEEE 802.15.4. A collection of time slots creates a superframe structure. Each superframe is repeated periodically at intervals proportional to the size of time slots used. It is possible to configure multiple superframes whose configuration is assigned to the network manager.

The data link layer assumes that the transmissions are beacon-oriented. The same procedure is used in the IEEE 802.15.4 data link layer. The joining process, inter-cluster management, and retransmissions occur in the CAP interval of the superframe where the medium access control is based on CSMA-CA. All other communications access the medium using a TDMA approach. During the CFP period, mobility devices are authorized to communicate with the cluster head (router). Note that the inactive period of the IEEE 802.15.4 superframe is also used for transmission in the WIA-PA superframe. It was divided into intra- and inter-cluster communications. The WIA-PA superframe also supports an inactive

period when the devices can minimize the energy consumption. However, it has a smaller size than the IEEE 802.15.4 inactive period.

To improve the network reliability, a frequency hopping mechanism was introduced to the medium access control. Basically, three hopping patterns are defined: Adaptive Frequency Switching (AFS), Adaptive Frequency Hopping (AFH), and Time slot Hopping (TH). The hopping pattern AFS is used during the transmission of beacons and CAP and CFP periods. In this pattern, all the devices use the same communication channel. If the channel suffers some interference (e.g. the packet loss rate increases) the network manager configures the devices to use another channel. On the other hand, the hopping pattern AFH is used during intra-cluster communication, where the changes of channels occur irregularly depending on the actual channel condition. Finally, the hopping pattern TH is used during inter-cluster communication, where the channels are changed per time slot.

Network Layer

The WIA-PA network layer is responsible for the following mechanisms: address assignment, routing, management of the life cycle of packets, joining and leaving of devices, fragmentation/reassembly of data, and end-to-end network monitoring. All the mechanisms are configured by the network manager.

Regarding address assignment, each network device has a 64-bit address in the physical layer whereas in the network layer the address has only 16 bits. These addresses are used in all communications (unicast, multicast, broadcast, intra- and inter-cluster).

The routing approach adopted is based on the network redundancy perspective. The network manager generates all routing tables after discovering the complete set of all neighbors of each network router. These tables are used to create a mesh topology where connections between routers and the gateway are made by redundant paths. Each device is configured to periodically transmit information about link failures, battery level, and the status of its neighbors to the gateway. Based on this information, the network manager can update the routing table of each device. Thus, the routing approach adopted can guarantee a resilient performance.

Another important functionality performed in the network layer is the fragmentation/reassembly of data. If a packet has a payload higher than 127 bytes it will be divided into smaller parts. When the parts reach the destination side, a reassembly mechanism is performed in the network layer.

Application Layer

The application layer defined in the WIA-PA standard is object-oriented. Devices and services are mapped to software objects whereas interconnections are managed by standardized methods. Beyond these features, the application layer is also responsible for providing the tunneling with legacy technologies, for example HART, Profibus, Modbus, and Foundation Fieldbus.

A COMPARISON OF INDUSTRIAL WIRELESS SENSOR NETWORK TECHNOLOGIES

The wireless sensor networks were designed to support devices with limited physical capabilities and resilient communications approaches. These networks enable the development of emerging industrial applications where the use of legacy wired technologies is difficult or impracticable, for example in tank farms, pipelines, distillation columns, wellheads, and rotation equipments (turbines and kilns). In this sense, all of the technologies described in the previous sections can be adopted as communication solutions for these emerging industrial applications. Thus, it is important to compare the main features of these technologies to aid the design of applications.

Considering the protocol stack, the more relevant information about the industrial wireless sensor network technologies is summarized in Table 3. All of them support a physical layer based on IEEE 802.15.4. However, implementation of the upper layers follows independent approaches. The WirelessHART, ISA100.11a and WIA-PA standards improved the medium access

Table 3. Protocol stack of industrial wireless sensor network technologies

Layers	Industrial Wireless Sensor Networks Technologies				
	IEEE 802.15.4	**IEEE 802.15.5**	**WirelessHART**	**ISA100.11a**	**WIA-PA**
Applications	–	–	Command-oriented	Object-oriented	Object-oriented
Transport	–	–	End-to-end reliability	UDP extension	–
Network	–	Mesh (energy saving mode)	Mesh (graph and source routing)	High level routing (backbone routers)	Star-mesh routing
Data Link	TDMA (limited), CSMA-CA, frequency hopping absent	IEEE 802.15.4	TDMA, CSMA-CA, 10 ms time slot, frequency hopping (1 profile)	TDMA, CSMA-CA, 10 ms or 12 ms time slot, frequency hopping (3 profiles), mesh (graph and source routing)	TDMA (IEEE 802.15.4 modification), frequency hopping (3 profiles)
Physical	2.4 GHz, 250 kbps	IEEE 802.15.4	IEEE 802.15.4	IEEE 802.15.4	IEEE 802.15.4

control protocol implemented in IEEE 802.15.4, highlighting the TDMA and frequency hopping approaches. Regarding the TDMA approach, the WirelessHART and ISA100.11 standards implement a similar solution with a flexible energy saving operation. Additionally, ISA100.11a implements a frequency hopping scheme more flexible than the WirelessHART standard. The TDMA approach implemented in the WIA-PA standard uses a modified version of the IEEE 802.15.4 superframe, where the energy saving operation is reduced.

As described in the previous sections, routing mesh protocols can be used to improve the network reliability. Regarding this issue, only the IEEE 802.15.4 standard does not support mesh routing. The IEEE 802.15.5 standard was developed exclusively to mitigate this limitation; however, the communications are limited for a beaconless scenario. The mesh routing implemented in IEEE 802.15.4 relies on a tree structure generated during the network formation. The performance of this structure in terms of huge scalability need be evaluated in more detail. On the other hand, the WirelessHART and ISA100.11a standards implement the same mesh routing algorithms (graph and source). Additionally, the ISA100.11a standard supports subnets. The segregation of the network is implemented by backbone routers. However, the specification of high level routing between the backbone routers is still an open issue. Finally, the WIA-PA standard uses a mesh-star routing approach where the field devices are organized in a cluster. From a high level viewpoint, a WIA-PA cluster is similar to an ISA100.11a subnet. Note that only in the WirelessHART standard is it possible for a field device to accumulate the routing function.

When considering a communication protocol it is also important to analyze the application requirements. These issues are found in the application layer. Only the WirelessHART, ISA100.11a, and WIA-PA standards implement the application layer. The WirelessHART standard was designed to perform only HART applications. Thus, its application layer is limited to commands supported by a HART network. On the other hand, a flexible object-oriented approach was developed in the application layers of ISA100.11a and WIA-PA standards. Thus, it is possible to use legacy applications (HART, Modbus, Foundation Field Bus, Profibus) over ISA100.11a and WIA-PA networks.

CONCLUSION

Industrial applications are known as a very conservative environment where reliability issues are always required. Adoption of new communication paradigms is viewed with great skepticism by plant managers. This context does not differ when considering the emerging industrial wireless sensor network technologies. In the last 10 years this technology has become sufficiently mature to allow its adoption in industrial environments. The main improvements are related to redundant routing protocols, real time scheduling, and efficient frequency hopping mechanisms.

In this chapter, the main industrial wireless sensor network technologies were described in detail. The features described in the chapter can be used to aid the design of applications to develop more resilient networks. From the standards mentioned, it is possible to note that they are all based on the IEEE 802.15.4 standard. The standards differ from each other when considering the upper layers.

From the commercial viewpoint, a wireless battle is on the horizon. Currently, WirelessHART networks dominate because the WirelessHART standard was approved first. However, ISA100.11a networks have more flexible features than WirelessHART ones, mainly those related with the tunneling of legacy applications, segregation of network (subnets), and more frequency hopping profiles. On the other hand, in the Chinese market it is expected that the WIA-PA networks will dominate. To increment the industrial wireless technology competition, the task group IEEE

802.15 (TG4e) is developing a new wireless standard specific to the industrial environment named IEEE 802.15.4e.

REFERENCES

Angrisani, L., Bertocco, M., Fortin, D., & Sona, A. (2008). Experimental study of coexistence issues between IEEE 802.11b and IEEE 802.15.4 wireless networks. *IEEE Transactions on Instrumentation and Measurement*, *57*, 1514–1523. doi:10.1109/TIM.2008.925346.

Bai, H., & Atiquzzaman, M. (2003). Error modeling schemes for fading channels in wireless. *IEEE Communications Surveys & Tutorials*, *5*, 2–9. doi:10.1109/COMST.2003.5341334.

Chang, K.-D., & Chen, J.-L. (2012). A survey of trust management in WSNs, internet of things and future internet. *KSII Transactions on Internet and Information*, *6*, 5–23.

Colpo, J., & Mols, D. (2011). No strings attached. *Hydrocarbon Engineering*, *16*, 47–52.

Gungor, V., & Hancke, G. (2009). Industrial wireless sensor networks: challenges, design principles, and technical approaches. *IEEE Transactions on Industrial Electronics*, *56*, 4258–4265. doi:10.1109/TIE.2009.2015754.

Han, S., Zhu, X., Chen, D., Mok, A. K., & Nixon, M. (2011). Reliable and real-time communication in industrial wireless mesh networks. In *Proceedings of the 17th IEEE Real-Time and Embedded Technology and Applications Symposium (RTAS)* (pp. 3–12).

IEC-62601. (2011). *IEC/PAS 62601: Industrial communication networks – Fieldbus specifications – WIA-PA communication network and communication profile*. International Electrotechnical Commission.

IEC-62734. (2012). *IEC 62734: Industrial communication networks – Fieldbus specifications – Wireless systems for industrial automation: process control and related applications (based on ISA 100.11a)*. International Electrotechnical Commission.

IEEE. IEC-62591. (2010). *IEC 62591: Industrial communication networks – Wireless communication network and communications profiles – WirelessHART*. International Electrotechnical Commission (IEC).

IEEE-802.15.4. (2006). Part 15.4: Wireless medium access control (MAC) and physical layer (PHY) specifications for low-rate wireless personal area networks (WPANs). *Revision of IEEE Std 802.15.4-2003*. IEEE.

IEEE-802.15.5. (2009). *Part 15.5: Mesh topology capability in wireless personal area networks (WPANs)*. IEEE.

Lee, J. M., Zhang, R., Zheng, J., Ahn, G.-S., Zhu, C., Rim, T. P., & Sun, J. R. (2010). IEEE 802.15.5 WPAN mesh standard-low rate part: Meshing the wireless sensor networks. *IEEE Journal on Selected Areas in Communications*, *28*, 973–983. doi:10.1109/JSAC.2010.100902.

Neves, P., & Rodrigues, J. (2010). Internet protocol over wireless sensor networks, from myth to reality. *The Journal of Communication*, *5*, 189–196.

Petersen, S., & Carlsen, S. (2011). WirelessHART versus ISA100.11a: The format war hits the factory floor. *IEEE Industrial Electronics Magazine*, 23–34.

Sauter, T. (2010). The three generations of field-level networks – Evolution and compatibility issues. *IEEE Transactions on Industrial Electronics*, *57*, 3585–3595. doi:10.1109/TIE.2010.2062473.

Young, S. S., Seong, H. P., Choi, S., & Hyun, W. K. (2007). Packet error rate analysis of ZigBee under WLAN and bluetooth interferences. *IEEE Transactions on Wireless Communications, 6,* 2825–2830. doi:10.1109/TWC.2007.06112.

ADDITIONAL READING

Akyildiz, I., & Su, Y. (2002). Wireless sensor networks: A survey. *Computer Networks, 38,* 393–422. doi:10.1016/S1389-1286(01)00302-4.

Anastasi, G., Conti, & Di Francesco. (2011). A comprehensive analysis of the MAC unreliability problem in IEEE 802.15.4 wireless sensor networks. *IEEE Transactions on Industrial Informatics, 7*(1), 52-65.

Bhatt, J. (2010). Wireless networking technologies for automation in oil and gas sector. In *Proceedings of the International Conference on Management of Pretroleum Sector (ICOMPS-2010)* (pp. 51-71). ICOMPS.

Costa, D., & Guedes, L. (2010). The coverage problem in video-based wireless sensor networks: A survey. *Sensors (Basel, Switzerland), 10*(9), 8215–8247. doi:10.3390/s100908215 PMID:22163651.

Decotignie, J.-D. (2009). The many faces of industrial ethernet [past and present]. *IEEE Industrial Electronics Magazine, 3*(1), 8–19. doi:10.1109/MIE.2009.932171.

Emerson. (2008). *Emerson wireless technology safely monitors temperatures in railcars at Croda Inc.* Emerson Process Management.

Emerson. (2009). *Emerson smart wireless transmitters monitor river water temperatures at lenzing fibers.* Emerson Process Management.

Emerson. (2012). *Emerson's smart wireless network delivers maintenance savings, prevents unscheduled shut downs at heavy plate steel mill.* Emerson Process Management.

Felser, M., & Sauter, T. (2004). Standardization of industrial ethernet - The next battlefield? In *Proceedings of the IEEE International Workshop on Factory Communication Systems* (pp. 413-420). IEEE.

Gill, K., & Yang, F., & Lu. (2009). A zigbee-based home automation system. *IEEE Transactions on Consumer Electronics, 55*(2), 422–430. doi:10.1109/TCE.2009.5174403.

Murray, J. (n.d.). Wireless finds new uses offshore. *Intelligent Fields - A supplement to E&P,* 17-24.

Silva, I., Guedes, L., Portugal, P., & Vasques, F. (2012). Reliability and availability evaluation of wireless sensor networks for industrial applications. *Sensors (Basel, Switzerland), 12,* 806–838. doi:10.3390/s120100806 PMID:22368497.

Willig, A. (2008). Recent an emerging topics in wireless industrial communications: A selection. *IEEE Transaction on Industrial Informatics, 4*(2), 102–124. doi:10.1109/TII.2008.923194.

Yang, D., Xu, & Gidlund. (2011). Wireless coexistence between IEEE 802.11-and IEEE 802.15.4-based networks: A survey. *International Journal of Distributed Sensor Networks,* 17.

KEY TERMS AND DEFINITIONS

Blacklist Channel: A mechanism used to eliminate the bad channels in an industrial wireless network.

Coexistence Problem: Since the transmission medium of wireless technology is open, different technologies may share the same frequency range. This scenario is known as the coexistence problem.

Field Networks: Traditional technology for industrial communication.

Frequency Hopping: A channel scheduling technique used to improve the resilience of communications.

Industrial Wireless: A special kind of wireless technology developed for operation in harsh environments.

Mesh Network (Topology): A kind of networking where the data can be relayed/disseminated by any device.

Reliability: A concept used to indicate that a component or system is working properly according its specification during a specific period of the time.

Chapter 18
Numerical Simulation of Distributed Dynamic Systems using Hybrid Tools of Intelligent Computing

Fethi H. Bellamine
University of Waterloo, Canada & National Institute of Applied Sciences and Technologies, Tunisia

Aymen Gdouda
National Institute of Applied Sciences and Technologies, Tunisia

ABSTRACT

Developing fast and accurate numerical simulation models for predicting, controlling, designing, and optimizing the behavior of distributed dynamic systems is of interest to many researchers in various fields of science and engineering. These systems are described by a set of differential equations with homogenous or mixed boundary constraints. Examples of such systems are found, for example, in many networked industrial systems. The purpose of the present work is to review techniques of hybrid soft computing along with generalized scaling analysis for the solution of a set of differential equations characterizing distributed dynamic systems. The authors also review reduction techniques. This paves the way to control synthesis of real-time robust realizable controllers.

INTRODUCTION

A large number of processes in electrical, chemical, and petroleum industries are distributed in nature. Tubular reactors, electrical furnaces, are typical examples of distributed dynamic systems. The proliferation of mobile actuators and sensor networks (Estrin, 2001; Akyilidz, 2002) has con-

tributed to the development of more distributed dynamic systems. Because of the diversity of distributed patterns, distributed dynamic systems can be highly nonlinear and time varying, and thus their modeling can be quite challenging. Thus, a significant number of modeling, control, and optimization applications arise for distributed dynamic systems. The mathematical description

DOI: 10.4018/978-1-4666-3922-5.ch018

of distributed dynamic systems may be in the form of partial differential equations, integral equations, integro-differential equations.

The simulation of distributed dynamic systems is an essential part in the control design and optimization of many physical processes. Most used simulation tools are typically based on discretization oriented numerical techniques. These techniques provide accurate results but are highly CPU intensive, and thus are not feasible for online optimization and control studies. This solution time makes it inconvenient to generate and manage in a timely manner required engineering decisions. The unavailability of methods appropriate for online optimization of complex systems prompted the use of look up tables and curve fitting based on data obtained by off-line extensive simulations. Curve fitting can only handle mild nonlinearity variations and few variables at one time. Look-up tables are powerful since they require only a query on the table, and this is fast. However, they are bulky, costly, and memory intensive and are not easy to maintain and upgrade. Interpolation of a point in look up tables does not make use of the entire input-output data since only values in the neighborhood of the point are used. In addition, asymptotic and approximations techniques have often underlying assumptions, and therefore their accuracy is compromised.

The use of hybrid intelligent soft computing tools is an efficient method to create system solutions which are capable of learning relationships and then use this knowledge for further computations. Fuzzy logic is a research area that received considerable attention, and has been successfully used in system control and identification, as well as many other areas. A fuzzy system is developed in this chapter for the scaling of the mesh-based solution from another dynamic distributed system to another.

The objectives of the present work is to investigate the use of hybrid soft computing techniques along with generalized scaling analysis for the simulation of distributed dynamic systems in an interactive CAD and optimization providing faster on-line solutions and speeding up design guidelines, and then to develop reduced order models with the aim of formulating control solutions. The remainder of the paper is organized as follows. First an overview of generalized similarity analysis is presented. This is followed by specific details of the implemented fuzzy neural network. Demonstration of the proposed approach is illustrated on two distributed dynamic systems. The first involves the modeling of oil reservoirs. Reduced order models are then presented based on the neural network linear and nonlinear principal component analysis. The last section covers briefly control synthesis of low order distributed dynamic systems.

BACKGROUND

An input-output process model is a set of equations to predict the future outputs of a system based on input data. The model should closely represent the relationships between inputs, outputs, and system variables to reduce the error caused by plant-model mismatch. Distributed dynamic systems are often represented by partial differential equations. For example, a large number of processes in different industries are distributed in nature, thus a significant number of modeling, control, and optimization applications arise for these types of systems. The state variables depend on at least two independent variables (i.e. time and space). For example, a tubular reactor may be modeled by a second order partial differential equation describing the change in axial position in the reactor and in time. Partial differential equations can be discretized so the system is represented by ordinary differential equations at separate discrete spatial points, which can then be used to synthesize a model-based control.

Because of the diversity of distributed patterns, distributed dynamic systems can be highly nonlinear and time varying, and thus their modeling can be quite challenging. There are mainly two approaches to model the process dynamics as closely as possible. The first one is to develop a PDE model based on the physics and knowledge of the process or the plant. The second approach is to develop an empirical model based on experimental data using system identification techniques. The solution of a PDE is in general an infinite order solution that leads to a control solution that is not realizable. In addition, satisfactory of control of the infinite-dimensional system must be achieved using a finite order controller and a finite set of actuators and measurement devices.

To solve PDEs, there are two classical kinds of solution categories: analytical and numerical. Typical techniques of analytical class of methods include separation of variables and spectral methods using eigenfunctions (Butkovskiy, 1982; Balas, 1983; Balas, 1986; Beard, 1998), and are more suitable for PDEs that are linear and self-adjoint. For nonlinear or not self-adjoint systems, spectral methods may require a very high order of basis functions approximation, or even fail to represent the system. Disadvantages of a higher-order solution involve computational burden, stability and realizable controllable synthesis

It is probably worth-mentioning that an inertial manifold may be computed analytically in some cases of distributed dynamic systems involving the domain of the flows. The fast modes of the system will converge to the inertial manifold much faster than the slow dominant modes. However in most cases, it is approximated by numerical methods leading to the approximate inertial manifold. The Approximate Inertial Manifold (AIM) (Christofides, 1997; Foas, 1983), an approach based on nonlinear Galerkin's method, is used to construct a finite-dimensional ODE system. AIM solution is a low-order model that captures dominant modes. A singular perturbation to construct AIM is proposed to find a low-order model suitable for the design of controllers with well-characterized closed-loop stability and performance. A mutiresolution approach can also be used to develop a low-order

model (Chen, 1997) where the dominant behavior is found from a multiscale decomposition. This model is appropriate for controller synthesis.

The second approach is to employ discretization-based numerical methods (Guo, 2006; Joshi, 2004). These methods are more flexible and powerful than spectral methods. For example, a finite difference or a finite element can be used to find a numerical solution. But to obtain satisfactory approximation, the number of nodes has to be very high, which makes the computation expensive. These techniques provide accurate results but are highly CPU intensive, and thus are not feasible for online optimization and control studies. This solution time makes it inconvenient to generate and manage in a timely manner required engineering decisions. The unavailability of methods appropriate for online optimization of complex systems prompted the use of look up tables and curve fitting based on data obtained by off-line extensive simulations. Curve fitting can only handle mild nonlinearity variations and few variables at one time. Look-up tables are powerful since they require only a query on the table, and this is fast. However, they are bulky, costly, and memory intensive and are not easy to maintain and upgrade. Interpolation of a point in look up tables does not make use of the entire input-output data since only values in the neighborhood of the point are used.

If the PDE model is difficult to develop, a data driven approach, named singular value decomposition-Karhunen-Loève (SVD-KL) (Bellamine, 2008; Zheng, 2002). KL (Dong, 1994; Li, 2000; Lu, 2003; Valle, 1999) was developed to arrive at a finite-order model. The approach relied on identifying empirical eigenfunctions using a combination of singular value decomposition (SVD) and Karhunen-Loève expansion. The SVD-KL uses input/output data obtained from tests on the open-loop system and will necessarily reflect the distributed behavior. One of the advantages of this method is that decoupling of the input/output interactions is possible. The SVD-KL method not only generated a model that is of low-order but this model emphasizes the dominant behavior of the system. In addition, similar to the KL-Galerkin and SVD method, the SVD-KL method not only generated a model that is of low order but this model emphasizes the dominant behavior of the system. This method identification method was applied to a non-isothermal tubular reactor with multiple reactions. The results showed the advantages of SVD-KL method in predicting the spatial input/output behavior. It may be concluded that when an exact model is not available, the SVD-KL approach can provide a low-order model with high quality comparable to the true solution for systems where the eigenspectrum has a clear separation.

Modeling, control and identification methods for distributed dynamic systems typically depend on the system type, for example, whether it is hyperbolic, or parabolic. A general model is lacking. Control od distributed dynamic systems must be achieved by accounting for the spatial nature of the system. Research in this area include geometric control methods (Jurdjevic, 1997), modal control techniques (Chen, 2000), sliding-mode control (Herrmann, 2003), Lyapunov based control (Byrnes, 1994; Jovanovic, 2003), infinite dimensional systems theory (Bensoussan, 2007; Luo, 1993). Stability and optimizability of infinite-order systems with finite dimensional controllers is investigated (Jacob, 1999). The infinite dimensional systems can be split into stable and unstable but controllable subsystems.

Many published results on the control of a distributed dynamic system start from a linear PDE model. H∞ controller design for robust control of a linear distributed system is studied by (Keulen, 1993). In (Armaou, 2001), the nonlinear PDE system is linearized around a nominal operating point to produce a linear time-varying model. The linear model provides a basis for robust control design. (Palazoglu, 2000) constructed an invariant solution space using infinitesimal transformation based on the Lie group transform. The control is synthesized in a solution space which is invariant along a time-invariant trajectory. The method of characteristics is one control solution for nonlinear first-order PDE systems. The characteristic index of the first order PDE gives the order of the interaction between inputs and outputs. A finite input output equivalent linear controller is designed. From the index, a sufficient condition for closed loop stability is derived in which the controlled poles are in the open left half of the complex plane. A major limitation of the method of characteristics is that the PDE system is required to be open-loop minimum phase which means the uncontrolled poles must be stabilizable. Another method to control DPS is to design an infinite-dimensional controller and then employ a reduction algorithm to arrive at a low dimensional control solution. This research was addressed by (Balas, 1983) and (Atwell, 2001). (Burns, 1999) compared the control design of both the distributed high and low dimensional dynamic system. They concluded that when the KL expansion method is integrated into the distributed dynamic controller, the closed-loop performance will be improved. An interesting discussion of closed-loop stability is by (Godasi, 1999). In that work, he employed Lie group to develop a linear local group of transformations. The control problem is then to find the control action that makes the transformed space invariant under perturbations to guarantee bounded input bounded output stability.

If an exact mathematical model of the DPS is available, model based control strategies can be applied. (Cheng, 2009) discussed optimal adaptive control theory to control a distributed dynamic system. (Curtain, 2003) proposed a finite control strategy for infinite order systems in which the dominant characteristics are represented by finite stable and low stable modes. The integrity of the approximation determines the controller performance. A discontinuous output feedback control method based on sliding modes is developed in (Orlov, 2003) for a class of linear infinite-dimensional systems with finite dimensional unstable part using finite-dimensional sensing and actuation. (Banks, 1997) demonstrated a PDE model based controller on a PDE system. The controller was designed based on a reduced order ODE model which approximated the original PDEs model.

Also in the category of model-based control is the class of model predictive controllers. Model-based controllers in the form of dynamic matrix control, quadratic dynamic matrix control, and model predictive control. Most of the applications use linear model. The model predictive concept is attractive because the controller actions that regulate the process at the current instance are simultaneous. This is achieved by solving an optimal open loop control problem that accounts for constraints on the inputs and outputs, and the effect of unmeasured disturbances. The MPC formulation necessarily required a model. It then follows that the model integrity affects the optimal predictive control solution, which in turn impacts the closed-loop system performance. (Rawlings and Muske, 1993) discussed stability of receding horizon controllers for linear systems. The model predictive control formulation using quadratic programming methods when the model is a convolution is solved. The models may be formulated as state space models (Lee, 1994). If a reduced order model of the distributed dynamic system is available, conventional model predictive control can be applied directly. Closed-loop stability of the control system is not guaranteed since constraint handling necessarily implies a nonlinear control law. This is true whether the system being controlled is linear or nonlinear.

ISSUES AND PROBLEMS

Modeling, reduced order modeling and control of distributed dynamic systems are the main issues. In the area of modeling, discretization oriented techniques provide accurate results but are highly CPU intensive, and thus are not feasible for online optimization and control studies. This solution time makes it inconvenient to generate and manage in a timely manner required engineering decisions. The unavailability of methods appropriate for online optimization of complex systems prompted the use of look up tables and curve fitting based on data obtained by off-line extensive simulations. Curve fitting can only handle mild nonlinearity variations and few variables at one time. Look-up tables are powerful since they require only a query on the table, and this is fast. However, they are bulky, costly, and memory intensive and are not easy to maintain and upgrade. Interpolation of a point in look up tables does not make use of the entire input-output data since only values in the neighborhood of the point are used. In addition, asymptotic and approximations techniques have often underlying assumptions, and therefore their accuracy is compromised. We propose in this chapter soft computing techniques with generalized dimensional analysis as a means to simulate distributed dynamic systems modeled by partial differential equations.

Reduction techniques are organized into one of the two methodologies: (i) "reduce-then-design"(ii)"design-then-reduce". "Reduce-then-design" approaches involve direct model reduction of the PDE. Model reduction means a lower-order finite dimensional approximation of the numerical PDE. Model reduction are achieved using, for example, projection based methods such as the proper orthogonal method, and capture the domainant havehior of the system. Then, a controller is designed using this low order approximation. Our interest is in the design of real-time robust realizable controllers which stabilize the low-order appromation. For the class of "design-then-reduce" techniques, a PDE finite controller (and a finite set of actuators and measurement devices) is designed after developing the PDE model. This controller is large-scale and is designed on the high order approximation of the PDE and then is reduced to obtain a low order controller. LQG balanced truncation is one such technique used in the "design-then-reduce". Each of these two methodologies has weaknesses and strengths. For example, some may argue that some loss of physical information prior to the controller design is an inherent weakness of "reduce-then-design", although we prove in this chapter that this loss could be controlled to be insignificant. But, on the other hand, the use of balanced truncation coupled with control design techniques (such as central control, minmax, etc) used in the "design-then-reduce" do not delete the unobservable uncontrollable states from the controller, and so a minimum realization of the controller is not guaranteed. So, in a nutshell in this chapter linear and nonlinear neural network principal component analysis is implemented to reduce the model.

SOLUTIONS AND RECOMMENDATIONS

Generalized Scaling Analysis

Scaling analysis reduces the number of unknown variables of the system under experimental investigation. The idea is to replace for an unknown relation between n quantities a relationship between a smaller number, $n - m$, of dimensionless groups, and m is generally the number of fundamental units (actually m is the rank of the dimensional matrix which is generally equal to the number of fundamental units but not always). As mentioned by (Mendez, 1999), the techniques of dimensional analysis, scaling, and appropriate use of orders of magnitude are powerful engineering judgment tools. Generalized scaling analysis consists of many steps and makes use of the inspection method and the order of the magnitude (Mazzeo, 1996; Dresner, 1983; Szirtes, 1983) has a number of advantages:

1. The ability to find scaling laws which provides insight knowledge about the necessary assumptions we need to make, and also to reduce the number of parameters involved in solving the problem once we know which groups are dominant.

2. The results obtained can predict the performance of a system from that the results of another system working under similar conditions (geometrical, dynamic, kinematics, electrical/thermal similarities). So laboratory experiments on a smaller scale can be transferred to the real-life field.

3. System comparisons can be made without actually determining the value of the unknown function relating dimensionless group, and so physical insight governing the phenomena is gained.

4. Experimental investigation is simplified and the presentation of results is in the form of a family of graphs. Also, tabular presentations are simplified. An additional advantage of the dimensionless presentation of data is that it is independent of the units employed, and thus can be used worldwide independent of the adopted system of units.

5. It is not necessary to assume idealized sets of conditions.

6. Determination of the minimum parametric representation of the physical phenomena.

For example, to illustrate the generalized scaling analysis, let's say we have the following governing differential equation:

$$\frac{\partial}{\partial x}(k_x \frac{\partial P}{\partial x}) + \frac{\partial}{\partial y}(k_y \frac{\partial P}{\partial y}) + \frac{\partial}{\partial z}(k_z \frac{\partial P}{\partial z}) = 0 \quad (1)$$

The boundary conditions are:

$$P(x = L - r_x, y = W - r_y) = P_L \quad (2)$$

$$\frac{\partial P}{\partial z}(z=0) = 0; \frac{\partial P}{\partial z}(z=H)=0 \qquad (3)$$

$$\frac{\partial P}{\partial x}(x=0, y > r_y) = 0; \frac{\partial P}{\partial x}(x=L, y < W - r_y) = 0 \qquad (4)$$

$$\frac{\partial P}{\partial y}(x>r_x, y = 0) = 0; \frac{\partial P}{\partial y}(x<L - r_z, y = W) = 0 \qquad (5)$$

where $0 < x < r_x < L$ and $0 < y < r_y < W$. The output quantity called injectivity [10]-[11] in a homogenous reservoir is defined as:

$$I = \frac{q}{\Delta p} \qquad (6)$$

where

$$q = \frac{W}{\mu} \int_h^H k_x (\frac{\partial P}{\partial x}(x = 0) dz \qquad (7)$$

$$\Delta p = \bar{P}(r_1 = r_w) - \bar{P}(r_2 = r_w) \qquad (8)$$

$$\bar{P}(r_1 = r_w) = \frac{1}{H-h} \int_h^H P(r_1 = r_w) dz \qquad (9)$$

$$\bar{P}(r_2 = r_w) = \frac{1}{H-h} \int_h^H P(r_2 = r_w) dz \qquad (10)$$

r_1 and r_2 are such that $r_1^2 = x^2 + y^2$ and $r_2^2 = (x - L)^2 + (y - L)^2$. In what follows we assume that $k_x = k_y = k_h$. The relevant list of

dimensional parameters on which the injectivity depend is: k_x, k_z, μ, L, H, h, H_T, W, r_w, q. At this point, we apply step 3 which is defining scale factors. So we will use the transformation of the form $a = a_1^* a_D + a_2^*$ where a is the dimensional variable, a_D is the dimensionless variable, a_1^* and a_2^* are the scale factors. This transformation permits us to move the equations into the general dimensionless space. So for example,

$$x = x_1^* x_D + x_2^*; P = P_1^* P_D + P_2^* \qquad (11)$$

and so on. The next step would be to non-dimensionalize the equations and the boundary conditions by replacing the transformations in the equations and associated boundary conditions, and then in order to preserve the form of the original equations, we set some terms to 1 and others to 0. For example, Equation (1) becomes:

$$k_h \frac{P_1^*}{x_1^{*2}} \frac{\partial^2 P_D}{\partial x_D^2} + k_h \frac{P_1^*}{y_1^{*2}} \frac{\partial^2 P_D}{\partial y_D^2} + k_z \frac{P_1^*}{z_1^{*2}} \frac{\partial^2 P_D}{\partial z_D^2} = 0 \qquad (12)$$

(12) can be rewritten as:

$$\frac{\partial^2 P_D}{\partial x_D^2} + \frac{x_1^{*2}}{y_1^{*2}} \frac{\partial^2 P_D}{\partial y_D^2} + \frac{k_z}{k_h} \frac{x_1^{*2}}{z_1^{*2}} \frac{\partial^2 P_D}{\partial z_D^2} = 0 \qquad (13)$$

Comparing (13) to (1), we can define the dimensionless group $\frac{k_z}{k_x} \frac{x_1^{*2}}{z_1^{*2}}$. Applying the same procedure to Equations (1)-(10), we can define 16 dimensionless groups which are:

$$\frac{k_z}{k_x}\frac{x_1^{*2}}{z_1^{*2}}, \frac{P_1^*}{z_1^*}\frac{\partial P_D}{\partial z_D}, \frac{P_1^*}{y_1^*}\frac{\partial P_D}{\partial y_D}, \frac{P_1^*}{x_1^*}\frac{\partial P_D}{\partial x_D}, \frac{x_1^{*2}}{y_1^{*2}},$$

$$\frac{H_T - z_2^*}{z_1^*}, \frac{W - y_2^*}{y_1^*}, \frac{L - x_2^*}{x_1^*}, \frac{z_2^*}{z_1^*}, \frac{y_2^*}{y_1^*}, \frac{x_2^*}{x_1^*},$$

$$\frac{r_y - y_2^*}{y_1^*}, \frac{r_x - x_2^*}{x_1^*}, \frac{W - r_y - y_2^*}{y_1^*}, \frac{L - r_x - x_2^*}{x_1^*},$$

$$\frac{P_L - P_2^*}{P_1^*}$$

To preserve the form of the Equations (1)-(10), we set the ninth, tenth, and eleventh dimensionless groups to zero, and the sixth, seventh, and eighth to 1. We also assume that $r_x = r_y = r_T$. So that we have:

$$D_1 = \frac{h}{H_T}, D_2 = \frac{H}{H_T}, D_3 = \frac{H - h}{H_T}, D_4 =$$

$$\frac{L^2}{H^2}\frac{k_z}{k_h}, A_d = \frac{4L^2}{\pi r_T^2}$$

Now, the 5th step is to apply inspectional analysis to reduce further the number of dimensionless analysis. The injectivity is, and when $L = W$:

$$I = \frac{q\mu L}{2\pi k_h H_T(\bar{P}(r_1 = r_w) - P_L)} \quad (14)$$

Next, we need to reduce further the dimensionless groups, so we have to search for dependencies by finding the rank of the following coefficients

$$\begin{bmatrix} 1 & 0 & -1 & 0 & 0 & 0 & 0 \\ 0 & 1 & -1 & 0 & 0 & 0 & 0 \\ 0 & 0 & -1 & 1 & 0 & 0 & 0 \\ 0 & 2 & 0 & 0 & 2 & -1 & 1 \end{bmatrix}$$

The rank of this matrix is four, so there are only four dimensionless groups which are:

$$h_d = \frac{h}{H_T}, R_L = \frac{L^2}{H^2}\frac{k_z}{k_h}, \Delta H = \frac{H - h}{H_T},$$

$$A_d = \frac{4L^2}{\pi r_T^2}$$

So, we conclude that (14) can be rewritten as a function of the following four dimensionless groups $R_L, h_d, \Delta H, A_d$ so that $I = f(R_L, h_d, \Delta H, A_d)$.

Fuzzy Neural Network

When the values of the dimensionless groups are crisp, then we use neural network techniques (Minai, 1992; Hornik, 1989; Poggio, 1990; Williamson, 1995) combined with generalized dimensional analysis to simulate distributed dynamic systems (Bellamine, 2006; Bellamine, 2008). Dimensionless groups may be inherently fuzzy. For example, the Reynolds number of value equal to 2320 constitutes the borderline between laminar and turbulent flow. A slightly higher or lower value does not reflect the flow type. There is a grey zone within which the transition occurs from one flow type to another. A fuzzy logic based inference system has been developed to handle this situation. There are a number of hybrid soft computing techniques (Mittra, 2000; Jang, 1994) of which we use the Fuzzy Neural Network described below.

We consider the so-called multi-input single-output fuzzy systems. In our problem, the inputs are the dimensionless groups. Both inputs and the output have to be transformed and interpreted to and from fuzzy variables in order to use fuzzy logic to solve our problem. So, the basic configuration of the fuzzy system used in this chapter is is made of four principal components: a fuzzification interface, a fuzzy-rule base (fuzzy-logic operation), a fuzzy inference engine or machine, and a defuzzification interface. The fuzzification interface performs a scale mapping that transforms the observed nonfuzzy input space to the fuzzy sets. Thus, the fuzzification interface provides a link between the nonfuzzy outside world and the fuzzy system framework. The fuzzy rule base is a set of m rules in general linguistic or conditional statements in the form of: "IF a set of conditions is satisfied, THEN a set of consequences are inferred". The fuzzy inference machine is the decision making logic which employs fuzzy rules from the fuzzy rule base to determine fuzzy to determine fuzzy outputs of a fuzzy system corresponding to its fuzzified. In this chapter, a fuzzy inference machine of the form suggested by Takagi-Sugeno-Kang is used, where fuzzy sets are involved only in the premise part (IF-part) of the rules, while the consequent part (THEN-part) is described by a nonfuzzy function of the input variables. The aim of the nonfuzzy function is to describe the local behavior of the system. The idea of a linear function in the TSK method has a foundation in the canonical realization of the system known as "the control canonical form". Usually the function is a polynomial in the input variables, but it can be any function as long as it can approximately describe the output of the model within the fuzzy region specified by the antecedent of the rule (check reference). The max-min composition is utilized as the choice for the t-norm and t-conorm operations.

The jth rule R^j may be described as follows:

R^j : If the dimensionless groups D_1 and D_2 belong to the jth membership functions μ_x^j and μ_y^j correspondingly then

$$A^j = \lambda_0^j + \lambda_{D_1}^j D_1 + \lambda_{D_2}^j D_2 \tag{15}$$

where R^j $(j = 1, \ldots, m)$ are the fuzzy rules, D_1 and D_2 are the input variables to the fuzzy system,

A^j is the output proposed by the jth rule, and μ_x^j, μ_y^j are the membership functions which characterize the jth rule fuzzy sets defined in the space of the dimensionless groups. The selected membership functions selected are Gaussian.

$$\mu_x^j(x) = \exp\left[-\frac{1}{2}\left(\frac{x - \overline{\sigma}_x^j}{\sigma_x^j}\right)^2\right] \tag{16}$$

where σ_x^j and $\overline{\sigma}_x^j$ are respectively the mean value and the standard variation of the membership function. The factors $\lambda_{D_2}^j$, $\lambda_{D_1}^j$ and λ_0^j of the consequent part of the jth rule need to be determined. Fuzzy if-the rules are used to capture the imprecise modes of human reasoning when making decision in an environment of imprecision and uncertainty.

The defuzzification interface defuzzifies the fuzzy outputs of the fuzzy inference engine and generates a nonfuzzy crisp output, which is the actual output of the fuzzy system. The weighted average defuzzification, the most commonly used, is used here. This method is one of the most widely adopted defuzzification strategies for the TSK model:

$$A = \frac{\sum_{j=1}^m A^j \mu^j}{\sum_{j=1}^m \mu^j} \tag{17}$$

μ^j gives the degree of fulfillment of rule R^j by the input vector and A^j is given in (15). Due to the similarity of such a fuzzy system to a three layer network, it is called a fuzzy neural network whose training is described in the next section.

A suitable training database for the FNN is used to construct the fuzzy rule base. Fuzzy rule base parameters are determined by a training process, so that the output of the FNN adequately matches the mesh-based computations. Once trained, the FNN may be used to compute the output for other cases. The parameters of the FNN to be adjusted, i.e. the tuning parameters, through its training are σ_x^j, σ_x^j $(j = 1, ..., m)$ and λ_x^j $(j = 1, ..., m)$. Let z denote the vector of tuning parameters. Initially, it is assumed that the number of rules m is fixed.

The FNN is trained by presenting it with a set of q input/desired output pairs (scaling groups, A_t^p), $(p = 1, ..., q)$ (q is the number of nodes). A gradient algorithm is then used to tune the FNN, so as to minimize the FNN mean square error

$$J(z) = \frac{1}{q} \sum_{p=1}^{q} J^p \tag{18}$$

where J^p is the squared difference between the computed values of the FNN A^P and the data derived from mesh-based results A_t^P.

The minimization of $J(z)$ in (18) through a gradient algorithm leads to the learning rule which is expressed by the following formula:

$$z(\nu + 1) = z(\nu) - \alpha \nabla_z J \tag{19}$$

where α is an acceleration factor and ν is the iteration index.

The rule creation consists first of initializing the FNN rules. The number of rules m can be arbitrarily determined. This may in general lead to large errors and long training times. To reduce errors and improve the training time m is determined by a sequential procedure. We start with a certain initialization of rules with a single rule $(m = 1)$, and we use a rule adaptation procedure. The parameters of $m = 1$ fuzzy rule are initialized on the basis of the first input ε and desired output sample pair as follows:

$$\bar{\sigma}_\varepsilon^1 = \varepsilon^1 \tag{20}$$

$$\sigma_\varepsilon^1 = \frac{1}{2m}[\max(\varepsilon^P) - \min(\varepsilon^P)] \tag{21}$$

$$\lambda_0^1 = A_1^t; \lambda_\varepsilon^1 = 0 \tag{22}$$

Let us denote the firing strength of the fuzzy rule base as:

$$S_\mu = \sum_{j=1}^{m} \mu^j \tag{23}$$

We also define a threshold β as the least acceptable firing strength of the fuzzy rule base. If $S_\mu < \beta$, a new rule R^{m+1} must be added to the rule base. Let μ_ε^{m+1} denote the new membership in the ε th premise axis. Then, the parameters of μ_ε^{m+1} are selected as follows:

$$\bar{\alpha}_\varepsilon^{m+1} = \varepsilon^P \tag{24}$$

$$\sigma_\varepsilon^{m+1} = \gamma(\varepsilon^P - \alpha_\varepsilon^{nearest}) \tag{25}$$

$\alpha_\varepsilon^{nearest}$ is the mean value of an existing membership closest to the incoming pattern vector ε^P and γ is an overlapping factor which has been chosen equal to two from computer experiments. The generation of new rules establishes the rule base adaptation mechanism whose steps are covered in the computational algorithm covered in the next section.

Computational Algorithm

The computational algorithm is summarized below:

Step 1: Write the complete differential governing equations and the associated initial and boundary conditions.

Step 2: List all variables and constants relevant to the physical process also called relevance list.

Step 3: Nondimensionalize the equations and the associated boundary and initial conditions.

Step 4: Inspectional analysis is carried out to combine and reduce dimensionless groups. At this stage, scale and reference factors are determined by setting dimensionless groups to one or zero. So that, we have a minimum parametric representation in the form $F(\pi_1, \pi_2, \pi_3, ...) = 0$ where π_k denotes a dimensionless group.

Step 6: The number of groups can be reduced further when π_k is very large or small by expanding the functional relationship F in a Taylor series and keeping the first lowest order or higher if need be.

Step 7: Generate training and test data set.

Step 8: Select the number of hidden layer neurons.

Step 9: Initialize the weights and biases with small random numbers. Select initial values for the learning rate and the momentum.

Step 10: Set $k = 1$.

Step 5: Provide training sample (x_k, a_k) and let

$x = x_k$.

Step 11: Feed forward the new pattern and compute the corresponding firing strength of the fuzzy rule base.

Step 12: If the firing strength is greater than the threshold or the least acceptable firing strength of the fuzzy rule base, then leave the rule base unmodified and go to step 14.

Step 13: If the firing strength is less than the threshold, create a new fuzzy rule, and select parameters using equations (24)-(25).

Step 14: Back-propagate the error and adjust weights, i.e. compute the error given in (2) and the gradients. Then, adjust the weights of the network.

Step 15: Increment k and go to step 5.

Step 16: Compute the FNN error.

Step 17: If the error is less than a given training tolerance, then we halt training, and we compute and evaluate test sample response.

Step 18: If the model performance is acceptable, then end the program.

Step 19: If the error is larger than its previous value, then decrease the learning rate and momentum. Go to step 10.

Step 20: If the error decreases, then increase the learning rate and momentum. Go to step 10.

The most important parameters that influence our computational algorithm are the number of similarity groups, the firing strength of the fuzzy rule base, The threshold of the firing strength, The membership function and the training tolerance

Application

The proposed approach is demonstrated for numerical reservoir characterization and more particularly for breakthrough time in an immiscible displacement in three dimensions (Novakovic, 2002; Bellamine, 2006). Breakthrough time is defined as the fraction of the recovered mobile displaced phase when the fractional flow of the displacing phase is one percent. Rather than varying more than 30 variables, only 7 dimensionless groups can be used to describe the behavior. The full range of system variability can be assessed using these 7 groups. It is easier to carry out a sensitivity study in 7 dimensions instead of 30. A 2-level factorial analysis leads to 128 simulations as opposed to 2 to the power 30 simulations.

This approach shows the potential benefits of the proposed FNN technique. The scaling groups have physical interpretation. The integration of scaling with FNN provides rapid numerical simulations. Boundary conditions are also included in the process of transformation from dimensional to dimensionless space. At the end of the training procedure, the FNN rule base contains ten rules on the average. The performance of the FNN is tested for cases which the FNN is not trained for. The deviations between mesh-based and FNN computations are nearly the same in all cases, and is negligeable (or less than 1%)

The computing time is negligibly small in comparison with the time needed for mesh-based calculations. The governing differential equations used for the oil reservoir are in (Bellamine, 2006), and will not be repeated in this chapter for the sake of brevity. These equations involve 32 relevant parameters. According to step 3, we need to nondimensionalize the equations. So, we define each of the target dependent variable in the form of $a = a_1^* a_D + a_2^*$ where a is the dimensional variable, a_D is the dimensionless variable, a_1^* and a_2^* are the scale factors. This transformation permits us to move the equations into the general dimensionless space. Nondimensionlizing must not change the form of the equations. We choose the dimensionless time to start at zero. Carrying out steps 4 and 5, we find out that there are 15 dimensionless groups. They are not all independent. So, we use step 6 to obtain the minimum parametric representation, i.e. the minimum number of dimensionless groups. One systematic way to perform this is to write the dimensional matrix relating the logarithmic of the dimensionless groups to the logarithmic of the relevant parameters, and find the rank of the matrix. The rank is the number of independent dimensionless groups. So, we get 11 dimensionless groups. However, the rank of the matrix is not the minimum number of groups that we are looking for. We applied further physical insight to find out that there are three redundant groups, and thus the dimensionless groups that describe the flow is provided by 8 groups which are: the aspect ratios in the following three directions x, y, z are respectively N_{RX}, N_{RY} given respectively by

$$\frac{L^2}{H^2}\frac{k_z}{k_x}, \quad \frac{W^2}{H^2}\frac{k_z}{k_y},$$

the x and y-directions tilt numbers N_{TX} and N_{TY} given respectively by

$$\frac{W}{H}\tan\alpha_X$$

and

$$\frac{L}{H}\tan\alpha_Y,$$

the density number N_ρ given by

$$\frac{\Delta\rho}{\rho_1},$$

the gravity number N_g given by, the mobility ratio M^0 given by

$$\frac{\lambda_{r1}^0}{\lambda_{r2}^0},$$

the capillary number N_c given by

$$\frac{k_z\lambda_{r1}^0}{u_T H}\sigma\sqrt{\frac{\varphi}{k_z}}$$

The last step is to find the order of magnitude of each dimensionless group to gain insight into which groups are important, and to reduce their numbers. There are several techniques to do that. Table 1 shows the statistical results when simulating the dimensionless breakthrough versus the gravity number for an aspect ratio in the

Table 1. Statistical training and testing results of the reservoir case

Statistics	Trained	Tested
R^2	0.99157	0.98756
Average absolute error	2.57654	5.06745
Minimum Absolute error	0.01897	0.00237

x-direction equal to 10. We conducted a number of simulations such as that shown in Figure 1 and the results obtained prove that the proposed approach is valid, and that is orders of magnitude faster than other discretization-based techniques.

Reduced Order Model of Distributed Dynamic Systems

There are a number of reduction techniques that concentrate on useful information, reduce variable redundancy, and increase computational efficiency. For example, principal component analysis finds the subspace that has the largest percent-

age of variation. In brevity, linear principal component analysis is a technique that project high-dimensional data to a lower dimensional subspace by finding the most "important" principal directions. The projection directions are orthogonal and uncorrelated. The principal components lie in the directions of the axes of a constant density ellipsoid. The principal components are arranged in a descending order according to their significant contribution to the overall data variations. This is achieved by understanding the covariance structure through a few significant combinations of the original variables. In other words, the utility of PCA as a dimensionality reduction technique can be realized by monitoring a set of uncorrelated scores rather than a large set of m correlated variables. The l eigenvectors of R (corresponding to the largest eigenvalues) are the loadings in the principal component space, and the eigenvectors corresponding to the remaining $m - l$ eigenvalues are the loadings in the residual space. In this way, more physical meaning and insight of the data is obtained. In addition, multi-collinearity between data points is reduced,

Figure 1. Comparison between finite difference numerical simulation and FNN-GSA training of the breakthrough recovery time as a function of the gravity number and the aspect ratio in the y-direction

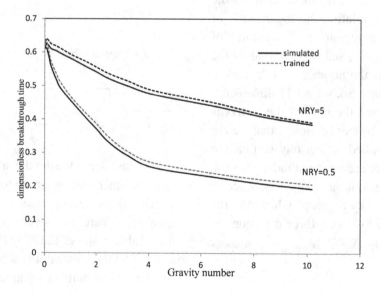

and combinations of data patterns that show a maximal informative significant content is retained. PCA has the following advantages: (1) the Hessian matrix of the error performance index of the neural network is diagonal since the principal components are uncorrelated. (2) Orthogonalization of input data speeds up the training of the neural network.

The classical PCA is not appropriate for applications requiring online data processing. The computation of eigenvalues and eigenvectors need to be repeated for additional incoming data and is very sensitive to data outliers. So, in this chapter, the PCA layer is embedded in the neural network and is sandwiched between the input and the hidden layers. The number of neurons in the PCA layer is equal to the number of selected principal components. Each neuron in the PCA layer has a linear transfer function. The eigenvectors obtained from the PCA are the weights on the connections between the input nodes and the neurons in the PCA layer. So, the data fed to the first hidden layer are the uncorrelated principal components of the data. PCA could be performed on the correlation matrix rather than the covariance matrix when the variables are used in different units.

For real time applications (on-line process control), PCA is an intrinsically linear projection method, and so non-linear effects cannot be accounted for. So, in this chapter, we use the nonlinear principal component analysis NPCA. There are many varieties of nonlinear PCA. For example, it is possible to get the nonlinear principal components by projecting data onto the principle curve which is a smooth one-dimensional curve that passes through the middle of multidimensional data, and its shape reflects the structure of the nonlinear structure of the data (Dong, 1994; Li, 2000). A nonlinear PCA method (Kramer, 1991) is proposed based upon the auto-associative neural network topology, which has been successfully applied for the extraction of nonlinear features from a dataset. It is based on 3-hidden layer feed-forward neural networks called respectively

"encoding", "bottleneck", and "decoding". Data compression is achieved by the bottleneck. For example, a 1-neuron bottleneck gives the first nonlinear principal component. The number of encoding and decoding neurons is adjustable for the optimal fit. A simpler 2-hidden layer may be used so that the encoding layer is eliminated and the bottleneck linear activation function is replaced by a non-linear one. This algorithm alleviates the over-fitting and non-uniqueness issues of Kramer's technique, although its non-linear modeling capability is reduced. Recursive PCA (Li, 2000) updates the correlation matrix. Then, the computation of the loading matrices is performed in the same manner as ordinary PCA. There are computational shortcuts for recursively determining the eigenvalues of the correlation matrix, for example, by rank-one modification. A method (Valle, 1999) is suggested to select the right number of principal components. If too few components are retained, the model will not capture all of the information in the data leading to a poor representation of the process. On the other hand, if too many components are chosen, then the model will be over parameterized, and dataset is redundancy is not eliminated. In this chapter, the nonlinear principal components are extracted using the work of (Kramer, 1991). First, we construct the auto-associative NN illustrated in Figure 2 to extract the nonlinear factors, then we take the first two layers and use them instead of the PCA layer.

The neural network adjusts its weights and thresholds so that the quadratic error between neural-network estimated output and model outputs is minimized

$$E(w,b) = \sum_{k=1}^{N} e^T e = \sum_{k=1}^{N} (T_k - a_k^r)^T (T_k - a_k^r)$$

(26)

Figure 2. The auto-associative NPCA neural network architecture

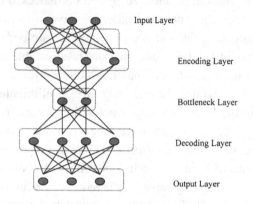

Input Layer

Encoding Layer

Bottleneck Layer

Decoding Layer

Output Layer

where T_k is the target output of the input x_k. N is the total number of samples. a_k^r is the output of an $r-$ layer feed-forward network. w and b are respectively the weights and the bias of the network. The error in Equation (26) which is defined in the least square sense is the most commonly used. However, other types of errors can be defined, for example, in the least p^{th} sense, or minimax. The powerful optimization Levenberg-Marquardt (LM) algorithm which is a variation of Newton's method is used. LM was designed for minimizing functions that are sums of squares of other nonlinear functions. This is well suited to neural network training where the performance index is the mean squared error. The algorithm approaches the steepest descent algorithm with a small learning rate. The conjugate gradient algorithm does not require the computation of the Hessian matrix which involves second derivatives, and converges to the minimum of a quadratic function in a finite number of iterations. Under other conditions, the LM algorithm approaches the Gauss-Newton, which should provide faster convergence. So, generally, the Levenberg-Marquardt (LM) algorithm is a good compromise between the speed of Newton's algorithm and the guaranteed convergence of steepest descent.

The NPCA is implemented by a multilayered auto-associative neural network as shown in Figure 2, which is composed of an input layer, three hidden layers, and an output layer. This structure is trained to produce the identity mapping. The input layer is driven by linear PCA factors and not by data inputs created from the dimensional analysis as is usually done. The hidden layers consist of the encoding layer, followed by the bottleneck layer, which is then followed by the decoding layer. The sigmoid nodal transfer function is used when mapping data from a layer to another, and is required from the input to the encoder and from the decoder to the output. Linear activation functions can be used instead to transfer from the encoding layer to the bottleneck layer and from the decoding to the output layer. Essentially the NPCA auto-associative neural network reproduces at its output the input data. Mathematically,

$$\hat{X} = I(X) \tag{27}$$

where $\hat{X}$ is the $n-$ dimensional output vector, and X is the $n-$ dimensional input vector consisting of all the variables necessary to get $\hat{X}$. The forward mapping is supplied by the encoding layer, and the inverse mapping is supplied by the decoding layer. There are a number of approaches to select the right number of the neurons of different hidden layers to obtain the required accuracy. Unfortunately, there are no established methods to choose the suitable number of the neurons of each of the hidden layers. One of the approaches is to account for the fact that the number of adjustable parameters (weights and biases) to be less than the number of entries in the input data matrix. The number of adjustable parameters is a direct function of the number of nodes in the encoding, decoding, and bottleneck layers. When the number of nonlinear principal factors is much less than the number of input variables and the number of samples, then the number of neurons of either the decoding or encoding layer is much less than the number of samples (Kramer, 1991). Generally, the number of neurons in both the decoding and encoding layers is the same. In addition, the number of neurons of the bottleneck layer is initially selected as that of the input layer, and then decreased one at a time until the network ceases to converge. Then, a sensitivity analysis is conducted to select the right number of neurons of both the encoding and decoding layers. It follows then that the number of the nonlinear factors is the minimum number of neurons of the bottleneck layer that ensures the convergence of the network. When the network converges, the outputs of the bottleneck layer are saved, and used subsequently to compute the desired parameters.

NPCA provides at bottleneck layer a reduced representation of the input from which it would be possible to restore the input data. Nonlinear principal components are extracted at the bottleneck layer which has a smaller dimension than either the input or output layers. For example, if the bottleneck layer has one neuron, then the output of that neuron is the primary nonlinear principal component. If the bottleneck has two neurons, then two leading nonlinear principal components are computed.

During learning, the neural network adjusts its weights and biases so that the sum of squared errors *sse* is minimized. The training algorithm employed is based on the multilayered Levenberg-Marquardt backpropagation. The most important principal components whose relative contributions is shown in Figure 3. The figure shows that 5 principal components or 5 dimensionless groups contribute to 99.89% of the data content information and that 4 dimensionless groups contribute to 91.91% of the data content information. In order to illustrate the effect of choosing only 4 dimensionless groups, we need to transform back the principal components to the original data. However, the retrieved data lost some information, and this loss is minimal. Figure 4 illustrate the

Figure 3. Contribution of different principal factors in percentage to data content information

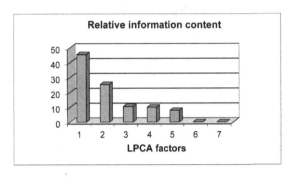

good agreement as compared to the finite difference simulation.

Control Synthesis

Control of distributed dynamic systems has been an active subject of research. As an example, a control objective is to regulate the concentration profile along the length of the reactor or to maintain the temperature and to prevent the propagation of the disturbances. A summary of theoretical developments on optimal open-loop controller synthesis is covered in (Fax, 2004; D'Andrea, 2003; Butkovskii, 1969; Tay, 1989). In (Tay, 1989), a summary of controller designs of linear distributed dynamic system in terms of linear lumped processes was provided. Developments on control of hyperbolic and parabolic partial differential equations systems are presented in (Christofides, 2001).

Traditional multivariable control theory can be used to synthesize a control solution with stable properties by reducing the PDE system to a set of ordinary differential equations of finite dimension. A novel nonlinear geometric feedback linearization controller is synthesized (Christofides, 2001), which makes the closed-loop system stable. More specifically, the novel nonlinear controller displays a two-time scale. Application of this control strategy subject to unmeasured disturbances and parameter uncertainty showed that the nonlinear

Figure 4. Comparison between finite difference numerical simulation and GDA-NN-PCA verification in the computation of breakthrough recovery time as a function of the buoyancy number and the mobility ratio (- - - - trained, ——— simulated)

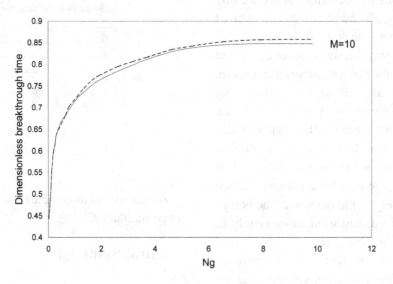

controller gave better closed-loop performance, i.e. robustness than that of a fixed proportional-integral PI controller. The latter was tuned for one set of input disturbances.

Two Model Predictive Control (MPC) strategies—Dynamic Matrix Controller (DMC) and Quadratic DMC (QDMC)—were applied to control the low order dynamic distributed system (Zheng, 2002). Quadratic Dynamic Matrix Control (QDMC) predicts the performance of the controlled variables over a prediction horizon, by solving an optimization problem using a quadratic programming approach to find the controller actions for a number of steps less than that of the prediction horizon. The predicted process behavior is calculated using a model of the process. Conventionally, the predicted control actions minimize an objective function. In this manner, the projected error between the desired trajectory and the predicted response is used to determine future control actions. Sufficiency conditions were provided to show that proper selection of the controller tuning parameters will provide closed-loop asymptotic stability.

Because the model contained the spatial correlations among the inputs and outputs, the QDMC approach gave better performance when compared to a linear controller (e.g. PI). A spectral radius analysis of the closed-loop system established a sufficient condition for stability of the QDMC control configuration (Zheng, 2002).

The QDMC controller is synthesized using a reduced order model. Nonlinear MPC (NLMPC) can be designed to minimize the objective function. To solve the NLMPC problem, one must solve a nonlinear optimization formulation to find the optimal solutions. However, in practice, the available nonlinear programming methods may yield multiple optima or not converge at all. In most applications, the nonlinear model is linearized at each sampling time. This modeling strategy results in a Linear Time-Varying (LTV) model. The resulting linear optimization problem is solved using a quadratic programming method at each sampling time. Convergence for the linear problem is guaranteed, but the computation may be expensive. Let this approach be the second modeling strategy.

Another alternative is to linearize the nonlinear system only once at the nominal case and assume that this model is valid over the expected range of disturbances. This yields a linear time-invariant LTI model. Let this approach be the third modeling strategy. The QDMC controller gave superior performance (speed of response and settling time) in the response of unmeasured disturbances.

Compared to the LTV and LTI QDMC controllers, the reduced order QDMC controller gives much better performance with a faster response. This is attributed to the quality of the low order model. The low order QDMC control strategy gave superior closed-loop performance in the face of unmeasured disturbances compared to DMC or PI. The QDMC control strategy is also superior to that of a linear Time varying QDMC or a linear time-invariant QDMC. For example, The LTI-QDMC controller output displays oscillations because of the model mismatch. It was stated that closed-loop stability of this type of model-based controller is a function of the tuning parameters. Different tuning configurations are tested on the SVD-KL QDMC controller strategy. The effects of the tuning parameters on stability can be observed by the spectral radius of the closed-loop matrix.

FUTURE DIRECTIONS

In this section, future directions in modeling techniques are provided (Bellamine, in press; Mehrkanoon, 2012). When the dataset is not available, neural network approaches including the Multi-Layered Perceptron (MLP) differential approximator, generalized hybrid power series, discrete Hopfield neural network, and the hybrid Galerkin numerical maybe used for constructing neural network models for solving a priori knowledge in the form of differential equations for distributed dynamic engineering processes. These approaches have a number of advantages over other traditional mesh-based methods such as reduction of the computational cost, speed up

of the execution time, and data integration with the a priori knowledge. Furthermore, the neural network techniques are applicable when the differential equations governing system or dynamic engineering processes are not fully understood. The proposed neural network architecture learns to compute the unknown or free parameters of the equation from observations of the process behavior; hence a more precise theoretical description of the process is obtained. Additionally, there will be no need to solve the differential equation each time the free parameters change. More work is needed in this area because the approaches outlined above cannot handle very complex, or a large number of differential equations. The authors recently conducted work to evaluate the most appropriate candidate approach. It was found that the hybrid Galerkin neural network is more robust than other techniques but require more complex neural network architectures.

CONCLUSION

First, FNN combined with generalized scaling analysis is used to simulate numerically distributed dynamic systems. This method offers several advantages. GDA simplifies the way of characterizing a physical problem and reduces the amount of data needed to train a fuzzy neural network. The number of input variables is reduced compared with the initial number of design parameters. This reduction was obtained through the application of scaling analysis to the partial differential equations to determine the minimum number of independent scaling groups used as inputs to the FNN. In addition, the application of generalized scaling analysis help in extracting general rules about the behavior of the systems, and allows for the quick settings of design guidelines. This technique leads to fast simulation times, and particularly when evaluating changes in the physical properties of the distributed systems. Once trained, the computation time of the modeled outputs is negligible and is orders of magnitude faster than any single fine mesh simulation.

A novel nonlinear neural network principal component analysis combined with the generalized scaling analysis is presented to derive reduced order models of dynamic distributed systems. For the case study we had, the number of input variables are reduced from 30 variables to only 4 variables in the case that linear principal component analysis is used, and to only 3 when nonlinear principal component analysis is utilized. In other words, our proposed method lead to a 90% reduction in input vector space and this translates in the same amount of required simulation time. The results demonstrate that much less CPU time was needed to achieve the same model accuracy than traditional techniques such as fine-mesh finite difference. The new approach results in a more efficient model development, and can be used in conjunction with an interactive CAD and optimization to provide faster on-line solutions and to speed up the decision and design cycles. This reduced model can be used to design robust controllers.

REFERENCES

Akyilidz, I. F., Su, W., Sankarasubramaniam, Y., & Cayirci, E. (2002). A survey on sensor networks. *IEEE Communications Magazine*, *40*(8), 102–114. doi:10.1109/MCOM.2002.1024422.

Armaou, A., & Christofides, P. D. (2001). Finite-dimensional control of nonlinear parabolic PDE systems with time dependent spatial domains using empirical eigenfunctions. *International Journal of Applied Mathematics and Computer Science*, *11*(2), 287–317.

Atwell, J., Borggaard, J. T., & King, B. B. (2001). Article. *International Journal of Applied Mathematics and Computer Science*, *11*(6), 1311–1330.

Balas, M. (1983). The galerkin method and feedback control of linear distributed parameter systems. *Journal of Mathematical Analysis and Applications*, *91*, 527–546. doi:10.1016/0022-247X(83)90167-1.

Balas, M. (1986). Finite dimensional control of distributed parameter systems by galerkin approximation of infinite dimensional controllers. *Journal of Mathematical Analysis and Applications*, *114*, 17–36. doi:10.1016/0022-247X(86)90062-4.

Banks, H. L., Smith, R. C., & Brown, D. E. (1997). Experimental confirmation of a PDE based approach for the design of feedback controls. *SIAM Journal of Optimization and Control*, *35*(4), 1263–1296. doi:10.1137/S0363012995285909.

Beard, R., & McLain, T. (1998). Successive galerkin approximation algorithms for nonlinear optimal and robust control. *International Journal of Control*, *71*(5), 717–743. doi:10.1080/002071798221542.

Bellamine, F. H. (2013). *Applications of neural networks approaches for incorporating a priori knowledge in dynamic engineering process*. Applied Mathematics and Computations.

Bellamine, F. H., & Elkamel, A. (2006). Numerical characterization of distributed dynamic systems using tools of intelligent computing and generalized dimensional analysis. *Applied Mathematics and Computation*, *182*(2), 1021–1039. doi:10.1016/j.amc.2006.05.002.

Bellamine, F. H., & Elkamel, A. (2008). Model order reduction using neural network principal component analysis and generalized dimensional analysis. *International Journal for CAE and Software*, *25*(5), 443–463.

Bensoussan, A., Giuseppe, D., Delfour, M., & Mitter, S. (2007). *Representation and control of infinite dimensional systems* (2nd ed.). Birkhauser.

Burns, J. A., & King, B. B. (1999). On the design of feedback controllers for a convecting fluid flow. In *Proceedings of the International Conference on Control Applications*, (vol. 2, pp. 1157-1162). IEEE.

Butkovski, A. G. (1982). *Green's functions and transfer functions handbook*. Chichester, UK: Ellis Herwood.

Byrnes, C. A., Gilliam, D. S., & Shubov, V. I. (1994). Global lyapunov stabilization of a nonlinear distributed parameter system. In *Proceedings of the 33rd IEEE Conference on Decision and Control*. IEEE.

Cagalaban, G., Soh, W., & Kim, K. (2011). Devising an optimal scheme for wireless sensors for patient report tracking and monitoring in ubiquitous healthcare. *International Journal of Software Engineering and its Applications, 5*(4), 63-76.

Chen, C. F., & Hsiao, C. H. (1997). Haar wavelet method for solving lumped and distributed parameter system. *IEEE Proceedings on Control Theory and Applications, 144*(1).

Chen, Y. H., & Piontek, E. D. (2000). *Robust modal control of distributed-parameter systems with uncertainty*. Paper presented at the American Control Conference. New York, NY.

Cheng, M. B., Radisavljevic, V., Chang, C. C., Lin, C. F., & Su, W. C. (2009). A sampled-data singularly perturbed boundary control for a heat conduction system with noncollocated observation. *IEEE Transactions on Automatic Control, 54*(6), 1305–1310. doi:10.1109/TAC.2009.2015522.

Christofides, P. D. (2001). *Nonlinear and robust control of partial differential equation systems: Methods and applications to transport-reaction processes*. Boston: Birkhauser.

Christofides, P. D., & Daoutidis, P. (1997). Finite-dimensional control of parabolic PDE systems using approximate inertial manifolds. In *Proceedings of the 36th Conference on Decision & Control*. San Diego, CA: IEEE.

Curtain, R. F. (2003). On model reduction for control design for distributed parameter systems. In *Research Directions in DPS* (pp. 95–121). Philadelphia: SIAM. doi:10.1137/1.9780898717525. ch4.

D'Andrea, A., & Dellurude, G. E. (2003). Distributed control design for spatially interconnected systems. *IEEE Transactions on Automatic Control, 48*(9), 1478–1495. doi:10.1109/TAC.2003.816954.

Dong, D., & McAvoy, T. J. (1994). Nonlinear principle component analysis-based on principal curves and neural network. In *Proceedings of the American Control Conference*. Baltimore, MD: ACC.

Dresner, L. (1983). *Similarity solutions of nonlinear partial differential equations*. London: Pitman.

Estrin, D., Girod, L., Pottie, G., & Srivastava, M. (2001). Instrumenting the world with wireless sensor networks. In *Proceedings of the IEEE International Conference on Acoustics, Speech, and Signal Processing*, (pp. 2033-2036). IEEE.

Fax, A. J., & Murray, R. M. (2004). Information flow and cooperative control of vehicle formations. *IEEE Transactions on Automatic Control, 49*(9), 1465–1476. doi:10.1109/TAC.2004.834433.

Foias, C., Jolly, M. S., Kevrekidis, I. G., Sell, G. R., & Titi, E. S. (1989). On the computation of inertial manifolds. *Physics Letters. [Part A], 131*, 433–437. doi:10.1016/0375-9601(88)90295-2.

Godasi, S., Karakas, A., & Palazoglu, A. (1999). A study of the control on nonlinear distributed parameter systems. In *Proceedings of the American Control Conference*, (vol. 2, pp. 1096-1100). ACC.

Guo, L., & Billings, S. A. (2006). Identification of partial differential equations models for continuous spatio-temporal dynamical systems. *IEEE Transactions on Circuits and Wystems. II, Express Briefs, 53*(8).

Herrmann, G., Spurgeon, S. S., & Edwards, C. (2003). A model-based sliding mode control methodology applied to the HDA-plant. *Journal of Process Control*, 2014–2019.

Hornik, H., Stinchcombe, M., & White, H. (1989). Multilayer feedforward networks are universal approximators. *Neural Networks*, 2, 359–366. doi:10.1016/0893-6080(89)90020-8.

Jacob, B., & Zwart, H. (1999). Equivalent conditions for stabilizability of infinite dimensional systems with admissible control operators. *SIAM Journal on Control and Optimization*, 37(5), 1149–1455. doi:10.1137/S036301299833344X.

Jang, J. S. R. (1993). ANFIS: Adaptive-network-based fuzzy inference system. *IEEE Transactions on Systems, Man, and Cybernetics*, 23(3), 665–685. doi:10.1109/21.256541.

Joshi, A., & Sevick-Muraca, E. M. (2004). Adaptive finite element methods for distributed parameter system identification: Applications in fluorescence enhanced frequency domain optical tomography. In *Proceedings of the American Control Conference*, (vol. 3, pp. 2263-2267). ACC.

Jovanovic, M. R., & Barnieh, B. (2003). Lyapunov-based state-feedback distributed control of systems on lattices. In *Proceedings of the American Control Conference*, (pp. 101-106). ACC.

Jurdjevic, V. (1997). *Geometric control theory*. New York: Cambridge University Press.

Keulen, B. V. (1993). *H∞ control for distributed parameter systems: A state space approach*. Boston: Birkhauser. doi:10.1007/978-1-4612-0347-6.

Kramer, M. A. (1991). Nonlinear principal component analysis using auto-associative neural networks. *AIChE Journal. American Institute of Chemical Engineers*, 37, 234–243. doi:10.1002/aic.690370209.

Lasiecka, I., & Triggiani, R. (2000). *Control theory for partial differential equations. Cambridge, UK*. Cambridge: University Press.

Lee, J. H., Morari, M., & Garcia, C. E. (1994). State-space representation of model predictive control. *Automatica*, 30(4), 707–717. doi:10.1016/0005-1098(94)90159-7.

Li, W. (2000). Recursive PCA for adaptive process monitoring. *Journal of Process Control*, 10, 471–486. doi:10.1016/S0959-1524(00)00022-6.

Lu, B., & Hsieh, W. (2003). Simplified nonlinear principal component analysis. In *Proceedings of the International Joint Conference on Neural Networks 2003*, (vol. 1, pp. 759-763). IEEE.

Luo, Z. H., Guo, B. Z., & Morgul, O. (1999). *Stability and stabilization of infinite dimensional systems with applications*. Berlin: Springer. doi:10.1007/978-1-4471-0419-3.

Luyben, M., Tyreus, B. D., & Luyben, W. (1999). *Plantwide process control*. New York: McGraw Hill.

Mahadevan, N., & Hoo, K. A. (1998). Model reduction and controller development for a class of a distributed systems. In *Proceedings of the American Control Conference*, (pp. 2315-2320). ACC.

Mayne, D., & Michalska, H. (1993). Receding horizon control of nonlinear systems. *IEEE Transactions on Automatic Control*, 38(10), 1512–1516. doi:10.1109/9.241565.

Mazzeo, N.A., & Venegas. (1997). An application of generalized similarity analysis to atmospheric diffusion. *Atmospheric Research*, 43, 157–166. doi:10.1016/S0169-8095(96)00028-2.

Mehrkanoon, S., Falck, T., & Suykens, J. A. K. (2012). Approximate solutions to ordinary differential equations using least squares support vector machines. *IEEE Transactions on Neural Networks and Learning Systems*, (99).

Mendez, P. F., & Eager, T. W. (1999). Order of magnitude scaling of complex engineering problems. In *Proceedings of the Seventh Symposium on Energy and Engineering Science*, (pp. 106-113). IEEE.

Michalska, H., & Mayne, D. Q. (1993). Robust receding horizon control of constrained nonlinear systems. *IEEE Transactions on Automatic Control, 38*(11), 1623–1633. doi:10.1109/9.262032.

Minai, A. A. (1992). *The robustness of feedforward neural networks: A preliminary investigation.* (Ph.D. Dissertation). University of Virginia, Charlottesville, VA.

Mitra, S., & Hayachi, Y. (2000). Neuro-fuzzy rule generation: Survey in soft-computing framework. *IEEE Transactions on Neural Networks, 11*(3), 748–768. doi:10.1109/72.846746 PMID:18249802.

Motee, N., & Jadbabaie, A. (2006). Distributed receding horizon control of spatially invariant systems. In *Proceedings of the American Control Conference*, (pp. 731-736). ACC.

Novakovic, D. (2002). *Numerical reservoir characterization using dimensionless scale numbers with application in upscaling.* (Ph.D. dissertation). Louisiana State University. Baton Rouge, LA.

Orlov, Y., Yiming, L., & Christofides, P. D. (2003). Robust stabilization of infinite dimensional systems using discontinous output feedback control. *International Journal of Control, 1*, 821–826.

Palazoglu, A., & Karakas, A. (2000). Control of nonlinear distributed parameter systems using generalized invariants. *Automatica, 36*, 697–703. doi:10.1016/S0005-1098(99)00196-X.

Poggio, T., & Girosi, F. (1990). Networks for approximating and learning. *Proceedings of the IEEE, 78*(9). doi:10.1109/5.58326.

Rawlings, J. B., & Muske, K. R. (1993). The stability of constrained receding horizon control. *IEEE Transactions on Automatic Control, 38*(10), 1512–1516. doi:10.1109/9.241565.

Szirtes, T. (1997). *Applied dimensional analysis and modeling.* New York: McGraw-Hill.

Valle, S. et al. (1999). Selection of the number of principal components: A new criterion with comparison to existing methods. *Industrial & Engineering Chemistry Research, 38*, 4389–4401. doi:10.1021/ie990110i.

Williamson, R. C., & Helmke, U. (1995). Existence and uniqueness results for neural network approximations. *IEEE Transactions on Neural Networks, 6*(1), 2–13. doi:10.1109/72.363455 PMID:18263280.

Zheng, D., Hoo, K. A., & Piovoso, M. J. (2002). Finite dimensional modeling and control of distributed parameter system. In *Proceedings of the American Control Conference.* Anchorage, AK: ACC.

ADDITIONAL READING

Abid, S., Fnaiech, F., & Najim, M. (2001). A fast feedforward training algorithm using a modified form of the standard backpropagation algorithm. *IEEE Transactions on Neural Networks, 12*(2), 424–430. doi:10.1109/72.914537 PMID:18244397.

Bamieh, B., Paganini, F., & Dahleh, M. A. (2002). Distributed control of spatially invariant systems. *IEEE Transactions on Automatic Control, 47*(7), 1091–1107. doi:10.1109/TAC.2002.800646.

Cooke, T. (2002). Two variations on Fisher's linear discriminant for pattern recognition. *IEEE Transactions on Pattern Analysis and Machine Intelligence, 24*(2), 268–273. doi:10.1109/34.982904.

Demetriou, M. A. (2005). Robust sensor location optimization in distributed parameter systems using functional observers. In *Proceedings of the 44th IEEE International Conference on Decision and Control*, (pp. 7187 – 7192). IEEE.

Fazio, R. (1999). Numerical applications of the scaling concept. *Acta Applicandae Mathematicae, 55*(1), 1–25. doi:10.1023/A:1006197920463.

Filici, C. (2008). On a neural network approximator to ODE. *IEEE Transactions on Neural Networks, 19*(3), 539–543. doi:10.1109/TNN.2007.915109 PMID:18334374.

Haykin, S. (1994). *Neural networks –A theoretical foundation*. Upper Saddle River, NJ: Prentice Hall.

Hu, & Zeigler, B.P. (2005). Model continuity in the design of dynamic distributed real-time systems. *IEEE Transactions on Systems, Man, and Cybernetics, Part A, 35*(6), 867-878.

Hyvarinen, A., & Oja, E. (2000). Independent component analysis: Algorithms and applications. *Neural Networks, 13*, 411–430. doi:10.1016/S0893-6080(00)00026-5 PMID:10946390.

Jang, J. S. R. (1993). ANFIS: Adaptive-network-based fuzzy inference system. *IEEE Transactions on Systems, Man, and Cybernetics, 23*(3), 665–685. doi:10.1109/21.256541.

Karnik, A., & Kumar, A. (2007). Distributed optimal self-organization in ad hoc wireless sensor networks. *IEEE/ACM Transactions on Networking, 15*(5), 1035–1045. doi:10.1109/TNET.2007.896227.

Kolmogorov, A. N. (1957). On the representation of continuous function of many variables by superposition of continuous functions of one variable and addition. *Doklady Akademii Nauk, 144*(5), 679–681.

Mahadevan, N., & Hoo, K. A. (1998). Model reduction and controller development for a class of a distributed systems. In *Proceedings of the American Control Conference*, (pp. 2315-2320). ACC.

Okba, T., Ilyes, E., & Hassani, M. (2012). Online identification of nonlinear system using reduced kernel principal component analysis. *Neural Computing & Applications, 21*(1), 161–169. doi:10.1007/s00521-010-0461-x.

Ramuhalli, P., Udpa, L., & Udpa, S. S. (2005). Finite element neural networks for solving differential equations. *IEEE Transactions on Neural Networks, 16*(6), 1381–1392. doi:10.1109/TNN.2005.857945 PMID:16342482.

Shaocheng, T., Changliang, L., Yongming, L., & Huaguang, Z. (2011). Adaptive fuzzy decentralized control of large-scale nonlinear systems with time-varying delays and unknown high-frequency gain sign. *IEEE Transactions Systems Man Cybernetics. Part B, 41*(2), 474–485.

Sirovich, L. (1987). Turbulence and the dynamics of coherent structures part I-part III. *Quarterly of Applied Mathematics, 45*(3), 561–590.

Staffans, O. (2005). *Well-posed linear systems*. London: Cambridge University Press. doi:10.1017/CBO9780511543197.

Tucsnak, M., & Weiss, G. (2009). *Observation and control for operator semigroups*. Boston: Birkhauser. doi:10.1007/978-3-7643-8994-9.

Wang, Y., Inman, D. J., & Slater, J. C. (1992). Variable coefficient distributed parameters system models for structures with piezoceramic actuators and sensors. In *Proceedings of the 31ˢᵗ IEEE Conference on Decision and Control*, (vol. 2, pp. 1803-1808). IEEE.

Wu & Li. (2008). H^∞ Fuzzy observer-based control for a class of nonlinear distributed parameter systems with control constraints. *IEEE Transactions on Fuzzy Systems, 16*(2), 502–516. doi:10.1109/TFUZZ.2007.896351.

Yanan, Song, & Feiqi, Deng, Qi, & Luo. (2005). Simulation of a class of delay stochastic system with distributed parameter. *Journal of Systems Engineering and Electronics, 16*(4), 843–846.

Yu-Te, C., & Bor-Sen, C. (2010). A fuzzy approach for robust reference-tracking control design of nonlinear distributed parameter time-delayed systems and its application. *IEEE Transactions on Fuzzy Systems*, *18*(6), 1041–1057. doi:10.1109/TFUZZ.2010.2058809.

Zhang, Li, & Li. (2008). Analytical study and stability design of a 3-D fuzzy logic controller for spatially distributed dynamic systems. *IEEE Transactions on Fuzzy Systems*, *16*(6), 1613–1625. doi:10.1109/TFUZZ.2008.2005934.

Zidong, W., Bo, S., Huisheng, S., & Guoliang, W. (2012). Quantized H^∞ control of nonlinear stochastic time-delay systems with missing measurements. *IEEE Transactions on Automatic Control*, *57*(6), 1431–1444. doi:10.1109/TAC.2011.2176362.

Chapter 19
Multi–Core Embedded Systems

Ricardo Chessini Bose
University of Mons, Belgium

Laurent Jolczyk
University of Mons, Belgium

Georgios Fourtounis
University of Mons, Belgium

Paulo Da Cunha Possa
University of Mons, Belgium

Naim Harb
University of Mons, Belgium

Carlos Valderrama
University of Mons, Belgium

ABSTRACT

Multiple processors, microcontrollers, or DSPs have been used in embedded systems to distribute control and data flow according to the application at hand. The recent trends of incorporating multiple cores in the same chip significantly expands the processing power of such heterogeneous systems. However, these trends demand new ways of building and programming embedded systems in order to control cost and complexity. In this context, the authors present an overview on multi-core architectures and their inter-core communication mechanisms, dedicated cores used as accelerators, and hardware reconfiguration providing flexibility on today's multi-core embedded systems. Finally, they highlight tools, frameworks, and techniques for programming multi-cores and accelerators in order to take advantage of their performance in a robust and cost effective manner.

1. INTRODUCTION

Embedded systems comprise diverse devices, ranging from consumer multimedia devices to industrial controllers. These systems are designed to perform specific tasks with high reliability requirements, low power consumption, real-time response demands, functional flexibility and low cost. In the case of multimedia processing and high-speed telecommunications, the real-time constraints and quality of service demanded require intensive computation capabilities and careful system design.

Multiprocessor architectures have become the foundation of most common appliances, such as digital TV, navigation systems and wireless devices. During the last four decades the drive for performance has resulted in microprocessors becoming faster, clocked at higher-frequencies, and having a more complex architecture. Indi-

DOI: 10.4018/978-1-4666-3922-5.ch019

vidual processors that integrate many processing elements in the same chip have recently become mainstream, spreading to embedded systems with advanced performance requirements. Apart from being an opportunity to use more processing power for demanding applications, distributing computations on many processors also addresses the problem of power dissipation, which is critical for small embedded systems that run on batteries or other limited power sources.

The transition from the single processor (*uni-processor*) to the multi-core as a component for building embedded systems means that system design and building must adapt. Current system building techniques must be updated and new ones must be developed to match the new hardware capabilities.

This chapter aims at giving an overview of the current state of incorporating multi-cores into embedded systems. We give the basic background (Section 2) needed for understanding embedded multi-cores at the hardware level and from the programmer's view. We describe (Section 3) the main changes that they bring to embedded systems design and the issues that arise, followed by the practices and tools that researchers and the industry have found effective in addressing these problems. We then give an overview of the emerging trends related to embedded multi-cores in Section 4 and we conclude in the last section.

2. BACKGROUND

In this section we describe the current state of multi-core hardware for embedded systems, both homogeneous and heterogeneous. We then proceed to give the basic elements of the programmer's view over multi-core hardware.

2.1. Multi-Core Hardware

Moore's law is an observation that has predicted hardware development for more than 40 years. It states that the number of transistors that can be placed on an integrated circuit roughly doubles every two years. This became the basis for the uniprocessor scaling of the 1970s-2000s, where the frequency of the chips increased by orders of magnitude, boosting performance and giving system designers headroom for building efficient systems on a decreasing budget.

Due to physical limitations related to heat dissipation and power consumption in high operating frequencies, it was recently realized (Kish, 2002) that current techniques for building integrated circuits cannot sustain frequency scaling. Since Moore's law still holds, the industry switched to placing more microprocessors, known as *cores*, into so-called *multi-core processors*, or *multi-cores*. Assuming that Moore's law will continue to hold, it is expected that the number of cores contained in a System-on-Chip (SoC) will double approximately every two years (Paulin, 2010).

The mainstream adoption of multi-cores has recently pushed such microprocessors inside embedded systems, promising to speed up computations and improve power consumption. Since embedded systems were already heterogeneous, using many custom processors in the same system, these new multi-cores, often integrated in a multiprocesor System-on-Chip (MPSoC), add an extra dimension to embedded system design, as homogeneous components in a heterogeneous environment.

Homogeneous multi-cores consist of the same processing element repeated on the die, to be used as a conventional symmetric multi-processor. For example, the Tilera TILEPro64 processor (TILERA, n.d.) contains 64 identical interconnected cores targeting high-performance embedded applications with scalable performance, power efficiency, and low processing latency. The TMS320C6678 multi-core DSP from Texas Instruments (Texas Instruments, n.d.b) contains eight TMS320C66x DSP Core Subsystems, each with a C66x Fixed/Floating-Point core, shared memory and a network coprocessor. The Parallax Propeller chip contains eight processors that can operate simultaneously, either independently or cooperatively, sharing common resources through a central hub (Parallax Inc., n.d.). The Massively Parallel Processor Array (MPPA) is a regular multi-core architecture targeting embedded systems. MPPAs provide scalability to processing power and real-time data flow for streaming media applications with hard real-time requirements (Hannig & Jurgen, 2001). The architecture is a Multiple-Instruction Multiple-Data (MIMD) parallel array of CPUs and memories interconnected by a 2D-mesh configurable network. The memory is distributed and individual CPU/RAM blocks are located in tiles stacked up to form the array.

The massively parallel hardware of Graphics Processing Units (GPUs), comprising hundreds of streaming processors, can also be programmed to solve computationally intensive problems involving data parallel computations. This has led to general-purpose computing on graphics processing units (GPGPU), effectively presenting GPUs as coprocessors in embedded systems. For example, the OMAP3530 SoC offers the GPU as a programmable coprocessor.

Heterogeneous multi-cores include in the same die General Purpose Processors (GPPs), Digital Signal Processors (DSPs), memory and custom chips (IP cores). For instance, the TI OMAP4430 SoC bundles a dual-core ARM Cortex A9 CPU, an Imagination Technologies PowerVR GPU, and a multimedia hardware accelerator with a programmable DSP that supports 1080p Full HD and multi-standard video encoding and decoding. NVIDIA provides the five-core ARM architecture Tegra3 for use in tablets and smartphones; from the five cores, one is a low power companion core that functions as a battery saver, while the other four can be used as a typical quad-core ARM MPSoC to run heavyweight parallel tasks, such as multimedia, or to run many applications in parallel. The Cell Broadband Engine used in the Sony Playstation 3 game console combines a Power Architecture processor (the Power Processing Element, or PPE) with eight streaming coprocessors (the Synergistic Processing Elements, or SPEs), each with its own memory. Each SPE has

several SIMD (Single Instruction Multiple Data) units that can process from 2 double-precision floating-point values up to 16-byte values per instruction and it is controlled by the PPE. The Software Scalable System on Chip architecture (3SoC) (Meng & Chaudhary, 2004) consists of dozens of high performance RISC-like and DSP processors on a single chip.

Field-Programmable Gate Arrays (FPGAs) (Compton & Hauck, 2002) are reconfigurable hardware that can be used to implement one processor core (*soft-core*) or more (*multi-soft-cores*). Altera Nios II and Xilinx Microblaze are examples of two soft-core designs that provide a pre-designed and pre-verified extensible instruction set architecture and are widely used in both prototyping and building actual embedded systems (Fernandez-Alonso, Castells-Rufas, Risueno, Carrabina, & Joven, 2010). The CUSTARD (Dimond, Mencer, & Luk, 2005) architecture is based on configuring a set of soft-cores, with parameterisable numbers of threads, threading type, datapath widths, and custom instructions. Multi-soft-cores are a promising platform for exploring current multi-core designs and they offer a flexible solution for many applications due to their reconfiguration capabilities.

FPGAs can be viewed as heterogeneous parallel computing substrates, where hardware compilers take the task of accepting programs in a high-level language and produce the hardware description language (HDL) description that will configure the FPGA (Martin & Smith, 2009). For specific applications, they compare favorably to traditional multi-cores, having lower power consumption and better performance.

A recent trend is bundling CPU cores with FPGAs, where the CPU runs a part of the software, and the accompanying FPGA acts as an accelerator, being configured for the custom task at hand, either before the execution, or during runtime (the case of *partial dynamic reconfiguration*). Such examples are the Intel Atom E6x5C (Intel, n.d.a) which combines an Intel Atom CPU and an Altera FPGA, and the Xilinx Zynq-7000 EPP, which bundles a dual-core ARM Cortex-A9 MPCore with a Xilinx 28nm FPGA. The Rad-hard Unified Scalable Heterogeneous (RUSH) architecture (Beresini, Ricketts, & Taylor, 2011) is a radiation resistant heterogeneous platform with both a 49-core processor (the Maestro) and an FPGA, for use in space applications. It is also possible that computations in these hybrid systems can migrate during runtime from the CPU to the FPGA or vice versa (Pellizzoni & Caccamo, 2007).

In general, FPGAs and GPUs are orthogonal solutions but they can also be combined as in the case of the Axel (Tsoi & Luk, 2010) heterogeneous cluster.

Except from homogeneous vs. heterogeneous, multi-cores in embedded systems can also be categorized according to their memory architecture: if there is a single memory that is visible to all cores, it is a *shared-memory* system; if each core sees its own memory address space, it is a *distributed memory* system.

2.2. Programming Embedded Multi-Cores

To develop software for multi-cores, the parallel hardware resources must be exploited in a safe and efficient way, taking into account the characteristics of the intended system. In programming embedded systems, we distinguish between *concurrency* and *parallelism*. Concurrency describes the behavior of many events appearing to happen at the same time. Parallelism is events occurring simultaneously. Concurrency is therefore what the user sees; it may be implemented by parallelism (where the hardware runs many processes in parallel) or not (for example, operating systems can appear to run multiple tasks at the same time on uniprocessors, scheduling the tasks in an interleaved fashion). On the other hand, parallel hardware may be used to implement a concurrent system, or to speed up a computation that appears indivisible from the user's perspective, such as a long-running computation. The following para-

graphs will examine using multi-cores for parallel execution, either for concurrent systems, or for parallel computation.

Concurrent software is pervasive in embedded systems, for example mobile phones must run a communication stack in real-time, while at the same time another part of the system communicates with the mobile data packet network or runs the device's user interface with minimum latency.

Programming parallel software has been based on the notion of the *thread*, which is an operating system concept that represents a piece of running code together with its local and global storage. A program may use many threads, each carrying out different work (*coarse grain parallelism*); these can then be scheduled by the operating system among the available cores according to system load, required power consumption, job priority, or real-time demands.

On a different level than threads, is *task parallelism*. It abstracts over threads, asking the programmer to provide the necessary tasks to be executed: these are then assigned to real threads, frequently on a ratio of many tasks per thread, and are managed by a runtime system that schedules them automatically on the available cores. This distribution lets the programmer split computations in smaller pieces (*fine-grain parallelism*), depending on the tasking mechanism to efficiently run them. Higher-level synchronization structures are usually provided, like task pools and concurrent data structures.

Data parallelism is another approach to parallelize computations that is similar to task parallelism but focuses on the distribution of the data among the multiple cores. For specific applications that involve data sets amenable to distribution, such as vectors or matrices, data parallelism can prove very efficient and is widely used in scientific computing. Data parallelism may also be fine-grain, as in the case of GPU computations.

An even finer-grain of parallelism is *dataflow programming*, where the programmer splits the program in as small nodes as possible. The compiler and the runtime system then examine the dependencies between the different dataflow nodes and schedule them in a way that the computations that are needed are always evaluated first compared to the other computations that need their results. For applications such as signal processing, multimedia, or pipelined algorithms, this can be very close to their actual, flow-based description.

Communication between the different parts running in parallel depends on the system architecture: if done through a shared memory, special data structures must be used for mutual exclusion and synchronization; if the parts are distributed, they must exchange messages with each other in order to synchronize.

3. BUILDING MULTI-CORE SYSTEMS

In this section we examine the problems of building multi-core systems and solutions that address these issues.

3.1. Problems

Multi-cores demand new techniques from system builders: hardware designers have to build systems taking care of scalable synchronization and communication between the processing elements, while programmers must write software that can efficiently distribute its computations among the available cores, using suitable design patterns. We will examine these two issues in the following sections.

3.1.1. Inter-Core Communication Mechanisms

As resource density is constantly increasing to respond to application needs, SoC design must exploit the full potential of every Processing Element (PE) available. This crucially depends on the dataflow management between an important number of PEs, storage elements and I/O in a multi-core architecture.

The two traditional interconnection techniques that are extensively used in small SoC design, bus-based and Point to Point (P2P) connection, present some limitations in handling efficiently the dataflow of complex multi-core architectures.

A bus interconnection is a shared communication architecture. Only one PE can transmit data at the same time. When the number of PEs increases, the available bandwidth is split between them. Moreover, the performance of the bus architecture depends on the number of peripherals that will use it. As the number of PEs increases, the maximal speed of the implemented interconnection decreases. This limitation is shown in Figure 1. This plot presents the evolution of the

Figure 1. Implementation results of a bus and a mesh network-on-chip

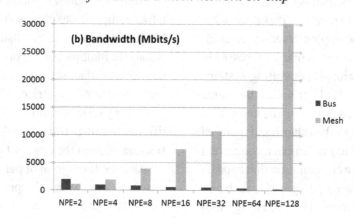

maximal bandwidth of a bus implemented in an FPGA chip when the number of PEs increases.

P2P connections are dedicated interconnections. A private communication pathway connects only two elements in the chip. The communication protocol is only constrained by the two elements connected together. Using P2P private links offers better performance because different data can pass through all the links at the same time. The communication becomes parallel. However, a communication scheme that uses only P2P links cannot be as flexible in terms of connectivity as a shared communication architecture. It is not possible to reach two PEs with the same link.

In this context, the Network-on-Chip architecture (NoC) (Dally & Towles, 2001; Amde, Felicijan, Efthymiou, Edwards, & Lavagno, 2005; Bartic, Mignolet, Nollet, Marescaux, Verkest, Vernalde, & Lauwereins, 2003) was introduced. NoCs are flexible interconnection architectures that can be seen as a trade-off between bus and P2P architectures. A NoC is made of routers connected together and to the PEs (Beigne & Vivet, 2006). Application data is transmitted in data-packets which contain routing information. P2P links are used to connect the routers. Thanks to the routing infrastructures, these private links are shared by all PEs. A NoC architecture has better behavior than a bus interconnection in huge multi-core system. The NoC infrastructure evolves with the number of PEs. More PEs lead to more routers able to process data in parallel. The maximum bandwidth of a standard Mesh implementation is represented in Figure 1. When the number of PEs is low, NoC and bus performance is similar.

There are many NoC architectures; to analyse the background of NoC implementations we adopt a 3D view of the design space (see Figure 2). At the origin of this representation stands the typical Mesh representation. The level of customization increases along the axis (x, y and z). The communication paradigm corresponds to the x-axis. This dimension captures how the packets are transferred through the network (such as deter-

ministic vs. adaptive routing). The communication infrastructures are represented along the y-axis, which defines how nodes are interconnected. The examples shown are regular networks, semi-customized networks and fully customized networks. Finally, the third dimension, the application axis, defines the dependence relation between the NoC and the target application. Close to the origin, the network solution is application-independent; another application can be easily mapped onto the same architecture. Far from the origin, the characteristics of the implemented network depend mainly on the application constraints. Mapping another application becomes a complicated or even impossible task. For instance, this can be achieved if the network is composed of two sub-networks that cannot communicate with each other.

Bus and P2P communication architectures are located in the NoC design space to allow another comparison point. The bus solution is located at the origin of the representation. The regular and deterministic NoC is the closest architecture to the bus. The P2P communication solution is highly customized, deterministic and application dependent. It is situated far from the origin in the YZ plane.

The main issue in using NoC architectures with multi-core embedded systems consists in designing the appropriate architecture that satisfies the application needs. NoCs offer more flex-

Figure 2. Network-on-chip design space

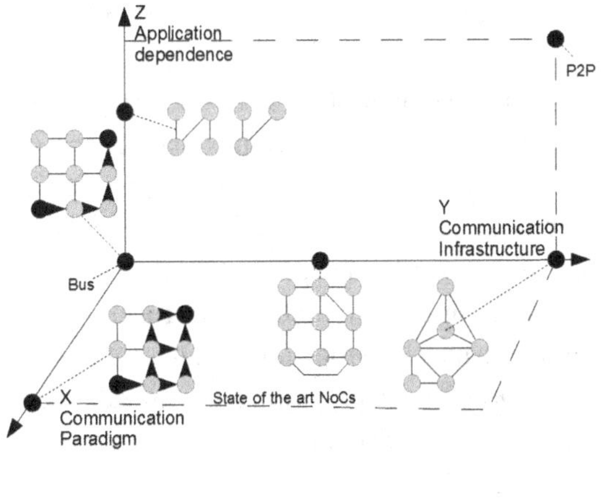

ibility. This also means that parameters such as topology selection, router design, and application mapping have to be taken into account during the design process of the multi-core architecture. The design goal is to find the best tradeoff between performance and resource or power consumption (Ogras, Hu, & Marculescu, 2005). This requires an adapted design methodology that will affect the application and platform decisions, all the way down to the circuit and layout-level considerations.

3.1.2. Parallel Programming Problems

Building and programming multi-cores is still considered difficult for many applications. Traditional uniprocessors that follow the von Neumann architecture are well-understood: we have decades of experience programming them, there is a standard theoretical model of computation that faithfully describes the cost and complexity of programming them, and their hardware architectures have been extensively analyzed. Multiprocessors on the other side, are less familiar: although they have been long used in big applications such as bioinformatics or military systems, only recently did multi-cores become commodity hardware, accessible by many programmers, and usable in small systems. The lack of experience regarding their use explains why we still do not have a standard model of multi-core computation, while in practice the landcape of multi-core programming solutions is fragmented with many competing frameworks and technologies.

In practice, thread-based programming is often found to be too low-level since computations must be represented on the operating system level. Thread synchronization is manual and can be subtle: two or more threads may block each other with no chance for progress (*deadlock*), enter a constantly changing state that does not let them progress (*livelock*), or the result of their interaction may be wrong for timing reasons (*race condition*). Often a program using threads seems to work correctly, failing unexpectedly on rare

cases, for no apparent reason. Threads are also expensive for the operating system to create and destroy and for this reason are only used to split work into few and big pieces of computation.

Threads are however the basic building block of many higher-level parallel programming frameworks, which abstract over them in order to provide the programmer a more convenient, efficient or productive view of the underlying hardware. These abstractions will be mentioned in the next section, where we describe solutions to effectively manage parallelism.

3.2. Solutions and Recommendations

In the following sections we describe solutions along two dimensions in multi-cores: the interconnection architectures and the programming tools.

3.2.1. Multi-Core Interconnection

NoC design implies dealing with several research problems thoroughly assessed in the literature (Marculescu, Ogras, Peh, Jerger, & Hoskote, 2009). Solutions provided are NoC design methodologies and computer-aided design algorithms

Figure 3. Generic network-on-chip design flow

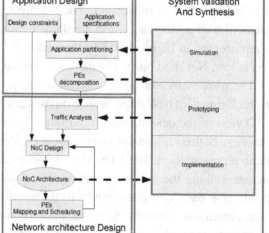

aimed at system, microarchitecture, and circuit levels of abstraction.

Figure 3 presents a generic development methodology for multi-core embedded systems. This generic solution presents all the factors to be taken into account and their inter-relation (Bertozzi, Jalabert, Murali, Tamhankar, Stergiou, Benini, & de Micheli, 2005). The methodology can be divided in three main parts: application design (Balfour & Dally, 2006), network architecture design and system validation and synthesis.

1. **Application design:** The first part of the design flow consists in finding the adequate set of PEs. This receives as inputs the design constraints and the application specifications. Based on these factors, it's possible to split the application into a set of tasks to be mapped onto the PEs of the NoC (Ascia, Catania, & Palesi, 2004). When the application is unknown, this part of the design consists in establishing reference traffic patterns that will be used for the NoC design (Grecu, Ivanov, Pande, Jantsch, Salminen, Orgas, & Marculescu, 2007).

2. **Network architecture design:** The second part of the design flow consists in defining the NoC infrastructure. A good understanding of the traffic patterns and design constraints helps determine the optimal network topology; this has a huge impact on design costs, power, and performance, and helps designers choose an efficient routing algorithm and flow control scheme in order to manage the incoming traffic (Bjerregaard & Sparso, 2004). Communication bandwidth and network latency are the key performance metrics, while area, power, and reliability are the key cost metrics.

3. **System Validation and Synthesis:** Many times during the design process, the embedded SoC has to be evaluated. In addition to performance, early and efficient floorplanning and accurate estimation of area and

power are necessary for optimizing the design and ensuring quick convergence of the design flow. This can be done with the help of simulation, prototypes, or measured in the implementation.

NoC design is a multifaceted process involving both application and communication architecture. The additional reading section of this chapter provides references to a comprehensive introduction to existing NoC design practices and current research topics.

3.2.2. Software Programming for Multi-Cores

Developing software for multiprocessors depends on the hardware architecture and the parallelism potential inherent in the software, combined with the programming language and framework used.

There are programming languages that offer a high-level view of the parallel resources of the underlying machine. The OpenMP standard (OpenMP Architecture Review Board, n.d.) provides extensions of the C and FORTRAN programming languages in the form of compiler directives; it offers parallel for-loops, data and task parallelism, work-sharing and synchronization primitives. It targets shared-memory multiprocessors, extended to use DSPs (Texas Instruments, n.d.a), multi-core DSPs (Texas Instruments, n.d.a), the Cell BE (O'Brien, O'Brien, Sura, Chen, & Zhang, 2008), the M32R chip multiprocessor (Hotta, Sato, Nakajima, & Ojima, 2004), and heterogeneous MPSoCs (Liu & Chaudhary, 2003; Margongiu & Benini, 2009; Chapman, Huang, Biscondi, Stotzer, Shrivastava, & Gatherere, 2009). The Erlang (Armstrong, 2007) language by Ericsson is based on message-passing processes and has been used to program parallel and distributed systems such as high-performance phone and ATM switches.

Another approach to express parallelism is to use a framework that provides the necessary parallel building blocks. Thread-based programming can be based on POSIX threads (Butenhof, 1997). The Intel Threading Building Blocks library contains C++ data and control structures that can be used to build programs where concurrent access to data is safe and parallel computations are handled by a scheduler. The MPI standard provides a framework for expressing distributed computations and message-passing between different parts of the system and can be used on an MPSoC with a NoC (Joven, Angiolini, Castells-Rufas, de Micheli, & Carrabina-Bordoll, 2010). The MSA framework (Li, Wang, Hsu, Chen, & Lee, 2010) provides a compact programming model for distributed multi-core embedded systems featuring remote procedure calls (RPC), message-passing and data streaming. MPOpt-Cell (Franceschelli, et al., 2011) is another framework for programming the Cell BE. The Multicore Association offers MCAPI (Multicore Communications API Working Group, 2012), a powerful API for communication and synchronization between cores in embedded systems. MCAPI is a compact message-passing API optimized for low-latency inter-core networks and small-scale distributed embedded systems. For some application types, there are specialized software frameworks that can take advantage of parallel hardware such as the Open Source Computer Vision (OpenCV) (Texas Instruments, 2011) library of programming functions for real-time computer vision. Besides pure software frameworks, there are also mixed hardware-software frameworks that combine a programming model with an underlying architecture; for example, an adaptive message passing framework for programming MPSoC systems is given by Almedia et al. (Almeida, Sassatelli, Benoit, Saint-Jean, Varyani, Torres, & Robert, 2009).

Heterogeneous multi-cores can be used by an umbrella framework like OpenCL (Grewe & O'Boyle, 2011) or Intel Parallel Building Blocks (Intel, n.d.b). OpenCL in particular aims to be the industry standard and is open.

A higher-level approach to programming embedded systems is to write a high-level model of the system in a suitable formalism and have a tool generate the actual program and map it onto the multi-core hardware. Environments such as LabVIEW (National Instruments, n.d.), Simulink (MathWorks, n.d.), and Matlab (Bartosinski, Hanzalek, Struzka, & Waszniowski, 2007) let the user describe the program in an expressive higher-level formalism; this description is then translated to a system suitable for parallel implementation. Model-based synchronous languages such as Lustre (Halbwachs, Caspi, Raymond, & Pilaud, 1991), Esterel (Berry & Gonthier, 1992), and Signal (Le Guernic, Gautier, Le Borgne, & Le Marie, 1991) have been used to build control systems and in avionics applications, providing high-level programming models that can run on distributed systems (Girault, 2005). Another model is stream programming, which is suitable for multimedia and signal processing applications; such languages are StreamIt (Thies, Karczmarek, & Amarasinghe, 2002), SPIR (Choi, Lin, Chong, Mahlke, & Mudge, 2009), SPUR (Zhang, Li, Song, & Liu, 2005), Baker (Chen, Li, Lian, Lin, Liu, Liu, & Ju, 2005), and Spidle (Consel, Hamdi, Reveillere, Singaravelu, Yu, & Pu, 2003).

A middle ground between explicit control of parallelism and model-driven program generation, is the automatic extraction of parallelism, using *parallelizing compilers*. Such tools accept a sequential program and analyze it to find hidden parallelism – they then produce an equivalent program that can use the parallel resources available. An example is the Par4All parallelizing and optimizing compiler for C and FORTRAN, that has been used by Thales in embedded systems (Keryel, 2009). On a similar note, tools like Parkour (Jeon, Garcia, Louie, & Taylor, 2011) can predict the parallel speedup of a serial program.

FPGA-based multi-soft-cores may be programmed like classic multi-cores, either using the techniques mentioned above, or using vendor-specific frameworks, such as Altera's Hardware Abstraction Layer (HAL) (Altera, n.d.b) for the case of the Nios II soft-core. In general, programming models are connected to the machine architecture: for heterogenerous embedded systems, distributed approaches like MPI are more popular since the mismatch between the characteristics of their processing elements makes it easier to program them transferring data between the processors; for homogeneous systems it may be easier to schedule data parallel computations among the cores.

3.3. Using FPGAs and GPUs

Hardware synthesis tools are the prime tools used for configuring FPGAs: they take a description in an HDL and produce a description that can be used by vendor-specific tools to configure the logical elements in an FPGA. There has been significant research on programming FPGAs with C or derivatives of C; examples of these hardware compilers are Catapult C (Mentor Graphics, n.d.), ChipCflow (Silva & Lopes, 2010), Handel-C (Loo, Wells, Freije, & Kulick, 2002), and ROCCC (Buyukkurt, Guo, & Najjar, 2006). Other languages are also possible, like the object-oriented Virgil (Kou & Palsberg, 2010). A fundamental problem of hardware compilers is mapping the programming model to the available hardware resources. This calls for careful analysis of the parallelism potential and the resources needed by the input program. The OpenCL framework has been used to program FPGAs (Altera, n.d.a). FPGAs can also be configured by model-driven design environments, such as the Compaan/Laura tools which interface with Matlab (Stefanov, Zissulescu, Turjan, Kienhuis, & Deprettere, 2004).

GPUs can be programmed using custom languages such as Brook (Buck & Hanrahan, 2003), or Cg (Mark, Glanville, Akeley, & Kilgard, 2003). NVIDIA provides the CUDA platform, which supports GPU programming in traditional languages such as C (NVIDIA, n.d.) and Python (Klockner, 2012), and in frameworks such as OpenMP (Ohshima, Hirasawa, & Honda, 2010).

4. FUTURE RESEARCH DIRECTIONS

Research on multi-core systems continues, both on hardware interconnection, to address core scaling, and on software models, to bridge the gap between the programmer's view and the hardware.

Recently, a new issue is considered as the ultimate limit for scaling multi-core systems, *dark silicon* (Esmaeilzadeh, Blem, St. Amant, Sankaralingam, & Burger, 2012). Dark silicon is an expression derived from "dark fiber," which refers to unused optic fiber. Different to dark fiber that originated from a market limit, dark silicon is a technological limit and refers to the amount of transistors that cannot be simultaneously powered up in a silicon die to avoid exceeding the maximum junction temperature. The solution for the dark silicon issue lies on researching new transistor technologies with better power efficiency. However, new power efficient architectures are a wide research field to be explored in order to reduce the dark silicon effects (Goulding-Hotta, et al., 2011; Possa, Schaillie, & Valderrama, 2011).

An answer to the restrictions of dark silicon is specialization: systems will have to be heterogeneous in order to successfully adapt to different workloads and power budget requirements (Suleman, Patt, Sprangle, Rohillah, Ghuloum, & Carmean, 2007). However, we need smart tools to deal with this heterogeneous future: while programming models provide good abstractions of the architecture, the tools that will map system descriptions to real architectures lack information such as communication and interconnection details.

While the number of the cores in embedded systems steadily increases, problems in scaling the interconnection and instruction sets become more complex. This has set the trend for simplifying cores; we anticipate that in future systems, parallelism will be provided by a cloud of very simple cores (Marowka, 2011). Moreover, power consumption has now become a critical metric of performance: uniprocessors consumed power exponentially with frequency, while multi-cores consume power linearly with the number of cores. For programming models, there is a trend of transferring the established models of High-Performance Computing (HPC) on smaller-scale, embedded systems, which are rapidly catching up in complexity with traditional parallel machines. HPC research on shared-memory parallelism, message-passing, and massive parallelism must be adapted for smaller systems, to exploit embedded parallel hardware capabilities.

CONCLUSION

Multi-cores continue to spread in embedded systems, with the aim to increase performance and limit power consumption, as well as serve the growing needs of multimedia and mobile applications.

Core interconnection will become more elaborate as communication costs come to be more important than computation costs (Moore, 2011), while programming models become more effective and smart. Moreover, heterogeneous systems have emerged, which have an advantage in utilizing their resources for parallel computations. Regular and flexible archichtectures, such as FPGAs, GPUs, and MPPAs, are part of a shift towards easy-to-use, regular and scalable systems.

In conclusion, as long as suitable programming platforms and tools are available, we will continue observing the growing use and benefits of multi-cores in embedded systems.

REFERENCES

Almeida, G. M., Sassatelli, G., Benoit, P., Saint-Jean, N., Varyani, S., Torres, L., & Robert, M. (2009). An adaptive message passing MPSoC framework. *International Journal of Reconfigurable Computing*, 242981.

Altera. (n.d.a). *Implementing FPGA design with OpenCL - A future look*. Retrieved April 11, 2012 from http://www.altera.com/education/Webcasts/all/source-files/wc-2011-opencl/player.html

Altera. (n.d.b). *Nios II software developer's handbook*. Retrieved April 11, 2012 from http://www.altera.com/literature/hb/nios2/n2sw_nii5v2.pdf

Amde, M., Felicijan, T., Efthymiou, A., Edwards, D., & Lavagno, L. (2005). Asynchronous on-chip networks. *IEE Proceedings. Computers and Digital Techniques*, *152*(2). doi:10.1049/ip-cdt:20045093.

Armstrong, J. (2007). *Programming erlang: Software for a concurrent world*. Raleigh, NC: Pragmatic Bookshelf.

Ascia, G., Catania, V., & Palesi, M. (2004). Multi-objective mapping for mesh-based NoC architectures. In *Proceedings of the Second IEEE/ACM/IFIP International Conference on Hardware/Software Codesign and System Synthesis* (pp. 182–187). IEEE.

Balfour, J., & Dally, W. J. (2006). Design tradeoffs for tiled CMP on-chip networks. In *Proceedings of the 20th ACM International Conference on Supercomputing (ICS)* (pp. 187–198). ACM.

Bartic, T. A., Mignolet, J.-Y., Nollet, V., Marescaux, T., Verkest, D., Vernalde, S., & Lauwereins, R. (2003). Highly scalable network on chip for reconfigurable systems. In *Proceedings of the International Symposium on System-on-Chip* (pp. 79–82). IEEE.

Bartosinski, R., Hanzalek, Z., Struzka, P., & Waszniowski, L. (2007). Integrated environment for embedded control systems design. In *Proceedings of the IEEE International Parallel and Distributed Processing Symposium (IPDPS 2007)* (pp. 1-8). IEEE.

Beigné, E., & Vivet, P. (2006). Design of on-chip and off-chip interfaces for a GALS NoC architecture. In *Proceedings of the 12th IEEE International Symposium on Asynchronous Circuits and Systems (ASYNC'06)* (pp. 172–183). IEEE.

Beresini, B., Ricketts, S., & Taylor, M. B. (2011). Unifying manycore and FPGA processing with the RUSH architecture. In *Proceedings of the NASA/ESA Conference on Adaptive Hardware and Systems (AHS)* (pp. 22-28). NASA.

Berry, G., & Gonthier, G. (1992). The ESTEREL synchronous programming language: Design, semantics, implementation. *Science of Computer Programming, 19*(2), 87–152. doi:10.1016/0167-6423(92)90005-V.

Bertozzi, D., Jalabert, A., Murali, S., Tamhankar, R., Stergiou, S., Benini, L., & De Micheli, G. (2005). NoC synthesis flow for customized domain specific multiprocessor systems-on-chip. *IEEE Transactions on Parallel and Distributed Systems, 16*(2), 113–129. doi:10.1109/TPDS.2005.22.

Bjerregaard, T., & Sparsø, J. (2004). Virtual channel designs for guaranteeing bandwidth in asynchronous network-on-chip. In *Proceedings of the IEEE Norchip Conference (NORCHIP 2004)*. IEEE.

Buck, I., & Hanrahan, P. (2003). *Data parallel computation on graphics hardware*. Retrieved April 11, 2012 from http://hci.stanford.edu/cstr/reports/2003-03.pdf

Butenhof, D. R. (1997). *Programming with POSIX threads*. Boston, MA: Addison-Wesley Longman Publishing Co..

Buyukkurt, B. A., Guo, Z., & Najjar, W. (2006). *Impact of loop unrolling on throughput, area and clock frequency in ROCCC: C to VHDL compiler for FPGAs*. Paper presented at the International Workshop on Applied Reconfigurable Computing (ARC 2006). Delft, The Netherlands.

Chapman, B., Huang, L., Biscondi, E., Stotzer, E., Shrivastava, A., & Gatherer, A. (2009). Implementing OpenMP on a high performance embedded multicore MPSoC. In *Proceedings of the 2009 IEEE International Symposium on Parallel & Distributed Processing (IPDPS '09)* (pp. 1-8). Washington, DC: IEEE Computer Society.

Chen, M. K., Li, X. F., Lian, R., Lin, J. H., Liu, L., Liu, T., & Ju, R. (2005). Shangri-la: Achieving high performance from compiled network applications while enabling ease of programming. In *Proceedings of the 2005 ACM SIGPLAN Conference on Programming Language Design and Implementation (PLDI '05)*. New York, NY: ACM.

Choi, Y., Lin, Y., Chong, N., Mahlke, S., & Mudge, T. (2009). Stream compilation for real-time embedded multicore systems. In *Proceedings of the 7th Annual IEEE/ACM International Symposium on Code Generation and Optimization (CGO '09)*. Washington, DC: IEEE Computer Society.

Compton, K., & Hauck, S. (2002). Reconfigurable computing: A survey of systems and software. *ACM Computing Surveys, 34*(2). doi:10.1145/508352.508353.

Consel, C., Hamdi, H., Réveillère, L., Singaravelu, L., Yu, H., & Pu, C. (2003). Spidle: A DSL approach to specifying streaming applications. In *Proceedings of the 2nd International Conference on Generative Programming and Component Engineering (GPCE '03)*. New York, NY: Springer-Verlag New York, Inc.

Dally, W. J., & Towles, B. (2001). Route packets, not wires: On-chip inteconnection networks. In *Proceedings of the 38th annual Design Automation Conference, DAC '01* (pp. 684-689). New York, NY: ACM.

Dimond, R., Mencer, O., & Luk, W. (2005). CUSTARD - A customisable threaded FPGA soft processor and tools. In *Proceedings of the International Conference on Field Programmable Logic and Applications* (pp. 1-6). IEEE.

Esmaeilzadeh, H., Blem, E., St. Amant, R., Sankaralingam, K., & Burger, D. (2012). Dark silicon and the end of multicore scaling. In *Proceedings of the 38th International Symposium on Computer Architecture (ISCA)*. New York, NY: ACM.

Fernandez-Alonso, E., Castells-Rufas, D., Risueno, S., Carrabina, J., & Joven, J. (2010). A NoC-based multi-softcore with 16 cores. In *Proceedings of the 17th IEEE International Conference on Electronics, Circuits, and Systems (ICECS)* (pp. 259-262). IEEE.

Franceschelli, A., Burgio, P., Tagliavini, G., Marongiu, A., Ruggiero, M., & Lombardi, M. … Benini, L. (2011). MPOpt-cell: A high-performance data-flow programming environment for the CELL BE processor. In Cascaval, Trancoso, & Prasanna (Eds.), *Proceedings of the 8th Conference on Computing Frontiers*. New York, NY: ACM.

Girault, A. (2005). A survey of automatic distribution method for synchronous programs. In F. Maraninchi, M. Pouzet, & V. Roy (Eds.), *International Workshop on Synchronous Languages, Applications and Programs, SLAP'05*. Elsevier Science.

Goulding-Hotta, N., Sampson, J., Venkatesh, G., Garcia, S., Auricchio, J., & Huang, P. et al. (2011). The GreenDroid mobile application processor: An architecture for silicon's dark future. *Micro, 31*(2), 86–95.

Grecu, C., Ivanov, A., Pande, P. P., Jantsch, A., Salminen, E., Ogras, U. Y., & Marculescu, R. (2007). Towards open network-on-chip benchmarks. In *Proceedings of the First International Symposium on Networks-on-Chips, NOCS*. Washington, DC: IEEE Computer Society.

Grewe, D., & O'Boyle, M. F. P. (2011). A static task partitioning approach for heterogeneous systems using OpenCL. In *Proceedings of the 20th International Conference on Compiler Construction (CC2011)* (pp. 286-305). Berlin: Springer-Verlag.

Halbwachs, N., Caspi, P., Raymond, P., & Pilaud, D. (1991). The synchronous dataflow programming language LUSTRE. In *Proceedings of the IEEE* (pp. 1305-1320). IEEE.

Hannig, F., & Jurgen, T. (2001). Design space exploration for massively parallel processor arrays. *Lecture Notes in Computer Science, 2127*, 51–65. doi:10.1007/3-540-44743-1_5.

Hotta, Y., Sato, M., Nakajima, Y., & Ojima, Y. (2004). OpenMP implementation and performance on embedded Renesas M32R chip multiprocessor. In *Proceedings of the 6th European Workshop on OpenMP (EWOMP 2004)*. EWOMP.

Intel. (n.d.a). *Intel® Atom™ processor E6x5C series*. Retrieved April 11, 2012 from http://www.intel.com/p/en_US/embedded/hwsw/hardware/atom-e6x5c/overview

Intel. (n.d.b). *Parallel building blocks*. Retrieved April 11, 2012 from http://software.intel.com/en-us/articles/intel-parallel-building-blocks/

Jeon, D., Garcia, S., Louie, C., & Taylor, M. B. (2011). Parkour: Parallel speedup estimates for serial programs. In *Proceedings of the 3rd USENIX Workshop on Hot Topics in Parallelism (HotPar)*. HotPar.

Joven, J., Angiolini, F., Castells-Rufas, D., De Micheli, G., & Carrabina-Bordoll, J. (2010). QoS-ocMPI: QoS-aware on-chip message passing library for NoC-based many-core MPSoCs. In *Proceedings of the 2nd Workshop on Programming Models for Emerging Architectures (PMEA'10)*. PMEA.

Keryel, R. (2009). *GPU & open source*. Paper presented at the Forum Ter@tec 2009. New York, NY.

Kish, L. B. (2002). End of Moore's law: Thermal (noise) death of integration in micro and nano electronics. *Physics Letters. [Part A], 305*(3-4), 144–149. doi:10.1016/S0375-9601(02)01365-8.

Klöckner, A. (2012). *PyCUDA*. Retrieved April 11, 2012 from http://mathema.tician.de/software/pycuda

Kou, S., & Palsberg, J. (2010). From OO to FPGA: Fitting round objects into square hardware? In *Proceedings of OOPSLA'10, ACM SIGPLAN Conference on Object-Oriented Programming Systems, Languages and Applications*. ACM.

Le Guernic, P., Gautier, T., Le Borgne, M., & Le Maire, C. (1991). Programming real-time applications with SIGNAL. *Proceedings of the IEEE*, 79(9), 1321–1336. doi:10.1109/5.97301.

Li, J. J., Wang, S. C., Hsu, P. C., Chen, P. Y., & Lee, J. K. (2010). A multi-core software API for embedded MPSoC environments. In *Proceedings of the Second Russia-Taiwan Conference on Methods and Tools of Parallel Programming Multicomputers (MTPP'10)*. Berlin: Springer-Verlag.

Liu, F., & Chaudhary, V. (2003). A practical OpenMP compiler for system on chips. In *Proceedings of the OpenMP Applications and Tools 2003 International Conference on OpenMP Shared Memory Parallel Programming (WOMPAT'03)*. Berlin: Springer-Verlag.

Loo, S. M., Wells, E., Freije, N., & Kulick, J. (2002). Handel C for rapid prototyping of VLSI coprocessors for real time systems. In *Proceedings of the 34th Southeastern Symposium on System Theory (SSST 2002)*. SSST.

Marculescu, R., Ogras, U. Y., Peh, L. S., Jerger, N. E., & Hoskote, Y. (2009). Outstanding research problems in NoC design: system, microarchitecture, and circuit perspectives. *IEEE Transactions on Computer-Aided Design of Integrated Circuits and Systems*, 28(1), 3–21. doi:10.1109/TCAD.2008.2010691.

Mark, W. R., Glanville, R. S., Akeley, K., & Kilgard, M. J. (2003). Cg: A system for programming graphics hardware in a C-like language. *ACM Transactions on Graphics*, 22(3). doi:10.1145/882262.882362.

Marongiu, A., & Benini, L. (2009). Efficient OpenMP support and extensions for MPSoCs with explicitly managed memory hierarchy. In *Proceedings of Design, Automation & Test in Europe Conference & Exhibition, 2009 (DATE '09)* (pp. 809-814). DATE.

Marowka, A. (2011). Back to thin-core massively parallel processors. *IEEE Computer*, 44(12), 49–54. doi:10.1109/MC.2011.133.

Martin, G., & Smith, G. (2009). High-level synthesis: Past, present, and future. *Design & Test of Computers*, 26(4), 18–25. doi:10.1109/MDT.2009.83.

MathWorks. (n.d.). *Simulink - Simulation and model based design*. Retrieved April 11, 2012 from http://www.mathworks.nl/products/simulink/

Meng, X., & Chaudhary, V. (2004). Bio-sequence analysis with Cradle's 3SoC software scalable system on chip. In *Proceedings of the 2004 ACM Symposium on Applied Computing (SAC '04)*. New York, NY: ACM.

Mentor Graphics. (n.d.). *Catapult C synthesis*. Retrieved April 11, 2012 from http://www.mentor.com/esl/catapult/overview

Moore, S. (2011). *Prototyping massively parallel architectures: Computing beyond a million cores*. Paper presented at the Microsoft Software Summit. Paris, France.

Multicore Communications API Working Group. (2012). *The multicore communication API V2.015 (MCAPI)*. Retrieved April 11, 2012, from http://www.multicore-association.org/workgroup/mcapi.php

National Instruments. (n.d.). *LabVIEW system design software*. Retrieved April 11, 2012 from http://www.ni.com/labview/

NVIDIA. (n.d.). *CUDA: Parallel programming made easy*. Retrieved April 11, 2012 from http://www.nvidia.com/object/cuda_home_new.html

O'Brien, K., O'Brien, K., Sura, Z., Chen, T., & Zhang, T. (2008). Supporting OpenMP on cell. *International Journal of Parallel Programming, 36*(3). PMID:22582009.

Ogras, U. Y., Hu, J., & Marculescu, R. (2005). Key research problems in NoC design: A holistic perspective. In *Proceedings of the 3rd IEEE/ACM/IFIP International Conference on Hardware/Software Codesign and System Synthesis, CODES+ISSS* (pp. 69-74). New York, NY: ACM.

Ohshima, S., Hirasawa, S., & Honda, H. (2010). OMPCUDA: OpenMP execution framework for CUDA based on omni OpenMP compiler. In Sato, Hanawa, Müller, Chapman, & de Supinski (Eds.), Beyond Loop Level Parallelism in OpenMP: Accelerators, Tasking and More. Berlin: Springer-Verlag.

OpenMP Architecture Review Board. (n.d.). *OpenMP application program interface 3.1*. Retrieved April 11, 2012 from http://www.openmp.org/mp-documents/OpenMP3.1.pdf

Parallax Inc. (n.d.). *Propeller general information*. Retrieved April 11, 2012 from http://www.parallax.com/propeller/

Paulin, P. (2010). *A component-based multicore programming environment*. Paper presented at the Workshop on Fundamentals of Component-Based Design, ESWeek 2010. New York, NY.

Pellizzoni, R., & Caccamo, M. (2007). Real-time management of hardware and software tasks for FPGA-based embedded systems. *IEEE Transactions on Computers, 56*(12), 1666–1680. doi:10.1109/TC.2007.70763.

Possa, P., Schaillie, D., & Valderrama, C. (2011). FPGA-based hardware acceleration: A CPU/accelerator interface exploration. In *Proceedings of the 18th IEEE International Conference on Electronics, Circuits and Systems (ICECS)* (pp. 374-377). IEEE.

Silva, J. L. E., & Lopes, J. J. (2010). A dynamic dataflow architecture using partial reconfigurable hardware as an option for multiple cores. *WSEAS Transactions on Computers Archive, 9*(5), 429–444.

Stefanov, T., Zissulescu, C., Turjan, A., Kienhuis, B., & Deprettere, E. (2004). System design using kahn process networks: The compaan/laura approach. In *Proceedings of the Conference on Design, Automation and Test in Europe (DATE '04)*. Washington, DC: IEEE Computer Society.

Suleman, M. A., Patt, Y. N., Sprangle, E., Rohillah, A., Ghuloum, A., & Carmean, D. (2007). *Asymmetric chip multiprocessors: Balancing hardware efficiency and programmer efficiency*. The High Performance Systems Group.

Texas Instruments. (2011). *OpenCV on TI's DSP+ARM®*. White paper.

Texas Instruments. (n.d.a). *OpenMP programming for TMS320C66x multicore DSPs: Delivering the industry's first multicore DSPs to support the OpenMP API*. Retrieved April 11, 2012 from http://www.ti.com/lit/ml/sprt620/sprt620.pdf

Texas Instruments. (n.d.b). *TMS320C6678, multicore fixed and floating-point digital signal processor, data manual*. Retrieved April 11, 2012 from www.ti.com/lit/ds/sprs691c/sprs691c.pdf

Thies, W., Karczmarek, M., & Amarasinghe, S. P. (2002). StreamIt: A language for streaming applications. In *Proceedings of the 11th International Conference on Compiler Construction (CC '02)*. London, UK: Springer-Verlag.

TILERA. (n.d.). *The TILEPro64 processor*. Retrieved April 11, 2012 from http://www.tilera.com/products/processors/TILEPRO64

Tsoi, K. H., & Luk, W. (2010). Axel: A heterogeneous cluster with FPGAs and GPUs. In *Proceedings of the 18th Annual ACM/SIGDA International Symposium on Field Programmable Gate Arrays (FPGA '10)*. New York, NY: ACM.

Zhang, D., Li, Z. Z., Song, H., & Liu, L. (2005). A programming model for an embedded media processing architecture. In *Proceedings of the 5th International Conference on Embedded Computer Systems: Architectures, Modeling, and Simulation (SAMOS'05)*. Berlin: Springer-Verlag.

ADDITIONAL READING

Amini, M., Ancourt, C., Coelho, F., Creusillet, B., Guelton, S., & Irigoin, F. Jouvelot,… Villalon, P. (2011). PIPS is not (just) polyhedral software: Adding GPU code generation in PIPS. In *Proceedings fo the 1st International Workshop on Polyhedral Compilation Techniques, Impact (in conjunction with CGO 2011)*. CGO.

Andrews, D., Niehaus, D., & Ashenden, P. (2004). Programming models for hybrid CPU/FPGA chips. *Computer, 37*(1), 118–120. doi:10.1109/MC.2004.1260732.

Augonnet, C., Thibault, S., Namyst, R., & Wacrenier, P. A. (2011). StarPU: A unified platform for task scheduling on heterogeneous multicore architectures. *Concurrency and Computation, 23*(2), 187–198. doi:10.1002/cpe.1631.

Bellens, P., Perez, J. M., Badia, R. M., & Labarta, J. (2006). CellSs: A programming model for the cell BE architecture. In *Proceedings of the 2006 ACM/IEEE Conference on Supercomputing (SC '06)*. New York, NY: ACM.

Bjerregaard, T., & Mahadevan, S. (2006). A survey of research and practices of network-on-chip. *ACM Computing Surveys, 38*(1). doi:10.1145/1132952.1132953.

Blume, H., von Livonius, J., Rotenberg, L., Noll, T. G., Bothe, H., & Brakensiek, J. (2008). OpenMP-based parallelization on an MPCore multiprocessor platform – A performance and power analysis. *Journal of Systems Architecture, 54*(11), 1019–1029. doi:10.1016/j.sysarc.2008.04.001.

Butts, M., Jones, A. M., & Wasson, P. (2007). A structural object programming model, architecture, chip and tools for reconfigurable computing. In *Proceedings of the 15th Annual IEEE Symposium on Field-Programmable Custom Computing Machines (FCCM 2007)* (pp. 55-64). IEEE.

De Micheli, G., & Luca, B. (2008). *On-chip communication architectures: System on chip interconnect*. San Francisco, CA: Morgan Kaufmann Publishers Inc..

Deepak Shekhar, T. C., Varaganti, K., Suresh, R., Garg, R., & Ramamoorthy, R. (2011). Comparison of parallel programming models for multicore architectures. In *Proceedings of the 2011 IEEE International Symposium on Parallel and Distributed Processing Workshops and Phd Forum (IPDPSW)* (pp. 1675-1682). IEEE.

Ghica, D. R., Smith, A., & Singh, S. (2011). Geometry of synthesis IV: Compiling affine recursion into static hardware. *ACM SIGPLAN Notices, 46*(9), 221–233. doi:10.1145/2034574.2034805.

Hamblen, J. O., & Hall, T. S. (2007). Rapid prototyping of digital systems: SOPC Ed. New York, NY: Springer.

Holland, B., Vacas, M., Aggarwal, V., DeVille, R., Troxel, I., & George, A. (2005). *Survey of C-based application mapping tools for reconfigurable computing*. Paper presented at the 8th International Conference on Military and Aerospace Programmable Logic Devices (MAPLD). New York, NY.

Hübner, M., & Becker, J. (Eds.). (2010). Multiprocessor system-on-chip: Hardware design and tool integration. New York, NY: Springer Science+Business Media.

Jojczyk, L., Possa, P. D. C., & Valderrama, C. (2010). Design of a low latency spectrum analyzer using the goertzel algorithm with a network on chip. In *Proceedings of the ICECS* (pp. 954-957). IEEE.

Kornaros, G. (Ed.). (2010). *Multi-core embedded systems*. Boca Raton, FL: CRC Press. doi:10.1201/9781439811627.

Kunzman, D. M., & Kale, L. V. (2011). Programming heterogeneous systems. In *Proceedings of the International Symposium on Parallel and Distributed Processing Workshops and Phd Forum (IPDPSW)* (pp. 2061-2064). IEEE.

Li, J. J., Wang, S. C., Hsu, P. C., Chen, P. Y., & Lee, J. K. (2010). A multi-core software API for embedded MPSoC environments. In *Proceedings of the Second Russia-Taiwan Conference on Methods and Tools of Parallel Programming Multicomputers (MTPP. '10)* (pp. 40-50). Berlin: Springer-Verlag.

Liu, T., Ji, Z., Wang, Q., Xiao, D., & Zhang, S. (2009). Research on evaluation of parallelization on an embedded multicore platform. In *Proceedings of the 8th International Symposium on Advanced Parallel Processing Technologies (APPT '09)* (pp. 330-340). Berlin: Springer-Verlag.

Lucena, J., Plata, O., & Guil, N. (2010). *Mapping a class of applications in heterogeneous multithreading architectures*. Paper presented at the Second Workshop on Programming Models for Emerging Architectures (PMEA). New York, NY.

Moron, C. E., & Malony, A. D. (2011). Development of embedded multicore systems. In *Proceedings of the IEEE 16th Conference on Emerging Technologies Factory Automation (ETFA)* (pp. 1-4). IEEE.

Pellerin, D., & Thibault, S. (2005). *Practical FPGA programming in C*. Upper Saddle River, NJ: Prentice Hall Modern Semiconductor Design Series.

Pericas, M., Cristal, A., Cazorla, F. J., Gonzalez, R., Jimenez, D. A., & Valero, M. (2007). A flexible heterogeneous multi-core architecture. In *Proceedings of the 16th International Conference on Parallel Architecture and Compilation Techniques (PACT '07)* (pp. 13-24). Washington, DC: IEEE Computer Society.

Rauber, T., & Rünger, G. (2010). *Parallel programming for multicore and cluster systems*. Berlin: Springer-Verlag. doi:10.1007/978-3-642-04818-0.

Singh, S. (2011). Computing without processors. *Communications of the ACM, 54*(8), 46–54. doi:10.1145/1978542.1978558.

Terman, L., & Lanzerotti, M. (Eds.). (2007). The impact of Dennard's scaling theory. IEEE Solid-State Circuits Society News, 12(1).

Ventroux, N., & David, R. (2010). SCMP architecture: An asymmetric multiprocessor system-on-chip for dynamic applications. In *Proceedings of the Second International Forum on Next-Generation Multicore/Manycore Technologies (IFMT '10)* (pp. 6:1-6:12). New York, NY: ACM.

KEY TERMS AND DEFINITIONS

Field-Programmable Array (FPGA): An integrated circuit containing programmable logic elements (*logic blocks*) that can be configured by the user after manufacturing.

Heterogeneous System: A system containing many different computing components, such as General Purpose Processors (GPPs), DSPs, FPGAs, or GPUs. Heterogeneous systems target applications where different parts of the system have different requirements and can therefore run on some processing elements better than others. For a specific application, a suitable heterogeneous system may improve performance and power consumption in a cost-effective way. The opposite, a system with uniform processing elements, is called a Homogeneous system.

Multiple-Instruction, Multiple-Data (MIMD): Running a computation using many different processing elements performing each a different operation on different data items. In multi-cores, this is the most general view of the system. See also: SIMD.

Network-on-Chip (NoC): A Network on Chip (NoC) is an approach to designing the communication subsystem between cores in a System-on-a-Chip (SoC). NoC applies networking theory and methods to on-chip communication. Cores are connected to routers, and routers are connected together following a topology to form a network.

Partial Dynamic Reconfiguration: The process of reconfiguring part of an FPGA while the rest of the circuit is still running.

Processing Element (PE): A processing element is a generic term used to refer to a hardware element that executes a stream of instructions. The context defines what unit of hardware is considered a processing element (for example, a core, a processor, or a computer).

Single Instruction, Multiple Data (SIMD): Running a computation using many processing elements performing the same operation on multiple data items in parallel. SIMD is frequently used in homogeneous massively parallel systems, for example in data-parallel problems. See also: Multiple-Instruction, Multiple-Data (MIMD).

System-on-Chip (SoC): An integrated circuit that integrates all components of a computer system into a single chip substrate. It may contain analog, digital and mixed-signal components. If it contains multiple processing cores, it is a Multiprocessor System-on-Chip (MPSoC).

Chapter 20
Securing Embedded Computing Systems through Elliptic Curve Cryptography

Elisavet Konstantinou
University of the Aegean, Greece

Yannis C. Stamatiou
University of Patras, Greece

Panayotis E. Nastou
University of the Aegean, Greece

Christos Zaroliagis
University of Patras, Greece

ABSTRACT

Embedded computing devices dominate our everyday activities, from cell phones to wireless sensors that collect and process data for various applications. Although desktop and high-end server security seems to be under control by the use of current security technology, securing the low-end embedded computing systems is a difficult long-term problem. This is mainly due to the fact that the embedded systems are constrained by their operational environment and the limited resources they are equipped with. Recent research activities focus on the deployment of lightweight cryptographic algorithms and security protocols that are well suited to the limited resources of low-end embedded systems. Elliptic Curve Cryptography (ECC) offers an interesting alternative to the classical public key cryptography for embedded systems (e.g., RSA and ElGamal), since it uses smaller key sizes for achieving the same security level, thus making ECC an attractive and efficient alternative for deployment in embedded systems. In this chapter, the processing requirements and architectures for secure network access, communication functions, storage, and high availability of embedded devices are discussed. In addition, ECC-based state-of-the-art lightweight cryptographic primitives for the deployment of security protocols in embedded systems that fulfill the requirements are presented.

DOI: 10.4018/978-1-4666-3922-5.ch020

INTRODUCTION

Today we are witnessing a proliferation of all kinds of inexpensive, portable computing and communication devices with complex versatile wireless connection capabilities. This has as a consequence that Internet is accessible from everywhere by anyone who carries such devices. Internet services proliferate, accordingly, offering services of increasing sophistication and coverage of user needs. However, this ubiquitous existence of devices and services, which exchange volumes of, possibly, sensitive user data and information has given rise to an unprecedented demand for security measures capable of protecting users and service providers alike.

Despite the enhancements in memory and speed capabilities of devices, which came through the technological advances in chip manufacturing processes, most of the portable wireless devices in the market today (Smart phones, VoIP phones, portable computers etc.) do not have sufficient resources for the execution of computationally expensive, multi-step cryptographic protocols essential for the security of the users. In view of the resource limitations of wireless devices modern mobile network protocols involve the heavy use of lightweight private key data encryption algorithms as well as *Elliptic Curve based* public key protocols.

The main objective of this chapter is to discuss the basic principles of the cryptographic primitives and protocols employed for the security of *resource limited devices*, which may be generally seen as belonging to the general class of *embedded systems*. A central theme of our discussion is the mathematical construct of Elliptic Curves and its applications to cryptography. Elliptic Curve Cryptography, or ECC for short, offers an attractive alternative to the classical public key cryptography protocols such as RSA (Rivest, Shamir & Adleman, 1978) and ElGamal (ElGamal, 1985). One of the main advantages of ECC is that ECC-based protocols use smaller key sizes

than traditional cryptosystems for achieving the same security levels. For instance, an ECC system with a key size of 160 bits is roughly equivalent, in terms of security, to an RSA system with a key size of 1024 bits. As the key size is much smaller, the requirements in space and memory are also small, rendering ECC an excellent candidate for implementation in embedded devices.

The chapter is organized in three parts. The first part presents some of the most frequently employed cryptographic primitives and protocols, which include block and stream ciphers, private and public key ciphers, digital signatures and key exchange. The second part is focused on Elliptic Curves and ECC and presents the basic definitions and primitives. The third part builds on the first and second parts and presents real world security protocols for embedded devices that employ the primitives discussed in these parts.

Given the space constraints, our aim is not to provide an in depth coverage on all issues pertaining to embedded systems security, but to raise awareness in a (possibly) non-expert audience to security solutions and provide pointers for more extensive information.

A BRIEF INTRODUCTION TO CRYPTOGRAPHIC PRIMITIVES

We briefly review in this part the basic cryptographic primitives and protocols. For more in-depth information on the concepts discussed in this chapter, the reader may consult the excellent book (Stallings, 1999).

A message to be subjected to encryption is called the *plaintext* or *cleartext*. *Encryption* is the process that transforms the message into a form so that it cannot be understood by parties who do not possess a special *key*. The transformed message is called *ciphertext*. *Decryption* is the process of transforming back the ciphertext into its original (plaintext) form. The science of keeping messages secure from being understood by unauthorised persons is *cryptography*. *Cryptanalysis* is the process of discovering the plaintext from the ciphertext without initial knowledge of the key.

A *cipher (cryptographic algorithm)* is a process for the encryption and decryption of messages. *Symmetric-key* algorithms use the same, secret key for encryption and decryption while *public-key* algorithms are designed in such a way that the key used for encryption is publicly available and different from the secret key used for decryption which is private. Moreover, the decryption key cannot be calculated in any reasonable amount of time from the encryption key (this is an essential requirement since the encryption key is publicised). Using the public key, one may send a message to the owner of the key while the decryption of the message is only possible by the owner of the public key, through the use of the private (decryption) key. It is assumed that the attackers have total access to the communications channel between the sender and the receiver.

In what follows, we present the basic encryption and decryption methods and algorithms, both for public and private key encryption systems, along with a comparative study of their relative advantages and disadvantages.

Block and Stream Ciphers

Symmetric-key block ciphers are the most prominent and important elements in many cryptographic systems. Individually, they provide confidentiality. As a fundamental building block, their versatility allows construction of pseudorandom number generators, stream ciphers, MAC (Message Authentication Code) and hash functions. They may, furthermore, serve as a central component in message authentication techniques, data integrity mechanisms, authentication protocols and symmetric-key digital signature schemes.

With few exceptions the best measure of security for practical ciphers is the complexity of the best currently known attack. Various aspects of such complexity are *data complexity, storage complexity* and *processing complexity*. The attack processing complexity is the dominant of these. When parallelization is possible, processing complexity may be divided across many processors reducing attack time. Given a data complexity of 2^n, an attack is always possible, since these many different n-bit blocks completely characterize the encryption function for a fixed n-bit key. Similarly, given a processing complexity of 2^k an attack is possible by exhaustive key search. Thus as a minimum, the effective key size should be sufficiently large to preclude exhaustive key search, and the block size sufficiently large to preclude exhaustive data analysis. A block cipher is considered computationally secure if these conditions hold and no known attack has both data and processing security significantly less than 2^n and 2^k respectively.

For symmetric-key block ciphers, data complexity is beyond the control of the adversary and is passive complexity. Processing complexity is active complexity that typically benefits from increased resources. A cipher provides *perfect secrecy* (unconditional security) if the ciphertext and plaintext blocks are statistically independent. There are a number of criteria for evaluating block ciphers and modes of operations that include the following: *Estimated security level, Key size, Throughput, Block size, Complexity of cryptographic mapping, Data expansion*. It is often desirable, and often mandatory, that encryption does not increase the size of plaintext data. Homophonic substitution and randomized encryption techniques result in data expansion, and *Error propagation*.

A *block cipher* encrypts plaintext in fixed-size n-bit blocks (often $n=64$). For messages exceeding n bits, the simplest approach is to partition the message into n-bit blocks and encrypt each separately. This electronic-codebook (ECB) mode has disadvantages in most applications, motivating other methods of employing block ciphers (*modes of operation*) on larger messages. The four most common modes are ECB, CBC, CFB and OFB.

A *product cipher* combines two or more transformations in a manner intending that the resulting cipher is more secure than the individual components. A *substitution-permutation* (SP) *network* is a product cipher composed of a number of stages involving substitutions and permutations. An *iterated block cipher* involves the sequential repetition of an internal function called *round function*. Parameters include the number of rounds r, the block bit size n, and the input key K from which r subkeys K_i (round keys) are derived. For invertibility (allowing unique decryption), for each value K_i the round function is a bijection on the round's input. A *Feistel cipher* is an iterated cipher mapping a $2t$-bit plaintext (L_0, R_0) to a ciphertext (R_r, L_r), through an r-round process where $r \geq 1$. For $1 \leq i \leq r$, round i maps $(L_{i-1}, R_{i-1}) \rightarrow (L_i, R_i)$ as follows: $L_i = R_{i-1}$, $R_i = L_{i-1} \oplus f(R_{i-1}, K_i)$, where each *subkey* is derived from the cipher key K. The function f of the Feistel Cipher may be a product cipher, though f itself needs not to be invertible to allow inversion of the Feistel cipher. Typically in a Feistel cipher $r \geq 3$ and often r is even. The Feistel structure specifically orders the ciphertext output as (R_r, L_r) rather than (L_r, R_r); the blocks are exchanged from their usual order after the last round. Decryption is thereby achieved using the same r-round process but with subkeys used in reverse order, K_r through K_1. For example, the last round is undone by simply repeating it. A notable example of a Feistel Cipher is the historic DES (DES, 1977).

Today, many modern cryptographic protocols employ the *Advanced Encryption Standard* or AES (Daemen & Rijmen, 2002) which replaced DES. This block cipher is composed of a substitution-permutation network (unlike DES which is Feistel cipher) and it is considered as one of the fastest ciphers for both hardware and software implementations. AES has a 128-bit block size and a key of variable of 128, 192, or 256 bits. The AES cipher operates on a 4×4 column-major order byte matrix, which is termed the *state* and the majority of AES computations are performed within a specially chosen finite number field (Galois field). The computations are performed in a series of iterations (whose number depends on the key length) composed of certain non-linear transformations taking into account the input as well as the key bits. Decryption is obtained by applying the same iterations in reverse order using the same key with which data was encrypted.

Stream ciphers are another important class of encryption algorithms. They encrypt individual characters (usually in binary digits) of a plaintext message one at a time, using an encryption transformation which varies with time. By contrast, block ciphers, as we have seen above, tend to simultaneously encrypts groups of characters of a plaintext message using a fixed encryption transformation. In real world, block ciphers seem to be more general and stream ciphers seem to be easier to analyze mathematically. There is a large body of theoretical work on the analysis and design of stream ciphers as they have been used by the world's militaries since the invention of electronics. This, however, gradually changed since the last two decades numerous theoretical papers have been written on block cipher design principles. Otherwise the differences between stream ciphers and block ciphers are in implementation. Stream ciphers that only encrypt and decrypt data one bit at a time are not really suitable for software implementation. Block ciphers can be easier to implement in software, because they often avoid time-consuming bit manipulation and they operate on data in computer-sized blocks. On the other hand, stream ciphers can be more suitable for hardware implementation because they can be implemented very efficiently on silicon.

Public Key Encryption Algorithms

Public key encryption algorithms dictate the use of two keys: a private and a public one. Public key encryption schemes can be defined over a suitably chosen group. RSA (Rivest, Shamir & Adleman, 1978) has been one of the most popular public-key algorithms for encryption and digital signature applications due to its simplicity and speed of operation. The security of RSA relies on the presumed computational intractability of the integer factoring problem on a suitably defined multiplicative group. Elliptic Curve based encryption schemes, on the other hand, rely on suitably defined additive groups of points on the two dimensional integer grid. In this section we focus on conventional public key schemes while Elliptic Curve based ones are discussed in a separate section.

For the RSA scheme, to generate the two required keys (private and public) we first choose two large random prime numbers p and q of about equal number of digits and compute their product $n=pq$. We then choose at random the encryption key e, making sure that e and $(p-1)(q-1)$ are relatively prime, i.e., their greatest common divisor is equal to 1. Finally, we compute the decryption key d so that e and d are *modular inverses*, i.e., $d=e^{-1}$ $mod\ ((p-1)(q-1))$. Note that d and n are relatively prime. Then e and n comprise the public key and d is the private key. Now p and q may be discarded but *not* revealed since their knowledge leads to the recovery of the decryption key d.

To encrypt a message m, we first divide it into blocks smaller than n. For example, if both p and q are 100-digit primes, then n will have at most 200 digits. Thus, if our message is longer than n, it will be divided into blocks with less than 200 digits. If we must encrypt a fixed number of blocks, we can pad them with few zeros on the left to ensure that they will always be less than n. The encrypted message c, will contain roughly equally sized message blocks c_i. The encryption formula is simply $c_i=m_i^e\ mod\ n$. Note that modular exponentiation can be performed fast by repeated squaring techniques. Now to decrypt a message, we take each encrypted block c_i and compute $m_i=c_i^d$ $mod\ n$. Since $c_i^d=m_i^{ed}=m_i m_i^{k(p-1)(q-1)}=m_i\ 1=m_i$ all mod n, the original message can be recovered. Note that the original message might, as well, have been encrypted with d and decrypted with

e and this observation has many applications in electronic signature applications.

DSA (Kravitz, 1993) is a public-key digital signature algorithm suitable for digital signature applications and it is part of the Digital Signature Standard (DSS). DSA uses the following parameters and operations:

1. An L-bit prime number p, where $512 \leq L \leq 1024$ and L=64k, k=1, 2,…,
2. a 160-bit prime number q, which is a factor of $p-1$,
3. a number g, given by g=h$^{(p-1)/q}$ mod p where h<(p-1) such that h$^{(p-1)/q}$ mod p >1,
4. a number x such that x<p, and
5. a number y, given by y=g^x mod p.

The DSA scheme also uses a *hash function* H(m). A hash function is a cryptographic construct that takes as input a block of data of arbitrary size (also called the «message») and outputs a fixed-size bit string which is the hash value (also called the «digest») of the input. The main property of hash functions is that any change of the input value results in (possibly) many changes in the hash value.

The first three parameters p, q and g of DSA are publicly available and can be shared among many users of a network, while x and y denote the private and public keys respectively. Let m be a message. In what follows we will describe how one person (say Alice) can sign m and how another person (say Bob) may verify her signature.

First, a random number k is generated by Alice such that k<q. Alice's signature is composed by the parameters r and s defined by r=(g^k mod p) mod q and s=(k^{-1}(H(m)+xr)) mod q. Bob, in order to verify Alice's signature, computes the following numbers: w=s^{-1} mod q, a=(H(m)*w) mod q, b=(rw) mod q and v=(g^a*y^b) mod q. If v=r then Alice's signature is verified by Bob.

Discrete Logarithm based signature schemes are digital schemes relying on the presumed intractability of the Discrete Logarithm Problem.

One of the most popular such schemes, is the DSA-like scheme we describe next. Two large prime numbers p and q (a 160-bit prime factor of $p - 1$) and either $p - 1$ or a large prime factor of $p - 1$ are chosen. Then a number g such that $1 \leq g \leq p$ and $g^p = 1 \bmod p$ is chosen. These numbers are publicly known and can be shared among users of some group. Let also x be the private key with $x < q$ and the public key y given by $y = g^x \bmod q$. To sign a message m, a random number k less than and relatively prime to q must be chosen. Also if q is a prime, any k less than q can be chosen instead. We first compute $r = g^k \bmod p$. Then, the *generalised signature equation* is $ak \equiv b + cx \bmod q$, with a, b and c suitably chosen numbers.

To verify the signature, the recipient checks the *verification equation* $r^a = g^b y^c \bmod p$. Note that by using RSA for digital signatures a nice feature called *message recovery* can be exploited. After verifying an RSA signature, m is computed. Then m is compared to the message and it is examined whether the signature is valid for that message. With the previous DSA-like scheme, m cannot be recovered when the signature is computed and some candidate m must be used in the verification equation. However, a message recovery variant is possible. In order to sign a message m, we first compute $r = mg^k \bmod p$ and then we replace m by 1 in the signature. Then the verification equation can be reconstructed so that m can be computed directly.

Finally, we state the key-exchange protocol of Diffie and Hellman (Diffie and Hellman, 1976). Suppose two communicating parties, Alice and Bob, want to agree on a shared secret key. Then they may execute the following steps. They, first, agree on a finite cyclic group G as well as one of its generators g (it is not necessary to keep g secret). Alice initiates the protocol by generating a secret random positive integer a. Bob also generates a secret random positive integer b. Then Alice's public value is computed as $g^a \bmod p$ while Bob's public value as $g^b \bmod p$. Next Alice and Bob exchange their public values, Alice computes $g^{ab} =$ $(g^b)^a \bmod p$, and Bob computes $g^{ba} = (g^a)^b \bmod p$. It is easy to check that $g^{ab} = g^{ba} = k$, which is taken by Alice and Bob as their secret shared key which they can, subsequently, use to communicate by means of a shared key block cipher.

ELLIPTIC CURVE CRYPTOGRAPHY

Elliptic curve based cryptosystems were introduced independently by Koblitz (1987) and Miller (1985) in 1985 as an alternative to conventional public key cryptosystems such as RSA (Rivest, Shamir & Adleman, 1978) and DSA (Kravitz, 1993). In particular, the cryptographic schemes that are based on elliptic curves are analogues of the corresponding ElGamal schemes (ElGamal, 1985) in which the group F_p is replaced by the group of points on an elliptic curve defined over a finite field. Since 1985, elliptic curves have become a major subject of research in cryptography and in number theory in general. In this part, we will define the parameters of an elliptic curve cryptosystem and present the most well-known encryption and signature schemes.

Elliptic Curve Properties and Generation Methods

There are many important decisions that one should make before starting the implementation of an elliptic curve cryptosystem (ECC). These include the type of the underlying finite field, the algorithms for implementing the basic algebraic operations, the type of the elliptic curve to be used as well as its generation, and finally the elliptic curve protocols. The fields usually used are either prime or binary fields. For simplicity, we shall restrict this section to elliptic curves over prime fields F_p, where p is a prime greater than 3.

An *elliptic curve* (EC) over the prime field F_p, denoted by $E(F_p)$, is the set of points $(x, y) \in F_p^2$ (represented by affine coordinates) which satisfy the equation

$$y^2 = x^3 + ax + b \qquad (1)$$

where $4a^3 + 27b^2 \neq 0$ (this condition guarantees that Equation (1) does not have multiple roots in F_p), along with a special point denoted by O, called the *point at infinity*. An addition operation $+$ is defined over $E(F_p)$ such that $(E(F_p), +)$ defines an Abelian group, called the *EC group*, with O acting as its identity.

A fundamental operation of cryptographic protocols based on EC is the *scalar (or point) multiplication*, i.e., the multiplication of a point P by an integer k (an operation analogous to the exponentiation in multiplicative groups), that produces another point $Q = kP$ (the point resulting by adding P to itself for k times). Several algorithms exist for the fast and efficient implementation of the scalar multiplication operation. Most of them are based on the binary representation of the integer k.

The *order m* of an elliptic curve is the number of points in $E(F_p)$. Hasse's theorem (see e.g., (Blake, Seroussi & Smart, 1999; Schoof, 1995)) gives upper and lower bounds for m that are based on the order p of F_p:

$$p + 1 - 2p^{1/2} \leq m \leq p + 1 + 2p^{1/2} \qquad (2)$$

The *order of a point P* is the smallest positive integer n for which $nP = O$. Application of Langrange's theorem (stating that the exponentiation of any group element to the power of the group's order gives the identity element) on $E(F_p)$, gives that $mP = O$ for any point $P \in E(F_p)$, which in turn implies that the order of a point cannot exceed the order of the elliptic curve.

Two important quantities associated with $E(F_p)$ are the *curve discriminant* Δ and the *j-invariant*, defined by

$$\Delta = -16(4a^3 + 27b^2) \qquad (3)$$

and

$$j = -1728(4a)^3/\Delta \qquad (4)$$

Given a *j*-invariant $j_0 \in F_p$ ($j_0 \neq 0, 1728$), two elliptic curves can be easily constructed. The first EC is of the form defined by Equation (1) and can be constructed by setting $a = 3k$ mod p, $b = 2k$ mod p, where $k = j_0/(1728 - j_0)$ mod p. The second EC, called the *twist* of the first, is defined as

$$y^2 = x^3 + ac^2x + bc^3 \qquad (5)$$

where c is any quadratic non-residue in F_p. If m_1 is the order of an EC and m_2 is the order of its twist, then $m_1 + m_2 = 2p + 2$, i.e., if one curve has order $p + 1 - t$, then its twist has order $p + 1 + t$, or vice versa (Blake et al., 1999, Lemma VIII.3).

Many of the security properties of elliptic curve cryptosystems depend on the order of the EC group and this is determined by the generated EC. If this order is *suitable*, i.e., it obeys some specific good properties, then there is a guarantee for a high level of security. The order m of an EC is called *suitable*, if the following conditions are satisfied:

1. m must have a sufficiently large prime factor (greater than 2^{160}).
2. $m \neq p$.
3. For all $1 \leq k \leq 20$, it should hold that $p^k \neq 1$ mod m.

The above conditions ensure the robustness of cryptosystems based on the *discrete logarithm problem for EC groups* (ECDLP), since it is very difficult for all known attacks to solve this problem efficiently, if m obeys the above properties. ECDLP asks for determining the value of t when two points P, Q in $E(F_p)$ are given such that P is of order n and $Q = tP$, where $0 \leq t \leq n - 1$. The best algorithm for attacking this problem takes time exponential in the size of the EC group, while for (conventional, non-EC) groups generated by prime numbers (e.g., the discrete logarithm problem – DLP) there are algorithms that take subexponential time. This implies that one may use smaller parameters for the EC cryptosystems than the parameters used in RSA or DSA, obtaining the same level of security. A typical example is that a 160-bit key of an EC cryptosystem is equivalent to RSA and DSA with a 1024-bit modulus. As a consequence, smaller keys result in faster implementations, less storage space, as well as reduced processing and bandwidth requirements. This advantage is really crucial when we are interested in implementations on constrained devices, such as smart cards, pagers or sensors.

There are three methods for generating the parameters of an EC: the point counting method (see Schoof, 1995), the method based on the constructive Weil descent (Galbraith, 2001), and the Complex Multiplication (CM) method (see Blake et al., 1999). The point counting method does not necessarily construct an EC of suitable order, but it may achieve this by repeated applications of the method. The other two methods construct ECs of a suitable order. In (Galbraith, 2001) it was shown that the method based on the constructive Weil descent suffers from a major drawback that is not easy to handle: it samples from a very small subset of the set of possible elliptic curves. For this reason, in almost all applications the other two methods are used. The point counting method was presented in 1985 by Schoof (1995) and it was the first polynomial time algorithm for computing the order of an ordinary EC. The algorithm computes the values m mod l for small prime numbers l and then determines the order m using the Chinese Remainder Theorem. In practice, the method is inefficient for values of p that are used in practical cryptosystems, but since 1985 it has been improved by many researchers – more details on the improvements of Schoof's method can be found in (Blake et al., 1999).

The theory of complex multiplication (CM) of elliptic curves over the rationals can be used

to generate elliptic curves of a suitable order m, resulting in the so-called *CM method*. The CM method computes j-invariants from which it is then easy to construct the EC. The method is based on the following idea (for more details see for example [Blake et al., 1999]). Hasse's theorem implies that $Z = 4p - (p + 1 - m)^2$ is positive. This in turn implies that there is a unique factorization $Z = Dv^2$, where D is a square free positive integer. Consequently,

$$4p = u^2 + Dv^2 \qquad (6)$$

for some integer u satisfying

$$m = p + 1 \pm u \qquad (7)$$

D is called a *CM discriminant for the prime* p and the elliptic curve has a *CM by D*. The CM method uses D in order to determine the j-invariant and constructs an EC of order $p + 1 - u$ or $p + 1 + u$.

The method starts with a prime p and then chooses the smallest D along with an integer u to satisfy Equation (6). Then, it checks whether $p + 1 - u$ and/or $p + 1 + u$ is suitable. If neither is suitable, the process is repeated. Otherwise, the so-called *Hilbert polynomials* have to be constructed (based on D) and their roots have to be found. A root of the Hilbert polynomial is the j-invariant we are seeking. The EC and its twist are then constructed as explained previously. Since only one of the ECs has the required suitable order, the particular one can be found using Lagrange's theorem by picking random points P in each EC until a point is found in some curve for which $mP \neq O$. Then, the other curve is the one we are seeking.

Concluding, the CM method is much faster than the best algorithms known for counting the points of randomly selected ECs over prime fields.

For ECs over binary fields, variations of Satoh's algorithm (Satoh, 2000) for point counting can find cryptographically secure ECs in few seconds.

Elliptic Curve Based Protocols

The security of cryptographic protocols based on ECs, is guaranteed by the intractability of ECDLP (Elliptic Curve Discrete Logarithm Problem). In particular, in EC-based protocols, each user selects his pair of public and private keys as follows: suppose that the base point P has prime order n. Then each user selects an integer k uniformly at random in the interval $[1, n-1]$ and computes the point $Q = kP$. His private key is k and his public key is the point Q. It is clear that the security of the private key is based on the difficulty of solving ECDLP.

Because of the straightforward correspondence of ECDLP and DLP, all cryptographic protocols that are based on DLP have their analogues in elliptic curve cryptosystems. For example, the Diffie-Hellman key agreement protocol (Diffie & Hellman, 1976), the ElGamal cryptosystem (ElGamal, 1985) and Digital Signature Algorithm (DSA) can be easily transformed to their elliptic curve analogues. In the Elliptic Curve Diffie-Hellman (ECDH) key agreement protocol, the two users A and B agree on the same elliptic curve parameters and compute the points $Q_A = k_A P$ and $Q_B = k_B P$ correspondingly. The point P is the base point, while the values k_A, k_B are randomly chosen integers in $[1, n-1]$. Then, the final shared key is calculated by the user A as $K = k_A Q_B = k_A k_B P$ and by user B as $K = k_B Q_A = k_A k_B P$.

A simple analogue of ElGamal encryption can similarly be created:

1. The plaintext m is first represented as a point M in $E(F_p)$. Then, an integer k is randomly selected such that $0 < k < n-1$, where n is the largest prime factor of the EC order m.

2. The point $C_1 = kP$ is computed, where P is the base point.

3. A second point $C_2 = M + k Q_B$ is computed. Q_B is the public key of the intended recipient.

4. The ciphertext is the pair (C_1, C_2).

The decryption procedure is the following:

1. Using his private key k_B the recipient of the ciphertext computes the point $k_B C_1$.

2. The point M is retrieved by $C_2 - k_B C_1$. Finally, the plaintext m is extracted from M.

A variant of the ElGamal encryption scheme is also the Elliptic Curve Integrated Encryption Scheme (ECIES) which was proposed by Bellare and Rogaway in 1997 (Bellare & Rogaway, 1997). The algorithm has been standardized in ANSI X9.63 and ISO/IEC 15946-3 standards, and is the most widely used elliptic curve based encryption scheme.

The Elliptic Curve Digital Signature Algorithm (ECDSA) (Johnson & Menezes, 1999) is the elliptic curve analogue of the Digital Signature Algorithm (DSA). It is the most well-known elliptic curve based signature scheme and it has been standardized in ANSI X9.62, FIPS 186-2 and several other standards. In the following, H(.) denotes a cryptographic hash function whose outputs have bit length smaller than the bit length of n (the largest prime factor of the EC order m). The steps of the signature generation are:

1. Choose a random integer k with $1 \leq k \leq n-1$.

2. Compute the point $kP = (x_1, y_1)$ where P is the base point. Next, compute $r = x_1 \bmod n$. If $r = 0$ return to the first step.

3. Compute the value $k^1 \bmod n$.

4. Use a hash function H to compute $e = H(M)$, where M is the message to be signed.

5. Compute $s = k^{-1}(e + dr) \bmod n$, where d is the signer's private key. If $s = 0$ then return to the first step.

6. The pair (r, s) is the signature.

The steps of the signature verification are the following:

1. Compute $e = H(M)$, where M is the signed message.

2. Compute $w = s^{-1} \bmod n$.

3. Compute the values $u_1 = ew \bmod n$ and $u_2 = rw \bmod n$.

4. Calculate the point $X = u_1P + u_2Q$, where Q is the signer's public key. If X is equal to the point at infinity, then reject the signature. Otherwise, compute $u = x_1 \bmod n$ where x_1 is the x-coordinate of the point X.

5. The signature is accepted only if $u = r$.

ECC BASED EXTENSIONS OF SECURITY PROTOCOLS AND THEIR APPLICATIONS ON EMBEDDED SYSTEMS

In this section, we present the main characteristics of some of the most widely employed protocols within the embedded systems domain and we show how such protocols can benefit from ECC. Furthermore, we show how a specially tailored port of a general purpose library, ECC-LIB (Kon-stantinou, Stamatiou & Zaroliagis, 2002) can be used in an ECC based extension of the Wireless Protected Access Protocol (Papaioannou, Nastou, Stamatiou, & Zaroliagis, 2009).

Generally, the client-server model is the standard model for most network applications. The majority of the embedded devices are equipped to support electronic applications for online banking, trading and voting. Peer applications on network devices can communicate over an insecure network through standard communication channels named sockets. The security of the e-commerce applications are based mainly on the Secure Sockets Layer protocol (SSL) originally developed by Netscape Communications Corporation and which evolved as a Web security standard since most Internet Browser developers adopted it for Web security. Later, the Transport Layer Security (TLS) working group was formed in the Internet Engineering Task Force (IETF) to develop a common standard and the TLS Internet standard for Web security was ratified (Dierks & Rescola, 2008).

Both protocols implement security above the Transport Control Protocol (TCP), as it is shown in Figure 1a. There is a number of specific applications that embeds the SSL protocol in order to provide application specific security services. SSL/TLS is considered as an inexpensive way to establish a secure connection between pairs of hosts when the demand for communication is occasional and it requires little user participation.

Figure 1. Levels of network security

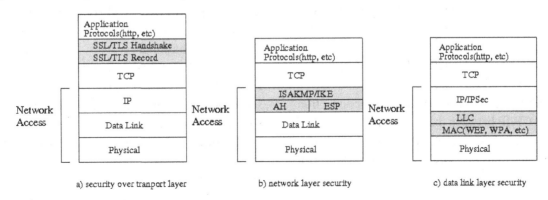

a) security over tranport layer   b) network layer security   c) data link layer security

Instead of adding security facilities to Web applications, there is the alternative of providing end-to-end security at the network layer. The initial version of the IP protocol (IPv4) did not support security mechanisms (Stallings, 1999). Thus, IETF formed a working group named IPSec that developed a protocol suite for providing security services in the IP protocol. In some sense, the IPSec group provided extensions to the IP protocol. In the IPv6, the IPSec security mechanisms have been adopted as mandatory. Actually, IPSec provides network layer security (Figure 1b) where any application can exploit it while transferring data through the network. A mobile device can be connected to a network device of a private or public network through an insecure network by using IPSec (Shneyderman & Casati, 2003).

However, for wireless mobile devices where the medium is considered absolutely insecure, data link layer security is important in addition to the network layer security (Raza, Voigt, & Jutvik, 2012). IPSec that provides network security is an end-to-end protocol which means that any attack can be detected at the end nodes. A data link layer security protocol (Figure 1c) controls the access to the insecure wireless medium. It is obvious that providing security at the link level any attack can be detected earlier. An example of this situation is the IEEE 802.11 standard for Wireless LANs (WLANs) where the members of the 802.11i Task Group have paid particular attention to provide WLAN users with a powerful security protocol at MAC layer.

Next, the architecture of the SSL/TLS, IPSec and WPA security protocols along with the involvement of the Elliptic Curve Cryptography in these protocols are presented.

The SSL/TLS Protocol

The idea is to establish a peer-to-peer connection over TCP/IP between the client and the server of an application. So, if an embedded device is to run more than one application concurrently, it must establish one SSL/TLS connection per application. SSL/TLS architecture is composed of the Handshake Protocol and the Record Protocol (Figure 1a). The Handshake protocol is used by the server and the client in order to establish a secure connection by authenticating each other, negotiating cipher suites and agreeing on cryptographic keys. The established secure connection is used by the Record Protocol to provide secure communication to the application required the secure connection.

A list of supported public-key and symmetric cryptographic algorithms, signature schemes, MAC schemes and hash functions forms the cipher suite. The generation of the keys that will be used by the symmetric cryptographic algorithms and the keyed hashed functions is based on a master key agreed by the server and the client through the Handshake Protocol. Thus, the Handshake protocol provides to the Record protocol the negotiated cipher suite and the agreed master key. The specification in (Dierks & Rescorla, 2008), recommends some cipher suites, e.g. TLS_DH_RSA_WITH_AES_128_CBC_SHA indicates the use of RSA Diffie Hellman key exchange mechanism, the AES with a key of 128-bit in CBC mode of operation for the encryption and decryption in the record protocol and SHA for hashing. Blake-Wilson et al. (2006) presented new ECC based key exchange algorithms for the TLS protocol. As for example, the EC cipher suite TLS_ECDH_ECDSA_WITH_AES_128_CBC_SHA indicates the use of Elliptic Curve Diffie-Hellman (ECDH) key agreement mechanism, the use of Elliptic Curve Digital Signature Algorithm (ECDSA) as a new authentication mechanism, the AES with a key of 128-bit in CBC mode of operation for the encryption and decryption in the record protocol and SHA for hashing.

The SSL/TSL handshake scheme is shown in Figure 2. As it is also pointed out in Figure 2, the server and the client initially negotiate the cipher suite that will be used for master key agreement and by the record protocol and they exchange two random numbers N_c and N_s through SSL/TLS Hello messages. The server sends to the client its certificate which contains its public key signed by the issuing certification authority. If the negotiated cipher suites are ECDSA_fixed_ECDH for the client and ECDH_ECDSA_WITH_AES_128_ CBC_SHA for the server, the server sends to the client its certificate that contains its ECDH-capable public key signed with ECDSA.

The server requests the client's certificate by sending a CertificateRequest in order to authenticate the client. The client responds by sending its certificate which contains its ECDH-capable public key on the same elliptic curve as the server's ECDH key (this scheme is computationally more efficient). The server and the client authenticate each other by verifying the signature of the received ECDH public keys. At the end of authentication, the client sends an empty KeyExchange message (this happens only when the TLS_ECDSA_fixed_ECDH cipher suite for the client has been negotiated) and both the server and the client generates the master key (MK) as it is presented in Figure 2. Finally, the client and the server verify that they possess the same mas-

ter key by exchanging the hash value of their MK through the *Finished* message of SSL/TLS protocol.

Gupta et al. (2005) presented Sizzle (Slim SSL), the world's smallest secure Web server on Mica2 motes implemented by Sun microsystems. Sizzle does not request client's certificate by CertificateRequest which eliminates the transmission of the certificate. The processor of Mica2 motes was the 8-bit Atmel ATmega 128L with 128KB flash, 4KB EEPROM, 4KB of RAM.

The IPSec Protocol Suite

The IPSec protocol suite provides security services through the Authentication Header protocol (AH), the Encapsulating Security Payload Protocol (ESP), the Internet Security Association and Key Management Protocol (ISAKMP) and the Internet Key Exchange protocol (IKE) (Figure 1b).

The AH protocol provides data origin authentication and data integrity through the AH header which is added either between the IP header and

Figure 2. SSL/TLS handshake scheme

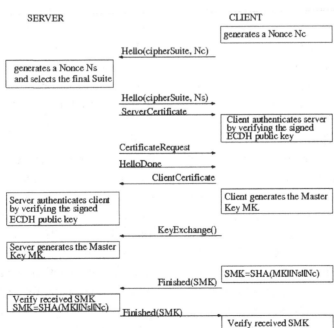

the transport layer payload in the transport mode or between the new IP header and the initial IP header of the IP packet in the tunnel mode. Similarly, the ESP protocol provides authentication and confidentiality through the ESP header added either between the IP header and the transport layer payload in the transport mode or between the new IP header and the initial IP header of the IP packet in the tunnel mode (Yuan & Strayer, 2001). The transport mode protects an upper-layer protocol while in the tunnel mode the original IP packet, which either encrypted or subjected to other security measures, is encapsulated into another IP packet by forming a new IP header that steers the packet in the network. Moreover, the ESP protocol appends an ESP trailer and authentication data in both tunnel and transport mode. The ESP protocol is used, either in tunnel or in transport mode, in the majority of Virtual Private Network (VPN) approaches whereas in Mobile IP the AH protocol in transport mode is used (Shnyderman & Casati, 2003).

Each IPSec device should support the Security Policy Database (SPD) and the Security Association Database (SAD). The SPD contains an ordered list of certain rules that should be applied to IP packets e.g. which encryption algorithm should be used for encryption. These rules are determined by the IPSec device administrator. A source device in order to send data to a destination device negotiates with the destination the security parameters that should be used to protect the IP traffic based on the rules of the SPD of the destination. The agreed security services form a Security Association (SA) which is recorded in the SAD of the source and the destination device. An IPSec SA is uniquely determined by the IP address of the destination device, the IPSec protocol identifier (AH or ESP) and the Security Parameter Index (SPI). If a bidirectional communication is needed the two devices should form a second IPSec SA for the other direction. A device establishes an IPSec SA with its peer dynamically by ISAKMP (Harkins & Carrel, 1998). ISAKMP determines

the procedures for securing the communication channel between two communicating devices.

Version 2 of IKE – IKEv2 (Harkins & Carrel, 1998; Kaufman, 2005) – is a protocol that uses the ISAKMP framework for mutual authentication and key exchange. Initially, IKE establishes an IKE Security Association (IKE_SA) that includes the shared secret information for establishing IPSec SAs between communicating devices and the cryptographic algorithms that should be used to protect traffic while establishing an IPSec SA. Actually, an IKE establishes a secure channel between two communicating devices through which the devices establish its IPSec secure channel for data transfer. An IKE_SA is established after the exchange of two pairs of messages, the IKE_SA_INIT and IKE_AUTH, between communicating devices. The IKE_SA_INIT pair of messages negotiate the cryptographic algorithms, exchange nonces and the public information in DH key exchange, (i.e., the large prime p that defines the modular exponentiation group, a generator g of this group and two powers of g or the EC parameters a, b and m, a point B on EC and the public key $P_e = K_d$ B) and establish the key of IKE_SA which is the master key, since it is used as a seed for the construction of keys used for encryption and integrity protection of the IKE_AUTH pair of messages. By IKE_AUTH messages the recipients verify that they hold the right master key and negotiate the cryptographic algorithms that should be used by IPSec SA established in the next phase of IKE.

Upon the completion of IKE_SA, the two communicating parties in order to establish the IPSec SA exchange the CREATE_CHILD_SA pair of messages. One of the two communicating devices sends to its peer the details of SA, a nonce, a DH value for the IPSec SA key generation and the traffic selectors. The peer responds by sending a message that contains its corresponding data to the initiator. Both messages are encrypted and authenticated using the cryptalgorithms negotiated in the IKE_SA establishment and the keys generated by the IKE_SA key. The result of this exchange is the IPSec SA and its master key which is considered as the user master key since it is used by the IPSec SA for the protection of the data traffic.

Fu and Solinas (2010) described for use in IKEv2 new elliptic curve groups which provide efficiency advantages in hardware applications. Although, the RFCs recommend the use of EC groups, the current IKE implementations use the RSA in DH for key exchange. Raza, Voigt and Jutvik (2012) suggested an implementation of ECC in DH based on standardized ECC algorithms and NIST recommended EC and prime numbers using the uIP stack and Contiki OS, which runs on networked embedded systems and wireless sensor networks.

The Wireless Protected Access Protocol

In 802.11i specification, the operation of a Robust Security Network (RSN) is defined in an Extended Service Set (ESS) or an Independent Basic Service Set (IBSS), which is the ad-hoc case. The operation of an RSN is based on the establishment of RSN Associations between Stations which can be based on Pre-Shared Key (PSK) or on IEEE 802.1X AKM (Authentication and Key Management). In an ESS, the Access Point (AP) is the Authenticator, and associated devices are the Supplicants.

Upon completion of an RSN association between Authenticator and Supplicant, the Authenticator initiates the 4-way Handshake protocol (802.11i). This is a Key Management protocol through which the existence of the PMK is confirmed, as well as that it is current, then a unique Pairwise Transient Key (PTK) from the PMK is derived, and the unicast encryption and message integrity keys are generated. Those keys are used in the 802.11 MAC Layer symmetric block ciphers (mainly AES) in various modes of operation. Initially, the Authenticator sends a nonce-value to the Supplicant (ANonce), and the Supplicant

constructs the PTK. The Supplicant responds by sending its own nonce-value to the Authenticator along with a Message Integrity Code (MIC) and the Authenticator generates the PTK and if it is needed the Group Temporal Key (GTK). Finally, the Authenticator sends to Supplicant the GTK and a sequence number along with MIC and the Supplicant sends a confirmation to Authenticator and establishes the PTK and GTK (if it was transmitted by Authenticator).

The software library ECC-LIB, presented in (Konstantinou, Stamatiou & Zaroliagis, 2002), was applied in (Papaioannou, Nastou, Stamatiou & Zaroliagis, 2009) for the implementation of an EC Diffie-Hellman Key Exchange Protocol that imitates the operation of the 802.11 4-way handshake protocol. This library is suitable for embedded systems since it contains implementations of new algorithms for the Complex Multiplication (CM) method, which are based on the use of the lightweight Weber polynomials instead of the computationally heavy Hilbert polynomials, thus resulting in faster and space-efficient methods compared to implementations with Hilbert polynomials for generating secure ECs over a prime field F_p, i.e., ECs of a suitable order. The details of these new algorithms and their experimental evaluation are reported in (Konstantinou, Stamatiou & Zaroliagis, 2007) and (Konstantinou, Kontogiorgis, Stamatiou & Zaroliagis, 2010). The ECC-LIB code has been successfully ported to Windows CE (one of the most commonly used operating systems for PDAs) and details can be found in (Argyroudis, 2004). For the implementation of an EC Diffie-Hellman Key Exchange Protocol that imitates the operation of the 802.11 4-way handshake protocol, only the code related to CM method variant has been ported to µcLinux which is a widely used operating system for embedded network devices (for example WLAN Access Points). Similar ports of ECC-LIB can be produced for other limited resource devices as well as embedded systems by simply compiling it with the right compilation switches.

The idea presented in (Papaioannou et. al, 2009) was simply to construct a protocol based on Elliptic Curve cryptography that will create PTK in a more secure way. A simple client-server application was written in standard ANSI C in (Papaioannou et al., 2009). The server part of the application runs on the AT76C520 device, an ATMEL's 802.11 WLAN Access Point, while the client part runs on a notebook. Since the EC generation and the construction of a public and private key pair using the ECC-LIB requires much time, a scenario was considered where the authenticator creates an EC with certain characteristics and a pair of private K_a and public P_a keys during its initialization instead of generating them in real time. The PMK now is the discriminant D and the size of prime p that the authenticator needs for the EC generation using the CM method.

After a successful association between the authenticator and the supplicant, the latter requests from an 802.11 authenticator an elliptic curve as it is shown in Figure 3.

The authenticator sends to the supplicant the EC parameters a, b and m, the prime number p, the coordinates of the base point B and its public key $P_a = K_a B$. The supplicant then creates its own set of private and public keys (K_s, P_s) where $P_s =$

$K_s B$ based on the received EC and transmits P_s back to the authenticator to complete the Diffie-Hellman protocol. The shared key of the two devices is then calculated on these devices: $PTK_a = K_a P_s$ and $PTK_s = K_s P_a$. In order to assure both the authenticator and the supplicant that $PTK_s = PTK_a$, the supplicant sends to the authenticator along with the public key, an ECDSA signature using PTK_s. The authenticator verifies the received public key, installs the constructed PTK and sends to the supplicant its public key ECDSA signature using PTK_a. Finally, the supplicant verifies that the received signature is the correct one and installs the constructed PTK. The above protocol was tested (Papaioannou et. al, 2009) using an Ethernet connection between a notebook (supplicant) and the AT76C520 embedded device.

CONCLUSION AND FUTURE RESEARCH

In this chapter, we presented an overview of cryptographic primitives and protocols that can be implemented on embedded systems. We focused on the promising cryptographic constructs based on Elliptic Curves that can lead to performance

Figure 3. An EC Diffie-Hellman key management protocol in 802.11

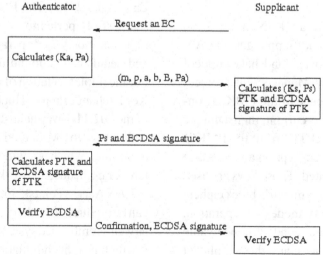

improvements when properly implemented on hardware, since their security can be assured with key sizes smaller than the ones required by conventional cryptographic schemes such as ElGamal or RSA. Our aim was to demonstrate the potential of ECC cryptography as well as the range of applications that can benefit from it and provide pointers that lead to more in depth information. To this end, we described the cryptographic primitives of ECC and how they are used in building security protocols. Then we showed how standard security protocols can be enhanced to use ECC and what improvements are obtained. Finally, we discussed open source software libraries for ECC that can be tailored to the needs of practical security problems in embedded systems using as an example the port of ECC-LIB to certain operating systems. As future work, we plan to explore the use of ECC in other types of embedded platforms and devices such as TPMs (Trusted Platform Modules) and eIdentity smart cards. Our goal is to contribute to the development and performance evaluation of a single, comprehensive library that can be tailored to the needs of a wide range of devices based on the settings of compilation switches.

REFERENCES

Argyroudis, P. (2004). *NTRG ECC-LIB WINCE – A WinCE port of ECC-LIB*. Retrieved from http://ntrg.cs.tcd.ie/~argp/software/ntrg-ecc-lib-wince.html

Bellare, M., & Rogaway, P. (1997). Minimizing the use of random oracles in authenticated encryption schemes. In *Proceedings of Information and Communications Security '97 (LNCS)* (*Vol. 1334*, pp. 1–16). Berlin: Springer. doi:10.1007/BFb0028457.

Blake, I., Seroussi, G., & Smart, N. (1999). *Elliptic curves in cryptography*. London: Cambridge University Press.

Blake-Wilson, S., Bolyard, N., Gupta, V., Hawk, C., & Moeller, B. (2006). *Elliptic curve cryptography (ECC) cipher suites for transport layer security (TLS). RFC 4492*. IETF.

Daemen, J., & Rijmen, V. (2002). *The design of Rijndael: AES - The advanced encryption standard*. Berlin: Springer. doi:10.1007/978-3-662-04722-4.

DES. (1977). *Data encryption standard*. Washington, DC: Federal Information Processing Standards Publication.

Dierks, T., & Rescorla, E. (2008). *Transport layer protocol version 1.2 (TLS). RFC 5246*. IETF.

Diffie, W., & Hellman, M. E. (1976). New directions in cryptography. *IEEE Transactions on Information Theory*, *22*, 644–654. doi:10.1109/TIT.1976.1055638.

ElGamal, T. (1985). A public key cryptosystem and a signature scheme based on discrete logarithms. *IEEE Transactions on Information Theory*, *31*, 469–472. doi:10.1109/TIT.1985.1057074.

Fu, D., & Solinas, J. (2010). *Elliptic curve groups modulo a prime for IKE and IKEv2. RFC 5903*. IETF.

Galbraith, S. (2001). Limitations of constructive Weil descent. In Public-Key Cryptography and Computational Number Theory.

Gupta, V., Wurm, M., Zhu, Y., Millard, M., Fung, S., & Gura, N. et al. (2005). Sizzle: A standards-based end-to-end security architecture for the embedded internet. *Pervasive and Mobile Computing*, 425–445. doi:10.1016/j.pmcj.2005.08.005.

Harkins, D., & Carrel, D. (1998). *The internet key exchange (IKE). RFC2409*. IETF.

IEEE. (n.d.). 802.11i, IEEE medium access control (MAC) security enhancements. IEEE Task Group I P802.11i.

Johnson, D., & Menezes, A. (1999). *The elliptic curve digital signature algorithm (ECDSA) (Technical report CORR 99-06)*. Waterloo, Canada: University of Waterloo.

Kaufman, C. (2005). *Internet key exchange (IKEv2) protocol. RFC 4306*. IETF.

Koblitz, N. (1987). Elliptic curve cryptosystems. *Mathematics of Computation, 48*, 203–209. doi:10.1090/S0025-5718-1987-0866109-5.

Konstantinou, E., Kontogiorgis, A., Stamatiou, Y. C., & Zaroliagis, C. (2010). On the efficient generation of prime order elliptic curves. *Journal of Cryptology, 23*(3), 477–503. doi:10.1007/s00145-009-9037-2.

Konstantinou, E., Stamatiou, Y. C., & Zaroliagis, C. (2002). *On the efficient generation of elliptic curves over prime fields*. Berlin: Springer-Verlag.

Konstantinou, E., Stamatiou, Y. C., & Zaroliagis, C. (2007). Efficient generation of secure elliptic curvers. *International Journal of Information Security, 6*(1), 47–63. doi:10.1007/s10207-006-0009-3.

Kravitz, D. W. (1993). *Digital signature algorithm*. U.S. Patent #5,231,668. Washington, DC: US Patent Office.

Miller, V. (1985). Uses of elliptic curves in cryptography. In *Proceedings of Advances in Cryptology – Crypto '85 (LNCS)* (Vol. 218, pp. 417–426). Berlin: Springer. doi:10.1007/3-540-39799-X_31.

Papaioannou, P., Nastou, P., Stamatiou, Y., & Zaroliagis, C. (2009). Secure elliptic curve generation and key establishment on a 802.11 WLAN embedded device. In *Proceedings of the 9th IEEE International Symposium on Autonomous Decentralized Systems*, (pp. 41-48). IEEE.

Raza, S., Voigt, T., & Jutvik, V. (2012). Lightweight IKEv2: A key management solution for both the compressed IPSec and the IEEE 802.15.4 security. In *Proceedings of the IETF International Workshop on Smart Object Security*. IETF.

Rivest, R., Shamir, A., & Adleman, L. (1978). A method for obtaining digital signatures and public-key cryptosystems. *Communications of the ACM, 21*, 120–126. doi:10.1145/359340.359342.

Satoh, T. (2000). The canonical lift of an ordinary elliptic curve over a prime field and its point counting. *Journal of the Ramanujan Mathematical Society, 15*, 247–270.

Schoof, R. (1995). Counting points on elliptic curves over finite fields. *Journal Theorie des Nombres de Bordeaux, 7*, 219–254. doi:10.5802/jtnb.142.

Shneyderman, A., & Casati, A. (2003). *Mobile VPN: Delivering advanced services in next generation wireless systems*. Indianapolis, IN: Wiley.

Silverman, J. H. (1986). *The arithmetic of elliptic curves*. Berlin: Springer. doi:10.1007/978-1-4757-1920-8.

Stallings, W. (1999). *Cryptography and network security: Principles and practice*. Upper Saddle River, NJ: Prentice Hall.

Yuan, R., & Strayer, T. (2001). *Virtual private networks: Technologies and solutions*. Boston, MA: Addison Wesley.

KEY TERMS AND DEFINITIONS

Cipher: A cryptographic algorithm for the encryption and decryption of messages.

Ciphertext: An encrypted plaintext.

Decryption: A process that transforms back the ciphertext into its original (plaintext) form.

Embedded System: A networked computing system characterized by limited computing and storage resources.

Encryption: A process that transforms a message into a form so that it cannot be understood by parties who do not possess a special key.

Plaintext: A message to be subjected to encryption.

Protocol: A set of rules that two or more communicating parties should follow in order to establish communication channels and to exchange data messages.

Security Protocol: A protocol for the establishment of secure channels and the secure exchange of messages between communicating parties.

Chapter 21
Security and Cryptographic Engineering in Embedded Systems

Apostolos P. Fournaris
University of Patras, Greece & Technological Educational Institute of Patras, Greece

Paris Kitsos
Technological Educational Institute of Patras, Greece & Hellenic Open University, Greece

Nicolas Sklavos
Technological Educational Institute of Patras, Greece

ABSTRACT

Strong security is a necessity in the modern IT world and is broadly provided though Hardware Security Modules (HSM) capable of realizing a wide variety of security algorithms and protocols. Such modules are no longer only found in expensive computer systems like servers, corporate PC, or laptops but also in every device where security is required, including embedded systems like smart cards or smart grid, smart environment, automobile, game station, and aviation processors. The chapter provides to the reader the necessary information on how strong security is structured in a hardware embedded system environment from cryptographic engineering point of view. The focus is efficient design on symmetric, asymmetric cryptography and hash function systems, and design approaches that can be used in order to provide strong security to the embedded system user.

INTRODUCTION

The immense growth of portable and mobile systems (smart phones, tablets, netbooks) and the increasing integration of computational logic into any devices through initiatives like future Internet and Internet of things have led to a flourish in embedded system technology stemming the creativity of the IT market to new levels. Wireless, mobile and portable devices are gradually replacing many traditional computer systems due to the increasing user need for mobility in high-end technology

DOI: 10.4018/978-1-4666-3922-5.ch021

applications while a new generation of intelligent machines that include embedded processor systems have hit the market, capable of providing very sophisticated functionality to users. So, from cars to mobile devices, video equipment to mp3 players and dishwashers to home thermostats, embedded computer systems have invaded our lives and are capable of collecting-processing a wide variety of information. Some of that information are sensitive to the user, like passwords, keys, credentials, even confidential data and life habits. This creates the need for protecting those data and calls for strong security features realized in the embedded system's structure.

In the IT world, strong security demands are satisfied by cryptographic solutions providing personal certificate for each communicating entity, encrypting the transmitted message or the communication channel in general and by generating/managing appropriate keys or certificates for encrypted transactions, authentication and privacy. For message encryption-decryption, a fast cryptographic algorithm, usually a symmetric key cryptographic algorithm is required. For the rest of the security operations, public key digital signatures schemes are employed along with corresponding key agreement and hash function mechanisms.

There are several approaches on how to provide strong security characteristics to a computer system. Most of them involve hardware structures that are physically connected to the computer system like usb tokens, smart cards or specialized security chips (Anderson et al., 2006; Potlapally, 2011). We can discriminate such devices by the level of protection they can provide to a user. Basic protection devices offer user authentication and identification by providing unique identification numbers or PINs stored or generated inside a USB token or smart card system. More advanced protection devices offer data integrity, data confidentiality and user digital signature/sign-on services. High end security protection devices can enforce security and trust in a target computer system and provide trust guarantees as well as malicious user evidence, detection, protection and resistance. However, in an embedded system, security functionality cannot be provided by independent structures. The security structure must be embedded inside the system along with any other functionality that the system needs to service. This means that security for embedded systems involves additional issues that are beyond the problems currently being addressed for enterprise and desktop computing. Those issues are related to the fundamentally different design and implementation approach of embedded systems, to their highly constrained resource technological environment (processing power, battery lifetime, chip covered area, etc.) and to their high vulnerability to attacks.

Cryptographic engineering offers solutions to the above concerns since it views cryptography and therefore security from a practical perspective, always in relation to the system at hand. One of the main goals of a cryptographic engineer is to design a cryptographic function in a secure yet efficient way so as to match the functional and non-functional requirements of the system (Koc, 2008). Using this approach, a cryptographic primitive (which is the structural element of a security system) is designed taking into account its hardware, software performance, its resistance against attacks on it (not only the crypto-algorithm but also its implementation) and how the resulted structure can be fitted into the overall system. Thus, cryptographic engineering principles can be very useful when adding security features and associated hardware structures in an embedded computing system where the constrains are very strict and the environment the system works is very hostile.

In this chapter, an account of the current approaches toward designing secure embedded systems is provided, the problems of realizing strong security functionality on embedded systems are highlighted and cryptographic engineering methodologies on providing attack resistant tamperproof, performance efficient cryptographic primitive accelerators are presented. We describe and analyze symmetric, asymmetric key approaches that are currently adopted by the IT security community focusing on how such approaches are implemented in hardware structures for embedded systems. We also present the most popular attacks (invasive, semi-invasive and non-invasive) that can be mounted on the hardware structure of cryptographic primitive accelerators and discuss protection mechanisms for such attacks.

The remaining of this book chapter is organized as follows. Initially, background information on Hardware Security modules are presented and the functional and non-functional specification of embedded systems are described. Then, a generic secure embedded system architecture is presented and analyzed. Approaches on designing specialized hardware accelerators for symmetric and asymmetric key cryptosystems are described later and hardware attacks are specified along with associated countermeasures. Further research trends are also presented and conclusions are provided in the final book chapter's section.

BACKGROUND

The increasing need for strong security applications that are fast and compromise resistant has led to the development, over time, of a wide range of hardware cryptographic processor devices capable of working independently as autonomous security modules that embed into their structure security related hardware and software units. A typical cryptographic processor is a physically tamper-resistant embedded processor which communicates to a conventional general purpose system and offers a predefined set of cryptographic services. (Anderson et al., 2006)

The first commercial uses of cryptographic processors or Hardware Security Modules (HSM), were made for financial transactions. Traditionally, in such applications, HSMs enforced a policy on

key usage along with a series of key protection measures. Electronic payment systems use the HSM for secure communication between the banks and the merchants and to securely store all needed authentication information. This financial system also involves the customer side by providing to the customer a cheap autonomous HSM (smart card) along with a Personal Identification Number (PIN). This smart card solution guarantees end-to-end security in the communication between the bank and its clients.

After the introduction of Internet banking in the financial world, the above security solution was not enough since the user no longer needed to be physically present in a prearranged place to use the bank services. The ubiquitous nature of banking through the Internet, created the need for an island of trust regardless of the user's location or the means by which a potential transaction is made. This challenge is currently met by issuing tamper resistant authentication – authorization devices (e.g. the RSA SecurID) that can provide time-dependent or random passwords based on unique registered key in the device.

HSMs are also used in military-government applications where strong security is of paramount importance. Military cryptographic processors have been used from the Cold War era for encrypting sensitive communications, messages and for authorizing people as well as high importance military operations. Some of these technologies have been replicated in crisis management situations where civil protection agencies (police, fire brigade, ambulance staff) need to communicate over secure channels. Proprietary closed architecture secure communication channels have been used in such applications, (TETRA, TETRAPOL e.t.c) that strongly rely on dedicated HSMs in an attempt to create a trusted-secure communication environment over an untrusted infrastructure (wireless links, telephone network e.t.c).

The emerging trend of embedded system designs for a wide variety of commercial products (smart grid, automotive, game station applications e.t.c.) has also created a need for strong security (Potlappy, 2011). In such systems, security is managed and maintained by hardware means. HSM for embedded systems need to incorporate a great number of security characteristics in order to instill trust to the user and stakeholder community. Public Key Infrastructure, Digital signature verification, key agreement-distribution, secure storage, tamper evidence, detection and resistance are key services that the upcoming new generation of HSMs will offer.

In general, a secure embedded system must be able to perform the following security related activities as part of its main functionality (Ravi et al., 2004; Kocher et al. 2004):

- **User identification:** Validate user's identity before allowing access to embedded system's resources – assets.
- **Secure access:** Provide access to a service only after identification and authorization.
- **Secure communication:** Provide confidentiality and integrity of sensitive data through system's communication channels.
- **Secure storage:** Provide confidentiality and integrity of stored data within the embedded system.
- **Content security (DRMs):** Provide Digital Rights Management of embedded device content by appointing usage access control.
- **Availability:** Provide guarantees that the system will be available at all times to service its legitimate users.

To meet the above objectives, the security IC must be able to realize a series of security protocols for authentication, authorization, key distribution, key establishment and secure data exchange. The means to achieve this realization is through advanced, modern cryptographic functions that need to be implemented within the security embedded Hardware system (Gebotys, 2010). Necessary cryptographic functions are the following (Menezes et al. 2001):

1. **Symmetric key encryption-decryption:** In these algorithms, the encryption key can be calculated from the decryption key and vice versa. In most symmetric key algorithms, the encryption key and the decryption key are the same. These algorithms, also called secret-key algorithms, single-key algorithms, or one-key algorithms, require that the sender and receiver agree on a key before they can communicate securely.

2. **Asymmetric key encryption–decryption:** These algorithms are designed so that the key used for encryption is different from the key used for decryption. Furthermore, the decryption key cannot (at least in any reasonable amount of time) be calculated from the encryption key. The algorithms are called "public-key" because the encryption key can be made public: A complete stranger can use the encryption key to encrypt a message, but only a specific person with the corresponding decryption key can decrypt the message. In these systems, the encryption key is often called the public key, and the decryption key is often called the private key. The private key is only known to the entity who issues it.

3. **Hash Functions:** These algorithms can generate from a variable bit length value a constant bit length value. Knowledge of the outcome value is impossible to provide knowledge of the input value (one time pads). Hash functions can be used in digital signature schemes.

4. **Digital signature schemes:** These schemes provide a digital signature of data series thus binding uniquely the data owner to its data and are an extension of Asymmetric key cryptography. Digital signature is a digital string for providing authentication. Commonly, in Asymmetric Key Cryptography, it is a digital string that binds a public key to a message in the following way: only the person knowing the message and the

corresponding private key can produce the string, and anyone knowing the message and the public key can verify that the string was properly produced. A digital signature may or may not contain the information necessary to recover the message itself. A digital signature is the value that plays the role of regular signature and is based on public key encryption-decryption algorithms and Hash functions. Digital signature can be generated and verified within the embedded system core.

When embedding the HSM functionality into an embedded system a series of new problems arise. Such problems derive from functional specifications of the currently used embedded systems (Ravi et al., 2004; Kocher et al., 2004) and constitute a series of non-functional specifications that can be summed up in the following categories:

- **Security processing:** The embedded system main processor does not always have the necessary processing power to run security demanding operations. Thus, special care must be paid by the system's designer to enhance system's processing power or provide alternative processing sources.
- **Power dissipation (battery problem):** On battery constrained embedded systems, the extra processing cost due to security functionality has a very negative impact to the system's overall power dissipation. Low power dissipation design is a major requirement in embedded system devices especially when running on battery.
- **Flexibility:** Due to ever evolving security status, the need for interoperability in different environments and the versatility of security objectives, the embedded system's security characteristics must be very flexible and adaptable.
- **Resistance Against attacks:** Embedded system devices can be easily targeted for

compromise by potential attackers. There exist a wide variety of attacks, both software and hardware ones, that due to restrictions in processing and power dissipation can be successful in embedded systems. Special structures within the embedded system hardware and software environment must be devised to overcome the above dangers.

- **Cost:** One of the most important things when designing embedded systems is the overall cost to put such systems on the market. The embedded system security can strongly influence that cost. The highest the level of security instilled in the embedded system device, the highest is the overall cost of implementing such device. Thus, the embedded system designer must come up with an appropriate, affordable, tradeoff between security and cost.

SECURE EMBEDDED SYSTEM ARCHITECTURE

In order to handle the security specific functionality described in the previous section, an embedded computing system must have a compatible hardware architecture capable of supporting all security specifications but also taking into account the restrictions-problems that the system itself imposes in the design (Anoop, 2001; Fournaris et al., 2011). Since, embedded processors do not have enough processing power to support strong security functionality, the computational laboring cryptographic operations needed by security protocols have to be performed by specially designed hardware accelerator units. Furthermore, storage of sensitive data must be taken into account thus leading in the design of special secure memory structures. Figure 1 presents a generic secure embedded system design where the above directives are put into effect.

Figure 1. Secure embedded system architecture

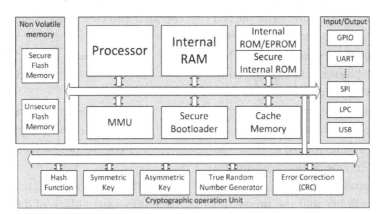

As described in Figure 1, a secure embedded system has a single core (or a dual-multi core in some cases) processor along with internal RAM and ROM units in order to support embedded software running on the system. There is also a secure internal memory area that is thoroughly protected from hardware attacks and is tamper-proof so that physical access to it by an attacker is impossible. Usually, additional protection to such memory is achieved by keeping its data in encrypted form. The processor's embedded Operating System and associated software may also be protected by a secure bootloader structure. Such module is executed during system boot and guarantees that a genuine, untampered version of the OS or firmware is loaded and starts up. The secure bootloader uses the secure internal memory of the system in order to retrieve secret information like public and private keys.

Depending on the embedded system's application, the architecture may have a Non-Volatile Memory (NVRAM) unit so as to store and retrieve data for processing. If the embedded system is used for gathering and processing sensitive information then the non-volatile memory needs to be realized in a secure way. So, this memory unit is split between unsecure NVRAM unit where non sensitive data are stored and secure NVRAM where user keys, passwords, credentials, certificates and any other sensitive data are stored.

The embedded system can have a variety of input/output components so that it can communicate to the external environment in various ways. In general, the input/output components are specified by the embedded system's application and are not directly related to security.

The most important embedded system architecture's component, from security point of view, is the cryptographic operating unit. This unit is responsible for performing all cryptographic operations of the embedded system's security protocols. Such operations are symmetric key encryption/decryption, asymmetric key encryption/decryption, digital signature generation/verification, random number generation and hash functions. Each operation is assigned to a specific hardware module that is responsible for providing to the embedded processor and therefore to the embedded software, a cryptographic operation result. All cryptographic operation modules are connected through a common bus interface to the main embedded system's bus and are controlled by the processor.

Cryptographic operations are structured over a complex mathematical background and require arithmetic and logical operations that are computational complex and intensive. This is the main reason why there is a need for accelerators hardware structure as are depicted in the cryptographic unit. This design approach helps overcoming the low processing power problem that many embedded systems have. The burden of performing cryptographic operations is lifted from the system's main processor that usually has small processing capabilities, and is assigned to the cryptographic operation unit. However, embedding in the system an additional Hardware unit (the cryptographic operation unit) has an impact to the overall system's behavior and design. The cryptographic unit affects the power consumption of the system (extra power dissipation), the chip covered area, the flexibility and the protection against attacks. Therefore, the cryptographic operation unit must be designed in an efficient way so that the embedded system remains competitive and secure. To achieve that, cryptographic engineering principles are applied to each of the modules composing the cryptographic unit. The main focus of such approach is the symmetric and asymmetric key modules where the most complex functionality of the cryptographic operation unit is performed. In the following section we point out the most widely accepted algorithms for each module and describe techniques on how to efficiently realize them in hardware in terms of computation speed, low power dissipation and chip covered area.

CRYPTOGRAPHIC ACCELERATORS FOR EMBEDDED SYSTEMS

Symmetric Key Accelerator Design

Symmetric key cryptography consists of two main types of algorithms, block ciphers and stream cyphers. The first type encrypts/decrypts a plaintext as a sequence of n bit blocks of data while the second type encrypts/decrypts a plaintext as a continuous sequence in a bit serial (or digit serial) fashion.

Symmetric-key block ciphers are used in several operating modes. From the point of view of

hardware implementations, these modes can be divided into two major categories (Koc, 2008):

1. Non-feedback modes, such as electronic code book mode (ECB) and counter mode (CTR).
2. Feedback modes, such as cipher block chaining mode (CBC), cipher feedback mode (CFB), and output feedback mode (OFB).

In the non-feedback modes, encryption of each subsequent block of data can be performed independently from processing other blocks. In particular, all blocks can be encrypted in parallel and no connection exists between them. Two blocks with the same data encrypted under the same key, result in the same ciphertexts. An attacker can trace patterns in a ciphertext to find similar parts of the plaintext and gain a foothold to mount cryptanalytic attacks.

In the feedback modes, during block encryption the ciphertext of the previous block is also used as input. Thus, two blocks with the same data do not result in the same ciphertext blocks. It is not possible to start encrypting the next block of data until encryption of the previous block is completed As a result, all blocks must be encrypted sequentially, with no capability for parallel processing.

There is a wide range of existing block cipher symmetric key algorithms. They follow the diffusion and confusion principles proposed by C. Shannon (Shannon, 1949). As block cipher implementations go, confusion and diffusion are generally implemented with substitution and permutation, respectively. Both operations are needed to achieve strong block cipher security. While permutation is easily implemented in hardware through proper wiring connections, substitution is nonlinear and has implementation difficulties.

Most block ciphers work in an iterative way in rounds of the main functionality. Usually, in parallel to the algorithm's round, a key generation procedure is executed (also iteratively, in rounds) that accepts a master key as input and provides round keys to the main functionality. There is also an initial transformation (which accepts the plaintext as input) feeding its outcome to the first round of the main functionality and there is also a final transformation operation that processes the final round's result and outputs the ciphertext.

In general, most block ciphers fall under the class of Feistel networks. In such a network, introduced by H. Feistel in 1973, a block is divided into two halves, the left L_i and the right R_i (where i is the round number) and perform in parallel iteratively (for a defined number of rounds) the following equations:

$$L_i = R_{i-1}$$

$$R_i = L_{i-1} \oplus f\left(R_{i-1}, Key_i\right)$$

Function $f()$ is called round function and uses the right half of the previous round along with round key that is provided by the key generation operation. Feistel's approach guarantees that the block cipher is reversible. In other words, decryption follows the same algorithm as encryption using the same key thus the design of the block cipher is simplified (decrypting is done using the encryption implementation). In Feistel net-

work block ciphers, the round function, the key generation, the block and round number as well as the key size determines the security level of the algorithm and its ease of implementation. Not all block ciphers follow Feistel networks, there are also block cipher algorithms that follow more generic Substitution-Permutation networks. One such block cipher is Advanced Encryption Standard (AES) algorithm, formerly known as Rijndael (Daemen et al.,2002), that constitute the most widely accepted symmetric key block cipher solution in embedded systems. However, since the non-functional specifications of embedded systems are very strict, lightweight block ciphers have also been proposed in open literature. Such algorithms are the Feistel network based CAST, DESL, DESXL, HIGHT, XTEA or the Substitution-Permutation network based PRESENT, PUFFIN CURUPIRA 1-2 (Kitsos et al., 2012).

The substitution operation of block ciphers consists of braking the processed message in specific bit length digits (e.g. 8 bits in AES) and replacing them with values from well-defined set of numbers through a strongly non-linear function. Such substitution set of numbers are referred as SBOXs and are implemented in various ways including their precomputation and storage as lookup tables in protected memory units, calcu-

Figure 2. Block cipher iterative loop hardware architecture

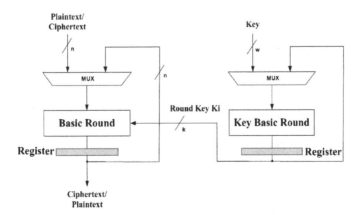

lating them on the fly when a request arises or a trade-off between the two approaches.

The realization of a fully functional block cipher in hardware can be done as an iterative loop architecture, as described in Figure 2, where one round of the algorithm is implemented and stored in one or several registers (depending on the algorithm). This stored outcome in a consecutive round is fed back to the round implementation as an input in order to come up with the next rounds result. This process is repeated for all the algorithm's rounds. In this approach, only one block of data is encrypted at a time and the number of clock cycles necessary to encrypt a single block of data is equal to the number of cipher rounds. However, the hardware resources used for iterative loop architecture are fairly small which makes this approach ideal for embedded systems where chip covered area and power dissipation is restricted.

To further increase computation speed of the above approach, instead of implementing one round of the block cipher, one can implement k rounds (where $k < total\ round\ number$). By applying this unrolling technique, the needed clock cycles to come up with a result is decreased by a factor of k. Obviously, if $k=total\ round\ number$ then the block cipher result can be outputted in one clock cycle. The main drawbacks of this approach is the high number of used hardware resources and the decrease in maximum frequency due to excessive circuit critical path delay that increases considerable for big k values. The high critical path delay can be reduced by applying the pipelining technique however, unrolling and pipelining are not easily applicable in embedded systems since they add a big overhead to chip covered area.

Stream ciphers typically operate serially by generating a stream of pseudorandom key bits, the keystream (stream ciphers are also called pseudorandom number generators). The stream cipher takes two parameters, the secret key, K, and the initialization vector, IV, and produces

the keystream bits, zt, as presented in Figure 3. In stream encryption each plaintext symbol, Pt, is encrypted by applying a group operation with a keystream symbol, zt, resulting in a ciphertext symbol ct. In modern cipher the operation is the simple bitwise XOR. Decryption takes the subtraction of the keystream symbol from the ciphertext symbol. With the bitwise XOR this is the same operation.

A stream cipher generates the keystream based on an internal state (St). This state is updated in essentially two ways. If the state changes independently of the plaintext or ciphertext messages, the cipher is classified as a synchronous stream cipher. Well known synchronous stream ciphers are E0, ZUC and SNOW3G. (Kitsos et al., 2012)

In contrast, if the ciphers update their state based on previous ciphertext digits, they are called self-synchronizing stream cipher as shown in Figure 4. The most recent self-synchronizing stream cipher is Moustique (Daemen et al., 2006).

Asymmetric Key Accelerator Design

The security strength of the Asymmetric Key Cryptography lies in the computational infea-

Figure 3. Synchronous stream cipher process

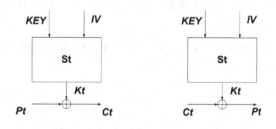

Figure 4. Self-synchronizing stream cipher process

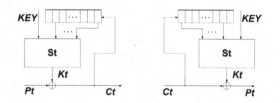

sibility of finding an Entity's Private Key from information about the Public Key or the Public Key itself. The problem of deriving the Private Key from the Public Key is equivalent to solving a computational problem that is considered intractable. Three such problems are used in Public Key Cryptography:

- **Integer Factorization Problem (IFP):** If n is a positive integer, find its prime factorization: meaning $n = p_1^{e_1} p_2^{e_2} .... p_k^{e_k}$ where the p_i are pair wise distinct prime integer numbers and each $e_i \geq 1$.

- **Discrete Logarithm Problem (DLP):** If p is a prime number, a is a generator element of Z_p^* ($0 < a < p$), and β is an element of Z_p^*, find integer x, $0 \leq x \leq p - 2$, such that $a^x \equiv \beta (\mod p)$.

- **Elliptic Curve Discrete Logarithm Problem (ECDLP):** It is a generalization of the DL problem. If there is an elliptic curve E defined over a Field F and if there is a point $P \in E(F)$ of order n, and a point $Q \in E(F)$, find an integer s, $0 \leq s \leq n - 1$, such that $Q = sP$, provided that such an integer exists.

Asymmetric Key algorithms use a complex mathematical background and require a considerable amount of modulus operations (addition, multiplication, inversion). Due to the fact that such operations are performed over very big numbers (e.g. 1024 bit length at least, in the case of RSA), a resulting Asymmetric Key Cryptosystem is considered slow and with considerable hardware resource needs. That is the reason why Asymmetric Key Cryptography is not used for message encryption-decryption but rather in coherence with Symmetric Key Cryptography or for Digital Signature schemes. In the first case, a Asymmetric Key Cryptosystem is used for encryption-decryption of the Secret Key of a Symmetric Key algorithm. Therefore, Asymmetric Key Cryptography is employed only once per session for encryption-decryption of a small value (the Secret Key is usually 128-256 bits long in Symmetric Key Cryptography). So, the time demanding message encryption-decryption handling is appointed to the Symmetric Key algorithms that require less hardware resources and are usually very fast. In the case of Digital Signature schemes, Public Key Cryptography is employed for certifying the owner authenticity of a message.

Schaumont and Verbauwhede presented the cryptographic engineer's view on the security domain in the form of a security pyramid as shown in Figure 5 (Schaumont et al., 2001). The pyramid form represents the design space of a Public Key cryptosystem at multiple levels of abstraction. The most abstract representation of a cryptographic application (Level 1) is the security protocol architecture, which details what steps make up a secure transaction. Level 2 represents the Asymmetric Key security algorithms. The operations related to the hard mathematical problems used for the Public Key security algorithms are derived from number theory and constitute the next level (Level 3). Beyond the level of number theory exist levels that deal with implementation issues. The outcome of Level 4 is a detailed hardware architecture with specific components that have distinct roles in the overall structure of the system and constitutes a detailed model described by a

Figure 5. Asymmetric key system design plan

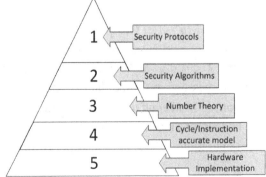

Hardware Description Language. This model specifies every aspect of the cryptographic system including accurate timing and control logic/ instructions that are used in the implementation of an Asymmetric Key Cryptosystem. Finally, on Level 5, we express all aspects of a security algorithm in terms of targeted platform technology including relevant circuitry and hardware technology specific optimization techniques.

There is a wide variety of Asymmetric key protocols that apart from encryption/decryption are used for security operations like digital signatures, key agreement, identity management, authentication, certificate authorities e.t.c. All protocols are based on the above mentioned hard mathematical problems and their associated algorithms. Most up-to-date secure embedded system manufacturers have adopted RSA algorithm (Rivest, Shamir, Adleman) as their main Asymmetric key scheme that is based on the IFP. However, it is expected that gradually in the future, Elliptic Curve Cryptography (ECC) based on the EDLP will become the dominant asymmetric key scheme since it can retain the same security level as RSA but with considerably smaller key sizes. Both approaches are based on number theory arithmetic and use cyclic groups. Both algorithms require modulus operations to provide a cryptographic result.

In the RSA scheme, the public key consists of a pair of integers *(n, e)* where the RSA modulus *n* is a product of two randomly generated (and secret) primes *p* and *q* of the same bit length. The encryption exponent *e* is an integer satisfying $1 < e < \varphi$ and $\gcd(e, \varphi) = 1$ where $\varphi = (p-1)^2(q-1)$. The private key *d*, also called the decryption exponent, is the integer satisfying $1 < d < \varphi$ and $e^2 d \equiv 1 (mod\, \varphi)$. To encrypt a message *m*, a modular exponentiation operation, $c = m^e mod\, n$, is performed. Similarly, to decrypt a message *c*, a modular exponentiation operation, $m = c^d mod\, n$, is performed.

Modular exponentiation is the main operation that the RSA scheme uses. This operation is analyzed in a series of modular multiplication and modular squaring (as a special case of modular multiplication) operations. In that case, cryptographic engineering aims mainly in optimizing modular multiplication and consecutively modular exponentiation in order to come up with efficient RSA implementations that fit well in hardware and are protected against hardware attacks.

In the ECC scheme, there exist several approaches that can be used for encryption, digital signature, authentication or key agreement. However, since ECC is based on the ECDLP, the main cryptographic operation used in this scheme is point multiplication. Assuming there exists a base EC point *P* and a secret random number *s*, the point multiplication result $Q = s^2 P$ along with *P* and the employed EC parameters constitute the cryptosystem's public key while the number *s* is the private key.

Point multiplication is the major design bottleneck in ECC. It requires a series of other mathematical operations that have increased mathematical complexity. Point multiplication can be realized as a series of other EC point operations. Those operations are point addition $(P_1 + P_2)$ and point doubling $(P_2 = 2P_1)$.

Point addition and doubling use the mathematical framework of the Finite Field on which the EC is defined ($\mathbb{F}_p$ or $\mathbb{F}_{2^k}$) following a series of rules denoted as the Group Law. Therefore, all mathematic operations between the coordinates *(x, y)* of EC Points P_1, P_2, as is dictated by the Group Law, are performed using $\mathbb{F}_p$ or $\mathbb{F}_{2^k}$ arithmetic (Menezes et. al, 2001).

In Finite Field arithmetic, four mathematical modulus operations can be identified. Those operations are addition-subtraction, multiplication, squaring and inversion-division. Each such operation has a different computational and hardware resources cost (measured in throughput, critical path delay, gate – storage element number, power dissipation). Inversion-division has the higher such cost, while addition-subtraction the lowest. The notable cost of multiplication in Finite Fields is of great importance since this mathematic operation can also be used under certain circumstances for inversion-division (using Fermat's Little Theorem) (Fournaris et. al, 2007). Main goals of a cryptographic engineer toward designing an efficient ECC system is the optimization of the point multiplication algorithm, the replacement of inversion/division with finite field multiplication during computations of point addition or doubling and the design of efficient finite field multipliers.

Optimizing Asymmetric Key Modulus Operations using Montgomery Modular Multiplication

As described in the above subsection, modulus operations are necessary, both in RSA and ECC schemes, and their realization in hardware is very important in order to design an efficient asymmetric key accelerator system. There exist several techniques on how to optimize such operations and they fall under two categories, algorithmic optimizations and circuit optimizations.

Modular multiplication either in $\mathbb{F}_p$ (used for RSA and ECC schemes) or $\mathbb{F}_{2^k}$ (for ECC) Fields plays a very important role on the efficient asymmetric key accelerator design. Many researchers have indicated that Montgomery modular multiplication (MMM) algorithm is one of the best approaches for designing modular multipliers for RSA and ECC. The MMM algorithm (Montgomery, 1985) calculates the value $Mont(X,Y) = X \cdot 2 Y \cdot 2 R^{-1} mod N$ where R is a constant number, usually $R=2^n$. The n-bit value N has to be an integer filling the condition $gcd(R,N)=1$. In RSA, N value is odd as the product of two primes therefore the above constrain is always true. In the original proposal of P. Montgomery (Montgomery,1985), after each multiplication a reduction is needed. If the result T of one MMM is $T > N$, N must be subtracted so that the

output can be used as input of the next multiplication (in RSA, modular exponentiation consists of repeated modular multiplications). To avoid this subtraction a bound for R is proposed by Walter in (Walter, 1999) such that for inputs X,Y<2N also the output is bounded $T<2N$. In (Walter, 1999), which is further improved in (Walter, 2002), it was shown that the Montgomery exponentiation method requires no final subtraction, which is very important for fast implementations.

A multiplier architecture based on Montgomery's algorithm is probably the best studied architecture for hardware. There are many variation of the algorithm, proposed by researchers in order to avoid long carry chains. Proposed ways to do so are based on circuit optimizations like systolic array and redundant representation optimizations like Residue Number System (RNS), Carry Save format, Signed Digit (Batina et al., 2003).

Montgomery multiplication also exists for $\mathbb{F}_{2^k}$ fields (Koc et al., 1998). The algorithm is simpler compared to $\mathbb{F}_p$ fields and does not include any final subtraction. Along with Most Significant bit and Least significant bit multiplication algorithms it is used in ECC systems in bit serial, digit serial and bit parallel multiplier structures (Fournaris et. al, 2007).

HARDWARE ATTACKS ON SECURITY EMBEDDED SYSTEM

An embedded system operates in hostile environment from security perspective. It can be stolen and manipulated in order to give out any sensitive information that may be stored or processed in it. While the system might be protected from cryptanalytic attacks by the use of strong security schemes, it can still be compromised when an adversary applies a hardware attack, an attack on the implementation itself. Even if secret information cannot be learned, attackers may be able to disrupt the hardware or deny service leading to failures in the security system. We can discriminate 3 types of such hardware attacks:

1. **Invasive attacks:** These attacks aim at physically disrupting the correct operation of an embedded chip. They involve removing chip packaging, micro probing of the chip's activity (memory, registers, buses) and physically tampering - interfering with the chip functionality. Invasive attack techniques begins with chip depackaging, removal of on-chip protection layers (depassivation) and modifications through probing tools. Through such tools one can modify the executed code or change values in Registers or simply observe the behavior of static/dynamic RAM blocks after power off since such units tend to "remember" values long after no power is applied to them. Invasive attacks are not easily mounted, require attackers with considerable on-chip expertise and expensive, specialized equipment like laser cuter microscope, micro probes e.t.c.

2. **Semi invasive Attacks:** These attacks aim at observing the behavior of the embedded system chip after an attacker specialized triggering. Like invasive attacks, they require depackaging the chip in order to get access to its surface. However, the passivation layer of the chip remains intact, as semi-invasive methods do not require depassivation or creating contacts to the internal lines. The goal is to induce a fault in the computation flow of the chip during a cryptographic operation and observe the cryptographic result as the fault propagates. The attacker can deduce sensitive information from such result on an unprotected embedded chip. In these attacks, also called Fault attacks, faults are injected using power or clock glitches, extreme variations in temperature, UV radiation or even optical laser beam induction. Depending on the attacker's equipment and expertise,

the fault attacks are moderately difficult to mount.

3. **Non-invasive Attacks:** Such attacks, also called side channel attacks (SCA), exploit an embedded system's hardware characteristics leakage (power dissipation, computation time, electromagnetic emission e.t.c) to extract information about the processed data and use them to deduce sensitive information (cryptographic keys, messages etc.). An attacker does not tamper with the chip in any way and needs only make appropriate observations to mount a successful attack. Side channel attacks can be mounted very easily, cheaply, using a PC, a digital oscilloscope and some probes. Therefore, they can be mounted to an embedded system device by even the most inexperienced attacker. This ease of use, makes SCA very potent. Some of the most widely used side channel attacks are the following:

    a. **Timing Attacks:** The attacker observes the computation time (clock cycle number) needed by the embedded system to provide a cryptographic result. Depending on the secret/private key that is employed, this time delay may vary and it can provide info about the key's Hamming weight. Furthermore, an attacker can start guessing key bits and observe which hypothesis results have the strongest correlation between the predicted results and the actual ones. Collecting enough samples the attacker can recover the whole key.

    b. **Power Attacks:** These attacks involve physical measurement of the power dissipation emitted from the chip during cryptographic operations. Simple power signal analysis can reveal what mathematical operation is performed in the chip (e.g. modular multiplication or squaring during an RSA operation) and since in most cases the operation is related to the secret/private keys this action can reveal the key itself. Even if the chip is protected against simple power analysis, it is not fully resistant against power attacks since differential power analysis can still lead to compromise. In differential power analysis, the attacker perform guesses about a secret/private key bit, collects the related to this hypothesis power signal and correlates it with the actual power signal. The strongest correlation between the hypothesis and the actual measurement is the correct guess. Taking enough power samples and correlations the secret/private key can be revealed.

c. **Electromagnetic attacks:** These attacks use the electromagnetic radiation emitted from the embedded system chip for simple analysis or differential analysis in a similar way as power attacks. In electromagnetic attacks, specific chip areas can be targeted and no physical access to the chip is strictly required (they can be mounted from afar). On the other hand, the existence of physical noise, RF interference or measurement error limits the attack's effectiveness.

Countermeasures

Designing countermeasures for Hardware attacks is not an easy task. Each security and cryptographic algorithm has its own vulnerabilities when implemented in hardware and therefore a ubiquitous approach toward Hardware attack resistance is impossible. In general, two approaches for countermeasures are used in practice, algorithmic based countermeasures and circuit based countermeasures. Algorithmic countermeasures aim at modifying the cryptographic algorithm and

associated computer algebra operations so that when implemented in hardware, the associated leaked information will be minimized thus being of no use to an attacker. Such countermeasures are more focused to semi-invasive and non-invasive attacks. Circuit countermeasures are hardware structures added to a cryptographic algorithm's hardware architecture, implementation or packaging, capable of detecting or thwarting a hardware attack. Such countermeasures can be used to protect an embedded system against all kinds of hardware attacks.

Invasive attack resistance is achieved by designing special structures during chip packaging and assembling in order to provide tamper evidence, detection and resistance. This may include mesh sensors implemented in the metal layer after packaging consisting of serpentine patterns of ground and power lines that are shortcircuited if attempts on depackaging or depassivation are done thus destroying the chip. Also, the on chip silicon layers can be designed in such a way that visual chip surface analysis through microscope is very difficult. Adding multiple layers with metal layers in between is such a technique applied during chip fabrication. All the invasive attack countermeasures are circuit based countermeasures.

Semi-Invasive attack resistance can be achieved by using some of the countermeasures for thwarting chip depackaging attempts (used in invasive attack resistance), however, usually such countermeasures are not enough or are too expensive. So, semi-invasive attack countermeasures are focused on detecting fault injection during cryptographic algorithm execution. One approach toward this end is to modify the cryptographic algorithm so as to support infective computation. The basic concept of infective computation is that any computational errors introduced by a fault will propagate throughout the cryptographic computation, thus ensuring that the final result appears random and useless to the attacker in the end. Another approach that can be combined with infective computation is the design of specialized fault detection units in the cryptographic algorithm hardware architecture capable of detecting single or multiple faults. Such units involve elegant circuit design as well as modifications in the cryptography algorithmic flow to include specific conditions between intermediate values that the fault detection unit must detect after the computations are concluded but before the cryptographic result is released. When faults are detected then a random number or zero value is released thus denying an attacker any useful information about secret/private keys.

There is a wide variety of non-invasive countermeasures depending on what side channel attack they thwart. The basic goal of all countermeasures is implementing the cryptographic architecture in such a way that the implementation's characteristics like power consumption, timing or electromagnetic radiation, leaks as little as possible of the secret keys or data. This can be achieved either by scrambling the leakage signal in such a way that is unrelated to the secret information that it is computed in the cryptographic unit or by minimizing the leakage as a whole so that it is very difficult for an attacker to use it for a side channel attack. The first approach is related to algorithmic countermeasures that aim at inserting randomization through the cryptographic algorithm computation flow by providing Boolean, or arithmetic (multiplicative or additive) masking of the secret information (multiplication or addition with a random number). These countermeasures, also known as blinding, is very useful against Differential attacks since they aim at decorrelation of the secret data with the leakage itself. The second approach is related to algorithmic and mostly circuit countermeasures. Through special circuitry, like double rail technique, power rebalancing or additional dummy operations (redundancy), we aim at normalizing the leaked signals so that they remain unchanged during cryptographic operations. In general, it should be mentioned however, that protection against side channel attacks is never expected to be absolute: a determined attacker with a vast amount of resources can eventually, given enough time and effort compromise an implementation. The goal from cryptographic engineering perspective is to realize in the cryptographic accelerator enough side channel attack countermeasures so that an attack on the system becomes too expensive in effort or cost to be interesting (Mangard et al., 2007).

FUTURE RESEARCH DIRECTIONS

In the near future, the notion of trust is going to play an important role in applications where security is needed. In a trusted system the user must be able to attest that the information provided by his device or another user's device is not tampered with or compromised. HSMs for providing a trust island in an existing untrusted environment have already hit the market with some success and hardware specifications have been defined, mostly by the Trusted Computing Group (TCG) industry consortium. TCG is responsible for formalizing, applying, and extending the trusted computing ideas to well-known and established computer systems either by introducing new hardware or software modules or by proposing appropriate protocols for those modules. Trusted Computing can be viewed as a collection of technologies capable of constantly monitor the behavior of a given computer system for indication of a possible compromise. The core of this technology is embodied in a HSM, denoted as Trusted Platform Module (TPM). The TPM (TPM v. 1.2) currently uses AES, RSA algorithms for encryption/decryption, authentication and privacy. It is expected that Elliptic Curve cryptography will be soon adopted in the standard as well. TCG has established a work group that explicitly works on applying the trust directives to the embedded system world.

Furthermore, new approaches on cryptography are expected to be applied to embedded systems. Bilinear pairing operations (Weil pairing, Tate pairing, Eta pairing, Ate pairing etc.) can be a very promising tool for providing advanced security services like short signatures, identity based encryption and signature, identity based authenticated key agreement, Tripartite Diffie-Hellman or self-blindable credentials (Barreto et al., 2002). Pairing Based Cryptography (PBC) is a fast growing research field and the latest published implementation results show that PBC applications are possible for a resource constrained environment where there is a need for compact and power efficient designs (Scott et al. 2006; Van Herrewege, 2009). Also, strongly secure self-synchronizing stream ciphers that are still under development (Daemen et al., 2006) as well as the finalist contenders (phase 3) of the eSTREAM project (Anashin, 2005) are bound to be realized in embedded systems.

CONCLUSION

Strong Security in Embedded systems is a complex issue from Hardware designer's perspective due to the non-functional specification that the embedded system's applications set. Cryptographic Engineering, however, provides the means of matching all systems' constrains by the efficient design and realization of symmetric and asymmetric key cryptographic accelerators. In the book chapter, we provided the design methodology toward efficient secure embedded systems and highlighted existing approaches for achieving that task. Special care was made to describe why the embedded system must be hardware attack resistant due to the existence of Hardware specific attacks that target the implementation itself rather than security algorithms. Such attacks

were categorized, analyzed briefly and associated countermeasures were sketched.

REFERENCES

Anashin, V., Bogdanov, A., Kizhvatov, I., & Kumar, S. (2005). *eSTREAM: A new fast flexible stream cipher.*

Anderson, R., Bond, M., Clulow, J., & Skorobogatov, S. (2006). Cryptographic processors-A survey. *Proceedings of the IEEE, 94*(2), 357–369. doi:10.1109/JPROC.2005.862423.

Anoop, M. (2008). *Security needs in embedded systems.* Retrieved from http://eprint.iacr.org/2008/198

Barreto, P., Kim, H., & Lynn, B. (2002). Efficient algorithms for pairing-based cryptosystems. In *Proceedings of the 22nd Annual International Cryptology Conference on Advances in Cryptology (CRYPTO '02)*. Springer-Verlag.

Batina, L., Berna Örs, S., Preneel, B., & Vandewalle, J. (2003). Hardware architectures for public key cryptography. *Integration (Tokyo, Japan), 34*(1-2), 1–64.

Daemen, J., & Kitsos, P. (2006). *The self-synchronizing stream cipher Moustique. eSTREAM Phase 2, the ECRYPT Stream Cipher Project.* ECRYPT NoE.

Daemen, J., & Rijmen, V. (2002). *The design of Rijndael — AES, the advanced encryption standard.* Springer-Verlag. doi:10.1007/978-3-662-04722-4.

Fournaris, A. P. (2010). Fault and simple power attack resistant RSA using montgomery modular multiplication. In *Proceedings of the IEEE International Symposium on Circuits and Systems (ISCAS 2010)* (pp. 1875-1878). IEEE.

Fournaris, A. P., & Hein, D. M. (2011). Trust management through hardware means: Design concerns and optimizations. In N. Voros, A. Mukherjee, N. Sklavos, K. Masselos, & M. Huebner (Eds.), *VLSI 2010 Annual Symposium* (Vol. 105, pp. 31-45). Springer.

Fournaris, A. P., & Koufopavlou, O. G. (2007). *Hardware design issues in elliptic curve cryptography for wireless systems*. CRC Press.

Gebotys, C. H. (2010). *Security in embedded devices*. Berlin: Springer. doi:10.1007/978-1-4419-1530-6.

Joye, M., & Tymen, C. (2001). Protections against differential analysis – An algebraic approach. In *Proceedings of the Third International Workshop on Cryptographic Hardware and Embedded Systems* (pp. 377-390). IEEE.

Kitsos, P., Sklavos, N., Parousi, M., & Skodras, A. N. (2012). A comparative study of hardware architectures for lightweight block ciphers. *Computers & Electrical Engineering, 38*(1), 148–160. doi:10.1016/j.compeleceng.2011.11.022.

Kitsos, P., Sklavos, N., Provelengios, G., & Skodras, A. (2012). FPGA-based analysis of stream ciphers ZUC, Snow3g, Grain v1, Mickey v2, Trivium and E0, accepted with minor revisions. In *Microprocessors and Microsystems: Embedded Hardware Design*. London: Elsevier.

Koc, C. (2008). *Cryptographic engineering*. Berlin: Springer.

Koc, C. K., & Acar, T. (1998). Montgomery multiplication in GF(2^k). *Designs, Codes and Cryptography, 14*(1), 57–69. doi:10.1023/A:1008208521515.

Kocher, P., Jaffe, J., & Jun, B. (1999). Differential power analysis. [Springer-Verlag.]. *Advances in Cryptology Proceedings of Crypto, 1999*, 388–397. doi:10.1007/3-540-48405-1_25.

Kocher, P., Ravi, S., Lee, R., McGraw, G., & Raghunathan, A. (2004). Security as a new dimension in embedded system design. In *Proceedings of the 41st Annual Conference on Design Automation - DAC '04* (pp. 753). New York: ACM Press.

Mangard, S., Oswald, E., & Popp, T. (2007). *Power analysis attacks: Revealing the secrets of smart cards*. Berlin: Springer.

Menezes, A. J., Oorschot, P. C. V., Vanstone, S. A., & Rivest, R. L. Menezes, & Van Oorschot, S. A. V. (2001). Handbook of applied cryptography. Boca Raton, FL: CRC Press.

Montgomery, L. P. (1985). Modular multiplication without trial division. *Mathematics of Computation, 44*(170), 519–521. doi:10.1090/S0025-5718-1985-0777282-X.

Potlapally, N. (2011). Hardware security in practice: Challenges and opportunities. In *Proceedings of the 2011 IEEE International Symposium on Hardware-Oriented Security and Trust* (pp. 93-98). IEEE.

Ravi, S., Raghunathan, A., Kocher, P., & Hattangady, S. (2004). Security in embedded systems. *ACM Transactions on Embedded Computing Systems, 3*(3), 461–491. doi:10.1145/1015047.1015049.

Schaumont, P., & Verbauwhede, I. (2001). A reconfiguration hierarchy for elliptic curve cryptography. In *Proceedings of the 35th Asilomar Conference on Signals, Systems, and Computers*. Asilomar.

Schneier, B. (1996). *Applied cryptography – Protocols, algorithms and source code in C*. New York: John Wiley & Sons.

Scott, M., Costigan, N., Abdulwahab, W., Goubin, L., & Matsui, M. (2006). Implementations of cryptographic pairing on smart cards. In Goubin, L., & Matsui, M. (Eds.), *Cryptographic Hardware and Embedded Systems - CHES 2006* (*Vol. 4249*, pp. 134–147). Berlin: Springer. doi:10.1007/11894063_11.

Shannon, C. E. (1949). Communication theory of secrecy systems. *The Bell System Technical Journal, 28*(4), 656–715.

Van Herrewege, A., Batina, L., Knezevic, M., Verbauwhede, I., & Preneel, B. (2009). Compact implementations of pairings. In *Proceedings of the 4th Benelux Workshop on Information and System Security - WISSec 2009*. Louvain-la-Neuve, Belgium: WISSec.

Walter, C. (2002). Precise bounds for Montgomery modular multiplication and some potentially insecure RSA moduli. *Topics in Cryptology- CT-RSA 2002*, 30-39.

Walter, C. D. (1999). Montgomery exponentiation needs no final subtractions. *Electronics Letters, 35*(21), 1831–1832. doi:10.1049/el:19991230.

ADDITIONAL READING

Brickell, E., Chen, L., & Li, J. (2008). A new direct anonymous attestation scheme from bilinear maps. In Trusted Computing - Challenges and Applications, (vol. 4968, pp. 166-178). Springer.

Coron, J.-S. (1999). Resistance against differential power analysis for elliptic curve cryptosystems. In *Proceedings of the First International Workshop on Cryptographic Hardware and Embedded Systems* (pp. 292-302). London, UK: Springer-Verlag.

Elbirt, A., Yip, W., Chetwynd, B., & Paar, C. (2001). An FPGA-based performance evaluation of the AES block cipher candidate algorithm finalists. *IEEE Transactions on VLSI, 9*(4), 545. doi:10.1109/92.931230.

Fournaris, A., & Koufopavlou, O. (2007). Hardware design issues in elliptic curve cryptography for wireless systems. In *Wireless Security and Cryptography: Specifications and Implementations*. CRC Press.

Fournaris, A. P., & Hein, D. M. (2011). Trust management through hardware means: design concerns and optimizations. In N. Voros, A. Mukherjee, N. Sklavos, K. Masselos, & M. Huebner (Eds.), *VLSI 2010 Annual Symposium* (Vol. 105, pp. 31-45). Springer.

Group, T. C. (2007). *TCG TPM specification version 1.2*. Retrieved from https://www.trusted-computinggroup.org/specs/TPM/

Guilley, S., Sauvage, L., Danger, J.-L., & Selmane, N. (2010). Fault injection resilience. In *Proceedings of the 2010 Workshop on Fault Diagnosis and Tolerance in Cryptography* (pp. 51-65). IEEE.

Hwang, D., Chaney, M., Karanam, S., Ton, N., & Gaj, K. (2008). Comparison of FPGA-targeted hardware implementations of eSTREAM stream cipher candidates. In *Proceedings of State of the Art of Stream Ciphers Workshop, SASC 2008*. Lausanne, Switzerland: SASC.

Kitsos, P., Sklavos, N., Galanis, M. D., & Koufopavlou, O. (2004). 64-bit block ciphers: Hardware implementation and comparison analysis. *Computers & Electrical Engineering, 30*(8), 593–604. doi:10.1016/j.compeleceng.2004.11.001.

Kitsos, P., & Zhang, Y. (2008). *RFID security: Techniques, protocols and system-on-chip design*. ISBN-10: 0387764801

Mamiya, H., Miyaji, A., & Morimoto, H. (2004). Efficient countermeasures against RPA, DPA, and SPA. In Joye, M., & Quisquater, J.-J. (Eds.), *Cryptographic Hardware and Embedded Systems- CHES 2004* (*Vol. 3156*, pp. 243–319). Springer. doi:10.1007/978-3-540-28632-5_25.

Ravi, S., Raghunathan, A., & Chakradhar, S. (2004). Tamper resistance mechanisms for secure embedded systems. In *Proceedings of the International Conference on VLSI Design*, (pp. 605 -611). VLSI.

Sklavos, N. (2010). On the hardware implementation cost of crypto-processors architectures. *Information Security Journal: A Global Perspective, 19*(2), 53-60.

Sklavos, N., & Koufopavlou, O. (2002). Architectures and VLSI implementations of the AES-proposal Rijndael. *IEEE Transactions on Computers, 51*(12), 1454–1459. doi:10.1109/TC.2002.1146712.

Sklavos, N., & Zhang, X. (2007). *Wireless security and cryptography: Specifications and implementations*. Boca Raton, FL: CRC Press. doi:10.1201/9780849387692.

Verbauwhede, I. M. R. (2010). *Secure integrated circuits and systems*. Berlin: Springer. doi:10.1007/978-0-387-71829-3.

Wollinger, T., Guajardo, J., & Paar, C. (2004). Security on FPGAs: State of the art implementations and attacks. *ACM Transactions on Embedded Computing Systems, 3*(3), 534–574. doi:10.1145/1015047.1015052.

KEY TERMS AND DEFINITIONS

Block Ciphers: Symmetric key cryptographic algorithms that process plaintext or ciphertext data in blocks of data. The block bit number influences the security of the algorithm.

Ciphertext: The outcome of a cryptographic encryption process. When decrypted it should provide a plaintext.

Elliptic Curve Cryptography: Type of cryptography that is based on an Elliptic Curve defined over finite fields. Each point P of the Elliptic Curve is defined by its coordinates (x, y). Usually, depending on the algorithm, the plaintext is inserted to the x coordinate of P and the resulting point is encrypted.

Finite Fields: Arithmetic fields with a finite set of elements. In cryptography, two types of finite fields are used, prime fields or $\mathbb{F}_p$, where p is a prime number and binary extension fields or $\mathbb{F}_{2^k}$ where k is an integer.

Hardware Attacks: Attacks meant to retrieve the secret/private key of a cryptosystem by targeting the implementation of a cryptographic algorithm and not the algorithm itself.

Plaintext: A numerical or alphanumerical message to be encrypted using a cryptographic algorithm.

Side Channel Attacks: Hardware attacks that aim at collecting signals leaking from a security implementation and use them to deduce sensitive information about the operation that is performed in that implementation at a given time.

Stream Ciphers: Symmetric key cryptographic algorithms that combine plaintext digits with a pseudorandom cipher digit stream in order to return ciphertext digits.

Chapter 22
Flash–Based Storage in Embedded Systems

Pierre Olivier
Université de Bretagne Occidentale, France

Jalil Boukhobza
Université de Bretagne Occidentale, France

Eric Senn
Université de Bretagne Sud, France

ABSTRACT

NAND Flash memories gained a solid foothold in the embedded systems domain due to its attractive characteristics in terms of size, weight, shock resistance, power consumption, and data throughput. Moreover, flash memories tend to be less confined to the embedded domain, as it can be observed through the market explosion of flash-based storage systems (average growth of the NVRAM is reported to be about 69% up to 2015). In this chapter, the authors focus on NAND flash memory NVRAM. After a global presentation of its architecture and very specific constraints, they describe the different ways to manage flash memories in embedded systems which are 1) the use of a hardware Flash Translation Layer (FTL), or 2) a dedicated Flash File System (FFS) software support implemented within the embedded operating system kernel.

INTRODUCTION

Nowadays, flash memory is widely used in embedded systems, serving as main storage system in numerous devices such as mp3 players, smartphones and various kind of mobile computers such as tablet computers and netbooks (Maleval, 2010). Moreover, flash memory tends to be less confined to this domain, replacing traditional hard disk drives in general computer systems and complementing them in large data centers. This tendency can be observed through the explosion of flash-based Solid State Drives (SSDs) in the market. 25 years after that Toshiba announced its invention, NAND flash memory is shipping almost 8 times more gigabytes in 2011 than DRAM.

DOI: 10.4018/978-1-4666-3922-5.ch022

Flash memory provides benefits in terms of size, power consumption, shock resistance, weight, and I/O performance (Macronix International Co., Ltd., 2012). The fast growth of the embedded market brings about a similar interest in both flash memory industrial production and academic/industrial research. For example, the company Anobit shipped 20 Millions of embedded flash controllers during the first semester of 2011 (Storage Newsletter, 2011). Generally speaking, the annual average growth of the non-volatile memory is reported to be about 69% up to 2015, according to MarketResearch.com (EETimes, 2011).

There are many types of flash memory cells, named after the logic gate used as their main building block. Nevertheless, one can identify two main types: NOR and NAND flash memory. NOR flash memory is used for code storage and is considered as a cheap DRAM alternative used for instance in mid-range mobile phones, while NAND flash memory is designed for data storage. This chapter focuses on NAND flash based storage systems and their management techniques.

Because of its intrinsic characteristics, flash memory presents some specific constraints that need to be taken into account in order to achieve efficient storage system integration. Some of these constraints, related to electrical properties of NAND flash memory cells, can be summarized as follows: 1) the necessity to perform an erase operation before a write, 2) the impossibility to perform in-place data updates, 3) the limited number of realizable write/erase cycles (limited lifetime), and 4) the I/O performance asymmetry between read and write operations. Those properties will be detailed farther in this chapter.

NAND flash memory can be managed in different ways in an embedded system, in order to cope with the aforementioned constraints and to abstract the hardware intricacies to the applicative layers.

Flash-based cards like SD cards, USB sticks, and SSDs use a specific hardware layer called the Flash Translation Layer (FTL) (Chung, Park, Park, Lee, Lee, and Song, 2009 ; Gal and Toledo, 2005). The FTL is located into the controller of the flash device. Its main functionalities are: 1) to provide a logical to physical address mapping for the applicative layer, 2) to achieve a good wear leveling algorithm, 3) to perform garbage collection operations, and 4) to emulate a block device so that the flash-based peripheral can be formatted using a standard (hard drive designed) file-system.

Bare flash chips, which can be embedded on many devices such as smartphones and tablet computers, are generally directly controlled by the operating system kernel. This is done by the means of a dedicated Flash File-System (FFS) (Opdenacker and Petazzoni, 2010). In addition to providing wear leveling and garbage collection management schemes, FFSs have to perform all the standard file-system functions: management of file and directory hierarchies, user access rights, etc.

In the first section of this chapter, we present some flash memory generalities, then we focus on the main flash memory type used for data storage, that is NAND. In the second section we describe the Flash Translation Layer (FTL) by depicting popular implementations (Lee and al., 2007 ; Park, Debnath and Du, 2010 ; Gupta, Kim and Urgaonkar, 2009 ; Chiang, Lee and Chang, 1999). In the next section, we present dedicated Flash File Systems (FFSs), implemented into embedded operating systems all along with implementation examples (Manning, 2010 ; Woodhouse, 2001 ; Bityutskiy, Havasi, Loki and Sogor, 2008 ; Engel, 2005).

FLASH STORAGE BASICS

Background

Flash memories are floating gate transistors based NVMs. They can be mainly of two types (even though other types exist such as divided bitline NOR, AND type, and other specific embedded technologies): NOR and NAND flash memories. They are named after the logic gates used, as the basic component for their design. 1) NOR flash memories are more reliable as they do not need Error Correction Code (ECC). They support bytes random access and have a lower density and a higher cost as compared to NAND flash memories. NOR flash memories are more suitable for storing code (Brewer & Gill, 2008). 2) NAND flash memories are block addressed, but offer a higher storage density at a lower cost. They provide good performance for large read/write operations. Those properties make them more appropriate for storing data (Brewer & Gill, 2008).

In this chapter, we focus on flash memories used as data storage devices i.e. NAND flash memories.

NAND flash memories can be classified into three categories: 1) Single Level Cell (SLC), 2) Multi Level Cell (MLC) and 3) Triple Level Cell (TLC). In SLC flash memories, only one bit can be stored in one cell, while in MLC, two bits can be stored, and 3 bits in TLC (see Table 1).

While TLC is more used for non critical data applications that do not require frequent updates (low end media players, mobile GPS, etc.), MLC and SLC are used for more data intensive appliances such as SSDs, mobile phones, memory cards, etc.

As one can see in Figure 1, flash memory is structured as follows: it is composed of one or more chips; each chip is divided into multiple planes. A plane is composed of a fixed number of blocks, each of them encloses a fixed number of pages that is multiple of 32 (typically 64). Current versions of flash memory have between 128 KB and 1024 KB blocks (with pages of 2-8KB). A page consists of user data space and a small metadata area also called Out-Of-Band (OOB) area that can contain information on ECC, page state, etc. (Roberts, Kgil & Mudge, 2009; Winter, 2008).

Three operations can be performed on flash memories: read and write operations are applied at the page level while the erase operation is achieved on block level.

Flash Memory Characteristics and Constraints

NAND flash memories present some specific I/O characteristics. Some of those peculiarities can be considered as advantages while some others are seen as constraints to consider at the design stage.

The advantages of flash memories over traditional Hard Disk Drives (HDD) result from the absence of mechanical elements and are the following:

- **Shock resistance and lightweight:** These characteristics are mainly due to the absence of mechanical parts.

Table 1. This table summarizes the characteristics of different NAND flash memory types

	SLC	MLC	TLC
Reliability	++	+	-
Bit density	-	+	++
Price/Gbit	-	+	++
Performance	++	+	-

Figure 1. Flash memory architecture

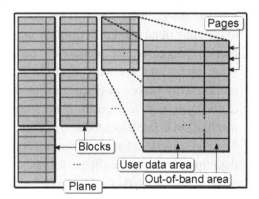

- **Low power consumption:** Flash based storage systems are more energy efficient than HDDs, even though their power consumption highly depends on their internal architecture and on the applied I/O workload (Park, Kim, Urgaonkar, Lee, & Seo, 2011).
- **Random read performance:** Read access latency does no more depend on the physical location of data, as a consequence, random reads are to perform as good as sequential ones. This makes flash memories more efficient and predictable for reads as compared to HDDs.

The constraints that a system designer has to deal with when implementing a flash memory based solution are the following:

- **Performance asymmetry:** In NAND flash memories reads are much faster that writes. This is due to electrical properties of the basic flash memory cell as it takes more time to program (write) the cell to reach a stable state than simply to read it.
- **Write/Erase operation granularity asymmetry:** Write operations are performed on pages while erase operations are achieved on blocks.
- **Erase-before-write limitation:** This is one of the most important constraints. In order to modify data in-place, the system should perform a costly erase operation before the data can be modified (in addition to the copy of all valid data from the erased block). Moreover, as mentioned earlier, erase operations are only performed on blocks. This makes in-place data modification operation very costly if no specific mechanism is implemented to overcome it. The consequence of such a behavior is that data updates are generally performed out-of-place (as detailed afterward).

- **Limited number of Erase/Write cycles:** The average number of write/erase (W/E) cycles depends on the flash memory technology. It is approximately 10^5 for SLC, 10^4 for MLC, and 5000 for TLC. When the maximum number of erase cycles is reached, a memory cell can no more be used. Some spare storage cells are available to cope with such a wearing out.
- **Sequential writes in a block:** In order to avoid write errors (due to some electrical organization), writes must be performed sequentially within one block. ECC are implemented in hardware to cope with such errors.

Flash Memory Support Mechanisms

In order to cope with NAND flash memory constraints mentioned earlier, some specific management techniques are employed.

- **Logical to physical block mapping:** Because of the erase-before-write limitation, data updates should be performed out-of-place meaning that the system must search for some free pages to write on the updated data. A mapping scheme is then necessary to keep track of the physical location of the data. As it will be discussed later, the mapping granularity can be as large as one block or as small as a page.
- **Garbage collection or cleaning policies:** Out-of-place data update induces the copy to another page/block and the invalidation of the previous data version. Over the time, invalid data tend to accumulate and in order to recycle some free blocks, garbage collection mechanisms should be employed. Such mechanisms scan the flash memory for invalid space to recover/erase (erase-before-write constraint).

- **Wear leveling:** Due to data temporal and spatial locality properties observed in most I/O workloads, writes can be concentrated in some subsets of flash memory blocks. Since each memory cell supports only a limited number of W/E cycles, if no special action is undergone, a subset of cells would wear out very quickly as compared to the others. In order to prevent this problem, wear leveling policies are implemented to spread evenly the W/E cycles over the whole flash memory surface.

As one can see in Figure 2, the aforementioned techniques can be either implemented in the flash memory controller through a hardware layer called the Flash Translation Layer (FTL), or through a software layer implemented by the hosting operating system that is a Flash File System (FFS).

HARDWARE SUPPORT OF FLASH STORAGE SYSTEMS (THE FLASH TRANSLATION LAYER)

The Flash Translation Layer (FTL) is a hardware/software layer that implements the three abovementioned management functionalities. We explore, in this section, some of the main implementations by focusing on one of the more discussed issue in the literature that is the mapping scheme.

Basic Mapping Schemes

As mentioned earlier, the mapping process consists in translating addresses coming from the applicative layer into physical addresses. This mapping is performed through a specific table managed by the FTL.

Basic mapping schemes depend on the granularity with which mapping information is managed. We can mainly classify them into page, block and hybrid mapping schemes (Chung et al., 2009).

- **Page mapping scheme:** With page mapping scheme (Ban, 1995), each logical page is mapped to a physical page independently from the other block's pages. Page mapping is very flexible and gives very good performance. The main drawback of this scheme is the mapping table large size that would hardly fit into the FTL embedded RAM as the number of table entries equals to the number of pages.
- **Block mapping scheme:** The block mapping scheme considers the granularity of a block rather than a page (Shinohara, 1999). The logical page address is composed of the logical block number and a page offset that is not modified by the mapping translation process. The number of mapping table entries in this case equals the number of blocks for the flash memory (remember that there is generally 64 pages in a block). The main drawback of block mapping is that updating data of a given page can induce a whole block copy as all the valid data of the block are remapped to another one.
- **Hybrid mapping schemes:** Hybrid schemes use both block and page mapping. They are designed to overcome the limitations of page and block mapping schemes. Many of them use a global block map and maintain a page mapping for some specific blocks. Only the block mapping table and a limited page mapping table are maintained in the FTL RAM (see Figure 3).

Advanced FTL Schemes

Most of the mapping schemes one can find in the literature are hybrid, nevertheless some pure page mapped FTLs can also be found.

The main drawback of page mapping schemes is the table size. To overcome such a shortcoming, the system can store the mapping table in the flash memory itself and only a part of it is pushed into the FTL embedded RAM acting like a cache for

Figure 2. Flash memory subsystems. Examples of the first (a) configuration are SSDs, USB sticks, compact flash, etc. while the second (b) configuration concerns embedded bare flash memories.

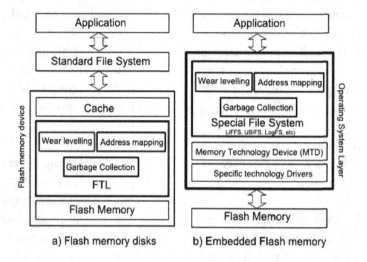

a) Flash memory disks   b) Embedded Flash memory

Figure 3. Basic mapping schemes example. For clarity of presentation, we suppose a flash memory of 3 blocks of 4 pages each. The hybrid mapping example uses a main block mapping scheme that can use an additional page mapping scheme for some blocks or store the physical page number into the OOB.

LPN: Logical Page Number, LBN: Logical Block Number, PPN: Physical Page Number, PBN: Physical Page Number

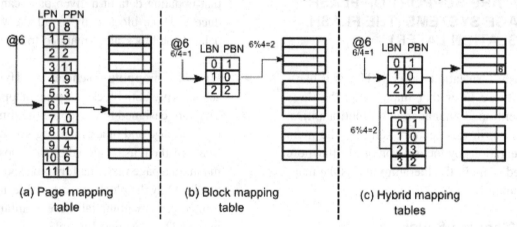

(a) Page mapping table   (b) Block mapping table   (c) Hybrid mapping tables

the mapping table. DFTL (Gupta, Kim & Urgaonkar, 2009) and SFTL (Jiang, Zhang, Yuan, Hu & Chen, 2011) are examples of such a system.

The objective of hybrid mapping schemes is to approach the flexibility and the performance of page mapping with the resource usage of block mapping scheme. Most hybrid mapping schemes are based on a primary block mapping while some of them partition the flash memory into two spaces each one using a different mapping scheme.

Hybrid mappings based on a primary block mapping scheme make use of log-pages or log-blocks. Log-pages are spare pages located in each block. They allow avoiding a block copy when a page data modification happens. A block copy is only triggered when all log-pages within a block have been written and a new update is requested (Shinohara, 1999).

Log-blocks are a more extensively studied concept, rather than having some log-pages in each block, log-pages are gathered in log-blocks. A log-block can be either dedicated to one data block like in M-Systems (Ban, 1999), AFTL (Wu & Kuo, 2006), CNFTL (Hsieh, Tsai, Kuo & Lee, 2008), BAST (Kim, Kim, Noh, Min & Cho, 2002), or shared between many of them like in RNFTL (Wang, Liu, Wang, Qin & Guan, 2010), FAST (Lee et al., 2007), or KAST (Cho, Shin & Eom, 2009). The associativity of pages in log-blocks is also crucial in mapping performance. While first FTLs use log-blocks that are directly mapped to data blocks as in ANAND (Ban, 1999), most of recent FTLs are fully associative i.e. FAST, LAST (Lee, Shin, Kim & Kim, 2008) and allow to write pages at any offset of the log-block (see Figure 4 for an example).

In this type of hybrid FTLs, page mapping is used to map the pages of the (or some) log-blocks (FAST, BAST). The more data pages (from a given block) are spread on different log-blocks, the higher is the cost of the merge operation (putting all valid pages in the data block). This issue has been partly leveraged by dedicating some log-blocks to subsets of data blocks. Data pages

can then be written to a reduced set of log blocks and symmetrically, a reduced number of data blocks pages can be present in a log-block which is the case in KAST (Cho, Shin & Eom, 2009) and SAST (Park, et al., 2008). If log-blocks contain both frequently (hot) and rarely modified (cold) data, cold data tend to be frequently moved from block to block without being modified which decreases the performance. Some FTLs, like LAST and FASTer (Lim, Lee & Moon, 2010), try to separate log-blocks according to update frequency.

The second type of hybrid FTLs partitions the flash memory space into a page mapped and a block mapped region like WAFTL (Wei et al., 2011) and CFTL (Park, Debnath, & Du, 2009). According to data access type and pattern, pages are directed toward the adequate region of the flash memory.

Caching Mechanisms

In order to optimize performance of flash memories, especially write operations, many cache sys-

Figure 4. Log-block example for different associativity schemes

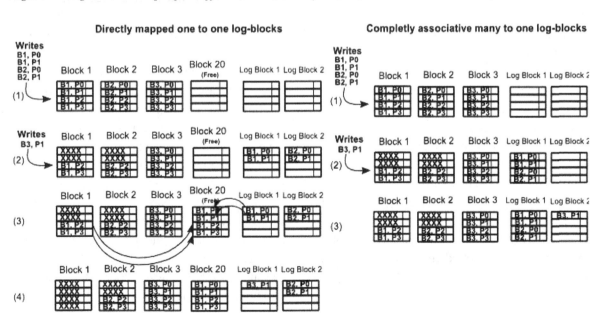

tems placed above FTLs have been designed (see Figure 2). They perform two main optimizations:

1. They absorb some page/block write operations at the cache level and thus avoid reporting them to the flash media.
2. They try to reveal sequentiality by buffering write operations and reorganizing them before flushing them to the flash media.

Most of those cache systems try to reflect the granularity of the erase operation by dealing with groups of pages rather than pages: FAB (Jo, Kang, Park, Kim & Lee, 2006), CLC (Kang, Park, Jung, Shim & Cha, 2009), BPAC (Wu, Eckart & He, 2010), LB-Clock (Debnath, Subramanya, Du & Lilja, 2009), BPLRU (Kim & Ahn, 2008), and C-lash (Boukhobza, Olivier & Rubini, 2011). Some of them even use two or more sets of page groups (CLC, C-lash, BPAC), generally to order the groups according to different parameters such as recency and size.

Wear Leveling Algorithms

The objective of wear leveling is to keep the whole flash memory volume usable as long as possible thus avoiding some flash memory cells to wear out more quickly than the others.

Wear leveling algorithms are based on the number of erase or write operations performed on a given block. If this number is smaller than the computed average of all the flash memory blocks, the block is said to be cold. Conversely, if it is higher than the average, it is said to be hot. Wear leveling algorithms try to maintain the gap between hot and cold blocks as small as possible. This can be achieved by swapping data from hot blocks (more exactly data that made that block to be hot) and cold blocks. This operation is costly and cannot be performed many times. In fact, one has to compromise between wear leveling and performance.

We can group wear leveling algorithms into two categories: those based on the erase count, and those based on write count.

Erase count based wear levelers: In these algorithms the erase count is maintained for each block and stored whether in the mapping table or in the block metadata space. The wear leveler is launched whenever a given difference is observed between blocks erase count. It is easier to monitor such algorithms when the count is stored in the FTL embedded RAM, otherwise partial read/write operations have to be performed on the block metadata area.

One of the wear leveling techniques based on erase count was described by (Assar, Namazie & Estakhri, 1995) and called dual pool. It refers to two additional mapping tables used with the standard block mapping scheme: hot-block and cold-block table. The hot-block table contains a given number of overused empty blocks sorted according to the number of erase count in descending order, while the cold-block table contains underused free blocks sorted in the ascending order. In dual pool algorithm, each time a free block is required, it is taken from the cold block table and the hot blocks stay unused. Periodically, the system recalculates the average erase count number and the difference between each block's erase count and the calculated average. It then compares the difference with a given threshold and according to the result; it puts the respective block into the corresponding table. The smaller the threshold, the better the wear leveling and the more it impacts performance because of the generated data movements. Some wear levelers do only take into account the erased (free) blocks in the wear leveling (global wear levelers) process while others consider the entire space. More specifically, if one block contains rarely modified data (called static or cold data), some wear levelers (Assar, Namazie & Estakhri, 1995; Chang, Qawami & Sabet-Sharghi, 2006) copy that data into hot/dynamic regions.

Write count based wear levelers: These algorithms maintain a count of write operations performed on blocks or set of blocks. In (Achiwa, Yamamoto & Yamagata, 1999), a write count is preserved in the embedded RAM, in addition to block erase count, and is updated each time a write operation is performed on the block. Blocks with a close erase count are grouped together. The objective of the wear leveler is to store highly written data to the least frequently erased blocks and to store rarely written data into the most frequently erased blocks.

A possible optimization consists in considering groups of blocks as cold/hot rather than blocks which allows to reduce the RAM usage necessary to control the wear leveling (Lofgren, Norman, Thelin & Gupta, 2005; Conley, 2005).

Garbage Collection Algorithms (Or Cleaning Policies)

Garbage collection is the process used to recycle free space from previously invalidated pages in blocks.

A garbage collector should answer a given number of questions: 1) when should it be launched, 2) which blocks should be concerned by the garbage collection and how many of them should be chosen, 3) How should valid data be written out in the new blocks.

A good garbage collector should minimize the cleaning costs while maximizing the recycled space without being very intrusive. Cleaning costs include the erase operations and the valid data copies.

Garbage Collectors (GC) are generally automatically launched when the number of free blocks passes under a predefined threshold. GC are optionally triggered during I/O timeouts.

One of the main metric considered when choosing a block as victim for the garbage collection operation is the ratio of invalid pages it contains. Some garbage collectors maintain the page state table in the FTL embedded RAM while others just use the page's Out-Of-Band area. Basic garbage collectors copy valid pages from the victim blocks into newly allocated blocks and erase the previous ones.

Yet again, the hot/cold data separation is very important to achieve garbage collection, and this partly answers the question about how data should be written to new blocks. In order to perform a good garbage collection, the system must separate cold and hot data into different blocks. Indeed, if cold and hot data coexist in a given block, there is a higher chance that garbage collector will be called due to the hot data updates. This would induce a costly and useless copy of cold data. Conversely, if the block contains only hot data, there is a high probability that only an erase operation is needed (no data copy) since all the pages are hot (thus modified and invalid).

Many contributions were based upon this hot/cold data separation. For instance, Dynamic dAta Clustering (DAC) (Chiang, Cheng & Wu, 2008) partitions the flash memory into many regions according to the update frequency. The two levels LRU (Chang & Kuo, 2002) uses two lists: one containing hot block address list managed in LRU and another one containing candidate (to be hot if accessed once again) block addresses.

Having an efficient hot/cold separation helps in the selection of the dirty block/group to clean up. The main objective of the selection policy is to free the higher amount of blocks at the lower cost, which implies selecting the block/group containing the less valid data and less usable space. The greedy policy simply selects the block with the higher number of invalid pages. This policy can be very efficient if the workload is accessing the flash memory blocks uniformly.

The number of dirty pages contained in the block/group is however always taken into consideration when calculating the cost benefit of cleaning some blocks. In (Kawaguchi, Nishioka & Motoda, 1995), the percentage of valid data

(1-u) is taken into consideration in addition to the elapsed time since the most recent modification (*age* in the equation): age * (1-u)/2*u. The block(s) with the highest score is/are chosen to be cleaned. In Cost Age Times (CAT) policy (Chiang, Chang, 1999), hot blocks are given more time to accumulate invalid data, the equation that calculates the score is: Cleaning_cost * (1/age) * Number_of_cleaning, where the cleaning cost is u/(1-u) and the number of cleanings is the number of erase operations.

Every garbage collection policy has its own advantages and drawbacks and can be very closely related to the wear leveling mechanism and the underlying mapping scheme.

SOFTWARE SUPPORT OF FLASH MEMORY SYSTEMS (FLASH FILE SYSTEMS, THE CASE OF LINUX)

In this section a general presentation of Flash File Systems (FFSs) is given. Next, we try to present some details about FFS performance evaluation and comparison. Finally, some current embedded Linux FFS implementations are described.

Flash File Systems Overview

The main goal of FFSs is to provide an efficient and reliable way to store and retrieve data in the underlying secondary flash storage. It is a software layer implemented inside the operating system. FFSs are very often used in embedded environments, so they need to have limited hardware resource consumption: it is true for CPU and RAM usage, but one can also cite the storage space overhead generated by the use of a FFS. They also have to provide efficient methods to manage unclean unmounts operations, for example in the case of power failure (Bityutskiy, 2005).

Moreover, FFSs must deal with the specific flash constraints cited earlier: the erase-before-

write rule preventing in-place data updates, and the wearing of the flash memory cells. Thus, address mapping and wear leveling techniques must be implemented in FFS. FFS should also recycle previously invalidated pages through the implementation of a garbage collector, noted GC in the rest of the section (Engel & Mertens, 2005).

Bad blocks can result from factory process (Micron Technology, Inc., 2005) and may appear during the flash memory lifetime. The FFS has to detect these blocks and prevent them from being used for data storage in the future. Bad blocks are generally identified with specific markers in the out-of-band (OOB) area of a given page. On NAND flash chips, bit errors can also occur: read and write operations can disturb adjacent data cells, so FFSs have to implement some ECC, especially in the case of MLC and TLC flash memories.

Another common function to most of the FFSs is the ability to compress stored data. Compression does not only lower the stored data size, but also reduces the load on the storage system, allowing a small decrease of the number of W/E cycles.

In the Linux kernel software architecture, FFSs are located between the *Virtual File System* (VFS) layer and the *Memory Technology Device* (MTD) layer, as depicted on Figure 5.

MTD is a software layer providing a generic interface to various NAND and NOR flash-based devices coming from different constructors. MTD

Figure 5. FFS integration in the Linux kernel

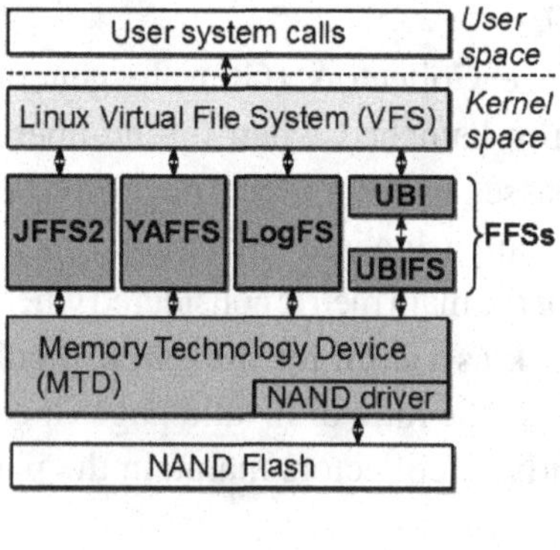

offers, amongst other things, a NAND driver used by the above FFS to perform raw flash accesses.

VFS (Bovet, Cesati, & Oram, 2002) is a generic layer located on top of the FFS layer. It is designed to abstract the file-systems (FS) complexity to the user space. VFS allows multiple FS to coexist on the same operating system, and to present the same interface to the user. To that end, VFS uses multiple data structures that are maintained in the RAM. One of the most important structures is the *inode*, representing a set of metadata describing a unique file. In order to create a given *inode*, VFS relies on the information of the underlying FS structures and each FS can manage its own information differently.

Some Flash File-System Performance Considerations

Many studies focus on FFS performance analysis, benchmarking and comparison (Liu, Guan, Torg & Cheng, 2010; Free Electrons 2012; Opdenacker & Petazzoni 2010; Toshiba 2009; Olivier, Boukhobza & Senn, 2012). The performance metrics analyzed in these works can be classified in two categories: 1) *flash memory* and 2) *file-systems* related ones.

An important flash memory related performance metric is the efficiency of the wear leveling. It allows to measure the impact of the FFS on the flash lifetime. It can be estimated by counting the number of erase operations performed when applying a given workload to the FFS. More relevant studies rely on the difference and/or the standard deviation of erase blocks counters (Liu, Guan, Torg & Cheng, 2010) which give more information about the leveling of write and erase cycles. There are other flash related performance metrics such as the impact of garbage collector on performance and lifetime (Liu, 2010).

Examples of file-system related metrics are mount time and RAM consumption. As the mount time is easy to measure, obtaining the amount of memory used by the file-system itself can be complex. Then, for comparison purposes, several studies simply measure the amount of memory used by the whole system for each FFS (Liu, Guan, Torg & Cheng, 2010; Free Electrons 2012; Opdenacker & Petazzoni 2010). One important point to take into account for a FFS is how these metrics vary when increasing the size of the file-system (i.e. the size of the managed partition). Some FFS are known to scale in a linear way with the size of the underlying flash partition. Others scale logarithmically, which is a great benefit compared to the first ones, especially for managing large sized flash chips.

Linux Flash File-Systems

In this section, we briefly describe JFFS2, YAFFS2, UBIFS and LogFS that are the most used Linux FFS.

The *Journaling Flash File system version 2* (JFFS2) (Woodhouse, 2001) is one of the most widely used FFSs. It is the successor of JFFS, a NOR-specific FFS. JFFS2 added, amongst other things, NAND support, as well as compression and hard linking functionalities. The compression algorithms *Zlib*, *LZO* and *Rtime* are supported. JFFS2 is integrated to the kernel sources since Linux 2.4.10 (2001).

The storage unit in JFFS2 is a *node*. A node either represents 1) a file; 2) part of a file or 3) a FS update (log). The minimum size that a node can manage is one flash page, and the maximum is half an erase flash block. New nodes are sequentially written in a block.

JFFS2 maintains three main lists of blocks: The *free* list links together all the erased blocks, the *clean* list contains blocks with only valid nodes, and the *dirty* list contains blocks with at least one invalid node. When the current block is full, a new block is taken from the free list.

The GC is performed by a background thread taking blocks from the dirty list for erasure and placing them into the free list. The GC can occasionally choose a victim from the clean list in order to perform global wear leveling (see the wear leveling section).

At mount time, a JFFS2 volume is entirely scanned, and a direct mapping table of the stored files and their locations on the flash memory is created. This procedure's execution time scales linearly with the size of the underlying flash partition, as do the amount of RAM usage for JFFS2 metadata. This can be a serious issue when dealing with large flash devices. A mount time of about 15 minutes (Engel & Mertens, 2005) was reported for a 1 Gigabyte flash chip using JFFS2.

When a power failure occurs, the entire flash space is scanned and JFFS2 restores the FS to a consistent state. JFFS2 manages bad blocks by inserting them into the specific *bad* list, containing blocks which must not be used.

YAFFS2, UBIFS and LogFS have all been designed to replace JFFS2 by coping with its scalability issues in terms of RAM consumption and mount time.

Yet Another Flash File-System version 2 (YAFFS2) (Manning, 2010; Wookey, 2007) is a NAND-only FFS. The first version dates back to 2001 and supported only 512 bytes pages flash memories. The current version supports flash pages of up to 2 KB. YAFFS2 is not officially integrated in Linux sources, although the activation is simply made by patching a standard kernel source tree. YAFFS2 does not support compression.

Files are represented with data structures called *chunks*. The *header* chunk contains metadata about the file (access rights, etc.), and *data* chunks store the file's data. The default value of the chunk size is the flash page size. Chunks are written sequentially on flash memory as one log.

At mount time, a direct map is created in RAM, mapping files to the corresponding chunks. Like JFFS2, YAFFS2 mount time and RAM usage scale linearly with the size of the managed flash volume. Nevertheless, YAFFS2 implements a mechanism called *checkpointing*, allowing the indexing data structures (the mapping table) to be stored on flash

at unmount time. The execution time of the next mount operation is then considerably reduced.

GC in YAFFS2 is triggered in two situations: 1) during a data update operation, if the block containing the previous version of the updated data is completely invalid, it is erased; 2) when the amount of free space falls under a given threshold, blocks containing the largest number of invalid pages are selected as victims and erased after the copy of valid data to another location.

After a power failure, the flash device is fully scanned and the FFS is restored to a consistent state. YAFFS2 identifies bad blocks by writing a specific code into the OOB area.

Unsorted Block Image File System (UBIFS) (Hunter, 2008): As shown in Figure 5, UBIFS relies on the UBI (Gleixner, Haverkamp, & Bityutskiy, 2006) layer placed between the FFS and the MTD level. UBI performs a logical to physical mapping with a block granularity. It provides wear leveling and bad block management functionalities, discharging UBIFS from those functions. UBIFS can support both NAND and NOR flash memories. It was developed by Nokia, and is integrated in the kernel mainline since Linux 2.6.27 (2008). UBIFS supports the *LZO* and *Zlib* compression algorithms.

UBIFS uses a write unit called a node, representing a file or part of a file. Indexing data structures are stored on flash in special type of nodes called *index nodes* coexisting with *data nodes* on the flash memory.

The indexing structure of UBIFS is a B+ tree: It is composed of index nodes. The tree leaves points to on-flash data nodes. As flash does not allow in-place updates, any update of a node in the tree requires to modify all the ancestors of the node up to the root of the tree (see Figure 6 for an example). Because of such an out-of-place tree modification, the update method is called a *wandering B+ tree*. As FFS modification may cause many flash updates, they are buffered in RAM and periodically flushed on flash. This operation is called a *commit*.

Figure 6. Update of an index node in a wandering B+ tree

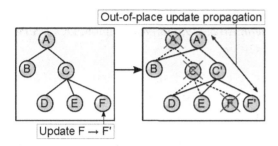

The managed flash partition is divided into multiple sections. The *superblock* contains global metadata about the FS. The *main area* stores data and index nodes. The *master nodes area* maintains the location of the root node of the indexing tree. In the *log,* all changes made during a commit are written, in order to replay or rollback the modifications in case of power failure. The *Logical erase block Property Tree* contains metadata about flash blocks: erase and dirty counters, used by the GC. UBIFS GC reclaims blocks with invalid data.

With the use of tree structures, UBIFS scales logarithmically with the size of the underlying UBI partition, in terms of RAM usage and mount time. UBI initialization time scales linearly.

LogFS (Engel & Mertens, 2005): LogFS is part of the kernel sources since Linux 2.6.34 (2010), and can be used on both NAND and NOR flash. Compression is supported through the *Zlib* library.

LogFS uses, like UBIFS, a wandering tree-based structure for file indexation, with index and data nodes.

In addition to *Superblock*, the flash device is partitioned into two main sections: the *journal* contains on-flash location of the root node of the index tree and the *object stores* that contains all the FS data and index nodes.

At mount time, the journal is scanned and the index tree rebuilt. Like UBIFS, LogFS buffers the journal into RAM to prevent frequent flash accesses. The journal can also be moved to different locations on flash to avoid rapid wearing.

Both mount time and RAM usage scale logarithmically in LogFS. LogFS GC is a very complex process which can cause heavy slowdowns when the flash is nearly full (Engel, Bolte, & Mertens, 2007).

Bad blocks are handled at the FS creation, but blocks turning bad later are not considered. LogFS still lacks of important features and stability, as reported in (Toshiba Corporation, 2009; Free Electrons 2012).

Various functionalities and properties of the FFSs studied in this document are summarized in Table 2.

Table 2. Summary of various properties for the presented FFSs

	JFFS2	YAFFS	UBIFS	LogFS
Supported flash type(s)	NOR, NAND	NAND	NOR, NAND	NOR, NAND
Supported device type(s)	MTD	MTD	UBI	MTD, Block
File indexing structure	Table	Table	Wandering tree	Wandering tree
Compression algorithm(s)	Zlib, LZO, Rtime	None	Zlib, LZO	Zlib
Scaling (mount time)	Linear	Linear	Linear (because of UBI)	Logarithmic
Scaling (memory usage)	Linear	Linear	Logarithmic	Logarithmic
Integration in the Linux Kernel mainline?	Yes	No	Yes	Yes

CONCLUSION

Flash memory is widely used in embedded systems because of its attractive characteristics. Nevertheless, its specific constraints require some dedicated management systems. Such systems can be either implemented in hardware, through the use of the Flash Translation Layer, or through a dedicated Flash File System, a software layer responsible for flash management in an operating system.

FTL and FFSs implement the same mechanisms as they deal with the same constraints: managing logical to physical mapping to bypass the erase-before-write rule, and implementing wear leveling and garbage collection techniques in order to maximize the flash memory lifetime.

In this chapter, we proposed an overview of NAND flash memory systems throughout 1) the description of its internal structure and specificities, and 2) the different implementations of its specific management techniques. Considering the peculiarities of such memory is necessary to understand their performance issues and integration possibilities.

Flash memory is currently the most mature NVM technology and studies achieved to optimize its usage will probably help in making other NVM technologies emerge quickly even though some of the constraints are different. PCRAM, FeRAM, MRAM are all new candidates that open up new opportunities to explore and challenges to tackle in this data centric era.

REFERENCES

Achiwa, K., Yamamoto, A., & Yamagata, O. (1999). Memory systems using a flash memory and method of controlling the memory system. *United States Patent, No 5,930,193*. Washington, DC: US Patent Office.

Assar, M., Namazie, S., & Estakhri, P. (1995). Flash memory mass storage architecture incorporation wear leveling technique. *United States Patent, No 5,479,638*. Washington, DC: US Patent Office.

Ban, A. (1995). Flash file system. *United States Patent, No 5,404,485*. Washington, DC: US Patent Office.

Ban, A. (1999). Flash file system optimized for page-mode flash technologies. *United States Patent, No 5,937,425*. Washington, DC: US Patent Office.

Bityuckiy, A. (2005). *JFFS3 design issues*. Retrieved June, 2012, from http://www.linux-mtd.infradead.org/doc/JFFS3design.pdf

Boukhobza, J., Olivier, P., & Rubini, S. (2011). A cache management strategy to replace wear leveling techniques for embedded flash memory. In *Proceedings of the 2011 International Symposium on Performance Evaluation of Computer & Telecommunication Systems (SPECTS)*. SPECTS.

Bovet, D., & Cesati, M. (2005). *Understanding the Linux kernel*. O'Reilly & Associates, Inc..

Brewer, J. E., & Gill, M. (Eds.). (2008). *Nonvolatile memory technologies with emphasis on flash*. Wiley-Interscience.

Chang, L. P., & Kuo, T. W. (2002). An adaptive striping architecture for flash memory storage systems of embedded systems. In *Proceedings of the 8th IEEE Real-Time and Embedded Technology and Applications Symposium*, (pp. 187-196). IEEE.

Chang, R. C., Qawami, B., & Sabet-Sharghi, F. (2006). Method and apparatus for managing an erase count block. *United States Patent, No 7,103,732*. Washington, DC: US Patent Office.

Chen, F., Koufaty, D. A., & Zhang, X. (2009). Understanding intrinsic characteristics and system implications of flash memory based solid state drives. In *Proceedings of the Eleventh International Joint Conference on Measurement and Modeling of Computer Systems* (pp. 181–192). IEEE.

Chiang, M., Cheng, C., & Wu, C. (2008). A new FTL-based flash memory management scheme with fast cleaning mechanism. In *Proceedings of the International Conference on Embedded Software and Systems (ICESS '08)*, (pp. 205-214). ICESS.

Cho, H., Shin, D., & Eom, Y. I. (2009). KAST: K-associative sector translation for NAND flash memory in real-time systems. In Proceedings of Design, Automation, and Test in Europe (DATE), (pp. 507-512). DATE.

Chung, T., Park, D., Park, S., Lee, D., Lee, S., & Song, H. (2009). A survey of flash translation layer. *Journal of Systems Architecture, 55*, 332–343. doi:10.1016/j.sysarc.2009.03.005.

Conley, K. M. (2005). Zone boundary adjustment for defects in non-volatile memories. *United States Patent, No 6,901,498.* Washington, DC: US Patent Office.

Darling, P. (2010). *Intel, micron first to sample 3-Bit-Per-Cell NAND flash memory on industry-leading 25-nanometer silicon process technology.* Retrieved August, 2012, from http://newsroom.intel.com/community/intel_newsroom/blog/2010/08/17/intel-micron-first-to-sample-3-bit-per-cell-nand-flash-memory-on-industry-leading-25-nanometer-silicon-process-technology

Debnath, B., Subramanya, S., Du, D., & Lilja, D. J. (2009). Large block CLOCK (LB-CLOCK): A write caching algorithm for solid state disks. In *Proceedings of the 2009 IEEE International Symposium on Modeling, Analysis & Simulation of Computer and Telecommunication Systems (MASCOTS).* IEEE.

Electronic Engineering Times. (2011). *Non-volatile memory market to boom by 2015.* Retrieved August, 2012, from http://www.eetindia.co.in/ART_8800647303_1800009_NT_f00693e1.HTM

Engel, J., Bolte, D., & Mertens, R. (2007). Garbage collection in logfs. In *Proceedings of Linyx Conference 2007.* Linyx.

Engel, J., & Mertens, R. (2005). *LogFS-finally a scalable flash file-system.*

Free Electrons. (2012). *Flash file system benchmarks.* Retrieved August, 2012, from http://elinux.org/Flash_Filesystem_Benchmarks

Gal, E., & Toledo, S. (2005). Algorithms and data structures for flash memories. *ACM Computing Surveys, 37*(2), 138–163. doi:10.1145/1089733.1089735.

Gleixner, T., Haverkamp, F., & Bityutskiy, A. (2006). *UBI-unsorte, d block images.* Retrieved August, 2012, from http://linux-mtd.infradead.org/doc/ubidesign/ubidesign.pdf

Gupta, A., Kim, Y., & Urgaonkar, B. (2009). DFTL: A flash translation layer employing demand-based selective caching of page-level address mappings. In *Proceedings of the 14th International Conference on Architectural Support for Programming Languages and Operating Systems (ASPLOS).* ASPLOS.

Hsieh, J., Tsai, Y., Kuo, T., & Lee, T. (2008). Configurable flash-memory management: Performance versus overheads. *IEEE Transactions on Computers*, *57*(11), 1571–1583. doi:10.1109/TC.2008.61.

Jiang, S., Zhang, L., Yuan, X., Hu, H., & Chen, Y. (2011). SFTL: An efficient address translation for flash memory by exploiting spatial locality. In *Proceedings of 2011 IEEE 27th Symposium on Mass Storage Systems and Technologies (MSST)*. IEEE.

Jo, H., Kang, J., Park, S., Kim, J., & Lee, J. (2006). FAB: A flash-aware buffer management policy for portable media players. *IEEE Transactions on Consumer Electronics*, *52*(2), 485–493. doi:10.1109/TCE.2006.1649669.

Kang, S., Park, S., Jung, H., Shim, H., & Cha, J. (2009). Performance trade-offs in using NVRAM write buffer for flash memory-based storage devices. *IEEE Transactions on Computers*, *58*(6), 744–758. doi:10.1109/TC.2008.224.

Kawaguchi, A., Nishioka, S., & Motoda, H. (1995). A flash memory based file system. In *Proceedings of the USENIX 1995 Technical Conference*. USENIX.

Kim, H., & Ahn, S. (2008). BPLRU: A buffer management scheme for improving random writes in flash storage. In *Proceedings of the 6th USENIX Conference on File and Storage Technologies (FAST)*. USENIX.

Kim, J., Kim, J. M., Noh, S. H., Min, S. L., & Cho, Y. (2002). A space-efficient flash translation layer for compact flash systems. *IEEE Transactions on Consumer Electronics*, *48*(2), 366–375. doi:10.1109/TCE.2002.1010143.

Lee, S., Shin, D., Kim, Y., & Kim, J. (2008). LAST: Locality aware sector translation for NAND flash memory based storage systems. *ACM SIGOPS Operating Systems Review*, *42*(6), 36–42. doi:10.1145/1453775.1453783.

Lee, S. W., Park, D. J., Chung, T. S., Lee, D. H., Park, S., & Song, H. J. (2007). A log buffer based flash translation layer using fully associative sector translation. *ACM Transactions on Embedded Computing Systems*, *6*(3), 1–27. doi:10.1145/1275986.1275990.

Liu, S., Guan, X., Tong, D., & Cheng, X. (2010). Analysis and comparison of NAND specific file systems. *Chinese Journal of Electronics*, *19*(3).

Lofgren, K. M. J., Norman, R. D., Thelin, G. B., & Gupta, A. (2005). Wear leveling techniques for flash EEPROM systems. *United States Patent, No 6,850,443*. Washington, DC: US Patent Office.

Maleval, J. (2010). *Notebooks without anymore optical disc or HDD?* Retrieved August, 2012, from http://www.storagenewsletter.com/news/flash/notebooks-without-optical-disc-hdd-ssd

Manning, C. (2012). *How YAFFS works*. Retrieved August, 2012, from http://www.yaffs.net/sites/yaffs.net/files/HowYaffsWorks.pdf

Micron Technology, Inc. (2005). *TN-29-07: Small-block vs. large-block NAND flash devices*. Retrieved August, 2012, from http://www.micron.com/~/media/Documents/Products/Technical%20Note/NAND%20Flash/136tn2907.pdf

Olivier, P., Boukhobza, J., & Senn, E. (2012). On benchmarking embedded linux flash file systems. *ACM SIGBED Review*, *9*(2), 43–47. doi:10.1145/2318836.2318844.

Opdenacker, M., & Petazzoni, T. (2010). *Flash filesystems*. Retrieved August, 2012, from http://free-electrons.com/doc/flash-filesystems.pdf

Park, C., Cheon, W., Kang, J. U., Roh, K., Cho, W., & Kim, J. S. (2008). A reconfigurable FTL (flash translation layer) architecture for NAND flash based architectures. *ACM Transactions on Embedded Computing Systems*, *7*(4), 1–23. doi:10.1145/1376804.1376806.

Park, D., Debnath, B., & Du, D. (2009). *CFTL: A convertible flash translation layer with consideration of data access patterns* (Technical Report 09-023). Minneapolis, MN: University of Minnesota.

Park, S., Kim, Y., Urgaonkar, B., Lee, J., & Seo, E. (2011). A comprehensive study of energy efficiency and performance of flash-based SSD. *Journal of Systems Architecture, 57*(4), 354–365. doi:10.1016/j.sysarc.2011.01.005.

Roberts, D., Kgil, T., & Mudge, T. (2009). Integrating NAND flash devices onto servers. *Communications of the ACM, 52*(4), 98–106. doi:10.1145/1498765.1498791.

Shinohara, T. (1999). Flash memory card with block memory address arrangement. *United States Patent, No 5,905,993*. Washington, DC: US Patent Office.

Storage Newsletter. (2011). *Anobit shipped 20 million MSP-based embedded flash controllers in 2011*. Retrieved August 2012, from http://www.storagenewsletter.com/news/business/anobit-msptm-flash-controllers

Toshiba Corporation. (2009). *Evaluation of flash file systems for large NAND flash memory*. Retrieved August, 2012, from http://elinux.org/images/7/7e/ELC2009-FlashFS-Toshiba.pdf

Toshiba Corporation. (2009). Evaluation of UBI and UBIFS. In *Proceedings of CE Linux Forum 2009*. Linux.

Wang, Y., Liu, D., Wang, M., Qin, Z., & Guan, Y. (2010). RNFTL: A reuse-aware NAND flash translation layer for flash memory. In *Proceedings of the ACM SIGPLAN/SIGBED 2010 Conference on Languages, Compilers, and Tools for Embedded Systems (LCTES)*. ACM.

Wei, Q., Gong, B., Pathak, S., Veeravalli, B., Zeng, L., & Okada, K. (2011). WAFTL: A workload adaptive flash translation layer with data partition. In *Proceedings of 2011 IEEE 27th Symposium on Mass Storage Systems and Technologies (MSST)*. IEEE.

Winter, R. (2008). *Why are data warehouses growing so fast?* Retrieved June 2012, from http://www.b-eye-network.com/view7188

Woodhouse, D. (2001). JFFS: The journaling flash file-system. In *Proceedings of Ottawa Linux Symposium*. Ottawa, Canada: Linux.

Wookey. (2007). YAFFS: A NAND flash file system. In *Proceedings of the Free and Open Source Developer's European Meeting (FOSDEM 2004)*. FOSDEM.

Wu, C., & Kuo, T. (2006). An adaptive two-level management for the flash translation layer in embedded systems. In *Proceedings of the 2006 IEEE/ACM International Conference on Computer-Aided Design*. IEEE.

Wu, G., Eckart, B., & He, X. (2010). BPAC: An adaptive write buffer management scheme for flash-based solid state drives. In *Proceedings of 2010 IEEE 26th Symposium on Mass Storage Systems and Technologies (MSST)*. IEEE.

Chapter 23
EAST-ADL:
An Architecture Description Language for Automotive Software-Intensive Systems

Hans Blom
Volvo Technology, Sweden

Carl-Johan Sjöstedt
KTH Royal Institute of Technology, Sweden

Henrik Lönn
Volvo Technology, Sweden

De-Jiu Chen
KTH Royal Institute of Technology, Sweden

Frank Hagl
Continental Automotive GmbH, Germany

Fulvio Tagliabò
Centro Ricerche Fiat, Italy

Yiannis Papadopoulos
University of Hull, UK

Sandra Torchiaro
Centro Ricerche Fiat, Italy

Mark-Oliver Reiser
Technische Universität Berlin, Germany

Sara Tucci
CEA LIST DILS, France

Ramin Tavakoli Kolagari
Nuremberg Institute of Technology, Germany

ABSTRACT

EAST-ADL is an Architecture Description Language (ADL) initially defined in several European-funded research projects and subsequently refined and aligned with the more recent AUTOSAR automotive standard. It provides a comprehensive approach for defining automotive electronic systems through an information model that captures engineering information in a standardized form. Aspects covered include vehicle features, requirements, analysis functions, software and hardware components, and communication. The representation of the system's implementation is not defined in EAST-ADL itself but by AUTOSAR. However, traceability is supported from EAST-ADL's lower abstraction levels to the implementation level elements in AUTOSAR. In this chapter, the authors describe EAST-ADL in detail, show how it relates to AUTOSAR as well as other significant automotive standards, and present current research work on using EAST-ADL in the context of fully-electric vehicles, the functional safety standard ISO 26262, and for multi-objective optimization.

DOI: 10.4018/978-1-4666-3922-5.ch023

INTRODUCTION

EAST-ADL is an Architecture Description Language (ADL) initially defined in the European ITEA EAST-EEA project and subsequently refined and aligned with the more recent AUTOSAR automotive standard (AUTOSAR Development Partnership, 2012) in the European FP6 and FP7 ATESST projects (ATESST2 Consortium, 2010). Currently, it is maintained by the EAST-ADL Association (EAST-ADL Association, 2012). It is an approach for describing automotive electronic systems through an information model that captures engineering information in a standardized form. The language provides a wide range of modeling entities, including vehicle features, functions, requirements, variability, software components, hardware components and communication.

EAST-ADL clearly defines several abstraction levels (see Figure 1) and at each of these levels, the software- and electronics-based functionality of the vehicle is modelled with a different level of detail. The proposed abstraction levels and the contained modeling elements provide a separation of concerns and an implicit style for using the language elements. The embedded system is defined completely on each abstraction level, and identical parts of the model are linked across abstraction levels with various traceability relations. This makes it possible to trace an entity from feature down to components in hardware and software.

The features in the "TechnicalFeatureModel" at the vehicle level represent the content and properties of the vehicle from top-level perspective without exposing the realization. It is possible to manage the content of each vehicle and entire product lines in a systematic manner. A complete representation of the electronic functionality in an abstract form is modeled in the Functional Analysis Architecture (FAA). One or more entities (analysis functions) of the FAA can be combined and reused to realize features. The FAA captures the principal interfaces and behavior of the vehicle's subsystems. It allows validation and verification of the integrated system or its subsystems on a high level of abstraction. Critical issues for understanding or analysis can thus be considered, without the risk of them being obscured by implementation details.

Figure 1. The EAST-ADL's breakdown in abstraction levels (vertically) and in core, environment and extensions (horizontally)

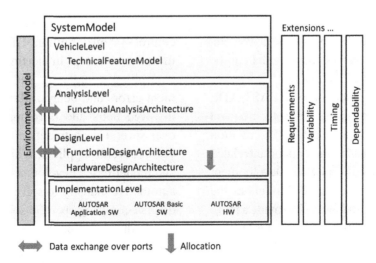

The implementation-oriented aspects are introduced while defining the Functional Design Architecture (FDA). The features are realized here in a function architecture that takes into account efficiency, legacy and reuse, COTS availability, hardware allocation, etc. The function structure is such that one or more functions can be subsequently realized by an AUTOSAR software component (SW-C). The external interfaces of such components correspond to the interfaces of the realized functions. The representation of the implementation, the software architecture, is not defined by EAST-ADL but by AUTO-SAR. However, traceability is supported from implementation level elements (AUTOSAR) to vehicle level elements. The Hardware Design Architecture (HDA) should be considered parallel to application development. On the design level and down, the HDA forms a natural constraint for development and the hardware and application software development needs to be iterated and performed together. There is also an indirect effect of hardware on the higher abstraction levels. Control strategies or the entire functionality may have to be revised to be implemented on a realistic hardware architecture. This reflection of implementation constraints needs to be managed in an iterative fashion. To verify and validate a feature across all abstraction levels, using simulation or formal techniques, an environment model is needed early on. This "plant model" captures the behavior of the vehicle dynamics, driver, etc. The core part of the environment model can be the same for all abstraction levels.

After this short introduction to the EAST-ADL concepts, we go on to discuss the motivation and modeling concepts in more detail. The relation between EAST-ADL and its most important related approach AUTOSAR (AUTOSAR Development Partnership, 2012) is explained throughout the following text. At the end, we will provide a more detailed discussion of other related approaches and how they compare to EAST-ADL.

CHALLENGES FOR MODELING AUTOMOTIVE EMBEDDED SYSTEMS

Automotive embedded systems have evolved enormously over the past decades. The use of electronics and software in automotive products has grown exponentially. For example, today vehicles in series production contain the same amount of electronics as an aircraft did two decades ago. To satisfy customer demands and competitiveness between OEMs, innovation will further drive the significance of software-controlled automotive electronics over the next decade. It is obvious, that the vehicle's electronic architecture will continue to grow in complexity, criticality and authority.

To manage some of the challenges of automotive software, the AUTOSAR consortium has developed a standardized automotive software architecture (AUTOSAR Development Partnership, 2012). One of its main features is a componentization of the software architecture, to favor reuse and assist collaboration and integration aspects. The software development effort is no longer bound to a specific hardware platform or a particular provider. A standardized software architecture and methodology is a first step towards meeting the challenges associated with the development of automotive systems, often distributed over several suppliers with different responsibilities. However, there still remains the critical issue of managing the overall engineering information to control system definition. This stage contains the most decisive steps in meeting safety challenges, controlling complexity and avoiding development errors and delays. Many stakeholders are involved here, and development is distributed over several departments and locations and involves several suppliers. While system modeling and model-based development is the trend in the automotive industry to solve this issue, there are diverse company-specific solutions. There is no standardized, comprehensive approach to support system modeling of the engineering information and therefore a federation of different modeling language initiatives is required to develop an automotive domain-specific language that is also in line with non-automotive approaches.

To support complexity and facilitate component development, an adequate organization of the system model is important. Representing the system in several "models" at different abstraction levels is a way to ensure separation of concerns and allow smooth interaction between disciplines. Supporting a functional decomposition of the system is also important to hide implementation aspects while the functional aspects are addressed. Another challenge is the capability to use product line engineering. The automotive industry is characterized by large model ranges and a high degree of customizability. In addition to end-customer configuration, also other important forms of variation occur, for example country variants arising from different legislation and variants for special purpose vehicles like ambulances or taxis. The organization and structuring of a comprehensive product line approach, from feature selection down to decomposition into components, requires innovative and efficient techniques. Finally, an important challenge is assessing the dependability of the application. In particular, means are required for early evaluation of system architecture, in terms not only of functional properties, but also of non-functional ones (such as timing, resource, safety level, etc.). In this context, the application of the upcoming standard for functional safety, ISO DIS 26262 (International Organization for Standardization, 2011), must be prepared by introducing new techniques and a structured development approach. An architecture description language provides means to represent the safety life-cycle information according to the requirements of the standard.

Last but not least, tool support for engineering development is organized today as a patchwork of heterogeneous tools and formalisms. A backbone environment using a standardized modeling language has to be harmonized to drive the tool market.

EAST-ADL META-MODELING APPROACH

The EAST-ADL language is formally specified as a meta model capturing domain specific, i.e. automotive, concepts. The meta-model follows guidelines originating from AUTOSAR (AUTOSAR Development Partnership, 2012) for definition of templates. Modeling concepts are represented by the basic notions of MOF (Object Management Group, 2011, August) supplemented by the AUTOSAR template profile. The meta-model thus fits as a specification of a domain specific tool environment, and also defines an XML exchange format. This *domain model* represents the actual definition of the EAST-ADL language and constitutes the heart of the EAST-ADL language specification.

In addition to the domain model, the EAST-ADL language is also implemented as a *UML2 profile*. UML profiles are standard extension mechanisms in the UML2 language, in which domain-specific concepts are provided as tags applicable to a selected subset of UML2 elements (such as classes, properties, ports, etc.) giving them different meaning and extra properties. The profile allows users to do system modeling according to the EAST-ADL semantics using off-the-shelf UML2 tools. Constraints are also part of the profile definition; this makes it possible to constrain the rich set of modeling constructs allowed by UML2 and to validate the conformance of the model. The EAST-ADL profile is delivered as an XMI file ready for use in UML2 tools. In the definition of the EAST-ADL profile, the general strategy has been to provide stereotype properties even for properties already populated within the UML2 superstructure. In other words, the property values that appear when defining a UML2 model are duplicated with semantic names in the stereotypes. This yields a model that is quite complete even without a profile. This approach is in line with the intention of UML2 that views and features of existing UML2 tools can be used readily, including for example, UML2 activity diagrams and related profiles such as SysML (Object Management Group, 2012) and MARTE (Object Management Group, 2011, June). The applied profile adds automotive semantics to this self-contained UML2 model.

EAST-ADL MODELING CONCEPTS

The modeling concepts of EAST-ADL fall into six areas: functional abstraction, timing modeling, requirements modeling, functional safety modeling, variability modeling and cooperative active safety systems.

Functional Abstraction

EAST-ADL provides the means to capture the functional decomposition and behavior of the embedded system and the environment.

At the analysis level, the "FunctionalAnalysisArchitecture" contains "Functions" that can be hierarchically composed and connected to each other. Functional devices represent sensors and actuators with their interface software and electronics, and these are connected to the environment. Figure 2 explains the entities involved and shows how they are connected. The "Functions" can have two types of ports, "FlowPorts" and "ClientServer" ports to represent data exchange and client-server interaction. The functions can be hierarchical, but the leaves have synchronous execution semantics, which means that they read inputs, calculate and provide outputs. They are triggered based on time or data arrival on ports. A function's internal behavior is typically defined by external tools and their techniques for behavioral descriptions. The behavior of the environment is captured in the "EnvironmentModel". The environment model also contains "Functions", but they represent vehicle dynamics, other vehicles, road-side IT systems, etc.

The design level (see Figure 2) contains a more detailed functional definition of the system. "Functions" and "LocalDeviceManagers" represent application software in the Functional Design Architecture. "BasicSoftwareFunctions" are used to capture middleware behavior affecting application functionality. HardwareFunctions represents the logical behavior of hardware components and

Figure 2. Functional decomposition in EAST-ADL on analysis and design levels

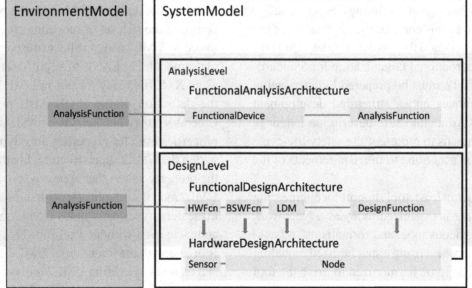

HWFcn=Hardware Function BSW=Basic Software LDM=LocalDeviceManager

complete the logical path to the environment model with the controlled "plant" and surrounding elements. The Hardware Design Architecture represent the resource platform with ECUs, busses, sensors, actuators and I/O to which the functions are allocated. The Hardware Design Architecture also reflects the physical topology of electrical elements and connectors.

Timing Modeling

EAST-ADL provides support for model-specific engineering information, including non-functional properties that are relevant for the timing of automotive functions. Conceptually, timing information can be divided into timing requirements and timing properties, where the actual timing properties of a solution must satisfy the specified timing requirements.

Modeling of timing requirements and properties on the functional abstraction levels of the architecture description language is done by means of the "Timing Augmented Description Language" TADL developed by the TIMMO project (TIMMO Consortium, 2012). In the implementation level, i.e. AUTOSAR, this is addressed by the "AUTOSAR Timing Extensions" which was introduced in AUTOSAR release 4.0 (AUTOSAR Development Partnership, 2012). Timing constraints are defined separately from the structural modeling and reference the structural elements of the EAST-ADL. The requirements modeling support in EAST-ADL allows for tracing from solutions as modeled in the structural model to requirements, and from verification cases to requirements. Form the perspective of the requirements support, TADL constraints can be perceived as refinements of the requirements.

The fundamental concept for describing timing constraints is that of Events and Event Chains. On every level of abstraction, observable events can be identified, e.g. events that cause a reaction, i.e. a stimulus, and resulting observable event, i.e. a response. Timing requirements can be imposed on Event Chains, for example, specifying that the time between the occurrence of a stimulus event and the occurrence of the expected response event shall not exceed a specific amount of time, e.g. an end-to-end delay from a sensor to an actuator. In addition, requirements regarding the synchrony of events can be expressed, stating that a number of events shall occur "simultaneously" in order to cause a reaction, or be considered as valid response of a system function. For example, in case of a passenger vehicle, its brake system shall apply the brakes simultaneously; or the exterior light system shall simultaneously turn on and off the rear and front turn signal indicators.

Figure 3 shows a simple example of an event chain with an annotated reaction constraint. A Functional Analysis Architecture with two functions builds up the structural model. The constraint with bound attributes has been defined. This refers to an Event Chain built up by an in event (stimulus) and an out event (response) referring to structural ports.

Requirements Modeling

In order to comprehensively support the development of complex automotive systems, EAST-ADL provides means for requirements specification, i.e. for specifying the required properties of the system (at varying degrees of abstraction). Furthermore, requirements can be refined by behavioral models, they can be traced between system refinement and system decomposition levels, and they can be related to verification and validation information and activities. Another important aim of EAST-ADL is to provide means for project-specific adjustments to requirements specification structures, which are inspired by the Requirements Interchange Format (Herstellerinitiative Software, 2007).

Methodically, EAST-ADL differentiates between functional requirements, which typically focus on some part of the "normal" functionality that the system has to provide (e.g. "ABS shall control brake force via wheel slip control"), and

Figure 3. Event chain with associated timing constraint

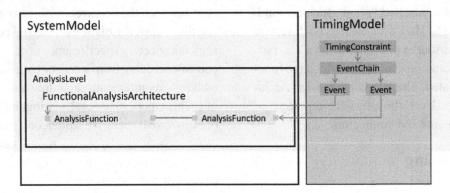

quality requirements, which typically focus on some external property of the system seen as a whole (e.g. performance, "ABS shall reduce stopping distance on snow by 40%"). EAST-ADL offers detailed means to model artifacts of verification and validation activities and to relate these artifacts to requirements. This allows us to explicitly and continuously plan, track, update and manage important V&V activities and their impact on the system parallel to the system's development.

Functional Safety Modeling

The overall objective of the support for functional safety modeling is to enforce explicit considerations of safety concerns throughout an architecture design process, which includes all safety related information that are necessary for developing a safety critical E/E system, in compliance with the Standard ISO 26262, an international standard dedicated to functional safety for road vehicles (International Organization for Standardization, 2011).

As an overall system property, safety is concerned with anomalies (e.g. faults, errors and failures) and their consequences under certain environmental conditions. It is one particular aspect of system dependability that normally also encompasses reliability, availability, integrity, maintainability and security. Functional safety

represents the part of system safety that depends on the correctness of a system in performing its intended functionality. In other words, it addresses the hazardous events of a system during its operation (e.g. component errors and their propagations).

EAST-ADL facilitates safety engineering in terms of safety analysis, specification of safety requirements, and safety design. While promoting safety in general through its intrinsic architecture modeling and traceability support, EAST-ADL provides explicit support for efficient integration of functional safety activities along with the nominal architecture design and evolution. As illustrated in Figure 4, EAST-ADL provides language-level support for the concepts defined in ISO 26262, including vehicle-level hazard analysis and risk assessment, the definition of safety goals and safety requirements, the ASIL (Automotive Safety Integrity Level) decomposition and the error propagation. The information is included in the Dependability package, as an extension of the nominal architecture model.

Following a top-down approach, the safety analysis starts at the VehicleLevel, beginning with the identification and description of the item. An item, as defined in ISO 26262, is a system or array of systems or functions that is of particular concern in regards to functional safety. Through hazard analysis and risk assessment activities, is possible to preliminarily evaluate at Vehicle-

Figure 4. Mapping of ISO26262 information to EAST-ADL abstraction levels

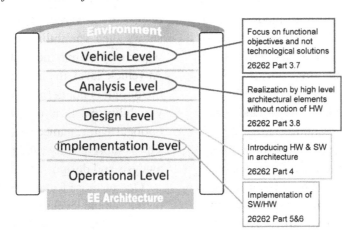

Level the "safety relevance" of the item under safety analysis, to define the safety goal (top-level safety requirement) for each hazardous event (hazard evaluated in different scenarios) and to classify them in terms of ASIL. Moreover, AnalysisLevel and DesignLevel of EAST-ADL support respectively the functional safety concept and the technical safety concept definition.

EAST-ADL error modeling allows to capture detailed information about the failure behavior of the system and thus enables a safety analysis to determine whether technical safety requirements are being met. This Error Model describes the generation and propagation of failures through the system. The relationships of local error behaviors are captured by means of explicit error propagation ports and connections. Within an error model, the syntax and/or semantics of existing external formalisms can be adopted for a precise description of the error logic. The specification captures what output failures of the target architecture component are caused by what faults of this component. This, together with the error propagation links, makes it possible to perform safety simulations and analyses through external analysis tools. In an architecture specification, an error is allowed to propagate via design specific architectural relationships when such relationships also imply behavioral or operational dependencies (e.g. between software and hardware).

The error modeling is treated as a separate analytical view (see Figure 5). It is not embedded

Figure 5. EAST-ADL error model as a separate architecture view extending the nominal architecture model

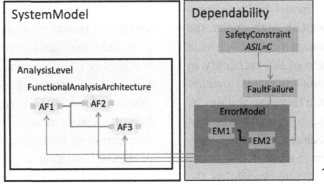

in a nominal architecture model but seamlessly integrated with the architecture model through the EAST-ADL meta-model. This separation of concerns in modeling is considered necessary in order to avoid some undesired effects of error modeling, e.g. relating to the comprehension and management of nominal design, reuse, and system synthesis (e.g. code generation).

Given an error model, the analysis of the causes and consequences of failure behaviors can be automated through tools. There is currently a (prototype) analysis plug-in in the Eclipse environment allowing the integration of the HiP-HOPS tool (Hierarchically Performed Hazard Origin and Propagation Studies1) for static safety analysis in terms of FFA, FTA, and FMEA (Papadopoulos et al., 2011). The analysis leverage includes fault trees from functional failures to software and hardware failures, minimal cut sets, FMEA tables for component errors and their effects on the behaviors and reliability of entire system.

In EAST-ADL, a safety requirement derived from the safety analysis has attributes specifying the hazard to be mitigated, the safety integrity level (ASIL), operation state, fault time span, emergency operation times, safety state, etc. The safety requirement is then traced to other nominal requirements or used to derive other nominal requirements from it, e.g. relating to safety functions and performance.

Variability Modeling

EAST-ADL variability management starts on the vehicle level, where model range features and variability are represented. At this point, the purpose of variability management is to provide a highly abstract overview of the variability in the system such as the complete system together with dependencies between these variabilities. A "variability" in this sense is a certain aspect of the complete system that changes from one variant of the complete system to another. "Abstract" here means that, for an individual variability, the

idea is not to specify how the system varies with respect to this variability but only that the system shows such variability. For example, the front wiper may or may not have an automatic start. At vehicle level, the impact of this variability on the design is not defined; only the fact that such variability exists is defined by introducing an optional feature named "RainControlledWiping." This is subsequently validated and refined during analysis and design.

One or more feature models may be defined on the vehicle level: the so-called core Technical Feature Model is used to define the complete system's variability on a global level from a technical perspective, whereas one or more optional Product Feature Models can be used to define views on this technical variability which can be tailored to a particular view-point or purpose, e.g. the end-customer perspective.

While the details of how variability is actually realized in the system are largely suppressed at the vehicle level, they are the focus of attention when managing variability in other areas of the development process. In fact, specific variability may lead to modifications in any development artifact, such as requirements specifications and functional models. Here, describing that a specific variability occurs is not sufficient; it is necessary to describe how each variation affects and modifies the corresponding artifact.

The purpose of feature modeling is to define the commonalities and variabilities of the product variants within the scope of a product line. Feature models are normally used on a high level of abstraction, as described above for vehicle level variability. However, in EAST-ADL, they are also used on analysis and design levels and acquire a much more concrete meaning there. Configuration decision modeling, on the other hand, is aimed at defining configuration: the configuration of a feature model f_T—i.e. the selection and deselection of its features—is defined in terms of the configuration of another feature model f_S. A configuration decision model can thus be seen as a link from f_S to f_T that allows us to derive a configuration of f_T from any given configuration of f_S. In EAST-ADL, this mechanism is used to define how a certain configuration on a higher abstraction level affects the binding of variability in lower-level components.

Variability management on the artifact level is driven by the variability captured on the vehicle level. This means that the main driver for variability and also variability instantiation is the vehicle-level feature model. Variability on the artifact level essentially consists of the definition of variation points within these artifacts. In addition, feature models can be attached to functions in order to expose the variability within these functions and hide the actual structuring, representation and binding of this variability within a function. This way, the benefits of information hiding can now be applied to the variability representation and variability binding within the containment hierarchy of functions in the EAST-ADL Functional Analysis Architecture and Functional Design Architecture (called compositional variability management).

Behavior Constraint Modeling

The reasoning and analysis of dependability and performance involve many aspects in a system's lifecycle. To this end, EAST-ADL allows precise and integrated annotations of various behavioural concerns related to requirements, application modes and functions, implementation and resource deployment, and anomalies. The approach is architecture-centric as all behaviour annotations are formally connected to a set of standardized system artefacts and lifecycle phases. This is fundamental for many overall design decisions, such as requirements engineering, component compositionality&composability, design refinements, safety engineering, maintenance, etc. From a wider perspective, this language support enables an integration of many existing modelling and analysis technologies, such as from computer science and electronic engineering, by making it

possible to trace and maintain the related engineering concerns and analytical information coherently using EAST-ADL.

Based on a hybrid-system semantics, the EAST-ADL support for the annotations of behavioural concerns consists of three categories of behaviour constraints:

1. **Attribute Quantification Constraint:** Relating to the declarations of value attributes and the related acausal quantifications (e.g., $U=I*R$).
2. **Temporal Constraint:** Relating to the declarations of behaviour constraints where the history of behaviours on a timeline is taken into consideration.
3. **Computation Constraint:** Relating to the declarations of cause-effect dependencies of data in terms of logical transformations (for data assignments) and logical paths.

Each of these behaviour constraints can be associated to time conditions given in terms of logical time, of which the exact semantics is given by the existing EAST-ADL support for timing definition (e.g. the triggering, and port data sending and receiving events of a function). Owing to the formal semantics, one can explicitly define the model transformation from EAST-ADL behavior model to other model formats of external analysis methods and tools, such as hazard analysis, response time analysis, model checking, test-case generation, etc.

METHODOLOGY

The purpose of the EAST-ADL methodology is to give guidance on the use of the language for the construction, validation and reuse of models for automotive embedded software. The purpose is thus not to impose a specific development process, but to show *one* sequence of steps that can produce sound and useful EAST-ADL models.

This provides understanding for the EAST-ADL language and serves as building blocks for a more complex and complete process definition.

The EAST-ADL methodology is defined as a core part which is complemented by extensions. The core is a top-down description of the most central steps in each phase:

- The Vehicle phase involves analysis of external requirements based on which a Technical Feature Model is constructed. This Feature tree shall be organized in an adequate way and also capture necessary or intended feature configurations. In addition, for each feature a set of requirements is specified.
- The Analysis phase results in a FunctionalAnalysisArchitecture which specifies a realization of the Features. The solution is a logical representation of the system to be developed. All the modeling in this phase will be on a logical behavior level, i.e. it will make no distinction between HW and SW or about the implementation of communication.
- The Design phase involves defining the FunctionalDesignArchitecture specifying a solution to the requirements in terms of efficient and reusable architectures, i.e. sets of (structured) HW/SW components and their interfaces, a hardware architecture,

and a mapping from functional components to HW/SW components. The architecture must satisfy more detailed constraints.
- The Implementation phase results in the HW/SW implementation and configuration of the final solution. This part is mainly a reference to the concepts of AUTOSAR which provides standardized specifications at this level of automotive software development (see Figure 6).

The core methodology is extended into a comprehensive methodology for automotive development projects by adding additional and orthogonal activities to each of these phases:

- Specification of Requirements and corresponding V&V cases to be executed and evaluated during the corresponding integration phase. V&V cases are most typically test cases, but can also include reviews etc.
- Verification of the model on a given abstraction level to the requirements of the model at the abstraction level directly above.
- V&V activities on the model artifacts of a given level itself, i.e. peer reviews, consistency checks, check of modeling guidelines etc.

Figure 6. The typical basic structure of automotive system development according to the V-model

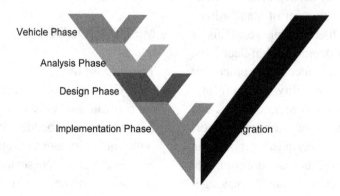

While the methodology tries to be comprehensive handling the construction phases, the integration activities are only covered inasmuch they involve V&V activities and the relation to V&V-artifacts defined in the construction phases.

The EAST-ADL methodology is extended beyond the core activities by means of a set of methodology extensions. In the first approach for EAST-ADL methodology, different methodology versions were defined depending on scope. Examples of scope were:

- **Environment Modeling:** Modeling of the (typically analog or discrete-analog) environment of the system to be developed.
- **Safety Assurance:** Development of Safety-critical systems.
- **Timing:** Detailed handling of timing requirements and properties.
- **Variability Modeling:** Detailed handling of variability modeling.
- **Behavior modeling:** Detailed handling of behavioral modeling.

The initial EAST-ADL methodology definition is using concepts of the Software & Systems Process Engineering Meta-model SPEM (Object Management Group, 2008), which means that the methodology is based on a set of elementary work tasks which are performed by a set of actors and produce a set output artifacts from a set of input artifacts. These tasks are structured into disciplines and then presented to the end user by a set of views. This leads of a highly linked network of methodological activities in which an end user can easily navigate to get information and guidance on the use of the language for particular development tasks.

The methodology definition is currently being restructured to follow a Generic Methodology Pattern, where the EAST-ADL phases are divided into a set of steps. The set of steps are the same for each phase, and also for each aspect (safety, timing, variability, etc.). The principle is that the user assesses the steps related to the core and each relevant aspect and then implicitly "weaves" an appropriate set of steps for his needs. The notation for this more recent methodology is Business Process Modelling Notation.

RELATED APPROACHES

One key aspect of the development of EAST-ADL is to benefit from existing methods and techniques and also to influence emerging approaches. Whenever possible, existing and state-of-the-art solutions were reused and integrated in the language. This favors the wide use of the language, allows the use of available tools and prepares for a sound standardization process. Efforts like AUTOSAR (AUTOSAR Development Partnership, 2012), TIMMO (TIMMO Consortium, 2012), and ISO 26262 (International Organization for Standardization, 2011) are sources both for the alignment of domain specific challenges and for the integration of technologies and methodologies in the development of EAST-ADL.

As a future de-facto standard for automotive embedded systems, AUTOSAR addresses the needs for a process-safe integration of functions. It provides a standardized platform for the specification and execution of application software, an integration method for software components and hardware resources, and also the interchange formats that these require. While adopting AUTOSAR for the implementation level abstractions, the EAST-ADL language complements the AUTOSAR initiative by providing higher-level abstractions, analysis and lifecycle management support. In effect, it allows an AUTOSAR-compliant software architecture being extended with models relating to the design of functionality, timing and safety, the structuring and allocation of application, as well as the management of variability, requirements, traceability and verification and validation.

EAST-ADL integrates the results of TIMMO, which is an ITEA project focusing on the timing constraints and timing properties in automotive real-time systems. TIMMO has developed a formal description language, TADL, and a methodology for dealing with the timing concerns on the basis of EAST-ADL 1. It has been developed in a close collaboration with AUTOSAR. The follow-up project TIMMO-2-USE is further developing the TADL language, in close collaboration with the MAENAD project (MAENAD Consortium, 2012), developing EAST-ADL.

The emerging international standard ISO 26262 (International Organization for Standardization, 2011) is carefully considered in EAST-ADL. The key content includes an automotive safety lifecycle, an automotive specific approach for determining risk classes and deriving safety requirements based on ASILs (Automotive Safety Integrity Levels), and a set of requirements for validation and confirmation measures to ensure a sufficient and acceptable level of safety being achieved.

To support behavior modeling, EAST-ADL provides dedicated behavior elements that facilitate the description of the relationship between behavioral and structural models. The EAST-ADL functions have synchrounous execution semantics, and language concepts are available to define their triggering and timing. By clearly distinguishing between component execution and component logical computation, EAST-ADL allows the integration of behavior models from off-the-shelf tools like SCADE, ASCET, Simulink, etc., according to lifecycle stages and stakeholder needs. For continuous-time behavior (e.g., for the vehicle dynamics under control), related modeling techniques from Modelica, which combines acausal modeling with object-oriented thinking,

have been adopted. The Functional Mockup interface, used for co-simulation and model exchange via Functional Mockup Units (FMUs) has been investigated, and a prototype transformation tool has been developed. EAST-ADL also provides tool prototypes for model transformation to Simulink and the SPIN (Simple PROMELA Interpreter) model checker.

A further standardization effort being taken into consideration is the SAE "Architecture and Analysis Description Language (AADL)" (Feiler et al., 2006), which has its roots in the avionics domain. Compared to EAST-ADL, AADL has a more narrow scope: no explicit support is provided for variability management or requirements refinements and traceability. Specifics for automotive systems such as the networks are weakly supported. The AADL is not designed for mass-produced systems and therefore has less emphasis on optimized overall solutions e.g. by considering compact runtime systems. For the automotive domain, the clash with AUTOSAR concepts is also a problem. However, wherever applicable, AADL concepts were reused, e.g. for dependability modeling.

EAST-ADL allows the adoptions of existing formalisms for the underlying semantics and provides support for model transformation and tool interoperability with the external safety analysis techniques. In particular, HiP-HOPS and the AADL's Error Model Annex have been carefully considered in the development of EAST-ADL. They both enable the modeling of system failure behavior and allow analysis of that behavior using tools.

A tool plug-in for HiP-HOPS has been developed to support both FTA and FMEA. Other approaches to model-based safety analysis and verification that have been investigated for the development of EAST-ADL include ISSAC and its predecessor ESACS in the aerospace industries (where the goal was to develop a formal methodology and tools for the safety analysis of complex aeronautical systems), the ASSERT project (with similar goals but more focused on software intensive systems specified in AADL), the SETTA project (focusing on the use of time-triggered architectures in automotive systems), and the SAFEDOR project (which aimed to develop new practices for the safety assessment of maritime systems).

SPEEDS (Speculative and Exploratory Design in Systems Engineering) is a European project aiming at providing support for modeling and analysis of complex embedded systems through the usage of formal analysis tools. EAST-ADL complements the SPEEDS approach with automotive architecture and lifecycle information. The techniques of SPEEDS have been considered in EAST-ADL for behavior modeling (i.e., with the hybrid automata variant) and for a more formal specification of requirements and constraints (i.e., with temporal logics scripts for contracts of functionality, safety, and timing).

MARTE (Object Management Group, 2011, June) is a UML profile for Modeling and Analysis of Real-Time and Embedded systems. MARTE models real-time constraints and other embedded systems characteristics, such as memory capacity and power consumption. MARTE supports modeling and analysis of component-based architectures, as well as a variety of different computational paradigms (asynchronous, synchronous, and timed). The EAST-ADL UML-profile is released as an annex to MARTE, done in the ATESST2 and ADAMS projects.

The OMG Systems Modeling Language (Object Management Group, 2012) is a general-purpose graphical modeling language for specifying, analyzing, designing, and verifying complex systems that may include hardware, software, information, personnel, procedures, and facilities. Compared with EAST-ADL, SysML is more generic and high-level, so EAST-ADL can be seen as a specialization and subset for automotive embedded systems. In fact, the first versions of EAST-ADL and SysML were defined in parallel with some interaction between the teams. The EAST-ADL function architecture with ports and datatypes are influenced by SysML, as well as the requirements modelling.

CONCLUSION

The main objective of EAST-ADL is to integrate and, where necessary, complement existing system development and modeling techniques in order to provide a comprehensive modeling language and methodology for the development of automotive software-intensive systems. Since its core parts are well consolidated by now, present and future focus will be put on extending EAST-ADL for other, more specialized applications within automotive development and providing improved tool support.

ACKNOWLEDGMENT

This work has been supported by the European FP7 project MAENAD under grant agreement number 260057.

REFERENCES

ATESST2 Consortium. (2010). *ATESST2 project web site*. Retrieved from http://www.attest.org/

AUTOSAR Development Partnership. (2012). *AUTOSAR web site*. Retrieved from http://www.autosar.org/

EAST-ADL Association. (2012). *EAST-ADL association web site*. Retrieved from http://www.east-adl.info/

Feiler, P., Gluch, D., & Hudak, J. (2006). *The architecture analysis & design language (AADL): An introduction. Technical Note CMU/SEI-2006-TN-011.* Pittsburgh, PA: Carnegie Mellon University.

Herstellerinitiative Software. (2007). *Requirements interchange format (RIF), version 1.1a.* Retrieved from http://www.automotive-his.de/rif/

International Organization for Standardization. (2011). *Road vehicles – Functional safety – Part 1 to 9. International Standard ISO/FDIS 26262.* ISO.

MAENAD Consortium. (2012). *MAENAD project home page.* Retrieved from http://www.maenad.eu/

Object Management Group. (2008). *Software & systems process engineering metamodel specification (SPEM) – Version 2.0. Document number: formal/2008-04-01.* OMG.

Object Management Group. (2011). *UML profile for MARTE: Modeling and analysis of real-time embedded systems – Version 1.1. Document number: formal/2011-06-02.* OMG.

Object Management Group. (2011). *Meta object facility (MOF) – Core specification – Version 2.4.1. Document number: formal/2011-08-07.* OMG.

Object Management Group. (2012). *SysML project web site.* Retrieved from http://www.omgsysml.org/

Papadopoulos, Y., Walker, M., Parker, D., Rüde, E., Hamann, R., Uhlig, A., … Lien, R. (2011). Engineering failure analysis & design optimisation with HiP-HOPS. *Journal of Engineering Failure Analysis.* DOI: 10.1016/j.engfailanal.2010.09.025

TIMMO Consortium. (2012). *TIMMO 2 USE project web site.* Retrieved from http://www.timmo-2-use.org/

Compilation of References

Abbasi, N., Hasan, O., & Tahar, S. (2010). Formal lifetime reliability analysis using continuous random variables. In *Proceedings of Logic, Language*[LNCS]. *Information and Computation, 6188,* 84–97.

Abeni, L., & Buttazzo, G. C. (1998). Integrating multimedia applications in hard real-time systems. In *Proceedings of the 19th IEEE Real-Time Systems Symposium (RTSS'98)*. Madrid, Spain: IEEE.

Abeni, L., & Buttazzo, G. C. (1999). Adaptive bandwidth reservation for multimedia computing. In *Proceedings of the 6th IEEE International Conference on Real-Time Computing Systems and Applications* (pp. 70–77). Hong Kong, China: IEEE.

Abeni, L., & Buttazzo, G. C. (2001). Hierarchical qos management for time sensitive applications. In *Proceedings of the IEEE Real-Time Technology and Applications Symposium*. Taipei, Taiwan: IEEE.

Abeni, L., & Buttazzo, G. C. (2004). Resource reservations in dynamic real-time systems. *Real-Time Systems, 27*(2), 123–165. doi:10.1023/B:TIME.0000027934.77900.22.

Abeni, L., Cucinotta, T., Lipari, G., Marzario, L., & Palopoli, L. (2005). QoS management through adaptive reservations. *Real-Time Systems, 29*(2-3), 131–155. doi:10.1007/s11241-005-6882-0.

Abrial & Cansell. (2005). *Formal construction of a nonblocking concurrent queue algorithm (a case study in atomicity).*

Abrial & Cansell. (2007). *Click'n'prove within set theory.*

Abrial. (1996). *The B-book: Assigning programs to meanings.* Cambridge, UK: Cambridge University Press.

Abrial. (1996). Extending B without changing it (for developing distributed systems). In H. Habrias (Ed.), *Proceedings of the 1st Conference on the B method,* (pp. 169–191). Academic Press.

Abrial. (2003). Toward a synthesis between Z and B. *Lecture Notes in Computer Science, 2651,* 168–177.

Abrial. (2006). *Using design patterns in formal development - Example: A mechanical press controler.*

Abrial, Cansell, & Mery. (2003). Formal derivation of spanning trees algorithms. *Lecture Notes in Computer Science, 2651,* 457–476. doi:10.1007/3-540-44880-2_27.

Abrial, Cansell, & Mery. (2003). A mechanically proved and incremental development of IEEE 1394 tree identify protocol. *Formal Aspects of Computing, 14*(3), 215–227. doi:10.1007/s001650300002.

Achiwa, K., Yamamoto, A., & Yamagata, O. (1999). Memory systems using a flash memory and method of controlling the memory system. *United States Patent, No 5,930,193.* Washington, DC: US Patent Office.

Akerholm & Fredriksson. (2004). *A sample of component technologies for embedded systems.*

Akyildiz, I. F., & Melodia, T. (2007). A survey on wireless multimedia sensor networks. *Journal Computer Networks, 51*(4).

Akyilidz, I. F., Su, W., Sankarasubramaniam, Y., & Cayirci, E. (2002). A survey on sensor networks. *IEEE Communications Magazine, 40*(8), 102–114. doi:10.1109/MCOM.2002.1024422.

Alexander. (1977). *A pattern language: Towns, buildings, construction.* Oxford, UK: Oxford University Press.

Alkan, M. (2010). *Interconnected FlexRay and CAN networks for invehicle communication: gateway implementation and end-to-end performance study*. Ankara, Turkey: Middle East Technical University.

Almeida, L., Fonseca, J. A., & Fonseca, P. (1999). Flexible time triggered communication system based on the controller area network: Experimental results. In *Proceedings of the Fieldbus Technology International Conference (FeT'99)*, (Vol. 99, pp. 24-31). FeT.

Almeida, G. M., Sassatelli, G., Benoit, P., Saint-Jean, N., Varyani, S., Torres, L., & Robert, M. (2009). An adaptive message passing MPSoC framework. *International Journal of Reconfigurable Computing*, 242981.

Al-Safi, Y., & Vyatkin, V. (2007). An ontology based reconfiguration agent for intelligent mechatronic systems. In *Proceedings of the 4th International Conference of Holistic Multi-Agent Systems Manufacturing* (LNCS), (vol. 4659, pp. 114-126). Regensburg, Germany: Springer.

Alsafi, Y., & Vyatkin, V. (2010). Ontology-based reconfiguration agent for intelligent mechatronic systems in flexible manufacturing. *Journal Robotics and Computer-Integrated Manufacturing*, *26*(4), 381–391. doi:10.1016/j.rcim.2009.12.001.

Altera. (n.d.). *Implementing FPGA design with OpenCL - A future look*. Retrieved April 11, 2012 from http://www.altera.com/education/Webcasts/all/source-files/wc-2011-opencl/player.html

Altera. (n.d.). *Nios II software developer's handbook*. Retrieved April 11, 2012 from http://www.altera.com/literature/hb/nios2/n2sw_nii5v2.pdf

Amde, M., Felicijan, T., Efthymiou, A., Edwards, D., & Lavagno, L. (2005). Asynchronous on-chip networks. *IEE Proceedings. Computers and Digital Techniques*, *152*(2). doi:10.1049/ip-cdt:20045093.

Anashin, V., Bogdanov, A., Kizhvatov, I., & Kumar, S. (2005). *eSTREAM: A new fast flexible stream cipher.*

Anderson, R., Bond, M., Clulow, J., & Skorobogatov, S. (2006). Cryptographic processors-A survey. *Proceedings of the IEEE*, *94*(2), 357–369. doi:10.1109/JPROC.2005.862423.

Andersson, B., & Tovar, E. (2009). The utilization bound of non-preemptive rate-monotonic scheduling in controller area network is 25%. In *Proceedings of the International Symposium on Industrial Embedded Systems (SIES)*, (pp. 11-18). IEEE.

Angelov, C., Sierszecki, K., & Marian, N. (2005). Design models for reusable and reconfigurable state machines. *Lecture Notes in Computer Science*, *3824*, 152–163. doi:10.1007/11596356_18.

Angrisani, L., Bertocco, M., Fortin, D., & Sona, A. (2008). Experimental study of coexistence issues between IEEE 802.11b and IEEE 802.15.4 wireless networks. *IEEE Transactions on Instrumentation and Measurement*, *57*, 1514–1523. doi:10.1109/TIM.2008.925346.

Anoop, M. (2008). *Security needs in embedded systems*. Retrieved from http://eprint.iacr.org/2008/198

Antonini, M., Barlaud, M., Mathieu, P., & Daubechies, I. (1992). Image coding using wavelet transform. *IEEE Transactions on Image Processing*, *1*(2), 205–220. doi:10.1109/83.136597 PMID:18296155.

Arcticus Systems. (n.d.). *Web-page*. Retrieved from http://www.arcticus.se

Aredo. (1999). Formalizing UML class diagrams in PVS. In *Proceedings of OOPSLA'99 Workshop on Rigorous Modeling and Analysis with the UML: Challenges and Limitations*. OOPSLA.

Argyroudis, P. (2004). *NTRG ECC-LIB WINCE – A WinCE port of ECC-LIB*. Retrieved from http://ntrg.cs.tcd.ie/~argp/software/ntrg-ecc-lib-wince.html

Arm. (2001). Retrieved December 19, 2001, from www.arm.com

Armaou, A., & Christofides, P. D. (2001). Finite-dimensional control of nonlinear parabolic PDE systems with time dependent spatial domains using empirical eigenfunctions. *International Journal of Applied Mathematics and Computer Science*, *11*(2), 287–317.

Armstrong, J. (2007). *Programming erlang: Software for a concurrent world*. Raleigh, NC: Pragmatic Bookshelf.

Ascia, G., Catania, V., & Palesi, M. (2004). Multi-objective mapping for mesh-based NoC architectures. In *Proceedings of the Second IEEE/ACM/IFIP International Conference on Hardware/Software Codesign and System Synthesis* (pp. 182–187). IEEE.

Assar, M., Namazie, S., & Estakhri, P. (1995). Flash memory mass storage architecture incorporation wear leveling technique. *United States Patent, No 5,479,638.* Washington, DC: US Patent Office.

ATESST2 Consortium. (2010). *ATESST2 project web site*. Retrieved from http://www.attest.org/

Atwell, J., Borggaard, J. T., & King, B. B. (2001). Article. *International Journal of Applied Mathematics and Computer Science, 11*(6), 1311–1330.

Audsley, N., Burns, A., Richardson, M., Tindell, K., & Wellings, A. (1993). Applying new scheduling theory to static priority pre-emptive scheduling. *Software Engineering Journal, 8*(5), 284–292. doi:10.1049/sej.1993.0034.

AUTOSAR Development Partnership. (2012). *AUTOSAR web site*. Retrieved from http://www.autosar.org/

AUTOSAR. (2012). *AUTOSAR specification release 4.0 rev. 3.0*. Retrieved from http://www.autosar.org/

Aydin, H., Melhem, R., Mossé, D., & Alvarez, P. M. (2001). Optimal reward-based scheduling for periodic real-time tasks. *IEEE Transactions on Computers, 50*(2), 111–130. doi:10.1109/12.908988.

Back & Sere. (1989). Stepwise refinement of action systems. In *Mathematics of Program Construction* (pp. 115–138). Berlin: Springer.

Back & Wright. (1998). *Refinement calculus: A systematic introduction*. Berlin: Springer-Verlag.

Badeau & Amelot. (2005). Using B as a high level programming language in an industrial project: Roissy VAL. *Lecture Notes in Computer Science, 3455,* 334–354. doi:10.1007/11415787_20.

Baier, C., Haverkort, B., Hermanns, H., & Katoen, J. (2003). Model checking algorithms for continuous time Markov chains. *IEEE Transactions on Software Engineering, 29*(4), 524–541. doi:10.1109/TSE.2003.1205180.

Baier, C., & Katoen, J. P. (2008). *Principles of model checking*. Cambridge, MA: MIT Press.

Bai, H., & Atiquzzaman, M. (2003). Error modeling schemes for fading channels in wireless. *IEEE Communications Surveys & Tutorials, 5,* 2–9. doi:10.1109/COMST.2003.5341334.

Baker, T. E., & Shobrys, D. E. (1985). *The integration of planning, scheduling, and control*. Paper presented at the National Petroleum Refiners Association Computer Conference. New Orleans, LA.

Baker, T. P. (1991). Stack-based scheduling of realtime processes. *Journal of Real-Time Systems, 3*(1), 67–99. doi:10.1007/BF00365393.

Balarin, F., Hsieh, H., Jurecska, A., Lavagno, L., & Sangiovanni-Vincentelli, A. (1996). Formal verification of embedded systems based on CFSM networks. In *Proceedings of the Design Automation Conference*, (pp. 568-571). Springer.

Balas, M. (1983). The galerkin method and feedback control of linear distributed parameter systems. *Journal of Mathematical Analysis and Applications, 91,* 527–546. doi:10.1016/0022-247X(83)90167-1.

Balas, M. (1986). Finite dimensional control of distributed parameter systems by galerkin approximation of infinite dimensional controllers. *Journal of Mathematical Analysis and Applications, 114,* 17–36. doi:10.1016/0022-247X(86)90062-4.

Balfour, J., & Dally, W. J. (2006). Design tradeoffs for tiled CMP on-chip networks. In *Proceedings of the 20th ACM International Conference on Supercomputing (ICS)* (pp. 187–198). ACM.

Ban, A. (1995). Flash file system. *United States Patent, No 5,404,485.* Washington, DC: US Patent Office.

Ban, A. (1999). Flash file system optimized for page-mode flash technologies. *United States Patent, No 5,937,425.* Washington, DC: US Patent Office.

Banks, H. L., Smith, R. C., & Brown, D. E. (1997). Experimental confirmation of a PDE based approach for the design of feedback controls. *SIAM Journal of Optimization and Control, 35*(4), 1263–1296. doi:10.1137/S0363012995285909.

Barkaoui, K. J., & Couvreur, K., & Klai. (2005). On the equivalence between deadlock freeness and liveness in Petri nets. *Lecture Notes in Computer Science, 3536*, 90–111. doi:10.1007/11494744_7.

Barkaoui, K., Couvreur, J.-M., & Dutheillet, C. (1995). On liveness in extended non self-controlling nets. *Lecture Notes in Computer Science, 935*, 25–44. doi:10.1007/3-540-60029-9_32.

Barkaoui, K., & Minoux, M. (1992). A polynomial-time graph algorithm to decide liveness of some basic classes of bounded Petri nets. *Lecture Notes in Computer Science, 616*, 62–75. doi:10.1007/3-540-55676-1_4.

Barkaoui, K., & Peyre, J.-F.-P. (1996). On liveness and controlled siphons in Petri nets. *Lecture Notes in Computer Science, 1091*, 57–72. doi:10.1007/3-540-61363-3_4.

Barreto, P., Kim, H., & Lynn, B. (2002). Efficient algorithms for pairing-based cryptosystems. In *Proceedings of the 22nd Annual International Cryptology Conference on Advances in Cryptology (CRYPTO '02)*. Springer-Verlag.

Barros, J. P., & Gomes, L. (2003). Modifying petri net models by means of crosscutting operations. In *Proceedings of ACSD'2003 - Third International Conference on Application of Concurrency to System Design*. ACSD. ISBN 0-7695-1887-7

Barros, J. P., & Gomes, L. (2004). Net model composition and modification by net operations: a Pragmatic approach. In *Proceedings of INDIN'2004 – 2nd IEEE International Conference on Industrial Informatics*. Berlin, Germany: IEEE.

Bartic, T. A., Mignolet, J.-Y., Nollet, V., Marescaux, T., Verkest, D., Vernalde, S., & Lauwereins, R. (2003). Highly scalable network on chip for reconfigurable systems. In *Proceedings of the International Symposium on System-on-Chip* (pp. 79–82). IEEE.

Bartolomeu, P., Ferreira, J., & Fonseca, J. (2009). *Enforcing flexibility in real-time wireless communications: A bandjacking enabled protocol*. Paper presented at the Emerging Technologies & Factory Automation, 2009. New York, NY.

Bartosinski, R., Hanzalek, Z., Struzka, P., & Waszniowski, L. (2007). Integrated environment for embedded control systems design. In *Proceedings of the IEEE International Parallel and Distributed Processing Symposium (IPDPS 2007)* (pp. 1-8). IEEE.

Baruah, S. (2005). The limited-preemption uniprocessor scheduling of sporadic task systems. In *Proceedings of the 17th Euromicro Conference on Real-Time Systems* (pp. 137–144). Palma de Mallorca, Spain: Euromicro.

Baruah, S., Rosier, L., & Howell, R. (1990). Algorithms and complexity concerning the preemptive scheduling of periodic real-time tasks on one processor. *The Journal of Real-Time Systems, 2*.

Baruah, S., & Goossens, J. (2004). Scheduling real-time tasks: Algorithms and complexity. In Leung, J. Y.-T. (Ed.), *Handbook of Scheduling: Algorithms, Models, and Performance Analysis*. Academic Press.

Baruah, S., Rosier, L., & Howell, R. (1990). Algorithms and complexity concerning the preemptive scheduling of periodic, real-time tasks on one processor. *Journal of Real-Time Systems, 2*(4), 301–324. doi:10.1007/BF01995675.

Batina, L., Berna Örs, S., Preneel, B., & Vandewalle, J. (2003). Hardware architectures for public key cryptography. *Integration (Tokyo, Japan), 34*(1-2), 1–64.

Bauer. (2008). Enhancing the dynamic meta modeling formalism and its eclipse-based tool support with attributes. (Bachelor thesis). University of Paderborn.

Beard, R., & McLain, T. (1998). Successive galerkin approximation algorithms for nonlinear optimal and robust control. *International Journal of Control, 71*(5), 717–743. doi:10.1080/002071798221542.

Bechtel. (1993). *PIMS (process industry modeling system) user's manual, version 6.0*. Houston, TX: Bechtel Corp.

Beck. (1997). *Smalltalk best practice patterns*. Upper Saddle River, NJ: Prentice-Hall.

Behm, B. Faivre, & Meynadier. (1999). METEOR: A successful application of B in a large project. In J. M. Wing, J. Woodcock, & J. Davies (Eds.), *Proceedings of FM'99: World Congress on Formal Methods* (LNCS), (pp. 369-387). Berlin: Springer-Verlag.

Beigné, E., & Vivet, P. (2006). Design of on-chip and off-chip interfaces for a GALS NoC architecture. In *Proceedings of the 12th IEEE International Symposium on Asynchronous Circuits and Systems (ASYNC'06)* (pp. 172–183). IEEE.

Bellamine, F. H. (2013). *Applications of neural networks approaches for incorporating a priori knowledge in dynamic engineering process*. Applied Mathematics and Computations.

Bellamine, F. H., & Elkamel, A. (2006). Numerical characterization of distributed dynamic systems using tools of intelligent computing and generalized dimensional analysis. *Applied Mathematics and Computation, 182*(2), 1021–1039. doi:10.1016/j.amc.2006.05.002.

Bellamine, F. H., & Elkamel, A. (2008). Model order reduction using neural network principal component analysis and generalized dimensional analysis. *International Journal for CAE and Software, 25*(5), 443–463.

Bellare, M., & Rogaway, P. (1997). Minimizing the use of random oracles in authenticated encryption schemes. In *Proceedings of Information and Communications Security '97 (LNCS)* (Vol. 1334, pp. 1–16). Berlin: Springer. doi:10.1007/BFb0028457.

Bensoussan, A., Giuseppe, D., Delfour, M., & Mitter, S. (2007). *Representation and control of infinite dimensional systems* (2nd ed.). Birkhauser.

Beresini, B., Ricketts, S., & Taylor, M. B. (2011). Unifying manycore and FPGA processing with the RUSH architecture. In *Proceedings of the NASA/ESA Conference on Adaptive Hardware and Systems (AHS)* (pp. 22-28). NASA.

Bernat, G., Broster, I., & Burns, A. (2004). Rewriting history to exploit gain time. In *Proceedings of the 25th IEEE Real-Time Systems Symposium*. Lisbon, Portugal: IEEE.

Bernat, G., & Burns, A. (2002). Multiple servers and capacity sharing for implementing flexible scheduling. *Real-Time Systems, 22*(1-2), 49–75. doi:10.1023/A:1013481420080.

Berry, G., & Gonthier, G. (1992). The ESTEREL synchronous programming language: Design, semantics, implementation. *Science of Computer Programming, 19*(2), 87–152. doi:10.1016/0167-6423(92)90005-V.

Berthelot, G. (1987). In Brauer, W., Reisig, W., & Rozenberg, G. (Eds.), *Transformations and decompositions of nets* (Vol. 254, pp. 359–376). Lecture Notes in Computer ScienceBerlin, Germany: Springer-Verlag.

Bertozzi, D., Jalabert, A., Murali, S., Tamhankar, R., Stergiou, S., Benini, L., & De Micheli, G. (2005). NoC synthesis flow for customized domain specific multiprocessor systems-on-chip. *IEEE Transactions on Parallel and Distributed Systems, 16*(2), 113–129. doi:10.1109/TPDS.2005.22.

Bianchi, G., Tinnirello, I., & Scalia, L. (2005). Understanding 802.11e contention-based prioritization mechanisms and their coexistence with legacy 802.11 Stations. *IEEE Network, 19*(4), 28–34. doi:10.1109/MNET.2005.1470680.

Bieber, P., Bougnol, C., Castel, C., Heckmann, J.-P., Kehren, C., Metge, S., et al. (2004). Safety assessment with AltaRica. In *Proceedings of IFIP Congress Topical Sessions* (pp. 505-510). IFIP.

Bini, E., Buttazzo, G. C., & Lipari, G. (2009). Minimizing CPU energy in real-time systems with discrete speed management. *ACM Transactions on Embedded Computing Systems, 8*(4), 31:1–31:23.

Bini, E., Buttazzo, G. C., & Buttazzo, G. M. (2003). Rate monotonic scheduling: The hyperbolic bound. *IEEE Transactions on Computers, 52*(7), 933–942. doi:10.1109/TC.2003.1214341.

Bini, E., Buttazzo, G. C., Eker, J., Schorr, S., Guerra, R., & Fohler, G. et al. (2011). Resource management on multicore systems: The ACTORS approach. *IEEE Micro, 31*(3), 72–81. doi:10.1109/MM.2011.1.

Bityuckiy, A. (2005). *JFFS3 design issues*. Retrieved June, 2012, from http://www.linux-mtd.infradead.org/doc/JFFS3design.pdf

Bjerregaard, T., & Sparsø, J. (2004). Virtual channel designs for guaranteeing bandwidth in asynchronous network-on-chip. In *Proceedings of the IEEE Norchip Conference (NORCHIP 2004)*. IEEE.

Blake, I., Seroussi, G., & Smart, N. (1999). *Elliptic curves in cryptography*. London: Cambridge University Press.

Blake-Wilson, S., Bolyard, N., Gupta, V., Hawk, C., & Moeller, B. (2006). *Elliptic curve cryptography (ECC) cipher suites for transport layer security (TLS). RFC 4492*. IETF.

Bodington, C. E. (1995). *Planning, scheduling, and control integration in the process industries*. New York: McGraw-Hill.

Bollinger, J. G., et al. (1998). Visionary manufacturing challenges for 2020. In *Proceedings of the Committee on Visionary Manufacturing Challenges, Board on Manufacturing and Engineering Design, Commission on Engineering and Technical Systems*. Washington, DC: National Research Council, National Academy Press.

Boneva, H. Kastenberg, & Rensink. (2007). Simulating multigraph transformations using simple graphs. In *Proceedings of the Sixth International Workshop on Graph Transformation and Visual Modeling Techniques, Electronic Communications of the EASST, 2007*. EASST.

Bosch GmbH. (1991). *Controller area network specification v2.0*.

Bottoni, K. Parisi-Presicci, & Taentzer. (2002). Working on OCL with graph transformations. In *Proceedings of APPLIGRAPH Workshop on Applied Graph Transformation*, (pp. 1–10). APPLIGRAPH.

Boukhobza, J., Olivier, P., & Rubini, S. (2011). A cache management strategy to replace wear leveling techniques for embedded flash memory. In *Proceedings of the 2011 International Symposium on Performance Evaluation of Computer & Telecommunication Systems (SPECTS)*. SPECTS.

Bovet, D., & Cesati, M. (2005). *Understanding the Linux kernel*. O'Reilly & Associates, Inc..

Bozzano, M., & Villafiorita, A. (2006). *The FSAP/NuSMV-SA safety analysis platform*. Paper presented at ECAI 2006. Riva del Garda, Italy.

Brennan, R., Fletcher, M., & Norrie, D. (2002). An agent-based approach to reconfiguration of real-time distributed control systems. *IEEE Transactions on Robotics and Automation, 18*(4), 444–451. doi:10.1109/TRA.2002.802211.

Brennan, R., Vrba, P., Tichý, P., Zoitl, A., Sünder, C., Strasser, T., & Marík, V. (2008). Developments in dynamic and intelligent reconfiguration of industrial automation. *Computers in Industry, 59*(6), 533–547. doi:10.1016/j.compind.2008.02.001.

Brewer, J. E., & Gill, M. (Eds.). (2008). *Nonvolatile memory technologies with emphasis on flash*. Wiley-Interscience.

Brinksma., et al. (2003). *ROADMAP: Component-based design and integration platforms*. Retrieved from http://www.artist-embedded.org

Bruno, G., Agarwal, R., Castella, A., & Pescarmona, M. P. (1995). In De Michelis, G., & Diaz, M. (Eds.), *CAB: An environment for developing concurrent applications* (Vol. 935, pp. 141–160). Lecture Notes in Computer Science Berlin, Germany: Springer-Verlag. doi:10.1007/3-540-60029-9_38.

Buck, I., & Hanrahan, P. (2003). *Data parallel computation on graphics hardware*. Retrieved April 11, 2012 from http://hci.stanford.edu/cstr/reports/2003-03.pdf

Burns, A. (1994). Preemptive priority based scheduling: An appropriate engineering approach. In Advances in Real-Time Systems (pp. 225–248).

Burns, J. A., & King, B. B. (1999). On the design of feedback controllers for a convecting fluid flow. In *Proceedings of the International Conference on Control Applications*, (vol. 2, pp. 1157-1162). IEEE.

Burns, A., & Baxter, G. (2006). Time bands in systems structure. In *Structure for Dependability: Computer-Based Systems from an Interdisciplinary Perspective*. London: Springer. doi:10.1007/1-84628-111-3_4.

Burns, A., & Wellings, A. J. (2001). *Real-time systems and programming languages: Ada 95, Real-time java, and real-time POSIX* (3rd ed.). Reading, MA: Addison Wesley.

Butenhof, D. R. (1997). *Programming with POSIX threads*. Boston, MA: Addison-Wesley Longman Publishing Co..

Butkovski, A. G. (1982). *Green's functions and transfer functions handbook*. Chichester, UK: Ellis Herwood.

Buttazzo, G. C., & Cervin, A. (2007). Comparative assessment and evaluation of jitter control methods. In *Proceedings of the 15th International Conference on Real-Time and Network Systems* (pp. 137–144). Nancy, France: IEEE.

Buttazzo, G. C., Abeni, L., & Lipari, G. (1998). Elastic task model for adaptive rate control. In *Proceedings of the IEEE Real Time System Symposium*. Madrid, Spain: IEEE.

Buttazzo, G. C., Bertogna, M., & Yao, G. (2012). Limited preemptive scheduling for real-time systems: A survey. *IEEE Transitions on Industrial Informatics*.

Buttazzo, G. C. (2005). Rate monotonic vs. EDF: Judgment day. *Real-Time Systems, 29*(1), 5–26. doi:10.1023/B:TIME.0000048932.30002.d9.

Buttazzo, G. C., & Abeni, L. (2002). Adaptive workload management through elastic scheduling. *Real-Time Systems, 23*(1), 7–24. doi:10.1023/A:1015342318358.

Buttazzo, G. C., Bini, E., & Wu, Y. (2011). Partitioning parallel applications on multiprocessor reservations. *IEEE Transitions on Industrial Informatics, 7*(2), 302–315. doi:10.1109/TII.2011.2123902.

Buttazzo, G. C., Lipari, G., Caccamo, M., & Abeni, L. (2002). Elastic scheduling for flexible workload management. *IEEE Transactions on Computers, 51*(3), 289–302. doi:10.1109/12.990127.

Buttazzo, G. C., Marti, P., & Velasco, M. (2007). Quality-of-control management in overloaded real-time systems. *IEEE Transactions on Computers, 56*(2), 253–266. doi:10.1109/TC.2007.34.

Buyukkurt, B. A., Guo, Z., & Najjar, W. (2006). *Impact of loop unrolling on throughput, area and clock frequency in ROCCC: C to VHDL compiler for FPGAs.* Paper presented at the International Workshop on Applied Reconfigurable Computing (ARC 2006). Delft, The Netherlands.

Byrnes, C. A., Gilliam, D. S., & Shubov, V. I. (1994). Global lyapunov stabilization of a nonlinear distributed parameter system. In *Proceedings of the 33rd IEEE Conference on Decision and Control*. IEEE.

Caben, K., & Gent, P. (2008). *Image compression and the discreet cosine transform.* Paper presented at International Conference on Machine Learning and Cybernetics. New York, NY.

Caccamo, M., Buttazzo, G. C., & Sha, L. (2000). Capacity sharing for overrun control. In *Proceedings of the IEEE Real-Time Systems Symposium*. Orlando, FL: IEEE.

Caccamo, M., Buttazzo, G. C., & Thomas, D. (2005). Efficient reclaiming in reservation-based real-time systems with variable execution times. *IEEE Transactions on Computers, 54*(2), 198–213. doi:10.1109/TC.2005.25.

Cagalaban, G., Soh, W., & Kim, K. (2011). Devising an optimal scheme for wireless sensors for patient report tracking and monitoring in ubiquitous healthcare. *International Journal of Software Engineering and its Applications, 5*(4), 63-76.

Cansell & Mery. (2006). Formal and incremental construction of distributed algorithms: On the distributed reference counting algorithm. *Theoretical Computer Science, 364.*

Cena, G., Seno, L., Valenzano, A., & Zunino, C. (2010). On the performance of IEEE 802.11e wireless infrastructures for soft-real-time industrial applications. *IEEE Transactions on Industrial Informatics, 6*(3), 425–437. doi:10.1109/TII.2010.2052058.

Cena, G., & Valenzano, A. (2006). On the properties of the flexible time division multiple access technique. *IEEE Transactions on Industrial Informatics, 2*(2), 86–94. doi:10.1109/TII.2006.875510.

Cena, G., Valenzano, A., & Vitturi, S. (2008). Hybrid wired/wireless networks for real-time communications. *IEEE Industrial Electronics Magazine, 2*(1), 8–20. doi:10.1109/MIE.2008.917155.

Cengarle, M., & Knapp, A. (2002). Towards OCL/RT. *Lecture Notes in Computer Science, 239*, 390–409. doi:10.1007/3-540-45614-7_22.

Chakeresa, I. D., & Klein-Berndtb, L. (2002). AODVjr, AODV simplified. *Mobile Computing and Communications Review, 6*(3).

Chang, L. P., & Kuo, T. W. (2002). An adaptive striping architecture for flash memory storage systems of embedded systems. In *Proceedings of the 8th IEEE Real-Time and Embedded Technology and Applications Symposium*, (pp. 187-196). IEEE.

Chang, R. C., Qawami, B., & Sabet-Sharghi, F. (2006). Method and apparatus for managing an erase count block. *United States Patent, No 7,103,732*. Washington, DC: US Patent Office.

Chang, K.-D., & Chen, J.-L. (2012). A survey of trust management in WSNs, internet of things and future internet. *KSII Transactions on Internet and Information, 6*, 5–23.

Chapman, B., Huang, L., Biscondi, E., Stotzer, E., Shrivastava, A., & Gatherer, A. (2009). Implementing OpenMP on a high performance embedded multicore MPSoC. In *Proceedings of the 2009 IEEE International Symposium on Parallel & Distributed Processing (IPDPS '09)* (pp. 1-8). Washington, DC: IEEE Computer Society.

Chen, C. F., & Hsiao, C. H. (1997). Haar wavelet method for solving lumped and distributed parameter system. *IEEE Proceedings on Control Theory and Applications, 144*(1).

Chen, F., Koufaty, D. A., & Zhang, X. (2009). Understanding intrinsic characteristics and system implications of flash memory based solid state drives. In *Proceedings of the Eleventh International Joint Conference on Measurement and Modeling of Computer Systems* (pp. 181–192). IEEE.

Chen, M. K., Li, X. F., Lian, R., Lin, J. H., Liu, L., Liu, T., & Ju, R. (2005). Shangri-la: Achieving high performance from compiled network applications while enabling ease of programming. In *Proceedings of the 2005 ACM SIGPLAN Conference on Programming Language Design and Implementation (PLDI '05)*. New York, NY: ACM.

Chen, Y. H., & Piontek, E. D. (2000). *Robust modal control of distributed-parameter systems with uncertainty*. Paper presented at the American Control Conference. New York, NY.

Cheng, M. B., Radisavljevic, V., Chang, C. C., Lin, C. F., & Su, W. C. (2009). A sampled-data singularly perturbed boundary control for a heat conduction system with noncollocated observation. *IEEE Transactions on Automatic Control, 54*(6), 1305–1310. doi:10.1109/TAC.2009.2015522.

Cheng, R.-G., Wang, C.-Y., Liao, L.-H., & Yang, J.-S. (2006). Ripple: A wireless token-passing protocol for multi-hop wireless mesh networks. *IEEE Communications Letters, 10*(2), 123–125. doi:10.1109/LCOMM.2006.02005.

Chen, H. X., Chu, C. B., & Proth, J. M. (1998). An improvement of the Lagrangian relaxation approach for job shop scheduling: A dynamic programming method. *IEEE Transactions on Robotics and Automation, 14*(5), 786–795. doi:10.1109/70.720354.

Chen, H., & Hanisch, H.-M. (2001). Analysis of hybrid system based on hybrid net condition/event system model. *Discrete Event Dynamic Systems: Theory and Applications, 11*(1-2), 163–185.

Chew, L. W., Ang, L. M., & Seng, K. P. (2008). Survey of image compression algorithms in wireless sensor networks. In *Proceedings of International Symposium on Information Technology (ITSim 2008)*. ITSim.

Chiang, M., Cheng, C., & Wu, C. (2008). A new FTL-based flash memory management scheme with fast cleaning mechanism. In *Proceedings of the International Conference on Embedded Software and Systems (ICESS '08)*, (pp. 205-214). ICESS.

Cho, H., Shin, D., & Eom, Y. I. (2009). KAST: K-associative sector translation for NAND flash memory in real-time systems. In Proceedings of Design, Automation, and Test in Europe (DATE), (pp. 507-512). DATE.

Choi, Y., Lin, Y., Chong, N., Mahlke, S., & Mudge, T. (2009). Stream compilation for real-time embedded multicore systems. In *Proceedings of the 7th Annual IEEE/ACM International Symposium on Code Generation and Optimization (CGO '09)*. Washington, DC: IEEE Computer Society.

Chokshi, D. B., & Bhaduri, P. (2010). Performance analysis of FlexRay-based systems using real-time calculus, revisited. In *Proceedings of the Symposium on Applied Computing*. IEEE.

Christensen, S., & Hansen, N. D. (1994). In Valette, R. (Ed.). Lecture Notes in Computer Science: *Vol. 815. Coloured petri nets extended with channels for synchronous communication*. Zaragoza, Spain: Springer-Verlag. doi:10.1007/3-540-58152-9_10.

Christensen, S., & Petrucci, L. (2000). Modular analysis of petri nets. *Computer, 43*(3), 224–242. doi:10.1093/comjnl/43.3.224.

Christofides, P. D., & Daoutidis, P. (1997). Finite-dimensional control of parabolic PDE systems using approximate inertial manifolds. In *Proceedings of the 36th Conference on Decision & Control*. San Diego, CA: IEEE.

Christofides, P. D. (2001). *Nonlinear and robust control of partial differential equation systems: Methods and applications to transport-reaction processes*. Boston: Birkhauser.

Chung, T., Park, D., Park, S., Lee, D., Lee, S., & Song, H. (2009). A survey of flash translation layer. *Journal of Systems Architecture, 55*, 332–343. doi:10.1016/j.sysarc.2009.03.005.

Ciardo, G., & Lindermann, C. (1993). Analysis of deterministic and stochastic Petri nets. In *Proceedings of the 5th International Workshop on Petri Nets and Performance Models*. Toulouse, France: PNPM.

Ciardo, G., & Trivedi, K. S. (1991). A decomposition approach for stochastic petri net models. In *Proceedings of the Fourth International Workshop on Petri Nets and Performance Models* (pp. 74-83). Melbourne, Australia: IEEE. doi: 10.1109/PNPM.1991.238780

Colpo, J., & Mols, D. (2011). No strings attached. *Hydrocarbon Engineering, 16*, 47–52.

Compton, K., & Hauck, S. (2002). Reconfigurable computing: A survey of systems and software. *ACM Computing Surveys, 34*(2). doi:10.1145/508352.508353.

Conley, K. M. (2005). Zone boundary adjustment for defects in non-volatile memories. *United States Patent, No 6,901,498*. Washington, DC: US Patent Office.

Consel, C., Hamdi, H., Réveillère, L., Singaravelu, L., Yu, H., & Pu, C. (2003). Spidle: A DSL approach to specifying streaming applications. In *Proceedings of the 2nd International Conference on Generative Programming and Component Engineering (GPCE '03)*. New York, NY: Springer-Verlag New York, Inc.

Consortium, L. I. N. (2012). *LIN - Local interconnect network*. Retrieved from http://www.lin-subbus.org/

Continental Automotive Gmb, H. (2012). *OSEK/VDX portal*. Retrieved from http://portal.osek-vdx.org/

Cooperation, M. O. S. T. (2011). *Media oriented systems transport*. Retrieved from http://www.mostcooperation.com/

Coplien. (1995). A generative development - Process pattern language. In J. Coplien & D. Schmidt (Eds.), *Pattern Languages of Program Design*, (pp. 183–237). Reading, MA: Addison-Wesley.

Costa, A. (2010). *Petri net model decomposition - A model based approach supporting distributed execution*. (PhD thesis). Universidade Nova de Lisboa, Lisbon, Portugal.

Costa, A., & Gomes, L. (2009). Petri net partitioning using net splitting operation. In *Proceedings of the 7th IEEE International Conference on Industrial Informatics* (pp. 204-209). Cardiff, UK: IEEE. doi: 10.1109/INDIN.2009.5195804

Costa, A., Gomes, L., Barros, J. P., Oliveira, J., & Reis, T. (2008). Petri nets tools framework supporting FPGA-based controller implementations. In *Proceedings of the 34th Annual Conference of the IEEE Industrial Electronics Society (IECON'08)*. Orlando, FL: IECON. doi: 10.1109/IECON.2008.4758345

Cottet, D. Kaiser, & Mammeri. (2002). Scheduling in real-time systems. New York: John Wiley & Sons Ltd.

Coxhead, R. E. (1994). Integrated planning and scheduling systems for the refining industry. In Ciriani, T. A., & Leachman, R. C. (Eds.), *Optimization in industry* (Vol. 2, pp. 185–199). New York: Wiley.

Crnkovic & Larsson. (2002). *Building reliable component-based software systems*. Boston: Artech House.

Crnkovic. (2003). *Component-based approach for embedded systems*.

Curtain, R. F. (2003). On model reduction for control design for distributed parameter systems. In *Research Directions in DPS* (pp. 95–121). Philadelphia: SIAM. doi:10.1137/1.9780898717525.ch4.

Czerwinski, C. S., & Luh, P. B. (1994). Scheduling products with bills of materials using an improved Lagrangian relaxation technique. *IEEE Transactions on Robotics and Automation, 10*(2), 99–110. doi:10.1109/70.282535.

D'Andrea, A., & Dellurude, G. E. (2003). Distributed control design for spatially interconnected systems. *IEEE Transactions on Automatic Control, 48*(9), 1478–1495. doi:10.1109/TAC.2003.816954.

Daemen, J., & Kitsos, P. (2006). *The self-synchronizing stream cipher Moustique. eSTREAM Phase 2, the ECRYPT Stream Cipher Project.* ECRYPT NoE.

Daemen, J., & Rijmen, V. (2002). *The design of Rijndael: AES - The advanced encryption standard.* Berlin: Springer. doi:10.1007/978-3-662-04722-4.

Dally, W. J., & Towles, B. (2001). Route packets, not wires: On-chip inteconnection networks. In *Proceedings of the 38th annual Design Automation Conference, DAC '01* (pp. 684-689). New York, NY: ACM.

Dang & Gogolla. (2009). On Integrating OCL and triple graph grammars. In *Models in Software Engineering* (pp. 124–137). Berlin: Springer-Verlag.

Darling, P. (2010). *Intel, micron first to sample 3-Bit-Per-Cell NAND flash memory on industry-leading 25-nanometer silicon process technology.* Retrieved August, 2012, from http://newsroom.intel.com/community/intel_newsroom/blog/2010/08/17/intel-micron-first-to-sample-3-bit-per-cell-nand-flash-memory-on-industry-leading-25-nanometer-silicon-process-technology

Dasgupta, S., & Yakovlev, A. (2009). Desynchronisation technique using petri nets. *Electronic Notes in Theoretical Computer Science, 245*, 51–67. doi:10.1016/j.entcs.2009.07.028.

David, R., & Alla, H. (1992). *Petri nets & grafcet, tools for modelling discrete event systems.* London, UK: Prentice-Hall International Ltd..

David, R., & Alla, H. (2001). On hybrid Petri nets. *Discrete Event Dynamic Systems: Theory and Applications, 11*(1-2), 9–40.

Davis, R. I., Burns, A., Bril, R. J., & Lukkien, J. J. (2007). Controller area network (CAN) schedulability analysis: Refuted, revisited and revised. *Real-Time Systems.* doi:10.1007/s11241-007-9012-7.

Davis, R. I., Zabos, A., & Burns, A. (2008). Efficient exact schedulability tests for fixed priority real-time systems. *IEEE Transactions on Computers, 57*(9), 1261–1276. doi:10.1109/TC.2008.66.

de Jonge. (2009). Developing product lines with third-party components. *Electronic Notes in Theoretical Computer Science,* 63–80.

De Pellegrini, F., Miorandi, D., Vitturi, S., & Zanella, A. (2006). On the use of wireless networks at low level of factory automation systems. *IEEE Transactions on Industrial Informatics, 2*(2), 129–143. doi:10.1109/TII.2006.872960.

Deb, K., Pratap, A., Agarwal, S., & Meyarivan, T. (2002). A fast and elitist multiobjective genetic algorithm: NSGA-II. *IEEE Transactions on Evolutionary Computation, 6*(2), 182–197. doi:10.1109/4235.996017.

Debnath, B., Subramanya, S., Du, D., & Lilja, D. J. (2009). Large block CLOCK (LB-CLOCK): A write caching algorithm for solid state disks. In *Proceedings of the 2009 IEEE International Symposium on Modeling, Analysis & Simulation of Computer and Telecommunication Systems (MASCOTS).* IEEE.

Decotignie, J.-D. (2005). Ethernet-based real-time and industrial communications. *Proceedings of the IEEE, 93*(6), 1102–1117. doi:10.1109/JPROC.2005.849721.

Deng, J., & Chang, R. S. (1999). A priority scheme for IEEE 802.11 DCF access method. *IEICE Transactions on Communications. E (Norwalk, Conn.), 82-B*(1), 96–102.

Dertouzos, M. L. (1974). *Control robotics: The procedural control of physical processes.* Information Processing.

DES. (1977). *Data encryption standard.* Washington, DC: Federal Information Processing Standards Publication.

Description, F. E. S. T. O. (2008). *Martin Luther University, Germany.* Retrieved from http://aut.informatik.uni-halle.de/forschung/testbed/

Desel, J. (1992). A proof of the rank theorem for extended free choice nets. *Lecture Notes in Computer Science, 616*, 134–153. doi:10.1007/3-540-55676-1_8.

Di Natale, M. (2000). Scheduling the CAN bus with earliest deadline techniques. In *Proceedings of the 21st IEEE Real-Time Systems Symposium* (pp. 259-268). IEEE.

Dierks, T., & Rescorla, E. (2008). *Transport layer protocol version 1.2 (TLS). RFC 5246.* IETF.

Diffie, W., & Hellman, M. E. (1976). New directions in cryptography. *IEEE Transactions on Information Theory, 22,* 644–654. doi:10.1109/TIT.1976.1055638.

Dimond, R., Mencer, O., & Luk, W. (2005). CUSTARD - A customisable threaded FPGA soft processor and tools. In *Proceedings of the International Conference on Field Programmable Logic and Applications* (pp. 1-6). IEEE.

Ding, S., Tomiyama, H., & Takada, H. (2008). An effective GA-based scheduling algorithm for FlexRay systems. *IEICE Transactions on Information and Systems.* doi:10.1093/ietisy/e91-d.8.2115.

Dong, D., & McAvoy, T. J. (1994). Nonlinear principle component analysis-based on principal curves and neural network. In *Proceedings of the American Control Conference.* Baltimore, MD: ACC.

Dresner, L. (1983). *Similarity solutions of non-linear partial differential equations.* London: Pitman.

D'Souza & Wills. (1998). *Objects, components and frameworks: The catalysis approach.* Reading, MA: Addison-Wesley.

Dugan, J. B., Sullivan, K., & Coppit, D. (2000). Developing a low-cost high-quality software tool for dynamic fault tree analysis. *IEEE Transactions on Reliability, 49*(1), 49–59. doi:10.1109/24.855536.

Dupuy. (2000). Couplage de notations semi-formelles et formelles pour la spécification des systèmes d'information. (PhD thesis). Université Joseph Fourier – Grenoble 1, Grenoble, France.

Duran-Faundez, C. (2009). *Transmission d'images sur les réseaux de capteurs sans fils sous la contrainte de l'énergie.* (Unpublished doctoral dissertation). Nancy University. Nancy, France.

EAST-ADL Association. (2012). *EAST-ADL association web site.* Retrieved from http://www.east-adl.info/

Eindhoven University of Technology. (2009). *SDF3 official website.* Retrieved from http://www.es.ele.tue.nl/sdf3/

Electronic Engineering Times. (2011). *Non-volatile memory market to boom by 2015.* Retrieved August, 2012, from http://www.eetindia.co.in/ART_8800647303_1800009_NT_f00693e1.HTM

ElGamal, T. (1985). A public key cryptosystem and a signature scheme based on discrete logarithms. *IEEE Transactions on Information Theory, 31,* 469–472. doi:10.1109/TIT.1985.1057074.

EN50126. (1999). *Railway applications – The specification and demonstration of dependability, reliability, availability, maintainability and safety (RAMS).* Comite Europeen de Nomalisation Electrotechnique.

EN50128. (2002). *Railway applications – Software for railway control and protection systems.* Comite Europeen de Nomalisation Electrotechnique.

EN50129. (2002). *Railway applications – Safety related electronic systems for signalling.* Comite Europeen de Nomalisation Electrotechnique.

EnAS. (2008). *Martin Luther University, Germany.* Retrieved from http://aut.informatik.uni-halle.de/forschung/enas_demo/

Engel, J., & Mertens, R. (2005). *LogFS-finally a scalable flash file-system.*

Engel, J., Bolte, D., & Mertens, R. (2007). Garbage collection in logfs. In *Proceedings of Linyx Conference 2007.* Linyx.

Engels, H. (1939). Heckel, & Sauer. (2000). Dynamic meta modeling: A graphical approach to the operational semantics of behavioral diagrams in UML. *Lecture Notes in Computer Science,* 323–337.

Erge, S. C. (2004). *ZigBee/IEEE 802.15.4 summary.* Retrieved July 29, 2009, from http://staff.ustc.edu.cn/ustcsse/papers/SR10.ZigBee.pdf

Ergen, M., Lee, D., Sengupta, R., & Varaiya, P. (2004). WTRP-wireless token ring protocol. *IEEE Transactions on Vehicular Technology, 53*(6), 1863–1881. doi:10.1109/TVT.2004.836928.

Ericson, C. A. (1999). Fault tree analysis - A history. In *Proceedings of the 17th International System Safety Conference*. Retrieved from www.fault-tree.net/papers/ericson-fta-history.pdf

Esmaeilzadeh, H., Blem, E., St. Amant, R., Sankaralingam, K., & Burger, D. (2012). Dark silicon and the end of multicore scaling. In *Proceedings of the 38th International Symposium on Computer Architecture (ISCA)*. New York, NY: ACM.

Esparza, J., & Silva, M. (1992). A polynomial-time algorithm to decide liveness of bounded free choice nets. *Theoretical Computer Science, 102*(1), 185–205. doi:10.1016/0304-3975(92)90299-U.

Estrin, D., Girod, L., Pottie, G., & Srivastava, M. (2001). Instrumenting the world with wireless sensor networks. In *Proceedings of the IEEE International Conference on Acoustics, Speech, and Signal Processing*, (pp. 2033-2036). IEEE.

Faggioli, D., Trimarchi, M., Checconi, F., & Scordino, C. (2009). An EDF scheduling class for the linux kernel. In *Proceedings of the 11th Real-Time Linux Workshop* (pp. 197–204). Dresden, Germany: IEEE.

Faller. (2004). Project experience with IEC 61508 and its consequences. *Safety Science, (42)*, 405-422.

Fax, A. J., & Murray, R. M. (2004). Information flow and cooperative control of vehicle formations. *IEEE Transactions on Automatic Control, 49*(9), 1465–1476. doi:10.1109/TAC.2004.834433.

Feiler, P., Gluch, D., & Hudak, J. (2006). *The architecture analysis & design language (AADL): An introduction. Technical Note CMU/SEI-2006-TN-011*. Pittsburgh, PA: Carnegie Mellon University.

Fernandez-Alonso, E., Castells-Rufas, D., Risueno, S., Carrabina, J., & Joven, J. (2010). A NoC-based multi-softcore with 16 cores. In *Proceedings of the 17th IEEE International Conference on Electronics, Circuits, and Systems (ICECS)* (pp. 259-262). IEEE.

FlexRay. (2011). *FlexRay communications system protocol specification version 3.0.1*. Retrieved from http://www.flexray.com/

Floudas, C. A., & Lin, X. (2004). Continuous-time versus discrete-time approaches for scheduling of chemical processes: A review. *Computers & Chemical Engineering, 28*(11), 2109–2129. doi:10.1016/j.compchemeng.2004.05.002.

Foias, C., Jolly, M. S., Kevrekidis, I. G., Sell, G. R., & Titi, E. S. (1989). On the computation of inertial manifolds. *Physics Letters. [Part A], 131*, 433–437. doi:10.1016/0375-9601(88)90295-2.

Fournaris, A. P. (2010). Fault and simple power attack resistant RSA using montgomery modular multiplication. In *Proceedings of the IEEE International Symposium on Circuits and Systems (ISCAS 2010)* (pp. 1875-1878). IEEE.

Fournaris, A. P., & Hein, D. M. (2011). Trust management through hardware means: Design concerns and optimizations. In N. Voros, A. Mukherjee, N. Sklavos, K. Masselos, & M. Huebner (Eds.), *VLSI 2010 Annual Symposium* (Vol. 105, pp. 31-45). Springer.

Fournaris, A. P., & Koufopavlou, O. G. (2007). *Hardware design issues in elliptic curve cryptography for wireless systems*. CRC Press.

Fowler. (1997). *Analysis patterns: Reusable object models*. Reading, MA: Addison-Wesley Publishing Company.

France & Bruel. (2001). *Rigorous analysis and design with the unified modeling language*. Retrieved from http://www.univ-pau.fr/bruel/Tutorials/etapsTut.html

France, B. Larrondo-Petrie, & Grant. (1997). Rigorous object-oriented modeling: Integrating formal and informal notations. In *Proceedings of the 6th International AMAST Conference* (LNCS), (vol. 1349). Sydney, Australia: Springer-Verlag.

Franceschelli, A., Burgio, P., Tagliavini, G., Marongiu, A., Ruggiero, M., & Lombardi, M. … Benini, L. (2011). MPOpt-cell: A high-performance data-flow programming environment for the CELL BE processor. In Cascaval, Trancoso, & Prasanna (Eds.), *Proceedings of the 8th Conference on Computing Frontiers*. New York, NY: ACM.

Free Electrons. (2012). *Flash file system benchmarks*. Retrieved August, 2012, from http://elinux.org/Flash_Filesystem_Benchmarks

Freescale. (2012). *MPC5567: Qorivva 32-bit MCU for powertrain applications*. Retrieved from http://www.freescale.com/Webapp/sps/site/prod_summary.jsp?code=MPC5567

Fu, D., & Solinas, J. (2010). *Elliptic curve groups modulo a prime for IKE and IKEv2. RFC 5903*. IETF.

Gaisler, J. (2001). *The LEON processor user's manual, version 2.4.0*. Retrieved December 19, 2001, from www.gaisler.com

Galambos, J. (1995). *Advanced probability theory*. New York: Marcel Dekker Inc..

Galbraith, S. (2001). Limitations of constructive Weil descent. In Public-Key Cryptography and Computational Number Theory.

Gal, E., & Toledo, S. (2005). Algorithms and data structures for flash memories. *ACM Computing Surveys, 37*(2), 138–163. doi:10.1145/1089733.1089735.

Gamma, H. Johnson, & Vlissides. (1995). Design patterns. Reading, MA: Addison-Wesley.

Gao, D., Cai, J., & Chen, C. W. (2008). Admission control based on rate-variance envelop for VBR traffic over IEEE 802.11e HCCA WLANs. *IEEE Transactions on Vehicular Technology, 57*(3), 1778–1788. doi:10.1109/TVT.2007.909286.

Gebotys, C. H. (2010). *Security in embedded devices*. Berlin: Springer. doi:10.1007/978-1-4419-1530-6.

Genrich, H. J. (1987). In Brauer, W., Reisig, W., & Rozenberg, G. (Eds.), *Predicate/transition nets (Vol. 254*, pp. 207–247). Lecture Notes in Computer ScienceBerlin, Germany: Springer-Verlag.

Genssler et al. (2002). *PECOS in a nutshell*.

Genßler, N. (n.d.). [Components for embedded software the PECOS approach.]. *Schonhage.*.

George, L., & Courbin, P. (2011). Reconfiguration of uniprocessor sporadic real-time systems: The sensitivity approach. In *Knowledge on Reconfigurable Embedded Control Systems: Applications for Flexibility and Agility*. Hershey, PA: IGI Global.

George, L., Rivierre, N., & Spuri, M. (1996). *Preemptive and non-preemptive real-time uniprocessor scheduling. Technical Report, INRIA*. INRIA.

Ge, X., Paige, R. F., & McDermid, J. A. (2009). Probabilistic failure propagation and transformation analysis. In *Proceedings of Computer Safety, Reliability and Security (LNCS) (Vol. 5775*, pp. 215–478). Berlin: Springer. doi:10.1007/978-3-642-04468-7_18.

Gharbi, Khalgui, & Hanisch. (2009). Functional safety of component-based embedded control systems. In *Proceedings of the 2nd IFAC Workshop on Dependable Control of Discrete Systems*. IFAC.

Gharsellaoui, H., Gharbi, A., Khalgui, M., & Ben Ahmed, S. (2011). Feasible automatic reconfigurations of real-time OS tasks. In *Handbook of Research on Industrial Informatics and Manufacturing Intelligence: Innovations and Solutions*. Academic Press.

Girault, A. (2005). A survey of automatic distribution method for synchronous programs. In F. Maraninchi, M. Pouzet, & V. Roy (Eds.), *International Workshop on Synchronous Languages, Applications and Programs, SLAP'05*. Elsevier Science.

Gleixner, T., Haverkamp, F., & Bityutskiy, A. (2006). *UBI-unsorte, d block images*. Retrieved August, 2012, from http://linux-mtd.infradead.org/doc/ubidesign/ubidesign.pdf

Glismann, K., & Gruhn, G. (2001). Short-term scheduling and recipe optimization of blending processes. *Computers & Chemical Engineering, 25*(4), 627–634. doi:10.1016/S0098-1354(01)00643-3.

Godasi, S., Karakas, A., & Palazoglu, A. (1999). A study of the control on nonlinear distributed parameter systems. In *Proceedings of the American Control Conference*, (vol. 2, pp. 1096-1100). ACC.

Gogolla, M., Büttner, F., & Richters, M. (2007). USE: A UML-based specification environment for validating UML and OCL. *Science of Computer Programming, 69*, 27–34. doi:10.1016/j.scico.2007.01.013.

Gogolla, Ziemann, & Kuske. (2003). Towards an integrated graph based semantics for UML. *Electronic Notes in Theoretical Computer Science, 72*(3). doi:10.1016/S1571-0661(04)80619-4.

Gokturk, M. S., & Gurbuz, O. (2008). *Cooperation in wireless sensor networks: Design and performance analysis of a MAC protocol.* Paper presented at the Communications, 2008. New York, NY.

Goldberg, D. E. (1989). *Genetic algorithms in search, optimisation, and machine learning.* Reading, MA: Addison-Wesley Professional.

Golestani, S. J. (1994). A self-clocked fair queueing scheme for broadband applications. In *Proceedings IEEE INFOCOM '94: The Conference on Computer Communications. Networking for Global Communications,* (vol. 2, pp. 636 - 646). IEEE.

Gomes, L. (2005). On conflict resolution in petri nets models through model structuring and composition. In *Proceedings of 2005 3rd IEEE International Conference on Industrial Informatics* (pp. 489-494). IEEE.

Gomes, L., & Costa, A. (2006). Petri nets as supporting formalism within embedded systems co-design. In *Proceedings of the International Symposium on Industrial Embedded Systems (IES'06).* IES. doi: 10.1109/IES.2006.357468

Gomes, L., Barros, J. P., Costa, A., & Nunes, R. (2007). The input-output place-transition petri net class and associated tools. In *Proceedings of the 5th IEEE International Conference on Industrial Informatics (INDIN'07).* Vienna, Austria: IEEE.

Gomes, L., Barros, J. P., Costa, A., Pais, R., & Moutinho, F. (2005). Formal methods for embedded systems co-design: The FORDESIGN project. In *Proceedings of ReCoSoC'05 - Reconfigurable Communication-Centric Systems-on-Chip.* ReCoSoC.

Gomes, L., Costa, A., Barros, J. P., & Lima, P. (2007). From petri net models to VHDL implementation of digital controllers. In *Proceedings of 33rd Annual Conference of the IEEE Industrial Electronics Society (IECON'07).* Taipei, Taiwan: IEEE.

Gomes, L., Rebelo, R., Barros, J. P., Costa, A., & Pais, R. (2012). From petri net models to C implementation of digital controllers. In *Proceedings of IEEE International Symposium on Industrial Electronics (ISIE'10).* Bari, Italy: IEEE.

Gomes, L., & Barros, J. P. (2005). Structuring and composability issues in petri nets modeling. *IEEE Transactions on Industrial Informatics, 1*(2), 112–123. doi:10.1109/TII.2005.844433.

Gomes, L., & Fernandes, J. M. (Eds.). (2010). *Behavioral modeling for embedded systems and technologies: Applications for design and implementation.* Hershey, PA: IGI Global.

Gomes, L., & Lourenco, J. P. (2010). Rapid prototyping of graphical user interfaces for petri-net-based controllers. *IEEE Transactions on Industrial Electronics, 57,* 1806–1813. doi:10.1109/TIE.2009.2031188.

Goulding-Hotta, N., Sampson, J., Venkatesh, G., Garcia, S., Auricchio, J., & Huang, P. et al. (2011). The Green-Droid mobile application processor: An architecture for silicon's dark future. *Micro, 31*(2), 86–95.

Grecu, C., Ivanov, A., Pande, P. P., Jantsch, A., Salminen, E., Ogras, U. Y., & Marculescu, R. (2007). Towards open network-on-chip benchmarks. In *Proceedings of the First International Symposium on Networks-on-Chips, NOCS.* Washington, DC: IEEE Computer Society.

Grenier, M., Havet, L., & Navet, N. (2008). Configuring the communication on FlexRay - The case of the static segment. In *Proceedings of the 4th European Congress Embedded Real Time Software (ERTS).* ERTS.

Grewe, D., & O'Boyle, M. F. P. (2011). A static task partitioning approach for heterogeneous systems using OpenCL. In *Proceedings of the 20th International Conference on Compiler Construction (CC 2011)* (pp. 286-305). Berlin: Springer-Verlag.

Griffault, A., Arnold, A., Point, G., & Rauzy, A. (1999). The AltaRica formalism for describing concurrent systems. *Fundamenta Informaticae, 34.*

Groove. (2012). *Graphs for object-oriented verification.* Retrieved from http://groove.cs.utwente.nl/

Grunske, L., & Neumann, R. (2002). Quality improvement by integrating non-functional properties in software architecture specification. In *Proceedings of EASY'02 Second Workshop on Evaluation and Architecting System Dependability*, (pp. 23-32). San Jose, CA: EASY.

Grunske, L., Kaiser, B., & Papadopoulos, Y. I. (2005). Model-driven safety evaluation with state-event-vased components failure annotations. In *Proceedings of the 8ᵗʰ International Symposium on Component-Based Software Engineering* (pp. 33-48). IEEE.

Grunske, L., & Kaiser, B. (2005). *An automated dependability analysis method for COTS-based systems. LNCS* (pp. 178–190). Berlin: Springer.

Güdemann, M., Ortmeier, F., & Reif, W. (2008). Computing ordered minimal critical sets. In *Proceedings of Formal Methods for Automation and Safety in Railway and Automotive Systems*. IEEE.

Guerra, M. L., & Stefanini, L. (2005). Approximate fuzzy arithmetic operations using monotonic interpolations. *Fuzzy Sets and Systems*, *150*, 5–33. doi:10.1016/j.fss.2004.06.007.

Gungor, V., & Hancke, G. (2009). Industrial wireless sensor networks: challenges, design principles, and technical approaches. *IEEE Transactions on Industrial Electronics*, *56*, 4258–4265. doi:10.1109/TIE.2009.2015754.

Guo, L., & Billings, S. A. (2006). Identification of partial differential equations models for continuous spatio-temporal dynamical systems. *IEEE Transactions on Circuits and Wystems. II, Express Briefs*, *53*(8).

Gupta, A., Kim, Y., & Urgaonkar, B. (2009). DFTL: A flash translation layer employing demand-based selective caching of page-level address mappings. In *Proceedings of the 14th International Conference on Architectural Support for Programming Languages and Operating Systems (ASPLOS)*. ASPLOS.

Gupta, V., Wurm, M., Zhu, Y., Millard, M., Fung, S., & Gura, N. et al. (2005). Sizzle: A standards-based end-to-end security architecture for the embedded internet. *Pervasive and Mobile Computing*, 425–445. doi:10.1016/j.pmcj.2005.08.005.

Ha, S. R.K. (Soft Hard Real-Time Kernel). (n.d.). *Home page*. Retrieved from http://shark.sssup.it/

Haddad, S., Ilie, J. M., & Klai, K. (2002). An incremental verification technique using decomposition of petri nets. In *Proceedings of IEEE International Conference on Systems, Man and Cybernetics*, (Vol. 2, pp. 381- 386). IEEE. doi: 10.1109/ICSMC.2002.1173442

Hagiescu, A., Bordoloi, U. D., Chakraborty, S., Sampath, P., Ganesan, P. V. V., & Ramesh, S. (2007). Performance analysis of FlexRay-based ECU networks. In *Proceedings of The Design Automation Conference (DAC)*, (pp. 284-289). ACM Press.

Haibo, Z., Di Natale, M., Ghosal, A., & Sangiovanni-Vincentelli, A. (2011). Schedule optimization of time-triggered systems communicating over the FlexRay static segment. *IEEE Transactions on Industrial Informatics*, *7*(1), 1–17. doi:10.1109/TII.2010.2089465.

Halbwachs, N., Caspi, P., Raymond, P., & Pilaud, D. (1991). The synchronous dataflow programming language LUSTRE. In *Proceedings of the IEEE* (pp. 1305-1320). IEEE.

Hall, A. (2007). Realizing the benefits of formal methods. *Journal of Universal Computer Science*, *13*(5), 669–678.

Hamidian, A., & Korner, U. (2006). An enhancement to the IEEE 802.11e EDCA providing QoS guarantees. *Telecommunication Systems*, *31*(2-3), 195–212. doi:10.1007/s11235-006-6520-z.

Han, J., Taylor, E., Gao, J., & Fortes, J. (2005). Faults, error bounds and reliability of nanoelectronic circuits. In Proceedings of Application-Specific Systems, Architecture Processors, (pp. 247–253). IEEE.

Han, S., Zhu, X., Chen, D., Mok, A. K., & Nixon, M. (2011). Reliable and real-time communication in industrial wireless mesh networks. In *Proceedings of the 17th IEEE Real-Time and Embedded Technology and Applications Symposium (RTAS)* (pp. 3–12).

Hannig, F., & Jurgen, T. (2001). Design space exploration for massively parallel processor arrays. *Lecture Notes in Computer Science*, *2127*, 51–65. doi:10.1007/3-540-44743-1_5.

Hantrakoon, S., & Phonphoem, A. (2010). *Priority based HCCA for IEEE 802.11e*. Paper presented at the Communications and Mobile Computing (CMC). New York, NY.

Hanzálek, Z., Benes, D., & Waraus, D. (2011). Time constrained FlexRay static segment scheduling. In *Proceedings of The 10th International Workshop on Real-Time Networks*. IEEE.

Harkins, D., & Carrel, D. (1998). *The internet key exchange (IKE). RFC2409*. IETF.

Harrison, J. (1998). *Theorem proving with the real numbers*. Berlin: Springer. doi:10.1007/978-1-4471-1591-5.

Harrison, J. (2009). *Handbook of practical logic and automated reasoning*. Cambridge, UK: Cambridge University Press. doi:10.1017/CBO9780511576430.

Hasan, O. (2008). *Formal probabilistic analysis using theorem proving*. (PhD Thesis). Concordia University, Montreal, Canada.

Hasan, O., Abbasi, N., Akbarpour, B., Tahar, S., & Akbarpour, R. (2009). Formal reasoning about expectation properties for continuous random variables.[]. Berlin: Springer.]. *Proceedings of Formal Methods*, *5850*, 435–450.

Hasan, O., Abbasi, N., & Tahar, S. (2009). Formal probabilistic analysis of stuck-at faults in reconfigurable memory arrays.[LNCS]. *Proceedings of Integrated Formal Methods*, *5423*, 277–291. doi:10.1007/978-3-642-00255-7_19.

Hasan, O., Patel, J., & Tahar, S. (2011). Formal reliability analysis of combinational circuits using theorem proving. *Journal of Applied Logic*, *9*(1), 41–60. doi:10.1016/j.jal.2011.01.002.

Hasan, O., Tahar, S., & Abbasi, N. (2010). Formal reliability analysis using theorem proving. *IEEE Transactions on Computers*, *59*(5), 579–592. doi:10.1109/TC.2009.165.

Hausmann. (2001). *Dynamische metamodellierung zur spezifikation einer operationalen semantik von UML.* (Masters thesis). Universitt Paderborn.

Hausmann. (2005). *Dynamic meta modeling: A semantics description technique for visual modeling languages.* (PhD thesis). University of Paderborn.

Hausmann, Heckel, & Sauer. (2002). Dynamic meta modeling with time: Specifying the semantics of multimedia sequence diagrams. *Electronic Notes in Theoretical Computer Science*, *72*(3).

Hausmann, Heckel, & Sauer. (2004). Dynamic meta modeling with time: Specifying the semantics of multimedia sequence diagrams. *Software & Systems Modeling*, *3*(3), 181–193. doi:10.1007/s10270-003-0045-7.

Heimdahl, M. P., Choi, Y., & Whalen, M. W. (2002). Deviation analysis through model checking. In *Proceedings of the 17th IEEE International Conference on Automated Software Engineering*. Edinburgh, UK: IEEE.

Herrmann, G., Spurgeon, S. S., & Edwards, C. (2003). A model-based sliding mode control methodology applied to the HDA-plant. *Journal of Process Control*, 2014–2019.

Herstellerinitiative Software. (2007). *Requirements interchange format (RIF), version 1.1a*. Retrieved from http://www.automotive-his.de/rif/

Hnninen, K., & Riutta, T. (2003). *Optimal design*. (Masters thesis). Mlardalens Hgskola, Dept of Computer Science and Engineering.

Holscher, Ziemann, & Gogolla. (2006). On translating UML models into graph transformation systems. Journal of Visual Languages and Computing Archive, 17(1).

Honkomp, S. J., Lombardo, S., Rosen, O., & Pekny, J. F. (2000). The curse of reality – Why process scheduling optimization problems are difficult in practice. *Computers and Chemical Engineering*, *24*(2-7), 323-328.

Hornik, H., Stinchcombe, M., & White, H. (1989). Multilayer feedforward networks are universal approximators. *Neural Networks*, *2*, 359–366. doi:10.1016/0893-6080(89)90020-8.

Hotta, Y., Sato, M., Nakajima, Y., & Ojima, Y. (2004). OpenMP implementation and performance on embedded Renesas M32R chip multiprocessor. In *Proceedings of the 6th European Workshop on OpenMP (EWOMP 2004)*. EWOMP.

Hsieh, J., Tsai, Y., Kuo, T., & Lee, T. (2008). Configurable flash-memory management: Performance versus overheads. *IEEE Transactions on Computers*, *57*(11), 1571–1583. doi:10.1109/TC.2008.61.

Hurd, J. (2002). *Formal verification of probabilistic algorithms*. (PhD Thesis). University of Cambridge, Cambridge, UK.

Hwang, G.-H., & Cho, D.-H. (2004). Fast retransmission mechanism for VoIP in IEEE 802.11e wireless LANs. In *Proceedings of the IEEE 60th Vehicular Technology Conference (VTC2004-Fall)*, (vol. 7, pp. 4996 - 5000). IEEE.

Hwang, G.-H., & Cho, D.-H. (2005). New access scheme for VoIP packets in IEEE 802.11e wireless LANs. *IEEE Communications Letters*, 9(7), 667–669. doi:10.1109/LCOMM.2005.1461699.

IEC 61508. (1992). *Functional safety of electrical/electronic programmable electronic systems: Generic aspects: Part 1: General requirements*. Geneva, Switzerland: International Electrotechnical Commission.

IEC. (2000). *61508 – Functional safety of electrical/electronic/programmable electronic safety-related systems*. Geneva, Switzerland: International Electrotechnical Commission.

IEC61513. (2002). *Nuclear power plants – Instrumentation and control for systems important to safety – General requirements for systems*. Geneva, Switzerland: International Electrotechnical Commission.

IEC-62601. (2011). *IEC/PAS 62601: Industrial communication networks – Fieldbus specifications – WIA-PA communication network and communication profile*. International Electrotechnical Commission.

IEC-62734. (2012). *IEC 62734: Industrial communication networks – Fieldbus specifications – Wireless systems for industrial automation: process control and related applications (based on ISA 100.11a)*. International Electrotechnical Commission.

IEEE P802.11e/D10.0. (2005). *Wireless LAN medium access control (MAC) and physical layer (PHY) specifications amendment 7: Medium access control (MAC) quality of service enhancements*. IEEE.

IEEE. (2005). *Standard for information technology - Wireless LAN medium access control (MAC) and physical layer (PHY) specifications amendment 8: Medium access control (MAC) quality of service enhancements. IEEE Std 802.11e-2005*. IEEE.

IEEE. (2007). Standard for information technology - Wireless LAN medium access control (MAC) and physical layer (PHY) specifications. ANSI/IEEE Std 802.11, 1999 Ed. (R2007). IEEE.

IEEE. (2012). *IEEE Xplore digital library*. Retrieved from http://ieeexplore.ieee.org/

IEEE. (n.d.). 802.11i, IEEE medium access control (MAC) security enhancements. IEEE Task Group I P802.11i.

IEEE. IEC-62591. (2010). *IEC 62591: Industrial communication networks – Wireless communication network and communications profiles – WirelessHART*. International Electrotechnical Commission (IEC).

IEEE-802.15.4. (2006). Part 15.4: Wireless medium access control (MAC) and physical layer (PHY) specifications for low-rate wireless personal area networks (WPANs). *Revision of IEEE Std 802.15.4-2003*. IEEE.

IEEE-802.15.5. (2009). *Part 15.5: Mesh topology capability in wireless personal area networks (WPANs)*. IEEE.

Ierapetritou, M. G., & Floudas, C. A. (1998). Effective continuous-time formulation for short-term scheduling, 1: Multipurpose batch processes. *Industrial & Engineering Chemistry Research*, 37(11), 4341–4359. doi:10.1021/ie970927g.

Intel. (n.d.). *Intel® Atom™ processor E6x5C series*. Retrieved April 11, 2012 from http://www.intel.com/p/en_US/embedded/hwsw/hardware/atom-e6x5c/overview

Intel. (n.d.). *Parallel building blocks*. Retrieved April 11, 2012 from http://software.intel.com/en-us/articles/intel-parallel-building-blocks/

International Electrotechnical Commission. (2005). *Function blocks: Part 1: Architecture*. Geneva, Switzerland: International Eectrotechnical Commission.

International Organization for Standardization. (2009). *ISO/DIS 26262*. Geneva, Switzerland: ISO.

International Organization for Standardization. (2011). *Road vehicles – Functional safety – Part 1 to 9. International Standard ISO/FDIS 26262*. ISO.

Ishii, H., Tada, M., & Masuda, T. (1992). Two scheduling problems with fuzzy due dates. *Fuzzy Sets and Systems*, 46, 339–347. doi:10.1016/0165-0114(92)90372-B.

ISO11898-1. (2003). *ISO 11898-1: Road vehicles—Interchange of digital information—Controller area network (CAN) for high-speed communication*. International Organization for Standardization.

Isograph Software. (2002). *Fault tree+ v11: Software tool*. Retrieved April 10, 2012 from http://www.isograph-software.com/index.htm

ITI. (2012). *SimulationX v3.5: Software tool*. Retrieved April 10, 2012 from http://www.itisim.com/

Jacob, B., & Zwart, H. (1999). Equivalent conditions for stabilizability of infinite dimensional systems with admissible control operators. *SIAM Journal on Control and Optimization*, 37(5), 1149–1455. doi:10.1137/S036301299833344X.

Jaikumar, R. (1974). An operational optimization procedure for production scheduling. *Computers & Operations Research*, 1(2), 191–200. doi:10.1016/0305-0548(74)90045-8.

Janapsatya, A., Ignjatovi, A., & Parameswaran, S. (2006). Finding optimal L1 cache configuration for embedded systems. In *Proceedings of the Asia and South Pacific Design Automation Conference*. IEEE.

Jang, J. S. R. (1993). ANFIS: Adaptive-network-based fuzzy inference system. *IEEE Transactions on Systems, Man, and Cybernetics*, 23(3), 665–685. doi:10.1109/21.256541.

Jensen, K. (1992). *Coloured petri nets: Basic concepts, analysis methods and practical use*. Berlin, Germany: Springer-Verlag.

Jeon, D., Garcia, S., Louie, C., & Taylor, M. B. (2011). Parkour: Parallel speedup estimates for serial programs. In *Proceedings of the 3rd USENIX Workshop on Hot Topics in Parallelism (HotPar)*. HotPar.

Jerraya, A. (2008). System compilation for MPSoC based on NoC. In *Proceedings of MPSoC '08, 8th International Forum on Application-Specific Multi-Processor SoC*. MPSoC.

Jiang, S., Zhang, L., Yuan, X., Hu, H., & Chen, Y. (2011). SFTL: An efficient address translation for flash memory by exploiting spatial locality. In *Proceedings of 2011 IEEE 27th Symposium on Mass Storage Systems and Technologies (MSST)*. IEEE.

Jia, Z., & Ierapetritou, M. (2004). Efficient short-term scheduling of refinery operations based on a continuous time formulation. *Computers & Chemical Engineering*, 28(6-7), 1001–1019. doi:10.1016/j.compchemeng.2003.09.007.

Jia, Z., Ierapetritou, M., & Kelly, J. D. (2003). Refinery short-term scheduling using continuous time formation: Crude oil operations. *Industrial & Engineering Chemistry Research*, 42(13), 3085–3097. doi:10.1021/ie020124f.

Jo, H., Kang, J., Park, S., Kim, J., & Lee, J. (2006). FAB: A flash-aware buffer management policy for portable media players. *IEEE Transactions on Consumer Electronics*, 52(2), 485–493. doi:10.1109/TCE.2006.1649669.

Johnson, D., & Menezes, A. (1999). *The elliptic curve digital signature algorithm (ECDSA) (Technical report CORR 99-06)*. Waterloo, Canada: University of Waterloo.

Jonsson, M., & Kunert, K. (2009). Towards reliable wireless industrial communication with real-time guarantees. *IEEE Transactions on Industrial Informatics*, 5(4), 429–442. doi:10.1109/TII.2009.2031921.

Joshi, A., & Sevick-Muraca, E. M. (2004). Adaptive finite element methods for distributed parameter system identification: Applications in fluorescence enhanced frequency domain optical tomography. In *Proceedings of the American Control Conference*, (vol. 3, pp. 2263-2267). ACC.

Jovanovic, M. R., & Barnieh, B. (2003). Lyapunov-based state-feedback distributed control of systems on lattices. In *Proceedings of the American Control Conference*, (pp. 101-106). ACC.

Joven, J., Angiolini, F., Castells-Rufas, D., De Micheli, G., & Carrabina-Bordoll, J. (2010). QoS-ocMPI: QoS-aware on-chip message passing library for NoC-based many-core MPSoCs. In *Proceedings of the 2nd Workshop on Programming Models for Emerging Architectures (PMEA'10)*. PMEA.

Joye, M., & Tymen, C. (2001). Protections against differential analysis – An algebraic approach. In *Proceedings of the Third International Workshop on Cryptographic Hardware and Embedded Systems* (pp. 377-390). IEEE.

Jubin & Friedrichs. (2000). *Enterprise javabeans by example*. Upper Saddle River, NJ: Prentice Hall.

Jurdjevic, V. (1997). *Geometric control theory*. New York: Cambridge University Press.

Kaiser, B., Gramlich, C., & Forster, M. (2007). State/event fault trees – A safety analysis model for software controlled systems. *Reliability Engineering & System Safety*, *92*, 1521–1537. doi:10.1016/j.ress.2006.10.010.

Kang, S., Park, S., Jung, H., Shim, H., & Cha, J. (2009). Performance trade-offs in using NVRAM write buffer for flash memory-based storage devices. *IEEE Transactions on Computers*, *58*(6), 744–758. doi:10.1109/TC.2008.224.

Karuppiah, R., Furmanb, K. C., & Grossmann, I. E. (2008). Global optimization for scheduling refinery crude oil operations. *Computers & Chemical Engineering*, *32*(11), 2745–2766. doi:10.1016/j.compchemeng.2007.11.008.

Kaufman, C. (2005). *Internet key exchange (IKEv2) protocol. RFC 4306*. IETF.

Kawaguchi, A., Nishioka, S., & Motoda, H. (1995). A flash memory based file system. In *Proceedings of the USENIX 1995 Technical Conference*. USENIX.

Keryel, R. (2009). *GPU & open source*. Paper presented at the Forum Ter@tec 2009. New York, NY.

Keulen, B. V. (1993). *H∞ control for distributed parameter systems: A state space approach*. Boston: Birkhauser. doi:10.1007/978-1-4612-0347-6.

Khalgui, M. (2008). A deployment methodology of real-time industrial control applications in distributed controllers. *Computers in Industry Journal*, *59*(5), 450–462. doi:10.1016/j.compind.2007.12.008.

Khalgui, M. (2010). NCES-based modeling and CTL-based verification of reconfigurable embedded control systems. *Computers in Industry Journal*, *61*(3), 198–212. doi:10.1016/j.compind.2009.09.004.

Khalgui, M. (2011). Reconfigurable multiagent embedded control systems: From modeling to implementation. In Khalgui, M., & Hanisch, H. M. (Eds.), *Reconfigurable Embedded Control Systems: Applications for Flexibility and Agility* (pp. 1–30). Academic Press. doi:10.1109/TC.2010.96.

Khalgui, M., & Mosbahi, O. (2010). Feasible distributed reconfigurable architecture for embedded IEC61499 function blocks. *International Journal of Discrete Event Control Systems*, *1*(1), 99–113.

Khalgui, M., & Mosbahi, O. (2011). Specification and verification of reconfigurable embedded architectures. *International Journal of Discrete Event Control Systems*, *1*(1), 1–18.

Khalgui, M., Mosbahi, O., Li, Z., & Hanisch, H.-M. (2010). Reconfiguration of distributed embedded-control systems. *IEEE/ASME Transactions on Mechatronics*.

Kim, H., & Ahn, S. (2008). BPLRU: A buffer management scheme for improving random writes in flash storage. In *Proceedings of the 6th USENIX Conference on File and Storage Technologies (FAST)*. USENIX.

Kim, B., & Park, K. (2009). Probabilistic delay model of dynamic message frame in FlexRay protocol. *IEEE Transactions on Consumer Electronics*. doi:10.1109/TCE.2009.4814417.

Kim, J., Kim, J. M., Noh, S. H., Min, S. L., & Cho, Y. (2002). A space-efficient flash translation layer for compact flash systems. *IEEE Transactions on Consumer Electronics*, *48*(2), 366–375. doi:10.1109/TCE.2002.1010143.

Kim, K., & Montenegro, G. (2007). *6LoWPAN ad hoc on-demand distance vector routing (LOAD). IETF Internet Draft: draft-daniel-6lowpan-load-adhoc-routing-03*. IETF.

Kim, K., & Park, S. (2007). *Dynamic MANET on-demand for 6LoWPAN (DYMO-low) routing. Internet Draft: draft-montenegro-6lowpan-dymolow-routing-03*. IETF.

Kim, K., & Yoo, S. (2005). *Hierarchical routing over 6LoWPAN (HiLow). IETF: Internet Draft: draft-deniel-6lowpan-hilow-hierarchicalrouting-00.txt*. IETF.

Kimura, N., & Latifi, S. (2005). A survey on data compression in wireless sensor networks. In *Proceedings of the International Conference on Information Technology: Coding and Computing (ITCC 2005)*, (vol. 2, pp. 8-13). ITCC.

Kish, L. B. (2002). End of Moore's law: Thermal (noise) death of integration in micro and nano electronics. *Physics Letters. [Part A], 305*(3-4), 144–149. doi:10.1016/S0375-9601(02)01365-8.

Kitsos, P., Sklavos, N., Parousi, M., & Skodras, A. N. (2012). A comparative study of hardware architectures for lightweight block ciphers. *Computers & Electrical Engineering, 38*(1), 148–160. doi:10.1016/j.compeleceng.2011.11.022.

Kitsos, P., Sklavos, N., Provelengios, G., & Skodras, A. (2012). FPGA-based analysis of stream ciphers ZUC, Snow3g, Grain v1, Mickey v2, Trivium and E0, accepted with minor revisions. In *Microprocessors and Microsystems: Embedded Hardware Design*. London: Elsevier.

Kjellsson, J., Vallestad, A. E., Steigmann, R., & Dzung, D. (2009). Integration of a wireless I/O interface for PROFIBUS and PROFINET for factory automation. *IEEE Transactions on Industrial Electronics, 56*(10), 4279–4287. doi:10.1109/TIE.2009.2017098.

Klir, G. J., St. Clair, U., & Bo, Y. (1997). *Fuzzy set theory-foundations and applications*. New Delhi: PHI Publishers.

Klöckner, A. (2012). *PyCUDA*. Retrieved April 11, 2012 from http://mathema.tician.de/software/pycuda

Koblitz, N. (1987). Elliptic curve cryptosystems. *Mathematics of Computation, 48*, 203–209. doi:10.1090/S0025-5718-1987-0866109-5.

Koc, C. (2008). *Cryptographic engineering*. Berlin: Springer.

Koc, C. K., & Acar, T. (1998). Montgomery multiplication in GF (2^k). *Designs, Codes and Cryptography, 14*(1), 57–69. doi:10.1023/A:1008208521515.

Kocher, P., Ravi, S., Lee, R., McGraw, G., & Raghunathan, A. (2004). Security as a new dimension in embedded system design. In *Proceedings of the 41st Annual Conference on Design Automation - DAC '04* (pp. 753). New York: ACM Press.

Kocher, P., Jaffe, J., & Jun, B. (1999). Differential power analysis.[Springer-Verlag.]. *Advances in Cryptology Proceedings of Crypto, 1999*, 388–397. doi:10.1007/3-540-48405-1_25.

Kondili, E., Pantelides, C. C., & Sargent, R. W. H. (1993). A general algorithm for short-term scheduling for batch operations—1: MILP formulation. *Computers & Chemical Engineering, 17*(2), 211–227. doi:10.1016/0098-1354(93)80015-F.

Konstantinou, E., Kontogiorgis, A., Stamatiou, Y. C., & Zaroliagis, C. (2010). On the efficient generation of prime order elliptic curves. *Journal of Cryptology, 23*(3), 477–503. doi:10.1007/s00145-009-9037-2.

Konstantinou, E., Stamatiou, Y. C., & Zaroliagis, C. (2002). *On the efficient generation of elliptic curves over prime fields*. Berlin: Springer-Verlag.

Konstantinou, E., Stamatiou, Y. C., & Zaroliagis, C. (2007). Efficient generation of secure elliptic curvers. *International Journal of Information Security, 6*(1), 47–63. doi:10.1007/s10207-006-0009-3.

Kopetz, H. (1998). Time-triggered model of computation. In *Proceedings of the Real-Time Systems Symposium*, (pp. 168 - 177). IEEE.

Koren, G., & Shasha, D. (1995). Skip-over: Algorithms and complexity for overloaded systems that allow skips. In *Proceedings of the IEEE Real-Time Systems Symposium*. Pisa, Italy: IEEE.

Kou, S., & Palsberg, J. (2010). From OO to FPGA: Fitting round objects into square hardware? In *Proceedings of OOPSLA'10, ACM SIGPLAN Conference on Object-Oriented Programming Systems, Languages and Applications*. ACM.

Kramer, M. A. (1991). Nonlinear principal component analysis using auto-associative neural networks. *AIChE Journal. American Institute of Chemical Engineers, 37*, 234–243. doi:10.1002/aic.690370209.

Kravitz, D. W. (1993). *Digital signature algorithm*. U.S. Patent #5,231,668. Washington, DC: US Patent Office.

Krishna, C. M., & Shin, K. G. (1997). *Real-time systems*. Singapore: McGraw-Hill.

Kudva, G. A., Elkamel, A., Pekny, J. F., & Reklaitis, G. V. (1994). A heuristic algorithm for scheduling multiproduct plants with production deadlines, intermediate storage limitations, and equipment changeover cost. *Computers & Chemical Engineering, 18*, 859–875. doi:10.1016/0098-1354(93)E0018-5.

Ku, H., & Karimi, I. (1991). Evaluation of simulated annealing for batch process scheduling. *Industrial & Engineering Chemistry Research*, *30*(1), 163–169. doi:10.1021/ie00049a024.

Kumar, B., Mesman, B., Theelen, H., & Corporaal, Y. (2008). Analyzing composability of applications on MPSoC platforms. *Journal of Systems Architecture*. doi:10.1016/j.sysarc.2007.10.002.

Kuske, G. Kollmann, & Kreowski. (2002). An integrated semantics for UML class, object and state diagrams based on graph transformation. Lecture Notes in Computer Science, 11–28.

Kweon, S.-K., & Shin, K. G. (2003). Statistical real-time communication over ethernet. *IEEE Transactions on Parallel and Distributed Systems*, *14*(3), 322–335. doi:10.1109/TPDS.2003.1189588.

Kwon, Y., Fang, Y., & Latchman, H. (2004). Design of MAC protocols with fast collision resolution for wireless local area networks. *IEEE Transactions on Wireless Communications*, *3*(3), 793–807. doi:10.1109/TWC.2004.827731.

Lahiri, K., Raghunathan, & Dey. (2000). Efficient exploration of the SoC communication architecture design space. *IEEE Computer Aided Design*.

Lamastra, G., Lipari, G., & Abeni, L. (2001). A bandwidth inheritance algorithm for real-time task synchronization in open systems. In *IEEE Proceedings of the 22nd Real-Time Systems Symposium*. London, UK: IEEE.

Lamastra, G., Lipari, G., Buttazzo, G. C., Casile, A., & Conticelli, F. (1997). HARTIK 3.0: A portable system for developing real-time applications. In *Proceedings of the 4th IEEE International Conference on Real-Time Computing Systems and Applications* (pp. 43–50). Taipei, Taiwan: IEEE.

Larman. (2001). *Applying UML and patterns* (2nd ed). Upper Saddle River, NJ: Prentice Hall.

Lasiecka, I., & Triggiani, R. (2000). *Control theory for partial differential equations. Cambridge, UK*. Cambridge: University Press.

Lautenbach, K., & Ridder, H. (1994). Liveness in bounded petri nets which are covered by T-invariants. In *Proceedings 15th International Conference* (LNCS), (vol. 815, pp. 358–375). Berlin: Springer.

Le Guernic, P., Gautier, T., Le Borgne, M., & Le Maire, C. (1991). Programming real-time applications with SIGNAL. *Proceedings of the IEEE*, *79*(9), 1321–1336. doi:10.1109/5.97301.

Ledang & Souquires. (2001). *Formalizing UML behavioral diagrams with B*. Paper presented in the Tenth OOPSLA Workshop on Behavioral Semantics: Back to Basics. Tampa Bay, FL.

Lee, J., Tiao, A., & Yen, J. (1994). A fuzzy rule-based approach to real-time scheduling. In *Proceedings of the FUZZ-IEEE*, (pp. 1394 – 1399). IEEE.

Lee, S., Ha, K. N., Park, J. H., & Lee, K. C. (2005). NDIS-based virtual polling algorithm of IEEE 802.11b for guaranteeing the real-time requirements. In *Proceedings of IECON*, (pp. 2427 - 2432). IECON

Lee, H., Pinto, J. M., Grossmann, I. E., & Park, S. (1996). Mixed integer linear programming model for refinery short-term scheduling of crude oil unloading with inventory management. *Industrial & Engineering Chemistry Research*, *35*(5), 1630–1641. doi:10.1021/ie950519h.

Lee, J. H., Morari, M., & Garcia, C. E. (1994). State-space representation of model predictive control. *Automatica*, *30*(4), 707–717. doi:10.1016/0005-1098(94)90159-7.

Lee, J. M., Zhang, R., Zheng, J., Ahn, G.-S., Zhu, C., Rim, T. P., & Sun, J. R. (2010). IEEE 802.15.5 WPAN mesh standard-low rate part: Meshing the wireless sensor networks. *IEEE Journal on Selected Areas in Communications*, *28*, 973–983. doi:10.1109/JSAC.2010.100902.

Leen, G., & Heffernan, D. (2002). TTCAN: A new time-triggered controller area network. *Microprocessors and Microsystems*, *26*(2), 77–94. doi:10.1016/S0141-9331(01)00148-X.

Lee, S. W., Park, D. J., Chung, T. S., Lee, D. H., Park, S., & Song, H. J. (2007). A log buffer based flash translation layer using fully associative sector translation. *ACM Transactions on Embedded Computing Systems*, *6*(3), 1–27. doi:10.1145/1275986.1275990.

Lee, S., Shin, D., Kim, Y., & Kim, J. (2008). LAST: Locality aware sector translation for NAND flash memory based storage systems. *ACM SIGOPS Operating Systems Review*, *42*(6), 36–42. doi:10.1145/1453775.1453783.

Lehoczky, J. P. (1990). Fixed priority scheduling of periodic task sets with arbitrary deadlines. In *Proceedings of the 11th Real-Time Systems Symposium*, (pp. 201-209). IEEE.

Leitão, P. (2004). *An agile and adaptive holonic architecture for manufacturing control.* (PhD Thesis). University of Porto.

Lemieux, J. (2001). *Programming in the OSEK/VDX environment.* CMP.

Leung, J.-T., & Merril, M. (1980). A note on preemptive scheduling of periodic real-time tasks. *Information Processing Letters*, *3*(11), 115–118. doi:10.1016/0020-0190(80)90123-4.

Leung, J., & Whitehead, J. (1982). On the complexity of fixed-priority scheduling of periodic real-time tasks. *Performance Evaluation*, *2*(4), 237–250. doi:10.1016/0166-5316(82)90024-4.

Leuschel & Butler. (2003). ProB: A model checker for B. In *Proceedings of FME 2003: Formal Methods* (LNCS), (vol. 2805, pp. 855–874). Berlin: Springer-Verlag.

Lewis, R. (2001). *Modelling control systems using IEC 61499.* London: Institution of Engineering and Technology.

Li, J. J., Wang, S. C., Hsu, P. C., Chen, P. Y., & Lee, J. K. (2010). A multi-core software API for embedded MPSoC environments. In *Proceedings of the Second Russia-Taiwan Conference on Methods and Tools of Parallel Programming Multicomputers (MTPP'10)*. Berlin: Springer-Verlag.

Li, W., Peng Pang, Z. Z., & Liu, J. (2010). *SPIHT algorithm combined with Huffman encoding.* Paper presented at the Third International Symposium on Intelligent Information Technology and Security Informatics. New York, NY.

Lin, C., & Brandt, S. A. (2005). Improving soft real-time performance through better slack management. In *Proceedings of the IEEE Real-Time Systems Symposium.* Miami, FL: IEEE.

Lipari, G., & Bini, E. (2003). Resource partitioning among real-time applications. In *Proceedings of the 15th Euromicro Conference on Real-Time Systems* (pp. 151–158). Porto, Portugal: Euromicro.

Lisagor, O., McDermid, J. A., & Pumfrey, D. J. (2006). Towards a practicable process for automating safety analysis. In *Proceedings of the 16th International Ship and Offshore Structures Conference (ISSC'06)*, (pp. 596-607). Albuquerque, NM: Systems Safety Society.

Litoiu, M., & Tadei, R. (1997). Real-time task scheduling allowing fuzzy due dates. *European Journal of Operational Research*, *100*, 475–481. doi:10.1016/S0377-2217(96)00094-X.

Litoiu, M., & Tadei, R. (2001). Fuzzy scheduling with application to real-time systems. *Fuzzy Sets and Systems*, *121*, 523–535. doi:10.1016/S0165-0114(99)00176-1.

Litoiu, M., & Tadei, R. (2001). Real-time task scheduling with fuzzy deadlines and processing times. *Fuzzy Sets and Systems*, *117*, 35–45. doi:10.1016/S0165-0114(98)00283-8.

Liu, F., & Chaudhary, V. (2003). A practical OpenMP compiler for system on chips. In *Proceedings of the OpenMP Applications and Tools 2003 International Conference on OpenMP Shared Memory Parallel Programming (WOMPAT'03)*. Berlin: Springer-Verlag.

Liu, J., Lin, K., & Natarajan, S. (1987). Scheduling real-time, periodic jobs using imprecise results. In *Proceedings of the IEEE Real-Time System Symposium* (pp. 210-217). San Jose, CA: IEEE.

Liu, T., Tanougast, C., & Weber, S. (2006). *Toward a methodology for optimizing algorithm-architecture adequacy for implementation reconfigurable system.* Paper presented at the 13th IEEE International Conference on Electronics, Circuits and Systems ICECS '06. New York, NY.

Liu, C., & Layland, J. (1973). Scheduling algorithms for multiprogramming in a hard-real-time environment. *Journal of the Association for Computing Machinery*, *20*(1), 46–61. doi:10.1145/321738.321743.

Liu, J. W. (2000). *Real-time systems.* Upper Saddle River, NJ: Prentice Hall.

Liu, J. W. S. (2001). *Real-time systems*. New Delhi: Pearson Education Asia.

Liu, J., Shih, W. K., Lin, K. J., Bettati, R., & Chung, J. Y. (1994). Imprecise computations. *Proceedings of the IEEE, 82*(1), 83–94. doi:10.1109/5.259428.

Liu, L., Hasan, O., & Tahar, S. (2011). Formalization of finite-state discrete-time Markov chains in HOL.[LNCS]. *Proceedings of Automated Technology for Verification and Analysis, 6996*, 90–104. doi:10.1007/978-3-642-24372-1_8.

Liu, S., Guan, X., Tong, D., & Cheng, X. (2010). Analysis and comparison of NAND specific file systems. *Chinese Journal of Electronics, 19*(3).

Liu, Y., & Karimi, I. A. (2008). Scheduling multistage batch plants with parallel units and no interstage storage. *Computers & Chemical Engineering, 32*(4-5), 671–693. doi:10.1016/j.compchemeng.2007.02.002.

Li, W. (2000). Recursive PCA for adaptive process monitoring. *Journal of Process Control, 10*, 471–486. doi:10.1016/S0959-1524(00)00022-6.

Li, W. K., Chi, W. H., & Hua, B. (2002). Scheduling crude oil unloading, storage, and processing. *Industrial & Engineering Chemistry Research, 41*(26), 6723–6734. doi:10.1021/ie020130b.

Lo Bello, L. (2011). The case for ethernet in automotive communications. *Tenth International Workshop on Real-Time Networks, 8*(4), 7-15.

Lo Bello, L., Kaczynski, F. S., & Mirabella, O. (2006). A wireless traffic smoother for soft real-time communications over IEEE 802.11 industrial networks. In *Proceedings of the 11th IEEE International Conference on Emerging Technologies and Factory Automation (ETFA)*, (pp. 1073-1079). IEEE.

Lo Bello, L., Kaczynski, G. A., & Mirabella, O. (2005). Improving the real-time behavior of ethernet networks using traffic smoothing. *IEEE Transactions on Industrial Informatics, 1*(3), 151–161. doi:10.1109/TII.2005.852071.

Lofgren, K. M. J., Norman, R. D., Thelin, G. B., & Gupta, A. (2005). Wear leveling techniques for flash EEPROM systems. *United States Patent, No 6,850,443*. Washington, DC: US Patent Office.

Loo, S. M., Wells, E., Freije, N., & Kulick, J. (2002). Handel C for rapid prototyping of VLSI coprocessors for real time systems. In *Proceedings of the 34th Southeastern Symposium on System Theory (SSST 2002)*. SSST.

Lopez-Aguilera, E., Casademont, J., Cotrina, J., & Rojas, A. (2005). Enhancement proposal for WLAN IEEE 802.11e: Desynchronization of its working procedure. In *Proceedings of the 14th IEEE Workshop on Local and Metropolitan Area Networks LANMAN*, (pp. 1-6). IEEE.

Lorenz, T. (2008). *Advanced gateways in automotive applications: Elektrotechnik und informatik der technische universität berlin*. Technische Universität Berlin.

Loria. (2005). Retrieved from www.loria.fr/nnavet/cours/DEA2004-2005/slide1.pdf

Loria. (2005). Retrieved from www.loria.fr/nnavet/cours/DEA2004-2005/slide2.pdf

Lo, S. C., Lee, G., & Chen, W. T. (2003). An efficient multipolling mechanism for IEEE 802.11 wireless LANs. *IEEE Transactions on Computers, 52*(6), 764–768. doi:10.1109/TC.2003.1204832.

Lu, B., & Hsieh, W. (2003). Simplified nonlinear principal component analysis. In *Proceedings of the International Joint Conference on Neural Networks 2003*, (vol. 1, pp. 759-763). IEEE.

Lukasiewycz, M., Glafl, M., Teich, J., & Milbredt, P. (2009). Flexray schedule optimization of the static segment. In *Proceedings of the International Conference on Hardware/Software Codesign and System Synthesis (CODES+ISSS)*. Citeseer.

Luo, Z. H., Guo, B. Z., & Morgul, O. (1999). *Stability and stabilization of infinite dimensional systems with applications*. Berlin: Springer. doi:10.1007/978-1-4471-0419-3.

Luyben, M., Tyreus, B. D., & Luyben, W. (1999). *Plantwide process control*. New York: McGraw Hill.

MAENAD Consortium. (2012). *MAENAD project home page*. Retrieved from http://www.maenad.eu/

Mahadevan, N., & Hoo, K. A. (1998). Model reduction and controller development for a class of a distributed systems. In *Proceedings of the American Control Conference*, (pp. 2315-2320). ACC.

Mainwaring, J., Polastre, J., Szeczyk, R., Culler, D., & Anderson, J. (2002). *Wireless sensor networks for habitat monitoring*. Paper presented in International Workshop on Wireless Sensor Networks and Applications. New York, NY.

Makkaoui, L., Lecuire, V., & Moureaux, J. (2010). *Fast zonal DCT-based image compression for wireless camera sensor networks*. Paper presented at 2nd International Conference on Image Processing Theory, Tools and Applications, IPTA 2010. Paris, France.

Maleval, J. (2010). *Notebooks without anymore optical disc or HDD?* Retrieved August, 2012, from http://www.storagenewsletter.com/news/flash/notebooks-without-optical-disc-hdd-ssd

Mangard, S., Oswald, E., & Popp, T. (2007). *Power analysis attacks: Revealing the secrets of smart cards*. Berlin: Springer.

Manning, C. (2012). *How YAFFS works*. Retrieved August, 2012, from http://www.yaffs.net/sites/yaffs.net/files/HowYaffsWorks.pdf

Marcelloni, F., & Vecchio, M. (2009). An efficient lossless compression algorithm for tiny nodes of monitoring wireless sensor networks. *The Computer Journal*, *52*(8), 969–987. doi:10.1093/comjnl/bxp035.

Marculescu, R., Ogras, U. Y., Peh, L. S., Jerger, N. E., & Hoskote, Y. (2009). Outstanding research problems in NoC design: system, microarchitecture, and circuit perspectives. *IEEE Transactions on Computer-Aided Design of Integrated Circuits and Systems*, *28*(1), 3–21. doi:10.1109/TCAD.2008.2010691.

Marinoni, M., & Buttazzo, G. C. (2007). Elastic DVS management in processors with discrete voltage/frequency modes. *IEEE Transactions on Industrial Informatics*, *3*(1), 51–62. doi:10.1109/TII.2006.890494.

Mark, W. R., Glanville, R. S., Akeley, K., & Kilgard, M. J. (2003). Cg: A system for programming graphics hardware in a C-like language. *ACM Transactions on Graphics*, *22*(3). doi:10.1145/882262.882362.

Marongiu, A., & Benini, L. (2009). Efficient OpenMP support and extensions for MPSoCs with explicitly managed memory hierarchy. In *Proceedings of Design, Automation & Test in Europe Conference & Exhibition, 2009 (DATE '09)* (pp. 809-814). DATE.

Marowka, A. (2011). Back to thin-core massively parallel processors. *IEEE Computer*, *44*(12), 49–54. doi:10.1109/MC.2011.133.

Martin, G., & Smith, G. (2009). High-level synthesis: Past, present, and future. *Design & Test of Computers*, *26*(4), 18–25. doi:10.1109/MDT.2009.83.

Marzario, L., Lipari, G., Balbastre, P., & Crespo, A. (2004). IRIS: A new reclaiming algorithm for server-based real-time systems. In *Proceedings of the IEEE Real-Time and Embedded Technology and Applications Symposium*. Toronto, Canada: IEEE.

MathWorks. (2012). *MATLAB simulink R2012a: Software tool*. Retrieved April 10, 2012 from http://www.mathworks.co.uk/

MathWorks. (n.d.). *Simulink - Simulation and model based design*. Retrieved April 11, 2012 from http://www.mathworks.nl/products/simulink/

Mattfeld, D. C., & Bierwirth, C. (2004). An efficient genetic algorithm for job shop scheduling with tardiness objectives. *European Journal of Operational Research*, *155*(2), 616–630. doi:10.1016/S0377-2217(03)00016-X.

Mayne, D., & Michalska, H. (1993). Receding horizon control of nonlinear systems. *IEEE Transactions on Automatic Control*, *38*(10), 1512–1516. doi:10.1109/9.241565.

Mazzeo, N.A., & Venegas. (1997). An application of generalized similarity analysis to atmospheric diffusion. *Atmospheric Research*, *43*, 157–166. doi:10.1016/S0169-8095(96)00028-2.

Mehrkanoon, S., Falck, T., & Suykens, J. A. K. (2012). Approximate solutions to ordinary differential equations using least squares support vector machines. *IEEE Transactions on Neural Networks and Learning Systems*, (99).

Mendez, P. F., & Eager, T. W. (1999). Order of magnitude scaling of complex engineering problems. In *Proceedings of the Seventh Symposium on Energy and Engineering Science*, (pp. 106-113). IEEE.

Mendez, C. A., & Cerda, J. (2002). An efficient MILP continuous time formulation for short-term scheduling of multiproduct continuous facilities. *Computers & Chemical Engineering*, *26*(4-5), 687–695. doi:10.1016/S0098-1354(01)00789-X.

Mendez, C. A., & Cerda, J. (2003). Dynamic scheduling in multiproduct batch plants. *Computers & Chemical Engineering*, *27*(8-9), 1247–1259. doi:10.1016/S0098-1354(03)00050-4.

Mendez, C. A., Cerda, J., Grossmann, I. E., Harjunkoski, I., & Fahl, M. (2006). State-of-the-art review of optimization methods for short-term scheduling of batch processes. *Computers & Chemical Engineering*, *30*(5-6), 913–946. doi:10.1016/j.compchemeng.2006.02.008.

Mendez, C. A., Grossmann, I. E., Harjunkoski, I., & Kabore, P. (2006). A simultaneous optimization approach for off-line blending and scheduling of oil-refinery operations. *Computers & Chemical Engineering*, *30*(4), 614–634. doi:10.1016/j.compchemeng.2005.11.004.

Menezes, A. J., Oorschot, P. C. V., Vanstone, S. A., & Rivest, R. L. Menezes, & Van Oorschot, S. A. V. (2001). Handbook of applied cryptography. Boca Raton, FL: CRC Press.

Meng, X., & Chaudhary, V. (2004). Bio-sequence analysis with Cradle's 3SoC software scalable system on chip. In *Proceedings of the 2004 ACM Symposium on Applied Computing (SAC '04)*. New York, NY: ACM.

Mennicke, S., Oanea, O., & Wolf, K. (2009). Decomposition into open nets. In T. Freytag & A. Eckleder (Eds.), *16th German Workshop on Algorithms and Tools for Petri Nets*, (Vol. 501, pp. 29-34). Karlsruhe, Germany: CEUR-WS.org.

Mentor Graphics. (n.d.). *Catapult C synthesis*. Retrieved April 11, 2012 from http://www.mentor.com/esl/catapult/overview

Mercer, C. W., Savage, S., & Tokuda, H. (1994). Processor capacity reserves for multimedia operating systems. In *Proceedings of IEEE International Conference on Multimedia Computing and Systems*. Boston, MA: IEEE.

Mesarovic, M. D., Macko, D., & Takahara, Y. (1970). *Theory of hierarchical multilevel systems*. New York: Academic Press.

Mhamdi, T., Hasan, O., & Tahar, S. (2011). Formalization of entropy measures in HOL. In *Proceedings of Interactive Theorem Proving (ITP-11) (LNCS)* (Vol. 6898, pp. 233–248). Berlin: Springer. doi:10.1007/978-3-642-22863-6_18.

Michalska, H., & Mayne, D. Q. (1993). Robust receding horizon control of constrained nonlinear systems. *IEEE Transactions on Automatic Control*, *38*(11), 1623–1633. doi:10.1109/9.262032.

Micron Technology, Inc. (2005). *TN-29-07: Small-block vs. large-block NAND flash devices*. Retrieved August, 2012, from http://www.micron.com/~/media/Documents/Products/Technical%20Note/NAND%20Flash/136tn2907.pdf

Microsoft. (n.d.). *COM specification*. Retrieved from http://www.microsoft.com/com

Military, U. S. (1949). *Procedure for performing a failure modes effect and criticality analysis. United States Military Procedure MIL-P-1629*. Washington, DC: US Military.

Miller, V. (1985). Uses of elliptic curves in cryptography. In *Proceedings of Advances in Cryptology – Crypto '85 (LNCS)* (Vol. 218, pp. 417–426). Berlin: Springer. doi:10.1007/3-540-39799-X_31.

Minai, A. A. (1992). *The robustness of feedforward neural networks: A preliminary investigation*. (Ph.D. Dissertation). University of Virginia, Charlottesville, VA.

Miorandi, D., & Vitturi, S. (2004). Analysis of master-slave protocols for real-time industrial communications over IEEE 802.11 WLANs. In *Proceedings of the 2nd IEEE International Conference on Industrial Informatics*, (pp. 143 - 148). IEEE.

Mitra, S., & Hayachi, Y. (2000). Neuro-fuzzy rule generation: Survey in soft-computing framework. *IEEE Transactions on Neural Networks*, *11*(3), 748–768. doi:10.1109/72.846746 PMID:18249802.

Mki-Turja, J., & Nolin, M. (2004). Tighter response-times for tasks with offsets. In *Proceedings of theof the 10th International Conference on Real-Time Computing Systems and Applications (RTCSA04)*. RTCSA.

Mok, A. K., Feng, X., & Chen, D. (2001). Resource partition for real-time systems. In *Proceedings of the 7th IEEE Real-Time Technology and Applications Symposium* (pp. 75–84). Taipei, Taiwan: IEEE.

Montgomery, L. P. (1985). Modular multiplication without trial division. *Mathematics of Computation*, *44*(170), 519–521. doi:10.1090/S0025-5718-1985-0777282-X.

Moore, S. (2011). *Prototyping massively parallel architectures: Computing beyond a million cores*. Paper presented at the Microsoft Software Summit. Paris, France.

Moraes, R., Portugal, P., & Vasques, F. (2006). Simulation analysis of the IEEE 802.11e EDCA protocol for an industrially-relevant real-time communication scenario. In *Proceedings of the 11th IEEE International Conference on Emerging Technologies and Factory Automation (ETFA)*, (pp. 202 - 209). IEEE.

Moraes, R., Vasques, F., Portugal, P., & Fonseca, J. A. (2007). VTP-CSMA: A virtual token passing approach for real-time communication in IEEE 802.11 wireless networks. *IEEE Transactions on Industrial Informatics*, *3*(3), 215–224. doi:10.1109/TII.2007.903224.

Moro, L. F. L. (2003). Process technology in the petroleum refining industry – Current situation and future trends. *Computers & Chemical Engineering*, *27*(8-9), 1303–1305. doi:10.1016/S0098-1354(03)00054-1.

Mosbahi & Jaray. (2004). *Représentation du temps en B événementiel pour la modélisation des systèmes temps réel. Rapport interne*. LORIA.

Motee, N., & Jadbabaie, A. (2006). Distributed receding horizon control of spatially invariant systems. In *Proceedings of the American Control Conference*, (pp. 731-736). ACC.

Moutinho, F., & Gomes, L. (2011). State space generation algorithm for GALS systems modeled by IOPT petri nets. In *Proceedings of the 37th Annual Conference on IEEE Industrial Electronics Society* (pp. 2839-2844). Melbourne, Australia: IEEE. doi: 10.1109/IECON.2011.6119762

Moutinho, F., Pereira, F., & Gomes, L. (2011). Automatic generation of VHDL for controllers with graphical user interfaces. In *Proceedings of the 20th IEEE International Symposium of Industrial Electronics (ISIE'11)*. Gdansk, Poland: IEEE.

Moutinho, F., & Gomes, L. (2012). Asynchronous-channels and time-domains extending petri nets for GALS systems. In Camarinha-Matos, L., Shahamatnia, E., & Nunes, G. (Eds.), *IFIP AICT* (*Vol. 372*, pp. 143–150). Boston: Springer. doi:10.1007/978-3-642-28255-3_16.

Moyne, J. R., & Tilbury, D. M. (2007). The emergence of industrial control networks for manufacturing control, diagnostics, and safety data. *Proceedings of the IEEE*, *95*(1), 29–47. doi:10.1109/JPROC.2006.887325.

Muhuri, P. K., & Shukla, K. K. (2008). Designing optimal task schedule by membership functions choice in fuzzy real-time scheduling. In *Proceedings of the 2nd National Conference on Mathematical Techniques: Emerging Paradigms for Electronics and IT Industries (MATEIT-2008)*. MATEIT.

Muhuri, Pranab, K., & Shukla, K. K. (2008). Real-time task scheduling with fuzzy uncertainty in processing times and deadlines. *Applied Soft Computing*, *8*(1), 1–13. doi:10.1016/j.asoc.2006.06.006.

Muhuri, Pranab, K., & Shukla, K. K. (2009). Real-time scheduling of periodic tasks with processing times and deadlines as parametric fuzzy numbers. *Applied Soft Computing*, *9*(3), 936–946. doi:10.1016/j.asoc.2008.11.004.

Multicore Communications API Working Group. (2012). *The multicore communication API V2.015 (MCAPI)*. Retrieved April 11, 2012, from http://www.multicore-association.org/workgroup/mcapi.php

Murakami, Y., Uchiyama, H., Hasebe, S., & Hashimoto, I. (1997). Application of repetitive SA method to scheduling problem in chemical processes. *Computers & Chemical Engineering*, *21*(supplement), 1087–1092.

Murata, T., Ishibuchi, H., & Gen, M. (1997). Multi-objective fuzzy scheduling with the OWA operator for handling different scheduling criteria and different job importance. *Proceedings of the FUZZ-IEEE*, *2*, 773–778.

Nascimento, P. S. B., Maciel, P. R. M., Lima, M. E., Sant'ana, R. E., & Filho, A. G. S. (2004). A partial reconfigurable architecture for controllers based on Petri nets. In *Proceedings of the 17th Symposium on Integrated Circuits and Systems Design* (pp. 16-21). IEEE. doi: 10.1109/SBCCI.2004.240918

Natarajan, S. (Ed.). (1995). *Imprecise and approximate computation*. Dordrecht, The Netherlands: Kluwer Academic Publishers. doi:10.1007/b102247.

National Instruments. (n.d.). *LabVIEW system design software*. Retrieved April 11, 2012 from http://www.ni.com/labview/

Naumowicz, T., & Freeman, R. (2008). Autonomous monitoring of vulnerable habitats using a wireless sensor network. In *Proceedings of the Workshop on Real-World Wireless Sensor Networks, REALWSN'08*. Glasgow, UK: REALWSN.

Navet, N., & Simonot-Lion, F. (2008). *Automotive embedded systems handbook*. Boca Raton, FL: CRC Press. doi:10.1201/9780849380273.

Navet, N., Song, Y., Simonot-Lion, F., & Wilwert, C. (2005). Trends in automotive communication systems. *Proceedings of the IEEE, 93*(6), 1204–1223. doi:10.1109/JPROC.2005.849725.

Neves, P., & Rodrigues, J. (2010). Internet protocol over wireless sensor networks, from myth to reality. *The Journal of Communication, 5*, 189–196.

Ng & Butler. (2003). Towards formalizing UML state diagrams in CSP. In Proceedings of the 1st IEEE International Conference on Software Engineering and Formal Methods. IEEE Computer Society.

Notomi, M., & Murata, T. (1994). Hierarchical reachability graph of bounded petri nets for concurrent-software analysis. *IEEE Transactions on Software Engineering, 20*(5), 325–336. doi:10.1109/32.286423.

Novakovic, D. (2002). *Numerical reservoir characterization using dimensionless scale numbers with application in upscaling*. (Ph.D. dissertation). Louisiana State University. Baton Rouge, LA.

Nunes, R., Gomes, L., & Barros, J. P. (2007). A graphical editor for the input-output place-transition Petri net class. In *Proceedings of IEEE Conference on Emerging Technologies and Factory Automation, (ETFA'07)*. IEEE. doi: 10.1109/EFTA.2007.4416858

NVIDIA. (n.d.). *CUDA: Parallel programming made easy*. Retrieved April 11, 2012 from http://www.nvidia.com/object/cuda_home_new.html

O'Brien, K., O'Brien, K., Sura, Z., Chen, T., & Zhang, T. (2008). Supporting OpenMP on cell. *International Journal of Parallel Programming, 36*(3). PMID:22582009.

Object Management Group. (2008). *Software & systems process engineering metamodel specification (SPEM) – Version 2.0. Document number: formal/2008-04-01*. OMG.

Object Management Group. (2010). Object constraint language specification v2.2. *OMG Document Number: formal/2010-02-01*. Retrieved from http://www.omg.org/spec/OCL/2.0/PDF

Object Management Group. (2010). Unified modelling language: Superstructure specification v2.3. *OMG Document Number: formal/2010-05-05*. Retrieved from http://www.omg.org/spec/UML/2.3

Object Management Group. (2011). *Meta object facility (MOF) – Core specification – Version 2.4.1. Document number: formal/2011-08-07*. OMG.

Object Management Group. (2011). *UML profile for MARTE: Modeling and analysis of real-time embedded systems – Version 1.1. Document number: formal/2011-06-02*. OMG.

Object Management Group. (2012). *SysML project web site*. Retrieved from http://www.omgsysml.org/

Ogras, U. Y., Hu, J., & Marculescu, R. (2005). Key research problems in NoC design: A holistic perspective. In *Proceedings of the 3rd IEEE/ACM/IFIP International Conference on Hardware/Software Codesign and System Synthesis, CODES+ISSS* (pp. 69-74). New York, NY: ACM.

Ohshima, S., Hirasawa, S., & Honda, H. (2010). OMP-CUDA: OpenMP execution framework for CUDA based on omni OpenMP compiler. In Sato, Hanawa, Müller, Chapman, & de Supinski (Eds.), Beyond Loop Level Parallelism in OpenMP: Accelerators, Tasking and More. Berlin: Springer-Verlag.

Olivier, P., Boukhobza, J., & Senn, E. (2012). On benchmarking embedded linux flash file systems. *ACM SIGBED Review, 9*(2), 43–47. doi:10.1145/2318836.2318844.

Olsen, Wang, Ramirez-Serrano, & Brennan. (2005). Contingencies-based reconfiguration of distributed factory automation. *Robotics and Computer-integrated Manufacturing*, 379–390. doi:10.1016/j.rcim.2004.11.011.

OMG. (2003). Retrieved from http://www.omg.org

OMG. (2011). Retrieved from http://www.omg.org/spec/UML/2.4/Superstructure

OMG. (n.d.). Retrieved from http://www.omg.org/spec/OCL/2.3.1

Opdenacker, M., & Petazzoni, T. (2010). *Flash filesystems.* Retrieved August, 2012, from http://free-electrons.com/doc/flash-filesystems.pdf

OpenMP Architecture Review Board. (n.d.). *OpenMP application program interface 3.1.* Retrieved April 11, 2012 from http://www.openmp.org/mp-documents/OpenMP3.1.pdf

Orlov, Y., Yiming, L., & Christofides, P. D. (2003). Robust stabilization of infinite dimensional systems using discontinuous output feedback control. *International Journal of Control, 1,* 821–826.

Ortmeier, F., Reif, W., & Schellhorn, G. (2005). Deductive cause-consequence analysis (DCCA). In *Proceedings of the 16th IFAC World Congress.* IFAC.

Palazoglu, A., & Karakas, A. (2000). Control of non-linear distributed parameter systems using generalized invariants. *Automatica, 36,* 697–703. doi:10.1016/S0005-1098(99)00196-X.

Palencia, J. M. G. (2003). Harbour, offset-based response time analysis of distributed systems scheduled under EDF. In *Proceedings of the 15th Euromicro Conference on Real-Time Systems.* Porto, Portugal: Euromicro.

Pantelides, C. C. (1994). Unified frameworks for optimal process planning and scheduling. In *Proceedings of the 2nd International Conference on Foundations of Computer* (pp. 253-274). CACHE Publications.

Papadopoulos, Y., Walker, M., Parker, D., Rüde, E., Hamann, R., Uhlig, A., ... Lien, R. (2011). Engineering failure analysis & design optimisation with HiP-HOPS. *Journal of Engineering Failure Analysis.* DOI: 10.1016/j.engfailanal.2010.09.025

Papadopoulos, Y., Walker, M., Reiser, M.-O., Servat, D., Abele, A., & Johansson, R. ... Weber, M. (2010). Automatic allocation of safety integrity levels. In *Proceedings of the 8th European Dependable Computing Conference - CARS Workshop,* (pp. 7-11). Valencia, Spain: ACM Press. ISBN: 978-1-60558-915-2

Papaioannou, P., Nastou, P., Stamatiou, Y., & Zaroliagis, C. (2009). Secure elliptic curve generation and key establishment on a 802.11 WLAN embedded device. In *Proceedings of the 9th IEEE International Symposium on Autonomous Decentralized Systems,* (pp. 41-48). IEEE.

Parallax Inc. (n.d.). *Propeller general information.* Retrieved April 11, 2012 from http://www.parallax.com/propeller/

Park, D., Debnath, B., & Du, D. (2009). *CFTL: A convertible flash translation layer with consideration of data access patterns* (Technical Report 09-023). Minneapolis, MN: University of Minnesota.

Park, C., Cheon, W., Kang, J. U., Roh, K., Cho, W., & Kim, J. S. (2008). A reconfigurable FTL (flash translation layer) architecture for NAND flash based architectures. *ACM Transactions on Embedded Computing Systems, 7*(4), 1–23. doi:10.1145/1376804.1376806.

Park, I., & Sunwoo, M. (2010). FlexRay network parameter optimization method for automotive applications. *IEEE Transactions on Industrial Electronics, 99*(1).

Park, S., Kim, Y., Urgaonkar, B., Lee, J., & Seo, E. (2011). A comprehensive study of energy efficiency and performance of flash-based SSD. *Journal of Systems Architecture, 57*(4), 354–365. doi:10.1016/j.sysarc.2011.01.005.

Paulin, P. (2010). *A component-based multicore programming environment.* Paper presented at the Workshop on Fundamentals of Component-Based Design, ESWeek 2010. New York, NY.

Pedreiras & Almeida. (2007). *Task management for soft real-time applications based on general purpose operating system.*

Pedreiras, P., & Almeida, L. (2002). EDF message scheduling on controller area network. *Computing & Control Engineering Journal, 13*(4), 163–170. doi:10.1049/cce:20020402.

Pelham, R., & Pharris, C. (1996). Refinery operation and control: a future vision. *Hydrocarbon Processing, 75*(7), 89–94.

Pellizzoni, R., & Caccamo, M. (2007). Real-time management of hardware and software tasks for FPGA-based embedded systems. *IEEE Transactions on Computers, 56*(12), 1666–1680. doi:10.1109/TC.2007.70763.

Pereira, F., Moutinho, F., & Gomes, L. (2012). A state-space based model-checking framework for embedded system controllers specified using IOPT petri nets. In Camarinha-Matos, L., Shahamatnia, E., & Nunes, G. (Eds.), *IFIP AICT* (*Vol. 372*, pp. 123–132). Boston: Springer. doi:10.1007/978-3-642-28255-3_14.

Pérez, Priol, & Ribes. (2002). *A parallel CORBA component model*. Research report N 4552.

Perkins, C., Belding-Royer, E., & Das, S. (2003). *Ad hoc on demand distance vector routing (AODV). RFC 3561*. IETF.

Petersen, S., & Carlsen, S. (2011). WirelessHART versus ISA100.11a: The format war hits the factory floor. *IEEE Industrial Electronics Magazine*, 23–34.

Pinto, J. M., & Grossmann, I. E. (1997). A logic-based approach to scheduling problem with resource constraints. *Computers & Chemical Engineering*, *21*(8), 801–818. doi:10.1016/S0098-1354(96)00318-3.

Pinto, J. M., Joly, M., & Moro, L. F. L. (2000). Planning and scheduling models for refinery operations. *Computers & Chemical Engineering*, *24*(9-10), 2259–2276. doi:10.1016/S0098-1354(00)00571-8.

Poggio, T., & Girosi, F. (1990). Networks for approximating and learning. *Proceedings of the IEEE*, *78*(9). doi:10.1109/5.58326.

Ponnambalam, S. G., Jawahar, N., & Aravindan, P. (1999). A simulated annealing algorithm for job shop scheduling. *Production Planning and Control*, *10*(8), 767–777. doi:10.1080/095372899232597.

Popescu, C., Soto, M. C., & Lastra, J. L. M. (2012). A petri net-based approach to incremental modelling of flow and resources in service oriented manufacturing systems. *International Journal of Production Research*, *50*(2), 325–343. doi:10.1080/00207543.2011.561371.

Pop, T., Pop, P., Eles, P., Peng, Z., & Andrei, A. (2008). Timing analysis of the FlexRay communication protocol. *Real-Time Systems*. doi:10.1007/s11241-007-9040-3.

Possa, P., Schaillie, D., & Valderrama, C. (2011). FPGA-based hardware acceleration: A CPU/accelerator interface exploration. In *Proceedings of the 18th IEEE International Conference on Electronics, Circuits and Systems (ICECS)* (pp. 374-377). IEEE.

Potlapally, N. (2011). Hardware security in practice: Challenges and opportunities. In *Proceedings of the 2011 IEEE International Symposium on Hardware-Oriented Security and Trust* (pp. 93-98). IEEE.

Ramamritham, K., & Stankovic, J. A. (1994). Scheduling algorithms and operating systems support for real-time systems. *Proceedings of the IEEE*, *82*(1), 55–67. doi:10.1109/5.259426.

Ramanathan, P. (1999). Overload management in real-time control applications using (m, k)-firm guarantee. *IEEE Transactions on Parallel and Distributed Systems*, *10*(6), 549–559. doi:10.1109/71.774906.

Randell, B., Lee, P. A., & Treleaven, P. C. (1978). Reliability issues in computing system design. *Computing Surveys*, *10*, 220–232. doi:10.1145/356725.356729.

Rashid, M. M., Hossain, E., & Bhargava, V. K. (2008). Controlled channel access scheduling for guaranteed QoS in 802.11e-based WLANs. *IEEE Transactions on Wireless Communications*, *7*(4), 1287–1297. doi:10.1109/TWC.2008.060861.

Rausch, M., & Hanisch, H.-M. (1995). Net condition/event systems with multiple condition outputs. In *Proceedings of ETFA'95 - 1995 INRIA/IEEE Symposium on Emerging Technologies and Factory Automation*, (vol. 1, pp. 592-600). Paris: IEEE.

Ravi, S., Raghunathan, A., Kocher, P., & Hattangady, S. (2004). Security in embedded systems. *ACM Transactions on Embedded Computing Systems*, *3*(3), 461–491. doi:10.1145/1015047.1015049.

Rawlings, J. B., & Muske, K. R. (1993). The stability of constrained receding horizon control. *IEEE Transactions on Automatic Control*, *38*(10), 1512–1516. doi:10.1109/9.241565.

Raza, S., Voigt, T., & Jutvik, V. (2012). Lightweight IKEv2: A key management solution for both the compressed IPSec and the IEEE 802.15.4 security. In *Proceedings of the IETF International Workshop on Smart Object Security*. IETF.

Realff, M. J., & Stephanopoulos, G. (1998). On the application of explanation-based learning to acquire control knowledge for branching and bound algorithms. *INFORMS Journal on Computing*, *10*(1), 56–71. doi:10.1287/ijoc.10.1.56.

Reer, F., & Reif, W. (2007). Using deductive cause-consequence analysis (DCCA) with SCADE. In *Proceedings of the 26th International Conference in Computer Safety, Reliability and Security*, (pp. 465-478). IEEE.

Reisig, W. (1982). Deterministic buffer synchronization of sequential processes. *Acta Informatica, 18*, 117–134. doi:10.1007/BF00264434.

Reisig, W. (1985). *Petri nets: An introduction*. New York: Springer-Verlag.

Rejowski, R., & Pinto, J. M. (2003). Scheduling of a multiproduct pipeline system. *Computers & Chemical Engineering, 27*(8-9), 1229–1246. doi:10.1016/S0098-1354(03)00049-8.

Rensink & Kleppe. (2008). On a graph-based semantics for UML class and object diagrams. In *Proceedings fo ECEASST, 2008*. ECEASST.

Rensink, B. Kastenberg, & Staijen. (2011). User manual for the GROOVE tool set. Enschede, The Netherlands: Department of Computer Science, University of Twente.

Rivest, R., Shamir, A., & Adleman, L. (1978). A method for obtaining digital signatures and public-key cryptosystems. *Communications of the ACM, 21*, 120–126. doi:10.1145/359340.359342.

Roberts, D., Kgil, T., & Mudge, T. (2009). Integrating NAND flash devices onto servers. *Communications of the ACM, 52*(4), 98–106. doi:10.1145/1498765.1498791.

Rooker, M.-N., Sunder, C., Strasser, T., Zoitl, A., Hummer, O., & Ebenhofer, G. (2007). Zero downtime reconfiguration of distributed automation systems: The εCEDAC approach. In *Proceedings of the Third International Conference on Industrial Applications of Holonic and Multi-Agent Systems, 2007*. Berlin: Springer-Verlag.

RTSJ (Real-Time Specification for Java). (n.d.). *Home page*. Retrieved from http://www.rtsj.org/

Rust, C., & Kleinjohann, B. (2001). *Modeling intelligent embedded real-time systems using high-level petri nets*. Paper presented at the Forum on Specification & Design Languages - FDL. Lyon, France.

Rutle, Rossini, Lamo, & Wolter. (2012). A formal approach to the specification and transformation of constraints in MDE. *Journal of Logic and Algebraic Programming, 81*, 422–457. doi:10.1016/j.jlap.2012.03.006.

Sabuncuoglu, I., & Bayiz, M. (1999). Job shop scheduling with beam search. *European Journal of Operational Research, 118*(2), 390–412. doi:10.1016/S0377-2217(98)00319-1.

Saharidisa, G. K. D., Minouxb, M., & Dallery, Y. (2009). Scheduling of loading and unloading of crude oil in a refinery using event-based discrete time formulation. *Computers & Chemical Engineering, 33*(8), 1413–1426. doi:10.1016/j.compchemeng.2009.02.005.

Satoh, T. (2000). The canonical lift of an ordinary elliptic curve over a prime field and its point counting. *Journal of the Ramanujan Mathematical Society, 15*, 247–270.

Sauter, T. (2010). The three generations of field-level networks – Evolution and compatibility issues. *IEEE Transactions on Industrial Electronics, 57*, 3585–3595. doi:10.1109/TIE.2010.2062473.

Sauter, T., & Vasques, F. (2006). Editorial: Special section on communication in automation. *IEEE Transactions on Industrial Informatics, 2*(2), 73–77. doi:10.1109/TII.2006.875801.

Schaumont, P., & Verbauwhede, I. (2001). A reconfiguration hierarchy for elliptic curve cryptography. In *Proceedings of the 35th Asilomar Conference on Signals, Systems, and Computers*. Asilomar.

Schmidt, E. G., Alkan, M., Schmidt, K., Yuruklu, E., & Karakaya, U. (2010). Performance evaluation of FlexRay/CAN networks interconnected by a gateway. In *Proceedings of the International Symposium on Industrial Embedded Systems (SIES)*, (pp. 209-212). IEEE.

Schmidt, K., & Schmidt, E. G. (2010). Optimal message scheduling for the static segment of FlexRay. In *Proceedings of the Vehicular Technology Conference Fall (VTC 2010-Fall)*. Ottawa, Canada: IEEE.

Schmidt, K., & Schmidt, E. G. (2010). Schedulability analysis and message schedule computation for the dynamic segment of FlexRay. In *Proceedings of the Vehicular Technology Conference Fall (VTC 2010-Fall)*. Ottawa, Canada: IEEE.

Schmidt, K., & Schmidt, E. G. (2009). Message scheduling for the FlexRay protocol: The static segment. *IEEE Transactions on Vehicular Technology, 58*(5).

Schneier, B. (1996). *Applied cryptography – Protocols, algorithms and source code in C*. New York: John Wiley & Sons.

Schoof, R. (1995). Counting points on elliptic curves over finite fields. *Journal Theorie des Nombres de Bordeaux*, *7*, 219–254. doi:10.5802/jtnb.142.

Scott, M., Costigan, N., Abdulwahab, W., Goubin, L., & Matsui, M. (2006). Implementations of cryptographic pairing on smart cards. In Goubin, L., & Matsui, M. (Eds.), *Cryptographic Hardware and Embedded Systems - CHES 2006 (Vol. 4249*, pp. 134–147). Berlin: Springer. doi:10.1007/11894063_11.

Seno, L., Vitturi, S., & Zunino, C. (2009). Analysis of ethernet powerlink wireless extensions based on the IEEE 802.11 WLAN. *IEEE Transactions on Industrial Informatics*, *5*(2), 86–98. doi:10.1109/TII.2009.2019727.

Seo, S. H., Kim, J. H., Moon, T. Y., Hwang, S. H., Kwon, K. H., & Jeon, J. W. (2008). A reliable gateway for in-vehicle networks. In *Proceedings of the 17th World Congress The International Federation of Automatic Control*. IEEE.

Seo, S. H., Moon, T. Y., Kim, J. H., Kim, S. H., Son, C. W., Jeon, J. W., & Hwang, S. H. (2008). A gateway system for an automotive system: LIN, CAN, and FlexRay. In *Proceedings of the 6th IEEE International Conference on Industrial Informatics INDIN*. IEEE.

Seo, S. H., Moon, T. Y., Kim, J. H., Kwon, K. H., Jeon, J. W., & Hwang, S. H. (2008). A fault-tolerant gateway for in-vehicle networks. In *Proceedings of the 6th IEEE International Conference on Industrial Informatics INDIN* (pp. 1144-1148). IEEE.

Shah, N. (1996). Mathematical programming techniques for crude oil scheduling. *Computers & Chemical Engineering*, *20*(Suppl.), S1227–S1232. doi:10.1016/0098-1354(96)00212-8.

Shah, N., Saharidis, G. K. D., Jia, Z., & Ierapetritou, M. G. (2009). Centralized–decentralized optimization for refinery scheduling. *Computers & Chemical Engineering*, *33*(12), 2091–2105. doi:10.1016/j.compchemeng.2009.06.010.

Sha, L. (1994). Generalized rate-monotonic scheduling theory: A framework for developing real-time systems. *Proceedings of the IEEE*, *82*(1), 68–82. doi:10.1109/5.259427.

Sha, L. et al. (2004). Real-time scheduling theory: A historical perspective. *Real-Time Systems*, *28*, 101–155. doi:10.1023/B:TIME.0000045315.61234.1e.

Shannon, C. E. (1949). Communication theory of secrecy systems. *The Bell System Technical Journal*, *28*(4), 656–715.

Sha, Rajkumar, & Lehoczky. (1990). Priority inheritence protocols: An approach to real-time synchronization. *IEEE Transactions on Computers*, *39*(9), 1175–1185. doi:10.1109/12.57058.

Shen, W., Wang, L., & Hao, Q. (2006). Agent-based distributed manufacturing process planning and scheduling: A state-of-the-art survey. *IEEE Transactions on Systems, Man and Cybernetics. Part C, Applications and Reviews*, *36*(4), 563–577. doi:10.1109/TSMCC.2006.874022.

Sheu, J.-P., Liu, C.-H., Wu, S.-L., & Tseng, Y.-C. (2004). A priority MAC protocol to support real-time traffic in ad hoc networks. *Wireless Networks*, *10*(1), 61–69. doi:10.1023/A:1026292830673.

Shih, W., Liu, W., & Chung, J. (1991). Algorithms for scheduling imprecise computations with timing constraints. *SIAM Journal on Computing*, *20*(3), 537–552. doi:10.1137/0220035.

Shih, W., Liu, W., Chung, J., & Gillies, D. (1989). Scheduling tasks with ready times and deadlines to minimize average error. *Operating System Review*, *23*(3), 14–28. doi:10.1145/71021.71022.

Shin, I., & Lee, I. (2003). Periodic resource model for compositional real-time guarantees. In *Proceedings of the 24th Real-Time Systems Symposium* (pp. 2–13). Cancun, Mexico: IEEE.

Shinohara, T. (1999). Flash memory card with block memory address arrangement. *United States Patent, No 5,905,993*. Washington, DC: US Patent Office.

Shi, W., & Fuchs, W. K. (1992). Probabilistic analysis and algorithms for reconfiguration of memory arrays. *IEEE Transactions on Computer-Aided Design of Integrated Circuits and Systems*, *11*(9), 1153–1160. doi:10.1109/43.160001.

Shneyderman, A., & Casati, A. (2003). *Mobile VPN: Delivering advanced services in next generation wireless systems*. Indianapolis, IN: Wiley.

Shobrys, D. E., & White, D. C. (2000). Planning, scheduling and control systems: why can they not work together. *Computers & Chemical Engineering, 24*(2-7), 163-173.

Silva, J. L. E., & Lopes, J. J. (2010). A dynamic dataflow architecture using partial reconfigurable hardware as an option for multiple cores. *WSEAS Transactions on Computers Archive, 9*(5), 429–444.

Silva, M. (1985). *Las redes de petri: En la automática y la informática*. Madrid, Spain: Editorial AC.

Silva, M., & Recalde, L. (2002). Petri nets and integrality relaxations: a view of continuous Petri net models. *IEEE Transactions on Systems, Man, and Cybernetics. Part C, 32*(4), 317–327.

Silverman, J. H. (1986). *The arithmetic of elliptic curves*. Berlin: Springer. doi:10.1007/978-1-4757-1920-8.

Singhoff, F., Plantec, A., Dissaux, P., & Legrand, J. (2009). Investigating the usability of real-time scheduling theory with the cheddar project. *Real-Time Systems, 43*(3), 259–295. doi:10.1007/s11241-009-9072-y.

Singhoff, L. N. L. M. F., & Legrand, J. (2004). Cheddar: A flexible real time scheduling framework. *ACM SIGAda Ada Letters, 24*(4), 1–8. doi:10.1145/1046191.1032298.

Skyrianoglou, D., Passas, N., & Salkintzis, A. K. (2006). ARROW: An efficient traffic scheduling algorithm for IEEE 802.11e HCCA. *IEEE Transactions on Wireless Communications, 5*(12), 3558–3567. doi:10.1109/TWC.2006.256978.

Slany, W. (1996). Scheduling as a fuzzy multiple criteria optimization problem. *Fuzzy Sets and Systems, 78*, 192–222. doi:10.1016/0165-0114(95)00168-9.

Smiri, K., & Jemai. (2009). Migration methodology in MPSoC based on performance analysis via SDF graph. *Advances in Computational Sciences and Technology*, 149-166.

Sobrinho, J. L., & Krishnakumar, A. S. (1998). EQuB - Ethernet quality of service using black bursts. In *Proceedings of the Conference on Local Computer Networks*, (pp. 286 - 296). IEEE.

Sobrinho, J. L., & Krishnakumar, A. S. (1999). Quality-of-service in ad hoc carrier sense multiple access wireless networks. *IEEE Journal on Selected Areas in Communications, 17*(8), 1353–1368. doi:10.1109/49.779919.

Son, J., Lee, I.-G., Yoo, H.-J., & Park, S.-C. (2005). An effective polling scheme for IEEE 802.11e. *IEICE Transactions on Communications. E (Norwalk, Conn.), 88-B*(12), 4690–4693.

Souissi, Y. (1991). Deterministic systems of sequential processes: A class of structured petri nets. In *Proceedings of the 12th International Conference on Application and Theory of Petri Nets* (pp. 62–81). IEEE.

Spuri, M. (1996). *Analysis of deadline scheduled real-time systems (Technical Report -2772)*. Institut National de Recherche en Informatique et en Automatique.

Stallings, W. (1999). *Cryptography and network security: Principles and practice*. Upper Saddle River, NJ: Prentice Hall.

Stankovic, J., Spuri, M., Ramamritham, K., & Buttazzo, C. (1998). *Deadline scheduling for real-time systems*. Norwell, MA: Kluwer Academic Publishers. doi:10.1007/978-1-4615-5535-3.

Stefanov, T., Zissulescu, C., Turjan, A., Kienhuis, B., & Deprettere, E. (2004). System design using kahn process networks: The compaan/laura approach. In *Proceedings of the Conference on Design, Automation and Test in Europe (DATE '04)*. Washington, DC: IEEE Computer Society.

Steinbach, T., Korf, F., & Schmidt, T. C. (2010). Comparing time-triggered ethernet with FlexRay: An evaluation of competing approaches to real-time for in-vehicle networks. In *Proceedings of the IEEE International Workshop on Factory Communication Systems (WFCS)* (pp. 199-202). IEEE.

Stephanopoulos, G., & Han, C. (1996). Intelligence systems in process engineering: A review. *Computers & Chemical Engineering, 20*(6-7), 743–791. doi:10.1016/0098-1354(95)00194-8.

Stewart, Volpe, & Khosla. (1997). Design of dynamically reconfigurable real-time software using port-based objects. *IEEE Transactions on Software Engineering*, (23): 592–600.

Storage Newsletter. (2011). *Anobit shipped 20 million MSP-based embedded flash controllers in 2011*. Retrieved August 2012, from http://www.storagenewsletter.com/news/business/anobit-msptm-flash-controllers

Strasser, T., Muller, I., Sunder, C., Hummer, O., & Uhrmann, H. (2006). Modeling of reconfiguration control applications based on the IEC 61499 reference model for industrial process measurement and control systems. In *Proceedings of the IEEE Workshop on Distributed Intelligent Systems*. IEEE.

Stuijk, S. (2007). *Predictable mapping of streaming applications on multiprocessors*. (PhD thesis). Eindhoven University of Technology.

Stuijk, S. Geilen, & Basten. (2006). SDF3: SDF for free. In *Proceedings of ACSD 2006*, (pp. 276-278). ACSD.

Suleman, M. A., Patt, Y. N., Sprangle, E., Rohillah, A., Ghuloum, A., & Carmean, D. (2007). *Asymmetric chip multiprocessors: Balancing hardware efficiency and programmer efficiency*. The High Performance Systems Group.

Symonds, G. H. (1955). *Linear programming: The solution of refinery problems*. New York: Esso Standard Oil Company.

Szirtes, T. (1997). *Applied dimensional analysis and modeling*. New York: McGraw-Hill.

Szyperski, Gruntz, & Murer. (2002). *Component software beyond object-oriented programming*. Reading, MA: Addison-Wesley.

Tacken, J., Rust, C., & Kleinjohann, B. (1999). A method for prepartitioning of petri net models for parallel embedded real-time systems. In *Proceedings of the 6th Annual Australasian Conference on Parallel And RealTime Systems* (pp. 168-178). Melbourne, Australia: Springer-Verlag.

Tavakoli, A. (2009). *HYDRO: A hybrid routing protocol for lossy and low power networks. IETF Internet Draft: draft-tavakoli-hydro-01*. IETF.

Tavli, B., & Heinzelman, W. (2006). *Mobile Ad hoc networks*. Dordrecht, The Netherlands: Springer. doi:10.1007/1-4020-4633-2.

Taylor, E., Han, J., & Fortes, J. (2006). Towards the accurate and efficient reliability modeling of nanoelectronic circuits. In *Proceedings of the Nanotechnology Conference*, (pp. 395–398). IEEE.

Terrier, F., & Chen, Z. (1994). Fuzzy calculus applied to real-time scheduling. In *Proceedings of the FUZZ-IEEE*, (pp. 1905 –1910). IEEE.

Teruel, E., Recalde, L., & Silva, M. (1985). Modeling and analysis of sequential processes that cooperate through buffers. *IEEE Transactions on Robotics and Automation, 11*, 267–277.

Teruel, E., Recalde, L., & Silva, M. (2001). Structure theory of multi-level deterministically synchronized sequential processes. *Theoretical Computer Science, 254*(1-2), 1–33. doi:10.1016/S0304-3975(99)00112-7.

Teruel, E., & Silva, M. (1996). Structure theory of equal conflict systems. *Theoretical Computer Science, 153*(1&2), 271–300. doi:10.1016/0304-3975(95)00124-7.

Terzic, I., Zoitl, A., Rooker, M. N., Strasser, T., Vrba, P., & Marík, V. (2009). Usability of multi-agent based control systems in industrial automation. In *Proceedings of the Holonic and Multi-Agent Systems for Manufacturing, 4th International Conference on Industrial Applications of Holonic and Multi-Agent Systems*. Linz, Austria: IEEE.

Texas Instruments. (2011). *OpenCV on TI's DSP+ARM®*. White paper.

Texas Instruments. (n.d.). *OpenMP programming for TMS320C66x multicore DSPs: Delivering the industry's first multicore DSPs to support the OpenMP API*. Retrieved April 11, 2012 from http://www.ti.com/lit/ml/sprt620/sprt620.pdf

Texas Instruments. (n.d.). *TMS320C6678, multicore fixed and floating-point digital signal processor, data manual*. Retrieved April 11, 2012 from www.ti.com/lit/ds/sprs691c/sprs691c.pdf

Thies, W., Karczmarek, M., & Amarasinghe, S. P. (2002). StreamIt: A language for streaming applications. In *Proceedings of the 11th International Conference on Compiler Construction (CC '02)*. London, UK: Springer-Verlag.

Thramboulidis, K. (2004). Using UML in control and automation: A model driven approach. In *Proceedings of the 2nd IEEE International Conference on Industrial Informatics*. Berlin, Germany: INDIN.

Thramboulidis, K., Doukas, G., & Frantzis, A. (2004). Towards an implementation model for FB-based reconfigurable distributed control applications. In *Proceedings of the 7th International Symposium on Object-oriented Real-time Distributed Computing (ISORC 04)*. Vienna, Austria: ISORC.

TILERA. (n.d.). *The TILEPro64 processor*. Retrieved April 11, 2012 from http://www.tilera.com/products/processors/TILEPRO64

TIMMO Consortium. (2012). *TIMMO 2 USE project web site*. Retrieved from http://www.timmo-2-use.org/

Tindell, K., Burns, A., & Wellings, A. J. (1995). Calculating controller area network (CAN) message response times. *Control Engineering Practice*, *3*(8), 1163–1169. doi:10.1016/0967-0661(95)00112-8.

TinyAODV. (2009). *TinyAODV implementation under TinyOS-1.x source code*. Retrieved July 29, 2009, from tinyos-1.x/contrib/hsn/apps/TraceRouteTestAODV

Toscano, E., & Lo Bello, L. (2011). *A middleware for reliable soft real-time communication over IEEE 802.11 WLANs*. Paper presented at the Industrial Embedded Systems (SIES), 2011. New York, NY.

Toshiba Corporation. (2009). *Evaluation of flash file systems for large NAND flash memory*. Retrieved August, 2012, from http://elinux.org/images/7/7e/ELC2009-FlashFS-Toshiba.pdf

Toshiba Corporation. (2009). Evaluation of UBI and UBIFS. In *Proceedings of CE Linux Forum 2009*. Linux.

Transformation. (n.d.). Retrieved from http://www.program-Transformation.org/Tools/KoalaCompiler

Trsek, H., & Jasperneite, J. (2011). *An isochronous medium access for real-time wireless communications in industrial automation systems - A use case for wireless clock synchronization*. Paper presented at the Precision Clock Synchronization for Measurement Control and Communication (ISPCS). New York, NY.

Tsoi, K. H., & Luk, W. (2010). Axel: A heterogeneous cluster with FPGAs and GPUs. In *Proceedings of the 18th Annual ACM/SIGDA International Symposium on Field Programmable Gate Arrays (FPGA '10)*. New York, NY: ACM.

TTTech Computertechnik AG. (2011). *TTEthernet specification*. Retrieved from http://www.ttagroup.org

Tucker, S., Taft, R. A., Duff, R. L., & Brukardt, E. Ploedereder, & Leroy. (Eds.), Ada 2005 reference manual: Language and standard libraries. Lecture Notes in Computer Science, 4348.

Ulrich, K., Daniel, G., & Rolf, D. (2006). Complete formal verification of multi core embedded systems using bounded model checking. In Proceedings of Design, Applications, Integration and Software, (pp. 147-150). IEEE.

Ulusoy, A., Gurbuz, O., & Onat, A. (2011). Wireless model-based predictive networked control system over cooperative wireless network. *IEEE Transactions on Industrial Informatics*, *7*(1), 41–51. doi:10.1109/TII.2010.2089059.

Vaidya, N., Dugar, A., Gupta, S., & Bahl, P. (2005). Distributed fair scheduling in a wireless LAN. *IEEE Transactions on Mobile Computing*, *4*(6), 616–629. doi:10.1109/TMC.2005.87.

Valle, S. et al. (1999). Selection of the number of principal components: A new criterion with comparison to existing methods. *Industrial & Engineering Chemistry Research*, *38*, 4389–4401. doi:10.1021/ie990110i.

Valverde, J., Rosello, V., Mujica, G., Portilla, J., Uriarte, A., & Riesgo, T. (2012). Wireless sensor network for environmental monitoring: Application in a coffee factory. *International Journal of Distributed Sensor Networks*. doi:10.1155/2012/638067.

Van Herrewege, A., Batina, L., Knezevic, M., Verbauwhede, I., & Preneel, B. (2009). Compact implementations of pairings. In *Proceedings of the 4th Benelux Workshop on Information and System Security - WISSec 2009*. Louvain-la-Neuve, Belgium: WISSec.

van Ommering, van der Linden, Kramer, & Magee. (2000). The koala component model for consumer electronics software. *IEEE Computer*, 78-85.

Vector. (2012). *Vector informatik GmbH*. Retrieved from http://www.vector.com/

Vesely, W. E., Stamatelatos, M., & Dugan, J. Fragola, J., Minarick, J., & Railsback, J. (2002). Fault tree handbook with aerospace applications. Washington, DC: NASA Office of Safety and Mission Assurance.

Villallón, N. J., Cuenca, P., Orozco-Barbosa, L., & Garrido, A. (2008). B-EDCA: A QoS mechanism for multimedia communications over heterogeneous 802.11/802.11e WLANs. *Computer Communications, 31*(17), 3905–3921. doi:10.1016/j.comcom.2008.07.012.

Vissers, K. (1999). *The trimedia CPU64 VLIW media processor*. Paper presented at Session Invite ICCD'99. New York, NY.

Vogler, W., & Wollowski, R. (2002). In Agrawal, M., & Seth, A. (Eds.), *Decomposition in asynchronous circuit design (Vol. 2556*, pp. 336–347). Lecture Notes in Computer ScienceBerlin: Springer.

Volvo. (n.d.). *Construction equipment*. Retrieved from http://www.volvoce.com

Vyatkin, V. (2006). Execution semantic of function blocks based on the model of net condition/event systems. In *Proceedings of the 4th IEEE International Conference on Industrial Informatics*, (pp. 874–879). IEEE.

Vyatkin, V., & Hanisch, H.-M. (1999). A modeling approach for verification of IEC1499 function blocks using net condition/event systems. In *Proceedings of ETFA '99 - 1999 7th IEEE International Conference on Emerging Technologies and Factory Automation*, (pp. 261–270). IEEE.

Walker, M., & Papadopoulos, Y. (2009). Qualitative temporal analysis: Towards a full implementation of the fault tree handbook. *Control Engineering Practice, 17*(10), 1115–1125. doi:10.1016/j.conengprac.2008.10.003.

Wallace, M. (2005). Modular architectural representation and analysis of fault propagation. *Electronic Notes in Theoretical Computer Science, 141*(3), 53–71. doi:10.1016/j.entcs.2005.02.051.

Walter, C. (2002). Precise bounds for Montgomery modular multiplication and some potentially insecure RSA moduli. *Topics in Cryptology- CT-RSA 2002*, 30-39.

Walter, C. D. (1999). Montgomery exponentiation needs no final subtractions. *Electronics Letters, 35*(21), 1831–1832. doi:10.1049/el:19991230.

Wang, X., Khalgui, M., & Li, Z. W. (2011). Dynamic low power reconfigurations of real-time embedded systems. In *Proceedings of the 1st Pervasive and Embedded Computing Systems*. Algarve, Portugal: IEEE.

Wang, Y., & Saksena, M. (1999). Scheduling fixed-priority tasks with preemption threshold. In *Proceedings of the 6th IEEE International Conference on Real-Time Computing Systems and Applications* (pp. 328–335). Hong Kong, China: IEEE.

Wang, Y., Liu, D., Wang, M., Qin, Z., & Guan, Y. (2010). RNFTL: A reuse-aware NAND flash translation layer for flash memory. In *Proceedings of the ACM SIGPLAN/SIGBED 2010 Conference on Languages, Compilers, and Tools for Embedded Systems (LCTES)*. ACM.

Wang, C., Li, B., & Li, L. (2004). A new collision resolution mechanism to enhance the performance of IEEE 802.11 DCF. *IEEE Transactions on Vehicular Technology, 53*(4), 1235–1246. doi:10.1109/TVT.2004.830951.

Wang, J. (1998). *Timed petri nets: Theory and application*. Dordrecht, The Netherlands: Kluwer Academic Publishers.

Wei, Q., Gong, B., Pathak, S., Veeravalli, B., Zeng, L., & Okada, K. (2011). WAFTL: A workload adaptive flash translation layer with data partition. In *Proceedings of 2011 IEEE 27th Symposium on Mass Storage Systems and Technologies (MSST)*. IEEE.

Wiggers, M. H., Kavaldjiev, Smit, & Jansen. (2005). Architecture design space exploration for streaming applications through timing analysis. *Communicating Process Architectures*.

Williamson, R. C., & Helmke, U. (1995). Existence and uniqueness results for neural network approximations. *IEEE Transactions on Neural Networks, 6*(1), 2–13. doi:10.1109/72.363455 PMID:18263280.

Willig, A. (1997). A MAC protocol and a scheduling approach as elements of a lower layers architecture in wireless industrial LANs. In *Proceedings of the IEEE International Workshop on Factory Communication Systems (WFCS'97)*, (pp. 139 - 148). IEEE.

Willig, A. (2008). Recent and emerging topics in wireless industrial communications: A selection. *IEEE Transactions on Industrial Informatics, 4*(2), 102–124. doi:10.1109/TII.2008.923194.

Willig, A., Matheus, K., & Wolisz, A. (2005). Wireless technology in industrial networks. *Proceedings of the IEEE, 93*(6), 1130–1151. doi:10.1109/JPROC.2005.849717.

Winter, R. (2008). *Why are data warehouses growing so fast?* Retrieved June 2012, from http://www.b-eye-network.com/view7188

Wolforth, I. P., Walker, M. D., Grunske, L., & Papadopoulos, Y. I. (2010). Generalisable safety annotations for specification of failure patterns. *Software, Practice & Experience, 40*(5), 453–483.

Woodhouse, D. (2001). JFFS: The journaling flash file-system. In *Proceedings of Ottawa Linux Symposium*. Ottawa, Canada: Linux.

Wookey. (2007). YAFFS: A NAND flash file system. In *Proceedings of the Free and Open Source Developer's European Meeting (FOSDEM 2004)*. FOSDEM.

Worrell, R. B., & Stack, D. W. (1978). *A SETS user manual for the fault tree analyst. NUREG CR-04651*. Washington, DC: US Nuclear Regulatory Commission.

Wu, C., & Kuo, T. (2006). An adaptive two-level management for the flash translation layer in embedded systems. In *Proceedings of the 2006 IEEE/ACM International Conference on Computer-Aided Design*. IEEE.

Wu, G., Eckart, B., & He, X. (2010). BPAC: An adaptive write buffer management scheme for flash-based solid state drives. In *Proceedings of 2010 IEEE 26th Symposium on Mass Storage Systems and Technologies (MSST)*. IEEE.

Wu, N. Q., Bai, L. P., & Zhou, M. C. (2011). *A three-stage method to find refining schedules of crude oil operations in refinery*. Paper presented at the 2011 IEEE International Conference on Service Operations and Logistics, and Informatics. Beijing, China.

Wu, N. Q., Bai, L. P., & Chu, C. B. (2007). Modeling and conflict detection of crude-oil operations for refinery process based on controlled-colored-timed Petri net. *IEEE Transactions on Systems, Man, & Cybernetics. Part C, 37*(4), 461–472.

Wu, N. Q., Chu, F., Chu, C. B., & Zhou, M. C. (2008). Short-term schedulability analysis of crude oil operations in refinery with oil residency time constraint using Petri net. *IEEE Transactions on Systems, Man, and Cybernetics. Part C, 38*(6), 765–778.

Wu, N. Q., Chu, F., Chu, C. B., & Zhou, M. C. (2009). Short-term schedulability analysis of multiple distiller crude oil operations in refinery with oil residency time constraint. *IEEE Transactions on Systems, Man, and Cybernetics. Part C, 39*(1), 1–16.

Wu, N. Q., Chu, F., Chu, C. B., & Zhou, M. C. (2010). Hybrid Petri net modeling and schedulability analysis of high fusion point oil transportation under tank grouping strategy for crude oil operations in refinery. *IEEE Transactions on Systems, Man, and Cybernetics. Part C, 40*(2), 159–175.

Wu, N. Q., Chu, F., Chu, C. B., & Zhou, M. C. (2010). Tank cycling and scheduling analysis of high fusion point oil transportation for crude oil operations in refinery. *Computers & Chemical Engineering, 34*(4), 529–543. doi:10.1016/j.compchemeng.2009.11.007.

Wu, N. Q., Zhou, M. C., & Chu, F. (2005). Short-term scheduling for refinery process: bridging the gap between theory and applications. *International Journal of Intelligent Control and Systems, 10*(2), 162–174.

Wu, N. Q., Zhou, M. C., & Chu, F. (2008). A Petri net based heuristic algorithm for realizability of target refining schedules in oil refinery. *IEEE Transactions on Automation Science and Engineering, 5*(4), 661–676. doi:10.1109/TASE.2008.916737.

Wu, Y.-J., Chiu, J.-H., & Sheu, T.-L. (2008). A modified EDCA with dynamic contention control for real-time traffic in multi-hop ad hoc networks. *Journal of Information Science and Engineering, 24*(4), 1065–1079.

Wuyts, Ducasse, & Nierstrasz. (2005). A data-centric approach to composing embedded, real-time software components. *Journal of Systems and Software*, (74): 25–34. doi:10.1016/j.jss.2003.05.004.

Yager, R. R. (1979). On the measure of fuzziness and negation part I: Membership in the unit interval. *International Journal of General Systems, 5*, 221–229. doi:10.1080/03081077908547452.

Yang. (2004). *OCL 2.0 and its relationship to meta-modeling*. Modelling, Simulation and Design lab (MSDL) Presentations.

Yang, S. X., & Wang, D. W. (2001). A new adaptive neural network and heuristics hybrid approach for job-shop scheduling. *Computers & Operations Research*, 28(10), 955–971. doi:10.1016/S0305-0548(00)00018-6.

Yang, X., & Vaidya, N. (2006). Priority scheduling in wireless ad hoc networks. *Wireless Networks*, 12(3), 273–286. doi:10.1007/s11276-005-5274-y.

Young, S. S., Seong, H. P., Choi, S., & Hyun, W. K. (2007). Packet error rate analysis of ZigBee under WLAN and bluetooth interferences. *IEEE Transactions on Wireless Communications*, 6, 2825–2830. doi:10.1109/TWC.2007.06112.

Yuan, R., & Strayer, T. (2001). *Virtual private networks: Technologies and solutions*. Boston, MA: Addison Wesley.

Zhang, D., Li, Z. Z., Song, H., & Liu, L. (2005). A programming model for an embedded media processing architecture. In *Proceedings of the 5th International Conference on Embedded Computer Systems: Architectures, Modeling, and Simulation (SAMOS'05)*. Berlin: Springer-Verlag.

Zheng, D., Hoo, K. A., & Piovoso, M. J. (2002). Finite dimensional modeling and control of distributed parameter system. In *Proceedings of the American Control Conference*. Anchorage, AK: ACC.

Zhou, M. C., & Venkatesh, K. (1998). *Modeling, simulation and control of flexible manufacturing systems: A Petri net approach*. Singapore: World Scientific.

Zimmermann, A., German, R., Freiheit, J., & Hommel, G. (1999). *TimeNET 3.0 tool description*. Paper presented at the International Conference on Petri Nets and Performance Models. Zaragosa, Spain.

Zimmermann, H. J. (1996). *Fuzzy set theory and its applications*. New Delhi: Allied Publishers Limited. doi:10.1007/978-94-015-8702-0.

Zoitl, A., Lepuschitz, W., Merdan, M., & Vallee, M. (2010). A real-time reconfiguration infrastructure for distributed embedded control systems. In *Proceedings IEEE Emerging Technologies and Factory Automation*. IEEE.

Zrida, H. K., Abid, M., Ammari, A. C., & Jemai, A. (2009). A YAPI system level optimized parallel model of a H.264/AVC video encoder. In *Proceedings of ACS/IEEE International Conference on Computer Systems and Applications (AICCSA'09)*. IEEE.

Zuberi, K. M., & Shin, K. G. (1995). Non-preemptive scheduling of messages on controller area network for real-time control applications. In *Proceedings of Real-Time Technology and Applications Symposium* (pp. 240-249). IEEE.

Zurawski, R. (2005). *The industrial communication technology handbook*. Boca Raton: CRC Press. doi:10.1201/9781420037821.

About the Contributors

Mohamed Khalgui is a full-time researcher in computer science at Xidian University in China and a part-time researcher at Martin Luther University in Germany. He's also the Founder and Head of IC-TICA (www.ictica.net). He was a part time researcher at ITIA-CNR Institute in Italy, collaborator with SEG Group of Patras University in Greece, and a temporary lecturer at Henri Poincaré University in France. Dr. Khalgui obtained the Bachelor degree in Computer Science at Tunis University in 2001. The master degree was obtained in telecommunication and services at Henri Poincaré University in 2003. He made research activities in computer science at INRIA Institute to obtain the PhD at the French Polytechnic Institute of Lorraine in 2007. Mohamed Khalgui obtained in 2011 the accreditation from Martin Luther University in Germany to be a Full Professor and Senior Director of Research in Computer Science. Dr. Khalgui activates in several European Projects and also in other interesting international collaborations.

Olfa Mosbahi received the B.S. degree in Computer Science and the M.S. degree from Tunis University in 1999 and 2002, respectively. She did research in Computer Science at INRIA Institute to receive the Ph.D. degree at the French Polytechnic Institute of Lorraine, France, in 2008. She is an Assistant Professor in Computer Science at the University of Carthage, Tunisia. She was a part time researcher at INRIA, France, and a temporary lecturer at Nancy II University. She is active in several European Projects and also in other interesting international collaborations.

Antonio Valentini, after attending the Electrical Engineering courses at the university, he started in 1985 his experience in the manufacturing industry with an internship in Olivetti inside the R&D of the printer division (OPE). Afterwards he passed from the design of printers to the design of automatic packaging machines, G.D SpA. In this area, he has completed his technical formation and consolidated his professional experience (co-inventor of *7 patents*, 3 of them extended to other countries). In 2001, he became technical director in the Italian branch of ELAU, a control system provider. He has been O3NEIDA CEO since the establishment in 2004 of the not-for-profit incorporation, originated and supported inside the IMS program, and later, president of O3neida Europe since its foundation in 2007. Main research areas of interest are: software engineering, distributed control systems, RTOS, motion control, mechatronics, embedded systems, industrial agents, service oriented architectures, Web-services. Many papers published in journals and conference proceedings. Communication skills developed through supporting clients and suppliers worldwide and active membership at international institutions. As for his international experience, he has participated at the development teams of the *IEC-61131*, *IEC-61499*, and *IEC-61804* standards. He is registered as EU Framework Program Expert since 2004 and has acted as independent expert in the evaluation of Project Proposals and in the reviewing of European funded Network of Excellence and Projects. From 2008 to 2011, he has coordinated O3neida participation in the EU-FP7- MEDEIA project and, currently, in the IMS-MTP-IADP project. Finally, he is member of the IEC-SC65B-WG15, the IEEE-IES-Technical Committee on Industrial Agents, and the IEEE-IES-TC on Standards. His assignments at international conferences include: Keynote Speaker at the first ICOA'06 Conference in Shanghai, China; Advisory Board member at the IEEE-IES INDIN Conferences, since 2006; Co-Chair for the Industrial Day of the INDIN'07and INDIN'08 Conferences; Co-Chair for the Industrial Day of the ETFA'08 and ETFA'11Conferences; Co-chair for Industry Track at ISIE'10 and IECON'11; Co-Chair for workshops and special sessions at INDIN'08, ETFA'10, ISIE'10, ETFA'11, IECON'11, ETFA'12, and IECON'12 Conferences.

* * *

Mohamed Abid, Head of Computer Embedded System laboratory CES-ENIS, Tunisia. Mohamed ABID is working now as a Professor at the Engineering National School of Sfax (ENIS), University of Sfax, Tunisia (http://www.ceslab.org/eng/perso.php?id=27). He received the Ph. D. degree from the National Institute of Applied Sciences, Toulouse (France) in 1989 and the "thèse d'état" degree from the National School of Engineering of Tunis (Tunisia) in 2000 in the area of Computer Engineering & Microelectronics. His current research interests include: hardware-software co-design, System on Chip, Reconfigurable System, and Embedded System, etc. He has also been investigating the design and implementation issues of FPGA embedded systems. Currently, Dr. Abid occupies the post of director of doctoral school Sciences & Technologies, University of Sfax. He is founding member and Head of the research laboratory Computer Embedded System CES-ENIS, since 2006 (http://www.ceslab.org). He was Founding member of System on Chip at Computer, Electronic and Smart engineering system Laboratory at ENIS 2001-2005. He was also founding responsible of Hardware-Software co-design research Group at EµM-Lab-FSM, Monastir-Tunisia, 1991-2000. Dr. Abid is member of scientific committee at ENIS, since 2008, member of quality committee at ENIS, 2006-2007 and member of national committee of engineering pedagogy, since 2006. He was founding member and responsible of doctoral degree computer system engineering at ENIS, 2003-2010. Dr. Abid served in national and international conference organization and program committees at different organizational levels including Conference General Co-Chair, Technical program co-chair, organization co-chair and Member of several national and international conference Program Committees. He was Founding Member of several international conferences and school: SCS, SSD, ICECS, ComNet, GEI, IDT, ICM, SensorNetSchool. He was also Joint Editor of Specific Issues in two International Journals and Joint editor of many conference's articles nationals and internationals: ICM'2004, GEI'2006-07, SCS'2004. He is a co-editor of the best paper in the international conference EDAC-ETC-EuroASIC'96. Dr. Abid is joint coordinator or an active member of several International Re-search and Innovation projects: STIC/INRIA project since 2009, CMCU project and since 2009 and Head of Federator Research Project since 2009. Dr. Abid was Supervisor or Co-supervisor of more than 20 PhD doctors, most of them were in joint guardianship and Supervisor or Co-supervisor of more than 50 master students. He is Author or co-author of more than 30 publications in Journals and author or co-author of more than 180 papers in international conferences.

He is also author or co-author of many guest's papers, Joint author of many book's chapters. Dr. Abid has served also as Guest professor at several international universities and as a Consultant to research & development in Telnet Incorporation.

Samir Ben Ahmed is a Full Professor in Computer Science at Tunis-El Manar University and Head of MOSIC Research Unit in Tunisia. He was Founder of ISI Institute of Computer Science, and Head of IT Department of Faculty of Science at Tunis-El Manar University in Tunisia. Prof. Ben Ahmed obtained his PhD Thesis in Automation and Computer Science at Paul Sabatier University in France. The Engineering Diploma was obtained before from National School of Electrical Engineering, Electronic, Computer Science and Hydraulic in Toulouse (ENSEEIHT). Prof. Ben Ahmed is strongly active in several National and International Projects and Collaborations.

Amen Ben Hadj Ali received the Bachelor's degree in Computer Science and the Master's degree in 1998 and 2002, respectively, from Tunis University, Tunis, Tunisia, where she is currently working toward the Ph.D. degree in computer science under Prof. Samir Ben Ahmed and Prof. Mohamed Khalgui. Her research interests are software engineering technologies and functional safety of industrial embedded systems. In 2002, she joined Tunis University, where she is currently an assistant professor in the department of computer science.

Kamel Barkaoui received a Ph.D. degree in Computer Science in 1988 from the University Paris 6 (UPMC). He is currently a Full Professor at the Conservatoire National des Arts et Métiers (CNAM - Paris). His research interests include verification techniques and performance evaluation methods related to concurrent and distributed formalisms and their applications to computer and communication systems. Dr Barkaoui has served on PCs and as PC chair or OC chair for numerous international workshops and conferences as ICTAC 2008 or FM 2 012. He is the Steering Committee Chair of the International Workshop on Verification and Performance Evaluation of Computer and Communication Systems (VECoS). He was a guest editor of *Journal of Systems and Software* (JSS), *International Journal of Critical Computer-Based Systems* (IJCCBS), and *Formal Aspects of Computing Journal* (FACJ). He has received the 1995 IEEE Int. Conf. on System Man and Cybernetics Outstanding Paper Award.

João Paulo Barros received the Lic. and M.Sc. degrees in informatics engineering in 1993 and 1997, respectively, and the PhD degree in 2006, in Digital Systems all from New University of Lisbon, Portugal. He is Professor of Informatics at the Polytechnic Institute of Beja, in Beja Portugal, and a Researcher at UNINOVA-CTS Institute in Lisbon. His research interests include Petri nets, graphical specification languages, languages and tools for object-oriented and model-driven software development. He is also especially interested in mobile computing, software educational tools, computer science education, programming didactics, and curriculum development. Mr. Barros is author or co-author of more than sixty peer-reviewed papers on international events and journals and a member of ACM, ACM SIGCSE, ACM SIGSOFT, ACM SIGPLAN, and founding member of the Portuguese Society for Engineering Education.

Fethi Bellamine earned his B.Sc., M.Sc., and Ph.D. degrees in Electrical and Computer Engineering from Colorado State and University of Colorado at Boulder, USA, respectively. From 1995 to 2002, he was a senior staff member at Lucent Technologies, Alcatel Networks, and NESA in USA. He was a visiting faculty member at University of Waterloo, Canada in 2005, 2006, 2008, and at University of Aveiro, Portugal in 2009. He is currently a visiting faculty member at University of Waterloo. Since 2002, he is a faculty member at Carthage University, Institute of Applied Science and Technologies, Tunis, Tunisia. His current research interests are in simulation, modeling, and soft computing techniques.

Hans Blom has a M.Sc. in engineering physics and a tekn.lic. in theoretical physics from Chalmers University of Technology and Göteborg University, Sweden. From 1998 to 2003, he was a systems architect at Ericsson AB and worked with system level management and software design, including model based design and roundtrip engineering. He has been in the Volvo Group since 2003 where he has participated in development projects working with systems engineering, and international research projects with applications in the area of model based development. In particular, he has worked with the definition of architecture description languages.

Ricardo Chessini Bose received his BSc degree in Electronics Engineering from the University of Vale dos Sinos, São Leopoldo, Brazil, in 2000. In 2003, he received his MSc degree in Biomedical Engineering from the Federal University of Santa Catarina, Florianópolis, Brazil. Currently, he is a researcher at the University of Mons, in Mons, Belgium. His research interests lie in the area of embedded biomedical systems.

Jalil Boukhobza received his electrical engineering degree (with honors) from I.N.E.L.E.C (Institut Nationale d'Electricité et d'électronique), Boumerdès, Algeria, in 1999, and M.S and PhD degrees in computer science from the University of Versailles, France, respectively, in 2000 and 2004. He was a research fellow at the PRiSM lab (University of Versailles) from 2004 to 2006. Jalil Boukhobza is currently Associate Professor at the University of Occidental Brittany in Brest, France since 2006 and member of the Lab-STICC lab in the CACS team (Communication, Architecture, and Circuits). His main research interests include flash-based storage system design, performance evaluation and energy optimization, and embedded operating systems.

Giorgio Buttazzo is Full Professor of Computer Engineering at the Scuola Superiore Sant'Anna of Pisa. He graduated in Electronic Engineering at the University of Pisa in 1985, received a Master in Computer Science at the University of Pennsylvania in 1987, and a Ph.D. in Computer Engineering at the Scuola Superiore Sant'Anna of Pisa in 1991. From 1987 to 1988, he worked on active perception and real-time control at the G.R.A.S.P. Laboratory of the University of Pennsylvania, Philadelphia. Prof. Buttazzo has been Program Chair and General Chair of the major international conferences on real-time systems. He is Editor in Chief of Real-Time Systems (Springer), Associate Editor of the *IEEE Transactions on Industrial Informatics*, and Chair of the IEEE Technical Committee on Real-Time Systems. He has authored 6 books on real-time systems and over 200 papers in the field of real-time systems, scheduling algorithms, overload management, robotics, and neural networks. He is IEEE Fellow for contributions to dynamic scheduling algorithms in real-time systems.

De-Jiu Chen received his PhD degree in Mechanical Engineering with a research on embedded computer control systems from KTH in 2004. His research interests are on systems and software architecture, model-based engineering, dependability and self-adaptive embedded systems. Since 2006, he has been actively involved in the development of EAST-ADL with the focus on the integration of modelling and analysis technologies for functional safety and behaviour.

Feng Chu (M'07) received the B.S. in Electrical Engineering from Hefei University of Technology (China) in 1986, the M.S. degrees Institut National Polytechnique de Lorraine (France) in 1991, respectively, the Ph.D. degree in Computer Science from University of Metz (France) in 1995 and the Habilitation for Research Advising degree from the University of Technology of Compiègne, Compiègne, France, in 2006. She was with Jiangsu University of Technology, Zhengjiang, China, for two years and the National Research Institute in Computer Science and Automation (INRIA), Metz, for four years. From 199 to 2009, she was an Associate Professor with the University of Technology of Troyes, Troyes, France. In 2009, she joined the Laboratoire Informatique, Biologie Intégrative et Systèmes Complexes (IBISC) EA 4526, Université d'Evry Val d'Essonne, Evry Cédex, France, where she is currently a Full Professor. She has led or participated in ten research and industrial projects. She has published more than 50 papers in international journals and more than 60 papers in academic conference proceedings. Her research interests include the modeling, analysis, and optimization of complex systems, particularly intelligent transportation systems, logistic and production systems based on combinatorial optimization, operations research, and Petri nets. Dr. Chu is the Associate Editor for the *IEEE Transactions on Systems, Man, and Cybernetics—Part C* and served on the program committees for international conferences. She is the Program Co-Chair of IEEE ICNSC 2012 and will be the General Co-Chair of IEEE ICNSC 2013. She is TC member of IFAC and IEEE SMC.

Anikó Costa received her Electrotech. Eng. Degree from Ceské Vysoké Učení Technické v Praze, Praque, Czech Republic in 1992, a Master degree in Informatics Eng. from Faculty of Science and Technology of Universidade Nova de Lisboa, in 2003 and a PhD degree in Digital Systems from Universidade Nova de Lisboa, in 2010. She is a professor at the Electrical Engineering Department, Faculty of Sciences and Technology of Universidade Nova de Lisboa, Portugal and a researcher at UNINOVA Institute, Portugal. Her research interests include Petri nets, Digital systems design. Anikó Costa is co-author more than 60 papers and chapters published in journals, books, and conference proceedings. She is member of IEEE and IES societies and founding member of the Portuguese Society for Engineering Education.

Rômulo Silva de Oliveira is graduated in Electrical Engineering from Pontificia Universidade Catolica do Rio Grande do Sul (1983), Masters in Computer Science from Federal University of Rio Grande do Sul (1987) and Ph.D. in Electrical Engineering from Universidade Federal de Santa Catarina (1997). He is currently an associate professor in the Department of Automation and Systems, Federal University of Santa Catarina. The main topics of interest are: real-time systems, scheduling, and operating systems.

Apostolos Fournaris has received his diploma and PhD degree in Electrical and Computer Engineering Department of University of Patras, Greece, in 2001 and 2008 respectively. In January 2009, he has joint the Information and Communication Technologies Lab, Hitachi Europe SAS European R-D Centre in Sophia Antipolis, France as a research and European project consultant where he worked for two years. He is currently an adjunct faculty member (Assistant Professor), in the Computer Engineering & Informatics department, University of Patras as well as in the Departments of Electrical Engineering and Mechanical Engineering, Technical Educational Institute of Patras. He is also a research associate in Electrical and Computer Engineering Department, University of Patras. Dr. Fournaris has acted as a technical program committee member for the 4th IFIP NTMS 2011, 6th IFIP NTMS 2013 conferences as well as the IEEE Greece Gold ATHENA 2011 and 2012 Summer Schools. He has acted as a reviewer for many international journals and conferences. He has been actively involved in cryptographic engineering research on the topics of Public Key cryptography, Finite Field arithmetic, wireless network security, Hardware Attack resistance and Trusted systems. He has been involved in several national and EU funded research projects like FLEXINET, VITAL, VITAL++, and SECRICOM. He has published more than 31 research articles in international conferences and journals, he is the author of 3 book chapters on cryptographic engineering and several technical reports on security issues. His work has received more than 56 non self-citations on his work. He is a member of IEEE, IEEE Circuits and Systems society, IEEE Computer Society and the Technical Chamber of Greece.

Georglos Fourtounis is a researcher for the Electronics and Microelectronics Department of the University of Mons, in Mons, Belgium. He received a Diploma in Electrical and Computer Engineering from the National Technical University of Athens, Greece, in 2005. His research interests include compiler technology, programming languages theory, distributed programming, dataflow architectures, and middleware systems.

Olfa Gaddour was born in 1983. Currently, she is a Ph.D student at the National Engineering School of Sfax since January 2010. Her research activity is conducted within CES Laboratory. She has received the Engineering degree in Networks and Communication, from the Higher School of Telecommunications (Sup'Com), Tunis, Tunisia in 2007 and the Master degree in New Technologies of Dedicated Computer Science Systems, from the National Engineering School of Sfax, in 2009. Her current research interests are in the field of Wireless Sensor Networks (WSN) and the 6LowPAN protocol. They are focused on the adequacy of 6LoWPAN and RPL with wireless sensor networks properties. She has several publications in many conferences.

Aymen Gdouda is currently a PhD student in Automatic Control and Industrial Informatics, University Lille 1 Sciences et Technologies, affiliated with the Laboratory of Automation and Computer Engineering and Signals (LAGIS) at the Ecole Polytechnique de Lille. He holds the engineering degree in Instrumentation and Industrial Maintenance in 2006 at the National Institute of Applied Sciences and Technology in Tunis, in 2006. In 2008, he obtained a Master 2 Research in Advanced Instrumentation, measurement, quality, at Polytechnic School of Lille with a research internship at LAGIS Laboratory.

Atef Gharbi received his computer engineering Diploma from the National School in Computer Science (ENSI) of Tunisia, in 2005. After that, he received the Master degree from the National Institute of Applied Sciences and Technology (INSAT) of Tunisia in 2007. He is currently related to Mosic Research Laboratory in Tunisia in order to obtain a PhD thesis in the same institute. His research interests include specification of model, verification of properties related to functional safety, implementation of software solutions to ensure functional safety.

Hamza Gharsellaoui is a Computer Science Technologist, Computer Technologies Department of the High Institute of Technology Studies of Kairouan, Tunisia. He is also a PhD student and a researcher in computer science at the MOSIC Research Laboratory in Tunisia. He obtained the Bachelor degree in computer science at the Tunis ElManar University in 2004, the master degree was obtained in Industrial Informatique and Automatic in 2007 at the National Institute of Applied Sciences and Technology, Tunisia where he made research activities since 2010 in computer science to obtain the PhD. His research interests include the schedulability analysis of reconfigurable real-time embedded systems with minimization of energy consumption.

Oussama Ghorbel is a Ph.D student at the National Engineering School of Sfax since January 2011. Her research activity is conducted within CES research unit. He has received the Diploma degree in Computer Science, from the Faculty of Sciences of Sfax, Tunisia in 2007, the Engineering degree from the National Engineering School of Sfax, in 2009 and the Master degree in New Technologies of Dedicated Computer Science Systems, from the National Engineering School of Sfax, in 2010. Her current research interests are in the field of Wireless Sensor Networks (WSN) and Image Compression.

Luís Gomes received his Electrotech. Eng. degree from Universidade Técnica de Lisboa, Lisbon, Portugal, in 1981, and a PhD degree in Digital Systems from Universidade Nova de Lisboa, in 1997. He is a professor at the Electrical Engineering Department, Faculty of Sciences and Technology of Universidade Nova de Lisboa, Portugal and a researcher at UNINOVA Institute, Portugal. From 1984 to 1987, he was with EID, a Portuguese medium-sized enterprise, in the area of electronic system design, in the R&D engineering department. He was made a "Profesor Onorific," at Transilvanea University of Brasov, Romania in 2007. His main interests include the usage of Petri nets and other concurrency models applied to reconfigurable and embedded systems co-design. Dr. Gomes is author of more than 170 papers and chapters published in journals, books and conference proceedings. He was a coeditor of the books *Hardware Design and Petri Nets* (Kluwer, 2000), *Advances on Remote Laboratories and E-Learning Experiences* (University of Deusto Press, 2007), and *Behavioral Modeling for Embedded Systems and Technologies: Applications for Design and Implementation* (IGI Global, 2009). Dr. Gomes has been serving in different roles within Industrial Electronics Society (IES) of the Institute of Electric and Electronics Engineers (IEEE) since 2002, including Vice President for Conferences, Vice President for Workshops, founding member and Chair of the Technical Committee on Education in Engineering and Industrial Technologies, and Chair of the Technical Committee on Electronic Systems on Chip. He is a founding member of the Portuguese Society for Engineering Education and member of its first Board.

Dr. Gomes has been serving in different roles in the organization of several IEEE conferences, including General Co-Chair and Technical Co-Chair for several well-established and prestigious conferences. Dr. Gomes has been serving as Associate Editor for the *IEEE Transactions on Industrial Informatics*, between 2005 and 2008, and after 2011, as Associate Editor for the *IEEE Transactions on Industrial Electronics*, since 2009, and a member of the Editorial Board of LNCS ToPNoC - Transactions on Petri Nets and Other Models of Concurrency, since 2006, among other editorial boards.

Luiz Affonso Guedes has a graduate in electrical engineering from Federal University of Pará, Brazil, in 1987, and PhD degree in Computer Engineering from State University of Campinas, Brazil, in 1999. Since 2003, he is an associate professor in the Department of Computer Engineering at University Federal of Rio Grande do Norte, Brazil. His main research interests include performance and reliability analysis to wireless sensor networks and industrial systems.

Frank Hagl has received a Diploma in Informatics from University of Karlsruhe in 1987. He has been working as a software developer for various companies before joining Continental in 1998 where he was involved in the introduction of model based development techniques and tools. From 2004, he has been responsible for piloting model driven software development methods and tools and worked as a software architect in series and demonstrator projects at the Interior Division of Continental Autotmotive GmbH.

Naim Harb is a senior researcher for the Electronics and Microelectronics Department of the University of Mons, in Mons, Belgium. He has a Diploma in Computer and Communication Engineering from the Islamic University of Lebanon. He also has an Engineering Masters degree in Electrical and Computer Engineering from the American University of Beirut (Lebanon). In addition to that, he obtained a PhD degree in Informatics from the University of Valenciennes (France). His research interests are embedded systems, FPGAs, partial and dynamic reconfiguration, image and signal processing, bioinformatics, hardware system design, and optimizations.

Osman Hasan received in 1997 the BEng (Hons) degree from the N-W.F.P University of Engineering and Technology, Pakistan, and in 2001 and 2008 the MEng and PhD degrees from Concordia University, Montreal, Quebec, Canada, respectively. He worked as a postdoctoral fellow at the Hardware Verification Group (HVG) of Concordia University for one year until August 2009. Currently, he is an Assistant Professor in the School of Electrical Engineering and Computer Science, National University of Science and Technology (NUST), Islamabad, Pakistan. He is the founder and director of System Analysis and Verification (SAVe) Lab at NUST, which main focuses on the design and formal verification of embedded systems.

Abderrazak Jemai received an Engineer degree from the University of Tunis (ENSI), Tunisia, in 1988, and the DEA and "Doctor" degrees from the University of Grenoble (ENSIMAG-INPG), France, in 1989 and 1992, respectively, and he received his Habilitation Degree in 2012, all in computer sciences. From 1989 to 1992, he prepared his thesis on simulation of RISC processors and parallel architectures. Since 1993, his interests are focused on high level synthesis and simulation at behavioral and system levels within AMICAL and COSMOS at TIMA Laboratory in Grenoble. Dr Jemai became an assistant professor at the ENSI University in Tunis in 1993 and a Maitre-Assistant Professor at the INSAT University in Tunis since 1994. He was the principal investigator for the "Synthesis and Simulation of VLSI circuits" project at the ENSI/Microelectronic group. He was the principal investigator of the simulation module in AMICAL at TIMA in Grenoble. He is also the principal investigator for the "Performance evaluation of MPSoC: Time & Energy consumption" project in LIP2/FST Laboratory in Tunis. His last interest is focused on the use of codesign methodology to optimize generation of embedded systems on MPSoC. Dr Jemai is also working on Security of embedded systems.

Mohamed Wassim Jmal is a Ph.D student at the National Engineering School of Sfax, Tunisia, since 2008. His research activity is conducted within CES Laboratory. He has received the Engineering degree in Electrical Engineering, from the National Engineering School of Sfax in 2005 and the Master degree in Automatic and Industrial Informatics, from the same Engineering School, in 2007. His current research interests are in the field of Wireless Sensor Networks (WSN) and the Embedded Systems. They are focused on the implementation of wireless sensor networks applications in Reconfigurable System (http://www.ceslab.org/fr/perso.php?id=61). He has several publications in many conferences and Journals. He is working now as Assistant in Higher Institute of Applied Science and Technology of Gafsa, Tunisia. Mohamed Wassim JMAL served in national and international conference organization: IDT, ICM, TWESD, SensorNets.

Laurent Jojczyk is a PhD student and a teaching assistant for the Electronics and Microelectronics Department of the University of Mons, in Mons, Belgium. He has a Diploma in Electrical Engineering from the University of Mons. His research interests include signal processing, Networks on Chip and digital hardware systems.

Adel Khalfallah is an associate professor at the High Institute for Computer Sciences – Ariana, Tunisia. He obtained a Ph. D. from Université Henri Poincaré – Nancy, France, as he was part of the INRIA-Loria laboratory. He is actually part of MOSIC research team –Tunis. His research interest is in the modeling and analysis of software architecture with a special focus on real time and embedded software.

Paris Kitsos received the B.Sc. degree in Physics in 1999 and a Ph.D. in 2004 from the Department of Electrical and Computer Engineering, both at the University of Patras. Currently is research fellow with the Digital Systems & Media Computing Laboratory, School of Science & Technology, Hellenic Open University. His research interests include VLSI design, algorithms and architectures for data security and efficient circuit implementations. Dr. Kitsos has published more than 75 scientific articles and technical reports, as well as is reviewing manuscripts for International Journals and Conferences/ Workshops in the areas of his research. He has participated to international journals and conferences organization, as Program/Technical Committee Member, Program Committee Chair, and Guest Editor. Also, he is a member of the Institute of Electrical and Electronics Engineers (IEEE).

Ramin Tavakoli Kolagari works at the Georg-Simon-Ohm-Hochschule at the faculty of Computer Science being responsible for the software engineering field of teaching. He studied computer science and business administration at the Technical University of Berlin and received his PhD at the University of Ulm on the topic of automotive requirements engineering and software product lines. Prof. Tavakoli lectured at the University of Ulm and at the Technical University of Berlin. He researched and published in the area of software reuse in general and specifically in the area of software product lines for the automotive domain. Today, his research focus lies in the area of model-based development for describing the system and software architecture of embedded automotive systems, e.g., with EAST-ADL. After his studies, Prof. Tavakoli worked in the research departments of internationally operative carmakers in Germany and Sweden in the areas software development, software architecture, and model-based development. Beside his work in the business units, he was involved in many European research projects in the context of his research interests.

Elisavet Konstantinou holds a B.Sc. in Informatics from the University of Ioannina, a M.Sc. in Signal and Image Processing Systems and a PhD in Theory and Applications of Elliptic Curve Cryptosystems from the University of Patras, Department of Computer Engineering and Informatics. She is currently an Assistant Professor in the Department of Information and Communication Systems Engineering, University of the Aegean. Her research interests include elliptic curves cryptosystems and generation of their parameters, public key cryptosystems, group key management, random number generation, algorithm engineering, algebraic number theory.

Rodrigo Lange is graduated in Information Systems from Universidade Federal do Noroeste do Estado do Rio Grande do Sul (2008) and Masters in Automation and Systems Engineering from Federal University of Santa Catarina (2010). He is currently is a Ph.D. candidate in the Graduate Program in Automation and System Engineering from Federal University of Santa Catarina. The main topics of interest are: real-time systems, scheduling and operating systems.

ZhiWu Li received the B.S., M.S., and Ph.D. degrees in mechanical engineering, automatic control, and manufacturing engineering, respectively, all from Xidian University, Xi'an, China, in 1989, 1992, and 1995, respectively. He joined Xidian University, in 1992, where he is currently a Professor of School of Electro-Mechanical Engineering and the director of Systems Control and Automation Group. From June 2002 to July 2003, he was a Visiting Professor at the Systems Control Group, Department of Electrical and Computer Engineering, University of Toronto, Toronto, ON, Canada. From February 2007 to February 2008, he was a Visiting Scientist at the Laboratory for Computer-Aided Design (CAD) and Lifecycle Engineering, Department of Mechanical Engineering, Technion-Israel Institute of Technology, Technion City, Haifa, Israel. From November 2008, he has been a Visiting Professor in Automation Technology Laboratory, Institute of Computer Science, Martin-Luther University of Halle-Wittenburg, Halle (Saale), Germany. He was a senior visiting scientist in Conservatoire National des Arts et Métiers (CNAM), Paris, France, supported by the program *Research in Paris* in 2010. He serves as a host professor of Research Fellowship for International Young Scientists, National Natural Science of Foundation of China. He is the author or coauthor of over 180 publications including two book chapters in *Deadlock Resolution in Computer-Integrated Systems* (Marcel Dekker, 2005) and in *Reconfigurable Embedded Control Systems: Applications for Flexibility and Agility* (IGI Global Press, 2011). He is a coauthor with MengChu Zhou, *Deadlock Resolution in Automated Manufacturing Systems: A Novel Petri Net Approach* (Springer, 2009) and *Modeling, Analysis and Deadlock Control in Automated Manufacturing Systems* (Beijing, 2009, in Chinese), and with YuFeng Chen, *Optimal Supervisory Control of Automated Manufacturing Systems* (CRC Press, 2013). He is a Co-editor with Professor Abdulrahman Al-Ahmari of a book *Formal Methods in Manufacturing: Recent Advances* (IGI Global 2013). His current research interests include Petri net theory and application, supervisory control of discrete event systems, workflow modeling and analysis, and systems integration. He is the General Co-Chair of the IEEE International Conference on Automation Science and Engineering, August 23–26, Washington, DC, 2008. He is a financial Co-Chair of the IEEE International Conference on Networking, Sensing, and Control, March 26-29, 2009, a member of International Advisory Committee, 10th International Conference on Automation Technology, June 27-29, 2009, a Co-Chair of the program committee of the IEEE International Conference on Mechatronics and Automation, August 24-27, 2010, and members of the program committees of many international conferences. He serves an Associate Editor of the *IEEE Transactions on Automation Science and Engineering, IEEE Transactions on Systems, Man, and Cybernetics, Part A: Systems and Human Beings, International Journal of Discrete Event Control Systems, IST Transactions of Robotics, Automation & Mechatronics - Theory & Applications*, and *IST Transactions of Control Engineering-Theory and Applications*. He is a Guest Editor of Special Issue on "Petri Nets for System Control Automation" in *Asian Journal of Control*, Special Issue on "Petri Nets and Agile Manufacturing" in *Transactions of the Institute of Measurement and Control*, and Special Issue on "Modeling and Verification of Discrete Event Systems" in *ACM Transactions on Embedded Computing Systems*. He is a member of Discrete Event Systems Technical Committee of the IEEE Systems, Man, and Cybernetics Society, and a member of IFAC Technical Committee on Discrete Event and Hybrid Systems (2011-2014). He serves as a frequent reviewer for nearly 30 international journals including a number of the IEEE Transactions as well as many international conferences. He is listed in Marquis *Who's Who in the World*, 27th Edition, 2010. Dr. Li is a recipient of Alexander von Humboldt Research Grant, Alexander von Humboldt Foundation, Germany. He is a senior member of IEEE and is the founding chair of Xi'an Chapter of IEEE Systems, Man, and Cybernetics Society.

Henrik Lönn has a PhD in Computer Engineering from Chalmers University of Technology, Sweden, with a research focus on communication issues in safety-critical real-time systems. At Volvo, he has worked with prototypes, architecture modelling and communication aspects on vehicle electronic systems. He is also participating in national and international research collaborations on embedded systems development. Previous project involvement includes X-by-Wire, FIT and EAST-EEA, ATESST and TIMMO. He is currently coordinating the MAENAD FP7 project.

Saïd Mammar received the Dipl.-Ing. degree from École Supérieure d' Électricité, Gif-sur-Yvette, France, in 1989, the Ph.D. degree in automatic control from the Université Paris XI-Supelec, Orsay, France, in 1992, and the Habilitation to Direct Research (HDR) degree from Université d'Évry val d'Essonne, Evry, France, in 2001. From 1992 to 1994, he held a research position with the French National Institute on Transportation Research and Safety, Versailles, France, where he worked on traffic network control. From 1994 to 2002, he was an Assistant Professor with the Université d'Évry val d'Essonne, Évry, France, where he has been a Professor since 2002. From 2006 to September 2009, he was a Scientific and University Attaché with the French Embassy, The Hague, The Netherlands. He is the head of IBISC laboratory since January 2010 where IBISC stands for Informatics, Integrative Biology, and Complex Systems. His research interests include sensing and robust control, vehicle longitudinal and lateral control for driving assistance to human drivers, and intelligent transportation systems. He is a Member of the Editorial board of Transportation Research Part-C. He has lead and managed many national and European research projects. He has published over 100 publications in his research areas.

Prof. Ricardo Moraes is Associate Professor of the Federal University of Santa Catarina in Brazil (UFSC), since July 2010. He got his PhD in Electrical and Computer Engineering at University of Porto, Portugal, in 2007. He was postdoctoral fellow in Wireless Communication at the Telecommunication Institute at University of Aveiro, Portugal, from 2007 to 2008. His research interests include real-time communication systems, wireless industrial communications, and real-time system architecture.

Filipe Moutinho received the Eng. degree (in 2003) and the MSc degree (in 2009) in Electrical and Computer Engineering from the Faculty of Sciences and Technology (FCT), Universidade Nova de Lisboa (UNL) where, since 2009, he is a PhD student in Electrical and Computer Engineering. From 2002 to 2006, he was a junior teaching assistant in the area of Computational and Perceptional Systems at the Department of Electrical Engineering of FCT/UNL, and from 2006 to 2007, he was a teaching assistant in Escola Náutica Infante D. Henrique. Afterwards, he was a software engineering at the enterprise NewHotel Software until 2009. He worked in several research projects at the Center of Technology and Systems (CTS) of the UNINOVA Institute. Filipe Moutinho is currently a member of the R&D Group on Reconfigurable and Embedded Systems (GRES) at UNINOVA Institute.

Pranab K. Muhuri is an Associate Professor in the Department of Computer Science at South Asian University, New Delhi, India. He has 14 years of research and teaching experience. Dr. Muhuri has published more than 30 research papers in reputed international journals and conferences. He has co-authored a book *Fuzzy Uncertainty Models and Algorithms For Real-Time Task Scheduling*. Dr. Muhuri's current research interest is in the area of real-time embedded systems scheduling under energy constraints and fuzzy uncertainty. He is a member of the IEEE, ACM, IEEE Computer Society, and IEEE Computational Intelligence Society.

Panayotis Nastou is Lecturer of the Applied Mathematics and Engineering within the Department of Mathematics of the University of Aegean, Samos, Greece. His research interests lie in Wireless Sensor Networks, Embedded Systems Design, Cryptography, Distributed Computing, Design, and analysis of algorithms and Combinatorial Optimization.

Pierre Olivier received his B.S and M.S degrees in Computer Science at the University of Occidental Brittany (Université de Brest), Brest, France respectively in 2010 and 2011. He is currently a PhD student working in computer sciences at the University of South Brittany (Université de Bretagne Sud), Lorient, France, and the University of Occidental Brittany (Université de Brest), Brest, France. He is working at the Lab-STICC laboratory in the CACS (Communication, Architecture and Circuits) team. His research interests include flash memory based data storage, and power consumption in embedded systems.

Yiannis Papadopoulos is Professor of Computer Science and leader of the Dependable Systems research group in the University of Hull. He has pioneered a state-of-the-art method and tool for model-based dependability assessment and evolutionary optimisation of complex engineering systems known as HiP-HOPS, and contributed to EAST-ADL, an emerging architecture description language developed as standard by the automotive industry. HiP-HOPS is commercial and successfully deployed in safety engineering processes in organisations which include Honda, Honeywell and Germanischer Lloyd. He is actively involved in two technical committees of IFAC (TC 1.3 & 5.1) on design and control of distributed dependable systems.

David Parker is a Lecturer of Computer Science and member of the Dependable Systems research group in the University of Hull. His PhD thesis and speciality is the automatic optimisation of safety-critical systems. One of the beneficiaries of this research and development is HiP-HOPS, a state-of-the-art tool for model-based dependability analysis and optimisation, available commercially. He has also participated in several EU safety-focused research projects, including SAFEDOR, ATESST2, and MAENAD.

Fernando Pereira received his Electrotech. Eng. degree from Universidade Técnica de Lisboa, Lisbon, Portugal, in 1992. He is an assistant professor at the Electrical Engineering and Automation Department of Instituto Superior de Engenharia de Lisboa, Portugal. He is currently a PHD Student at the Faculty of Sciences and Technology of Universidade Nova de Lisboa, Portugal where he is working in the areas of Embedded Systems Design and Petri Nets. Since 2003, he has also been with InoCAM, a Portuguese company that develops CAD/CAM software, Automatic Nesting, Computer Numeric Controller Systems, and Control Electronics.

Paulo Portugal received the licenciatura, M.Sc., and Ph.D. degrees in electrical and computer engineering from the University of Porto, Porto, Portugal, in 1992, 1995, and 2005, respectively. Currently, he is an Assistant Professor in the Department of Electrical and Computer Engineering of the University of Porto. His research interests include dependability modeling and evaluation, real-time communication protocols and fault-tolerant systems.

Paulo da Cunha Possa received his BSc degree in Electronics Engineering from the University of Passo Fundo, Passo Fundo, Brazil, in 2005. In 2008, he received his MSc degree in biomedical engineering from the Federal University of Santa Catarina, Florianópolis, Brazil. Currently, he is a PhD student at the University of Mons, in Mons, Belgium. His research interests lie in the area of reconfigurable architectures for real-time video processing.

Mark-Oliver Reiser, after having received his degree in Computer Science in 2001 from the Technische Universität Berlin he worked for two years at DaimlerChrysler Research & Technology. From 2004 to 2008, he has been doing a PhD at Daimler AG. Currently he is working as a researcher at Technical University of Berlin. Among his main scientific interests lie software product line concepts, esp. variability management, requirements engineering and design modeling with a focus on applying and adapting these concepts to the automotive domain as well as other embedded system domains.

Eric Senn received the B.S. degree in Electrical Engineering from the University of Paris VI in 1991. He was student of the "Ecole Normale Supérieure de Cachan" from 1991 to 1992 and he succeeds the "Agrégation" of Electrical Engineering in 1992. In 1993, he received the M.S. Degree in Electronics and Computer Sciences from the University of Paris XI. He was Professor at the French Ministry of

Defense in the GIP (Geography Image and Perception) Laboratory for the DGA (Déléguation Générale de l'Armement) from 1995 to 1999. He received his Ph.D. degree in Electronics from the University of Paris XI in 1998. He is currently an Associate Professor at the University of South Brittany (Université de Bretagne Sud), Lorient, France, and member of the Lab-STICC since 1999. He received the HDR (Habilitation à Diriger des Recherches) Degree in 2008 from the UBS. His current works include research on high-level methods and tools for embedded systems design (encompassing hardware and software architectures, as well as real time operating systems), power and energy modeling, analysis and optimization, and Model Driven Engineering (Meta-models definition, and model transformations).

K. K. Shukla is professor of Computer Engineering at Indian Institute of Technology, BHU, India. He has 30 years of research and teaching experience. Professor Shukla has published more than 120 research papers in reputed journals and conferences and has more than 90 citations. 15 PhDs have been awarded under his supervision so far. Professor Shukla has to his credit, many projects of national importance at BHU, Hindustan Aeronautics and Smiths Aerospace U.K. Presently he has research collaboration with Space Applications Center, ISRO, Tata Consultancy Services, Institut National de Recherche en Informatique et en Automatique (INRIA), France and École de Technologie Supérieure (ÉTS), Canada. He has written 4 books on Neuro-computers, Real Time Task Scheduling, Fuzzy modeling, Image Compression and has contributed chapters to 3 books published in the U.S. Professor Shukla is a Fellow of the Institution of Engineers, Fellow of the Institution of Electronics and Telecommunications Engineers, Senior Member, ISTE and the Senior Member, Computer Society of India.

Ivanovitch Silva received the licenciatura degree (2006) and M.Sc. (2008) in Electrical and Computer Engineering at the Federal University of Rio Grande do Norte, Natal, Brazil. Currently, he is pursuing the Ph.D. degree at Federal University of Rio Grande do Norte, Natal, Brazil. His research interests include industrial wireless communications system, dependability evaluation, simulation models, and wireless sensor networks.

Carl-Johan Sjöstedt received his Masters degree in Mechanical Engineering from KTH (The Royal Institute of Technology, Sweden) in 2001, and his PhD degree in Mechanical Engineering with a research on Mechatronics/Embedded Control Systems also from KTH in 2009. Since 2003, he has been involved in several international research projects, including NFCCPP, ATESST, ATESST2, and MAENAD and worked on modeling and simulation of automotive electronic systems language development, and component IP-protection. He is now a researcher of the team lead by Prof. Martin Törngren at KTH. His research interests are modeling and simulation of Mechatronic systems and model-driven development.

Nicolas Sklavos received the Ph.D. Degree in Electrical & Computer Engineering, and the Diploma in Electrical & Computer Engineering, in 2004 and in 2000 respectively, both from the Electrical & Computer Engineering Dept., University of Patras, Hellas. Since 2008, he is an Assistant Professor with the Informatics & MM Dept, Technological Educational Institute of Patras, Hellas. He is also adjunct faculty, Assistant Professor, with the Computer Engineering & Informatics Dept., University of Patras, Hellas, from 2007. He holds an award for his PhD thesis on "VLSI Designs of Wireless Communications Security Systems" from IFIP VLSI SOC 2003. His research interests include System on Chip Design, Computers Architecture, VLSI Design, Security of Computers and Networks. N. Sklavos has participated to a great number of European and National projects both research & development, in the areas of his research. He serves as evaluator of both European Commission Projects (FP7) and General Secretary of Research and Development, Hellas. He is director of KNOSSOSnet Research Group. Since 2007, he is the Council's Chair of IEEE Hellas GOLD Affinity Group. He is the Editor-in-Chief for the *Information Security Journal: A Global Perspective Journal*, Taylor & Francis Group. He serves as Associate Editor for *IEEE Latin America Transactions*, IEEE Press, and *Computers & Electrical Engineering Journal*, Elsevier. He has been Guest Editor of Special Issues for Elsevier & Springer publishers. He was the General Co-Chair of ACM MobiMedia 2007 and General Chair of ATHENA 2011, 2012 Summer School. He has participated to the organization of up to 100 conferences organized by IEEE/ACM/IFIP, as Publicity, Publication Chair, Program Chair and Program Committee member. He has authored or co-authored up to 100 scientific articles, books, chapters, tutorials, in the areas of his research. His published works has received up to 750 citations. He is member of IEEE and IACR.

Habib Smei received an Engineer degree in Computer sciences of Industrial Systems from the National School of Engineers of Monastir (ENIM), Tunisia, in 1993. In 1995, he was awarded the Certificate of Specialized Studies in Computer sciences of Industrial Systems from the National School of Engineers of Computer Sciences of Tunis (ENSI). In 1997, he obtained the aggregation in Industrial systems of Computer sciences from the University of Sciences of Tunis (FST). Since 1995, it is permanent higher teacher in institutes of technological studies (ISETs). In 1997, he has held the post of Technologist. Since 2006, he served as master technologist at ISET Rades. He held the post of Director of Technology Department of Computer Science at ISET Rades from 2005 to 2011. He was a member of the MIRACL laboratory (Multimedia Information Systems and Advanced Computing Laboratory), where he published several papers in the field of Semantic Web.vCurrently, his focus on the use of codesign methodology to optimize the production of MPSoC embedded systems and more precisely assessing the performance of MPSoC: "Time & Energy."

Kamel Smiri was born in Tunis, Tunisia, on December 2, 1976. He received an engineering degree from the National School of Engineering in Monastir (ENIM), Tunisia, in 2001 and the Master degrees from the University of MANAR II, Faculty of Science of Tunis (FST), Tunisia, in 2005. From 2006, he prepared his thesis on Performance evaluation and MPSOC design flow based on performance estimation. Since 2007, he has been an assistant professor of computer engineering at the Faculty of Science of Tunis (FST) in Tunis, Tunisia.

Yannis Stamatiou was born in Volos, Greece, in 1968. In 1990, he graduated from the Computer Engineering and Informatics Department of Patras University, and in 1998, he was awarded the PhD degree from the same department. From 1998 to 1999, he was a postdoctoral fellow at Carleton University, in Ottawa, Canada, and from 1999 to 2003, he worked as a senior researcher at the Research Academic Computer Technology Institute in Patras where he served as technical manager in various R&D projects. He is now Associate Professor at the Business Administration department of the University of Patras. He is also consultant on Cryptography and Security at the Computer Technology Institute and Press - "Diophantus," in Patras. His main research interests lie in cryptography, cryptanalysis, privacy and anonymity, and ICT security with a focus in eVoting and eGovernemt related applications. He has been a Program Committee member in over 20 security/cryptography related conferences as well as a reviewer for several peer reviewed scientific journals. He has published over 50 research articles in peer reviewed international journals and conferences. He has also participated as proposal evaluation expert for four EU calls in security related areas.

Fulvio Tagliabò, his expertise started in the field of industrial automation as software/firmware expert and subsequently technical manager. From 1990, he has worked at CRF, and has covered many technical roles: Project Leader in a methodological European Project, "TOP;" Project manager in the field of energy and power capability management; and Project manager in CRF 42V program. He also covered the role of head of the group "network and reliability" and he was involved in projects of optimization of the local Plug & Play architectures and in "x By Wire projects," as well as being reference person for CRF in the IST DECOS. Furthermore, he has been the reference person for functional safety in developing of the Electrical Electronic Architectures for CRF's steer-by-wire, brake-by-wire and full-by-wire prototypes. He is holder of two patents and participated in the LIN consortium. Currently he holds the role of head of the new group "Functional Safety for Systems Design" of "Electric Power Systems Department." He participates in the ISO SC3/WG16/DIS26262 – Functional Safety effort, and moreover, he participates in Functional Safety Italian Working Group for the ISO DIS 26262 evaluation. Finally, he is reference person for CRF in the ATESST2 and CESAR projects and is involved in functional safety efforts related to FIAT and IVECO products.

SofièneTahar received in 1990 the Diploma degree in computer engineering from the University of Darmstadt, Germany, and in 1994 the Ph.D. degree with "Distinction" in computer science from the University of Karlsruhe, Germany. Currently he is Professor in the Department of Electrical and Computer Engineering at Concordia University, Montreal, Quebec, Canada, where he is holding a Senior Research Chair in Formal Verification of System-on-Chip. Prof. Tahar is founder and director of the Hardware Verification Group at Concordia University, which focuses on developing verification technologies in the fields of microelectronics, telecommunications, security, aviation, etc. He has received several awards and distinctions, including in 2010 a National Discovery Award, given to Canada's top 100 researchers in engineering and natural sciences. Prof. Tahar is Senior member of IEEE, Senior member of ACM and member of the Order of Engineers of Quebec, IEEE Computer, and IEEE Communications Societies.

Sandra Torchiaro graduated in Automation Engineering at "Università degli Studi della Calabria" in 2006. She joined CRF in 2007 focusing her expertise on functional safety for Electrical Electronic Architecture in the group "Functional Safety for Systems Design" of "Electric Power Systems Department." She was involved in activities devoted to the application of the Time Trigger Network Protocol "Flexray" in vehicle prototypes. She participates in Functional Safety Italian Working Group for the ISO DIS 26262 evaluation. She was involved in developing of EU Projects ATESST2 (harmonization of EAST-ADL2 with ISO 26262 activity, and definition of a model-based design approach based on EAST-ADL2 and compliant with the new automotive standard) and CESAR Artemis JU project. She is involved in in the EU Project MAENAD. She is also involved in functional safety efforts related to FIAT and Chrysler Group products (safety methodology development, functional safety analysis of vehicle dynamic control systems, E/E systems and for Electric Vehicle).

Sara Tucci-Piergiovanni is a research engineer at the CEA LIST's laboratory of model-driven engineering. She received her MS and PhD degrees in computer engineering from the Sapienza University of Rome, respectively, in 2002 and 2006. Her master's thesis was awarded in 2002 with the prize of the Confederation of Italian Industry for the best Italian thesis in ICT. At Sapienza, she held a lecturer position teaching a course on distributed systems until 2008. Since her master degree, she publishes regularly in peer-reviewed scientific forums and journals in the areas of distributed-, real-time-, mission critical-systems and software. She has served as a reviewer in numerous journals (TPDS, TCS, JSS, SoSym, etc.) and as a program committee member in several international conferences (ACM SAC, IEEE ICPS, EDCC, etc.). She also co-chaired the International Conference in Distributed Event Systems in 2008.

Carlos Valderrama is the director of the Microelectronics Department at the University of Mons, in Mons, Belgium, which is dedicated to the design of integrated electronic circuits and digital systems. Previously, he was leading projects in Coware NV. in Belgium, and was a visitor professor at Brazilian Universities. He received the EE engineer diploma from the UNC, in Cordoba, the MSc in Microelectronics from the UFRJ in Rio de Janeiro and the PhD diploma from the INPG in Grenoble in 1998.

Francisco Vasques is Associate Professor of the Mechanical Engineering Department (DEMec-FEUP), Faculdade de Engenharia, University of Porto, since 2004. He got his PhD degree in Computer Science at LAAS-CNRS, Toulouse, France, in 1996. He is director of the Integrated Master in Mechanical Engineering at UPorto (MIEM) since November 2006. Prof. Francisco Vasques is author or coauthor of more than 100 technical papers in the areas of real-time systems and industrial communication systems. His current research interests include real-time communication systems, industrial communication, fault-tolerant systems, and real-time embedded system architectures. Additionally, he is also interested in safety-critical computing systems and communications. Prof. Francisco Vasques is Associate Editor of the IEEE Transactions on Industrial Informatics for the topic Industrial Communications, since 2007. He is also Member of the Editorial Board for the following scientific journals: *International Journal of Discrete Event Control Systems* (SP Publishers), *ISRN Communications Journal* (Hindawi Publishing), and *Journal of Ubiquitous Systems and Pervasive Networks* (IASKS Publications). He served as Program Co-Chairman for the 2000, 2004, and 2006 editions of the IEEE Workshop on Factory Communication Systems (WFCS), which were held in, respectively, Porto, Vienna, and Torino, and since then he is member of the Steering Committee for this series of IEEE Workshops (WFCS). He also served as Program Co-Chairman for the 2008 edition of the IEEE Conference on Emerging Technologies and Factory Automation (ETFA) and the 2009 edition of the Workshop on Real-Time and Embedded Systems (WTR), which were held, respectively, in Hamburg, Germany, and in Recife, Brazil.

Martin Walker is a Computer Science lecturer at the University of Hull, working in the Dependable Systems research group. He has a PhD and MSc in Computer Science and his research is focused on the development of model-based safety analysis techniques and tools, particularly for dynamic systems. He has participated in EU projects on safety, including SAFEDOR, ATESST2, and MAENAD, and has contributed to the development of the HiP-HOPS analysis tool. Recently he challenged a duck to a duel and lost.

NaiQi Wu received the B. S. degree in Electrical Engineering from Huainan Institute of Technology, Huainan, China, in 1982, the M. S. and Ph. D. Degree in Systems Engineering both from Xi'an Jiaotong University, Xi'an, China in 1985 and 1988, respectively. From 1988 to 1995, he was with the Chinese Academy of Sciences, Shenyang Institute of Automation, Shenyang, China, and from 1995 to 1998, with Shantou University, Shantou, China. He joined Guangdong University of Technology, Guangzhou, China in 1998. From 1991 to 1992, he was a Visiting Scholar in the School of Industrial Engineering, Purdue University, West Lafayette, USA. In 1999, 2004, and 2007-2009, he was a visiting professor with the Department of Industrial Engineering, Arizona State University, Tempe, USA, the Department of Electrical and Computer Engineering, New Jersey Institute of Technology, Newark, USA, and Industrial Systems Engineering Department, Industrial Systems Optimization Laboratory, University of Technology of Troyes, Troyes, France, respectively. He worked at laboratory of Informatics, Integrative Biology, and Complex Systems (IBISC), Université d'Evry Val d'Essonne as a visiting professor in 2010 and 2011. He is currently a Professor of Industrial and Systems Engineering in the Department of Industrial Engineering, School of Electro-Mechanical Engineering, Guangdong University of Technology, Guangzhou, China. His research interests include production planning and scheduling, manufacturing system modeling and control, discrete event systems, Petri net theory and applications, intelligent transportation systems, and information assurance. He is the author or coauthor of many papers published in international journals, such as *International Journal of Production Research, IEEE Transactions on Systems, Man, and Cybernetics, IEEE Transactions on Robotics and Automation, IEEE Transactions on Automation Science and Engineering, IEEE/ASME Transactions on Mechatronics, IEEE Transactions on Semiconductor Manufacturing, IEEE Transactions on Intelligent Transportation Systems, Journal of Intelligent Manufacturing, Production Planning and Control*, and *Robotics and Computer Integrated Manufacturing*. Dr. Wu is an associate editor of the *IEEE Transactions on Systems, Man, & Cybernetics, Part C* and *IEEE Transactions on Automation Science and Engineering,* and editor in chief of *Industrial Engineering Journal*. He was a Program Committee Member of the 2003-2011 IEEE International Conference on Systems, Man, & Cybernetics, a Program Committee Member of the 2005-2011 IEEE International Conference on Networking, Sensing and Control, a Program Committee Member of the 2006, 2008-2011 IEEE International Conference on Automation Science and Engineering, a Program Committee Member of the 2006 IEEE International Conference on service systems and service management, a Program Committee Member of the 2007 International Conference on Engineering and Systems Management, and reviewer for many international journals. Program Committee co-chair of 2012 IEEE International Conference on Networking, Sensing, and Control.

Christos Zaroliagis received his PhD in computer science from the University of Patras, Greece, in 1991. He is currently a Full Professor in the Department of Computer Engineering & Informatics, University of Patras, Greece, and a Senior Researcher of Computer Technology Institute & Press – DIOPHANTUS, Patras, Greece. He held previous positions at the Max-Planck-Institute for Computer Science, Saarbruecken, Germany, and in the Department of Computer Science, King's College, University of London, UK. He is the head of the ALGOCUR Research Group specializing in the areas of efficient algorithms and data structures, algorithm engineering, parallel and distributed computing, combinatorial optimization, large-scale network optimization, multi-objective optimization, robust and online optimization, transport optimization, cryptography and information security, and Web searching and applications. He has extensively published in major international journals and conferences, and has received numerous invitations from international conferences and leading academic institutions to give talks about his work. He is editor of the *Journal of Discrete Algorithms* (Elsevier), and he has served in several Program and Organizing Committees of leading international computer science conferences. He has participated as a coordinator and/or key researcher in numerous research projects funded by EC or by the Greek State. He has also served as a scientific consultant in the public and private sectors. Since 2000, he is the Director of the Laboratory for Computing (Computer Center) at the Department of Computer Engineering & Informatics, which provides ICT infrastructure and services to more than 3500 users and which hosts one of the Grid Nodes of the Hellas Grid Network. He is a member of ACM, IEEE, and EATCS.

MengChu Zhou received his B.S. degree in Electrical Engineering from Nanjing University of Science and Technology, Nanjing, China, in 1983, M.S. degree in Automatic Control from Beijing Institute of Technology, Beijing, China in 1986, and Ph. D. degree in Computer and Systems Engineering from Rensselaer Polytechnic Institute, Troy, NY in 1990. He joined New Jersey Institute of Technology (NJIT), Newark, NJ, in 1990, and is a Professor of Electrical and Computer Engineering. He is presently a Professor of Tongji University, Shanghai, China. His research interests are in Petri nets, sensor networks, Web services, semiconductor manufacturing, transportation, and energy systems. He has over 480 publications including 10 books, 200+ journal papers (majority in IEEE Transactions), and 18 book-chapters. He is the founding Editor of IEEE Press Book Series on Systems Science and Engineering, Editor of *IEEE Transactions on Automation Science and Engineering*, and Associate Editor of *IEEE Transactions on Systems, Man and Cybernetics: Part A, IEEE Transactions on Industrial Informatics,* and *IEEE Transactions on Intelligent Transportation Systems*. He is a life member of Chinese Association for Science and Technology, USA, and served as its President in 1999. He is Fellow of both IEEE and American Association for the Advancement of Science (AAAS).

Najet Zoubeir is a Ph. D student at Faculté des Sciences de Tunis, interested on the design, formalization, and validation of real-time systems, using visual formalisms such as UML models and graph transformation systems.

Index